Bilingual Competence and Bilingual Proficiency in Child Development

Bilingual Competence and Bilingual Proficiency in Child Development

Norbert Francis

The MIT Press
Cambridge, Massachusetts
London, England

© 2012 Massachusetts Institute of Technology

All rights reserved. No part of this book may be reproduced in any form by any electronic or mechanical means (including photocopying, recording, or information storage and retrieval) without permission in writing from the publisher.

For information about special quantity discounts, please email special_sales@mitpress.mit.edu

This book was set in Sabon by Toppan Best-set Premedia Limited. Printed and bound in the United States of America.

Library of Congress Cataloging-in-Publication Data

Francis, Norbert.
Bilingual competence and bilingual proficiency in child development / Norbert Francis.
    p.   cm.
Includes bibliographical references and index.
ISBN 978-0-262-01639-1 (alk. paper)
1. Bilingualism in children. 2. Language acquisition. 3. Competence and performance (Linguistics)
I. Title.
P115.2.F73   2012
404′.2083—dc22
                                                            2011010003

10 9 8 7 6 5 4 3 2 1

Contents

Preface ix
Acknowledgments xiii
Abbreviations xv

1 **Introduction:** The Problem of Language Acquisition When There Are Two   1
   1.1 Bilingual Proficiency and Bilingual Competence   3
   1.2 Knowledge That Outstrips Experience   10
   1.3 Modularity   11
   1.4 A Study of Indigenous-Language Bilingualism in Mexico   16
   1.5 Looking Ahead: Overview of the Chapters   20

2 **Bilingualism in School**   25
   2.1 When Second Language Learning Is Not Optional   27
   2.2 Bilingualism, Diglossia, and Literacy   29
   2.3 A Componential Approach to Language Ability Solves a Practical Problem in Second Language Learning   33
   2.4 New Democracy in South Africa: The Challenge of a Multilingual Language Policy   35
   2.5 A Possible Counterexample from North Africa   38
   2.6 Program Design Based on a Concept from Sociolinguistics   44

3 **The Debate on the Nature of Bilingual Proficiency:** Distinguishing between Different Kinds of Language Ability   49
   3.1 First Language and Second Language in Literacy Learning   51
   3.2 Concepts of Bilingual Proficiency: Background to the Debate   53
   3.3 A Proposed Modification of Cummins's Model   56
   3.4 Literacy Learning at the San Isidro Bilingual School: A Follow-Up Study   61
   3.5 Comparing Results from Both Languages   63

- 3.6 Using the New Model to Describe Different Kinds of Interdependence 68
- 3.7 Components and Connections 76

4 Componential Approaches to the Study of Language Proficiency 79
- 4.1 Vygotsky and Luria: The Concept of "Inner Speech" 81
- 4.2 Metacognition: Language at the Service of Higher-Order Thinking 85
- 4.3 Compartmentalization of the Bilingual Mind 88
- 4.4 Bilingualism as a Showcase for the Internal Diversity of Language Proficiency 94
- 4.5 Advancing the Research Program on Bilingualism: The Need for Clarity and Reflection 101

5 Research on the Components of Bilingual Proficiency 107
- 5.1 Maximum Imbalance in Bilingualism 109
- 5.2 Separation of the Linguistic Subsystems 115
- 5.3 How Bilingual Speech Constitutes Evidence of Language Separation 118
- 5.4 Contradictions of an Integrativist Approach 124
- 5.5 A Bilingual Version of the Tripartite Parallel Architecture 125
- 5.6 More Opportunities for Research on Uneven Development 132

6 The Critical Period, Access to Universal Grammar in First and Second Language, and Language Attrition 141
- 6.1 Overview of the Chapter 142
- 6.2 The Concept of Language Attrition 144
- 6.3 What the Research Says about First Language Attrition 146
- 6.4 The Critical Period Hypothesis 151
- 6.5 Is Second Language Competence Universal Grammar–Constrained? 159
- 6.6 Acquisition and Learning in the Second Language 166
- 6.7 A Wider Discussion: Applying Concepts to New Research 171

7 An Analysis of Academic Language Proficiency 177
- 7.1 Secondary Discourse Ability + Metalinguistic Awareness 179
- 7.2 The Development of Narrativization and Levels of Narrative Ability 183
- 7.3 Language Development—Grammar 187
- 7.4 Access to Shared Academic Proficiencies in Biliteracy 192
- 7.5 Linking Secondary Discourse Ability and Metalinguistic Awareness at the Discourse, Sentence, and Word Levels 197

8 Metalinguistic Awareness, Bilingualism, and Writing 203
- 8.1 Metalinguistic Development and Bilingualism 204
- 8.2 Metalinguistic Awareness in Literacy and Second Language Learning 206
- 8.3 A Study of Children's Perceptions of Focus on Form 207
- 8.4 Children's Development of a Reflective Posture toward Writing: Results from Spanish 210
- 8.5 Metalinguistic Awareness as a Component of Literacy Ability—Writing in Particular 213
- 8.6 Possible Implications for Teaching Writing Skills 217
- 8.7 Children's Development of a Reflective Posture toward Writing: Results from Nahuatl 218
- 8.8 The Revision/Correction Assessment in Nahuatl 220
- 8.9 A Comparison of Performance between the Languages 222
- 8.10 Internal Resources and External Factors 223
- 8.11 Applying Different Kinds of Knowledge in Literacy Development 227

9 Metalinguistic Awareness, Bilingualism, and Reading 231
- 9.1 Modular Approaches to the Study of Reading 232
- 9.2 A Study of Focus on Form in Reading 234
- 9.3 The Development of a Reflective Posture toward Reading Comprehension 237
- 9.4 One Way in Which Children Learn to Use Context Strategically 240
- 9.5 Future Research on Literacy Learning, Metalinguistic Awareness, and Bilingualism 244
- 9.6 Does the Use of Context Contradict Modularity in Reading? 247

10 Conclusion: Results and Prospects 253
- 10.1 Parts to Whole: What's Natural and What's Unnatural in Language Learning? 254
- 10.2 Versions of Modularity and Pending Questions in Bilingual Research 266
- 10.3 Language Diversity, Cognition, and Culture 275

Appendix 1 Assessment of Metalinguistic Awareness Related to Bilingualism 281
Appendix 2 Indices of Additive Bilingualism 289
Appendix 3 Early Childhood Borrowing and Codeswitching 295
Appendix 4 Writing Samples, including the Assessment of Revision/Correction 307
Glossary 313
Notes 325
References 343
Index 383

Preface

This book is about the development of bilingual proficiency and the different kinds of underlying competence that come together in making up its component parts. When two or more languages are part of a child's world, we have a rich opportunity to learn something about language in general and about how the mind works. The same is true (some opportunities richer, others less so) for bilingualism in adults. This explains in part why recent years have seen such an upsurge of interest in this area of research. We will barely lift the cover on this voluminous body of investigation. In fact, we will restrict ourselves mainly to problems of language ability (proficiency) when children use two languages for tasks related to schooling, especially in learning how to read and write.

Describing kinds of knowledge (competence) as "underlying" involves no idea that there is anything deep or occult about them. Rather, it seems like a good way to begin to frame some of the problems of language use—thinking about, for example, what the component parts of bilingual proficiency might be so as to understand it better.

Our main concern in looking at the research discussed here will be the questions that second language and bilingual educators ask. This includes research that addresses issues of competence: how it develops, how knowledge is organized mentally, and how it is processed. As we get a better idea about the knowledge and processing components that come together in performance, we should better understand how two languages are used for different purposes. At the same time, findings from research specifically oriented toward aspects of learning and teaching pose interesting problems for other applied subfields, and even for work on theoretical models.

That language learning and literacy might be enriched by including second languages, alongside the use of first languages, is one idea that we will explore. Another research proposal that makes this idea somewhat more interesting (because as it stands it's rather unremarkable) is that this manner of language inclusion might apply without exception, for example, in school. But not all languages (i.e., the people who speak them) have access to the same resources for developing learning materials and texts, and this clearly imposes certain limitations and practical constraints. So the question might better be formulated like this: how and to what extent might an inclusive bilingual or multilingual educational approach be applied even in cases where distribution of resources is sharply unequal?

The discussions about child bilingualism are all based on research or take research-based proposals as a beginning framework. They also take a direction that is influenced by a point of view, or just a view, that in some ways is more like a long view of where things might lead us somewhere down the road, someday. For now, it would be safe to say that most researchers in the field of bilingualism today have concluded that exclusionary (deliberately monolingual) approaches to language learning result in one or another kind of missed opportunity: one kind for children who already know the customary or official language of instruction when they enter elementary school, and a related but different kind for children who know a language that isn't used for instruction and who need to learn a second. One perspective on this state of affairs takes very seriously the following possibility: that scientific studies of language learning might contribute to clearing away unnecessary limitations on human development related to knowledge of one language or another. In theory, we would like to be able to say, it shouldn't matter what language a child knows or knew first.

Much of the research reported on here comes from a project on child bilingualism in which an indigenous language is part of the picture. The full picture, when an indigenous or minority vernacular comes into contact with a national or official language, more often than not involves missed opportunities of significant proportion. A major UNICEF-sponsored study of the developmental potential for children in developing countries (Grantham-McGregor et al. 2007) reminds us of this enduring asymmetry in the world today. The researchers estimated, conservatively, that over 200 million children in these countries are affected by loss of cognitive potential. In early childhood, contributing factors included extreme poverty, poor health, and poor nutrition, along one dimension, and deficient care and impoverished experience along another. Together, according to the authors, these factors predict not only low attendance and achievement in school, but overall attenuated cognitive attainment on a vast scale. With 50% of the world's population sharing about 1% of global wealth (Davies et al. 2006), the 200 million estimate may correspond only to the infant population at *greatest* risk of lost learning potential.

Concentrated in the most marginalized and impoverished regions of sub-Saharan Africa, Latin America, and southern Asia, these children often are speakers of indigenous and minority languages with limited access to their respective national/official languages, and even less so to instruction in a language they understand. Despite significant advances since the year 2000, particularly in Latin America, girls are much more likely to suffer from limited access to a language of schooling, worldwide, than boys (UNESCO 2007). These unhappy correlations are not the subject of this book. But, as certain related and tangential issues are examined in the coming chapters, we might want to consider adding this language-learning circumstance to the ones cataloged by the UNICEF investigators as a predictor of academic failure during the middle childhood years. A number of different kinds of extreme social and economic disparity have been shown to be serious obstacles to school achievement; and the unequal distribution of language-learning resources is one among them that needs to be better understood. In the end, all of this should prompt us to think about the language policy implications that research on bilingualism and second language learning has called attention to over the years.

Acknowledgments

Many people are owed thanks for helping shape the research project that I will report on here, first and foremost the bilingual elementary students with whom I had the privilege of working in a number of rural communities in Central Mexico. It is to them and their families that the first acknowledgment is most sincerely extended. As a guest and visitor to their communities, I want to express my gratitude for the hospitality and generous understanding that they extended to me, always. Thanks go especially to the teachers and principals of the following schools for access to their classrooms and for the many interesting discussions about bilingualism and language learning that we shared: the Escuela Xicohténcatl (municipality of San Pablo del Monte, Tlaxcala state), the elementary schools of Pozuelos and Santa Teresa (municipality of Cardonal, Hidalgo state), and the elementary schools of San Isidro and Uringuitiro (municipality of Los Reyes, Michoacán state).

I would like to thank the colleagues and coworkers who have collaborated as coauthors on a number of reports published over the years, and who have been especially close to the work of the project: Rainer Enrique Hamel, Pablo Rogelio Navarrete Gómez, Rafael Nieto Andrade, Jon Reyhner, and Phyllis Ryan. Especially helpful as well were valuable consultations and extended discussions with Antonio Carrillo Avelar, Pedro Aztatzi Rugerio, Colin Baker, Rebeca Barriga Villanueva, Hintat Cheung, Karen Dakin, Yi Jhen Du, Kerim Friedman, Chieh-Fang Hu, Kent Johnson, Sam-Po Law, John McClure, Mercedes Montes de Oca Vega, Ishmael Munene, Timothy Murphy, Carol Myers-Scotton, Judith Oller Badenas, Akiyo Pahalaan, Kent Parks, Charles Perfetti, Sungok Serena Shim, Navin Kumar Singh, Tasaku Tsunoda, Chih-Hsiung Tu, Monkol Tungmala, Jiang Xia, Jin Xue, Jia-Ling Yau, and Emiko Yukawa. I owe special gratitude to Juan Carlos Sierralta and the other staff members of the Dirección General de Educación Indígena (DGEI), Mexico's national department of indigenous education; my thesis director when I was a student at the UNAM, Martha Corenstein Zaslav; and, in Tlaxcala and neighboring Puebla in particular, María de Carmen Flores Vázquez, Enriqueta Vicenta Saucedo, Filiberto Pérez, Angel Pérez, Floriberto Pérez, Reyes Arce, María

Fernanda Magdalena Arce, Víctor Arce Luna, Rubén Sanchez, Avelino Zepeda, Miguel Zepeda, Trinidad Zepeda, and Scott Hadley, in addition to other members and friends of the Seminario de Estudios Modernos y de Cultura Acallan (SEMYCA) in San Miguel Canoa. As is customary and required, all persons mentioned from whom a language sample was taken are indicated with a pseudonym, for which I ask their forgiveness. Thanks also go to Natalia and Zoraida for their patience and forbearance during the years of research and writing.

Portions of earlier versions of chapters appeared in the following journals: *Applied Linguistics*, *International Journal of Applied Linguistics*, *International Journal of Bilingual Education and Bilingualism*, *International Journal of Bilingualism*, *Language Awareness*, *Language Learning*, *Language Problems and Language Planning* (where "Democratic Language Policy for Multilingual School Systems" appeared in vol. 19, pp. 211–230), and *Linguistics and Education*.

I extend great appreciation to the anonymous reviewers of this book for their observations, suggestions, and corrections, and for posing hard questions and challenging critiques. I am also grateful to MIT Press editor Ada Brunstein and her assistant Marc Lowenthal for keeping everything together for me, in more ways than one, and to editors Sandra Minkkinen and Anne Mark who did the same for this book.

Finally, thanks go to the US/Mexico Fund for Culture, the Ford Foundation, and the Office of Grants and Contracts of Northern Arizona University for supporting an earlier phase of the work that started things going, many years back.

Abbreviations

ASL	American Sign Language
BICS	Basic Interpersonal Communication Skills
CALP	Cognitive Academic Language Proficiency
CLI	Cross-Linguistic Interface
CPS	Central Processing System
CS	Conceptual Structure
CS ↔ L$_{a+b}$	Conceptual Structure ↔ linguistic structures interface
CUP	Common Underlying Proficiency
EL	embedded language
FL	Faculty of Language
IL	indigenous language
ISN	Idioma de Signos Nicaragüense
L1	first language
2L1	bilingual acquisition of two primary languages in early childhood
L2	second language
L$_a$ and L$_b$	the two languages of a bilingual when neither can be clearly shown to be L2
L$_a$↔L$_b$	interlinguistic interface (between the two languages of a bilingual)
LAD	Language Acquisition Device
LSQ	Langage de Signes Québécoise
MA	metalinguistic awareness
ML	matrix language
MT	mother tongue
NL	national language
PLD	primary linguistic data
PS	Phonological Structure
RHM	Revised Hierarchical Model
RL	replacing language
SDA	secondary discourse ability

SLI	Specific Language Impairment
SS	Syntactic Structure
TE	translation equivalent
ToM	Theory of Mind
TPA	Tripartite Parallel Architecture
UG	Universal Grammar

1

Introduction

The Problem of Language Acquisition When There Are Two

Explaining how language acquisition unfolds in young children continues to elude consensus among investigators, even when we consider only one mother tongue. Children exposed to two languages, beyond a minimum threshold, develop bilingual competence and bilingual proficiency to some degree, usually to a degree that is surprising to both the casual observer and the student of language development. Contact with more than two languages may result in multilingual competence and multilingual proficiency. Increasingly considered as a normal and even typical developmental outcome, child bilingualism is attracting growing interest among investigators from many fields. Part of the interest stems from the marvel and admiration that adults, including researchers, experience when we listen to young children alternate fluently between one language and another.

Major lines of research have opened up around several important questions:

• How might second language (L2) learning differ from first language (L1) acquisition? Implied here is a kind of "sequential" bilingualism. Is L2 learning different from monolingual L1 acquisition if it begins in early childhood, in middle childhood, or in the post–elementary school years?

• If bilingualism is "simultaneous" (i.e., if two first languages develop during early childhood), how might it differ from monolingual development? And how might it differ from "sequential" bilingualism?

• It is commonly observed that L2 grammatical development in older learners is uneven while L1 development is uniform. Might this difference apply as well to child L2s?

• What are the general cognitive correlates of bilingualism in children? These will not be the same as in the case of late (adult) bilingualism, for obvious reasons. But again, it may turn out that they do not differ qualitatively. Is thought affected in any way by knowing more than one language?

• In L2 learning, especially for academic purposes, what are the effects of L1 knowledge, and how is conceptual knowledge available to bilingual learners?

- To what degree are the L1 and L2 subsystems independent, and how do they interact? How can we explain language mixing in child bilingualism?
- In regard to the topic of general cognitive correlates of bilingualism, how do metalinguistic abilities associated with school-related language use develop when the child knows two languages?

These are the topics that the next nine chapters will address.

Educators, who in the past have often viewed any language spoken in the classroom other than the official one as a deviation from the ideal, are today more interested in the opportunities that bilingualism and early L2 learning offer, both

- for children who are monolingual speakers of the national language or official language of instruction, and
- for children who speak another language and are still learning the customary or official language of instruction.

Perhaps because of their different circumstances (for them, L2 learning is not optional), the second group of language learners have often been viewed as suffering from a deficiency in need of correction. In fact, a persistent problem that continues to plague bilingual and second language education, despite clear policy guidelines in most school systems, is the disproportionate assignment of L2 learners to special education programs (i.e., assigning children who do not suffer from an intrinsic language disability). Although they may overlap, the school populations served by speech and language therapy and by L2 instruction should be considered different. Less egregious "dis-ability" approaches to child bilingualism, but unfortunately just as widespread, include assessment of learning outcomes exclusively through the L2, and uninformed and informal characterizations of "semilingualism," when the corresponding monolingual condition normally would apply only in cases of true language impairment. The identification of such linguistic deficits requires a formal clinical diagnosis based on appropriate assessment.

Even though few educators today would consider young L2 learners as suffering from a kind of impairment, in practice most pedagogical approaches fail to take into account the existing linguistic knowledge of bilingual children. Curriculum models and teaching methods are often based on the idea that L2 learners' L1 knowledge is either an irrelevant factor or an obstacle to achieving advanced levels of language proficiency. Indeed, much early research on child bilingualism concluded that early exposure to two languages counts as a potential risk factor with regard to normal linguistic and cognitive development (for a historical overview, see C. Baker 2006).

While few language development specialists today would warn bilingual parents and second language teachers against promoting bilingualism in children, might there be under some circumstances a secondary or transitory "cost" to processing two languages that in turn could affect learning and performance in school-related tasks? D. K. Oller and Eilers (2002) ask this interesting question. Of far-reaching theoretical importance, it also comes up often in the real world when teachers are asked to counsel parents whose children are experiencing delays in language development and initial literacy learning. This is in fact one of the language-learning problems about which we want to keep an open mind.

A good place to start this discussion would be around the complex issue of literacy learning, complex enough in just one language. It quickly becomes difficult to sort out the interacting factors when we consider all the possibilities: literacy in the child's primary language, in both primary languages if bilingualism is simultaneous, and in the second if bilingualism is sequential, to mention just some of the broad categories. Since this is the aspect of bilingual proficiency with which this book will be most preoccupied, another major theme will be that of children's development of language awareness. What is the connection between this kind of awareness, on the one hand, and bilingualism, L2 learning, and literacy, on the other? The problems of bilingual literacy will be introduced in the next two chapters. The setting that we want to consider in particular is the minority language community where children learn to read and write in their L2.

1.1 Bilingual Proficiency and Bilingual Competence

The title of this book refers to both "competence" and "proficiency." The suggestion is that there is an important distinction here. At first, this may seem to be simply a matter of sorting out terms that in common usage are interchangeable. A "competent teacher" usually refers to someone who is skillful and able and demonstrates a high level of performance. But this is not the way that competence is understood by most linguists.

In this book, "proficiency" will refer to aspects of skill and performance, synonymous with "ability." A language proficiency test measures performance on a given set of skills. Bilingual children might demonstrate degrees of proficiency in more than one language. Moreover, in discussing proficiency we usually need to be specific—that is, to talk about skill or ability in using language for a specific purpose: reading, writing, listening, or speaking in L1 or L2.

Proficiency or ability, then, is skill in performance, adeptness in using language in comprehension or expression. The idea of a "specific purpose," or any purpose for that matter, also implies that the use to which language is put is meaningful or potentially meaningful in some way. For bilingual children, it is the ability to use one or the other language that they know, or even both together, for some meaningful purpose. The studies reported on here from the Mexican research project have in fact taken one particular set of purposes as a major point of reference: those linked to school achievement, literacy, and other academic uses of language.

"Competence" will refer to something different: knowledge. For a user of a language to be able to understand a question or respond with a coherent answer, he or she must possess linguistic knowledge (among other kinds of knowledge). In this book, this knowledge will be viewed as being specific to a particular language, or particular languages. (Note that this aspect of the definition is different from that of many linguists.) Competence, then, is about underlying cognitive structures that store knowledge. The intuition that knowledge is not the same as ability comes from the frequently observed inability to put knowledge to use. The most dramatic examples are of people who have lost some aspect of language proficiency but who demonstrably have not lost at least some underlying component of the knowledge needed for the ability. Under this category, the most interesting cases are those in which impaired language ability is recovered within such a short time that we would not want to say that the relevant knowledge structures were acquired or learned a second time around. In other words, competence is based on mental representations that have a "content."

Considering other examples of language breakdown, a patient may suffer from a condition in which normal speech production is impaired, but in which, in a more controlled setting, he or she can perform perfectly on judgments of grammaticality. In an aphasia that affects only expression or comprehension, but not both (some aphasias do affect both), or a dyslexia that affects reading but not auditory comprehension, the most likely explanation for the differing performance is that the underlying knowledge of grammar, in part or as a whole, has been spared (Obler and Gjerlow 1999, 144). This also assumes that the same basic grammatical competence underlies both production and comprehension (put to use, to be sure, by different processing mechanisms). Otherwise, we would be forced to assign a different kind of grammatical knowledge for every kind of language use.

To recap: proficiency = ability, competence = knowledge. Note that according to the way the distinction between competence and proficiency is presented here, language breakdown could conceivably be traced to one, to the other, or to both in varying proportions.

In practice, the distinction between competence and proficiency is much more complex—a topic of ongoing debate among professional linguists and psychologists, even within the theoretical approaches that accept the distinction in the first place. The problem is not new, either. A particularly illuminating early attempt to frame the broader question we owe to Plato's allegory of the cave from part III of the *Republic*: how do we attain progressively better understanding of the world through experience? A more modern reading of the allegory might ask us to consider a specific problem. In regard to how we experience the world around us, there appears to be an interesting relationship between perception and how information is stored in memory. The input to our senses is passed to a first line of processing mechanisms, eventually finding its way to internal mental structures where the essential properties of this information are stored. We could think of these as "more internal" than the "outer layer" of input/output processing mechanisms. For example, visual input is received from all sorts of circular objects in an infinite variety of presentations and in all degrees of degradation, as in their orientation, projecting elliptical images. From this inconstancy the mind constructs constant representations, as if it possessed ideal models for different categories of phenomena. In Plato's cave, projections of constant forms (themselves models of real objects), now deformed and impoverished, are all that the captive perceivers have access to. Plato speculates on the possibility of one prisoner first ascending out of this den of shadows and studying the invariant forms themselves, then climbing out of the darkness to study higher sources of knowledge, in the manner of philosophers and psycholinguists. Plato then asks us to consider a pedagogical implication:

Then if he called to mind his fellow prisoners and what passed for wisdom in his former dwelling-place, he would surely think himself happy in the change and be sorry for them. They may have had a practice of honouring and commending one another, with prizes for the man who had the keenest eye for the passing shadows and the best memory for the order in which they followed or accompanied one another. . . . Would our released prisoner be likely to covet those prizes or to envy the men exalted to honour and power in the Cave? (Plato 1941, 230)
If this is true, then, we must conclude that education is not what it is said to be by some, who profess to put knowledge into a soul which does not possess it. . . . (p. 232)

How, from impoverished input, do both our perceptions and our concepts come to be as rich and complex as they are? In other words, how is it that knowledge is underdetermined by experience? There appear to be two ways, at least, of making the connection to our distinction between proficiency and competence.

First, previous knowledge enriches the input processed through the senses. While for native speakers of a language, negotiating a transaction over a bad telephone connection may present no insurmountable difficulty, the L2 learner may require a face-to-face meeting. The L2 learner's knowledge is insufficient to upgrade the input. Newmeyer (2008, 119–122) gives a different kind of example of the same general idea: how sentence fragments are understood. Even though in actual speech we may use truncated forms, underlying mental representations embody all the relevant principles and help us make sense of "incomplete" phrases. Possible answers to the question "Who does Betty want to wash?" could be any of these:

"Herself."

"Her." (not Betty)

"Him."

"Me."

But these are not possible (coherent) answers:

"Myself."

"Her." (referring to Betty)

The well-formed fragment fits into a pattern that aligns with the form and meaning of a full sentence:

"Betty wants to wash *herself*."

"Betty wants to wash *her*." (i.e., someone else)

"Betty wants to wash *him*."

"Betty wants to wash *me*."

Fragments aligning with the following sentences are not well-formed (in the sense of being either ungrammatical or incoherent) or cannot be assigned the intended meaning:

"Betty wants to wash *myself."

"Betty wants to wash *her." (referring to Betty)

A related practical problem in language teaching is the common misconception among inexperienced second language teachers that "sentence fragments" are ungrammatical. Apparently neglecting to reflect on their own, generally grammatical, use of "incomplete sentences," native-speaking instructors sometimes give learners misleading advice. They often take L2 students to task for pragmatically appropriate truncated forms, instructing them to "speak in full sentences." Of course, practice in formulating complete sentences, in the appropriate language use context, is of undeniable pedagogical value for improving academic writing. But if corrective feedback is to be effective, teachers should try not to confuse well-formed fragments and true errors.

Second, the competence-performance (proficiency) distinction comes up when an inability to process input or produce well-formed utterances may not necessarily reveal the full contours of a listener's or speaker's competence. An interesting inverse relationship observed among bilinguals (perhaps unforeseen by Plato) highlights the distinction in this regard. Skill in managing information (a hyperability perfected by some L2 learners) partially compensates for incomplete knowledge of grammar. Literacy tasks in L2 lend themselves ideally to the application of such a strategy. This L2 learner "trick" often creates the impression that competence is more advanced than in fact it is (Lebrun 2002). In this example, competence doesn't advance, yet; rather, performance is boosted by more highly developed processing skills.

Many years after Plato, Descartes again posed the problem of how knowledge and experience are related: specifically, suggesting that the former is not likely to be simply a matter of induction, of forming generalizations and concepts from examples provided by sensory input alone:

> But as for the essences we know clearly and distinctly, such as the essence of a triangle or any other geometric figure, I can easily make you admit that the ideas of them which we have are not taken from particular instances. . . . [When] in our childhood we first happened to see a triangular figure drawn on paper, it cannot have been this figure that showed us how we should conceive of the true triangle studied by geometers, since the true triangle is contained in the figure only in the way in which a statue of Mercury is contained in a rough block of wood. . . . Thus we could not recognize the geometrical triangle from the diagram on the paper unless our mind already possessed the idea of it from some other source. (Descartes 1984, 261–262)

Modern-day psychologists, some of them following Plato's and Descartes's lead, have suggested that young children begin to categorize objects by developing an understanding, on some level, about objects' more fundamental properties, beyond their outward appearance. For Bloom (2001, 1102), the research on early concept formation and language development points to a "rationalist account" of word learning; that "children's categorization, and their use of words, is governed by an essentialist conceptual system." In childhood, surely, there are many examples of how we seem to "know" much more than we should, given what experience provides. If correct, this would be true twice over in bilingualism. Consider the following mixed utterances from a 2;5-year-old Spanish-English bilingual (Elizabeth in appendix 3):

Oo ta Papi's coins?
Titas de agua in the baby tree.
One *arriba*, one *abajo*, one *abajo*, one *arriba*, one here.

Baby talk for:

[*Where is* Daddy's coins?]
[*Little drops of water* in the baby tree.]
[One *up*, one *down*, one *down*, one *up*, one here.]

Researchers studying child bilingual development have pointed to similar systematic patterns of switching and borrowing from numerous language pairs as evidence for the early separation of the grammatical systems. For example, phrases tend to be kept intact, in the same language; and word order patterns generally match up at switch points. This differentiation of language subsystems, internal to the Faculty of Language,[1] appears to complete its course far in advance of any declarative knowledge or conscious awareness of the differences between the languages (Genesee, Paradis, and Crago 2004). Switching appears to be rule-governed, an expected consequence of early separation of the two grammatical subsystems. For example, balanced Spanish-English bilingual 2-year-olds would tend not to produce patterns like "Where *ta* Papi's *monedas*" or "*Titas de* water in *el bebé* tree" (although such utterances that contravene the word order of one or the other language are by no means impossible, especially if one language is dominant). This kind of internally regulated interaction between language subsystems is further evidence that young children's developing mental grammar is more elaborate and structured than their utterances suggest (Newmeyer 2008). Research has shown that this specialized linguistic knowledge emerges spontaneously despite the fact that the child receives language input from "competing" sets of examples, input that one might suspect is at least potentially confusing. In addition, mixing tends to be systematic even in the absence of well-formed codeswitching models, or any model of language mixing if parents do not codeswitch in the child's presence, as attested in Elizabeth's case (see appendix 3).

In different ways, then, knowledge enriches and upgrades the input we receive from the outside world. However, just as the higher domains of Plato's cave were not hermetically closed off from the shadow world, so abstract categories, geometrical concepts, and existing linguistic knowledge should work closely with incoming information. Indeed, the distinction between knowledge structures and processing modules may not be as clear-cut as it is portrayed here. However, it makes a good starting place, one we will pick up on in the chapters to come.

In sum, the way the relationship between knowledge and ability is being conceived here is that there *is* a relationship, in fact a close one. From the point of view of understanding a particular category of related abilities (e.g., school-related), it would be odd to start with the idea of a sharp disconnect between ability and knowledge. Taking an example of a specific academic language ability among the many that children learn in school, reading comprehension, one proposal would be that competence is an integral component of proficiency. But it is apparent that competence itself should be disaggregated. In reading comprehension, a number of interacting competencies must come together, be accessed, and be coordinated, very quickly. Processing mechanisms and interfaces of different kinds must effect this coordination. Some may be specific to certain knowledge structures, and others may be nonspecific processors of the type called "domain-general."

The same type of relationship should apply to an ability that is acquired without instruction, such as proficiency in conversation. In the case of a bilingual, this would include the ability to sustain a coherent face-to-face conversation using two languages. Proficiency in this kind of communication also requires the concurrence of various competencies (of both linguistic and nonlinguistic knowledge), coordinated with the help of the information-processing components of the skills in question. In this sense, perhaps, a more precise title for this collection of studies would have been *Bilingual Competencies and Proficiencies*, plural. Or, from another point of view, one could say that in the study of any one bilingual proficiency, considered in isolation from others, the former is singular, the latter plural: "competencies." But none of this makes for a good book title.

On a related note, years of research on the effects of social, cultural, and economic factors on language development have made clear that "language" is in fact a broad umbrella term. In regard to some aspects of "language," the effects of these external factors have been difficult to observe or measure in a reliable way. In fact, their influence on certain core components of grammatical knowledge can be shown to be indirect and even secondary. But in regard to other aspects (including even some components of what we call "grammar"), the effects are more demonstrably broad and thorough-going. If this is true, it should be cause for serious reflection about the possible componential nature of language ability and language knowledge. How does the research panorama on these very hard questions change when we consider two languages instead of just one?

A full discussion of these questions goes far beyond the scope of the coming chapters. The idea behind this overview of the problem is to lay out the first of several tentative proposals: that while knowledge/competence should not be equated with ability/proficiency, it would be unwise to draw the distinction out to the point where the two are completely divorced. When competence is actually put to use, typically multiple competencies come together to serve a given ability. A necessary implication of this relationship (and for the study of language development, a happy one) is that evidence from performance always reveals something about competence, to varying degrees of indirectness. For example, findings from psycholinguistic research that call into question a theory of linguistic competence should be taken into account seriously. The evidence may turn out to be too indirect; in the experiment too many cognitive general factors could not be controlled for, maybe. But findings from rigorously conducted studies of language use that plausibly bear on questions of language knowledge are important for theorists even when results are inconclusive.

So far, three working hypotheses have been proposed as a way of setting the stage for the discussions to come:

- knowledge structures and processing mechanisms underlie language ability,
- linguistic knowledge (competence) depends only partly on experience, and

- the early separation of the language subsystems in bilingual children is an example of how competence does not depend completely on experience and how it in turn may be separable into components.

In the coming chapters, we will weigh some of the evidence that might support these proposals. In doing so, we will consider whether certain strong claims associated with some of them might be too strong. If empirical findings compel us to retreat toward weaker hypotheses, this cannot be a bad thing, for one because it allows us to pursue more seriously an interdisciplinary approach to the problems of bilingualism.

1.2 Knowledge That Outstrips Experience

A twenty-first-century controversy that Plato and Descartes anticipated in the passages quoted earlier turns on different approaches to what is called the *poverty-of-stimulus* problem. To take one example: the knowledge acquired by all normally developing children appears to far outstrip the evidence available to them from the environment alone (the so-called *primary linguistic data*). In other words, the knowledge attained seems to be underdetermined by the totality of positive examples encountered in the primary linguistic data. The number of alternative sets of grammatical principles that are consistent with the regularities that an "empiricist learner" would notice are just too numerous. Given how quickly children show evidence of knowledge of one particular set of patterns, there is good reason to start with the hypothesis that some kind of acquisition mechanism helps them zero in on what they have to know.

For children who receive input in two languages, the language subsystems are differentiated at an earlier age. This suggests the operation of language acquisition mechanisms that not only are specialized for processing linguistic input but also can accommodate this input from two different grammars at the same time. Even if the separation is not complete at a given stage of development, the degree to which young children begin to form autonomous linguistic subsystems along the way is difficult to account for with a model based on the application of purely inductive learning strategies. We could even venture to say that for dual-language acquisition the "stimulus" suffers from a different kind of "poverty," one that is potentially more difficult to surmount: too much data from which to construct two separate grammars. Nevertheless, young bilinguals hit on the right hypotheses separately for each language subsystem. Thus, the poverty-of-stimulus problem has led to the postulation of acquisition processors that are domain-specific (S. Anderson and Lightfoot 2002; Laurence and Margolis 2001). We will encounter this idea again in chapters 5 and 6, specifically with regard to how it might apply to bilingualism and L2 learning. In the meantime, a question to keep in mind is this: might there be some domains of language and language-related knowledge to which the poverty-of-stimulus problem does not apply?

This tradition of theorizing about how language is acquired poses an alternative to the idea that a single generic associative learning process can account for the richness and complexity of human knowledge of language. It would be incorrect to deny that associative learning and inductive strategies play a role in language development. Indeed, such a denial would be unsustainable in the face of self-evident facts regarding language ability in a number of domains. Rather, the argument is that there needs to be a certain minimum level of built-in cognitive machinery for young children to be able to process linguistic input for acquisition as rapidly and effectively as they do. Linguistic data have to be processed in such a way that the result is not only linguistic competence, but multilingual competence—all this in cognitively immature learners who still have trouble figuring out things that appear to be much less challenging.

The modern-day version of the alternative to associationism is described by Pinker (2002) as the "computational theory of the mind." Sense organs transduce physical energy into patterns of activity and initial configuration: information. Intermediate processors structure these patterns further. In turn, thinking and reasoning can also be thought of in terms of computation and transformation. These kinds of cognitive procedure require the concurrence of different kinds of information-processing system, each internally structured for specialized mental operations that transform information. Basic capacities that underlie the construction of linguistic knowledge include:

- distinguishing between a kind and an individual;
- compositionality, and operating on variables (grammatical combination involves forming patterns of sequences that are structure-dependent);
- recursion (patterns embedded in patterns); and
- the ability to make categorical distinctions (see Pinker 2002, 73–83).

1.3 Modularity

1.3.1 Analysis of Language Abilities

The proficiency-competence distinction and the poverty-of-stimulus problem lead to the second recurring theme of the book: the concept of modularity—how an ability, for example, can be analyzed componentially. "Components" of language ability can be understood in two ways. We could refer to components simply as a matter of terminological convenience, to make it easier to talk about grammar (the "parts of speech") or to analyze it as an object of formal description. An example would be to describe the rules of a certain dialect for the purpose of prescribing "proper usage." The second way to understand "components" is that they are good for more than just chapter titles in books about language. They are actual cognitive structures, materially: subsystems of cognition that are psychologically real—that is, correspond to neural networks in the brain. Modular approaches to the study of bilingualism all share the second notion of "component."

Bilingual development in children should offer greater possibilities for testing different hypotheses related to the claim that language proficiency and language competence are modular in some way. The emergence of two distinct linguistic subsystems in child bilingualism (what we call "two languages"—e.g., French and Spanish) presents the first set of research questions related to the concept of modularity. If each language subsystem, by itself, can be further analyzed into component subsystems (i.e., if the different domains of linguistic knowledge and processing capability can be broken down into components), which of these subsystems in each language develops independently, and which might have components shared in common? Or are all aspects of language in bilinguals represented in a completely integrated and undifferentiated manner? Or are all components and subcomponents language-specific, with no shared domains? In other words, how and to what degree might the two language subsystems of a bilingual be separate, if in fact they are? Is this separation manifested, (micro)anatomically, in actual neurolinguistic differentiations; and if so, how is it achieved developmentally?

A few informal examples might help to make the notion of modularity more concrete. First, we could compare the abilities of two bilingual children in a hypothetical 3rd-grade classroom in an isolated mountainous region in South America. Both speak the indigenous language of their community, and both started to learn Spanish in 1st grade. In regard to mastery of the basic grammar of their L1 and L2, they are indistinguishable. However, Asención (A) has been steeped in the oral tradition of his community through daily exposure to it in his family from an early age. Bonifacio (B) has had virtually no contact with traditional narratives, ceremonial discourse, religious sermons, or popular poetry and songs. In and out of school, A demonstrates exceptionally high levels of mastery in tasks related to academic-type discourse ability. For example, in Spanish (his L2) he can produce, coherently and skillfully, a complex narrative with multiple characters, attributing internal psychological states to them, and he can generate embedded story lines. But at the "sentence level," his knowledge of Spanish grammar is rudimentary. Meanwhile, B exhibits exactly the converse profile in his L1: flawless grammar and rudimentary narrative ability. University students sometimes comment on this kind of "double dissociation" in comparing a favorite professor, a nonnative speaker of the language of instruction, with a native-speaking professor whose lectures are hard to follow (not because of faulty grammar or difficult pronunciation).

In another domain of language, we could compare our eloquent foreign college professor with a native speaker of the professor's L2—say, one who has never received formal education. Since the professor studied the L2 throughout her secondary school, university, and postgraduate years, she has built up a sizable vocabulary, more extensive in fact than is typical of native speakers of the language. However, while her absolute number of L2 lexical entries is large, at the word level she experiences persistent difficulties with inflectional affixes and other aspects of grammar related to word formation. The non-university-educated speaker of the language displays error-free mastery of L1 inflectional morphology, as we would expect, but for reasons that are also easy to explain he has access to a less extensive vocabulary. But independent of the absolute number of entries in his L1, and in contrast to the L2 learner, each entry in the native speaker's lexicon is more complete and well-formed. (Van de Craats (2003) analyzes what "lexical knowledge" consists of, in L1 and L2, and Lebrun (2002) explains how different aspects of the lexicon develop (and break down) unevenly.) This dissociation is also related to the distinction between implicit and explicit knowledge systems. We will consider a similar illustrative anecdote in chapter 5 after we see how this kind of internal bilingual differentiation might be represented graphically (in figures 5.2–5.4).

As we discuss literacy learning, the idea that an ability can be analyzed componentially will be useful in a number of ways. Coltheart (2006), for example, emphasizes the need to study the "individual components of the reading system," especially in trying to understand the causes of reading disability:

When children are learning to read, they are acquiring a mental information-processing system that they previously lacked, and that has some particular functional architecture or other: the system will have as components distinct modules, each responsible for one of the different information-processing jobs that have to be carried out for an act of reading to be successfully accomplished. (p. 124)

Beginning in this introductory chapter and continuing in chapters 3, 4, 8, and 9, I will present findings from an ongoing research project on bilingual literacy development that colleagues and I carried out. Comparisons between measures of children's performance on school-related literacy tasks, in both languages that they understand, called our attention to the concept of modularity. The question that came up very quickly in this work was how a truly analytical approach can be applied to the study of literacy development in children's L1 and L2. What are the components and subsystems that make up this one aspect of bilingual proficiency? In an attempt to get a grip on this question, we made this provisional assumption: understanding the complex interactions among these component domains calls for a working model that at least tentatively assumes that some of them enjoy some degree of autonomy.

How this working hypothesis fares will depend on future investigations very different in kind from the studies we were able to conduct in school settings, far from the controlled conditions of experimental research. In the end, the hypothesis may turn out to be wrong. But the idea was to start with a reasonably plausible framework and then take it as far as it will allow us to go, until it breaks down and leads to different questions. Basic questions that still need to be formulated properly include these:

- Which components can in fact be identified as potentially autonomous?
- To what degree or in what sense are they independent?
- What is the nature of the interfaces that enable communication between components?
- How are these kinds of interaction constrained?

1.3.2 The Idea of Components Applied to the Problem of Language Learning in School

The starting point for discussing a working model of this sort was Cummins's framework for how bilingual proficiency in the academic realm should be understood. In its current version (Cummins 2000, 191), the *Common Underlying Proficiency/Central Processing System (CUP/CPS*—henceforth *CUP*) model suggests an interdependence between L1 and L2. "Interdependence" means that some components are more language-specific (have separate representations for each language) and that others belong to domains that are shared or "overlapping." This distribution between language-specific domains and shared domains is consistent with research on the cognitive architecture of bilingualism, in particular, with many of the seemingly contradictory findings. For example, in bilinguals, some aspects of language ability appear to be based on a common, undifferentiated store of knowledge, while other aspects appear to depend on knowledge structures that are specific to L1 or L2 (for reviews of the literature, see Heredia and Brown 2004; M. Paradis 2004).

Chapter 3 will show how the CUP model accounts for key aspects of interdependence between L1 and L2 in the performance of language tasks related to literacy. In an attempt to portray the language-specific and shared domains more precisely, a first approximation of a modified version of Cummins's model will be proposed. Chapters 4 and 5 will then review current research, leading to the conclusion that the modified version is inadequate in important respects. The guiding idea in this evolution of proposed models is the need to seriously examine the distinction between language-specific and shared domains, and how and to what extent they are interconnected. The concepts of modularity, poverty of stimulus, and the competence-performance distinction are most commonly associated with Universal

Grammar and generativist approaches to the study of language. But none of these concepts draw a sharp line that should lead us to question the applicability of research findings from the various functionalist approaches, in particular in the applied fields. Keeping this in mind is especially important given our primary interest in bilingual proficiency, aspects of performance, and L1-L2 language use. From this starting point, the possibilities for exploring new and unexpected intersections of consensus might be more promising than they first appear. It is no secret, even among its most fervent proponents, that Universal Grammar–oriented research on bilingualism and L2 learning has suffered a growing isolation within the field. Numerous investigators find nothing relevant in either the specific theoretical models or the general concepts outlined so far in this introduction. Starting with chapter 3, as we begin to consider what kind of evidence might falsify the claims of modularity, poverty of stimulus, and the competence-performance distinction, there will be occasion to reflect on why these notions have fallen into disfavor. As noted earlier, part of the reason might lie in the tendency to insulate some of the guiding constructs of the Universal Grammar approach from potentially disconfirming findings in the broader realm of the cognitive and social sciences.

In fact, functionalist-oriented (emergentist, connectionist) researchers have contributed in two important ways to better understanding the issues in the study of bilingual proficiency: (1) Some lines of criticism have undermined versions of modularity, the competence-performance distinction, and parameter-setting models of acquisition that can be characterized as too narrow or too radical. Most functionalists might wish to point out that their intention has been to question the assumptions of generative grammar in a more fundamental way. But for our purposes, these critical observations have helped clarify basic constructs related to dual-language ability, mainly by suggesting that we might want to step back from hypotheses that are too strong. E. Bates, E. Clark, H. Diessel, A. Goldberg, A. Karmiloff-Smith, and M. Tomasello belong to this first group. (2) The actual empirical findings and analyses from connectionist and functionalist research bearing on important applied questions have coincided—unexpectedly, I might add—with Universal Grammar–oriented researchers' conclusions about the same questions. Specifically, these coincidences have appeared in the areas of L2 learning and literacy learning. Explanations may not be converging in the strict sense, but the concurrences raise important questions. For one, might there be a certain common ground, conceptually (not just in regard to practical applications), that accounts for these points of contact? Among this group, B. MacWhinney, M. Schleppegrell, and M. Seidenberg come to mind. Readers will recognize other authors mentioned in the coming chapters who fall into one of these two categories. This theme deserves an extensive discussion of its own. Introducing it in this book, albeit in a very summarized way, I hope encourages some much-needed reflection on future directions in bilingual research.

1.4 A Study of Indigenous-Language Bilingualism in Mexico

1.4.1 Evaluation of Academic Language Proficiency and Literacy Learning

What makes child bilingualism especially informative in studying the components of language proficiency is the wide variation in types of contact situation between L1 and L2, and all subsequent L2s. The extensive variability in social context as it affects the use of two or more languages can push certain language-learning circumstances to the limit. In this regard, we can take the ideal situation of social equilibrium between languages as a hypothetical standard against which to compare varying degrees of disequilibrium.

In North America, for example, there is generally a lesser degree of imbalance in French literacy learning in Anglophone Canada than in Spanish literacy learning in most places in the United States. And the relation between Spanish and indigenous languages in Latin America represents a qualitatively different order of imbalance. Even among the indigenous languages, a clearly discernable hierarchy vis-à-vis Spanish ranks major, officially recognized, and historically valued autochthonous languages above those with fewer speakers, diminished ethnolinguistic vitality, and lower prestige. In an interview done many years ago, an elderly gentleman from the town in which our study was carried out offered his view of the local hierarchy. Beginning with a comparison between his mother tongue, Nahuatl, and another indigenous language spoken in a nearby town, Nhähñu, he remarked that the former was much more useful in the immediate vicinity of the rural towns of the region. More importantly, it was a language of higher culture, of a former grand empire, with a literature. Nhähñu was more like the "dialect" of a "tribe," one that happened to be also in an advanced stage of extinction in his state of Mexico. Spanish stood above all as the national language, useful especially for schooling; English, now immensely popular among young people, for communication globally; and Latin for the highest spheres on Sunday mornings. Similar social disequilibrium in regard to different realms of language use is evident in virtually all multilingual societies. These relations allow the possibility of studying, at the level of the individual language learner,

- how the language-specific components in L1 and L2 might develop differently,
- how shared domains might be accessed differently, and
- how the interface modules and other connections might behave differently, under different bilingual learning circumstances (e.g., involving codeswitching).

The studies of bilingual literacy learning that will be reported on here and in chapters 3, 4, 8, and 9 come from a long-term project in Central Mexico. The indigenous towns of San Isidro Buensuceso, San Miguel Canoa, and neighboring localities form a large Nahuatl-speaking community on the outskirts of the city of

Puebla (figure 1.1). Not far from a major industrial corridor that runs in a number of directions connecting other major urban areas, and home to one of Latin America's largest auto assembly plants, this community is distinguished by a high level of bilingualism. This contact situation appears to be related to the coincidence of extensive daily access to the national language (especially on television) with a not yet fully explicable maintenance of the indigenous language. The specific locality of San Isidro and San Miguel where the study was undertaken is the most linguistically conservative of all indigenous-language-speaking communities in this region. For example, systematic assessment of language dominance among a sample of older children (in 4th and 6th grades) revealed a surprising profile: no monolinguals or incipient L2 learners of either Spanish or Nahuatl. Balanced bilingual conversational ability was the norm, with no evidence of nonnative grammatical competence among the older children except for one Spanish-dominant 4th grader who, nevertheless, could be described as an intermediate speaker of Nahuatl. Extensive assessment in both languages, confirmed by child and parent interviews, provided the

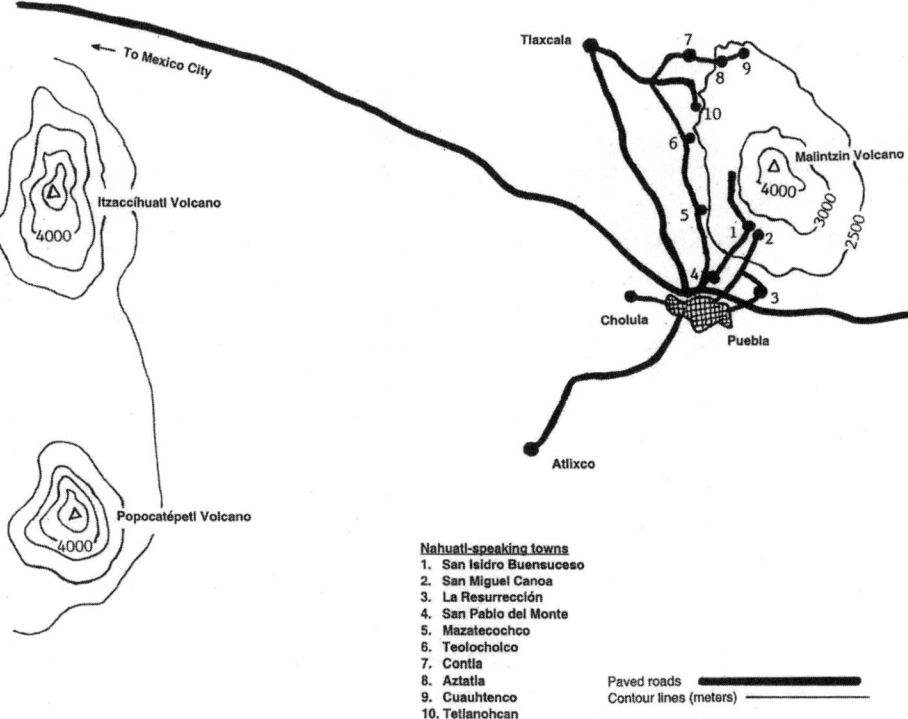

Figure 1.1
The Puebla-Tlaxcala valley

following profile: the few children who enter 1st grade with nonnative or incipient knowledge of Nahuatl (typically "passive bilinguals") acquire at least intermediate conversational proficiency by 4th or 5th grade. Similarly, Nahuatl-dominant 1st graders (also a minority, but more numerous than the Spanish-dominant speakers) rapidly approach levels of balanced bilingualism.

Three sets of literacy-related language assessments were administered in one of the public elementary schools, designated officially as "bilingual,"[2] that draws students from both of the above-mentioned adjacent towns that form part of the community:

1. a broad descriptive survey of language and literacy performance, in both languages, in a selected cohort of 2nd, 4th, and 6th graders;
2. a follow-up assessment to confirm observed tendencies in an unselected group of 3rd and 5th graders;
3. among the original cohort, a more narrowly focused evaluation of one aspect of proficiency in reading and writing: self-correction.

This chapter will set the stage with a summary of the first part of the study: a description of tendencies across grades 2, 4, and 6, in conversational discourse, oral narrative (coherence and completeness of story construction), written narrative (same criteria), and reading in Spanish and Nahuatl (oral miscue analysis, retelling, and a cloze test). Participants were selected by teachers with the purpose of examining normal grade-level achievement. Therefore, performance on academic language tasks was expected to show upward tendencies from 2nd to 6th grade in Spanish, the medium of instruction, as in fact it did. These tendencies were statistically significant between 2nd and 6th grades in all three literacy-related areas (not in conversational discourse, which should not be expected to show variation after early childhood). Conversational abilities in both languages were sampled as part of the assessment of language dominance, and predictably, no grade-level trends and no appreciable differences between Spanish and Nahuatl appeared.

In school, the indigenous language received positive recognition, was broadly tolerated and respected, and was the object of a demonstrably forthright symbolic valorization, in line with official national educational policy for bilingual programs. Perhaps because most children entering 1st grade in this community command at least passive comprehension abilities in Spanish, and because of other pressures and constraints internal to the community, literacy instruction is almost exclusively carried out in the national language. Exceptions include occasional writing contests in Nahuatl and introduction to the Nahuatl alphabet.

To reiterate, especially given the teachers' selection criteria, literacy testing in Spanish, the language of instruction, was expected to show typical grade-level progressions. In comparison, two equally plausible outcomes in response to the parallel Nahuatl assessments could be predicted:

1. Performance in the sociolinguistically disfavored indigenous language, virtually excluded from day-to-day literacy instruction and practice, lacking any compensatory reading material in the community or at home, and with minimal presence in "environmental print," would show weak, nonsignificant advances across the grade levels, or none at all.

2. Statistically significant ascending curves would be found, commensurate with the achievement curves in Spanish, despite the sociolinguistic imbalance.

Results revealed, for all three academic language measures, without exception, tendencies consistent with hypothesis #2 (see figure 1.2). Between 2nd and 6th grade, none of the curves for Nahuatl patterned as hypothesis #1 would predict. The negative effects of minimal language-specific literacy instruction and practice in the socially disfavored language appear to be much weaker than might have been anticipated. In other words, the overall absence of the indigenous language from literacy-related learning activities in school might have (or should have) had a greater depressing effect on performance on literacy tasks when these were evaluated

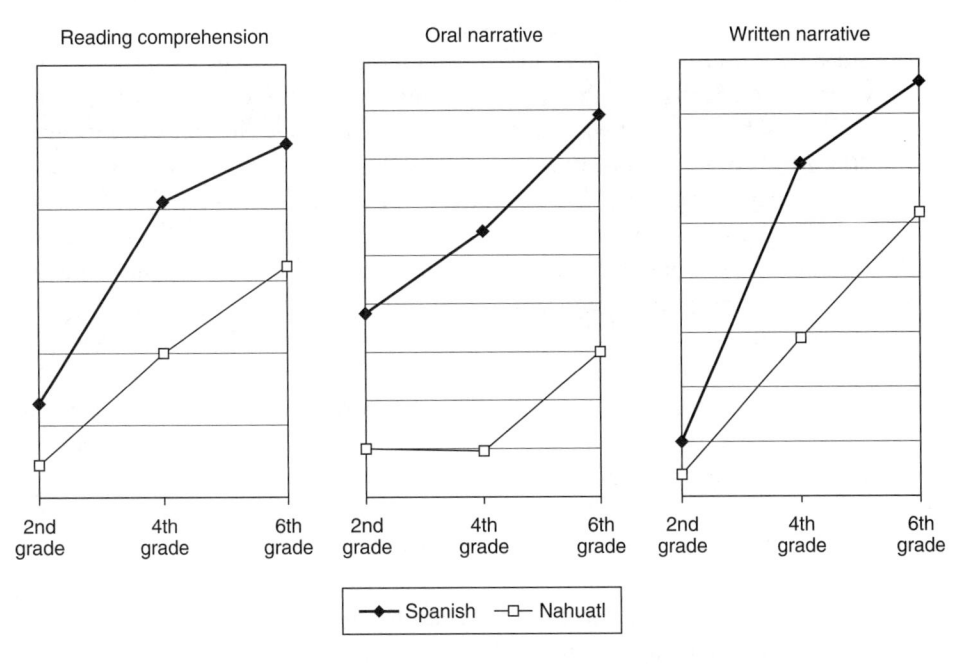

Figure 1.2
Performance of bilingual students on academic tasks in Spanish and Nahuatl

in the indigenous language. However, a different result would have been expected if students were beginning L2 learners of Spanish or beginning L2 learners of Nahuatl, or one-time native speakers who had experienced early attrition and were now strongly Spanish-dominant. Note also that while Nahuatl performance on school-related tasks "parallels" Spanish performance in the sense that significant differences resulted in all three grades, impressionistically Nahuatl appears to advance less robustly than Spanish. In every case, the "scissors" open toward 6th grade (N. Francis and Nieto Andrade 1996). Speculations regarding this effect will be taken up in chapter 3. Summing up for now: In some respects, the sociolinguistic situation of these bilingual children affects their performance in noteworthy ways. But in certain more important ways, it offers lessons and examples that all bilingual educators and researchers should find applicable to their work. In some important ways, their performance is not that exceptional after all.

1.4.2 Special Circumstances of Language Learning

In other ways, indigenous languages do provide special opportunities to study language contact and bilingualism in part because the social inequalities that separate the languages in contact vary widely, sometimes in the extreme. Exceptional circumstances of material economy and access to technology even pose the question of cognitive and linguistic exceptionality. With this in mind, the reader is encouraged to consider the results from a field study of an indigenous-language-speaking community very different from the one described here: the Pirahã of the Amazon region (Everett 2005). In fact, the two communities differ radically in almost every way; but this is not of primary concern to us yet. Everett's findings should be consulted first because they point to general conclusions that differ fundamentally from the model of language ability that we will consider here. In this way, they stand as a pointed challenge. Second, in keeping with the idea of evaluating functionalist-oriented research in order to self-critique traditional generative approaches to language competence, we want to try to account for some of the strong conclusions of the Pirahã study. One question that Everett raises is, what are the basic, indispensable design features of grammar shared by all languages? For example, is recursion one of them? Pinker and Jackendoff (2005) present an interesting discussion of Everett's claims on this point.

1.5 Looking Ahead: Overview of the Chapters

There are two threads in the discussion that will follow this introduction, like parallel story lines of a narrative. One is the report and analysis of findings from a comprehensive evaluation of literacy-related abilities in two languages in the special circumstances of national language–indigenous language bilingualism. In some ways, this thread is indeed like a story, as it opens a window onto the life in school of a group of bilingual children, profiles their abilities in each language, and samples what they themselves think about the languages they know. The other thread, interwoven among the chapters of the first, is a survey and assessment of the research literature that bears more directly on the theoretical topics introduced earlier: modularity, the poverty-of-stimulus problem, and the relationship between competence and proficiency. The first thread should be most useful to bilingual educators and researchers who work in school settings. But in the end, the book comes down to a proposal for looking seriously at the three concepts in the second thread. While the research findings reported here do not prove that any one version of modularity is correct, they do raise the possibility that further research might. In any case, proposals about concepts that have yet to attain broad consensus are useful in describing and beginning to understand things. The second thread invites researchers from outside the confines of bilingualism and bilingual education to look at new opportunities in the applied disciplines of language learning and language teaching.

The discussion in chapter 2 continues the themes of this introduction. Researchers interested in cognitive science approaches to bilingualism often lose sight of why anyone else might be interested in the internal workings of mental entities. We should not forget about the potential broader applications of work centered on developmental issues involving school-age children, to name just one area of concern to practitioners. For example, if a better understanding of bilingualism and L2 learning eventually could lead to a consensus on more efficient L2 teaching approaches, this would represent a major practical contribution of linguistic and psychological science. This advance would have a cascading effect in a number of areas, including facilitating literacy learning in L2s, providing earlier and more complete access to academic content, and developing other higher-order cognitive abilities associated with schooling. Both applied and theoretical researchers would benefit. The advance would open up discussion in the field of educational practice to new ideas (in short supply in some parts). At the same time, it would provide a real-world corrective in regard to which scientific questions are truly important. Finally, well-designed studies of language teaching and related macrolevel sociolinguistic phenomena can contribute to formulating critical alternative hypotheses for psychologists and linguists. This chapter's discussion of bilingual education policy worldwide sets the stage for looking at a local example in chapter 3.

The Mexican study of academic language ability in Spanish and Nahuatl, reported in chapter 3, provides some confirming evidence for Cummins's CUP model. Chapter 3 also presents the first attempt at a more explicit version of this model. Although the proposed modification will have to be abandoned in chapter 5, it deserves a moment's consideration, the idea being that the conceptual subcomponents of language proficiency, which are not language-bound, need their own domain. If something is really "shared," it shouldn't reside with or be the property of either component. The options are belonging to neither or to both. This problem only gets a partial solution in chapter 3, but with the door left open for the proposed model's next, more elaborated, version. All the versions, by the way, owe their usefulness in modeling bilingual proficiency to one idea: the many multidirectional interactions between L1 and L2 are not all of the same kind. The metaphor of "transfer" has captured the nature of these interactions; at the same time, it has introduced a simplification that sometimes makes things harder to understand.

The Mexican study raised more questions than a descriptive investigation of limited scope could even begin to approach. Chapters 4 and 5 start to look beyond the confines of that project. The studies of bilingualism that are reviewed in these chapters are of an order that our project could never have gathered the resources for, materially or theoretically. Hence, our most sincere gratitude goes to the many authors cited in this book for the meticulous reconstruction, for our benefit, of their investigations. The most suggestive are those that delve into the fascinating realm of exceptional bilingualism, in which atypical conditions of language development are truly pushed to the limit. Chapter 5 concludes with a presentation of a bilingual version of Jackendoff's (1997) Tripartite Parallel Architecture.

Chapter 6 takes up one of the big topics in the study of bilingualism today: the question of critical period effects in L2 learning. It is proposed that the debate around nearly every aspect of this question might benefit from a new lens: results from the emerging field of study into child language attrition. Far from merely documenting a phenomenon restricted to small, endangered languages, the study of how language loss unfolds reveals universal properties of linguistic competence. Bilingual educators might recognize this phenomenon under the name of "subtractive bilingualism." For many years, the field has shied away from a serious examination of this particular outcome of child bilingualism, treating it as something simply to avoid in its commitment to the "additive" alternative. One unfortunate side effect has been failure to recognize fully how pervasive, normal, and even typical the subtractive variant actually is in many L2-learning situations. Neglecting the scientific study of L1 attrition in this way has led many practitioners to flirt with unclear notions such as "semilingualism." This happens, for example, when trying to make the (at times exaggerated) case that subtractive bilingualism is always disruptive and damaging to children's development. For minority language communities concerned about preserving their linguistic heritage, understanding language attrition should be important from the point of view of designing an effective language preservation program.

Chapter 7 proposes that academic language proficiency rests upon a foundation formed by two major dimensions of ability: secondary discourse ability and metalinguistic awareness. The chapter focuses on studies of bilingual and L2 literacy and provides a framework for distinguishing one kind of ability from another. It also concludes the discussion of the competence-performance distinction with some concrete examples.

Chapters 8 and 9 return to the original study of the Nahuatl-speaking community in Mexico. Chapter 8 examines an aspect of literacy learning for which metalinguistic awareness—reflection on language forms—should figure in an important way: self-correction. How do bilingual children respond when asked to shift their attention to orthographic, grammatical, and discourse-level patterns in their own writing? How do they respond when asked to do this both in the language in which writing skills are normally practiced in school, and in their "nonacademic" language? Chapter 9 then explores how children shift to a focus on form in reading.

Chapter 10, aside from giving cause for optimism about future directions in research, questions the usefulness of some popular approaches to bilingualism in school that run counter to the modular perspective. Current evidence from various quarters argues rather convincingly that this perspective should at least be considered with an open mind. Specifically, the critique in chapter 10 centers on strong versions of the "whole-language" philosophy. This book proposes that the study of bilingualism might advance more productively if it began with an analysis of the components of bilingual ability. These components are best thought of as internally structured subsystems, in interactive connections of different kinds. Crucially, however, the components and connections cannot do whatever they want; and "central" cognitive domains cannot direct the lower-level components any way they want to, either. This componential approach should provide a better understanding of bilingual children's abilities, more reliable and meaningful assessments of their abilities in school, and more effective teaching models, above all in literacy and L2 learning.

The appendices offer new data to contemplate, data that students of bilingualism are invited to try their own hand at analyzing. The data illustrate key concepts discussed in the chapters, along with some preliminary interpretations. The appendices include (1) procedures for evaluating an aspect of metalinguistic awareness related to children's knowledge of two languages; (2) a summary of findings from a broad range of measures of developing additive bilingualism, including indices of lexical borrowing, shifts in language dominance, ethnolinguistic loyalty, and observations of language use in conversation; (3) codeswitching data from early simultaneous bilingualism; and (4) writing samples from Nahuatl-Spanish bilingual students.

With all of these topics in mind, the reader is asked to critically evaluate the usefulness of the three guiding concepts introduced in this chapter: the competence-proficiency distinction, the poverty-of-stimulus problem applied to bilingualism, and modularity. This is the overarching objective of the next nine chapters. A good starting place is to consult the glossary entry for each concept.

Before we take up the evidence from studies of bilingual competence and bilingual proficiency as these develop within individuals, it is important to look at the broader implications of language contact and multilingualism. Why should the problems (the details, in particular) of development and learning matter to people who make decisions about language policy, especially in school? The next chapter will explore this question.

2
Bilingualism in School

This chapter outlines the basic principles for understanding bilingual and L2 learning, applicable to multilingual and multicultural educational institutions. Chapter 3 will bring this focus down to one bilingual school in particular.

The study of how children learn second languages and how the L1 and L2 subsystems interact under different conditions of development should be an important part of an informed discussion of language-teaching practices. Often, though, debates on school language policy suffer from a restricted perspective that elevates sociopolitical questions above all others. Setting aside the developmental principles of bilingualism in this way renders the discussion incomplete and incoherent. Language policy-making needs to reckon with the internal constraints on language learning in addition to external social factors. On the other hand, the application of language-learning principles in real time, in actual language-learning situations, and across diverse populations, offers important evidence for cognitive scientists.

Converging conclusions from research are not far off on three important practical applications:

1. A consensus is emerging on the most productive approaches to L2 teaching. Inefficient and unreliable methods impose an onerous cost when valuable resources are squandered. What are the conditions that maximize the learning potential of young L2 learners?

2. Since language is an indispensable tool for higher-order thinking, the most advantageous conditions for intellectual and academic development are closely related to the optimal development of language abilities. Specifically, when there is a "mismatch" between language of instruction and the child's linguistic competence, what measures are necessary to ensure comprehension and maximize engagement with meaningful instruction?

3. Especially in situations of intense contact among languages resulting in language shift and attrition, what policies and practices might yield tangible results for revitalizing or preserving a national, regional, or ethnic minority language?

If the promotion of a nondiscriminatory societal bilingualism comes to be an actual planning objective, basic acquisition and learning principles, especially concerning child bilingual development, should be at the heart of any public policy debate. Critical social justice issues come to the fore when language-learning resources are not distributed equitably and when sociolinguistic imbalances coincide with economic inequalities. These issues are easier to understand if research findings from cognitive science are included in the discussion.

As globalization increasingly leads to labor force migration, fewer and fewer school systems in labor-receiving countries can afford to maintain their former "one state–one language" educational policies (J. Anderson 2008; Wright 2007). The progressive shift toward more pluralistic language policies is an irresistible consequence of the new immigration trends. (See the discussion in Spolsky 1999 on the breakdown of the monolingual ideal of early Zionist language policy in Israel; Glastra and Schedler 2004 on the question of citizenship and language in Europe; and T. Wiley 2002 for a historical note on language pluralism in the United States that puts the current "English-only" restrictions into a broader perspective.) Among the labor-exporting countries, recent proposals for pluralistic language models have offered alternatives to highly centralized integrationist educational models inherited from the past. The continuing crisis of equal access to school literacy in receiving and exporting countries alike will require a better understanding of both social relations in language contact and the principles of language learning. Especially in regard to the latter, questions related to child development during the primary-school years most urgently demand our attention.

Two dimensions of child language development in bilingual and multilingual contexts are fundamental to the debate over language policy. The debate is often framed in terms of linguistic rights to which all individuals should be able to lay claim: access to effective L2-learning opportunities, and the use and development of one's own primary language. In the literature on this question, often the second prerogative is emphasized. However, as this chapter will show, a one-sided emphasis would result in only partially affirming the school's responsibility in language learning.

For multilingual institutions that face changing relations of language contact (e.g., a new official-national language), a continuing challenge is to ensure unimpeded access to academic texts and other didactic materials, especially Internet resources. This problem will continue to be critical in the coming years in a number of countries as they apply the above-mentioned principles. The recent language policy reforms in South Africa offer the broadest lessons, in part because the scope of the reforms is so ambitious. This chapter will consider the options that the concept of diglossia allows for, and how it might be applied to language-teaching curricula to meet the challenges of linguistic diversity.

2.1 When Second Language Learning Is Not Optional

Which language or languages are to be designated as medium of instruction and which as language-learning objectives (keeping in mind that these categories overlap) involves policy decisions with broad repercussions. For example, exclusionary language policies lead to persistently unequal levels of literacy learning and academic achievement. School language policy also has consequences for children's ability to maintain competence in a natively acquired language and successfully learn a second. For the communities to which individual language learners belong, language policy affects tendencies in language preservation and language shift.

Studies of language policy and planning normally focus on community, regional, and nationwide issues; sociolinguistic concepts are naturally at the center of discussion. In this regard, for most multilingual states there remains an inescapable distinction between national-official-language-of-wider-communication and vernacular, indigenous, or minority language. This distinction raises the need to take account of both language-learning constraints and linguistic rights. These rights apply most directly to child language learners. A narrow view of the relevant prerogatives, which for example might encompass solely social and political considerations of language policy, would result in a partial and distorted perspective. Much of the current debate on multilingualism and schooling in fact suffers from this defect. Thus, taking developmental psycholinguistic factors into consideration in analyzing language contact situations will inform policy and planning on fundamental concepts. The complexity of these multilingual situations, especially those where sharp sociolinguistic inequalities persist, simply cannot be addressed by any one social science discipline on its own. Most notably, in the literature from the fields of cultural studies and multiculturalism, the disparagement of what are variously referred to as "technical" questions or "positivist" and "scientific experimental" approaches only serves to narrow the field of inquiry and debate (for one example, see Zentella 2005).

In multilingual school systems, the stakes are raised along a number of critical dimensions. Two that immediately present themselves are L2 learning and L1 development. Both invoke questions about the language-learning needs and the linguistic rights of individual learners:

1. Multilingual and multicultural educational institutions face the need to prioritize the most effective and efficient methods of learning second languages, within an optimal time period, for three purposes:
    - Access, without unnecessary delay, in developmental terms, to available didactic materials and texts, and the national language of schooling. This timely access

to a L2 is especially critical if the local community language lacks the resources to provide a full complement of academic texts and learning materials, in particular at levels beyond the first years of primary school. Where these resources are lacking, multilingual school systems have few alternatives to shifting more and more teaching resources toward languages-of-wider-communication as medium of instruction.[1]

• L2 learning for the recuperation or revitalization of a minority language, if this objective comes to be identified and assumed by the minority speech community itself.

• Learning regionally prominent languages of wider communication (e.g., a lingua franca necessary for interethnic/interlinguistic communication) not spoken natively by speakers of a national language (NL)[2] and/or local vernacular.

Under all three categories, considerations of effectivity and efficiency of L2 learning are more pressing than most commentators have acknowledged. For example, the consequences of inadequate achievement for the North American English-speaking foreign language student are such that the incentives for maximizing pedagogical efficacy can even come to be viewed as secondary. This in fact would not be an implausible explanation for the relatively deficient state of students' performance. Such a luxury cannot be entertained, for example, by monolingual indigenous-language speakers and child immigrants not at liberty to neglect the development of proficiency in the national language of schooling. For them, the stakes in L2 learning are high. The need for access to texts and high motivation on the part of students and their families should prompt educational planners to consider only the most productive and effective program models.

2. In one sense, the dimension of L1 development can be reformulated more fundamentally as simply *language development*. Core linguistic competence and primary discourse ability evolve and attain their steady (complete) states even under the most adverse conditions where schooling and literacy learning are denied. However, in all cultures the development of higher-order literacy-related discourses and specific academic language abilities requires active engagement through the medium of a language that can be processed grammatically and understood (keeping in mind that the language that is best understood is not necessarily a child's L1). This aspect of language development is often facilitated, most effectively and efficiently, with the significant participation of the child's primary language, in conjunction with early L2-medium instruction. This traditional principle of mother tongue (MT) inclusion in early literacy development (UNESCO 1953), to date unrefuted, follows self-evidently in the case of young preliterate children who understand no other language. In addition, if language revitalization figures among a community's planning objectives, L1 development in primary school cannot be left unattended, abandoning the field to exclusive NL-medium instruction.

This dual-language learning right (consisting of dimensions #1 and #2 above) has provided a unifying conceptual framework for our research team's work over the years in bilingual indigenous education in Mexico and the United States (Carrillo Avelar 2004; N. Francis and Navarrete Gómez 2009; N. Francis and Reyhner 2002; Hamel 2003; Hamel and Francis 2006). Here, it is being extended to all bilingual and multilingual instruction for which child L2 learning is not optional. For example, language policies whose purpose it is to consolidate a national identity may conceive of this consolidation in a way that contravenes one dimension or the other of this right. Specifically, the imposition of a language as medium of instruction that is neither the MT/L1 nor facilitates broad access to texts and learning resources often sparks widespread resistance among families, for good reason in many cases.

Optimizing dimension #1 (L2 learning) hastens unfettered access to academic texts and other materials if children's L1 does not allow for access to these resources. Efficient L2 learning also frees up instructional resources for L1 development (dimension #2) if this has become the actively assumed objective of the bilingual speech community. Sustained advances along dimension #2, aside from contributing to the stability of a pluralistic bilingual/multilingual school system, help ensure the most favorable conditions for L2 learning and literacy (Benson 2002; Fillol and Vernaudon 2004; Molyneux 2009). Crucially, L2 learning needs to be advanced for the purpose of facilitating L2 literacy tied to academic texts where this is necessary. As C. Baker (2003) points out, bilingual education cannot be justified solely as a means of language preservation. In some cases, from the perspective of the speech community itself, it may not even turn out to be a high priority. In the end, the most fundamental language right consists of unimpeded development of higher-order language abilities and literacy. In turn, this development provides the most favorable conditions for successful L2 learning. Since previous theories that viewed early L2 learning as somehow detrimental to children have been largely discounted (De Houwer 2006; Kovelman, Baker, and Petitto 2008), combining MT/L1-medium instruction and a strong L2 learning strand from the very beginning of primary schooling need not be avoided. Thus, even L2 literacy teaching for child beginning learners of the L2 can be initiated much earlier than previous "MT/L1 literacy first" models had envisioned.

2.2 Bilingualism, Diglossia, and Literacy

For vernacular-language speakers and speakers of "smaller" languages, the need to develop proficiency in a L2–NL-of-wider-communication is conditioned by the degree of diglossic separation in the realm of literacy between the NL and their native language. Today, in some areas of academic study, even a strong NL (a language of international communication, spoken by hundreds of millions, laying claim to centuries of literary tradition) may be insufficient[3] in regard to the important consideration of access to specialized texts in the upper grades. Along the continuum of text/literacy diglossia, the following degrees of separation are possible:

1. At one extreme, in relation to a NL of extensive material and cultural resources, lies an isolated indigenous language (IL), lacking even an externally introduced writing system.

2. At the other extreme lies the language contact situation of a NL and an IL of differing degrees of literary tradition, current text production, and accessibility.

3. The contact between a less populous language/nationality or language minority with a long-standing literary tradition and a NL with overwhelmingly superior resources represents a different kind of diglossic separation. In some newly independent states in Eastern Europe and the former Soviet Union, for example, bilingualism/diglossia continues to evolve in an imbalanced way, between a former NL and the new official language of the newly sovereign state, formerly subordinate language of an autochthonous nationality. In other regions, a similar evolution is found within the borders of a single state. This broad category admits wide variation—for example, the differences between these contact situations:

- Spanish-Catalan, Spanish-Basque (Juarros-Daussà and Lanz 2009; Solé i Durany 2004);
- Russian-Latvian, Russian-Lithuanian, Russian-Estonian (Hogan-Brun et al. 2007; C. Schmid 2008); and
- in North America, English-French, English-Spanish (Bourhis, Montarule, and Amiot 2007; D. C. Johnson 2009; McGroarty 2006).

For a discussion of diglossia, see Ferguson 1959, Fishman 1967, and (with respect to literacy) Hornberger 2002 and Romaine 2001.

Not all languages of a multilingual school system spoken by children and their families can, or should under all circumstances, be afforded the same status in the language-learning curriculum. This principle applies regardless of the absolute number of languages spoken; that is, it is not simply a practical consideration of "too many languages." Taking up again the two dimensions of children's language-learning needs and language rights, and beginning with dimension #2, primary-language development: specific pedagogical provisions follow from determining which language children understand, or understand more completely. In the case of initial literacy teaching, for example, not just any combination of languages that could serve as medium of instruction may conform to language learners' developmental needs. To take one example, sociopolitical considerations related to preserving or revitalizing the disfavored or threatened language of a nationality will usually require elevating the status of the nationality's threatened language above all others. Affirmative or preferential measures may even include the setting of specific language-learning objectives and standards for both the language's native-speaking children and child L2 learners enrolled in the new bilingual or multilingual school system.

In regard to dimension #1 (effective learning of a NL/L2), even the most pluralistic educational system will eventually converge upon the languages of wider communication, both national and international, that can permit learners to fulfill the requirements of discipline-specific curricula. Students need to meet academic objectives in line with international standards and gain access to prerequisite texts. Preferably, this convergence would be initiated in a conscious and systematic way in the early primary grades. (As noted earlier, there is no language development justification for not initiating L2 learning, in proper proportion to MT/L1-medium instruction, as early as possible.) Depending on the circumstances, such a convergence will vary in proportion and tempo; as a case in point, consider the official language education policy for Tanzania.[4] Of course, the above considerations of utility and access to texts are not value-free, neutral, or unrelated to ideological orientation; but no aspect of this important qualification overrides them.

A particularly instructive example of the need to provide for a multidisciplinary perspective is the dilemma that confronts formerly subordinate language groups now in a position of language policy and planning authority (e.g., Catalonia, Quebec, the Baltic states). In these cases, where the new NL is still under the displacing pressures of the former NL (Spanish, English, and Russian, respectively) and is spoken by sizable minorities of monolinguals within the new autonomous jurisdictions, school language policy is often guided by the need to normalize the new NL's use. This normalization typically requires all students to demonstrate successively advanced levels of proficiency in the new NL as they progress through the grades. Under such circumstances, understanding developmental constraints and the principles of language acquisition and learning, of L1 and L2, is indispensable for informing school language policy. One starting point could be the preservation and revitalization of the (still) disfavored new NL, essential emblem of the newly reconstituted nation. In many cases, however, the dilemma is not easily resolved. In the case of imposing a language that is neither the MT/L1 of a given minority nor a language of wider communication, applying the principle of dual-language learning rights becomes more complex. All variants of linguistic cleansing are always and under all circumstances excluded. Therefore, a dual-language transitional program is proposed such that the linguistic rights and language-learning needs of the new language minority are taken into account. Fortunately, from the perspective of the new language minority (the Spanish-speaking Catalonian, the Anglophone native of Montreal, the Russophone Estonian, etc.), "rights" and "language-learning needs" coincide completely. From the perspective of language-planning authorities, as cooler heads continue to prevail, such a coincidence is more widely accepted as also preserving the nation's linguistic heritage. Integrating minority-language speakers into pluralistic educational settings also facilitates the learning of L2s, in this case a new NL. For example, providing Russian speakers in the former Soviet republics with extended bilingual instruction, a long-term transitional program consisting of Russian-medium content teaching in the primary and secondary levels facilitates their academic integration. In the long run, such integration is also compatible with L2 learning of Lithuanian, Ukrainian, Armenian, and so on.

Specifically, a policy that is informed by the two fundamental dimensions of language development will favor the following outcomes:

1. It will create the curricular foundation for the most effective and efficient L2 learning of the new NL by applying the concepts that have emerged from research on child bilingualism.

2. At the same time, it will ensure the most favorable conditions for language development. All other factors being equal, initial literacy development proceeds most effectively with the significant participation of the language the child understands. This also applies to developing skilled reading and writing in the highly decontextualized and cognitively demanding curricular areas. In the meantime, proficiency in the L2 develops through predictable stages, though students traverse timetables and attain milestones at highly varying rates; ultimate attainment varies as well. Dual-language transitional programs that foresee this variation have been well-advised to reserve significant portions of the early core curriculum for primary-language-medium instruction for monolingual speakers. Such a policy of early bilingual instruction could be significantly extended, easing the transition to predominantly L2-medium instruction, and guarding against a (politically motivated or pedagogically uninformed) exclusion of the former NL at the higher grade levels. Another example might be to allow some qualifying exams to be taken in Russian by L2 learners of Latvian and Estonian, in Spanish by L2 learners of Catalan, and so forth.

Again, inclusionary measures that respond to sociopolitical concerns of minority communities (families whose L2 beginner children are at the same time struggling with new NL-medium instruction) coincide with language-learning theory and current L2 pedagogy. To this end, Artigal (1997) and Siguán (1991) sketch the outlines of best-practice content-based immersion in the L2 teaching of Catalan in the elementary grades, as do Cormier and Turnbull (2009) and Wesche (2001) for French immersion in Canada. Thus, the policy dilemma on this specific question is resolved because the imperatives of normalizing the use of the new NL do not need to be "balanced against" the developmental needs of the beginning L2 learner, speaker of the previously favored language.

2.3 A Componential Approach to Language Ability Solves a Practical Problem in Second Language Learning

A better understanding of the components of bilingual proficiency contributes to resolving another L2 learning problem that many children face in school. In the last section, we considered the problem of L2 learning on the part of language minority students in new political situations where majorities have gained the right to establish their previously subordinate language as medium of instruction. The new language policy applies not only for native speakers of the new NL but often also for children who had never learned it, and for new immigrants into the now autonomous state or region. Similar, in some ways, is the requirement that children learn an official language (as a L2) that is rarely spoken by anyone outside of the capital city, as in the case of many newly independent countries in Asia and Africa. Several questions immediately arise: To what level or standard of proficiency should child L2 learners be held? What general expectations should be established in regard to mastery of academic objectives in the L2 (for both native speakers and L2 learners)? What expectations should be set for different entrance requirements for secondary and higher education? The dilemma is this: normally, the rate of L2 learning in situations in which the school is the primary (sometimes only) source of L2 input is highly variable, with many learners advancing toward mastery slowly. In response to this predictable lag in L2 learning, a common solution is to intensify the teaching of the linguistic subcomponents of the L2. This emphasis takes up a great percentage of available instructional time and resources—time and resources that are now less available for work in the content area curriculum. Integration of L2 and content teaching is a necessary part of the solution, but insufficient by itself.

Returning to the question of what standards should be required, we can begin with a functional analysis of the different domains and subsystems of language proficiency. Taking complete native-speaker proficiency of the target L2 as a hypothetical standard, mastery of which linguistic subsystems is most essential for a given purpose? For example, in order to access L2 academic texts (as if L2 learning were needed only for this purpose), it would be necessary to master a highly circumscribed set of language skills—but not all the skills that characterize certain aspects of native-speaker proficiency. This specific instrumental goal would lie at one extreme of a series of "proficiency sets" that progressively incorporate other domains of the target L2. The final consensus on this difficult question of educational language policy would depend on a host of factors, many of which are often largely independent of children's developmental needs. But optimally, external requirements should be evaluated with these developmental constraints in mind. In any case, curricular efficiency would advise against intensive direct teaching and extensive practice dedicated to certain lower-level skills—for example, those whose only purpose might be to approximate native-like pronunciation. These considerations are relevant to the interesting broader questions posed in regard to appropriate L2 learning objectives from researchers in the rapidly growing field of World Englishes (He and Li 2009).

The appropriate question to ask is not "how closely" the L2 learner can approach target norms. Rather, it is which components of the L2 grammar are most useful and most easily attainable, at each stage of L2 development and at each stage of *academic achievement*. The adoption of content-based L2 teaching models helps resolve this issue by focusing the greatest attention on those aspects of grammar that students need for specific text comprehension and expressive tasks (Haley and Austin 2004; Hamel and Francis 2006; Stoller 2004). In contrast, a prescriptive approach to attaining native-speaker "norms" in the abstract suffers from two serious difficulties:

1. It fails to recognize that advances in L2 learning are systematic, in some ways analogous to the stages that children pass through in L1 acquisition. In other words, even L2 learners' grammatical errors are evidence of constructed knowledge, termed "interlanguage." While at the beginner levels it is still incomplete and deficient, advanced levels of interlanguage competence easily and completely serve certain academic purposes. For example, many L2 tasks can be carried out without any loss of comprehension, even if expressive skills lag behind. But even at beginner levels, the L2 competence that learners have constructed is usable for many academic purposes, an insight that is lost if students' deficiencies are simply viewed as evidence of being more or less distant from an arbitrarily fixed target-level standard. (For more discussion on how content-based L2 teaching is implemented, see Hernández 2005, Snow 2001, and Stoller 2007.)

2. The inordinate time and resources devoted to certain lower-level linguistic features that are of marginal academic utility is wasteful and inefficient. (NB: This advisory does not apply to the mastery of lower-level abilities required for skillful decoding and fluent reading in the L2, which happen to be of paramount academic utility. We will return to this topic in chapters 7 and 9.)

The concept of modularity can be applied to L2 teaching because of the kind of unevenness in L2 development that is not characteristic of primary-language development to the same degree. The same components and modules make up both L1 and L2 knowledge and ability. However, in the case of L1 the greater evenness of development of the components of language ability obscures the underlying heterogeneity of its organization. Uneven development in L2, on the other hand, is usually the rule. It would not be considered exceptional, for example, for a literate L2 speaker to have acquired an extensive vocabulary (usable and functional entries for a large number of words that are "defective" in some respects) and to have mastered aspects of the L2 grammar useful for written discourse, but to experience continued difficulties related to the use of certain core grammatical domains. This heterogeneity in L2 learning can even be turned to the learner's advantage, strong subsystems bootstrapping the weaker ones. But even short of leveraging the development of these late-emerging subsystems, the more developmentally advanced components may compensate for incompleteness elsewhere. (Note that this approach differs from those that deny that interlanguage competence is incomplete in any way.)

2.4 New Democracy in South Africa: The Challenge of a Multilingual Language Policy

The experiment in multilingual educational policy in South Africa offers a unique counterpoint to the cases mentioned in the previous section, those of the former subordinate languages that today benefit from official language-planning authority in Europe and North America. Despite the many contrasts, the same dual-language learning right considerations apply. To review:

1. availability to child language learners of the most efficient and effective L2 instruction, especially when the L2 is a NL of wider communication and of academic literacy, or a NL newly granted official status and required for full citizenship; and

2. optimal conditions for childhood development of higher-order language abilities through the medium of the language(s) in which comprehension is adequate.

South Africa's 1996 constitution provides for 11 official languages, English and Afrikaans carried over from the pre–majority rule period, plus 9 of the major ILs: Sepedi, Sesotho, Setswana, siSwati, Tshivenda, Xitsonga, isiNdebele, isiXhosa, and isiZulu (Bamgbose 2000, 108–110). The final report of the Language Plan Task Group (LANGTAG), released the same year, sets out an ambitious multilingual policy (LANGTAG 1996, cited in Reagan 2001):

- Each citizen should have access to all spheres of society through the development and maintenance, in both speech and writing, of any official language.
- All South Africans should have access to L2 learning of another national language.
- An affirmative developmental program should be established for the previously disfavored IL.

The accelerating ascendancy of English in postapartheid South Africa, however, poses a unique challenge for democratic language policy. For example, the progressive displacement of Afrikaans within the realm of public education, eventually reducing it to a rightful place alongside the other national, indigenous languages, appears to be a necessary and inevitable task for the new South African democracy.

Much more than simply a lingua franca of interethnic communication, English appears poised in the short term to occupy a commanding position in all levels of the public education system. Kamwangamalu (2003) reports that in addition to Afrikaans, other ILs have been subject to the pressures of a shift to English, in this case within their traditional areas of use. Few scholars seem to explicitly view the emerging South African multiglossia in these terms. Nevertheless, any objective assessment of the trends over the past decade—prefigured, in fact, almost 30 years ago by the language-conscious rebellious youth of Soweto—point inescapably toward such an outcome (Bersten 2001; Louw 2004). For now, English remains as one of 11 official languages, perhaps a temporary and politically expedient designation in accord with the present transitional period.

In South Africa today, a *long-term transitional* bilingual instructional program (combination of transitional and maintenance, with an emphasis on transitional) for Afrikaans-speaking L2 English learners is posed as a linguistic right and citizen responsibility. This objective is analogous to the rights and responsibilities of Russophone Latvians, Lithuanians, and Estonians; Spanish speakers in Catalonia; and English-speaking residents of Quebec. Such a rationalization of multilingual policy and additive bilingual instruction, which openly projects the necessity of a transition to high levels of proficiency in the new de facto NL, is the most effective means for efficient L2 learning. Evidently, the same high expectations for English as a L2 should apply to speakers of all of the ILs.

The evolving compartmentalization of such a tiered multiglossia can still work to the benefit of the official ILs. In fact, it could provide for the most favorable language-learning program design for the continued development of South Africa's ILs. Specifically, a robust language development curriculum, based on children's complete knowledge of the core grammar of their primary MT/L1, could play a prominent role in early development of academic literacy. This language development objective would be complemented by the early introduction of L2-medium instruction in the new de facto NL:

- IL (mother tongue) + *English*,
- IL_1 (mother tongue) + IL_2 (L2) + *English*,
- *English* + second (or more) official heritage language(s), depending on the perspective of each language learner.

Unlike early-exit transitional programs, a long-term transitional bilingual program implies no extinction of non-NL-medium instruction from the bilingual curriculum even at the tertiary level, this being a critical program feature of a fully additive model. Transitional program models of the terminal variety, even of the early-exit type, may justifiably concentrate scarce bilingual teaching resources at the grade levels where they are most critical. This feature represents an advance over total exclusion of the nonofficial minority language. Nevertheless, aside from the pedagogical limitations of early-exit transition programs (Hovens 2002), they cannot fully serve a national policy of revitalizing previously disfavored languages (Hamel 2008; King 2004; López 2008; Skutnabb-Kangas 2003). In programs that follow Krashen's (1991) Multiple Threshold model, high-prestige, context-reduced, and cognitively demanding academic subject areas are allocated heavily to the MT/L1. Happily, again, this allocation represents an essential coincidence between optimal learning conditions and promoting a shift in sociolinguistic perceptions regarding functions of "high language" and "low language" in school. For example, in the case of a previously disfavored IL, for those children who speak it as their MT/L1, cognitively demanding, high-prestige, literacy-related content could be delivered through this language, at least in part, during the formative period of early literacy learning. Continued IL-medium instruction in the upper grades must be balanced against the need to progressively increase the weight of English-medium instruction. But in principle, nothing excludes the participation of the officially recognized ILs, in some measure, at all levels through university.

Specifically, narrowing the requirement of NL proficiency for higher education from two to one (Afrikaans or English to English) frees up resources for the development of the official ILs. "Resources" here include both those at the disposal of schools and the cognitive resources that individual language learners can call upon. As a complement to the idea that not all the languages of a multilingual nation can be afforded the same status, there is also a hard limit on the number of L2s for which effective instruction can be provided. There is also a limit on the number of L2s that children normally can be expected to learn. Hastening the elevation of English as the sole academic medium for which proficiency is *required* in all tertiary institutions rationalizes, and democratizes, important language-learning choices. Of course, the goal of higher-education language policy is to make all official languages *available* to students, even as medium of instruction where this is feasible. However, only one NL of wider communication will eventually be sufficient (as entrance requirement) for advanced study, in all fields, unambiguously, and without exception.[5] Without a doubt, knowledge of two or more official languages will enrich and broaden students' advanced study in many ways. In this respect, the new multilingual policy projects an equitable and practical alternative that also happens to be in the best interests of democratic nation building.

In this regard, Skutnabb-Kangas (2000, 498–502) makes a distinction between "necessary individual rights" and "enrichment individual rights." To the first category belongs access to instruction in the MT/L1 *and* the official language of schooling. Skutnabb-Kangas's approach differs in some respects from the dual-language learning right proposed in this chapter. Nevertheless, including *both* MT/L1 and official-NL in the first category represents an important corrective to language policy models that tend to minimize the learning of the official NL, implicitly shifting it to an "enrichment" category.

2.5 A Possible Counterexample from North Africa

One of the most instructive contrasting scenarios to the South African experiment in multilingual education is that of the North African countries of Tunisia, Algeria, and Morocco. Compared with South Africa, these countries are linguistically less diverse. The continued influence of the former colonial language aside (Bourdereau 2006), the principal policy question revolves around the relations between NL-status Arabic and Berber, spoken by a large minority throughout the region, crossing the borders of all three countries. Despite recent decrees that have granted it a limited measure of recognition (e.g., in education, in Morocco), Berber continues to occupy a strictly subordinate IL/vernacular position in regard to the higher realms of schooling and official literacy. Since independence, successive waves of activism on the part of the Berber-speaking communities have insistently called attention to deep-rooted linguistic and cultural discrimination (Errihani 2008; Tilmatine and Suleiman 1996). Demands for official recognition and equality have specifically included the proposal that Berber no longer be excluded from school (Faiq 1999; Iazzi 1998).

Studies by Wagner (1993, 1998) and Wagner, Spratt, and Ezzaki (1989), conducted in Morocco, are among the best-known attempts to address the question of medium of literacy instruction and schooling, comparing the achievement of Arabic- and Berber-speaking children. A recurring theme in these reports is a critique of the 1953 UNESCO recommendation in favor of L1 literacy instruction for speakers of vernacular languages. While Wagner is careful not to propose an outright rejection of the "L1 literacy advantage hypothesis," a clear tendency is discernable in the interpretation of the Arabic-Berber findings: that there may turn out to be no difference, or one that is of little consequence, between initial literacy instruction in children's primary language and initial literacy instruction in a language children do not understand upon school entry. This more cumbersome, but more precise, formulation of the distinction is preferable to the often confusing comparison between "L1 literacy" and "L2 literacy." In the L2 literacy research literature, the latter designation often leaves unspecified both previous exposure to L1 literacy and actual linguistic competence attained in the L2. The Moroccan studies avoid this confusion, allowing for independent examination of their findings. This is a welcome detail because the studies serve as an important contrast not only to the South African language policy objectives but also to research that views as problematic exclusive L2 literacy for vernacular-language speakers who are either monolingual or L2 beginners.

Before we examine the Moroccan studies, it is necessary to be explicit about what the current version of the "L1 literacy advantage hypothesis" would, or should, in fact propose, 50 years after the historic UNESCO paper. Let us begin with what, today, it would *not* claim:

1. That under all circumstances initial L1 literacy is the only viable alternative or even that it would be preferable, across the board, regardless of external sociolinguistic circumstances.

Without citing any, Wagner (1998, 181) asserts that "[m]any language specialists have come to regard mother-tongue literacy as the natural panacea for children from minority-language backgrounds who are at risk for school failure."

2. That exclusive initial L2 literacy cannot provide adequate conditions for successful learning of reading and writing, or that as a rule (e.g., "virtually always") it is inferior to primary language–medium instruction.

Yet Wagner (1998, 180) argues that "[t]he present findings provide an important counterexample to the generally accepted claim that schoolchildren who must study in a second language are virtually always at a disadvantage—or are *at risk* for failure—in their primary school years."

Even the most cursory survey of bilingual teaching alternatives for emergent readers around the world shows that both point #1 and point #2 are false (C. Baker 2006; Bialystok 2007; Peregoy and Boyle 2008). As it turns out, neither point is widely accepted in the field. Rather, a much more modest proposal (#3) is at the center of the debate between exclusionary and pluralist language policy perspectives on literacy teaching:

3. For the preliterate monolingual child or preliterate beginning L2 learner, an additional risk factor may be introduced when literacy is taught exclusively through the medium of a language in which the learner possesses only minimal linguistic competencies. Conversely, in principle, including the L1 in the literacy-learning curriculum stands as a facilitating resource.

To be sure, under favorable developmental conditions the simultaneous "dual-task," L2 learning plus literacy learning in L2 (Verhoeven 2000), may pose no insurmountable obstacle to either learning objective. Under certain highly favorable conditions, it may even make available the kind of cognitive challenge that *fosters* the development of higher-order language proficiencies in young children. K. Johnson and Swain (1997) describe such L2 immersion program options. But none of the previously mentioned sociolinguistic limitations that might preclude L1 literacy or reports of successful initial L2 literacy learning stand as decisive evidence for any version of the "no-difference" hypothesis. Nor do they constitute evidence against the claim that initial literacy learning that includes preliterate children's strongly dominant or only language facilitates the task of learning how to read and write. Presenting another alternative view, Rossell (2005) offers counterarguments that call into question the efficacy of bilingual instruction for literacy learning in general.

Given that nowadays the "stages theory" (the postponement of L2 literacy to provide exclusive L1 literacy during an initial primary-language "consolidation period") is largely discredited, the "L1 literacy advantage hypothesis" actually puts forward a more modest claim: The inclusion into the beginning literacy program of decodable texts and instructional materials that coincide with the preliterate child's language-specific knowledge represents an important learning advantage. The task of mapping linguistic forms (the phonemes and syllables of the sound system, and morphemes and morphological patterns) to an orthography presents fewer obstacles. Relevant grammatical knowledge at the sentence level and language-specific lexical knowledge expedite processing of written text and favor higher levels of comprehension.

This "advantage" may turn out to be more important in some bilingual circumstances than others. And certainly, the possible "risk factor" associated with excluding the primary language from initial literacy is to be weighed against external social and material determinants (no available texts that are decodable by beginning readers, minimal presence of the vernacular in print, community opposition to L1 literacy). Often these considerations are overriding and one-sidedly in favor of initial L2 literacy teaching. However, in the face of widespread cultural/political mobilization on the part of a disenfranchised language minority, it becomes more difficult to sustain the claim that sociolinguistic limitations preclude vernacular-medium literacy instruction in any proportion or to any degree. (For historical background regarding Arabization policies, the question of Berber language rights, and recent developments in Algeria and Morocco, see Maddy-Weitzman 2006, Marley 2005, and Mostari 2001.) One starting point, then, would be to contrast:

- a "weak L1 literacy advantage hypothesis" (as formulated in point #3, explicitly disavowing the evidently untenable points #1 and #2) and
- a "strong no-difference hypothesis" (it is not clear that Wagner actually argues for the strong version, which has recently gained currency in some quarters).

The authors of the Moroccan study pursue the "no-difference" hypothesis—although, again, they are careful to step back from its strongest claims—in their analysis of Arabic literacy achievement in a longitudinal study that began with 166 children in 1st grade (83 Berber-speaking and 83 Arabic-speaking upon school entry). However, a closer look at the study should prompt us to step back even further from a conclusion that the findings provide counterevidence to the claim that use of the MT/L1 in literacy instruction counts as a facilitative factor.

Comparing L1 and L2 literacy learning continues to be an important object of investigation. Among other things, it can provide practitioners with valuable guidelines on how to ensure the most favorable learning conditions for L2 literacy. In fact, the "L2 (literacy) first" alternative will continue to be the most feasible and practicable for large numbers of children whose vernacular language is not in a position to assume the role of medium of literacy learning. At any rate, it should be uncontroversial that recognizing the various limitations on the use of the L1 in school is different from proposing that the L1 cannot play any useful role in the development of literacy-related language proficiencies.

In this regard, the language contact situation selected for the Moroccan study makes for a test case that is less clear than one would hope for. At the time of the study (mid to late 1980s), by the authors' account Standard Arabic enjoyed a broad attraction for Berber and Moroccan Arabic speakers alike (as it does today, notwithstanding recent popular demands for upgrading Berber). Standard Arabic has no effective competitor as the official language of schooling and literacy, and it is the liturgical language of undisputed prestige and reverence shared by all. Arabic in Morocco is an imposed NL, but it is widely viewed as the target L2 by speakers of Berber—doubtless universally so by families who send their children to school. With motivation so high and opportunity at hand for L2 learning of Arabic, we should not be surprised that Berber-speaking children in contact with the NL of their country and the sacred language of their religion will mark consistent and even rapid advances in L2 learning. By all accounts, in any bilingual school setting similar to the one described by the authors, postponing L2 literacy would be entirely artificial, even inconceivable in some cases. At the same time, significant advances in L2 literacy by Berber-speaking children who remain enrolled in school, parallel to their learning of the L2, is more or less what we should expect. In other words, if it is the contribution of a linguistic factor that requires our scrutiny, a less extreme diglossic separation would make for a better test case.

This compartmentalization of language use in Morocco calls attention to another methodological question. If a well-defined contrast between L1 and L2 literacy is important to the analysis, the L2 part of this condition is probably satisfied for the young Berber speakers even if many of them had the benefit of prekindergarten contact with Arabic. But for the speakers of colloquial Moroccan Arabic, literacy in Standard Arabic may not count as the most typical case of L1 literacy. The authors in fact remark on the considerable variation from one country to another and the linguistic distance between the nonstandard Moroccan dialect and the Standard Arabic of writing and schooling. Wagner (1998, 176) goes on to compare the extent of this separation with that of English dialects, for example: "Moroccan Arabic speakers can be thought of as learning literacy in their mother tongue in the same sense that non-standard dialect English speakers...are learning mother-tongue literacy when they learn to read English." While it would be correct to describe the variation in Arabic in terms of a continuum, the structural divergence between standard and vernacular dialects might represent a significant linguistic factor, not to be easily dismissed. Versteegh (2001, 189), for example, likens it to that of a "hypothetical modern France, where all newspapers and books are written in Latin" (p. 189). As another example, Haeri (2003) points to the differences between Classical Arabic and the Egyptian vernacular.

The vernacular-standard divergence in Arabic as it affects language learning is in fact an important research question related to this particular case of L1 and L2 literacy. In her assessment of Palestinian Arabic speakers' reading skills, Saiegh-Haddad (2003b) describes the standard variety, typically first encountered by children in school "almost as a second language" (p. 432); Abu-Rabia (2000, 148) makes a similar observation. Saiegh-Haddad hypothesized that the structural differences between the two varieties, which extend beyond vocabulary to wide-ranging contrasts in phonology and morphosyntax, are an important factor in the development of basic reading skills. Results from examining children's performance on a series of phonemic awareness tasks in kindergarten and 1st grade showed that the difference between standard and nonstandard spoken forms did interfere with children's ability to isolate phonemes in both initial and final positions. Summarizing the results, Saiegh-Haddad (2003b, 444) emphasizes the "unique complexity present in learning to read in Modern Standard Arabic":

Whereas in other linguistic contexts, beginning readers come to the reading task with sufficient knowledge and experience with the phonological structures that they are taught to decode, Arabic native children are required to simultaneously master the oral representation of a set of diglossic structures that are not available to them from their oral language experience and to discover how these structures are mapped onto the specific orthography. The present results show this task to remain a serious challenge for children even at the end of the first grade.

In a related study, Abu-Rabia (2000) found that early exposure to Standard Arabic during preschool and kindergarten significantly enhanced children's performance on reading comprehension tasks two years later, over that of a control group that received exposure only to spoken Arabic. Along the same lines, Ibrahim and Aharon-Peretz (2005) present evidence from experiments that measured the priming effect within and between spoken Arabic, literary Arabic, and Hebrew. In regard to this index, literary Arabic maintains the status of a L2 in the cognitive system of adult Arabic speakers.

The core of the Berber-Arabic study involved tracking the original cohort of beginning readers through 3rd and 5th grades, carrying out a battery of measures including letter knowledge, word decoding, and sentence- and paragraph-level comprehension in Arabic. A graph of the results (see Wagner, Spratt, and Ezzaki 1989,

41, fig. 1) shows convergence in the later grades: a significant gap in achievement during year 1 between Berber speakers and Arabic speakers progressively narrows in years 3 and 5 (in both of the latter years, the difference in favor of the Arabic speakers becomes statistically nonsignificant). Here, the authors seem to distance themselves from the strongest version of the no-difference hypothesis, pointing out that the Arabic-speaking students maintained their superiority throughout the years despite the convergence in 3rd and 5th grades. This could be taken as evidence for some degree of "MT advantage" in the earlier years, which "diminishes substantially" by 5th grade (Wagner 1993, 176–180). This qualification (admitting the possibility of an "early" or "temporary" MT advantage) is underscored by the authors' breakdown of the Berber-speaking cohort between those who had benefited from Quraanic preschool instruction, in Arabic, and those who had not. The latter group visibly lags behind all others, appearing to maintain this disadvantage through to 5th grade (p. 42, fig. 2). In other words, entering 1st grade with preschool L2 instruction might facilitate L2 literacy development. Children having less preschool contact with the L2 appear not to benefit from L2 literacy instruction to the same degree as their Berber-speaking Quraanic-preschool peers.

To their credit, the researchers provide readers with these important details, specifying the actual composition of the cohort and how different subgroups performed on the experimental measures. And it is here that the most serious qualifications must be placed on the strength of their claims. Longitudinal studies present some of the most difficult challenges to investigators. A particularly troublesome factor in bilingual communities outside of the main urban centers is the interaction between sharp sociolinguistic imbalances and school nonattendance/abandonment. Universal obligatory school attendance is often not the norm. In the study of literacy and bilingualism in Mexico, our project faced these same limitations, compelling us to take a much more conservative approach to the kinds of hypothesis we could put forth. As it turns out, the grade-level comparison that appears to indicate the most visible convergence between Berber and Arabic speakers (year 5) is at least in part the product of successive stages of selection. To begin with, the 166 original 1st graders belong to that sector of the school-age population that is sent to school. Five years later, only 47 were in 5th grade (19 had advanced to 3rd grade; 51 had advanced to 4th grade; and 49 were lost outright, apparently having left school at some point along the way). Recognizing this problem, the authors point out that, in the end, the average grade level attained for both language groups was the same, as was the dropout rate for each (Wagner, Spratt, and Ezzaki 1989, 46). While this outcome, interesting as it is, helps control the damage, it does not allow us to dispense with the thorny detail of exactly who was left standing after five years of exclusive L2 literacy instruction. A sample attrition of such magnitude compels us to ask, for example: (1) At what grade level did each successive group of

Berber-speaking and Arabic-speaking school leavers drop out? (2) What level of Arabic literacy would each of them have attained upon leaving? (3) Among the 51 students in 4th grade, for whom apparently no test data are available, how might their inclusion among the 5th graders have affected the Berber-Arabic comparison, if they had been promoted along with their peers?

In the end, pursuing the elusive no-difference hypothesis will not be easy. On another level, it shifts our attention away from what is most interesting about the "L2 literacy first" scenario. Framing the question differently and starting with a more analytic approach toward different aspects of the "dual-task" problem of L2 literacy may lead to a better understanding of how child L2 learners actually overcome it (when they do). When all is said and done, this kind of research program might lead to maximizing the effectivity of L2 literacy—again the only practical option, for now, for many vernacular-language speakers. We should also keep in mind that a correctly implemented L2-literacy-teaching program provides an important source of target language input for learning L2 vocabulary and grammar, including for child L2 learners. Two questions immediately arise: If the key programmatic ingredient of successful L2 literacy instruction is an early and strong start on L2 learning, what are the key features of such an instructional model? What role can children's primary language play, for example, as part of a biliteracy approach?

2.6 Program Design Based on a Concept from Sociolinguistics

The concept of diglossia becomes pivotal in the rationalization of multilingual language policy in education. While static views of diglossia may envision a kind of "prescriptive" approach to maintaining the existing functional distribution of vernaculars and official languages, applying the concept of diglossia as an analytical tool for the purpose of democratizing language learning leads to a different set of proposals. The logic of the former approach has led advocates of language revitalization to question the inclusion of ILs in school, or to minimize the development of writing in an IL with a predominantly oral tradition. Applying diglossia with one eye on history and the other on multilingual school reform places language planning within an objective and scientific framework. It foresees the conflict and transitional instability of shifting boundaries and expectations, and charts a course that will manage and channel this conflict toward a new relative stability.

In her analysis of educational language policy in Haiti and in Trinidad and Tobago, Youssef (2002) applies this approach to the contact situations of French and English with their creole counterparts. Arguing against proposals for monolingual Haitian Creole education, she makes the case for a *bilingual* policy: (1) the consolidation of Haitian Creole as an independent language requiring continued status and corpus planning, and (2) early introduction of French-medium instruction. Continuing to view French as a foreign language *subject* simply contributes to perpetuating the linguistic gulf that separates the bilingual elite from the vast monolingual Haitian Creole–speaking majority. A bilingual elementary school curriculum could easily apply the same distribution of L1 and L2 that today represents a broad consensus among bilingual educators internationally. In this model, beginning in the early grades, core academic subjects are taught in the MT/L1, and the L2 is introduced in other subjects. L2-medium teaching begins in context-embedded content and nonacademic realms, gradually transitioning to parity in the context-reduced academic curriculum (see Echevarría and Graves 2007, 13–19; Krashen 1991). The L2 shifts from subject to *medium of instruction*. That is, this model promotes *content-based L2 instruction*, the most effective and efficient method for child L2 learning. Wesche and Skehan (2002) discuss strong and weak forms of content-based instruction, the strongest form of which (here taken as synonymous with immersion) integrates into the content-based curriculum the systematic teaching of the L2 grammar.

A dual-language program model that calculates precisely at which stage which school subject should transition to L2-medium instruction, based on an analysis of available context embedding and children's advancing L2 proficiency, puts an end to a particularly unfortunate debate: until what grade should L2-medium instruction be postponed (see Bamgbose 2000)? Properly contextualized comprehensible L2-medium instruction need never be postponed. It begins with the teacher's welcoming greeting on the first day of preschool. The initial choice of subject areas and ratio between MT/L1 and NL/L2 (90%-10%, 80%-20%, 70%-30%, etc.) is determined by teachers in consultation with their community. It will surely vary from school to school, on the basis of considerations that educators and parents are best qualified to judge.

Instructional compartmentalization, another key feature of immersion teaching, also provides the most favorable conditions for ensuring the future of Haitian Creole as an independent language of instruction. The peculiarities of French colonialism that excluded other European competitors from the western portion of Hispañola gave rise to a relatively homogenous Haitian Creole, clearly differentiated as well from the former colonial language. Today, this accident of history can be exploited as a bilingual asset—not, as it could have turned out to be, an insurmountable multilingual challenge. Diglossic separation applied to language learning in the classroom can now be pressed into the service of additive child bilingual development. In contrast, the difficulty of demarcating Standard English from Trinidad Creole, according to Youssef, tends to block the emergence of a bilingual, and specifically *biliterate*, curriculum—again, unlike the case of Haiti, where the additive bilingual objective does not face this particular obstacle.

Since not every language must serve every function, MT/L1 and NL/L2 are also distributed throughout the curriculum according to what learners actually need to promote the development of higher-order language abilities. If the NL/L2, or other L2 of international communication, primarily provides students access to academic texts, instruction can be streamlined, concentrating valuable teaching resources on those components of L2 proficiency that are fundamental for developing strong decoding skills in reading and for text comprehension. Eliminating standards of performance for certain nonessential (to this purpose) aspects of oral expression, for example, maximizes achievement by redirecting scarce pedagogical resources in a strategic way.

Along similar lines, recognizing the present stage of evolution and level of standardization of a previously excluded vernacular allows a more flexible approach, for example, toward written expression. Children's development in this essential academic language proficiency need never be held up pending orthographic reform or production of pedagogical manuals, teaching grammars, or primers. Similar guidelines would apply to student lexical borrowing and codeswitching (Schaengold 2003). Compartmentalization does not allocate language use for the purpose of imposing artificial norms and purist standards. In the case of an IL, it promotes the normal, unmarked use of the previously excluded language during specific parts of the school day. (The concepts of diglossia and compartmentalization have been applied in interesting ways to other conflictive multilingual situations in New Caledonia (Fillol and Vernaudon 2004), Taiwan (Yeh, Chan, and Cheng 2004), and Singapore (C. Tan 2006).)

The research on child bilingualism prompts us, today, to discard language-teaching models that restrict primary-grade instruction to any one language. Policy makers in multilingual systems are particularly ill-advised to impose such restrictions, even under the guise of promoting the development of subordinate, historically disfavored languages. Bilingual instructional models need to be based on current research that prioritizes both an early introduction of content-based L2 instruction (immersion) and the development of higher-order language abilities through a language, or languages, that children understand.

Material limitations (among others) may prevent offering bilingual instruction to all child L2 learners. Where such limitations are present, effective L2-medium instruction is still possible, but it faces the task of maximizing language development under conditions that may not be optimal for all learners. In this case, attention to research on the linguistic and cognitive aspects of language learning takes on greater importance because the pedagogical challenges are more formidable. Again, it would be an error to dismiss as unworkable, or unprincipled, all L2-medium instructional models that lack a L1 curricular component. In fact, research on the effectivity of this model, even if opinions differ in regard to the conclusions drawn by some of its proponents, offers important insights on how to improve L2 immersion methods. The most effective bilingual instructional models incorporate L2 immersion into their overall curriculum plan; therefore, any theoretical or practical advance from this field is welcome (Curtain and Dahlberg 2010; Herrera, Pérez, and Escamilla 2010; Muñoz 2006). The converse restriction, exclusive L1 instruction that postpones L2 immersion for an extended period, represents a different kind of obstacle, one that is easier to explain to bilingual educators who might continue to adhere to this outdated model.

Putting all this into a historical perspective, it must be said that UNESCO has not advanced significantly in its concept of bilingual literacy in the half-century since its 1953 declaration on vernacular languages in education. It was cited approvingly at the beginning of this chapter, and the declaration remains a point of reference today in the discussion of literacy development in L2s (International Reading Association 2001). But UNESCO persists in an important error that should have been corrected by now. An updated Principle II still argues for a version of the "stages approach," the postponement of content-based L2 teaching during the beginning stage of L2 learning: "the introduction of the second language ... as a subject of instruction the amount of which should be increased gradually and which should not become the medium of instruction until the pupils are sufficiently familiar with it" (UNESCO 2003, 32).

In this field, in which it often seems that many more things are at stake than just the question of optimal child language development, it is helpful to remember not to confound what we might want to believe about bilingualism with empirical evidence from research. For example, in the context of the highly charged debates about linguistic pluralism, it may be tempting to anticipate possible questions in dispute, and place a (+) where "the other side" might place a (–), and vice versa. This method, however, makes for very bad science.

The following chapter will review research from other subfields of child bilingual development that are directly relevant for educational language policy: the interaction between the child's languages, and how the child gains access to concepts and processing strategies through L1 and L2. From the examination of language-learning situations around the world, we return to the study of bilingualism in one community. The same basic principles outlined in this chapter should apply there as well.

# 3

The Debate on the Nature of Bilingual Proficiency
Distinguishing between Different Kinds of Language Ability

The previous chapter provided some background on the school language policy debate. That discussion opens the way for us now to consider the problems of bilingualism and literacy learning in a concrete language contact situation similar to some of those that we examined from afar. Here, we will examine the findings from a comparative follow-up to the study that was described in chapter 1. The follow-up study focused on the two skill areas that receive the most attention in school: reading and writing. Four classes of bilingual 3rd and 5th graders were chosen from the same school in Mexico to confirm the tendencies that emerged among the 45 children in 2nd, 4th, and 6th grades in the previous phase of the study (see figure 1.2). Since the 2nd-, 4th-, and 6th-grade cohort had been selected to reflect an average to above-average achievement range, the idea was to see if similar patterns of performance in Spanish and Nahuatl would hold up with the 3rd and 5th graders if the entire student body at each grade level were evaluated. Like the 2nd, 4th, and 6th graders, the 3rd and 5th graders were instructed in all subjects exclusively or almost exclusively in Spanish. This presented us again with the unique opportunity to examine the application of literacy skills learned through one language to literacy tasks in another language that children understand, but in which they have not had the opportunity to practice these skills.

Recall that in chapter 2 the discussion of bilingual instructional models centered on the closely related teaching objectives of effective L2 learning and development of academic-related language abilities. Implicit in this discussion is the problem of applying academic literacy skills learned through one language to school tasks that involve reading and writing in another language, a research problem that was not addressed directly. This is the question we will examine here.

As we will see, the results offer a new vantage point on the idea of interdependence between the linguistic domains of L1 and L2. We will also look at the related concepts of Common Underlying Proficiency, Central Processing System, Cognitive Academic Language Proficiency, and transfer. The researchers wanted to explore which aspects of language proficiency may be more interdependent and which aspects may be more autonomous in the way they are represented and put to use in actual performance. For example, what precisely does "interdependence" mean? What are the conditions under which skills stored in a Common Underlying Proficiency can be accessed? In particular, how can they be accessed under special circumstances of language contact—for example, those that involve indigenous languages (ILs)?

In the bilingual education literature, the term "transfer" appears to refer to a different kind of interaction between L1 and L2 than it does in the field of second language learning. In the first case, the focus appears to be on the use of shared resources. In the second, the interaction is between one grammatical subsystem and another. So, an attempt will be made in this discussion to find a common ground, at the level of terminology at least.

This chapter will also present an initial overview of the concept of Cognitive Academic Language Proficiency, primarily to introduce the controversy surrounding its application to child bilingualism. Chapter 7 will examine its components in more detail.

In field studies of language use, patterns of results often emerge and analyses produce findings that were predictable but interesting in some way; or neither hypothesized result turns out to be more predictable than the other. Sometimes results are unanticipated, and from time to time they are surprising—these are the most interesting. However, all results evoke broader discussions: about a theory in dispute, about how they might be related to a finding from another study, or about a practical application somewhere in the real world of language learners. In discussing implications and applications, the natural tendency is to go too far. Experts in each field who review and comment on research reports have the very important job of keeping this tendency under control. There are two options:

1. Authors can restrict the discussion of findings scrupulously to what the data allow for.

2. Same as #1 because anything else would be incoherent. However, after the authors have signaled clearly where the discussion of findings concludes, it is sometimes helpful to speculate about what the study might suggest for further research: to refine questions that are still too coarse-grained, to reformulate hypotheses, or to suggest new ones for the next phase of work. As a rule, in speculation, as in any long journey, the most conservative and parsimonious approach most clearly illuminates the next steps forward.

The findings from our descriptive study of the development of academic abilities in two languages fall in between the first two categories of result: "predictable but interesting" and "unanticipated – most interesting." As noted earlier, our interest was in taking a closer look at which aspects of language competence and language use may be more interdependent and which may be more autonomous. But a much more powerful research design will be required to provide data that can weigh in on this question directly. With this in mind, our hope is that the descriptions will help others construct such a research program. The following chapters will examine the results of other investigations that do bear more directly on the many related questions of L1-L2 interdependence. This chapter will need to keep the discussion of findings and the points of the broader controversy clearly separated, the first evoking the research questions and theoretical concepts raised in the second. These are the two parallel threads alluded to in chapter 1 that will run through the discussions to come.

3.1 First Language and Second Language in Literacy Learning

Learning to read and write in one's first or primary language is an opportunity that many literacy learners simply take for granted as the norm. However, in situations of extensive societal multilingualism it is more common than not that children are taught to read and write in a L2, one that they use less frequently than their L1, or over which they have only partial command, or even none at all. As we saw in chapter 2, no single prescription would be adequate to meet the learning needs of all bilingual beginning readers and writers.

For many investigators who study how children become literate, the circumstances of L2 literacy present the most interesting cases. They offer opportunities to examine situations in which the linguistic and cognitive variables and social relations interact in ways that reflect degrees of imbalance not present in the more typical L1 literacy scenario. (See Grabe 2002 for an introduction to some of the outstanding research questions, in particular, the Language Threshold Hypothesis. Also see Miller et al. 2006 on cross-linguistic interaction, for example, between oral language skills in L1 and literacy attainment in L2.) In the study of L2 literacy, key aspects of learning and development become salient. In some ways, this is the context of our study of literacy development in the indigenous communities of San Isidro and San Miguel: literacy learning in the NL, which is the L2 of many 1st graders. For most of them, probably, early exposure to Spanish in different ways (e.g., via radio and television) has ensured a minimal level of listening comprehension. A significant number are probably already proficient speakers. Another portion are beginners with little or no knowledge of Spanish. Of particular interest to us was the degree to which comprehension skills and literacy-related discourse competencies, learned in school through the medium of Spanish, would be available to the students when presented with similar tasks in Nahuatl. The idea was to examine the questions posed at the start of this chapter, taking as an example a situation of bilingual development where basically only one language is used for literacy learning.

In large part, the concepts Common Underlying Proficiency and Cognitive Academic Language Proficiency can be traced to the work of Cummins (1981, 1991, 2000). Two observations from the Mexican study suggested the need to refine the overarching concept of interdependence, depicted in the well-known model of the "double icebergs" (figure 3.1):

1. Parallel tendencies in both languages on measures of academic ability suggest that the basic idea of interdependence and the related construct of Cognitive Academic Language Proficiency are universally applicable.

2. Comparing the students' performance in Spanish and in their IL suggests a more fine-grained approach to analyzing how, in bilinguals, knowledge of one kind "depends on" knowledge of other kinds. One starting point could be to distinguish between language-*specific* components and language-*independent* components. This distinction appears to be entirely consistent with Cummins's model of autonomous and interacting domains of language proficiency. At the same time, it suggests that the model would benefit from elaboration and fine-tuning, the subject of the next section. The objective here is to extend Cummins's hypotheses—to ask how the different domains of language proficiency may be autonomous and how they interact.

In the following sections, an elaboration of Cummins's model is proposed as a tentative descriptive scheme for the purpose of interpreting results from assessments of language ability in bilinguals. The idea behind the proposal is that it might describe this category of ability along the same lines, but in a way that emphasizes

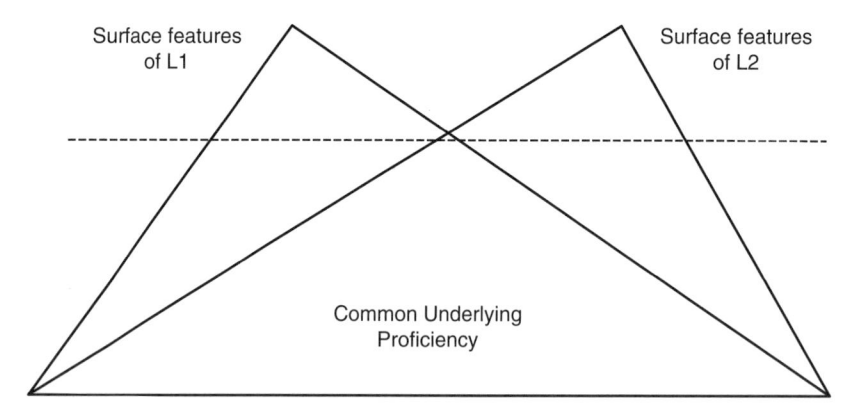

Figure 3.1
The Common Underlying Proficiency model (Cummins 1991)

the distinction between the linguistic knowledge components and conceptual knowledge. The findings of the Mexican study themselves fall short of lending support to the hypotheses associated with interdependence, Common Underlying Proficiency, and Cognitive Academic Language Proficiency; rather, they suggest directions for further research along the lines of a "three-component model" consisting of:

- the L1 linguistic knowledge components of language ability,
- the L2 linguistic knowledge components, and
- a Common Underlying Proficiency that is largely not "language-bound."

3.2 Concepts of Bilingual Proficiency: Background to the Debate

There is now a broad consensus among bilingual educators that a complex interdependence of some kind exists between L1 and L2 linguistic knowledge, and skills, of different kinds, learned through L1 and L2. Transfer is also widely viewed as one of the principal resources available to the L2 learner.

Both concepts are associated with the notion of a Common Underlying Proficiency (CUP), related in turn to the well-known distinction between Basic Interpersonal Communicative Skills (BICS) and Cognitive Academic Language Proficiency (CALP), first proposed by Cummins (1979b). Today, after undergoing a number of useful refinements, the BICS-CALP distinction continues to be an important point of reference among the contending models in the research on bilingualism. From the beginning, however, differentiating between BICS and CALP has met with vigorous challenge. Today Cummins's model is still subject to criticism, in large part from approaches that can be categorized as "social-interactionist" (Piper 2007). Before we take up the proposed elaboration of the CUP model, a brief summary of the arguments will help to frame the important issues.

The distinction between interpersonal face-to-face conversational ability and cognitively demanding academic language ability[1] (BICS and CALP) is questioned on a number of points. Critics focus on three in particular:

1. On the methodological level, discrete-point assessment of literacy skills and test score data that support the distinction are rejected in principle. According to this view, literacy cannot meaningfully be analyzed as consisting of separate component skills and cannot be evaluated as such by tests. Only integrative assessments (associated with "whole-language" approaches) can provide valid interpretations (Edelsky 1996; Edelsky et al. 1983). Damico (1991) presents a wide-ranging critique of modular theories and discusses why the related methods of discrete-point assessment purportedly lead to findings that lack validity.

2. The notion of cognitively demanding, context-reduced language proficiency is little more than an artifact of the way decontextualized language subskills are

evaluated in school by means of standardized tests. CALP can be reduced, basically, to "test-wiseness." "What Cummins calls skill with academic language is really skill in instructional nonsense" (Edelsky 1996, 76). Consistent with the social-interactionist inclination toward top-down models, apparently no aspect of language proficiency can be studied meaningfully apart from context-embedded and socially grounded events. Processing of language, according to this view, would be described as holistic and integrative in every way; the possibility of analyzing components or "separate skills," for any useful purpose, would be strongly rejected. At most, CALP would be a reflection of the "degree of acculturation to a culture-specific set of norms" rather than a set of abilities that children learn from experience with literacy-related discourse (Troike 1984, 49).

3. CALP is basically a "prescriptive" notion of language proficiency, specific to the cultural setting of school, a narrow definition that perpetuates the divide between school-based literacy and the cultural practices of socially marginalized groups in society. Thus, suggesting that "child input factors" (e.g., the development of higher-order discourse abilities) play a role in literacy learning constitutes a "deficit theory in the making" (Martin-Jones and Romaine 1986, 31); Piper (2007, 208–209) makes a similar claim.

Edelsky's critiques represent by far the strongest version of the whole-language-oriented objections. They basically liquidate all inquiry into component cognitive processes and the universals of language acquisition. Relativist conceptions assign to cultural and social circumstances the primary mechanism that imprints knowledge on a homogeneous and malleable mind. Faltis (2001, 105–106), citing C. Edelsky (personal communication), questions the evidence for viewing CALP as a distinct set of abilities:

Aren't students hypothesizing when they use BICS to say "Becha I win next time"; evaluating when they exclaim in BICS "You're cheating!"; inferring when they say in BICS "So, now you are going to get him, huh?"; generalizing when they say in BICS "It's gonna rain"; and classifying when they argue in BICS that "These over here are the freebies." If the answer is yes, then the distinction falls apart, and consequently so does the argument that achieving CALP is necessary to success in school.

The sharpness of Edelsky's disqualification tends to obscure the pertinent arguments. However, after stripping away side issues and misrepresentations, the substance of the critique appears to turn on the methodological questions related to language assessment outlined above in #1. Consistent with the whole-language-oriented approach, Edelsky et al. apparently eschew any index of language proficiency that focuses analytically on a subcomponent, specific skill, or bottom-up processing mechanism. Not surprisingly, any approach to the study of language proficiency that conceives of a diversity of autonomous and interacting processes will clash head-on with the strong integrativist/top-down theories. A third edition of *With Literacy and Justice for All* (Edelsky 2006) essentially repeats the earlier strident opposition to componential analysis of complex literacy-related abilities for instructional purposes.

Perhaps a more coherent critical assessment of Cummins's model is offered by Romaine (1995) and Martin-Jones and Romaine (1986). The authors seem to object to the idea that CALP-type proficiencies are found in the higher-order language use of all cultures. For them, the conversational discourse (BICS)-CALP distinction "constitutes a spurious language proficiency dichotomy" (p. 30) and a "deficit theory in the making" (p. 31):

> The type of literacy-related skills described by Cummins are, in fact, quite culture-specific: that is, they are specific to the cultural setting of the school. In this setting, only a narrow range of prescribed uses and functions of literacy is seen as legitimate. Moreover, school standards of literacy are seen as contributing in a very direct way to the cognitive development of the child. In our view, CALP can only be understood as appropriate display of schooled language, or as Edelsky et al. (1983) have more aptly put it: "test-wiseness" (1983, p. 6). (Martin-Jones and Romaine 1986, 30)

While more measured in tone than Edelsky's critique, this objection nevertheless suffers from the same basic defect. A strong top-down holistic perspective overrides and minimizes the consideration of component subskills and psycholinguistic factors. Cultural determinants, theoretically, and ethnographic research methods, procedurally, are viewed as paramount.

In an early reply, Cummins and Swain (1983) countered these objections as follows:

1. It is a serious oversimplification to claim that standardized assessment measures essentially test "out-of-context irrelevant nonsense." For a number of purposes, such as research, information from standardized measures is useful, and sometimes invaluable. Regarding questions of validity, evidence shows that "discrete-point" measures of literacy skills correlate highly with results from more "integrative" approaches (e.g., cloze, miscue analysis). In any case, when it comes to language assessment, the dichotomy between "discrete-point" and "integrative" is not as categorical as it is often portrayed.

2. CALP was never conceived of as an expression of "fixed IQ," or any other predetermined intrinsic capacity. Rather, experience with literacy-related discourse and language use that promotes reflection on texts is probably the determining factor in the early development of academic language proficiency.

3. Calling attention to the bottom-up and interactive processes in comprehension, Cummins and Swain point out that decontextualized language use requires a shift of attention on the part of the reader/listener toward language patterns themselves.

The usefulness of (top-down) dependence on different kinds of contextual information depends on the circumstances. Effective comprehension strategies shift between more and less dependence on context.

4. The "deficit theory" charge is unjustified and misleading. To claim that "learner attributes" are related to differential school achievement implies nothing about any purported immutable trait or intrinsic deficiency shared by students from a given social class. For example, variation in "learner attributes" could be related to differences in preschool contact with complex narrative and context-reduced academic-type discourse, early experience with reading and writing, quality of literacy instruction in kindergarten and 1st grade, access to books and the elevated oral genres of one's culture, and early practice with decodable independent-level reading materials. Lack of experience in these realms of language use does not lead to any kind of "deficit"; nor does it cause language impairment or developmental disability.

3.3 A Proposed Modification of Cummins's Model

For educators and researchers who continue to find the concepts CUP and CALP useful, some of the underlying constructs could benefit from a different kind of discussion. In the ongoing exchange with proponents of strong versions of social-constructivist theory, greater precision on some points might help to move it forward. The far-reaching implications of the debate should prompt us to draw out the defining arguments and try to identify where opposing models diverge and where they don't. For example, in the case of the Mexican study, as we attempted to outline the tendencies that emerged in terms of a CUP, the need to distinguish more clearly between two different kinds of transfer became apparent.

The graphic depiction of the "double iceberg" has been useful in contrasting the CUP to the hypothetical model of the Separate Underlying Proficiency, in which no ability network would be shared between L1 and L2. In Cummins's model, L1 and L2 overlap, with a common sector lying "below the surface" in figure 3.1. The separate sectors encompass the "surface features" of the respective linguistic subsystems. The idea behind depicting subsystems that are language-specific and a domain that is held in common (below the surface) goes a long way in explaining how bilinguals put all the different components of language ability to use. However, despite its usefulness, the metaphor of the double iceberg oversimplifies somewhat the complex relationships that are involved. To better portray bilinguals' access to both linguistic knowledge and general world knowledge, it would be useful to expand the model, maintaining a more explicit separation between the linguistic and conceptual domains. As the double iceberg indicates in figure 3.1, L1 and L2 are already represented separately to some important degree. As noted earlier, the two linguistic subsystems begin to differentiate long before young bilinguals are able to reflect upon language forms and be aware of the separation (Genesee 2003). At the same time, L1 and L2 also form part of a larger linguistic system, and they appear to share a single conceptual store.

It also seems that some languages "overlap" more than others in the domains that represent language-specific features (e.g., Spanish and Italian, more so; Italian and Hungarian, less so). For now, we will maintain this feature of the model; intuitively, the idea of overlap in this sense appears to be correct. In chapter 5, another way of looking at the relationship between L1 and L2 will suggest that this may not be the best way to conceptualize how the language subsystems interact and influence each other.

As a first attempt at portraying a more explicit separation between linguistic subsystems and the conceptual system, figure 3.2 suggests that the double iceberg (the separate and "overlapping" representations of L1 and L2) rests upon a Central Operating System (C. Baker 2006) or a Common Underlying Proficiency/Central Processing System (Cummins 2000).

Irrespective of the language in which a person is operating, the thoughts that accompany talking, reading, writing and listening come from the same central engine. When a person owns two or more languages, there is one integrated source of thought. . . . Information processing skills and educational attainment may be developed *through* two languages as well as *through* one language. Cognitive functioning and school achievement may be fed *through* one monolingual channel or equally successfully *through* two well developed language channels. Both channels feed the same central processor (C. Baker 2006, 169–170; emphasis added)

The modification depicted in figure 3.2 might help to get around some of the rough edges in descriptions of the mutual influences between L1 and L2 (interlinguistic connections) and the interactions with other, nonlinguistic, cognitive domains. In the field of bilingual education, all of these have for the most part gone under the single category of "transfer." In the bilingual teacher preparation literature, the shorthand formulation has become almost commonplace:

Bilinguals express their language proficiency in two modes, the native and the second language. Thus the concepts known in one language are transferable to the other. (Williams and Snipper 1990, 54)
A learner can immediately begin to transfer concepts from the first language to the second. (Díaz-Rico and Weed 2001, 37)
Relying on the idea that concepts and skills transfer from one language to another and that students with a strong cognitive base will easily make the transition to a second language, the thesis that CALP should be developed in a student's first language follows. (Lessow-Hurley 2009, 80)
[Students] who learn to read and write in their first language are able to readily transfer those abilities to a second language. (Herrera and Murry 2005, 100)

58   Chapter 3

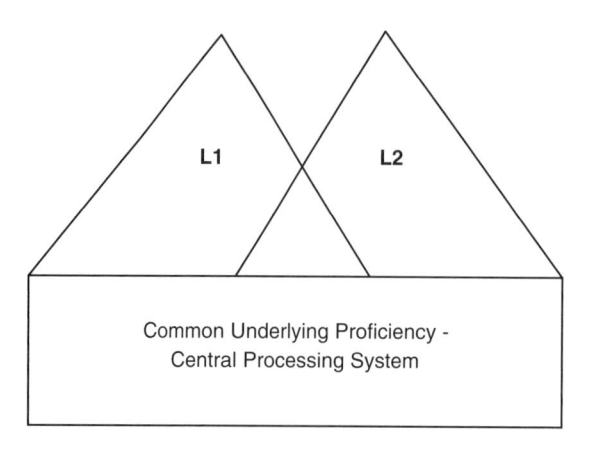

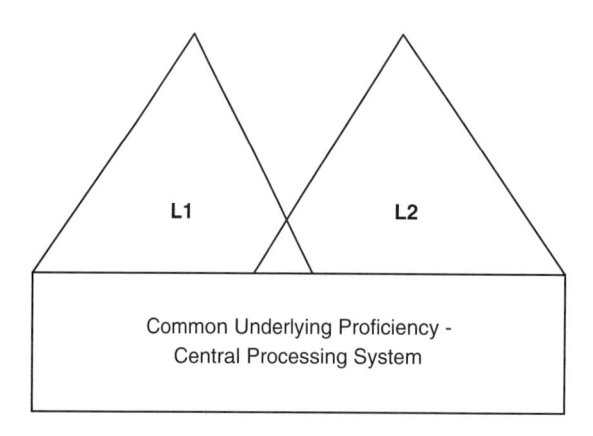

Figure 3.2
Modified Common Underlying Proficiency model. Variant 1: L1 and L2 are typologically "closely related." Variant 2: L1 and L2 are "less closely related."

In our own work, we have fallen into using the same abbreviated formula—for example, referring to "the transfer of encoding strategies from Spanish to the indigenous language" (N. Francis and Nieto Andrade 1996, 165). In the above cases, presumably, what all the authors are referring to (and in fact what Nieto Andrade and I intended) is that competencies that underlie discourse ability, text comprehension, and general language-processing skills are not language-bound.

Competencies that are not language-bound may be learned by means of language use in L1 or L2, or by nonlinguistic means. Subsequently, they are available for application to academic language tasks (or nonacademic tasks, for that matter) in either language. Rather than being "transferred" from L1 to L2, or L2 to L1, since

CALP-type skills do not "reside in" or "belong to" either in the strict sense, they are accessed from a CUP, a shared nonverbal conceptual store (C. Baker 2006; Paivio 1991; M. Paradis 2004; Sadowski and Paivio 1994). As another example, research suggests that key aspects of literacy-related metalinguistic ability are "shared" (Nakamoto, Lindsey, and Manis 2008). In her study of L2 reading, Walter (2007) also recommends that a distinction be made between "transfer" and "access," based on Gernsbacher's (1990) Structure-Building Framework, which we will discuss in chapter 7. For now, the main idea is that important components of comprehension ability, including lower-level processing skills, are nonlinguistic and strictly speaking don't pass directly between L1 and L2. Cheung and Lin (2005) have outlined a proposal that takes Cummins's model as its point of departure in a manner similar to figure 3.2. Using the term "cognitive mobilization" instead of "transfer," they also draw the distinction between "language-independent" and "language-specific processes" (p. 43) from a modular point of view. In the same vein, J. Oller (2008) presents an extended discussion of alternative models of bilingual proficiency and of how the notion of CUP might be reconceptualized, pending evidence from future investigation, along the lines of a componential model of this kind.

Sometimes the metaphors that are used to describe cognitive processes are important. The added emphasis on "through" in the above quotation from C. Baker 2006 underlines the idea that L1 and L2 can be visualized as channels *through* which cognitive-general competencies are developed. Informally, we may have all said something like, "A bilingual child learned the commutative property/how to tell a story in chronological order/effective comprehension strategies/how to read" *in* his or her L1 (or L2), but then maybe had the feeling that "in" is part of a shorthand formulation that is a little misleading.

With all this in mind, then, it would be better to reserve the term "transfer" to refer to interaction between one language subsystem and another. In this way, transfer would be a kind of cross-linguistic influence within the domain of the larger linguistic system (related to, for example, word forms that suggest cognates, similarities and differences in word order patterns, phonological patterns, and morphological forms in L1 and L2). In figure 3.2, the interaction is "direct" from one "iceberg" to the other. At the same time, "transfer" (now synonymous with "cross-linguistic influence") would not exclude the intervention of one or another general cognitive mechanism. In this regard, the outcome of these kinds of mutual influence between L1 and L2 is subject to degrees of awareness and deliberate reflection that can be useful to the L2 learner. Often they are not. But in any case, whatever it is that we as language users might be able to direct attention to (a syntax error, or a fortuitous choice of inflection in L2 speech) is restricted to the end product, not the inner workings of the interlinguistic transfer mechanism itself. We are able to monitor the output of language processing (e.g., after a message has been formulated and before it is spoken, in "inner speech") or the observable/audible input in comprehension, but not how the mechanisms of language processing work internally. By the same token, we cannot apply metalinguistic strategies to the actual mental representations of linguistic competence. The computational procedures of implicit grammatical knowledge are not available to introspection. Rather, attention and reflection can be directed to the overt forms in the output, or in the outcome of these procedures (M. Paradis 2004, 36–38).

As research in L2 learning has demonstrated, such interlinguistic transfers do not have to result in target language forms or native-speaker-like accuracy in production to be useful for the L2 learner. Sharwood Smith's (1994a, 43–81) discussion of "creative construction" and "analyzing interlanguage" is relevant to this way of thinking about transfer. For an alternative point of view, that of a "relativist" orientation to cross-linguistic influence, see Odlin 2002.

Understood in this way, both the CUP-interdependence model (figure 3.1) and the proposed elaboration (figure 3.2) fall under the broad category of modular approaches to the study of language proficiency. Recapping the working definition from chapter 1, modularity refers to an approach to the study of language ability in which autonomous and interacting components are specialized in some way. In contrast to approaches that view all aspects of language proficiency as holistically conformed (a homogenous, rather than a diverse and heterogeneous mental architecture), modular perspectives emphasize a componential organization. This componential nature of language ability is related in an interesting way to the distinction that is often made between top-down and bottom-up[2] processes, and how these actually work together. This is another topic that we will return to in later chapters.

The elaboration of Cummins's model in figure 3.2 is offered here as a way to move the discussion forward and perhaps clarify what might be the essential bone(s) of contention in the debate. In essence, the proposal seeks to emphasize the interconnectedness between L1 and L2 subsystems and how they, in turn, interact with the CUP. For educators working within the general framework proposed by Cummins, refining some of its key analytical categories should help make our descriptions more precise, as we hope will be the case in the following sections.

In the present study of literacy development in Spanish and Nahuatl, the "double-iceberg" model, in its modified version, served (1) as a guide for designing a series of literacy tasks for assessment in both languages, and (2) as a framework for portraying and summarizing the tendencies that emerged from students' responses. It is presented here as a proposal for discussion of future directions in research and will be taken up again in section 3.7.

3.4 Literacy Learning at the San Isidro Bilingual School: A Follow-Up Study

3.4.1 The Participants

Sixty-nine 3rd- and 5th-grade students (35 and 34, respectively; 28 girls, 41 boys), enrolled in the bilingual primary school of San Isidro, participated in the study. Given the high levels of bilingualism, community-wide, by the end of 3rd grade, the great majority of children possess age-appropriate conversational proficiency in both Spanish and Nahuatl. A small minority evidence Spanish or Nahuatl dominance, with receptive proficiency in the other language. As in the case of the 4th and 6th graders from the previous study (see figure 1.2), none of the 3rd and 5th graders demonstrated less than intermediate proficiency in Nahuatl; and none could be distinguished (aside from subtle phonological transfer features) from monolingual Spanish speakers of a similar age.

All students present during testing completed cloze tests and submitted writing samples for both Spanish and Nahuatl versions of the assessment (a complete set of responses for the cloze test, and actual narrative samples for the writing task). This aspect of the results (task completeness) confirmed classroom teachers' estimates of Spanish and Nahuatl proficiency among their students: that all children understand both languages and that, with few exceptions, all possess some measure of expressive ability in both. Of the 35 students in 3rd grade, 6 elected to complete the Nahuatl writing sample in Spanish. Interestingly, however, their scores on the Nahuatl cloze test do not suggest that this choice of language was due to a lack of proficiency in comparison to their 3rd-grade peers who elected to complete the writing sample in Nahuatl (see section 3.5).[3] This finding regarding 3rd- and 5th-graders' overall bilingual proficiency coincides with the results of the earlier study of 2nd, 4th, and 6th graders, proportions that are consistent with the last previous official federal census estimates for the community: Spanish speakers—79.9% (monolinguals—7.3%), Nahuatl speakers—92.7% (monolinguals—20.3%) (INEGI 2000).

3.4.2 The Assessment Measures

For Reading, a rational deletion cloze test scored for "acceptable response" was administered in both languages. For Writing, parallel story stems were presented for completion: one in Spanish, and a different one (not a translation of the first) in Nahuatl.

Cloze/Reading The choice of the cloze test and scoring procedure made for a reasonable match with the earlier Reading assessment of the 2nd-, 4th-, and 6th-grade cohort, which also included a cloze test plus an analysis of oral miscues utilizing a scoring rubric similar to the present one. Cloze passages in Spanish and Nahuatl were prepared with a ratio of deletions averaging approximately 20 words per blank, with a list of exact word replacements (15 high-frequency content words in all cases) displayed in random order along with 10 distractors. Texts were comparable in length and difficulty level, both drawn from the oral narrative tradition:

- Spanish cloze: "La bruja" [The Witch]. Seven children struggle to free themselves from their witch-mother whose turkey form is discovered as they spy on her during the night.
- Nahuatl cloze: "Soatl uan miko" [The Woman and the Monkey]. A young woman and her half-monkey progeny struggle against the prejudices of pure-blooded human society.

Scoring of responses followed a 7-point rating scale adapted from MacLean and d'Anglejan 1986: 6 = full grammatical compatibility at the sentence level plus full semantic compatibility at the text level, and 0 = a completely incongruent response, not forming part of even a grammatical fragment or semantic pattern.

Story Closure/Writing   Like the cloze passages, story prompts were chosen from the oral narrative tradition:

- Spanish writing task: "El señor Tlalocan y la señora Tlalocan" [Mr. and Mrs. Tlalocan]. A boy is chosen by his community to undertake a journey to an underworld kingdom of knowledge and plenty to transmit an important request. The prompt ends with the young traveler beholding the marvels of the land of the Tlalocans as he descends through a subterranean passageway.
- Nahuatl writing task: "Tetsitsilintlan." A young man betrays his dying father, contravening his wishes to be buried alongside his ancestors. The action is suspended as the unhappy pair interrupt their journey to rest on the magic rock, Tetsitsilintlan.

This procedure helped ensure that all writing samples submitted by students represented actual connected text, consistent with the indicated genre, as opposed to nontext responses, such as listing.

To ensure that the writing task was not completely dependent on reading comprehension (of the story prompt or "stem"), the first part of the truncated narrative was summarized orally along with an introduction that identified the protagonist, other principals, and the story problem. Students were then asked to read the prompt, reflect, and complete the story. Specifically, they were instructed to complete the story in the same language in which it began: "Tetsitsilintlan" in Nahuatl, "Tlalocan" in Spanish (see examples in appendix 4).

Scoring emphasized elements in the story endings that contributed to overall coherence, yielding a Sense-of-Story-Structure rating (0–10) adapted from Morrow 1988:

- 1 point for completing the unfinished second episode;
- 1 point for reference to the problem/theme;
- 1 point for reference to the "petition" (Spanish story—"Tlalocan") or the "magic rock" (Nahuatl story—"Tetsitsilintlan");
- 1 point for ending the story;
- a global rating of 2, 1, or 0 for sequence; and
- up to 4 points for intervening events/details.

All initial indications pointed to high acceptability ("face validity"), on-task behavior, and completion rates, particularly in the case of the Nahuatl assessments, reflecting a positive perception of the tasks on the part of the children. For reasons that will be explored in the following sections, the literacy tasks in the IL presented students with special circumstances—problems and complexities unique to the sociolinguistic situation in which speakers of the language find themselves.

3.5 Comparing Results from Both Languages

The most interesting comparison in this study was between students' performance in Nahuatl and their performance in Spanish:

1. internally, within the 3rd- and 5th-grade cohort on the cloze and writing tasks; and
2. in comparison with the findings from the previous study of 2nd-, 4th-, and 6th-grade bilinguals from the same school. (For brevity, this will be called the *first study*, and the study of 3rd and 5th graders will be called the *second study*.)

3.5.1 Reading in Nahuatl and Reading in Spanish: Parallels and Divergences

At first glance, figure 3.3 indicates an upward trend in developing abilities in Spanish that one would expect from tests of academic language proficiency. Importantly, the results support one of the two hypotheses from chapter 1 regarding performance in Nahuatl: the upward tendency in the case of the IL suggests that literacy skills learned through Spanish are applied to performance in the other language that children know. A significant tendency appears even though children only practiced these skills in Spanish. The alternative hypothesis was that performance in the IL would be stagnant across grade levels or would show a weak, nonsignificant advance.

Comparing the results for the two languages, the differences between 3rd and 5th grade appear to reflect a steeper learning curve for the language of literacy

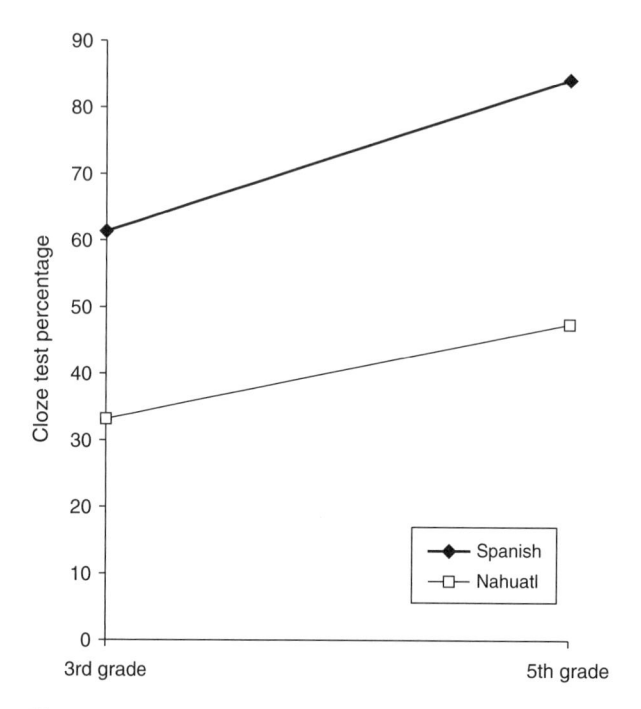

Figure 3.3
Reading in Spanish and Nahuatl

instruction (Spanish) than for Nahuatl: for the cloze results, the mean difference between 3rd and 5th grades for Spanish is 22.8 and for Nahuatl, 14.3 (an observation we will return to shortly). However, the difference between 3rd grade and 5th grade for *both* languages is statistically significant.

Comparing Spanish and Nahuatl globally, the separation between the Spanish and Nahuatl curves appears to indicate a real difference. Students' responses on the Spanish cloze are highly compatible with sentence grammar and context constraints, as high as 84% for 5th graders, as opposed to 47.5% for 5th graders on the Nahuatl cloze. This could reflect overall superior reading abilities in Spanish. However, it is possible that some unforeseen intervening variable temporarily augmented or depressed performance in one language or the other. It is, of course, plausible (even likely in this circumstance) that literacy skills are stronger across the board in Spanish; but let us set this possible interpretation aside for now. What is more interesting is the uniform, and so far exceptionless, tendency observed in the first study (figure 1.2) and confirmed in the second study (figures 3.3 and 3.4):

1. Performance on academic language proficiency tasks in Nahuatl improves across grade levels from 2nd to 6th, and from 3rd to 5th, all differences being statistically significant, parallel in this sense to the trends in Spanish.

2. In all cases, the "learning curve" for Spanish is "steeper," even though both languages advance at a significant rate (the "scissors effect"). In addition, the same groups of students who performed in the high range on the Spanish cloze test tended to do so on the Nahuatl cloze, the correlation being moderately significant. In other words, the direction and relative rate of advance for the two languages indicates parallel development.

3.5.2 Writing in Spanish and Writing in Nahuatl (Sense of Story Structure)

In Writing (scored on the 10-point scale for story construction), the same upward tendency in both languages marks significant differences between 3rd and 5th grade. The correlation between Sense-of-Story-Structure scores in Nahuatl and Spanish was moderately significant, as the correlation of scores was in the Reading assessment. In contrast to the relationship between Nahuatl and Spanish on the cloze test results, students' written expression in the IL appears to be superior, as reflected in higher average scores (figure 3.4). But for the same reasons discussed in regard to the Reading results, we will refrain from considering this interpretation (even though we are tempted to conclude that the level of performance is at least equivalent).[4]

More interestingly, however, we can still observe a sharper learning curve in Spanish ("catching up" by 5th grade). An average difference of 1.0 point in 3rd grade closes to 0.65 in 5th. The former difference is significant, the latter is not. This consistent "diverging" relation (even though in the case of Writing it takes the appearance of a "converging" tendency), now confirmed in both studies on all measures, merits further comment. For now, let us note that despite the contrast between cloze and story completion, the "scissors" continue to "open" for both measures, Reading and Writing: for the cloze task at the "blades" end (figure 3.3), on the Sense-of-Story-Structure measure at the "handle" (figure 3.4).

A final fact about the Nahuatl writing results is worth mentioning: the six missing values from the 3rd-grade samples. As noted earlier, all children submitted writing samples. All 34 of the 5th-grade students completed the Nahuatl story prompts in Nahuatl; however, only 29 of the 35 students in 3rd grade did so. The remaining 6 elected to switch languages, completing the narrative in Spanish. Notably, however, there is no evidence to suggest that these 3rd graders are less proficient in Nahuatl than their classmates. On the Nahuatl cloze test, they ($n = 6$) averaged 37.7%, whereas their 3rd-grade peers ($n = 29$) averaged 32.3%. The contrast with 5th

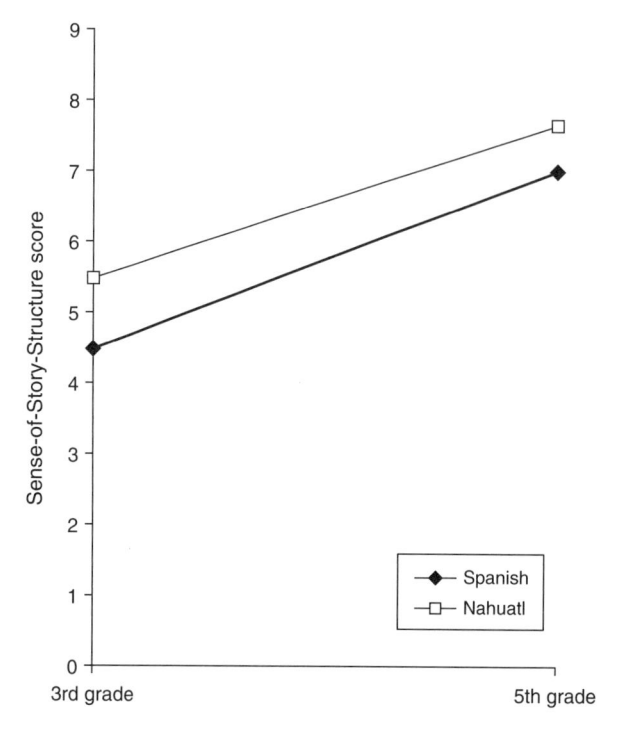

Figure 3.4
Writing in Spanish and Nahuatl

graders, none of whom switched entirely to Spanish, is consistent with other patterns of response by younger and older bilinguals. This difference between younger and older children confirms a finding from the first study, in which 6th graders tended to respond more consistently in Nahuatl than 4th and 2nd graders. On all measures, both academic and conversational, the increased "preference for Nahuatl" with age was in evidence regardless of the language used in administering the assessment or the perceived/actual bilingual proficiency of the examiner. This result is interesting given that the unmarked language for all classroom verbal interaction, and all academic discourse in particular, is Spanish. This diglossic relation holds regardless of the level of bilingual proficiency of student or teacher, and is true for all grade levels. (Chapter 5 returns to this aspect of metalinguistic awareness in a discussion of borrowing and codeswitching, and appendix 2 summarizes the patterns of language choice and preference in a wide range of performance measures.)

To sum up this section, the "scissors effect" is evidenced in all academic measures used in both the first and second studies. In 2nd grade (in the first study), the separation between the curves is either minimal, notable but not statistically significant, or significant at a low level. In all cases, the curves diverge in 4th and 6th grades; performance in Nahuatl also improves in all aspects of performance related to academic proficiency, but Spanish performance appears to improve more rapidly. The same relation in performance between the languages holds for the 3rd- and 5th-grade assessments (the second study). Notably, this "steeper learning curve" is in evidence despite the *opposite tendency* in actual use of Nahuatl among peers, and despite stated preference. In the first study (N. Francis 1998), all 6th graders showed a preference for Nahuatl when conversing with peers; younger students were divided between preference for one language or the other (appendix 2). To highlight the above observations, the significant upward tendency in performance that was observed in academic abilities in both languages was not evident in measures of conversational discourse in either language: these showed no variation across the grades, as should be expected.

The Use of Verbs of Cognition in Writing In the first study, an informal tally of verbs that indicate internal psychological states pointed to this category as another possible index of children's literacy development, following the suggestion by Torrance and Olson that "cognitive verbs are part of a system of concepts for decontextualizing language and thought" (1985, 268). The writing samples from the second study revealed an even more marked difference between beginners (3rd graders) and the more advanced 5th-grade writers.

Comparing the results for each language revealed the same tendency in both. In Spanish, only 6 of the 3rd graders used one or more cognitive verbs; 29 did not. The ratio was inverted for the 5th graders: 19 and 15, respectively. In Nahuatl, only 6 of the 3rd graders used cognitive verbs; 29 did not. The ratio was again inverted for the 5th graders: 24 and 10, respectively.

The number of different verbs is noteworthy as well: for Nahuatl, 3rd grade—3, 5th grade—15; for Spanish, 3rd grade—6, 5th grade—17. Here are five examples, the first three from Nahuatl and the last two from Spanish:

pur eso ineamo noteki
[for that reason it doesn't matter to me]
(Asención 501)

amo oquilnamic
[didn't remember]
(Constantina 561)

ocmomaca cuenta porque non tetl magico
[he realized why the rock was magic]
(Bonifacio 537)

que comfundieron con el venado
[that they confused with the deer]
(Jesús 533)

para que aprendiera sus costumbres y me gustaría que me las enseñaran
[so that I would learn your customs and I would like it if you would teach them to me]
(Bonifacio 537)

These examples, all but one taken from 5th-graders' writing samples, represent children's attempts to portray intentions; contradictory notions that characters entertain; counterfactual conditions; and representations of memory, learning, and understanding. The use of cognitive verbs correlates with descriptions that go beyond what is "directly observable" to what must be inferred, presupposed, or implied. (Chapter 7 will revisit this aspect of children's narrative performance.) Comparing the overall sense-of-story-structure scores for all writers (3rd and 5th graders) who used at least one cognitive verb and those who made no reference to the characters' thoughts, the difference is significant for both Nahuatl and Spanish.

3.6 Using the New Model to Describe Different Kinds of Interdependence

The results reported in the previous section are consistent with the logic of bilingual instruction in literacy learning: that the development of academic language proficiency for L2 learners proceeds effectively under optimal conditions of instruction in two languages—students' primary language and their L2. This was the question examined in chapter 2. Under the special circumstances of widespread bilingualism in the student population in the second study, L1 and L2 were not possible to determine for most children. In fact, this peculiar circumstance, which distinguishes the population of the Mexican study from the typical class of English as a Second Language students in English-speaking countries, motivated the proposed modification of the CUP model. Nevertheless, the same considerations apply to situations of bilingualism where one language is clearly dominant, with the L2 being the vehicle of much, if not all, of content instruction.

First let us consider how the concept of transfer may be applied most usefully to cross-linguistic aspects of bilingual proficiency.

3.6.1 Interactions between Knowledge Structures of the Same Type and between Knowledge Structures of Different Types

A separate study of the students' writing samples and cloze responses would surely reveal a number of interesting aspects of cross-linguistic influence (transfer) between the L1 and L2 representations depicted in figure 3.2. In fact, this is the way that the terms "transfer" and "cross-linguistic influence" are used (as synonyms) in the research literature on L2 learning.[5]

At the phonological/orthographic level, a pattern shows up that is frequently observed in the writing of Nahuatl-speaking learners of Spanish. A subdifferentiation in Nahuatl between /o/ and /u/ often affects pronunciation, reflected in turn in a highly visible spelling error, widespread and persistent among almost all of the bilingual participants in our study ("soelo" for "suelo," "pudu" for "pudo," "so" for "su," "poeblito" for "pueblito," and "pregonto" for "pregunto"). (How this category of cross-linguistic influence in the domain of phonology/orthography is manifested in children's writing will be examined further in chapter 8.)

Spanish cloze
dormían juntos en el soelo
[they slept together on the ground]
(Xema 339)

Quería pasar una vez más sobre sus hijos pero no pudu
[She wanted to pass over her children one more time but could not]
(Xema 339)

Spanish writing
lla llega va a so poeblito . . .y lo pregonta . . .
[now he arrives goes to his town . . . and (someone) asks him . . .]
(Alvaro 351)

Under the category of "lexical transfer," if one can call it that, it is interesting that switching or borrowing only occurs "in one direction," insertion of Spanish material into Nahuatl discourse:

Nahuatl cloze
okijtoya in chango
[(she) said to the monkey]
(Bonifacio 537)

oktitlan inauak se maestro
[he was sent to a teacher]
(Juan de Dios 535)

okuikak ompa ni pueblo
[he took her to his town]
(Patricio 530)

Nahuatl writing
Quilia onikpatia in no papan porque mokokoa
[(He) said I am curing my father because he is sick]
(Flor 540)

As pointed out in a previous analysis of bilingual children's literacy development (N. Francis and Navarrete Gómez 2003), even when mixing results in ungrammatical sequences, which it rarely did in the language samples in this study, for the beginning bilingual reader and writer, this type of cross-linguistic influence provides the learner with a useful set of expressive strategies. In the case of single-word insertion into a matrix language, as in these Spanish insertions into Nahuatl texts, we could speak of a kind of transfer. Other kinds of mixing that involve switching from one grammatical subsystem to another ("alternating" between one and the other) perhaps fall under a different category of transfer or interlinguistic interaction.

On the other hand, the interfaces that account for the interdependent relationship between Nahuatl and Spanish in regard to the application of text-processing skills (figures 3.3 and 3.4) are perhaps better described without reference to the notion of transfer. Unlike in transfer of the interlinguistic influence type, the core competencies associated with text comprehension and production are not stored in either L1 or L2. These are related to:

• knowledge of higher-order discourse patterns that characterize texts of different kinds;
• knowledge of logical, causal, temporal, hierarchical, and taxonomic relationships;
• strategies for inference and prediction;
• access to the universe of scripts, frames, and content schemas; and
• information-processing mechanisms in working memory related to text comprehension.

In the model depicted in figure 3.2, these competencies and skills are "accessible to both languages," being separate from the linguistic representations of L1 and L2. They are "below the surface," within the domain of the CUP. Thus, a more apt metaphor might be *access* to text-processing mechanisms and knowledge structures related to discourse ability rather than *transfer*. Much of what falls under the category of literacy-related discourse abilities and text-processing skills is certainly acquired by means of language use. At the same time, a major portion has as its source nonlinguistic input "fed" into cognitive development "through" different "channels," to borrow C. Baker's (2006) terms. Through experience with cognitively demanding language use, as well as nonlinguistic mental operations applied to different kinds of problem-solving tasks, the CUP sector depicted in figure 3.2 grows and develops.

Here it is important to reemphasize that nothing in a componential model need imply a rigid encapsulation; very early in the child's development, the ability to manipulate symbols and representations of successively more complex kinds depends on language. For example, the model would propose that along the "boundary" between language (in figure 3.2, the overlapping triangles of L1 and L2) and the CUP rectangular "base," language functions emerge that are closely tied to higher-order discourse abilities. Consider, for example, the development of uses of grammar for comprehending and producing the complex syntax of academic texts. These are part of "language" (part of "grammar") but perhaps not part of those subsystems or subcomponents that are universally available to all native speakers in their primary language.[6] Sharwood Smith (1991, 13) applies the concept of modularity to the grammar domain itself:

> If some aspects of linguistic knowledge share the same type of mental representation with other more general kinds of knowledge, this also means that they can be acquired and used following more general cognitive principles involving, presumably, inductive learning and some conscious manipulation during actual performance.

In other words, there appears to be a boundary or separation between the domains of linguistic knowledge and the domain of conceptual knowledge. But, along this boundary, we can point to the development of "aspects of linguistic knowledge [that] share the same type of mental representation" that characterizes domain-general conceptual knowledge. Along this boundary, as well, operate the various processing mechanisms, specialized for interfacing linguistic components with conceptual structures and vice versa. Whatever the nature of these processing components that connect linguistic domains and conceptual knowledge turns out to be, we should consider these interfaces to be an integral part of *language*, part of grammar.

3.6.2 Access to Underlying Proficiencies: Facilitating and Limiting Factors in Reading and Writing

For the students in the Mexican study, whose Nahuatl literacy skills appear, graphically, to be keeping pace with their Spanish skills (despite the "scissors effect"), the idea of access offers a more useful framework for future research than the idea of transfer; Walter (2008) argues along the same lines. In this way, we can reserve the term "transfer" for cross-linguistic influence. Text-processing skills, learned in school (through Spanish) and outside of school (sources would include television, in Spanish; traditional narrative, in Nahuatl), continue to advance from grade to grade. The knowledge structures and ability networks of CUP develop, becoming more elaborate and productive. Though subject to different kinds of limitations, short-circuits, and obstacles to free and unfettered access, they are available for literacy-related tasks in the other language that the student speaks or understands. To this point, it should be noted that the testing sessions in which reading and writing were assessed in Nahuatl were the first opportunity for the vast majority of the children in the second study to apply literacy skills to texts in this language. When children are working in their IL, under the category of limitations, short-circuits, and obstacles, we can speculate about a number of possibilities: (1) lack of familiarity with some orthographic patterns; (2) novelty of the activity associated with conflicting sociolinguistic/pragmatic expectations regarding language choice in the school setting; (3) on the reading task especially, temporary loss of automaticity of processing; (4) lack of previously established repertoire of "sight words." Impressionistically (contrast figures 3.3 and 3.4), it seems that some of the processing limitations that affect fluent *reading* do not apply to basic *writing* ability (at least not in the same way), suggesting an interesting question for further research.

From this point of view, "developing CALP in L2," or "academic L2" (Ovando, Combs, and Collier 2006, 129), serves as a shorthand formulation (not an inappropriate one, we might add) that summarizes a more complex idea. One possible expansion of "academic L2" could detail the different ways that language is used for purposes related to schooling and literacy:

1. the use of L2 in organizing and constructing context-reduced and cognitively demanding discourses;

2. the application of metacognitive strategies to academic texts in the L2; and

3. developing aspects of the L2 grammar that specifically serve these academic, advanced literacy-related uses of language.

If it can be shown that there are in fact domains of grammar development that are tied to literacy and academic discourse (i.e., beyond a hypothetical universal core grammar), then this aspect (#3) would be what we might refer to as "academic L2" in the narrow sense. In the broader sense, we could also include #1, #2, and academic content-specific L2 vocabulary. Strictly speaking, it would be #3 (plus new vocabulary knowledge) that is the "language component" of "academic L2"; #1 and #2 would correspond to the cognitive components that are accessible to the L2 learner during the performance of academic tasks *through the medium of* the L2. For example, it is often observed that bilingual students may require more years to develop academic language proficiency in their L2 than in their L1. The reason why this appears to be true for many L2 students, without the benefit of a significant L1 component, may be that through the medium of a language in which input is only partially comprehensible, the process of building up abilities associated with the CUP is abbreviated, delayed, or made more difficult in some way. The narrow sense of "academic L2" would refer to aspects of the L2 grammar that do not develop spontaneously in everyday conversation. Rather, these aspects of grammar develop through sustained contact with academic discourse. By the same token, we could refer to "academic L1" along the same lines (chapter 7 will return to this difficult question). But crucially, for these aspects of grammar to develop in the L2, language input must be comprehensible.

Under optimal conditions (such as full-time sheltered L2 teaching), comprehensible input is maximized and L2 learning is facilitated. Instruction is contextualized to a greater degree, information load is decreased, abstractions are made more concrete, the teacher's speech and grammar are modified for beginners, and so on—all considered appropriate and necessary L2-teaching adaptations. In fact, these teaching adaptations *are* appropriate and necessary. However, in the absence of any instruction in the student's primary language, modified L2 teaching often presents educators and learners with a dilemma. All things being equal, in L1 teaching, instructional discourse can be *more* cognitively demanding and *less* contextualized. Students' information-processing capabilities are advanced toward higher levels, at a faster rate, along the cognitively demanding axis and "across" the context support axis toward more decontextualized language tasks. However, when all content instruction is provided without any recourse to L1, the result may be a delayed or abated learning of higher-order academic proficiencies. Access to academic texts through the language that the beginning reader understands could compensate for one set of possible limitations. (NB: It doesn't always.)

With use of an instructional model that allows for access to beginning literacy materials in both L1 and L2, as opposed to exclusively in L2, CALP-type discourse and metacognitive abilities can be learned and consolidated more rapidly. Since higher-level academic content does not require contextualization and information reduction beyond what is normally needed, the development of abilities associated with CALP is more likely to proceed according to age-appropriate mileposts. This is possible, all things being equal, because students have complete command of the basic grammar of the language of instruction. Instruction in the L1 can dispense with the kind of extra context support and reduced information load that is characteristic of L2-medium content teaching. The proficiencies stored independently of language are subsequently *accessible* to the learner when he or she is presented with tasks in L2, L3, and so on. They are available to the learner subject to the degree of control over bottom-up processes, that is, a minimum threshold of grammatical competence in the language of instruction. Below this threshold, advanced comprehension strategies and metalinguistic abilities are more difficult to apply, and they themselves do not develop as rapidly as they normally would. Including decodable L1 materials and L1 direct instruction specifically targeted to cognitively demanding academic tasks should help to develop these strategies more efficiently and effectively. This traditional view of literacy and bilingualism (UNESCO 1953) happens to be consistent with the findings of a meta-analysis of studies on the question of "language of instruction" (D. Francis, Lesaux, and August 2006) and other recent major reports on the problem of L2 literacy learning (Guglielmi 2008; Short and Fitzsimmons 2007; Tong et al. 2008).

In principle, the same relationship between the development of CALP-type abilities and level of attainment of linguistic competence in L1 and L2 should apply to the findings from the Nahuatl-Spanish study. In the school where the study was carried out, as is also the rule in other bilingual communities, reading comprehension and text composition skills are developed through instruction in Spanish (unfortunately for many of the students who were Nahuatl-dominant in 1st grade, not under optimal conditions). Subsequently, in a series of quasi-experimental tasks (the second study) where proficiencies were tested in the IL, what appears to be "development of Nahuatl academic proficiency" shows a positive upward tendency. But strictly speaking, academic language proficiency tied to literacy "in Nahuatl" does not develop. To reiterate, in school, only occasional, symbolic uses of the IL were evident. Rather, the bilingual 5th and 6th graders found ways to get around, with varying degrees of success, the limitations, short-circuits, and obstacles imposed by this imbalance between the languages to gain access to CALP when the demands of the task required it.

3.6.3 "Language-Bound" Aspects of Academic Discourse Ability

It would be helpful here to return briefly to the observation of the "scissors effect": why the scores in Nahuatl begin to attenuate relative to Spanish. It is important not to fall into a simplification: that of an autonomous-components model that ignores the interaction between linguistic knowledge and the nonlinguistic competencies that underlie literacy-related abilities. The development of academic discourse and related metacognitive abilities also involves learning how to use grammar that is necessary for understanding and producing texts. For examples, see the chapters "Linguistic Features of Academic Registers" and "Functional Grammar in School Subjects" in Schleppegrell 2004, and, specifically with respect to advanced narrative development, Christie 2005. These same "text-related" grammatical patterns are of course in evidence in all structured discourse, oral and written. By the same token, they are encountered with less frequency in situation-dependent interactive discourse, such as e-mail chat. In her study of traditional formal speech styles of oral cultures, Feldman (1991) draws the distinction between primary and secondary discourses in a manner relevant to this idea:

Ordinary conversation is not as tightly patterned as the other genres discussed here; it does not focus the listener's attention on the locutions themselves but rather on illocution and perlocution, and it seems to help define the others by contrast as the oral base-level or pre-genre form.... Perhaps careful students of conversation would disagree, citing the complexity of conversational patterns, an observation with which I agree. But complexity is not structure, pattern, or rule, and that is what I am after here. (p. 63)

Some of the genres are seen as, and are in fact, different from everyday talk in having an element of artfulness or special skill. In this sense, special, beautiful, or elegant forms of talk in oral cultures may have characteristics similar to some of our literary genres. (p. 51)

For one thing, all that genres do—whether they are written or oral—is to create a text in which the words themselves, and not just their intended meaning, matter. . . . [Whether a] genre is written or spoken, it works much the same way, by fixing a form for expression. (p. 50)

Thus, not all CALP-related skills would be independent of the grammar-knowledge components of language. According to this view, some aspects of higher-order academic language proficiency are, in a way, language-specific. They are typically learned in school through experience with context-reduced language use. Following Feldman, they are also learned in traditional oral discourse settings that are formal and academic-like. For the Nahuatl-Spanish bilinguals, as their academic language proficiency develops, those aspects of Spanish grammar and lexical knowledge that are associated with CALP-type abilities are learned as well. Hence, the following research question arises: is this aspect of language ability, in the IL, not provided with the same opportunity to develop (or not made available through the mechanisms of interlinguistic transfer)?

A partial solution to the problem of incomplete development of these aspects of language ability in Nahuatl may be the extensive borrowing of grammatical and lexical resources from Spanish when writing in Nahuatl, as in the example of the borrowing of discourse connectors. Earlier studies from the Nahuatl-Spanish project showed a significant shift in lexical borrowing patterns in Nahuatl writing samples as children progress from 2nd to 6th grade (N. Francis and Navarrete Gómez 2003). Older, more mature writers begin to avoid borrowing Spanish *content* words; they appear to be replacing them with their Nahuatl equivalents. (Navés, Miralpeix, and Celaya (2005) report on similar tendencies across grade levels in experiments that involved learners of English.) At the same time, the children tend to increase their use of Spanish discourse connectors—this tendency, of course, accompanied by an increase in the use of discourse connectors in general. For example, the 3rd grader Pascuala (359) inserts "cuando" [when], "pero" [but], "porque" [because], "luego" [then] into her Nahuatl narrative (see appendix 4), "substituting for" IL connectors that are rarely used even in speech by proficient speakers of the language. Out of 63 students who completed the Nahuatl writing task in Nahuatl, 59 availed themselves of Spanish borrowings (content words—52%, discourse connectors 48%). The first study reported here, involving 2nd, 4th, and 6th graders, reflected the same tendency (only 1 child out of 45 avoided borrowing from Spanish). Oral narrative data in Nahuatl available from the first study show the same trend. Notably (although predictably), none of the children's Spanish writing samples from either study ($N = 69$ and $N = 45$) contain any borrowed items from Nahuatl ("historical" loanwords integrated completely into the Mexican Spanish lexicon aside).

To sum up this discussion on the "language-bound" aspects of literacy-related discourse abilities, we might conclude that access to CALP is not unfettered, regardless of which language is the medium of the academic task at hand. As the task requirements associated with more complex and informationally dense texts become more demanding—in 5th and 6th grade, for example—performance in Nahuatl begins to "lag." This less robust development, showing up graphically as the "scissors effect," occurs even though the bilingual may possess the relevant CUP-based proficiencies and enjoys full command of basic, age-appropriate linguistic competence in both languages. In this case, the aspects of (Nahuatl) grammar beyond those universally provided by the Faculty of Language and those gained by typical exposure to the language through normal primary socialization may develop at a slower rate. Perhaps within this domain of language ability, skill in putting to use certain aspects of grammatical knowledge is not developed to the same level as it is in Spanish. In this regard, sociolinguistic studies in Latin America have pointed to a narrowing of the range of discourse practices associated with ILs. This reduction might be related to the historical and ongoing displacement of the languages from the elevated genres and formal language use (Chiodi 1993). All of these findings, of course, should be taken as a proposal for further research.

3.7 Components and Connections

The provisional model of interacting L1, L2, and CUP depicted in figure 3.2 is a first attempt at conceptualizing a componential breakdown of a very big category: bilingual proficiency. Further investigation might (1) probe how different aspects of language proficiency and language use in bilinguals might actually be compartmentalized, and then (2) describe more precisely, and eventually explain, how the components and subsystems are interconnected. For example, an *interaction-among-components* model would attempt to account for both the positive/upward tendency in the Nahuatl writing task results *and* the relative lag, in relation to Spanish, of the Nahuatl results as a whole. In the first case, research could look for evidence of CUP competencies that are strictly non-language-specific. In the second case, it would focus on "missed opportunities" for developing language-specific grammar that is associated with literacy-related academic abilities. This difficult problem presents itself in all bilingual literacy-learning situations in which there is a social imbalance between the languages. That's one reason why the findings from the Mexican studies are interesting. Practical insights for educators working in similarly imbalanced language contact situations might emerge from more research attention to this problem.

Models of bilingual mental representation are complex, and resolving the nature and degrees of interconnectedness and interdependence of L1 and L2 in relation to nonverbal systems remains a major research problem in the field today.

At the root of the opposition to componential approaches are the proposals of the strong associationist theories that tend to view the architecture of the mind as largely undifferentiated, "uniform and omnicompetent in all cognitive domains" (Gregg 1989, 25). Theories that take experience and sociocultural context as their point of departure tend to favor cognitive homogeneity. In the field of bilingual education, for example, this approach appears to be largely taken for granted as a basic underlying assumption. Theoretical frameworks that view language from a holistic and strongly integrative perspective would question the distinctions between linguistic competence and general cognition (perhaps even with regard to the different subsystems of language). On the methodological plane, they would reject discrete-point assessment, and more generally the study of any aspect of language proficiency apart from "communicative contexts." Finally, they tend to resist differentiating between conversational ability and literacy-related academic proficiencies. On the other hand, accepting this differentiation inevitably entails a serious reckoning with theories of modularity. (A fuller discussion of modular approaches to bilingualism and L2 learning can be found in Bialystok and Cummins 1991; Bialystok and Hakuta 1994; Carroll 2001; Dekydtspotter, Sprouse, and Swanson 2001; Milicevic 2007; Sharwood Smith 1991, 1994a; and Towell 2004; and in chapters 4 and 5.)

At this point, we can reformulate the research question posed in the previous section. Academic abilities "in Nahuatl" appear to develop, although not strictly in parallel with the indices of performance in Spanish (i.e., they tend to begin to level out and slip relative to Spanish). Is this observation consistent with (1) an interactive model, some of whose components are specialized, or (2) a different kind of interaction (e.g., in line with emergentist accounts; N. Ellis 2008) that doesn't make use of dedicated domain-specific components?

The first approach will need to describe the nature and mechanisms of the interaction between the linguistic domains and the conceptual domains associated with general learning and "central" cognition. In regard to these "nonlinguistic" domains, it will be important to distinguish between (1) early-emerging competencies, and basic, universal, information-processing capabilities on the one hand, and (2) those that evidence wide variation within all speech communities, on the other hand. Along the boundary (as in figure 3.2) between language and the nonlinguistic domains, it will be necessary to examine the interface aspects of language proficiency in relation to all the linguistic subsystems. Different kinds of knowledge or sets of knowledge structures, in different combinations, underlie each kind of ability related to both "primary discourse" and "secondary discourse." In regard to lexical development, where we would expect to cross deeper into cognitive domains outside the Faculty of Language (narrowly defined), the use of mental verbs points to another aspect of the above-mentioned interaction, the development of metalinguistic awareness. Along these lines, Bloom (2004, 3–34) and Morgan and Kegl (2006) discuss the important related development of Theory of Mind.

An integrativist-holistic account of the findings would be supported by evidence that language acquisition (all aspects of it) is no different in kind from concept learning and general intellectual development. Also, if it can be demonstrated that in the development of literacy-related language proficiency, the learning of advanced discourse abilities and metalinguistic awareness is more "incremental" and continuous with earlier, more basic abilities, the modularity hypothesis might be weakened. In contrast, the modularity hypothesis would find support in degrees of discontinuity, compartmentalization, and dissociation.

The pedagogical implications of current theories and proposals remain unclear. As Sharwood Smith (1994a) points out, premature generalizations of research findings to classroom practice run the risk of promoting teaching approaches that are methodologically narrow, raising some applications to the level of principle, to the exclusion of all others. Nevertheless, the resolution of key research problems, and the elaboration of a general theory of bilingual language proficiency, will in the end have far-reaching consequences for L2 instruction and, more broadly, school language policy. And, again, the findings and speculations from the exploratory Nahuatl-Spanish investigation of bilingual literacy should be taken as a framework for designing more controlled and less open-ended assessments. As things stand, the findings do not provide unequivocal support for any one version of modularity. Rather, this approach to studying the components of language ability might offer one way of framing research questions that so far have been difficult to formulate in a useful way.

As mentioned in chapter 1, the proposed modification of Cummins's model of bilingual proficiency, figure 3.2, will undergo further modifications. In some respects, it turns out not to be modular enough; in other respects, not sufficiently interactive. The further modifications will try to account for the seemingly disparate findings from research on bilingual competence and bilingual proficiency. In any case, figure 3.2 is a necessary first approximation, coinciding with our first attempt to fine-tune the concepts of Common Underlying Proficiency/Central Processing System, interdependence, and language-bound and language-independent abilities. Soon we will see in what ways the model needs to be improved.

4
Componential Approaches to the Study of Language Proficiency

The previous chapter revisited an important theme in the study of language and language ability: Can a given proficiency be analyzed in terms of cognitive systems and subsystems? Might these components, or some of them, be specialized to some degree or to varying degrees (have "domain-specific" properties)? The question was posed in regard to concrete problems encountered by bilingual and second language educators as they grapple with how to conceptualize the development of knowledge and proficiency in academic settings. What is the most useful framework for understanding how school-related abilities develop when children know, or are learning, two languages? Modularity was proposed as one way of framing the problem.

This chapter and chapter 5 will take up the details of this proposal, starting with some historical background. In a direct way, we can trace the current discussion about models of bilingualism back to the contributions of Lev Vygotsky and A. R. Luria, who attempted to differentiate among the different components of language ability in child development. Certain themes of today's debate were anticipated by Vygotsky in particular:

- the distinction between interpersonal conversational discourse ability and literacy-related academic language abilities,
- the relationship between the development of linguistic knowledge in two languages and general cognitive development, and
- aspects of language development that are universal and aspects that show significant variation.

In this chapter, we will widen our discussion of the approach proposed in chapter 3 for the study of bilingual development. The hope is that it will help in finding common ground around results and interpretations that at times appear irreconcilable. For the student of language development and bilingualism, trying to make sense of the competing theories, and even conflicting research results, at times becomes truly discouraging. Still, exaggerated claims and counterclaims aside, the difficult and at times frustrating discussions are an important part of the advances that the science of language continues to make. In some ways, one might even say that the disparity of views among investigators reflects the internal diversity of the bilingual mind. As the confrontation of theories and research findings moves forward, the remaining contradictions in the first instance should yield, little by little, to the coherence and interconnectedness of the second.

It also seems that in the study of bilingualism, research is drawn toward multi-disciplinary approaches to a greater degree than in the study of language as a whole. Bilingualism research being tied closely to applied fields in bilingual education and L2 learning, investigators borrow freely from work outside their discipline. Since bilingualism involves additional layers of interaction among the cognitive systems, it turns out to be more difficult to limit research to any one field. This of course both offers opportunities and opens up many traps to fall into. On balance, however, the interchange (mostly in one direction for now) between the applied-oriented and theoretically oriented research programs is probably a good thing, and not just for the former.

The problem explored in this chapter concerns the relationship among the components of the school-related language abilities: proficiencies specifically related to literacy learning and other language skills needed for academic achievement. Two dimensions of this academic language ability are what we may call *secondary discourse ability*, learned through schooling and/or its extracurricular counterparts, and the set of abilities related to *metalinguistic awareness*.

With these two dimensions of academic language proficiency in mind, we will look at certain historical antecedents to the idea of modularity. After applying the modular approach to Cummins's Common Underlying Proficiency (CUP) model, we will assess MacSwan's (2000) critique of it, distinguished from most other critiques in its point of reference from within the cognitive sciences. Taking other applications of the modular approach to the study of bilingualism as examples of comparison, we will again look at findings from the studies of the Nahuatl-speaking community in Mexico. These descriptive studies of tendencies across the elementary grades in the area of literacy-related proficiencies raised interesting questions about how bilingual children develop these proficiencies through each language they know. Considering the two models that were presented in chapter 3 (see figures 3.1 and 3.2), one possibility is that the cognitive domains that *underlie proficiency* in L1 and L2, and that are shared in *common*, could be thought of as *processing systems* that are more *central* (Cummins's acronyms CUP and CPS, from chapter 1, slightly reshuffled).

4.1 Vygotsky and Luria: The Concept of "Inner Speech"

Even though Vygotsky and Luria framed their work in a way that appears different from the way the problems of bilingualism are presented in this book, they made the most important early contribution to understanding the componential nature of language ability in general. As mentioned in chapter 1, the concept of modularity is most often associated with Universal Grammar (UG) approaches to the study of language. The connection between the different versions of UG and the concept of modularity, the competence-performance distinction, and the poverty-of-stimulus problem goes back a long way. In broad terms, Fodor's (1983) modularity hypothesis describes a heterogeneous mental architecture a good part of whose internal structure is "built in" or set down, guided in development by human biological endowment. Whatever it is that is predetermined in this way, in fact, allows no other kind of mental architecture to emerge than that of a human mind with a human Faculty of Language and communication system. In any case, "preprogrammed" would probably more accurately describe this kind of unfolding, as opposed to the growth of a "hardwired" structure (Marcus 2004, 40–45). (For an overview of the major themes in this line of work over the years, see Coltheart 1999, Garfield 1987, Grodzinsky and Friederici 2006, Maratsos 1992, Pinker and Jackendoff 2005, R. Samuels 2006, and B. Schwartz 1999.)

Far from resulting in a unified approach to the problem of modeling linguistic competence and language proficiency, modularity has given rise to a great diversity of views. Perhaps, as a blessing in disguise, this divergence might in the future favor a greater openness for the coming together of new lines of discussion, especially in applied linguistics where some theoretical differences can at times be temporarily set aside.

Roughly, modules are the cognitive structures (their component parts) that operate in a "vertical" manner at least to some degree. According to Fodor, vertical processors coexist and interact with components that are nonmodular, or modular to a lesser degree. The "vertical" and highly modular structures are contrasted to components that are more "horizontal."[1] On the other hand, descriptions of language use from research currents outside the generativist tradition have at times called attention to contrasts and oppositions that we could study as an antecedent to the problems that modular approaches seek to address. Beginning with Vygotsky (1934/1986), an attempt was made to distinguish among cognitive domains that suggests the idea of interdependent faculties interacting in systematic ways. Of course, before the 1950s, observations and speculations on the internal diversity of language were couched in different terms than they are today. And even though the intent here is mainly to survey historical antecedents and approximations, many readers already steeped in the controversies surrounding these questions might object that this isn't the usual way of dividing up the sides.

In fact, a convergent reflection regarding Vygotsky's theories about language and literacy from a modular perspective will not be easy. Fodor's (1972) highly critical assessment of *Thought and Language* in the inaugural issue of *Cognition* surely discouraged friendlier readings. Perhaps his review was directed at contemporary interlocutors: proponents of social constructivism and other strong integrativist theories. For them, the idea of a single origin, in social and historical circumstances, of thought and language continues to exercise great attraction. This being an irresistible theory in his own time and political/intellectual climate, Vygotsky seems never to have seriously questioned it himself. If he had, such a heretical doubt would not have been entertained very widely, spoken out loud or in writing, among his colleagues. (Carruthers (in press) offers an evaluation of Vygotsky's views on the role of language in higher-order thinking that touches on some of the same themes.)

In any case, the motivation behind this review of Vygotsky and Luria is that it may be more interesting to put aside these secondary aspects of their work (even though at times they appear to be primary) and instead to examine the research observations they reported, some of which may be compatible, in some ways, with a modular point of view. This historical appreciation, especially of Vygotsky's ideas, will also offer some perspective on another theme introduced in chapter 1: the contribution of functionalist theorists to the current ferment in generative linguistics. Most observers today would trace the lineage of Vygotsky's work forward directly to the former school of thought. The suggestion here is that it should be reconsidered, rather as a possible bridge for further discussion.

Despite the constant temptation to fuse language and thought, Vygotsky struggled with his own observations that did in fact suggest differentiations—for example, in child development. In *Language and Thought*, he refers to the two in terms of parallel development, described by separate curves. He calls attention to both nonverbal cognition and aspects of language use in which the participation of higher-order cognitive abilities is minimized or overshadowed (e.g., in the expression of affective states, and "psychological contact with others of [one's] kind"). From "different genetic roots" (1934/1986, 78–79), the curves converge—for example, when children direct attention inward toward their own activity or toward resolving comprehension problems, and when their own language becomes the object of contemplation. "Mental drafts" in the form of internalized speech mark the development of the intellectual functions associated with complex cognition. The development of the abilities that are associated with this kind of reflective, nonverbalized discourse is discontinuous in many respects with the unfolding of the language abilities that are universally attainable, that emerge spontaneously and unreflectively.

It is from this point of view that we should consider Vygotsky's observations about the need for understanding how literacy learning is different from language acquisition (Fodor was especially critical on this point, for some reason). Vygotsky seemed to be arguing that as an intellectual attainment, learning to read and write calls upon the higher-order proficiencies, in opposition to the notion that literacy evolves, or should evolve, "naturally" and spontaneously, similarly to the way children acquire their mother tongue (pp. 179–184). Lately, among linguists and psychologists who have ventured into the debate on literacy learning, the idea that the development of reading skills does not follow the same course as primary-language acquisition has gained greater acceptance. Primary-language development is universal and natural (taken to mean "coming from nature in a preprogrammed way, and driven by a specific genetic endowment"). Reading and writing abilities are secondary acquisitions (Liberman and Whalen 2000). (This line of argument certainly does not imply, however, that anyone is proposing that literacy is unnatural for humans, or that all aspects of oral-language development are genetically preprogrammed.)

Luria, Vygotsky's colleague and coworker, shared his interest in the role of language in general cognitive operations. Contrary to a superficial reading of Vygotsky's conception of "inner speech," it doesn't appear that he meant this term to be synonymous with "thought." Rather, it refers to nondialogical discourse, applied to problem solving, deliberate planning, and metacognitive reflection. As such, monologic internalized speech, now a tool of what Luria referred to in terms of higher-order cognitive operations, organizes practical intellectual activity. It helps to overcome the perception of things and "take one beyond the world of sensory experience." One use of language is as a "powerful instrument for analyzing this world," elaborating abstract concepts, and formulating logical conclusions (Luria 1981, 38). For Vygotsky and Luria in their early research, "word" is not "concept," but "tool of abstraction" (today, for clarity, we would emphasize: not the only one).[2] For example, in regard to the operations that are called upon in solving a syllogism, the reasoner is asked to contemplate premises that are counterintuitive, or that contradict contextual information and cultural preconceptions. Luria often appears to tip in favor of a fusion of "word" and "concept": that is, language should be considered as the most essential mechanism that serves as a foundation for cognition.[3] Then he seems to hedge, referring to this "fusion" in relation to the functions of complex cognition and the secondary discourses, beyond the universal platform of conceptual development, attained by all cognitively nondisabled children.

Prefiguring the debate on orality and writing, Vygotsky and Luria proposed their typology of (1) oral discourse of the dialogic, interactive, and contextualized kind; (2) oral monologic discourse; and (3) monologic written discourse. It is in #1, colloquial-interpersonal oral discourse, where "extralinguistic factors" compensate for lesser degrees of self-sufficiency. (Certainly, the adjustment in regard to self-sufficiency in face-to-face conversation conforms to appropriate pragmatic constraints.) Relatively higher degrees of context independence (i.e., self-sufficiency) characterize #2 and #3. Work on discourse processing (Garrod and Pickering 2004), for example, has confirmed this distinction between monologic ability and the ability to engage in conversational dialog. Despite the complexity of the information that must be computed in everyday, face-to-face conversation, Garrod and Pickering propose that dialog is less cognitively demanding than nonconversational discourse because:

it takes advantage of a processing mechanism that we call "interactive alignment." We argue that interactive alignment is automatic and reflects the fact that humans are designed for dialogue rather than monologue. (p. 8)
This is a process by which people align their representations at different linguistic levels at the same time. . . . [Alignment] at one level leads to more alignment at other levels. (p. 9)

According to this view, interlocutors arrive at common representations ("an implicit common ground") largely in an unconscious way, without recourse to complex reasoning or explicit negotiation.

[Production] and comprehension become interdependent because they extensively draw on the implicit common ground. . . . As the conversation proceeds, it will become increasingly common to use exactly the same set of computations. (p. 10)

Garrod and Pickering's approach provides another interesting perspective on Cummins's analysis of Basic Interpersonal Communicative Skills (BICS) and Cognitive Academic Language Proficiency (CALP). From this point of view, there is no reason to privilege the interpersonal, communicative functions of language over those related, for example, to conceptualization and reasoning (M. Baker 2003; Carruthers 2002; Newmeyer 2008). Communicating intention and negotiating context-embedded meaning are not the only useful purposes to which language can be applied. In their study of Catalan-Spanish bilingualism, J. Oller and Vila (2010) also draw an explicit link between Vygotsky's conception of the role of language in higher-order thinking (e.g., metacognition) and Cummins's proposed distinction between literacy-related academic language proficiency and conversational ability.

As a footnote to this review, it is perhaps worth noting here that Luria (1981, 233–246) speculated about the neurological representations of what he saw as a heterogeneity of linguistic functions, making reference to subfaculties dedicated to serving different kinds of language use. These were suggested to him by his work on brain pathology, how lesions that his patients had suffered affected one or another language function.

Clearly, any assessment of Vygotsky's and Luria's early work on the different aspects of language proficiency should stand on its own, independent of the later evolution of Luria's own views, or speculations about which camp Vygotsky might have fallen into. In fact, Luria's later appraisal of modern linguistic theory associated with the modularity hypothesis was openly hostile (Luria 1994). But it would be a mistake to cede the legacy of this early work on the development of different kinds of discourse ability exclusively to the strong social-constructivist theories on language and literacy.

4.2 Metacognition: Language at the Service of Higher-Order Thinking

Bernstein (1964) references Vygotsky and Luria in his analysis of elaborated and restricted codes. For now, we can put aside the controversy around how these discourse abilities may correlate with social class, especially given the confusion, pointed out by Halliday (1978) and others, over distinguishing between aspects of variation related to dialect and register. To this point (of confusion), variation related to elaborated and restricted codes should be considered apart from, or above, individual differences in the development of the *primary* linguistic systems. Dialectal variation or individual differences among children in meeting developmental milestones in linguistic competence, and in the ability to put these to use in conversation, should be considered independently from the development of the kinds of discourse ability that can be characterized as *secondary*. This would be related to the division depicted in figure 3.2 between the modules of grammatical knowledge and the other domains of knowledge that underlie the ability to use language. Much of the misunderstanding that surrounds Bernstein's work and many of its misapplications might have been avoided had his findings been read in this more discerning way. On this view, proficiency in one or another register depends on networks of knowledge structures and processing mechanisms that in large part are not linguistic and are independent of dialect. Any lingering ambiguity regarding these categories notwithstanding, this is what the distinction between elaborated and restricted codes should refer to. Variation in regard to secondary discourse abilities is distributed among individuals in a different way than are the abilities that account for differences in dialect.

As an illustration, let us again consider our two hypothetical bilinguals from chapter 1, A(sención) and B(onifacio), who are learning Spanish as a L2. Let's suppose that A comes to learn a local nonstandard dialect of Spanish while B learns the standard variety spoken in the capital city. There might be something about A's knowledge of Spanish phonology and syntax, or his choice of words, that prompts many people to perceive him as less educated. But obviously there is nothing in principle about the nonstandard dialect that would prevent him from using *this* knowledge of Spanish for academic purposes and for developing high levels of skill in literacy. By the same token, learning the standard dialect will in no way ensure that B even learns how to read and write at all. The same dissociation could obtain in the case of a standard-nonstandard difference in the boys' L1. Certainly, extraneous factors such as social prejudice and discrimination against speakers of indigenous languages (ILs) and nonstandard dialects often tip the scales in one direction. But this result simply reminds us why the fact that dialect and literacy-related language ability are often correlated has more to do with historical circumstance than with any factor related to knowledge of grammar, per se.

Bernstein's category of reflexive monologic discourse at the service of reasoning and planning (the elaborated code) is taken directly from Vygotsky: the child begins to view language as a set of tools for the reorganization and analysis of experience. Fundamentally, mastery of this kind of nonconversational discourse proficiency is achieved through deliberate effort and sustained learning. Uncontroversially, the opportunity for engaging with this kind of learning experience is distributed unequally in all speech communities and cultures.

Bruner (1975), also following Vygotsky, assigned the use of language a preeminent role in the development of analytic, "context-independent" thinking. In turn, written language facilitates a distancing from concrete referents. Schooling and literacy help lay the basis for performing operations in the passageway between what is in the here and now and what is possible, in other worlds, for example. From the field of psychology, the interest in research on metalinguistic awareness is closely tied to previous speculations on the interaction between language development and the development of intellectual capabilities associated with complex cognition. Indeed, we need to acknowledge Vygotsky and Luria for the attention they gave to children's developing ability to reflect on language (awareness of language use and form) in their discussions of how orality and writing are related to all this.[4]

In the 1970s and 1980s, a strong emphasis is noticeable in the work on the theme of metalevel abilities (Olson 1977; Ryan and Ledger 1984; Scribner and Cole 1981; Tunmer and Myhill 1984). Independent of differences in emphasis and interpretation, what seems to emerge is a tendency toward separating metalinguistic knowledge from grammatical competence. "Grammatical competence" refers to implicit knowledge of grammar, implying a separation between two kinds of knowledge. This key distinction is clear, for example, in the studies of Scribner and Cole (1981), who found:

1. a uniform performance on the part of illiterates, nonschooled Vai literates, and schooled literates alike on tests of grammatical judgment, in contrast to

2. significant variation among the same three groups on a test that required them to justify their acceptability judgments (pp. 151–158).

The debate over the onset of metalinguistic awareness between proponents of "autonomous" and "interactive" models, reviewed by Gombert (1992), reflects the broader confrontation between modular and integrative perspectives. In the Mexican project, assessment of how students perceived different aspects of language use examined this question as it relates to different *levels* of awareness in younger and older children; examples of testing procedures are given in appendix 1.

The key distinctions discussed so far have evolved over the last 50 years, from Vygotsky to Olson (1991), leading us to their application to the study of bilingualism by Cummins and Swain (1986). Readers should take special note here of how Cummins and Swain themselves review the theoretical antecedents to their discussion of CALP and BICS (pp. 141–151).

In the interest of heading off certain misunderstandings that have grown up around these constructs, two clarifications are in order:

1. Mastery of interpersonal communicative ability—that is, skill in context-embedded conversational contexts (BICS)—should not be confused with the universal attainment of L1 grammatical competence. A possible source of the confusion is the observation that interpersonal communicative ability, the fluent use of a L1 or L2 in conversation, is also a "universal" of sorts. But it is a universal of a different kind, a "performance universal" or an ability that typically and normally is distributed evenly in any speech community, composed of an array of competencies and processing skills. "Grammatical competence" refers to children's knowledge of the linguistic system of their L1 (or L2) that underlies the construction of well-formed sentences in comprehension and expression. Grammatical competence, internally heterogeneous itself, could be said to consist of a network of interacting linguistic subsystems, knowledge structures of the linguistic kind. Conversational (primary) discourses depend on these competencies, but also require, for example, specific pragmatic knowledge related to interpersonal interaction, necessary for socially appropriate performance in everyday face-to-face communicative situations.[5]

2. Academic-type, cognitively demanding language ability also depends on grammatical competence (the linguistic knowledge that BICS requires). In addition, it consists of more and more complex kinds and levels of ability related to:

    a. nonlinguistic knowledge structures and skills that underlie secondary discourse ability, and

    b. specific kinds of metalinguistic awareness.

There is much more to the distinction between BICS and CALP than this. Performance in any kind of language use situation requires the participation of specialized processing mechanisms; and CALP-specific pragmatic knowledge is also applied to different types of academic discourse. The sets of specific processing mechanisms and kinds of pragmatic knowledge in BICS and CALP are not the same (though some components of course are shared). Chapter 7 will return to this topic and focus more closely on the relevant components.

This breakdown of the constructs in question accounts for the widely observed phenomenon of the L2 learner, with incomplete (nonnative) knowledge of the target language grammar, who nevertheless performs adequately or even more effectively than the average native speaker in a wide variety of language use contexts (e.g., involving written language) because of the participation of #2a and #2b, skillful mastery of CALP-specific pragmatic rules, and high performance levels in the domain of information processing.[6]

Despite the impression given by invoking the term "higher-order" (used by most of the authors cited in this review, from Vygotsky to Fodor) when referring to academic-type discourses or cognitive abilities, Cummins and Swain clarify that CALP-type abilities are not more "advanced" or more "difficult" in the abstract, or in any absolute sense. For example, for an adult, mastering the basic grammatical patterns of sentence construction in a L2 with native-like levels of skill in fluid and accurate performance is not "cognitively undemanding" in general, across all realms of language use.

4.3 Compartmentalization of the Bilingual Mind

In trying to better understand academic language proficiency in bilingual learners, focusing on its components is a good way to begin. It is in the study of bilingualism, in fact, where aspects of secondary discourse and metalinguistic awareness become especially prominent. And a modular approach might clear the way for a less sectarian assessment of research findings. At least some of the debate would come to be tempered by an accounting of sorts: which mental domains have a claim on which set of (apparently contradictory) research findings? However, the objective of this section goes beyond just dividing up the labor to avoid unnecessary arguments.

To review, Cummins's CUP model is associated with hypotheses in psychology and linguistics that suggest a differentiation between (1) representations of the respective grammatical subsystems of L1 and L2, and (2) aspects of language ability that are independent of L1 and L2.[7] Paivio (1991) offers a somewhat different version of this kind of "three-component" model, the Bilingual Dual Coding Model—on the face of it, modular to a greater degree (for an updated version, see Paivio 2007, 111–115). While Cummins's CUP explicitly encompasses academic language abilities and other aspects of literacy-related proficiency, Paivio's shared conceptual system appears to be more autonomous from the L1 and L2 verbal subsystems. Consistent with this separation, the connections between the nonverbal/conceptual domain and the two verbal subsystems, L1 and L2, differ in kind from the connections between the L1 and L2 subsystems themselves, what we are calling cross-linguistic influence (or transfer). Cross-linguistic influence between the L1 and L2 linguistic domains involves transfer of grammatical features (including phonology). On another level, according to Paivio, the separation and interaction between L1 and L2 may be conditioned by the bilingual's specific history of acquisition and learning, suggesting either two differing kinds of representation or two representations of the same kind. In contrast, the interactions between L1 or L2 (or both) and the nonverbal system would be qualitatively different from all types of cross-linguistic interactions between L1 and L2.

Along similar lines, M. Paradis's (2004) Three-Store Hypothesis proposes two dimensions of separation: the nonlinguistic cognitive store, autonomous from the language system; and within the language system, separate neurofunctional representations for each language (subsystems of L1 and L2). The same conceptual system interacts with the two grammars in performance—in comprehension and expression. In support of this aspect of modularity, Paradis points to the evidence from the study of aphasias. For example, patients suffering from severe disruptions of language ability have been shown to retain skills in nonverbal learning and memory functions, and to perform normally on assessments of nonverbal intelligence. From the idea of a shared conceptual system, it does not follow that exactly the same repertoire of concepts aligns with each language. Rather, the language subsystems share the same semantic features, the same primitive elements that are combined in the construction of fully formed concepts (M. Paradis 2004, 195–198). As we will consider further in the next chapter, grammar and general cognition appear to be doubly dissociated:

- deficits are found in which language ability is affected yet nonverbal cognitive abilities are spared, and
- defective intellectual development may coexist with well-preserved linguistic knowledge, manifested in fluent grammatical speech.

In regard to these "three-component" models, a better understanding of metalinguistic awareness should help us sort out some of the issues regarding how different kinds of knowledge are represented—in particular, how bilinguals' L1 and L2 grammatical competence may be interconnected with conceptual knowledge. Metalinguistic knowledge, which may be considered a type of conceptual knowledge about language, might potentially intervene more prominently in L2 development than in L1. In other words, the L2 learner might benefit to a greater degree from deliberate reflection on, and learning about, language forms and language use. Sharwood Smith (1994a) and Gregg (1996) discuss such a possibility. Chapter 7 will take up this important aspect of language learning. For now, the best way to think about metalinguistic awareness is to place it squarely into the category of explicit knowledge, separate and apart from linguistic competence, which is not accessible to awareness. This shifting balance between specialized acquisition mechanisms and domain-general learning resources is perhaps related to different patterns of development and ultimate attainment in L1 and L2; Birdsong (2006) surveys the relevant findings.

In addition to the ways in which Paivio's Bilingual Dual Coding Model and Paradis's Three-Store Hypothesis view "language" as internally diverse and heterogeneous, it may be diverse and heterogeneous in that some subsystems may be highly encapsulated and vertical, while others develop and function in a nonmodular fashion, allowing, at the same time, for intermediate degrees of encapsulation and "verticality." (This last proposal, by the way, is not necessarily favored by either Paivio or Paradis.) Thus, reference to "*a* language module" would be particularly unhelpful and misleading; Stowe, Haverkort, and Zwarts (2005) argue along similar lines. In principle, the distinction (on some level or another) between central processor and peripheral modules seems compatible with this kind of internal differentiation of language. The contrast between the development of L1 grammatical knowledge in children and the development of metalinguistic knowledge suggests that the idea of a differentiation along these lines is plausible. What seems to be under consideration is the possibility of two different kinds of knowledge, making one wish that there were different terms to distinguish between one kind of knowing and another.

Recalling the discussion in chapter 3 on this point, the distinction between the *primary*, implicit system of language knowledge and *secondary*, explicit knowledge may be especially useful in understanding L2 learning and the development of literacy-related academic language ability. Metalinguistic awareness, as proposed here, is strictly part of secondary explicit knowledge, within the domain of what psychologists term "declarative memory" (M. Paradis 2004, 36–38, 222–223). If it can be shown that the participation of metalinguistic awareness facilitates the development of some language abilities, and at the same time is irrelevant or plays no important role in the development of others, there will be more reason to pursue the idea of an internal differentiation, even more so when we specify that it is language *ability* that is the object of study.

To consider L1 grammatical knowledge first, a system that develops to a complete, fully formed representation by exposure to positive evidence alone achieves this by means of what have been described, for better or for worse, as parameter-setting-type mechanisms (Chomsky 1999; Eisenbeiss 2009). In contrast, for general-purpose learning, input that consists exclusively of positive evidence would be insufficient. Negative evidence, among other kinds of pertinent information, is needed in trial-and-error-type learning and hypothesis formation. A current debate, for example, centers on this far-reaching question: If L1 acquisition[8] depends basically on some kind of parameter-setting acquisition procedure (input composed of primary linguistic data with positive evidence being sufficient for it to do its work), is positive evidence sufficient for L2 learning in sequential bilingualism? Or are general learning strategies and negative evidence necessary as well? If input restricted to primary linguistic data (i.e., positive evidence alone) is not sufficient for development of higher-order discourse abilities (literacy in particular), then a common ground of sorts is suggested between the learning of these secondary discourse abilities and L2 learning.

Turning now to the development of metalinguistic awareness, UG-oriented approaches uniformly disavow any important role for deliberate reflection upon core grammatical patterns in the acquisition of L1.[9] The "options" or "settings" that are "selected" during language acquisition (alternatively, "constraints" or "biases" that guide acquisition) present themselves developmentally, independent of experience. This kind of deductive (prior-knowledge-driven) acquisition is effected outside of any systematic awareness or deliberative trial-and-error-type learning on the part of the young child. The development of other kinds of knowledge that underlie abilities in nonprimary language domains would not proceed in this way. Related also to the question of positive and negative evidence, how might metalinguistic operations participate in language development in the domains of secondary discourse abilities, literacy, and L2 proficiency?

A related line of research on the "interdependent" or "autonomous" development of syntax in bilingual children may shed important light on the question of the internal diversity of language. In early simultaneous bilingualism, (1) is the separation between L_a and L_b achieved from the beginning (the "continuity" or "dual-system" hypothesis) (Genesee, Nicoladis, and Paradis 1995; J. Paradis and Genesee 1996); or (2) are the mechanisms of the Language Acquisition Device programmed to unfold developmentally across the preschool years—in which case, the separation between L_a and L_b would also unfold developmentally? The latter hypothesis might imply that not all the principles of UG are necessarily at the child's full disposal from the beginning. (Schachter (1996) argues for a version of this "maturational hypothesis.")

An important change in our labeling scheme follows from these research questions: "L_a" and "L_b" refer to the bilingual acquisition of two primary languages (2L1s). In reference to the acquisition of two languages during early childhood, the subscripts "$_a$" and "$_b$" do not necessarily imply any differentiation in regard to type of mental representation and internal structure, as the terms "L1" and "L2" sometimes suggest. Further research will need to resolve, empirically, when and under what circumstances a L_a or a L_b might pass over to the status of a L2. And all of this in turn will be related to demonstrating a psychologically real difference between simultaneous and sequential bilingualism, the subject of chapter 6. The final resolution of this research problem will be of great theoretical import. However (at least as things stand now), both hypotheses are compatible with both a modular perspective and a parameter-setting-type explanation of L1 acquisition in early simultaneous bilingualism (L_a+L_b). The reason for this compatibility is that the poverty-of-stimulus problem applies to the language acquisition circumstances that both hypotheses assume.

Studying early differentiation of the preschool bilingual's two languages, during the critical period of L1(L_a+L_b) acquisition, allows us to examine the poverty-of-stimulus problem, also known sometimes as the "logical problem" of language acquisition (Gregg 1996), from a new perspective. As J. Paradis and Genesee (1996) point out, in the case of early simultaneous bilingualism, during the period when primary language development unfolds, bilinguals receive input that is "less complete" and even more "impoverished" in each language (L_a and L_b separately) than monolinguals receive in the only language through which they receive input. The young French-English bilinguals in their study established an early separation between the languages, notably free from mutual interference as each grammatical subsystem passed through the developmental stages typical for monolingual French- and English-speaking children. There are two possible scenarios: the emerging grammars of L_a and L_b are fixed autonomously, without interaction (the continuity hypothesis); or they come to be differentiated over time, but still within the critical period (the maturational hypothesis). In any case, the intervention of general cognitive learning strategies as the principal motor of development, and in particular of separation, would be out of the question. Confirming the achievement of a balanced bilingualism (native-level competence in both languages) in at least a significant subsample in the Paradis and Genesee study would be sufficient to lend support to the Bilingual Dual Coding Model, the Three-Store Hypothesis, or the proposed modification of Cummins's double-iceberg model from chapter 3 (figure 3.2). But now the L1 and L2 icebergs would be *nonoverlapping*. Separating the icebergs in this way so they do not overlap is the second approximation leading toward the final version of the modified double-iceberg model, in chapter 5.

In an attempt to distinguish between the unfolding of bilingual syntactic development and the development of other components, Paradis and Genesee contrast their results with those from studies of the growth of vocabulary knowledge in children. They cite Pearson, Fernández, and Oller (1993), who found (in contrast to early bilingual syntax) the productive vocabulary of the bilingual children in their study to be more limited in each language, counted separately, than that of monolinguals. In addition, total vocabulary in each language of the bilinguals was found to be related to the amount of input (in quantitative terms) received in each language. In regard to syntactic development, there surely also exists a threshold below which the child's bilingual competence would turn out to be imbalanced. But it would seem that the relationship between amount of input (in each language) and syntactic development is of a different kind than the relationship between amount of input, in each language, and this aspect of lexical development. Pinker (1999) makes a related observation: the acquisition of regular verbs and irregular verbs differs. Each may be associated with different subcomponents, encapsulated to a different degree or in a different way: for example, the acquisition of regular verbs might be guided by rule-type representations, that of irregular verbs by a more associative-type network.

Perhaps with this kind of variation in mind, in a review of studies on cognitive development and bilingualism, Bialystok and Cummins (1991) propose a discussion on modularity as a way of orienting research toward "a more differentiated conception of the competencies of bilingual children" (p. 228). Pointing out that the evidence to date has indicated both specialization of functions and interaction, they suggest that work on describing the different representational systems of language and cognition should help explain the wide-ranging individual differences in bilingual children's development. One dimension of the differentiation would be between the linguistic aspects of the languages children speak, on the one hand, and secondary discourse ability and metalinguistic awareness, on the other. They propose that these representations, and the operations associated with them, can indeed be discretely identified and studied. Such a componential organization, in fact, presupposes an extensive array of interfaces and interactivity that research has scarcely begun to describe.

Bialystok and Cummins specifically call attention to Jackendoff's (1987) assessment of Fodor's (1983) model. Jackendoff's representation-based modularity hypothesis envisions a "finer-grained" array of specializations, which in turn appears to allow for a greater degree of interaction across domains than more "bottom-up" modular models would allow for. For example, in reading and in the processing of sign languages, visual information signals lower-level grammatical distinctions that the linguistic modules operate upon. While lower-level operations may share some features of horizontal/cross-domain interaction and exchange, the "central" faculties may share some features of modular-type functioning—"not one great slush of central processes, totally interactive," either (Jackendoff 1987, 267). Weighing the relative merits of the competing perspectives on modularity, Bialystok and Cummins (1991) conclude:

There are indeed interactions between first- and second-language skills . . . but at the same time there is evidence for specialization for languages. Other problems, notably school tasks, seem impervious to the language in which the problem is presented and are solved equally by both languages, . . . although sometimes this too becomes an important feature as solutions to problems are more easily carried out in the language in which those problems were presented. (p. 229)

Descriptions of children's performance on linguistic tasks minimally demand that the task be characterized as being either conversational, contextualized, informal on the one hand, or academic, decontextualized, formal on the other, and each bears a different relation to central cognitive processes.

The primary implication of these highly differentiated descriptions of cognition is that there are cognitive and linguistic operations that can be discretely identified and that have the potential for functioning autonomously. But more importantly, they have the potential of developing autonomously. (pp. 230–231)

All of this, after many years, still awaits many more years of theoretical and experimental work before we can even begin to propose a consensus model of modularity. Nonetheless, research is now in a position to make out the broad contours of what such a model might look like.

4.4 Bilingualism as a Showcase for the Internal Diversity of Language Proficiency

The review of the research so far provides an opportunity to revisit the study of bilingualism and literacy in Central Mexico from a more fine-tuned perspective. A broad sample of assessments was carried out in both languages (Spanish and Nahuatl). On the surface, each task seems to be associated with either primary or secondary discourses, the latter associated with higher levels of metalinguistic ability.

1. Primary (early, preschool development):
   a. contextualized conversational dialog based on a shared graphic display of narrative scenes;
   b. independent oral narrative based on the same narrative scenes, scored for rudimentary narrative form (basic event sequence with interpretable descriptions of each of five episodes);
   c. knowledge of basic everyday vocabulary (vocabulary produced in response to open-ended stimulus items based on familiar everyday scenes of community life).
2. Secondary (later childhood, school-age):
   a. the same oral narrative task described in #1b, now evaluated for indices of textuality and narrative coherence;
   b. written narrative;
   c. reading comprehension.

To clarify, secondary discourses are a late-developing type of language ability. They do not "level off" during the first year or two of elementary school. That is, they are not developmentally "closed," but instead are "open" in relation to time and maturation. It is important not to conceive of a successive onset, secondary following primary. Rather, the two types of discourse can be traced to a parallel, preschool onset, although the secondary discourses typically depend for their further development on schooling and formal instruction (but not always or in all circumstances; see notes 4 and 5). (Chapter 7 will return to the important category of secondary discourse, a term and concept taken from Gee 1996.)

Under the category of primary discourse, all children from 2nd grade on in the Mexican study showed a uniform development: early, complete mastery after which no variation was evident. A native speaker of each language, Nahuatl and Spanish, judged virtually all responses of all students on tasks #1a and #1b as acceptable/age-appropriate for a child native speaker in both languages, except for 4 (out of 45) children who evidenced native levels of Spanish but L2-learner levels of Nahuatl. In addition to revealing uniform performance across all grade levels, results from tasks #1a and #1b failed to correlate (as would be predicted) with *any* index of secondary discourse or academic language proficiency. As described in the previous chapter, during the present stage of the expansion of the national language (NL) in the community, high levels of bilingualism persist among school-age children in part because of their extensive day-to-day contact with both languages during early childhood. Given these peculiar sociolinguistic circumstances of this bilingual, IL-speaking community, uniform performance in both languages on measures that more directly index native-speaker competence was to be expected. In contrast to the measures of primary discourse, *all* measures of secondary discourse indicated a systematic variation from 2nd to 6th grade and correlated positively with each other. As would be expected, scores on a separate test of metalinguistic awareness (appendix 1) only predicted performance on secondary-discourse and academic-language tasks, in addition to showing a late-developing tendency.

The general framework proposed by J. Paradis and Genesee (1996) helps us put these different patterns of variation into perspective, and put together a framework for subsequent analysis. In this community, characterized by high levels of child simultaneous bilingualism, despite individual variation regarding contact with Spanish and Nahuatl, it was not possible to register a series of incremental levels of core grammatical competence. Rather, the performance of the children appears to identify 41 native speakers of L_a and L_b, and 4 (native) Spanish-speaking L2 learners of Nahuatl. As in the case of Paradis and Genesee's French-English bilinguals, we can hypothesize that the Nahuatl and Spanish input that the children received was "less complete and even more impoverished" than the input typically received by either Nahuatl-speaking or Spanish-speaking monolinguals. Clearly, this speculation is only suggested by the results of our assessments; it awaits experimental and comparative studies of a different kind.

In other words, the speculation runs, the poverty-of-stimulus problem that applies to all children acquiring only one language applies with even greater force to young children exposed to two languages. Not only might the acquisition device receive less, and "less complete," positive evidence for each of L_a and L_b separately—it must also sort out potentially conflicting positive evidence. The research on early simultaneous bilingualism suggests that the acquisition device is indeed able to sort out the language-specific grammatical subsystems without much difficulty (Jusczyk

2001; Meisel 2004; Petitto and Kovelman 2003). As we will see in chapter 6, one language may begin to lag behind the other developmentally dominant primary language (another normal variant of early childhood bilingualism, namely, imbalanced). But this outcome does not call into question the Faculty of Language's *balanced bilingual capability*. In the same way, cross-linguistic influence—including manifestations of facilitation/acceleration, delay, or other types of transfer—is compatible in all respects with the separation of grammatical subsystems in early child bilingualism (Hulk and Müller 2000; Sánchez 2003; Werker and Byers-Heinlein 2008; Yip 2006). Evidence of temporary developmental delays, interference, and asymmetrical mixing (e.g., the L_a subsystem imposes its grammatical frames on mixed utterances) would only contradict a model of bilingualism in which each language subsystem is completely encapsulated and isolated from the other.

In contrast to the categorical difference (between fluent native speakers and L2 learners) that resulted from the evaluation of children's knowledge of Nahuatl, the development of secondary discourse abilities shows a markedly noncategorical, stepwise, and continuous variation. Hypothetically, performance in these abilities—#2a (oral narrative), #2b (written narrative) and #2c (reading comprehension)—is sensitive to a hierarchy of equally stepwise and continuous experiences with different kinds of higher-order language use. Consistent with the concept of a CUP that is not strictly "language-bound" (not integrally "bound" to either L1 or L2), performance on tasks #2a, #2b, and #2c improved across grade level (2nd through 6th) in both the NL (the language of instruction) and the IL. And as noted with respect to figures 1.2, 3.3, and 3.4, performance in the IL improves at a significant rate (although somewhat diminished relative to the NL) despite the virtual monopoly of the NL over the literacy-related language curriculum.

In other words, beyond a certain threshold of input during early childhood, the Language Acquisition Device imposes a uniform configuration in all normally developing children (none turn out to be less native-speaking than any others). This uniformity corresponds to mental domains that are most highly encapsulated and dedicated, in a preprogrammed way. In contrast, learning that does not proceed by means of this kind of deductive acquisition process responds to input in a different way. For example, the poverty of stimulus, or the "logical problem," that characterizes L1 acquisition, does not apply (at least not in the same way) to the learning and mastery of secondary discourses, the development of advanced metalinguistic abilities, and other aspects of academic literacy-related language proficiency.

On one level, these findings are entirely predictable: academic-discourse-related language tasks should show late-developing systematic variation across the elementary grades. Conversational, situationally embedded, interpersonal discourse will show early-developing, universal tendencies. However, upon comparing the 41 balanced bilinguals' uniform performance on the primary discourse tasks #1a and #1b with their performance on the measure of basic vocabulary knowledge in both languages (task #1c), we noted a disparity (between the NL and the IL) that did not have an obvious explanation. Why, in determining language dominance, does a sample of primary discourse that focuses on grammatical acceptability of responses produced during an interactive dialog turn out to be a more reliable measure than a sample of vocabulary knowledge? In this case, a componential approach helps to sort out issues related to a problem in the area of language assessment.

Returning to task #1a, the dialog-interview, grammatical processing of the verbal request for information about the display of narrative scenes would be obligatory, strictly speaking nondeliberative. General preconceptions, cultural expectations, previous world knowledge, and so on, may affect *how* a native speaker of a language interprets a particular question or request for information. However, the interpretive components of comprehension cannot normally block grammatical processing. Listeners may elect not to attend: cover their ears, tap their fingers very loudly, hum the national anthem. Children participating in an experiment may respond evasively, respond in a nonreciprocal manner, or decline to respond. They may be confused about how to respond owing to a pragmatic disconnect. However, none of this normally blocks the grammar modules from doing their work.

Again, in the Mexican study, all 41 balanced bilinguals revealed themselves to be competent speakers of both Spanish and Nahuatl. In contrast, the Nahuatl speakers' performance on the assessment of basic Nahuatl vocabulary showed a systematic upward progression across the grades. That is, it showed a variation that appears to reflect the relative autonomy of some subcomponents of this domain of language competence. In other words, some aspects of lexical knowledge seem to be independent of other aspects. If lexical knowledge in general turns out to be governed by the same kinds of mental structure that govern linguistic competence as a whole (as may indeed be the case), we might ask, what is different about the way some components of lexical knowledge are represented in contrast to others? Learning words is not simply a matter of building a larger and larger network of associations, item by item; and special acquisition devices of the Faculty of Language should play a role in lexical development, as they do for other domains of linguistic knowledge (Bloom 2000). But there seems to be at least one aspect of lexical development that departs from the pattern of automatic and modularized acquisition that is characteristic of the emergence of core grammar. When we attempt to sketch a model of the bilingual lexicon in chapter 5, we will speculate on an avenue of future research related to this question.

In effect, the Nahuatl speakers' performance on the assessment of basic Nahuatl vocabulary showed a systematic upward progression across the grades, as if they were responding to a measure of secondary discourse ability, which clearly they were not. Given that the semantic domains called upon in each graphic are associated with basic everyday vocabulary, no straightforward explanation of the findings immediately presents itself. In Spanish, the sociolinguistically unmarked language of school, the corresponding curve for 2nd-, 4th-, and 6th-graders' basic vocabulary is statistically flat (appendix 2). Again, this was to be expected since the graphic stimuli used for the evaluation were drawn from domains that form part of the everyday experience of the average 7- or 8-year-old 2nd grader.

In previous analyses of this disparity (why basic Spanish vocabulary development levels out early while basic Nahuatl vocabulary shows growth across the elementary grades; N. Francis, 1998, 2004, 2005), the following possible explanations were suggested:

1. the influence of Spanish that has imposed, historically, its own peculiar set of imbalances (e.g., the unequal interchange of loanwords between Nahuatl and Spanish);

2. cultural perceptions and sociolinguistic constraints regarding the diglossic distribution of the two languages (e.g., in school);

3. the development, in this particular school-age population, of metalinguistic awareness tied to a kind of de facto, limited, additive bilingual development (e.g., older bilinguals are more conscious of the "origin" of loanwords);

4. general growth of Nahuatl vocabulary (plus #3) on the part of child bilingual speakers. This growth of vocabulary might result in a gradual replacement of Spanish-origin terms (that form part of the young child's Nahuatl lexicon) by their IL equivalents. That is, as children progress through the grades in school, they are better able to reflect on the sociolinguistic factors in #1 and #2 and exercise greater control over a language task that requires them to focus on form related to language choice (this is where factor #3 comes in—the young bilinguals' growing sense of the differences between the languages they speak). As the bilingual children learn new words in their IL (factor #4) and become increasingly aware of how their languages are separate, these new lexical entries might begin to "replace" (in use) Spanish lexical entries that are perceived to be equivalent. This would occur, for example, when the children are specifically asked to comply with language tasks "in Nahuatl" or get the idea that they should try to differentiate between Spanish and Nahuatl (e.g., control the participation or "interference" of Spanish in an experiment). The relative level of activation, or ability to control the activation, of a bilingual's two languages, one of which functions as the "base language," is the object of continuing research related to the important concept of *language mode* (Grosjean 2001).

What is interesting here is that the four factors outlined above are associated with central domains of language proficiency, including aspects of language proficiency that are nonlinguistic. While they appear to affect performance on lexical tasks, in the circumstances of task #1a they would not intervene in syntactic processing in a significant way, if at all (for the native speaker of the language). According to this idea, online (automatic and implicit) grammatical analysis of the kind of context-embedded request for information described above proceeds rapidly and involuntarily. In a way, it is "encapsulated" from penetration of a good part of top-down influences (for an explanation, see Fodor 1983, 1990). In addition, to the extent that grammatically well-formed questions and requests also conform to culture-specific pragmatic constraints, comparably rapid and automatic comprehension would be ensured. Here we might take note of a different kind of imbalance: that between receptive and expressive abilities.

Findings from these descriptive studies point toward the next investigations, which would seek further evidence for a componential organization of lexical knowledge itself. This aspect of language competence is also likely to be internally diverse. We should expect the core components of all subsystems of the lexicon to be constrained by the specialized mechanisms of the Faculty of Language. At the same time, though, differences in the way the components behave suggest different levels of "openness" toward central domains—morphology and syntax more "restricted" and "closed," other subsystems of the lexicon more "open" (Bloom 1994). In the case of monolinguals, the disparities that we observe in bilingual competence are much less apparent: the different components seem to develop more evenly or in a more balanced way. In normal bilingual development, the same overall trend in lexical knowledge (a more even and balanced development) would also be observed:

1. in either L1 or L2,
2. in both, or
3. upon combining the total lexical store from the two languages, a procedure that is applied, preferably, to the assessment of bilingual vocabulary (Muñoz Sandoval et al. 1998).

It is the relative imbalance in some aspects of lexical knowledge that suggests a more heterogeneous or "open-ended" kind of mental representation for this domain, in contrast to other aspects of linguistic knowledge, which may be less imbalanced. Recent studies of early bilingual development have made similar observations. For example, D. K. Oller, Pearson, and Cobo-Lewis (2007) suggest that what is called "vocabulary" may be distributed between L1 and L2 in a different way than other components of language competence. Thordardottir et al. (2006) also discuss this complex issue, pointing to important implications for bilingual assessment.

Other experiments could explore this asymmetry observed in the bilingual lexicon, which does not appear to manifest itself in the same way in overall morphosyntactic development. While vocabulary knowledge might stabilize around a kind of complementary distribution between L1 and L2 (below the monolingual average in each language, measured separately; complete if the lexicons are combined), typical native-speaker knowledge of morphology and syntax would normally arrive at a complete steady state in at least one of the two languages. Note that the concept of "semilingualism" (temporary developmental imbalances aside) would therefore be reserved for cases of bilingual development that are pathological in some way—for example, resulting from deprivation of primary linguistic input below a minimum threshold. The emblematic case is that of deaf children denied access to sign language during the critical period of L1 acquisition. McLaughlin, Gesi Blanchard, and Osanai (1995) discuss the possibility of temporary developmental imbalances resulting from subtractive bilingualism; however, this kind of transitory distribution of grammatical resources should (sooner rather than later) tip toward one or the other core grammar system, leaving only one of them as incomplete or "nonnative."

A research program centered on these questions could begin to explain a number of apparently contradictory findings in the literature. In the performance domains of primary discourse, all measures of proficiency for all native speakers of a language should evidence an early attainment plateau at typical native-speaker ability levels. In the Mexican study, our initial assessment of these components indicated such homogeneity in all areas except basic lexical knowledge in the children's IL, Nahuatl (in Spanish, basic lexical knowledge did indicate homogeneity). As it turns out, the highly imbalanced diglossic bilingualism of this speech community might reveal more clearly a lexical subcomponent of linguistic competence that may be represented in a more open-ended fashion. This subcomponent would be more sensitive to general knowledge and other influences outside the core domains of the Faculty of Language—sometimes referred to as the Faculty of Language (Narrow). Further research might be able to propose a kind of continuity between this lexical subcomponent, closely tied to UG, and those aspects of lexical knowledge that should show themselves to be completely open. The latter would be dependent on the higher-order discourse proficiencies and learning, and largely independent of the mechanisms of the Language Acquisition Device.

L2 learning displays an analogous relationship: incremental development of vocabulary knowledge in close correlation with experience. With sufficient input, even of the passive variety (e.g., reading L2 texts), the learner can easily accumulate a lexical repertoire superior, in terms of number of discrete entries, to the average for the native-speaker community. In contrast, the development of other linguistic domains does not proceed in this manner. For older learners, morphology, syntax, and phonology are often stubbornly resistant despite deliberate learning and extensive everyday contact with the L2, usually falling far short of native-speaker levels (and apart from abnormal cases, are hardly ever learned by passive methods of simple immersion, without interaction or practice). (For a graphic portrayal of this interesting dissociation commonly observed in L2 learning, see figure 5.3.)

4.5 Advancing the Research Program on Bilingualism: The Need for Clarity and Reflection

The modularity of language can be viewed in a number of ways. We have touched on three:

1. developmentally;
2. in regard to the actual mental representation of different components and subsystems of language ability; and
3. in regard to processing (i.e., how comprehension and production proceed in real time).

In this way, a modular approach can be applied to the study of a particular proficiency, or to any one of its components (e.g., the subcomponents into which a competence structure might be analyzed). And it would be entirely possible that different aspects of bilingualism would evidence different combinations of encapsulation, speed, and domain specificity, or different degrees of modularity. For example, a highly modular structure, in regard to its mental representation (#2), may evidence a high degree of interactivity in processing (#3) (Sharwood Smith 1991).

In this regard, Fodor (1998) disfavors the idea of "massive modularity." The problem of integrating the computations coming up from the "peripheral processors" requires the intervention of some kind of "central operating system." This system would have some of the following characteristics: global rather than local functions that are more integrated, interpretive, and computationally horizontal. Information would circulate in a more diffuse and multidirectional manner than in a more encapsulated system. The "higher cognitive faculties" (Fodor 1990) would exchange information both among themselves and with lower-level processors. Which mental domains this exchange matches up with, and what characteristics this kind of interaction exhibits, will be the subject of research for years to come. For now, the idea is that there are restrictions on how central faculties intervene in the operation of systems dedicated to perception and other kinds of more encapsulated processing. And for now, it would seem reasonable to continue to explore, within the realm of the higher-order abilities, all the possible interactions between language and thought. "Massive-modularity" approaches, on the other hand, might tend to favor a more bottom-up kind of interactivity. Wilson (2005) presents a view of modularity that questions the distinction between local/modular and global/central processes as it has been applied to the study of pragmatics, for example.

For one exchange of views on all this, see Karmiloff-Smith's (1991) "Beyond Modularity" model, and Fodor's (1998) reply. An unfortunate missed opportunity this debate turns out to be. Coming from the study of atypical child development, which modularists should be keen on understanding, Karmiloff-Smith detects some cracks in the mainstream version of nativism. Two points are pertinent here: (1) innate principles cannot be highly detailed and complex in all domains of linguistic knowledge, and (2) we should keep open the possibility of greater intercomponent and interdomain communication than many theorists interested in modularity are willing to admit. For example, in development, knowledge structures, "in the mind," provide input to other knowledge structures, even of different types (an interactivity related to the idea of "representational redescription").

Following Luria, the study of abnormal language development presents a useful point of reference. Again, deaf children who have been severely isolated or deprived of language input present the most dramatic example. On the one hand, a significant degrading of language in these cases does not block all cognitive development, confirming the autonomy of thought from language at some level. On the other hand, the peculiar deficiencies in the development of abstraction and problem solving that require more cognitively demanding manipulation of symbols, reported in deaf children and adults deprived of access to sign language (Sacks 1990), seem to confirm Vygotsky's (1934/1962) observations in regard to the metacognitive functions of language. (For more discussion, see Edwards and Kirkpatrick 1999, Lasagabaster Herrate 1998, Hamers 1991, Sharwood Smith 1993; to sharpen the debate, see Olson 1991, Ong 1992; and see Jahandarie 1999 on the role that *written* language plays in the development of metalinguistic awareness and the intellectual capacities.) In any case, further study of bilingualism from a point of view that allows the kind of diversity and heterogeneity discussed so far may hold out new prospects for interdisciplinary communication. On the face of it, approaches that distinguish between degrees of modularity of peripheral processes and degrees of openness of central processes would seem to be more compatible with these prospects, but then that is not an argument against "massive modularity" either (Barrett and Kurzban 2006). Sperber (2001) favors a different slant on "domain-specific mechanisms" and "domain-general abilities"; in turn, Carruthers (2003) argues for an intermediate position between Fodor and Sperber, somewhat more inclined toward "massive modularity."

Cummins (2000) has applied to bilingualism the distinction between abilities that correspond to different language use contexts, which in turn depend on the participation of different clusters of competencies and processors. This viewpoint provides a framework that can move the research program on bilingualism forward along lines that have been suggested here. Until recently, opposition to this framework has primarily gravitated around holistic and integrativist (i.e., antimodular) theories of language and literacy (e.g., strong top-down "whole-language" theories). MacSwan (2000) questions it from a different vantage point, based on concepts derived from UG-oriented linguistic research. The critique centers on discrediting the notion of semilingualism, which throughout MacSwan attempts to link to Cummins's discussion of variation in literacy-related abilities. Clearing away the confusion that has enveloped the concept of semilingualism and pointing out how limited its application might be is a worthy objective. (A curious aspect of this confusion is the attraction that this category of language impairment seems to have, especially among educators who work with IL-speaking populations.) Since Cummins's (2000, 99–111) own reassessment on this point is more thorough, perhaps it will be better, for now, to set aside this especially unhelpful red herring.

As this chapter has argued so far, the distinction between conversational (primary) discourse ability and literacy-related, academic-type (secondary) discourse ability has been useful in understanding different kinds of variation in language use. A particular complex of linguistic and general cognitive subcomponents come together in school-related language proficiencies. Different complexes come together in other kinds of language ability. "Secondary" achievements might include these: development of reading and writing ability, especially for academic purposes; development of higher-order comprehension abilities (written and oral, especially in regard to expository genres); and even perhaps aspects of late childhood L2 learning. Different circumstances of bilingualism (e.g., subtractive) and varying conditions of L2 learning (e.g., submersion or exclusion of the child's L1 from instruction) add to the mix still more literacy-related factors tied to academic achievement. The consequences of different types of subtractive bilingualism and L2 submersion instruction continue to deserve serious consideration and are not easily dispensed with. After many years of research, it seems that the basic concepts are still not well understood. For example, what differing consequences do the following child bilingual development scenarios have for the development of academic language proficiency? (1) L1 attrition coincides with inadequate L2 instruction. (2) The L1 is not lost, but it plays no role in literacy learning. (3) L1 attrition proceeds "normally" (as it often does), and L2 instruction, including L2 literacy learning, is adequate.

Where MacSwan (2000) misses the mark in his hasty challenge to Cummins's model is in liquidating the question of variation in secondary discourse development and literacy-related academic proficiency by applying to this domain the defining characteristics of the development of L1 grammatical competence. To repeat: L1 grammatical competence is not the same as conversational discourse ability; rather, in most cases it is most reliably revealed by observing this ability. A modular approach would help us avoid confounding competence and performance, knowledge and ability. But more substantially, being mindful of the heterogeneity of what is loosely referred to as "language proficiency" helps us separate out the components that coincide with the implicit knowledge of grammar: the complete and uniform linguistic competence that is characteristic of all normally developing 10-year-old native speakers of any language. These components should be separated out from other competencies and processing modules that subserve secondary discourses and related academic language proficiencies. The same would be useful in regard to other competencies and processing modules that subserve all types of discourse ability, BICS included. These are competencies and knowledge structures that in large part lie outside the ("narrow," UG-based) Faculty of Language. Here, "complete" and "uniform" do not apply to learned abilities in the realm of literacy and school-related academic discourse abilities; rather, they apply to the attainment of the steady state of grammatical development as it is revealed in performance on primary-discourse-type tasks by all school-age children in their primary language.

It is absolutely correct to point out that the superficial grammatical differences that are noticeable to the ear and the eye, and that distinguish one speech community from another, obscure an underlying uniformity in the knowledge of more abstract principles of grammar. But the normal variation in the rate of grammatical development in children, and the variation in basic grammatical patterns related to dialect, are of a completely different kind than the variation under consideration in the domains of CALP and literacy. For example, a monolingual speaker of a socially disfavored (e.g., nonstandard) dialect may, because of social prejudice, suffer from being denied opportunity in school to develop advanced academic abilities related to language use. But, in principle, nothing in the grammar of such a dialectal variant poses any obstacle to developing advanced levels of mastery of CALP-related discourses. (This was the case of our hypothetical bilingual A in section 4.2.) Despite the complex interfaces that connect linguistic structures and conceptual structures, the cognitive domains to which these two sets of knowledge structure belong should be viewed as independent of each other. On the one hand, we have the components of linguistic knowledge related to dialectal variation, and on the other hand, knowledge structures that specifically subserve academic discourse abilities, metalinguistic awareness, and literacy.

Academic language proficiency encompasses more than the ability to read and write; and it can develop in language use contexts both outside of formal schooling and apart from contact with written language. But these CALP-type discourse abilities do not emerge automatically, "spontaneously" (to borrow Vygotsky's term), and uniformly in the same manner as primary discourse ability. Thus, studying the variation in the *learning* of these CALP-type discourse abilities and of the school-related metalinguistic abilities in no way amounts to endorsing a "deficit theory" of any kind. For example, children's early and sustained immersion in the oral tradition of their speech community, or in a literary tradition through the medium of books, might be associated with developing a more robust vocabulary beyond the core repertoire shared by all native speakers. Children would most likely vary discernably in this realm of CALP-type language ability. The "deficit theory" attribution fails because increments in this aspect of lexical knowledge beyond the core vocabulary, tied to exposure to secondary discourses, simply require experience and learning. There is no disability, intrinsic or otherwise, no critical period threshold, no impairment, no deficit. The "deficit theory" charge also fails with respect to variation in other literacy-related language abilities (e.g., text comprehension), for the same reason. Now, some children (bilinguals included) have been shown to suffer from intrinsic disabilities, and manifest symptoms of a true language impairment. In this case, one could unobjectionably discuss a *theory* that might help shed light on the etiology, for example, of a particular *deficit*. Therefore, it is useful to avoid the unreflective use of the term "deficit theory," as if it were part of an accusation.

Though correctly describing "linguistic development" as a "process that is inwardly directed and accomplished effortlessly and unerringly by all normal children ... by virtue of [their] biological makeup" (p. 18), MacSwan (2000) could help readers better understand this fundamental insight of cognitive science by circumscribing more explicitly (1) which components or aspects of "linguistic development" unfold in such an innately predetermined and genetically specified way, (2) which cognitive domains this "process" corresponds to, (3) which kind of proficiency (language ability, performance) might most reliably reveal completeness and universality, and (4) what the basic irreducible foundations of language are (Goldin-Meadow 2005).

In an otherwise well-argued critique of current assessment practices in bilingual education, MacSwan and Rolstad (2006) return to the theme of an implicit deficit theory that underlies the concept of CALP. Seizing on an unfortunately ambiguous formulation by Cummins (2000, 35) in reference to academic language ability ("Less knowledge of language itself is usually required to function appropriately in interpersonal communicative situations"), the authors gloss over a more complicated discussion, including an important and helpful self-criticism by Cummins (2000) of previous conceptions (1979a) related to the idea of semilingualism. A debater's point is scored at the expense of clarity in how we should better understand the development of literacy-related academic abilities in school. As late as 2008, MacSwan and Rolstad continued to press their case for tying Cummins to an incorrect application of the concept of semilingualism. Many readers might find it somewhat odd, at least unfair. What useful purpose is served by polemicizing against a view long after it has been retracted, and after a clarification of the original error has been offered for further discussion? Fairness aside, digging into the past while passing over current positions in scientific debate doesn't move it forward.

If some subcomponents of language develop automatically and are represented in a more encapsulated way than others, this may be related to the manner in which these linguistic subsystems are supported by domain-specific modules. In this way, they would contrast with other knowledge structures, which one day may be shown to be represented differently (e.g., may be shown to be more variable, more dependent on experience, and more sensitive to context). In other words, it is unlikely that all aspects of language ability are innately specified to the same extent and in the same way that some core components of it are. This is a big and complex question involving the balance between learned and "nonlearned" aspects of language ability that research is still far from resolving (see, e.g., S. Anderson and Lightfoot 2002; Bloom 2001; Foster-Cohen 1990; Jusczyk 2001; Lidz and Gleitman 2004; Pinker and Ullman 2002). That there is some kind of "balance" between UG-determined deduction and open-ended general learning induction is a view that has gained greater acceptance. Complex abilities related to performance on secondary-discourse and metalinguistic tasks appear to require the participation of deliberate learning strategies that are even more "open," and more dependent on instruction. If this assessment is correct, then all bets on parameter-setting-type completeness and universality are off. Paradoxically, what may lead us toward a more convergent discussion are methods that compartmentalize even more finely the way we have been studying what we call bilingual proficiency.

5

Research on the Components of Bilingual Proficiency

In this chapter, we will delve deeper into the idea that bilingual proficiency is componential—what it means to say that it is internally diverse. Along the way, we will see that the proposed modification to Cummins's Common Underlying Proficiency model (figure 3.2) turns out to be in need of some modification of its own. Paivio's (1991, 2007) Bilingual Dual Coding Model and M. Paradis's (2004) Three-Store Hypothesis will help move the task of elaboration and specification along.

A model of bilingual proficiency, depicting the competencies and processing mechanisms that make it up, should be able to account for the many ways in which its components appear both independent of each other and closely interconnected. In child development, we need to answer these questions:

1. Why, in some circumstances and in some respects, one language subsystem does not appear to affect another, whereas in other circumstances prolific interaction seems to take place (i.e., influences of L_a on L_b, L_b on L_a)?

2. Under similar conditions, why is it possible to find both balanced development of L_a and L_b, and unbalanced development (in reference to both acquisition and erosion)?

In processing and normal language use:

3. How are bilinguals able to keep their languages separate, and how are they able to allow the two subsystems to combine and interact in performance?

4. How are combining and mixing accomplished in a grammatically systematic way?

5. How do the strictly linguistic components of proficiency reveal themselves to be independent of the general conceptual systems? How, at the same time, do language and general cognition appear to be interdependent?

6. How do general cognitive operations intervene in language use in different ways that sometimes reveal separation and at other times appear to suggest integration?

In chapter 4, we focused mainly on the last two points: the way in which different kinds of language ability draw on different aspects of Central System knowledge structures. These knowledge structures are more "central" in a number of ways—for one, in bilinguals they are *shared*, accessible in performance through either linguistic "channel." In multilingual competence, the "centrality" of shared knowledge structures is easier to visualize. (Would a polyglot need to store separate conceptual structures for every language?) Culicover and Jackendoff (2005, 20) describe the conceptual structures as being part of a "central-system" of the mind. Access to these (shared/central) extralinguistic domains is subject to many limitations: some closely tied to the linguistic domains; others external, from general cognitive operations; and still others entirely removed from the mental realm, coming at us from the sociolinguistic world outside. Conversely, other factors and conditions facilitate or free up the channels that interconnect language and the resources of the Central System. In any case, "access" is still the most adequate metaphor for the idea of reachableness and availability. Unavoidably, it will get overused in the coming chapters.

In this chapter, we will consider more closely another dimension of connectedness and interaction, introduced by points #1–#4. This dimension of the interface relations of language is specific to bilingualism because it involves interactions between the grammatical components of two separate linguistic subsystems. By contrast, the language ↔ general cognition interfaces (introduced by points #5 and #6), though perhaps more clearly laid bare when two languages are observed in children, are of the same kind found in the monolingual condition.

With all these questions in mind, the descriptive generalizations from the Nahuatl-Spanish study have evoked concepts discussed in research in other bilingual settings. One of the main conclusions that this research has converged upon, which holds a key to understanding a whole range of observations, is that bilingual proficiency is internally differentiated in a number of interesting ways. This is what the last two chapters have tried to suggest. Analysis of the children's performance on the school-related tasks described so far in Nahuatl and Spanish now leads us to consider the findings of other bilingual research projects, all very different from the one conducted in Mexico. Specifically, we will focus on these topics: language separation, cross-linguistic interactions as in borrowing and codeswitching, the relationship between grammatical knowledge and literacy-related discourse abilities, and how lexical knowledge in two languages is related to other domains of linguistic knowledge. These important themes in research on bilingual proficiency have come to the fore in the attempts of the project to describe children's development in Spanish and in their indigenous language.

In the San Isidro circumstance, the social inequalities and conflicts that weigh heavily upon the contact between national language and vernacular apply pressures of varying degrees upon language use and language proficiency. As illustrated in the previous chapters, these pressures open a wider window, so to speak, onto the components of language proficiency and their interaction than does the monolingual condition. The study of exceptional bilingualism, in which extralinguistic pressures on the components of language and the associated processing mechanisms are multiplied, provides an especially acute viewpoint. It is to this area of investigation that we will turn first.

5.1 Maximum Imbalance in Bilingualism

When complex systems suffer breakdown, lose equilibrium, and get out of balance, what previously appeared to function as an integrated unit opens up to provide a vantage point onto components that once passed unnoticed. Compared with monolingual competence and performance, bilingualism affords more opportunities for examining the components of language because aside from simply being a more complex system, during development it seems to be more susceptible to different kinds of imbalance and tension. Examining dissociations of different kinds, especially "double dissociations," is an important tool for language researchers; bilingualism multiplies the possibilities. One starting point, among others, is to describe how language development proceeds under circumstances in which processing must be shifted to another modality (auditory → visual) or in which development is abnormal in some way.

5.1.1 Sign Language Development, Early and Late

Studies of sign language acquisition have provided the field of bilingualism with fresh perspectives on old questions. For example, in Quebec, Petitto (1997) was able to study the different combinations of bilingual-bimodal signers (e.g., hearing children born to deaf parents), bilingual-unimodal signers (ASL/LSQ, American Sign Language/Langue des Signes Québécoise), and two types of monolinguals (deaf ASL or LSQ signers, and hearing signers not exposed to speech).

Having confirmed previous findings that sign and speech pass through the same developmental milestones, Petitto went on to look more closely at the earliest stages in bilingual and bimodal subjects. Comparing ASL and LSQ in bilingual babblers, she found that initial stages showed no differentiation. By 12 months, however, language-specific sign-phonetic units began to emerge. Bimodal (e.g., ASL and English) infants produced both manual and vocal babbling within the same developmental time period. Petitto (1997, 59) proposes, "The infant's nascent sensitivity to aspects of language structure may reflect the presence of a neural substrate that is uniquely sensitive to the stimulus values specified in prosodic and syllabic structure." "A mechanism ready to differentially process input signals," dedicated uniquely to linguistic input, accounts both for early differentiation in ASL/LSQ bilinguals and for the finding that bimodal infants treat both speech and sign as language. For bimodal children with normal hearing, for example, an alternative possibility would be that auditory input is directed to the language acquisition mechanisms and visual input is automatically processed nonlinguistically. Apparently, this does not happen.

These acquisition-processing mechanisms are both "rigid" and "flexible." Rigidity is the hallmark of underlying linguistic templates sensitive to distributional patterns specific to natural language—"abstract features of language patterning." Flexibility is evident in how the "capacity for language can be potentiated in multiple ways" depending on available input-output resources and environmental pressures (Petitto 1997, 56–58). Domain specificity then refers to how structure-seeking modules analyze linguistic input at an abstract level beyond and independent of modality. That language cannot be derived solely from general cognitive capacities is suggested by deaf children's consistent separation of linguistic signs and nonlinguistic gestural communication, even though the two share properties of formation and reference (Petitto 1992, 28–31). For example, the high iconicity of many ASL signs does not appear to affect the normal time-course of language acquisition (i.e., during the same critical period that constrains other kinds of early child language development).

There seems to be an important differentiation between early prelinguistic gestures and early linguistic forms, lending support to the idea of a modular-type separation between general cognitive domains and a dedicated set of interacting special-purpose linguistic components (Lillo-Martin 1999). In this regard, Sandler (2003) points to a number of conceptual problems that theories of modularity need to account for. Input modules, for example, must be flexible and open-ended enough to be able to process both auditory and visual information. Sign language points to an ongoing interaction among the linguistic subsystems and the visual system, also allowing for top-down influences from the Central System. Coltheart (1999) makes a related proposal regarding the conditions necessary for a system to be considered modular, including the possibility of admitting *degrees* of encapsulation and interactivity among a set of smaller, more specialized modules.

Probably the most compelling evidence for the robustness of children's language-structure-seeking capacity comes from the groundbreaking investigation of sign language genesis among previously isolated deaf children in Nicaragua, brought together in newly established schools for the deaf. Since the early 1990s, child language development specialists have been able to get an unprecedented glimpse into the creation of a sign language creole arising from an exceptional multilingual concurrence of pidgins, homesign systems, and spoken language.

Unlike typical creoles, the new sign language, Idioma de Signos Nicaragüense (ISN), was formed apparently without access to a full-blown language substrate. In the study, a series of cohorts of previously linguistically isolated children were evaluated to determine the level of proficiency attained despite the absence of a fully formed language model.

Entering the school, none of the children had advanced beyond a primitive homesign gestural system. Upon contact with other deaf children, however, they created two new linguistic systems: (1) a highly variable peer-group pidgin that evolved into a communication form progressively incorporating shared signs and an incipient grammar; and (2) a distinct, fully formed sign language, ISN (Kegl, Senghas, and Coppola 1999, 180). Crucially, each stage of language development represented a qualitative leap forward over the previous stage, confirming previous observations of how children surpass impoverished models. Most interesting, however, was the finding that ISN, the signed creole, emerged precipitously when the peer-group pidgin became the input to young children. Thereupon, ISN became the target language for all other sign language learners in the community.

On the basis of findings from their study, Morford and Kegl (2000) discuss the question of a continuity between gestural communication and linguistic development. In the case of an isolated homesigner, exposure to conventional gestures used by hearing family members results in defective linguistic development—surpassing the impoverished model, but minimally. A community of homesigners, on the other hand, gives rise to a system that is rich enough to support the emergence of a full-fledged creole if children are exposed to it sufficiently during the critical period. Commenting on the stages through which the fully formed sign language emerged, A. Senghas and Coppola (2001) refer to earlier research (Goldin-Meadow 2000) that had already demonstrated the capacity of deaf children to build a grammar from significantly degraded input (degraded far below any level that would be considered "normal," recalling that the poverty-of-stimulus problem applies to all child language acquisition situations). In the case of ISN genesis, they speculate:

[The] time required to originate a language may exceed a child's sensitive period, which presumably evolved to enable learning from a full language model. Without rich input, an individual may still have the resources, but not enough time. . . . If time is the limiting factor, perhaps sequential cohorts of interacting individuals, successively building on the achievements of their predecessors, could effectively concatenate their individual sensitive periods into a combined period long enough to create a language. (p. 323)

In effect, age of contact with the peer-group pidgin turned out to be the critical variable: homesigners immersed before age 7 were the most successful in surpassing their models, whereas "slightly older" 8- to 14-year old learners made considerable progress, but consistently attained levels less native-like in comparison to the youngest acquirers. Late-immersion deaf students, past the critical period for language development, showed permanent effects of language deprivation. These late learners, whose first contact was initiated after 15 years, "[did] not acquire a signed language at native levels of fluency at all" (Kegl, Senghas, and Coppola 1999, 212). Most notably in regard to the nonnative, L2- learner-type performance of the late-childhood cohort (8–14 years), the Nicaraguan study represents a striking confirmation of Newport's (1990) findings that differentiated similarly among native, early, and late ASL learners. Herschensohn's (2000) discussion of modularity and the critical period in sign language and creole acquisition is particularly relevant here. The evidence for strong critical period effects in exceptional (i.e., delayed) L1 learning (Curtiss 1994) and double dissociations contrasting deficient intellectual development–normal grammar with normal intellectual development–deficient grammar (Rondal 1995; Tager-Flusberg 1999; Yamada 1990) all argue against an undifferentiated and holistic mental organization. If access to a Language Acquisition Device (LAD) is time- and maturation-sensitive, as the contrast between native and late (>7 years) signers shows, whatever this acquisition device turns out to consist of, it will likely be special-purpose and domain-specific to some important degree.

Eubank and Gregg (1999) and Gregg (1996) explain the connection between critical period effects and modularity in regard to L1 learning; and in regard to L2 learning, Foster-Cohen (1996) does the same. In a wide-ranging discussion of Specific Language Impairment (SLI), adult L2 learning, and creole formation, Newmeyer (1998) concludes:

Creolization itself is the work of children. . . . [While] adults may modify pidgins into something more creole-like, it is only children who literally have the ability to *create* creoles, that is, to create a new grammatical system. This contrast between the abilities of adults and children provides support for [the autonomy of grammatical knowledge]. (pp. 72–73)

The next chapter will revisit this question in the context of a fuller discussion of the critical period hypothesis in relation to L1 acquisition and the possibility of "access to Universal Grammar (UG)" in L2 learning. In the meantime, however, the pattern of language creation in Nicaragua seems to point to the importance of not overstating the capacity of the LAD to overcome the poverty-of-stimulus problem. What the ISN creole needed was an active "sign/speech community" that had upgraded the earlier individual homesign systems that children brought with them (R. Senghas, Senghas, and Pyers 2005). In other words, the input to the LAD cannot be too degraded (the interesting research question remains: what are the limits in this regard?). For example, the deaf children who lacked contact with a signing community surpassed but could not prevail over the impoverished input they received.

5.1.2 Multilingualism and Abnormal Development

Rounding out our review of research on exceptional bilingualism, the case study conducted by N. Smith and Tsimpli (1995) of the polyglot savant Christopher stands out as one of the most extensive and theoretically well-grounded analyses of the components of linguistic competence. To review, so far we have considered two dimensions of modularity: (1) the separation between the respective subsystems that are associated with representations of L_a and L_b and how this is manifested in development and language use ($L_a \leftrightarrow L_b$), and (2) the relative autonomy of central cognitive systems and Conceptual Structure (CS) from the linguistic components of phonology and morphology-syntax (CS $\leftrightarrow L_{a+b}$). Smith and Tsimpli's case study sharpens our focus on the second dimension.

The dissociation examined in Christopher's case contrasts his normal, native-speaker level knowledge of English, a "hyperability" in his mastery of 16 L2s (in a number of which he attained intermediate to advanced proficiency), and defective development in higher-order aspects of language use that reflected significantly diminished capacities in a number of Central System domains. Analysis of Christopher's performance on a wide range of language tasks suggested to the authors a reconsideration and elaboration of Fodor's (1990) modularity framework.

Despite full command of L1 (English) grammar and superior vocabulary knowledge, Christopher experienced difficulty with interpreting sentences that involved resolving an apparent contradiction, increased processing demands, discourse-level comprehension, and Theory of Mind (ToM) type problems (requiring second-degree interpretations of someone else's thought; e.g., imputing false belief) (N. Smith and Tsimpli 1995, 61–77). Although Christopher's conversational skills found support in the interactive and contextual scaffolding of turn taking (p. 171) and appeared normal, certain of his key discourse-level and cognitively demanding pragmatic abilities were clearly subnormal. N. Smith and Tsimpli conclude that these deficiencies "arise from processing difficulties which involve the interaction of his modular linguistic faculty with central system operations" (p. 79).

Given the pattern of assessment results, and evidence from the study of other abnormal conditions such as autism, the authors make the case that the Central System ToM competencies are quasi-modular—that at least some components of the Central System reveal modular-like characteristics (Tsimpli and Smith 1998). The stark discrepancy between Christopher's defective ToM capabilities and his superior vocabulary knowledge (Peabody Picture Vocabulary Test English: 121/100, German: 114/100, French: 110/100) (N. Smith and Tsimpli 1995, 8) indicates that the Central System may not be entirely integrated and holistic. However, this suggestion would be more convincing if Christopher had not failed, in addition to some ToM tasks,[1] other language tests that implicate the participation of Central System–

type operations. Superior vocabulary knowledge in L1, plus all the possible nonredundant entries in this polyglot's 16 L2s, implies Conceptual Structure components for each lexical item that meaning can be assigned to. This indicates strong development in at least some domains of general cognition, despite serious deficits in others. Drawing on these findings, Smith and Tsimpli argue for a model that views the Central System as richly structured but not massively modular. Some components may be domain-specific but not informationally encapsulated; for further discussion of this possibility, see R. Samuels 2006, and Gerrans and Stone 2008 specifically in relation to the question of modularity and ToM. ToM appears to depend on operations that are inferential and cognitively penetrable (as evidenced in Christopher's uneven performance), taking advantage of a free flow of information among the different Central System components.

Along these lines, drawing on an extensive review of the research, Garfield, Peterson, and Perry (2001) argue for a weak modularity claim for ToM development—namely, that it emerges with the recruitment of general-purpose learning mechanisms: "While some of the processes that subserve ToM are innately specified, and modular in some cases, the acquisition of ToM is dependent as well on social and linguistic accomplishment, and it is modular in only a weak sense" (p. 505). Early "pragmatic enrichment" appears to be a strong contributing factor in the development of children's understanding of mental states (Harris, de Rosnay, and Pons 2005). Thus, ToM is not likely to be subserved by "a module" or to be highly specialized and encapsulated.

Assessments of Christopher's L2 proficiency confirmed this approach to ToM development. On the one hand, Christopher displayed a remarkable ability to learn L2 vocabulary. (He showed demonstrably less ability in regard to syntax, and his language exhibited pervasive transfer of syntactic patterns from English—commonly observed imbalances among all L2 learners.) On the other hand, a seriously flawed performance on translation tasks coincided with difficulties in discourse processing and interpretive tasks in English. Christopher's translations, often incoherent, were far out of line with his overall conversational proficiency in the respective L2s, radically underestimating his linguistic knowledge in each of them. In other words, normal and typical abilities coexisted in Christopher with what were, by any standard, hyperabilities—supernormal language-learning skills. Contrasting with these abilities were surprisingly deficient performance patterns in domains that call upon a different set of interactions among the knowledge and processing components of other language proficiencies.

For the researchers in this case study, these disparate patterns are consistent with a componential view of language proficiency. They would be very hard to explain from a holistic point of view. The deficits are particularly noteworthy when we contrast them with the hyperabilities. What might someday explain this kind of unevenness in development is an approach that tries to ascertain which sets of interacting domains of language and general cognition are recruited for each kind of ability. Which combinations of components and which networks of connection are subject to selective breakdown?

Broad generalizations from exceptional cases (especially when, overall, something is very wrong with the way things are working) are always problematic, and we should avoid them here as well. But we still need to account for this kind of language development phenomenon, as atypical as it appears to be. If a system that is completely homogeneous (all of its emerging internal members, joints, and connections are equipotential) were to suffer an early trauma, how could it turn out later to be so variegated and irregular? With time, why don't the unaffected and exceptional capacities always bootstrap the developmentally disabled ones? However this line of inquiry turns out, it is the parallel to the typical, less extreme unevenness in L2 development that makes the comparison relevant to the study of normal bilingualism: the special unevenness in L2 development that afflicts normal learners is also hard to explain.

5.2 Separation of the Linguistic Subsystems

The research we have considered on exceptional bilingualism and exceptional (abnormally late) L1 learning in the case of the deaf children has shed some light primarily on the CS $\leftrightarrow$ L_{a+b} dimension of modularity. Now let us turn to the other dimension: L_a-L_b differentiation. Turning to the studies of early childhood bilingualism will recapitulate some of the terrain covered by Petitto (1997) on L_a-L_b differentiation, as in the related study by Holowka, Brousseau-Lapré, and Petitto (2002) that confirms language separation. A wide-ranging discussion has ensued from decades of work dating back to the beginnings of scientific studies of child bilingualism. Recent installments in the debate perhaps show a glimmer of consensus, in some quarters, between two potentially converging perspectives: early L_a-L_b differentiation, and very early differentiation. In a way, exactly when bilingual children's linguistic subsystems show signs of separation is secondary. That these subsystems should come to be represented autonomously at all during the preschool years is what is interesting, considering the combination of young children's immature metalinguistic abilities and the poverty of evidence at their disposal. The poverty-of-stimulus problem for bilingual development may even be more severe if we consider codemixing and potentially conflicting evidence in general from two different grammars (Yip and Matthews 2007). Besides, it is not likely that differentiation is "instantaneous," from the very outset of language acquisition. Within some modules and subsystems, separation may proceed rapidly, leaving others undifferentiated during a transitory period. Again, none of this would prompt us to overturn the main contours of any of the bilingual models discussed so far.

Specifically, research findings have steadily accumulated against the claim that a single unitary language system—a fusion or hybrid of L_a and L_b—is sustained for a prolonged period (or perhaps even an abbreviated period) prior to the separation of the language subsystems (De Houwer 2006; Genesee 2001; Meisel 2001; Mishina-Mori 2002; Nicoladis and Genesee 1997; Zwanziger, Allen, and Genesee 2005):

1. As soon as bilinguals[2] begin to have access to grammatical knowledge at the multiword stage around the age of 2, when language-specific word order properties and inflectional morphemes emerge, they show a strong tendency to separate the language subsystems. Whether or not a pregrammatical stage or period of rudimentary syntactic development precedes the multiword milestone will elude consensus for some time yet, owing to obvious methodological limitations. Therefore, a version of the unitary-system hypothesis might be compatible with early separation theories (Deuchar and Quay (2000) in fact suggest such a possibility). For example, in observing any given 2- or 3-year-old bilingual, how could we be sure whether that child was a case of simultaneous balanced development of L_a and L_b or that of an early dominance of one over the other? Perhaps some of the cases of early lack of differentiation reported in the literature are manifestations of the latter scenario. As we will see in chapter 6, from reports of research on early childhood bilingualism of the imbalanced variety, whether early bilingualism is 2L1 ($L_a + L_b$) or $L_{a(dominant)}$ + $L_{b(subordinate)}$ cannot be determined from observing the apparent distribution of each language in the child's sociolinguistic environment. This would be another example—in reverse, so to speak—of how input underdetermines competence. In any case, evidence against differentiation at the one- and two-word stages, prior to age 2, would have no bearing on the question of language separation following the emergence of functional categories. If syntax develops along a maturational timetable, an early undifferentiated stage would not be especially noteworthy. Nor would it call into question the capacity of young bilinguals to mentally separate L_a and L_b spontaneously, that is, with limited positive evidence and surely no usable negative evidence. Some children might receive a sort of corrective feedback directed at immature mixing or socially inappropriate language choice. But even if such unusual cases could be studied, the problem of how the child is to interpret such feedback arises just as it does in studies of negative evidence in L1 acquisition. Most bilingual 2-year-olds probably receive no such feedback anyway.

2. In early balanced bilingual development (2L1), it has been shown that each language marks the same norms across time as the single language in monolingual development. In other words, in balanced bilingualism, studies have found no evidence for either delay or significant facilitative effect for either language.

Simultaneous balanced bilingualism of the 2L1 type has been shown to unfold spontaneously and effortlessly to the same degree as monolingual development (Montrul 2008). Within the critical period, the parameters for each of L_a and L_b appear to be set with the same degree of automaticity, and based on the same amount of input that is sufficient for the monolingual child. Most bilingual children would probably have at their disposal even less input (in purely quantitative terms) for one language or the other than monolinguals.

3. Transfer of grammatical features, where it has been attested, is systematic. For example, cross-linguistic influence will tend to affect the weaker language more extensively. Unlike lexical development, phonological and morphosyntactic development in either L_a or L_b, or both, is complete (or age-appropriate for the relevant maturational stage) as opposed to "shared." Transfer of structural patterns from one language to the other in the case of balanced bilingualism tends to be temporary. Again, in the case of imbalanced bilingualism, transfer—even if it were permanent and prolific in the same proportion as the imbalance between L_a and L_b—would not count as disconfirming the idea that languages are represented separately (M. Paradis 2004). Persistent error patterns in the nondominant, developmentally "incomplete" language can be attributed to cross-linguistic influence only as one of a complex array of interacting underlying causal factors.

From whatever point of view, we should be surprised that there is any observable differentiation between L_a and L_b during the early childhood years. Why, as Meisel (2001) points out, is the LAD selective about which kinds of variation it treats as belonging to one linguistic subsystem and which it treats as distributed between two subsystems? It seems that a nonmodular bilingual mind and a nonmodular bilingual processor would have to labor under very adverse conditions for an extended period during which language acquisition would be significantly more difficult than in the monolingual condition. Such a hypothetical bilingual child would struggle with idiosyncratic cross-linguistic influences, fusion (and confusion) of the grammatical subsystems, and all manner of delayed learning and disruptive interference. J. Paradis, Crago, and Genesee (2005) make a similar observation. In fact, as we will see shortly, some nonmodular theories of bilingualism tend to view these potential afflictions as serious problems, even for normally developing bilinguals. This is not to say that bilinguals may not also suffer from abnormally delayed language acquisition or other type of impairment. In these cases, bilingualism may even be an important intervening factor that affects the course of development of an impaired language system. By the same token, child bilingualism may develop unevenly, with a dominant L1 "overcoming" a weaker language with which contact was also simultaneous. Significant and persistent interference and incomplete acquisition of the weaker language might even be traced, hypothetically, to the influence of the dominant L1. However, aside from trauma or inherent deficit, Language development (with a capital L) proceeds unimpeded, and unimpaired, even in the medium and short term.

5.3 How Bilingual Speech Constitutes Evidence of Language Separation

The two dimensions of modularity reveal themselves (impressionistically, at least) in children's performance when we focus on patterns of borrowing and codeswitching. These ubiquitous bilingual performance features could be taken as a kind of cross-linguistic influence, discussed in the previous section. As such, they present another example of how transfer is systematic and constrained by grammatical knowledge—as is the broadly accepted view today. That is, child borrowing and codeswitching patterns begin to conform to mature adult constraints early in development, earlier than we would expect considering children's limited experience with coordinating two linguistic subsystems in speech. Exposure to the grammatical patterns of adult language mixing could not possibly provide sufficient confirming and disconfirming evidence for preschool-age children to induce the constraints of rule-governed borrowing and switching.

In another series of assessments from our Nahuatl-Spanish study, focusing initially on the first dimension of differentiation (L_a-L_b), we found clear evidence that suggests the ability to keep the languages separate in specific contexts of use. This predictable observation was in line with the general consensus on this question (Genesee 2003; Hamers and Blanc 2000). When we shift our focus to the second dimension (CS $\leftrightarrow$ L_{a+b}), certain aspects of borrowing and switching ability appear to manifest themselves in a completely uniform way, across the board: we found no differences related to age, grade level attained, or sex, and no correlation with any measure or category of discourse style or academically related aspects of discourse. In contrast, other kinds of borrowing and switching ability appeared to vary in a systematic way among the same bilingual speakers (N. Francis and Navarrete Gómez 2000).

Observations of borrowing and switching patterns in the children's narratives, both oral and written, in both languages, are consistent with a L_a-L_b separation. Children were presented with a series of illustrations that depicted a short sequence of events for which they produced an oral narrative in Spanish, and another for which they produced an oral narrative in Nahuatl. In another assessment, children listened to a familiar narrative in Spanish (selected from the community's oral tradition) and then composed a written version of it; they completed the same task in Nahuatl with a different narrative. When the task required a Spanish-language narrative, no mixing was in evidence. In stark contrast, mixing was a feature that distinguished virtually all Nahuatl narratives, both oral and written. This pattern coincides closely with an observed diglossic distribution in conversation according to interlocutor and context, correlating systematically with self-reports of language use patterns (e.g., in response to questions like "In which language do you speak to teachers, family, and friends?"; N. Francis 1998). Pfaff (1999) reports a similar asymmetry in mixing patterns between German and Turkish among bilingual children living in Germany; Heredia and Altarriba (2001) discuss the same phenomenon.

Predictable as these results turn out to be (from a sociolinguistic point of view: *why* there is evidence of such an asymmetry), they do point to the need to explain *how* children are able to gate out the nonselected language in both spontaneous conversation and planned narrative performance. How is it that, when composing or narrating in Spanish, children are able to avoid the use of an entire class of words—words that belong to their Nahuatl lexicon? Whatever mechanism is responsible for this ability (one that all bilinguals are familiar with), in the case of Mexican Spanish this would be interesting from another point of view. A large number of established loanwords from Nahuatl "belong to" Spanish and are used even by monolinguals. Nahuatl-Spanish bilinguals who avoid switching (or when they avoid switching) seem to effect control only over certain lexical items of Nahuatl origin, those that would be perceived as nonce borrowings into Spanish. As the Nahuatl narratives show, children were perfectly capable of inserting grammatical constituents from the nonselected language (Spanish) into a text language (Nahuatl), no general prohibition being imposed on this particular discourse strategy. In addition, the particular type of mixing that children appeared to prefer in this language use context was highly constrained. Thus, the question shifts to describing the patterns of control, selective inhibition, and specific switching strategy, and also to describing when mixed speech is considered appropriate and when it should be suppressed. Whatever the relevant mechanisms turn out to be (an early language-specific selection, or non-language-specific activation and subsequent inhibition; Costa 2004), bilinguals appear to be working with structures and connections that call upon two separate representations, one for each language subsystem. That is the hypothesis, in any case. Emmorey et al. (2008) offer an important discussion of asymmetric inhibition in the case of bimodal bilingualism (speech-sign), both different from and similar to the asymmetric mixing patterns found in "unimodal" bilingualism in the Mexican study. (An interesting study on how language switching might be experimentally induced is reported in Holtzheimer et al. 2005; for a survey of the research on language control, see De Groot and Christoffels 2006.)

Turning now to the CS ↔ L_{a+b} dimension, we can examine the difference between the aspects of borrowing and switching ability that show themselves to be completely uniform and those that show systematic individual variation. The initial analysis of children's Nahuatl narratives sought to identify sentences containing

Spanish switches or borrowings that might result in grammatical incompatibility. Virtually none emerged from this assessment, and a parallel evaluation of adult narratives showing the same strong tendency (N. Francis and Navarrete Gómez 2000). The adult narratives showed the same overall uniformity; for example, literate adult bilinguals showed no superiority over nonliterates in their ability to maintain congruent grammatical patterns combining constituents from both languages (N. Francis and Navarrete Gómez 2003).

Given that mixing was largely restricted to insertion of single content words and discourse connectors, consistent grammatical compatibility was to be expected from a population of bilinguals with relatively high levels of proficiency in both languages. Still, the phenomenon needs to be accounted for: how are speakers able to implement the bilingual couplings in such a way as to maintain integral grammatical constructions containing two different linguistic subsystems? Even if it were a matter of avoiding insertion of more complex (Spanish) patterns into Nahuatl sentences (i.e., a preference for "safe" insertions of single content words and connectors), what kind of grammatical knowledge accounts for this selection ability? A similar mixing pattern was reported by Allen (2007) from a study of Inuktitut-English child bilinguals, reflecting "the child's knowledge that there are few points where the grammars of the two languages . . . permit codeswitching or alternational mixing" in the case of this language pair (p. 522). All participants demonstrated this ability, showing no variation as a function of any of the nonlinguistic factors mentioned above.

In contrast, frequency of content word insertion does vary systematically across grade level in children's written and oral expression: older children borrow content words from Spanish less frequently. This interesting result coincided with the finding on separate evaluations in which, in response to illustrations of everyday life, older children consistently provided a higher percentage of Nahuatl descriptive terms than younger children. When the task required providing Nahuatl vocabulary, 4th graders avoided Spanish terms to a greater degree than 2nd graders, and 6th graders to a greater degree than 4th graders. And generally, "Spanish borrowing avoidance" correlated positively with scores on a separate Metalinguistic Awareness assessment involving the identification of words as Spanish or Nahuatl (see appendices 1 and 2). Adults showed wide variation in switching frequency in their Nahuatl stories, ranging from zero Spanish insertion to frequencies higher than any child narrator's. In the case of the adult narratives, as might be expected, correlations with other indices did not show the same sharp tendencies as narratives provided by the 2nd, 4th, and 6th graders. However, in contrast to their ability to grammatically integrate Spanish insertion (to recap: equivalent and uniform to the same degree as children), frequency of Spanish insertion did correlate, negatively, with 6th-grade completion: 6th-grade graduates inserted fewer Spanish words (N. Francis and Navarrete Gómez

2003). Even though the relation is confounded by the result that adult female participants, who generally had not completed 6th grade, also switched more frequently to Spanish, the dissociation still holds up, making it an interesting object of further analysis.

The following examples illustrate the mixing patterns that characterize the narrative elicitation tasks: typically, insertion of Spanish content words into Nahuatl sentence patterns and of Spanish discourse connectors between Nahuatl independent clauses.

Adult Oral Narrative
In zoatzintli mopepehtla ica in *peine, mientras* in occe zoatzintli paca ni cone ica *jabón* huan *agua* noihqui in occe zoatzintli quitzquitoc ni piltzintli.
[The woman is combing herself with a *comb, while* the other woman washes her child with *soap* and *water* also the other woman is holding her baby.]
(S14)

Te *maman* caltia ni *alma*tzitzin *luego* tetlapatilia.
[Their *mother* bathes her *child (literally: soul-Spanish + endearment diminutive–Nahuatl) then* changes him.]
(C26)

Child Oral Narrative
Huan ye huitze ome tlatlacameh *entonces* umpa yeca yoyahqueh ce *día de campo* huan umpa quimtlamacaque *luego* in zoatzintli quimtlamaca huan mizton *igual* nehqui tlacuaz.

[And two men are already coming *then* there they went on a *picnic* and there they were given something to eat *then* the lady gave them something to eat and the cat *also* wants to eat.]
(AL606)

Occe ye tlapatilia ipiltzintli *porque* yazque in *fandango*, in occe ye mopepehtla.
[The other one is changing her child *because* they are going to a *party*, the other one is combing (herself).]
(MR404)

In Myers-Scotton's (2002) model, grammatical congruence is established through the emergence or selection of a matrix-language (ML) frame into which embedded-language (EL) constituents are inserted, the former dominating the formation of sentence patterns. EL counterparts are checked for integration into the grammatical frame of the language, the ML, that is "sufficiently activated to direct morphosyntactic procedures" (p. 21). Muysken (2000) calls attention to two ways besides *insertion* that L_a and L_b form integrated grammatical patterns: *alternation* (a shift, codeswitch, from the L_a to the L_b) and *congruent lexicalization* (in the sentence containing L_a and L_b, the languages share a common grammatical organization). MacSwan (1999) surveys the relative merits of prominent alternative theories (additional instructive overviews are Lüdi 2003 and Muysken 2004). Nevertheless, despite a wide divergence of approaches, researchers appear to converge on the need to explain the same phenomenon: how knowledge of two languages, and some kind of Cross-Linguistic Interface (CLI), underlie coherent and well-formed bilingual speech.[3] A consensus should form around a language production model in which the conceptualizer activates both L_a and L_b lexicons and L_a and L_b grammatical subsystems in such a way as to effect fluent intrasentential processing comparable in speed and structural well-formedness to typical monolingual speech (de Bot 2000, 438–441). For an interesting contrast, consider the examples provided by Fabbro (1999, 143–157) and Fabbro, Skrap, and Aglioti (2000) of pathological switching, resulting from dysfunction of neurological mechanisms that are responsible for selection and regulation of L_a and L_b (or L1 and L2, as the case may be).

In exploring the different patterns of CS ↔ L_{a+b} autonomy and interdependence, one avenue would be to take up the question of degrees of awareness, or accessibility to awareness, of the different mixing abilities. Here is one proposal for further research:

1. The processing mechanisms and interlinguistic interfaces responsible for maintaining grammatical compatibility in sentences and clauses that contain insertions from an embedded language are inaccessible to awareness. Attention to morphological and syntactic integration cannot normally be brought to bear on performance in either speaking or listening. When adults and children were telling stories in Nahuatl in the Mexican study, that they maintained Nahuatl as the ML throughout (with few exceptions) is perhaps related to the relatively low frequency of Spanish insertion. But the grammatical processing itself (which "inhibits" crossing over to Spanish grammatical patterns) cannot be subject to deliberate control and reflection.

2. On the other hand, potentially salient features such as frequency of borrowing, using marked word choices for borrowings, and so on, are noticeable, accessible to awareness, and subject to monitoring and control. The sharp diglossic division in regard to language choice in oral and written expression that was shown to operate among all the children at all grade levels is probably, on one level or another, accessible to monitoring. Correlations between frequency of borrowing, for example, and the measure of Metalinguistic Awareness that involved attention to structural features of each language, suggest the participation of CS-type knowledge, that again would play little if any role in establishing grammaticality, online, at the point of language mixing itself. Speakers and listeners can direct reflective-type monitoring only to the results of computational procedures, not the procedures themselves. The

intervening morphosyntactic processes, and competence itself, are inaccessible to awareness (M. Paradis 2004). In all this, it should be kept in mind that the separation of L_a and L_b (or L1 and L2) in the mental grammar of the bilingual child is not the same as *awareness* of how his or her languages are separate in language use. In discussing the development of metalinguistic reflection, Fodor (1998, 139) makes a related observation: "What children theorize about is not what's represented *in* their modules, but rather what's represented in the *outputs* that their modules compute.... What the child has increasing access to is information in the structural descriptions that the modules deliver, not intramodular information per se." Jackendoff (1997) makes a similar argument.

In a study of how some of these questions might be related to language loss and replacement, the topic of chapter 6, Gross (2004) points to an interesting parallel: content morphemes are more vulnerable to attrition than early- and late-system morphemes (grammatical elements, functional features). Since content morphemes are conceptually activated, they are "salient," accessible to awareness. Early-system morphemes are also conceptually activated, but indirectly via the first level of conceptual activation. Selection of late-system morphemes, on the other hand, depends on implicit procedural knowledge, is more encapsulated, and is inaccessible to awareness and control. As such, according to Gross, this subsystem, or component, is more resistant to attrition and replacement.

To return to issues of language mixing, a number of child bilingualism researchers have concluded that language separation is a prerequisite for grammatical intrasentential codeswitching: "one can only switch from one system into the other if the two are distinct" (Meisel 1994, 414). The ability to constrain insertion and switching from early childhood appears to depend on establishing early, and maintaining independent, grammars for L1/L_a and L2/L_b (Allen 2007). This view seems implicit in at least the insertion and alternation schemes of Myers-Scotton (2002) and Muysken (2004). On the other hand, Dijkstra and van Heuven (2002), Proverbio, Adorni, and Zani (2007), and Wei (2002) argue for an alternative point of view, one that appears to disfavor the idea of separate and autonomous linguistic subsystems. But as we will see in discussing MacWhinney's (2005) Competition Model in chapter 6, not all aspects of the emergentist model are incompatible with modular approaches to bilingualism (recall that this is one of the themes of the book).

Based on his studies of young bilinguals, Meisel proposes that constraints on codeswitching are most productively examined from the point of view of processing. The performance mechanisms that select, activate, inhibit, and couple constituents from each language reflect underlying linguistic knowledge in different ways, sometimes in ways that are surprising and hard to explain. As such, especially in the case of early childhood developing grammars (considering, in addition, that one cannot assume completely balanced growth of each language in the bilingual child), we can safely say that these processing constraints do not operate in a categorical manner. Nevertheless, findings point to an early convergence with adult codeswitching norms during the preschool years, between the ages of 2 and 5. The emergence of functional categories of the grammar appears to mark the beginnings of the qualitative turning point toward this convergence (Genesee 2002; Köppe and Meisel 1995; Meisel 1994).

5.4   Contradictions of an Integrativist Approach

That some aspects of borrowing and switching might vary across grade level and be subject to monitoring, while others appear to be uniform and inaccessible to awareness, prompted a review of results from language assessments given to children in other bilingual indigenous communities in Mexico (N. Francis 1997; N. Francis and Paciotto 2004). Just as in the original studies with Nahuatl-Spanish bilinguals, certain aspects of lexical development showed themselves to be open to learning and individual variation. In contrast, context-dependent dialogic tasks and core vocabulary in the unmarked language of school (Spanish) showed no variation from 2nd grade on.

Reflecting on the relative autonomy of the latter universally attainable language abilities brings to mind certain controversies in the field that continue to generate confusion among practitioners. A case in point is a theoretical proposal by Herdina and Jessner (2002) that strongly disfavors modular conceptions, arriving at a number of conclusions that flow from the authors' "holistic multicompetence" perspective. In this case in particular, failure to fully take into account the componential nature of language proficiency explains the seemingly contradictory review of the literature and serious misrepresentations of current theoretical models including UG and Cummins's construct of Cognitive Academic Language Proficiency. On the one hand, the authors refer to research findings that purportedly lend support to the contention that bilingualism contributes to linguistic and cognitive insufficiencies (pp. 7–11, 106–107) and that normal bilingual development can result in less than complete mastery of both L_a and L_b: "[If] the effort required to master a language is split between two, it is likely to result in a reduction of the mastery of both" (p. 13).[4] On the other hand, adherence to a holistic model, with its tendency to view the interaction between linguistic competence and general cognition as boundless and unrestricted, makes it difficult to critically evaluate the more exaggerated claims regarding bilinguals' superiority in metalinguistic awareness, cognitive "flexibility," "creativity," "divergent thought," and the like (p. 64). (The relationship between metalinguistic awareness and bilingualism will be discussed further in chapters 8 and 9.)

Taking a strong holistic/integrativist perspective as one's starting point leads to errors in both directions. For one, the purported likelihood of a "reduction of mastery" in both languages is impossible to assess in the abstract. To which components or subsystems might this degraded mastery refer? On the other hand, overstating the cognitive-general benefits of bilingualism flows from a failure to recognize that the interactions between the linguistic domains and general cognition are subject to some hard constraints. Not every aspect of linguistic knowledge and linguistic development affects thought processes and cognitive development. Both types of error are still prevalent today among educators who work with L2 learners: (1) in the first instance, a disposition toward language diversity that perceives deficit and underachievement in the normal variation of bilingual grammatical development, and (2) a defensive posture on the part of many advocates of pluralism who often argue for deep-rooted inherent cognitive advantages to knowing two languages. The apparent contradiction in sustaining both sets of hypotheses, at the same time, should be cause for serious reflection.

5.5 A Bilingual Version of the Tripartite Parallel Architecture

So far, this chapter has drawn together some common threads on exceptional bilingualism, language separation, and cross-linguistic interactions (in the form of codeswitching and borrowing). This section will propose a model of how two languages are represented in the bilingual, based on an extension of Jackendoff's (1997) Tripartite Parallel Architecture (TPA; see figure 5.1). The bilingual version is intended to make for a close match with a model of bilingual proficiency—how the linguistic components and their interfaces are deployed in actual language use (also an idea that flows from the TPA, now applied to bilingualism). How does the processing of L_a and L_b fit into a broader mental organization that accounts for meaningful comprehension and expression?

Jackendoff's model emphasizes the important role of interfaces that align and match up the correspondences in each modular component. The interfaces allow communication between Phonological Structure (PS), Syntactic Structure (SS), and Conceptual Structure (CS), each autonomous from the others and yet all richly interconnected. In comprehension, for example, such a modular organization accounts for both bottom-up processing and top-down effects, the latter operating in a constrained manner. In a way, PS, SS, and CS can maintain their strongly independent combinatorial systems and their specific formation rules thanks to the fast and modular-type operation of the interface connections. Modules are isolable and computationally autonomous, *and* interactive: internal functions of one module do not interfere with the internal functions of others; rather, dedicated interfaces are specialized for guaranteeing the proper alignments (M. Paradis 2004, 119–121).

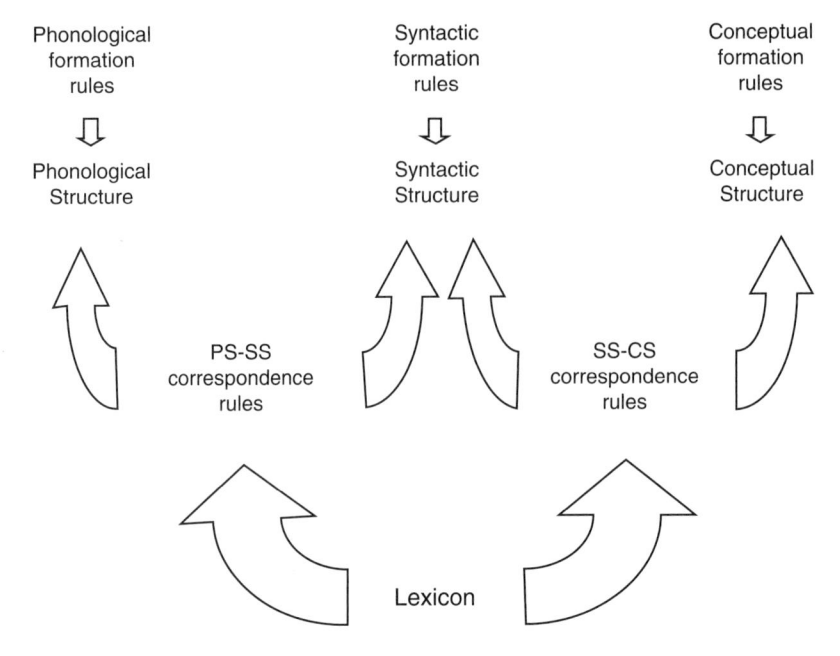

Figure 5.1
The Tripartite Parallel Architecture (Jackendoff 1997)

From the perspective of Lexical-Functional Grammar, Falk (2001, 22–24) outlines a similar approach to studying the components and interconnections of language:

> Information structure, semantic structure, argument (or thematic) structure, syntactic constituent structure, and phonological/phonetic structure are distinct subsystems of language, each with its own primitives and its own internal rules of organization. . . . These levels of representation all exist in parallel; no one is prior to any of the others. A theory of language that is based on such a model can be said to have a parallel architecture. . . . Besides different kinds of primitives and rules for each dimension of linguistic structure, a system of correspondence is required to map between the levels. Such a theory therefore needs correspondence functions, or "projection" functions. [Lexical-Functional Grammar] is said to have a projection architecture connecting the different levels of representation. Determining all the properties of a particular element in a modular system requires examining the corresponding item (or items) in each of the projections.

In the TPA model, the lexicon forms an integral part of the interfaces that keep the components of grammar and Conceptual Structure in registration with each other. In this sense, the lexicon is not a "subsystem" of language like syntax or phonology. Because they include features, or sublexical elements, that line up with PS, SS, and CS, lexical items are like interface rules (Jackendoff 2002, 131). They establish the proper correspondences among the components and subcomponents, linguistic and conceptual. The lexicon connects the PS and SS components (the "linguistic side") with CS—the "locus for understanding of linguistic utterances in context, incorporating pragmatic considerations, and world knowledge" (p. 123). This idea seems to be compatible with N. Smith and Tsimpli's (1995) distinction between "UG lexicon" and "conceptual lexicon." Thus, "Language" has one foot in the Central System and the other in the strictly linguistic domains. Discussing the evolution of lexical knowledge, Kenneally (2007, 122) sums it up this way: "[Words] are clusters of complex knowledge about sound, grammar and meaning. Human words don't exist by themselves. They are points in a series of intersecting systems, and when you hear or produce a word, all these systems come into play."

The bilingual version of the TPA (figure 5.2) portrays the separation between L_a and L_b by representing the two grammatical subsystems in parallel, with separate domains for the L_a lexicon and the L_b lexicon, each one integrated into the interface components of its language, linked closely, in turn, to the formation rules of its language's PS and SS. Since lexical knowledge straddles language (here PS+SS) and thought (CS), the double arrows show that the lexicon is an interface that connects these three domains. A crucial aspect of this network of interfaces is that the conceptual elements of lexical items connect to a single non-language-specific CS, shared between L_a and L_b. For example, exact translation equivalents would be connected to a common set of semantic features in CS. Under this proposal, the bilingual lexicon is not a simple listing of words from both languages in long-term memory, in which, for example, entries are "tagged" as belonging to one language or the other. The sets of linguistic components (PS+SS of L_a and PS+SS of L_b) for each of the two lexical networks (which are language-specific, L_a or L_b, unlike the non-language-specific CS) maintain their autonomy one from the other. This view of word knowledge should help to bring greater coherence to findings that sometimes suggest independent representations, and other times suggest an integrated lexicon serving both languages.

Credit goes first to Paivio's (1991) Bilingual Dual Coding Model for helping to correct a deficiency in the first elaboration of Cummins's Common Underlying Proficiency model (figure 3.2). In Bilingual Dual Coding, L1 and L2 are kept separate, without any overlap—connected, rather, by an interlinguistic interface. M. Paradis (2004) also maintains the independence of each language subsystem: "the morphosyntax module contains as many subsystems as the person speaks languages. . . . If two languages happen to legitimately contain a similar feature, that feature is represented twice, i.e., once in each language subsystem, because features do not exist in a void but are part of a system, with reciprocal relationships with other features within the language subsystem" (pp. 130, 135). This more mutually autonomous contact relationship between the two languages is now appropriated by the Bilingual TPA. It portrays more clearly the close and extensive interconnections

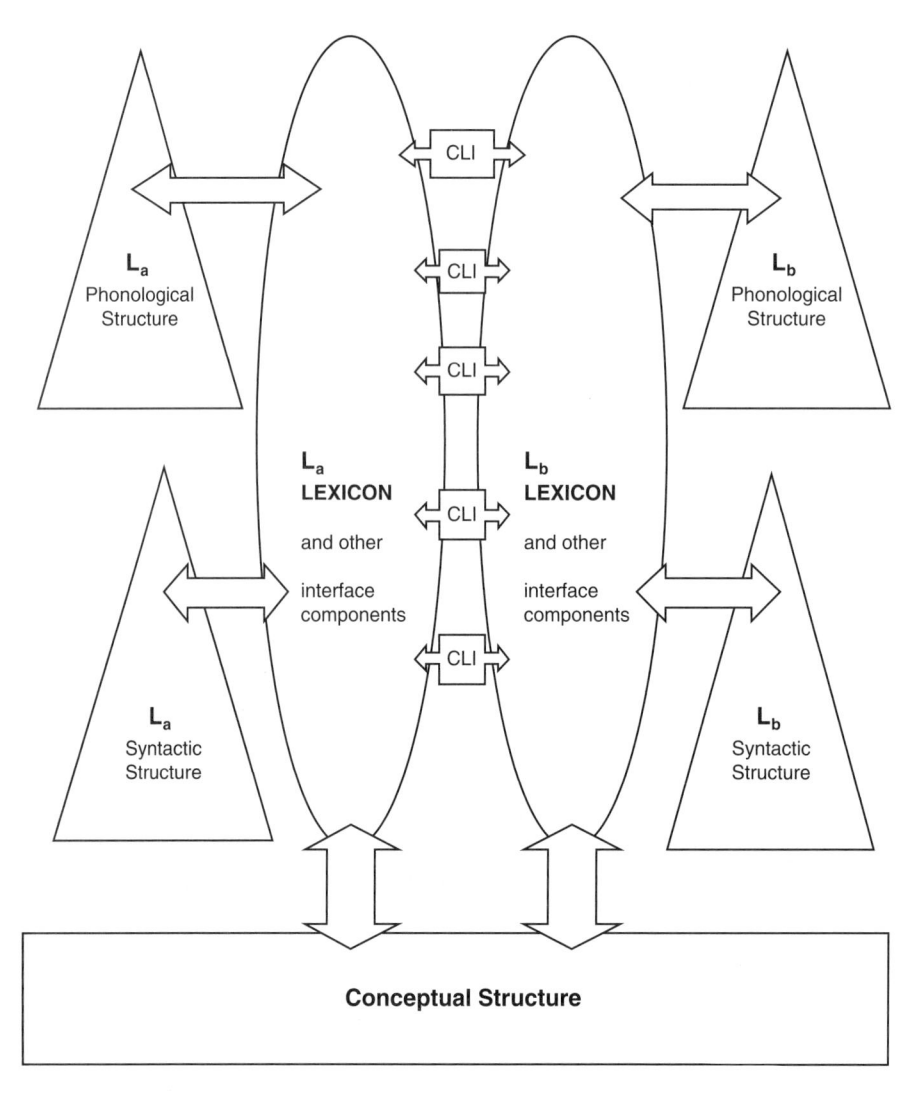

Figure 5.2
The Bilingual Tripartite Parallel Architecture

between the two languages and also how the interconnections are controlled and inhibited from time to time (probably most of the time). The suggestion of "overlap" in figure 3.2 made this more difficult to conceptualize.

Interaction between L_a and L_b (the double arrows labeled CLI) is constrained, responsive to the grammar of each language; that is, interlinguistic transfer is systematic and "rule-governed." The Faculty of Language imposes restrictions on how the CLI effects mutual influences between the language subsystems. This is evidenced in L2 interlanguage error patterns that can be traced to the L1 and to other sources, and in codeswitching. The CLI is productive and highly interconnective, sensitive to the full range of possible typological differences and parallels that may present themselves. The CLI has to function just as systematically and efficiently for Spanish-Italian bilinguals as for the English-speaking L2 learner of a polysynthetic language like Inuktitut. And, as just emphasized, this network of connections between L_a and L_b must also allow the suppression of all variety of transfer and cross-linguistic influence. Along these lines, in their study of English-Inuktitut bilingual children (ages 1;8–3;9), Zwanziger, Allen, and Genesee (2005) found that these children possessed knowledge of each target language that was language-specific. That is, they were able to maintain a separation between the languages and were able to control the effects of cross-linguistic influence. Costa (2004), in commenting on this "remarkable skill," summarizes the alternative proposals that have been advanced to explain it: "Regardless of whether the words of the non-response language enter into competition or not, the question still remains of how the lexical selection mechanism ends up selecting the intended word instead of its translation" (p. 207). Two possibilities are that inhibitory processes control lexical nodes from L_a and L_b activated nonselectively, or that a "selection mechanism" preempts interference from the nonresponse language. Either way, a common assumption seems to be that an external cognitive mechanism intervenes in some way upon a system composed of separate representations for each language.

Simplifying greatly, under the Bilingual TPA proposal, the semantic component, or CS, would constitute a shared domain. This proposal of a single CS, to which both sets of linguistic modules have access, follows the general idea that CS is independent, having its own combinatorial principles, very different from those of morphosyntax and phonology. Since CS formation rules are not linguistic in nature, semantic features that are connected to or belong to lexical items cannot be language (L_a or L_b) specific. In this view, for example, a Spanish-English bilingual stores separate phonological structures for translation equivalents "dormir" and "sleep"; a phrasal syntax structure that is the same in both cases; and differing word formation structures in the morphology tier of SS. In CS, the L_a and L_b lexical items link up to most (not all) of the same semantic features: for example, both link to the feature that indicates intransitivity, but only Spanish "dormir" links to the transitive feature ("I sleep"/*"I sleep the baby," in English, but "Yo duermo" [I sleep]/"Yo duermo al bebé" [I sleep the baby = I put the baby to sleep], in Spanish). If our hypothetical bilingual learns French, the French verb "dormir" would not need to generate a separate set of CS features specific to a third language; rather, it would simply link up to the features, already in place, that accord with its "French meaning"—in this case including only the intransitive, as in English. ("Endormir" is the French counterpart of the transitive Spanish "dormir.") De Groot (2002) explains how a "distributed model" accounts for nonequivalence of word meaning across languages. Tentatively, we could propose that L_a-specific and L_b-specific meaning elements, if such in fact exist, would be represented within the domain of the CS-SS interface. For further discussion, see Jackendoff 1996, 1997 and M. Paradis 1997.

In an adaptation of Levelt's (1999) speech production model, de Bot (2000) outlines a bilingual processing version that on several key points fits well with the proposed bilingual version of Jackendoff's TPA. The "blueprint" for the speaker consists of a *knowledge component* (discourse model, pragmatic knowledge, encyclopedia, etc.) plus three processing components: *conceptualizer*, *formulator*, and *articulator*. De Bot assumes a knowledge component that is not language-specific and proposes that the "macroplanning" tier of the conceptualizer forms a single subsystem shared between L_a and L_b. "Microplanning," in accordance with Levelt's view, is language-specific, at least to some degree. The output from the conceptualizer, a preverbal message/communicative intention, is preprocessed and passed on to the formulator. To account for bilinguals' ability to inhibit one or the other language in performance, de Bot seems to favor a differentiated formulator. Looking back to figure 5.2, we can tentatively draw a parallel, starting from the bottom and proceeding upward:

1. Preverbal message generation and macroplanning take place in CS.

2. Microplanning, in which the preverbal message begins to be converted into a speech plan and lexical items are activated, takes place in the CS-SS interface.

3. As lexical items are activated, their matching syntax, morphology, and phonology components are activated; in this way, partial structures are established in these domains (Jackendoff 2002, 201–202). The autonomy of the CS domains from the linguistic modules is evidenced in the separation of semantic and syntactic processing at this level. This stage of processing would be specific to L_a or L_b, or both, depending on the circumstances—that is, at which point along the continuum between monolingual mode and bilingual mode (Grosjean 1997) speakers find themselves.

What emerges from the formulator (in the bilingual adaptation of the model, a *dual* formulator) is a "grammatical unit." Phonological encoding provides the input to the articulator in the form of a phonetic plan. In figure 5.2, the separate sets of SS and PS components, interconnected through their respective interface components, correspond to the two separate formulators in the production model. Each of the bilingual's lexicons is an integral part of the interface components; and the CLI connections are the locus of all types and degrees of interlinguistic activation and inhibition.

Recalling our discussion of accessibility to awareness of different aspects of mixing ability, Levelt and de Bot's production model offers a graphic portrayal of the distinction between (1) CLI mechanisms not subject to awareness and deliberate control, and (2) aspects of bilingual production to which attention and monitoring can be directed. With respect to #1, interfaces between L_a and L_b are confined to the internal processes of the dual formulator. In contrast, #2 encompasses a "wider loop" including, crucially, the output from the formulator (a phonetic plan, "inner speech"). According to the blueprint: "this phonetic plan can be scanned internally by the speech-comprehension system, which provides the first possibility for feedback" (de Bot 2000, 423). Monitoring, whose domain is back in the conceptualizer, can perform operations on mixed constituents only because a full complex structure (CS+SS+PS) of the utterance-to-be is constructed in the form of the phonetic plan. Language choice, initial selection of a matrix frame, calls directly upon the knowledge component. (Sharwood Smith (1991) discusses the role of metalinguistic awareness in both processing and language development within a similar modular framework.)

On the question of separate lexicons and a dual formulator, de Bot poses two interesting challenges for future research: (1) Is separation maintained even in the case of languages that are typologically very close, as well as for bidialectical speakers? (2) How is level of L2 competence accounted for (assuming, for example, that in the initial stages of interlanguage development, L2 grammar is largely parasitic on L1, and thus manifests only the most embryonic autonomy)? The Bilingual TPA model should apply to both early bilingualism and L2 learning. In this regard, it suggests several research questions: (1) How, precisely, are L_a and L_b represented in a way that may be different from the way L1 and L2 are represented? This is one of the most interesting topics in the study of bilingualism, to be addressed in chapter 6. (2) Regarding late L2 learning, key research questions include whether L2 is constrained by the same principles as L1, and how the CLI might operate differently, especially at beginner L2 levels. (3) In early child bilingualism, why do L_a and L_b subsystems differentiate whereas the CS does not?

Various other outstanding issues remain to be worked out; for example, consider Jackendoff's (2002, 211–215) discussion on the status of lemmas. However, on the whole, reflection upon the points around which the TPA and the Bilingual TPA coincide should prompt a serious attempt at convergence.

On another front of potential dialog, the Bilingual TPA model implies different types of interface. Within the linguistic system (L_a and L_b), the CLI maintains different kinds of registration and correspondence between L_a and L_b than the interfaces necessary for integration of the subsystems and tiers within each language. Also, the CLI is activated and inhibited in a way that should be different from how intralanguage interfaces are deployed. In turn, both the CLI and the intralanguage interfaces are different from the interfaces that connect the modules of the linguistic system with the Central System CS. In this way, figure 5.2 attempts to depict the two dimensions of modularity discussed in previous sections: $L_a \leftrightarrow L_b$ and $CS \leftrightarrow L_{a+b}$. The idea behind the two dimensions of modularity is not new. "Three-component, two-level" models of bilingualism also portray lexical and grammatical links interconnecting L1 and L2 domains "cross-linguistically," and conceptual links connecting each linguistic domain to a shared conceptual level (Cheung and Lin 2005; Kroll and Tokowicz 2001; Paivio 1991; M. Paradis 2004). Logically, each of the two proposed dimensions of modularity does not necessarily presuppose the other, questions about $CS \leftrightarrow L_{a+b}$ in particular leaving the door open to a prosperous exchange of views with approaches to bilingualism outside the narrow confines of the fields covered in this discussion.

An important comparison here is the Competition Model (Hernández, Li, and MacWhinney 2005; MacWhinney 2005), which attempts to explain the various aspects of the CLI, or transfer, on the basis of completely different assumptions about the architecture of bilingual competence, or so it would seem. Interestingly, though, a number of observations appear to coincide. For example, the Competition Model postulates a fundamental link between transfer and age-related effects in L2 learning, one we will discuss at length in chapter 6. What is notable here is that this potential link does not seem to figure prominently in most leading UG-based models of critical period effects. In chapter 6, we will consider arguments that it should. Regarding aspects of bilingual processing, the Competition Model's explanations of how each language achieves "insulation against intrusion" are not incompatible with modular accounts. Perhaps we can attribute these insights on the part of the Competition Model to the greater attention that connectionists pay to the "I" part of "CLI."

5.6 More Opportunities for Research on Uneven Development

5.6.1 Different Kinds of Imbalance

Four areas of research present fair possibilities for testing a modular model like the Bilingual TPA.

1. Neurolinguistic investigation of normal bilinguals and of bilinguals who suffer from language disorders offers different opportunities. In regard to the latter, it will

be necessary to distinguish among different recovery patterns in aphasia, pathological mixing and switching, and translation disorder (Fabbro 2001). In regard to pathological mixing and switching, does each differ from normal patterns pragmatically, grammatically, or both? For example, further evidence supporting the Subsystem Hypothesis (M. Paradis 2001) would be compatible with models of the three-component, two-level type, to which the Bilingual TPA also belongs. In the Subsystem Hypothesis, L_a and L_b are subserved by different circuits interwoven in the same language domain, at the same gross anatomical level. If each language is susceptible to selective pathological inhibition, the "extended system hypothesis" (in which the linguistic components of L_a and L_b are represented in an undifferentiated way) can be definitively excluded. Simos et al. (2005) provide an overview of the key issues in this line of research.

2. Among exceptional bilinguals, deaf children represent the most important population. Study of sign language/speech development in the late L1 learner (after age 7) offers the possibility of evidence for early critical period effects. Early language deprivation reveals degrees of autonomy and interdependence between grammatical development and general intellectual development. The study of bilingual Specific Language Impairment is pertinent here as well. To what extent do successively degraded levels of linguistic competence affect overall cognitive development—in particular, with regard to the higher-order abilities associated with schooling?

3. Research on typical child bilingual development complements areas #1 and #2. If simultaneous balanced acquisition of L_a and L_b is marked by an early separation, subsequent L2 learning after age 7 (or even before) should evidence at least the same kind of separation, and perhaps additional kinds of differentiation not manifested in balanced 2L1 acquisition. On the other hand, data from early attrition of L_a or L_b should sharpen the separation hypothesis, calling attention to how the components of language-specific ability may deteriorate at different rates and with different ultimate steady states. Parallel insights should result from studying cases of early imbalanced bilingual development despite balanced input and opportunity for using each language from birth. Chapter 6 will pose the question, might it be possible that one of the simultaneous bilingual's languages (L_a or L_b) evolves differently than the other, in effect taking on the characteristics of a L2, even in childhood?

4. Along the same lines, examining the processing of mixed-language discourse under conditions of greater and greater imbalance (including advanced displacement of one language by the other) might begin to reveal more clearly the conditions and constraints on grammatical compatibility of insertions and alternations. Research should examine both naturalistic conversational utterances and controlled elicited production. Comparing language pairs whose word formation rules display varying

degrees of productivity might illuminate the difference in processing proposed by Jackendoff between the phrasal syntax and morphosyntax tiers of SS. Such a program of experimentation on language mixing should open up more lines of communication with the psycholinguistic research on lexical access and sentence- and discourse-level processing (cf. De Groot 2002). Again, bilingualism introduces another level of complexity and additional ways in which the language subsystems are subject to asymmetries and different kinds of uneven development. Thus, cross-discipline discussion should be favored by the division of labor that a modular approach could lay the groundwork for.

5.6.2 Lexical Knowledge in Second Language: A Puzzle
If we strip away all the interactive connections and focus on just the lexicons, in the case of a language learner with a fairly well-developed L2, we can explore a number of comparisons between the lexicons of primary language and interlanguage.

Figure 5.3 portrays aspects of lexical knowledge that might account for different kinds of disproportion in language proficiency. To take just three examples:

1. To start with an exceptional monolingual condition, consider the imbalance between syntax and vocabulary in the late-L1 learner "Genie," who was isolated almost without language input until the age of 13 (Curtiss 1994). Following intensive language remediation, her vocabulary development showed considerable initial advances and continued to progress adequately, in contrast to difficult progress and a permanent deficit in syntax.

2. In adult L2 learning, intensive study and immersion in the L2 can yield impressive results in vocabulary knowledge, often (depending on the circumstances) equal to or surpassing the typical everyday vocabulary of many native speakers of the target language. However, similar achievement with respect to L2 phonology, morphology, and syntax is not as common. Scherag et al. (2004, B106) propose that the development of syntactic competencies, for example, "might be more tightly linked to restricted times during development than the elaboration of semantic subfunctions. . . . The latter are based on associative learning mechanisms that permit learning throughout life. . . . [S]yntax is based on a computational mechanism that can be set up only during limited periods of life."

3. Recall that the Nahuatl-Spanish bilinguals in the Mexican study showed a superior performance on Spanish lexical retrieval even though the mental grammar of neither language subsystem was dominant (as revealed in the study participants' fluent, native-like command of both languages). This result indicates that measures of this aspect of lexical knowledge underestimate children's actual grammatical competence in each language.

L1   L2

Orthographic Form	Orthographic Form
Phonological Structure	Phonological Structure
Morphosyntax tier of SS	Morphosyntax tier of SS
Phrasal syntax tier of SS	Phrasal syntax tier of SS
Conceptual Structure	Conceptual Structure

Orthographic Form	Orthographic Form
Phonological Structure	Phonological Structure
Morphosyntax tier of SS	Morphosyntax tier of SS
Phrasal syntax tier of SS	Phrasal syntax tier of SS
Conceptual Structure	Conceptual Structure

Orthographic Form	Orthographic Form
Phonological Structure	Phonological Structure
Morphosyntax tier of SS	Morphosyntax tier of SS
Phrasal syntax tier of SS	Phrasal syntax tier of SS
Conceptual Structure	Conceptual Structure

Orthographic Form	Orthographic Form
Phonological Structure	Phonological Structure
Morphosyntax tier of SS	Morphosyntax tier of SS
Phrasal syntax tier of SS	Phrasal syntax tier of SS
Conceptual Structure	Conceptual Structure

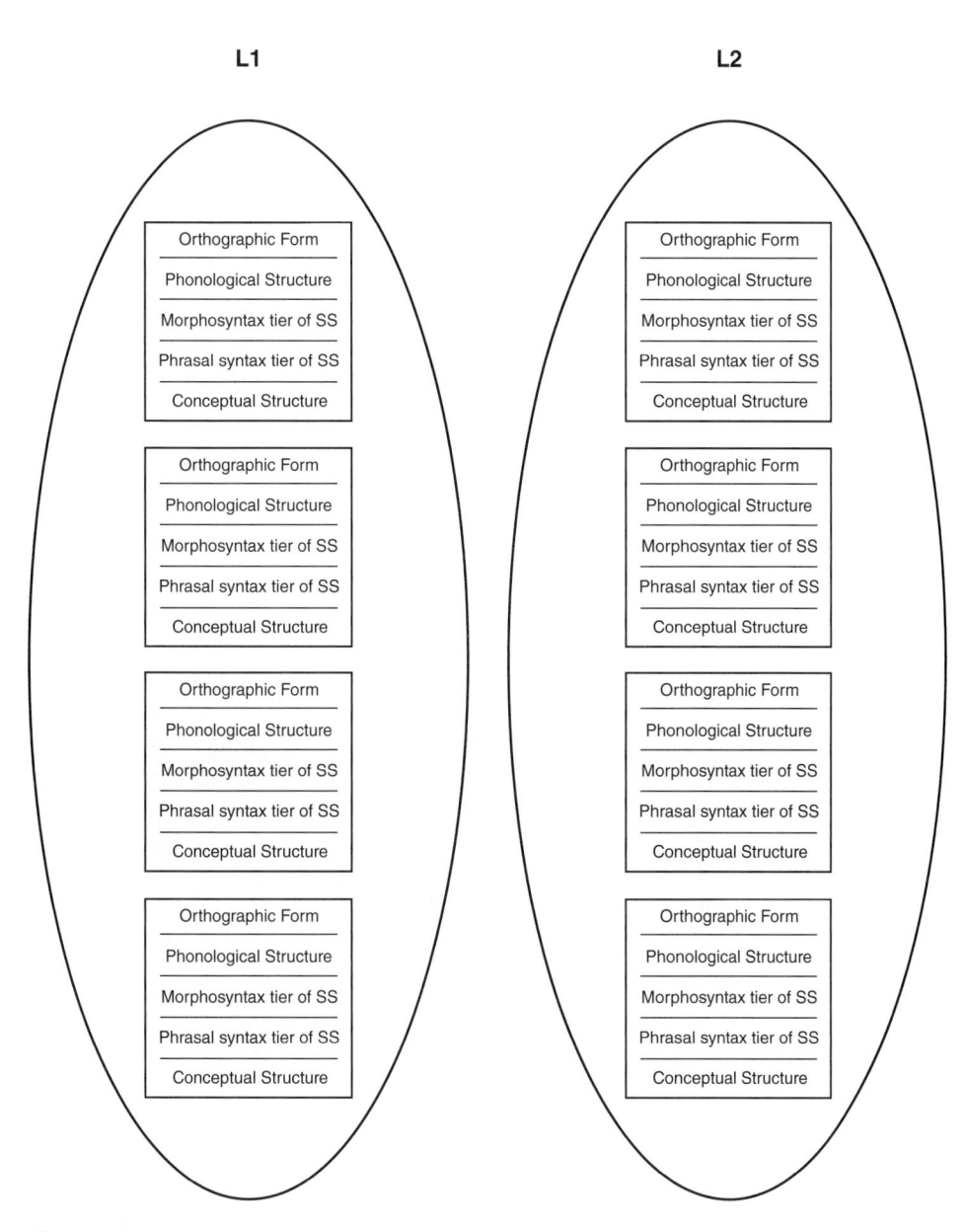

Figure 5.3
Aspects of lexical knowledge in L1 and L2

One starting point in approaching the problem of this kind of imbalance is to examine what we mean by knowledge of "vocabulary." What informally (e.g., in educational settings) is called a language learner's vocabulary is in reality just one aspect of lexical knowledge. The lexicon is intimately tied to the other linguistic subsystems, being part of the interface components that make the necessary connections among PS, SS, and CS in the TPA and the Bilingual TPA. In addition to meaning, each lexical entry that is a word (hypothetically, there are other kinds of lexical entry) typically must "include," or be linked to, information about its phonological structure, morphology, and syntax. In addition, for literate speakers there must be a connection to an orthographic representation. For each core lexical item in a bilingual's L1, the entry is normally complete: orthographic representations aside, all the required slots are filled. During L1 acquisition, "fast mapping" of each lexical item combined with rapid and spontaneous fixing of grammatical features ensures an early native-speaker completeness for core lexical entries. In L1 acquisition, mapping of a meaning representation and completing the entry with the right grammatical information appear to proceed as one integrated and seamless process.

In L2 learning, and in the curiously analogous examples of dissociation in abnormal L1 development, we can observe more easily how the components interact. In each case, the imbalances show how the components are in fact separate, and how their respective interface modules might work to interconnect them. Besides knowing fewer words than the average native speaker, typical L2 beginning-level learners rarely have complete entries for the words that they do know. Advanced L2 learners (e.g., adult students immersed in the L2 for several years in an academic setting) will most likely have accumulated an impressive target language "vocabulary." However, a significant portion may consist of "defective" entries: a complete CS element (although not necessarily) and an orthographic form, an incomplete phonological element, and partial or even empty morphology or syntax elements. Alternatively, a L2 entry may be "complete" but have the wrong features ("transferred" from the L1, constituting an interlanguage hypothesis about a L2 form, etc.), integrated into the morphology or syntax subcomponent (see examples in Van de Craats 2003). This kind of imbalanced knowledge of a L2 commonly shows itself, for example, when performance in spontaneous oral expression grossly underestimates proficiency in reading comprehension for students with advanced literacy skills.

If we continue focusing in closer, on the lexical entry itself (figure 5.4), the ways it can be defective become clearer. An array of sublexical elements, each connected to the knowledge structure that it is a part of, makes up the lexical entry. (Recall that all these connections are not depicted, and need to be drawn in by the reader.) Even in complete steady-state grammars, a number of them are naturally defective: items that contain sublexical elements for phonology and semantics, but not syntax

```
┌─────────────────────────────────┐
│      Orthographic Form          │
│     ━━━━━━━━━━━━━━━━━           │
│      Phonological Structure     │
│     ─────────────────           │
│      Morphosyntax tier of SS    │
│     ─────────────────           │
│      Phrasal syntax tier of SS  │
│     ─────────────────           │
│      Conceptual Structure       │
└─────────────────────────────────┘
```

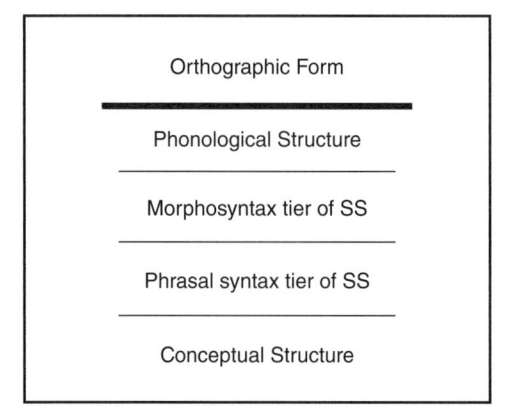

Figure 5.4
Lexical entry

("good-bye," "hooray"); and items that contain sublexical elements for phonology and syntax, but not semantics ("it" as in "it's snowing"). In some theories of syntax, the idea behind the "empty pronoun" (PRO) category ("Bill tried [PRO to talk]") is that it has syntax and semantics but no phonology (examples from Jackendoff 2002, 130–132).

The lexical entry in figure 5.4 is divided into elements for PS, the morphosyntax and phrasal syntax tiers of SS, and CS. Zooming in, we can add a bolder division, not depicted in figure 5.3, that separates Orthographic Form from the other elements or subcomponents. Note that for simplicity, figure 5.3 only depicts word entries of the lexicon. The idea here is that the lexicon must provide for fast and secure *connections* between orthography and the strictly linguistic elements. But we should hesitate to portray lexical items as *containing* orthographic forms. As Packard (2000) explains, the mental lexicon is fundamentally a natural-speech lexicon, with orthographic representations emerging during literary learning, only for speakers of a language who learn how to read. The linguistic elements are integrally, genetically, more closely related to each other than any of them are to Orthographic Form. The links that tie PS, SS, and CS together are not established through experience in the way that these linguistic components and meaning come to be linked to orthography.

The sublexical elements depicted in figure 5.4 may not be the right ones (e.g., they wouldn't be for a preliterate child). There could be others, and some might actually be part of a single undifferentiated element. But the basic idea should be compatible with most theoretical models of this domain of language knowledge. Following Jackendoff's concept of lexical items as multiway interface rules, we can now visualize the contrast between, say, a typical native speaker (NS) of a language and a L2 student of the same language who has built the latticework for a large "vocabulary." Because of his life circumstances, NS may have stored fewer entries in his lexicon, perhaps even very few beyond the basic lexical platform attainable by all members of his speech community. But, apart from the naturally defective entries, typically none of the sublexical slots for any item are empty or only partially filled. Each entry is richly and securely connected to its designated knowledge structures—PS, SS, and CS—and within the entry, among the other sublexical elements. During childhood language acquisition, the development of NS's lexical repertoire (though perhaps judged by some as "limited" against an arbitrary standard of "educated speech") more than sufficed for completely consolidating the parallel development of his linguistic subsystems. On the other hand, our highly literate L2 learner makes a surprising first impression on NS and his friends, but within minutes they realize that something isn't right. Lexical entries are associated reliably with orthographic forms, and conceptual structures for many are completely intact, but for others they are off by one or more semantic features. Syntactic structures and phonological structures for many items are defective to one degree or another or even empty. The connections to the PS, SS, and CS knowledge structures, themselves nonnatively incomplete, are unreliable and insecure. Recourse to a pidgin or interlanguage version of the L2 grammar, L1 grammatical templates, and efficient (non-language-specific) processing strategies allow for effective, even fluent, communication. Interestingly, though, the large number of entries in the "vocabulary" does not completely remedy the defects—apparently for most L2 learners, ever. This is the puzzle.

A possible explanation to explore is that each aspect of lexical knowledge is associated with different cognitive domains, components, and modules, each characterized by different degrees of openness and encapsulation, as proposed in chapter 4. This might help account for why certain classes of lexical entry in L2 tend to be more defective than others. Citing findings from a study by Van de Craats (2003) on L2 Dutch development on the part of L1 speakers of Arabic and Turkish, Towell (2004) discusses the author's "transfer and conservation hypothesis." Following this approach, "interlanguage lexical entries" can be analyzed applying the "defective entry" concept in a way that coincides with observations on how L2 grammatical competence is progressively restructured. For example, "The initial state of the learner's lexicon, home to lexical- and functional-category entries, is that specified by the L1; the transition to the L2 takes place on the basis of exposure to L2 forms" (p. 293). Along lines that are compatible with the Bilingual TPA model, Towell goes on to argue, rather persuasively, that Jackendoff's representational modularity view might be especially useful in understanding L2 development.

Returning to the lexical entry in figure 5.4, hypothetically, each sublexical element does not store *all* the information that words need for proficient use in understanding and expression, as this would result in massive redundancy. In the Bilingual TPA model, this is why connections are so rich and extensive, internally within each lexical entry, and outwardly between each sublexical element and its corresponding knowledge structure, PS, SS, and CS. This is one reason for portraying each of these component structures in the TPA (figure 5.1). This aspect of modularity, revealed in the uneven development of L2 competence, is a theme that will come up again in chapter 6 when we consider how L1 and L2 development are similar and how they differ.

6

The Critical Period, Access to Universal Grammar in First and Second Language, and Language Attrition

So far, the concepts of modularity and the competence-ability distinction have proved useful in a number of ways. We will continue applying them in two areas of language development. First, in this chapter we will apply them to aspects of grammatical development: how child language research has tried to explain simultaneous, sequential, and subtractive bilingualism, L2 learning, and L1 attrition. All of this will lead to the important debate, still current after many years, over critical period effects in L1 and L2. The interesting point is that the critical period question is not the same for L1 and L2. A closely related topic, among generativist-oriented researchers, is "access to Universal Grammar (UG) in L2 acquisition," also still controversial, but with recent signs of hope regarding a possible convergence around some proposals at least. Second, in chapter 7 we will apply the concepts of modularity and the competence-ability distinction to the development of academic language proficiency and L2 literacy. The same properties associated with modularity will also apply, but in a different way.

In regard to grammatical development, bilingualism in children may develop toward a steady state of balanced competence in two languages or toward an imbalanced competence in which one language begins to undergo attrition or early stabilization. For a number of good reasons (and some not as good), the first outcome has attracted more attention from researchers than the second. However, as we saw in chapter 5, it is the unbalanced, out-of-equilibrium condition that sometimes reveals more clearly what the components of language are, and how they interact. In child L2 learning, a similar distinction is often drawn between additive and subtractive bilingualism. The research review in this chapter focuses on the latter, keeping in mind that "attrition" and "subtraction" are not the best metaphors for characterizing the developmental shift toward one primary/dominant language. As this chapter will propose, pathological language development aside, all "attrited languages" in children have an accompanying "replacing language" (RL) that attains completeness in a timely manner. The studies of L1 attrition reviewed here also offer a new way of looking at the two related questions of critical period effects in L1 and L2 and access to UG in L2 learning. If, as will be proposed, RLs are not diminished versions of fully formed primary languages, language acquisition capacity must remain intact (i.e., not deteriorate) during the period in childhood after L1 acquisition is consolidated, and perhaps even beyond.

It is worth emphasizing, one last time, that the research on childhood bilingualism has resolved at least one important long-standing question, correcting previous misconceptions that early bilingual development was a potential source of cognitive confusion, possibly resulting in developmental lags or other dysfunctions. Cutting across theoretical perspectives, the consensus on this point stands as a major conceptual acquisition in the field: that knowledge of two or more languages in early childhood does not contribute to language deficiency (see note 4 in chapter 5 on "semilingualism").

The Faculty of Language (FL) appears to operate equally robustly and flexibly in both monolingual and bilingual development. Despite significant variation in cultural language socialization patterns, and assuming at least a threshold amount of passive or interactive input to the FL, complete acquisition of the child's primary language core grammar is assured. Primary language acquisition unfolds automatically, deflected or attenuated only by the most extreme degradation of usable primary linguistic data. A number of studies have shown that this capacity extends to bilingualism: that the Language Acquisition Device (LAD) is also equipped to process input from two languages such that simultaneous acquisition of two primary (first) languages is a normal and typical outcome (Genesee 2001). Again, this outcome is obtained despite considerable variation in the young child's bilingual experience (e.g., codeswitching by parents; unequal distribution of the two languages in different realms of language use in the home).

Does the FL, then, include among its innate capacities an "endowment for multilingualism"? The claim that the LAD is designed to accommodate bilingual and multilingual input just as easily as monolingual input appears to be well-founded; at the same time, it needs to be qualified. The challenge posed to researchers, based on the existing incomplete evidence, is to formulate a provisional working model that can help us explore in which ways the claim can be supported, and in which ways it might be too strong. In fact, a number of investigations of L1 attrition and imbalanced bilingualism point toward the conclusion that the distribution of grammatical competence in children exposed to two languages can be (even under normal language acquisition circumstances) "unstable" in interesting ways (Köpke 2004).

6.1 Overview of the Chapter

This chapter will evaluate research on the critical period, access to UG in L1 and L2, and language attrition. Its focus will first be narrow and then will branch out.

That is, it will start with a seemingly one-sided assessment of empirical findings for the purpose of taking care of some internal theoretical housecleaning, before reaching out to alternative and (on some points) potentially compatible approaches. First, the review of research findings on early imbalanced bilingualism and L1 attrition will show why we need to account for these phenomena, as well as balanced simultaneous bilingualism. A discussion of critical periods in L1 and L2 will then suggest a new way of assessing studies in this area—namely, that the concept of RL in L1 attrition can help reconcile at least some of the contradictory findings. All of this, in turn, goes to the heart of an important debate among researchers of L2 learning working within the UG framework. The attrition/replacement studies may even suggest a new way of aligning the competing hypotheses on the possible role of "parameter-setting and -resetting" mechanisms in L2 development. The poverty-of-stimulus problem will come up again, in a different guise: as a problem in explaining *erosion* of knowledge in situations where factors related to experience don't seem to tell the whole story. We will then contrast two conceptions of modularity that underlie the debate. As it turns out, the prospects for expanding the discussion beyond the confines of UG-oriented assumptions (something all linguists and psychologists should welcome) hinge on which of these conceptions ends up holding sway.

The chapter concludes with these questions for further research:

1. Why, under conditions of adequate/equal exposure to two languages in early childhood, may only one of them develop to form a complete L1?

2. If in subtractive bilingualism/replacement the "new L1–former L2" attains completeness, what does this imply for the possibility of "access to UG" in all L2 acquisition/learning situations?

3. Can we then still accept the idea of a "fundamental difference" between L1 acquisition and L2 learning?

4. If cognitive-general learning mechanisms are shown to play a more prominent role in L2 learning than strong "naturalistic" L2-learning models would suggest, might there be reason to consider a more important role for them in L1 acquisition as well (Bates 2001; Tomasello 2005)? Across all theoretical tendencies, there has been a trend toward recognizing that more of the constraints on grammar should be accounted for in terms of semantic principles (Goldberg 2003)—"cutting syntax down to size," as Culicover and Jackendoff (2005) propose. In development, acquisition might be more incremental and dependent on exposure to and learning of specific constructions (Clark 2003). Thus, the distinction between what is lexical and what is syntactic may have to be explained in a new way (Clark and Wong 2002).

6.2 The Concept of Language Attrition

The study of L1 attrition and the closely related study of early imbalanced bilingual development provide a unique perspective on the capacities of the FL in early childhood bilingualism. At the same time, they offer a new point of view on the continuing discussion on differences and similarities between L1 and L2 development.

An important subfield in the area of language attrition has focused on two cases:

1. middle childhood bilingualism in which a fully developed L1 begins to undergo attrition following normal monolingual development through age 5 or 6;
2. early childhood (< 5 years) bilingualism of the imbalanced type evidencing L_a or L_b dominance with concomitant stabilization of the nondominant language (analogous to a fossilized interlanguage), often precursor to attrition. Major studies by Montrul (2008) and Yip and Matthews (2007) have called attention to this important, but still largely neglected, research problem.

The distinction between #1 and #2 hinges on the ability to identify an age of first exposure to each language and to measure the onset of attrition or delayed development. But in all instances it would be an emerging dominant L_a or L_b, or L2, that either displaces a L1 in decline or continues its normal robust development in coexistence with a stabilized weaker language subsystem. Along similar lines, Polinsky (1995) distinguishes between "forgetters" and "incomplete learners"; Montrul (2004) and Sorace (2004) point out some of the methodological problems in drawing a clear line between these two categories. For now, let us set aside late L1 attrition, L2 attrition, and all types of abnormal incomplete[1] language development (e.g., Specific Language Impairment or denial of exposure to language during the critical period). In this chapter, the most pertinent and interesting case studies are those that provide evidence for balanced bilingual input during early childhood, beyond a minimum threshold in each language, L_a and L_b, such that it would allow, or should allow, for simultaneous balanced bilingualism instead of attrition of one or the other.

Findings from the attrition studies line up with research on simultaneous balanced bilingualism (Meisel 2001; J. Paradis and Genesee 1996) that argues for early separation of the bilingual child's languages. That is, the evidence for early differentiation between the two languages in child bilingualism helps explain both (1) the balanced development of L_a and L_b and (2) childhood bilingualism in which L_a-or-L_b undergoes stabilization, yielding, so to speak, to a dominant L1. Attrition or early stabilization of L_a should not affect L_b (neither delaying nor seemingly accelerating its development). Language competence (again, with a capital L) never erodes or fossilizes; simply, knowledge of one or the other instantiation of it is lost or develops at an unexpectedly slower rate (Schlyter 1993). That is, only (lowercase) language-specific knowledge might erode; at least one language system is always spared, remaining completely intact.

Provisionally, the metaphor of parameter setting appears to offer one way of modeling L1 attrition (Sharwood Smith and Van Buren 1991), in turn giving way to a discussion of the possibility of parameter *resetting* in child L2 learning. Notwithstanding the current debate on the continued usefulness of the parameter-setting concept (Newmeyer 2004), the general idea allows us to conceptualize, even if in an approximate way, the seemingly "complementary" relationship between L1 and L2 in this case. For example, do all of the components and mechanisms of the language acquisition capacity remain fully operative for a L2 as the L1 progressively converges on a complete steady state? And do they remain so for later L2 learning after the FL has completed its work in the construction of the L1? Closely related to these questions is the notion of a critical period or critical periods in language development. What *kind* of difference, or discontinuity, in terms of actual knowledge of language, might there be between L1s and L2s? If L1 attrition is formulated more precisely as displacement and replacement, the findings from this growing field of investigation (de Bot and Hulsen 2002; Hansen 2001; Isurin 2005; Köpke et al. 2007; M. Schmid 2009) will offer new evidence to consider in discussing the various critical period hypotheses. The same can be said for the question of access to the principles of UG and the LAD in L2 learning. In addition, evidence of how the components of linguistic competence undergo change differentially in attrition (Gross 2004; Montrul 2004) will contribute to a more precise conceptualization of modularity.

Researchers working in a broad range of theoretical models have contributed to the discussion of maturational constraints on language development. UG-oriented hypotheses are taken here as an initial framework because, first, the strongest claims against a L1-L2 discontinuity come from within the UG field: the "no transfer/full access" position that draws the broadest equivalence between L1 and L2 development (Epstein, Flynn, and Martohardjono 1996; Martohardjono and Flynn 1995). Second, if the present isolation of UG-oriented work on L2 learning within the applied linguistics field is to be remedied, a way must be found to allow new lines of research findings to be considered. A good starting point in constructing less impenetrable models would be to question the usefulness of noninteractive versions of modularity that excessively isolate the linguistic domains from the rest of cognition. Summaries of cognitive-functional theories (Bates 2001; Tomasello 2000) and emergentist models (MacWhinney 2006) are recommended here as counterpoint references. They tend to question the fundamental idea of modularity, but they have also served the debate among cognitive scientists by pointing to some interesting defects in the mainstream generativist research program. It needs to recognized, truth be told, that especially in the area of L2 learning, most work is being carried out within the framework of these nonnativist approaches (to mention only a few, Bardovi-Harlig 2000; Hulstijn 2002; Schmidt 2001; Tarone 2002). More cross-paradigm assessment of research findings would help clarify a number of long-standing controversies.

The following proposal will serve as a provisional working assumption, without any intention of prejudicing investigation of what probably remains an empirical question in one way or another: a RL may trace its origin to a L2; but upon effecting attrition of a L1, it takes on the status of a full-fledged (dominant) primary language, a "new L1." More succinctly, in all children (barring trauma or other pathology) attrition adheres to the "no semilingualism" condition— the linguistic knowledge that "lingual" refers to being the core grammatical competencies that underlie language ability of the typical 9- or 10-year-old monolingual speaker. Among the language development phenomena that should be excluded when considering RL completeness are temporary transitional states, lexical access that may appear to be "below average" in each language counted separately, and residual and superficial phonological L1 influences on the RL, now the "new L1." The "no semilingualism" condition applies to all bilingual children, simultaneous and sequential, and all child L2 learners, additive and subtractive. After considering research findings that are consistent with the idea of "RL/no semilingualism," the conclusion will take up one particular application of this working assumption, which of course still should be taken as a proposal for further investigation.

6.3 What the Research Says about First Language Attrition

We begin with category #1 of L1 attrition/delay above, where a fully developed L1 begins to undergo attrition following normal monolingual development. In a series of studies of early childhood L1 attrition, Kaufman (1995, 2001) presents the problem in an especially clear way. The bilinguals in this case were largely children born to recent immigrants to the United States whose use of the primary language (Hebrew) was maintained both in the home and within a closely knit speech community, with significant opportunities for extrafamilial use. All bilinguals in the study were native speakers of Hebrew, which was spoken at home as the primary or exclusive language, actively promoted within the family through kindergarten age and beyond. Within this highly ethnolinguistically vital and heritage-language-preservation-conscious community, we would nevertheless expect English, on average, to exercise a predominant influence upon exposure to television and enrollment in preschool. But from the author's account we might also conclude that the amount and quality of exposure to Hebrew should have more than sufficed for full and complete development of the language that parents actively transmitted, on par with or even exceeding development of English. That is, hypothetically, if exposure to English had been eliminated or significantly diminished, the same level of exposure to Hebrew would have easily ensured complete ultimate attainment together with timely meeting of all intermediate milestones along the way.

Investigating the second category of L1 attrition/delay (imbalanced early bilingualism assuming simultaneous exposure to L_a+L_b from birth or during early childhood), Kaufman and Aronoff (1991) and Bolonyai (1998) report on early onset of attrition/delay of Hebrew and Hungarian, respectively. In both cases, bilingual speech (mixing)—specifically, changing patterns of intrasentential mixing—serves as an index of attrition. Recall that mixing reflects attrition only sometimes and only in some bilingual circumstances (J. Anderson 2004); in this case, it does. Kaufman and Aronoff outline four stages of attrition in their case study:

1. onset, three months after initial contact with English (age 2;9–3;1);
2. a short, one-month bilingual period;
3. disintegration of the Hebrew verbal system (age 3;2–3;5); and
4. reconstruction of the derivational and inflectional system, reducing it to a single form, used productively by the child (age 3;5–4;6).

During the bilingual period, stage 2, mixing consists of English insertions into Hebrew sentence structures. All resulting mixed utterances show that the latter continues its normal course of development, including appropriate overgeneralizations that attest to the child's knowledge of Hebrew morphology. Stage 3 marks the shift to insertion of Hebrew verbs into English grammatical frames, "deviant but recognizable forms ... devoid of appropriate morphological inflections ... different from developmental forms used by younger children" (p. 182). Stage 4, during which incorporation of the eroding language into the dominant language advances, attests to the autonomous nature of attrition: the idiosyncratic modifications that emerge are individual creations without the benefit of a direct model (p. 187). Hebrew insertion into English patterns reflects grammatical knowledge of both languages (as it did, inversely, in stage 1), even in the context of the more advanced erosion of Hebrew.

Like Kaufman (1995, 2001), Bolonyai (1998) describes an active language-maintenance effort on the part of both parents in an attempt to compensate for the growing influence of English during their English-Hungarian bilingual child's preschool years (specifically ages 3–4). Applying Myers-Scotton's (2006, 233–287) Matrix Language Frame model to the changes in mixing patterns, Bolonyai describes a similar language shift: here, codeswitching reveals a *matrix language (ML) turnover*. Bolonyai describes three stages:

1. At age 3;7, two years after initial contact with English, the languages remain separated. Codeswitching is mainly intersentential. Of the few intrasentential switches recorded (seven), Hungarian is the ML in five.
2. At age 4;2, codeswitching increases significantly, and a shift begins toward English as the ML in mixed utterances (19 out of 50).
3. In what appears to be a partial and temporary regaining of Hungarian following a two-month visit to Hungary, "the Matrix Language turnover [takes] a different route" (p. 36)—a further increase in codeswitching. Hungarian is the preferred ML in 77% of mixed utterances, but such utterances show an increase in *composite ML* structures. The bilingual child demonstrates a greater effort to use Hungarian; but since her proficiency does not keep pace, performance is marked by a "compromise strategy of converging structures," surface morphemes drawn from Hungarian but with parts of the complex and modular lexical structure taken from English (p. 37).

According to the Matrix Language Frame model, the concept of ML turnover helps explain the intermediate stages of the development of the bilingual child's weaker grammar. During the phases of balanced bilingualism and initial loss of balance, the ML (in this case the original dominant L_a) still provides the grammatical frame for mixed-language utterances, as in adult "classic codeswitching." As the faster-developing language emerges, it more and more takes on the role of ML, and the now weaker language (the former ML) becomes the embedded language (EL) in bilingual speech. Lanza (1997) also shows how shifts in mixing patterns reveal asymmetries in the development of L_a and L_b in young bilinguals. Convergence, a different kind of $L_a \leftrightarrow L_b$ interaction, has the outward appearance of monolingual speech; all lexical items occurring in the sentence come from L_a, but not all components of the abstract lexical structures belong to L_a. (In the Bilingual TPA model of chapter 5, these would be the sublexical elements in figures 5.3 and 5.4.) Converging speech and mixing, which accompany attrition or imbalanced early bilingualism, require the construction of a composite ML (Bolonyai 1998; Myers-Scotton 2002; Schmitt 2000). Although not discussing actual erosion of L1 competence, Pfaff (1999) documents the course of mixing patterns (Turkish-German) in which the one-time L2, now the preferred language of the preschool bilingual, progressively becomes the dominant base language in bilingual speech, another example of "ML turnover." Finally, in a major study of incomplete acquisition in bilingualism, Montrul (2008) reports on additional case studies of "weaker language" development. In a number of these studies, from the subjects' language socialization profile one can surmise exposure to the attriting language theoretically sufficient to ensure complete ultimate attainment similar to the above, paradoxical, examples.

For an alternative, although not necessarily incompatible perspective, see the treatment of "bidirectional transfer" by Pavlenko and Jarvis (2002), who favor a *multicompetence* view of bilingualism. By contrast, Hall, Cheng, and Carlson (2006) elaborate the multicompetence view into a model explicitly at odds with the componential perspective presented so far in this book. The virtue of their position is that it draws the lines of debate clearly, based as it is on a strong usage-based account of the knowledge of language. We will have to leave this interesting discussion for another occasion.

The case study of a 5-year-old Japanese-English bilingual (Yukawa 1997) is testimony to how dramatic the onset of L1 attrition can be, and how rapidly it may proceed in early childhood. After only three months in an English-speaking environment, significant processing difficulties in production were in evidence in the bilingual child's dominant language, Japanese. While comprehension abilities appeared to be unaffected during the "attrition period," after four months English had come to predominate and "oral Japanese production [had] decreased to zero" (p. 16) in periodic assessments over the course of the study (natural conversations, storytelling, and language games). Rapid recovery (within two months) of all L1 abilities upon the child's return to Japan, and an absence of restructuring of the L1 grammar during the English-dominant period, were taken as evidence that L1 competence remained intact throughout. A follow-up study of the same subject at age 7;0–8;4 (Yukawa 1998), in a similar English-speaking non-Japanese setting, confirmed that he had surpassed a critical threshold for language maintenance. The boy's younger sister (age 3;10) revealed the same rapid and dramatic "processing failure" that characterized her brother's switch to English in the earlier study. Maintenance of L1 competence during the "erosion of ability" period distinguishes the findings in this study from the above descriptions of more advanced attrition. However, if the children's sojourns in English-speaking environments had been significantly extended, to include English-medium elementary schooling for example, the case could perhaps be made that the "processing failure" stage marks a potential onset for full-scale attrition of L1 language knowledge itself (E. Yukawa, personal communication). A similar speculation is in order in the descriptions of ML turnover by Bolonyai (1998), Pfaff (1999), and Schmitt (2000).

What distinguishes the Japanese-English study is the description of the "recuperation" of the child's primary language, and the evidence showing that the erosion could not have represented a loss of the knowledge of Japanese (or at most represented a very localized, marginal loss). This study thus makes for a good example of the competence-ability distinction. If, with time (under sustained conditions of English immersion and nonuse of Japanese), "erosion of ability" were to pass over to actual erosion of competence, many interesting questions could be posed about how competence is understood in relation to ability (performance). That is, as in the other studies just reviewed, the instantiation of knowledge of language in either L_a or L_b is in fact subject to attrition.

Summing up this section, we can pull together common themes from the research findings, which set the stage for the discussion to follow on critical period effects and the accessibility of UG in L2 learning. Attrition and replacement are integral parts of a single process. L1 loss is developmental and systematic in a manner similar to L1 acquisition, not "random forgetting" (Seliger 1996, 617). L1 attrition is "L2/RL-induced": the developing dominant language restructures elements of its grammatical subsystem and incorporates or introduces them into the receding L1 (Gürel 2004). In other words, erosion of a language subsystem can only proceed under the systematic interference of another, expanding language subsystem, the RL. Most importantly, it appears that external factors are not determinative and sufficient; that is, attrition is not driven exclusively by properties of the input. Therefore, external factors do not provide a full account of how the *development* of attrition/replacement unfolds. This development, then, is constrained by the mechanisms of the FL as language acquisition itself is constrained, only in a different way. As studies of attrition have noted, components of the grammar erode under the pressure of the expanding dominant language and also as a result of internal dynamics (internal to the attriting language), not directly attributable to RL influence (Isurin 2005; McCormack 2004). In other words, attrition is "L2/RL-induced," but it's not just a matter of transfer pure and simple, the way the search-and-replace function works in a word-processing program. While all of the authors cited in this section may not agree with this last interpretation of the findings, the proposal that characteristics of the input underdetermine the attrition process is not inconsistent with at least some of the findings. The studies that provide evidence for sufficient and sustained exposure to the child in the attriting language are most suggestive in regard to this proposal.

In an interesting case study of adult L1 attrition, Köpke (2001) analyzed contrasting profiles in three L1 German speakers who experienced late immersion in an English-speaking environment (age at arrival: 18, 25, and 26–age at assessment: 54, 64, and 55, respectively). The findings illustrate how input factors contribute to attrition in a complex way. While all three bilinguals reported English as their current dominant or preferred language, it was the two who had the *least* contact with German after immigration for whom measures of their previous L1 grammatical knowledge showed the least erosion. In contrast, for the third bilingual, weekly contact with the L1-speaking immigrant community appears to have contributed to an actual competence restructuring, evidenced in a significantly greater number of errors in all assessment categories. Presumably, a number of this bilingual's German-speaking friends and associates were also L1 attriters at a similar interlanguage stage of "language replacement/ML turnover." Regardless, it is the presence of a competing RL system, internally, that accounts for the effect of this environmental factor. Hypothetically, the core grammatical system of a monolingual speaker of German exposed to an even more highly pidginized input in his L1 (all the while, for example, in an English-speaking environment) would "insulate" itself, so to speak, against the effects of the nonnative model. A 3-year-old (very hypothetically, exposed to the same pidginized input, and isolated somehow from English as a L2) would construct a German-based creole. In both cases, we would certainly see a kind of restructuring. But it would be one in which the core L1 grammar would remain complete and well-formed, unlike in the replacement/attrition scenario described by Köpke.

6.4 The Critical Period Hypothesis

Now let us turn to research on the question of critical periods in language development. Here, we will take up the idea from the previous section that the attriting language and the RL interact in a systematic way. The encounter is not like two interlanguages simply passing each other in opposite directions, like the proverbial ships in the night; rather, they are in close contact with each other such that the RL systematically occupies ceded domains. If it is possible for the attrited language to be replaced at any age during the childhood years, how might this square with different proposals on critical period effects, especially in regard to L2 development? Given that the discussion of critical period effects focuses on factors that are maturational/biological or FL-internal (Eubank and Gregg 1999), there is a logical tie-in to findings on early L1 attrition—namely, that external factors alone cannot explain how a L_a evolves into a dominant L1, at the same time that its L_b counterpart undergoes early stabilization or erosion under comparable input conditions. As with the puzzle of the imbalance in borrowing patterns among Nahuatl-Spanish narrators in the Mexican study, social factors related to language use go a long way in explaining why. But here, again, our purpose is different.

Research on critical periods asks the question, what intrinsic factors might account for an ultimate attainment plateau in the development of a nonprimary or delayed L1 that differs significantly in some way from the normal and typical acquisition of primary languages? Formulated in this more general way, the critical period question now becomes pertinent to the problem of explaining L1 attrition and replacement. However, to be of any use to us, the findings on possible critical period effects need to be divided and considered separately: critical period for L1, critical period for L2.

Considering first a critical period for L1, while the studies of modern-day wild children have uncovered interesting imbalances in late L1 learning (e.g., vocabulary and basic word order versus functional categories), ultimate attainment deficiencies are difficult to attribute to FL-internal factors. In these cases, extreme deprivation potentially impinges on all mental faculties. In contrast, research on specifically language-deprived children, for whom other aspects of socialization and childhood experience are assumed to be normal, allows confounding variables to be delimited. For example, evidence from late sign language learning by deaf children (Mayberry and Lock 2003; Newport 1991; A. Senghas and Coppola 2001) argues convincingly for a critical period for L1 acquisition below age 5. Consistent with a modular view of language development, different components or subsystems of linguistic competence may be sensitive to maturational constraints at different stages (Schachter 1996), beginning as early as before 2 years. The work of Mayberry and her associates over the years has confirmed that only language input during early childhood ensures normal L1 development (Mayberry 2007; Mayberry and Lock 2003). Late exposure outside this narrow window results in long-term degraded L1 competence that tends to be impervious to remediation, and significant degradation in the capacity to learn any other language as a L2. Surely, attributing these observations to performance factors, processing failure, or some aspect of ability alone, would be out of the question. Normal language acquisition mechanisms atrophy, the disruption typically being irrevocable.

Investigations of age and *L2* learning are also often framed in terms of critical periods—alternatively, in terms of "multiple sensitive periods" (Kim 1997). Immediately, though, we see the need to separate out the complex question of critical periods in L2 learning from the very strong and straightforward evidence for a critical period in L1. Findings for L2 are less uniform and analyses are more controversial. While the contrasts between L1 acquisition and L2 learning are less contested, comparisons between child L2 and postpuberty L2 learners appear not to suggest a strong maturational constraint. Evidence for a clearly identifiable offset age and qualitatively pronounced deterioration at puberty is not conclusive (Bylund 2009). In regard to the L1-L2 contrast,, inevitable and spontaneous acquisition based on primary linguistic data alone, and universal completeness, independent of language, culture, and social circumstance, apply across the board only to early childhood L1 (Herschensohn 2000). On the other hand, in regard to L2 learning at different ages, inconsistent findings have come to undermine the puberty threshold. But pushing the critical period for L2 learning back to age 5 or 6, and proposing a gradual decline, strongly suggests (as Bialystok and Hakuta (1994) point out) that the relevant dimension may not be age; rather, it may be L1 versus L2. As a first approximation, we might propose that within a certain age range, before 5 years, the introduction of a "L2" is in effect a case of early L_a+L_b bilingualism, not one of child L2 learning.

To reiterate, the automaticity of normal L1 acquisition and the assurance of native-speaker ultimate attainment in response to "impoverished input" have prompted researchers to propose acquisition mechanisms unlike those children use in inductive learning: for example, triggering and parameter setting (Crain and

Pietroski 2002; Foster-Cohen 1990; Meisel 1995). Even though we still do not have a clear picture of what "triggering" or "setting" a parameter involves psychologically, the need to propose a different kind of acquisition paradigm for L1 appears to be warranted. While near-native and native-like L2 proficiency needs to be explained (a similar poverty-of-stimulus problem also applies to intermediate L2 ability), the benchmarks of uniformity, universal completeness, and spontaneous acquisition *without exception* do not apply to L2. This might be another case where research on the early stabilization or attrition of a developing L1 (in childhood bilingualism) should inform research on critical period effects.

Regarding the separate but related question of whether maturational factors confer any advantage to younger L2 learners (e.g., ages 6–12), the evidence points to a gradual decline, but no categorical cut-off as in normal L1 versus late L1 development. If L1 acquisition proceeds normally during early childhood, L2 learning outcomes range from native-like to rudimentary interlanguage competence. However, note that, overall, L2 ultimate attainment is qualitatively superior to late, abnormal L1 learning. That is, once engraved during an early critical period, the language acquisition capacity (even if it may be shown to begin to "deteriorate") does not atrophy (Eubank and Gregg 1999; Hyltenstam and Abrahamsson 2003; Mayberry and Lock 2003). Again, a categorical distinction appears to hold between early childhood L1 acquisition and L2 learning, but of a different kind.

On the other hand, analyses of L2 proficiency, comparing child beginners (age of onset 6–12 years) and older beginners (age of onset >12), do *not* reveal a categorical contrast. Rather, they reveal a linear decline, with no sharp discontinuity or salient offset. A critical period ending in early adolescence should allow all child L2 learners to attain complete native-speaker ability while late-adolescent and adult L2 learners should generally show wide variation skewed toward rudimentary proficiency. However, research to date, in addition to favoring the linear decline view, has documented both near-native performance by late learners (Bongaerts, Mennen, and Van der Slik 2000; Van Boxtel, Bongaerts, and Coppen 2005) and, most significantly, less than native-like ultimate attainment among many child L2 learners. The latter findings extend to some very early beginners. Even L2 learners with age of onset less than 5 years could be distinguished from native speakers of the L2 (Birdsong and Molis 2001; Marinova-Todd, Bradford Marshal, and Snow 2000; McDonald 2000; Scovel 2000; Singleton 2001). Strongly calling into question a maturational account for L2, these results relativize observations of a general decline in L2-learning *capacity* with age. In addition, external factors can often account for the overall tendency toward negative correlations between age of onset and L2 proficiency. Even controlling for length of residence, child immigrant L2 learners, for example, benefit from substantially upgraded experience with the L2, quantitatively and qualitatively: full-time L2-medium instruction, language-learner-appropriate television programming, and so on. Thus, not only does L2-learning capacity not atrophy (if L1 acquisition proceeded normally), the idea behind the term "deterioration" also fails to account for whatever it is that characterizes L2 learning.

The observation made by several investigators (Harley and Wang 1997; Herschensohn 2000; Hyltenstam and Abrahamsson 2003) that unlike L1 acquisition, L2 native-speaker attainment is not ensured at any age, including any age of onset below 5 years, is consistent with the early-language-attrition research surveyed in the previous section. It appears that this observation can be extended to include not only early child "L2s" but also any language, either the L_a or the L_b of simultaneous bilingual acquisition. In principle, this alternative must be entertained given that no case study of attrition considered so far has suggested any type of linguistic disability or impairment. If the FL is designed to ensure the rapid, preprogrammed development of Language in young children, it does not do so for an unlimited number of languages (assuming that the child is afforded the normal and typical opportunity to acquire each one). Researchers of early child multilingualism might come to agree on an upper limit of L1s that the LAD could accommodate simultaneously given sufficient exposure (perhaps three, or even four or five—an interesting question in its own right). But the evidence clearly (and surprisingly) indicates that the lower limit for normal childhood bilingualism is not two, but *one primary language*. There are thus three possibilities, neither of the last two implying any language deficit or degraded language acquisition capacity:

1. early L_a+L_b → balanced bilingualism (2L1);
2. early L_a+L_b → L1+L2; or even
3. early L_a+L_b → L1+ an attriting L2 (an early childhood L2 that lags behind L1 and subsequently shows signs of erosion).

Thus, we could formulate more precisely the idea of an "endowment for multilingualism" along the following lines: Under all normal circumstances of bilingual or multilingual input, the LAD ensures the complete development (full and mature native-speaker ultimate attainment) of one primary language. In addition, the LAD is capable of accommodating this bilingual/multilingual input, resulting in the ultimate development of full and mature native-speaker attainment in more than one language *or* in the primary language(s) plus a number of L2-like second(ary) languages (characterized by one degree or another of incomplete acquisition), all of which are UG-constrained.

Returning now to the problem posed earlier of distinguishing between early L2 learning (L1+L2) and simultaneous balanced bilingualism (2L1), we can see that our first approximation to a solution was incorrect. The rudiment of L1-L2 divergence and subsequent asymmetry[2] can now be traced to the very initial stages of grammatical development when the acquisition mechanism begins to fix the "settings" for the L1 and L2 subsystems in response to positive examples provided by primary linguistic data. At the same time, it is necessary to reemphasize that early L_a-L_b separation and divergence may evolve toward *either* symmetrical and equivalent knowledge in each language *or* imbalanced early bilingualism.

Keeping in mind now the reciprocal relationship between imbalanced early bilingualism or attrition and the resulting predominance of a soon-to-be-primary "L1," we can contemplate the possibility of another confounding variable in the research on age and L2 learning. For example, in comparing groups of child and adult L2 learners, for which members of the former group is the L2 in reality a RL? As Yukawa's (1997) study indicates, it is more likely that *child* L2s develop into RLs (the younger the child, the more likely this is). RLs (adhering still to our "no semilingualism" condition) are in fast transition toward full primary-language status. Here, we may want to draw a parallel with Myers-Scotton's (2006) ML turnover as it is revealed in codeswitching. The comparison, then, might have to be recast as one between children, many of whom have attained or are in transition toward a "RL–new L1," and older learners, for whom this shift is less likely to have been initiated or completed.

This potential methodological problem prompts further reflection on the fundamental research question regarding critical period effects: what intrinsic factors might account for diminished ultimate attainment in the development of a nonprimary or delayed L1 in comparison to normal and typical L1 acquisition? Excluding semilingualism in L1 attrition/replacement coincides with the position that language-learning capacity after L1 acquisition does not deteriorate. As long as the child's L1 maintains its predominance (e.g., is represented mentally as the ML into which constituents of the L2 are inserted in language mixing), it may *appear* that language-learning capacity (for L2) has deteriorated. But if RLs attain completeness, we would not want to say that the capacity as a whole, or any essential component of it, had eroded, to be reconstituted somehow for the purpose of replacing an attrited L1. Since we still face the task of trying to explain L1-L2 differences, we must now explore some other process (apart from erosion of the language-learning capacity), internal to the FL. We might begin by taking up the approach of Sharwood Smith and Van Buren (1991) that invokes parameter setting and resetting—in this case, presupposing a concurrent "unsetting" in the subsystems of the declining L1.

Along the lines of an interaction hypothesis proposed by Yeni-Komshian, Flege, and Liu (2000) and Harley and Wang (1997, 39), a developing L2 is mediated by L1. Mediation is a systematic influence of the established language system upon the developing L2, described by researchers in different terms: "filtering" (Doughty 2003; Pallier et al. 2003; White 2000), "providing a template for," "inhibiting," "blocking" (Newmeyer 1998), or "interfering with" (Pallier 2007) the fast triggering mechanisms of the language modules specialized for acquisition. In her discussion of early L1 attrition, Köpke (2004, 12) alludes to the effect of a "cognitive sieve" through which L_a or L_b may be acquired, even in simultaneous bilingualism. Truscott and Sharwood Smith (2004) take a very different approach toward bilingual competence than the one outlined in the last three chapters. Nevertheless, their explanation for why L2 learning rarely attains native-like completeness (an input competition view) is not totally inconsistent with the notion of filtering/blocking. Limits are imposed on L2 learning by "L1 involvement in L2 processing. During the parsing of an L2 utterance, L1 entries are also activated and therefore compete with the appropriate L2 entries for a place in the representations being constructed.... If L2 entries routinely lose out to their L1 counterparts, then L2 acquisition will be slow, or even non-existent" (pp. 14–15). In regard to the initial stages of imbalanced bilingualism, the metaphor of a "cognitive sieve" captures the essence of how the language systems might interact. The acquisition device, faced with indicators of L_a or L_b stabilization or attrition, under the pressure of a robust and predatory L2 development, allows for "filtering in reverse," facilitating the ceding (as opposed to "loss") of L_a or L_b settings in a systematic way.

Investigations of infant speech perception are also consistent with the filtering/blocking hypothesis. Kuhl et al. (2005) studied how 7-month-old children's phonetic discrimination skills might affect their rate of language development through 30 months, leading them to propose the Native Language Magnet theory. The crucial underlying mechanism is "neural commitment to the acoustic and statistical properties of native language phonetic units" (p. 238), a kind of narrowing of options in the construction of linguistic competence related to the critical period in L1 acquisition. Findings from their study supported the hypothesis that exposure to the child's native language produces dedicated neural networks, "committing" these networks to patterns that are language-specific. That is, the initial coding of native-language patterns eventually *interferes with* the establishment of patterns associated with a nonnative language. The researchers point to confirming findings from related studies that have shown an "inefficiency" in brain measures of L2 speech processing due to the possibility that L2 input is processed utilizing L1 strategies. In fact, Kuhl et al.'s infant speech perception experiments showed a negative correlation at 7 months between native and nonnative phonetic perception skills: the better young children were at perceiving native-language (English) phonetic contrasts, the less skilled they were at perceiving nonnative contrasts (in this experiment, from Chinese). The authors went on to make a further strong prediction: that "nonnative perception reflects the degree to which the system remains uncommitted ... [and that] an open system reflects uncommitted circuitry" (p. 243). In other words, children who continue to show an ability in nonnative phonetic perception would not advance as rapidly, at least initially, in their general language development, a prediction confirmed by the findings.

These hypotheses were tested in an actual bilingual speech community, characterized by high levels of individual bilingualism. Bosch and Sebastián-Gallés (2003) compared the performance of monolingual Catalan, monolingual Spanish, and bilingual infants on the perception of a Catalan-specific vowel contrast (that does not occur in Spanish). At 4½ months, all children were able to make the relevant discrimination. Consistent with Kuhl et al.'s findings, by 8 months the Spanish monolinguals failed to show sensitivity to the contrast, while the Catalan monolinguals maintained the ability to perceive it. Surprisingly, bilingual infants also lost the ability to discriminate the vowel contrast at 8 months, then regained it at 12 months.

Sebastián-Gallés, Echevarría, and Bosch (2005) went on to evaluate adult Spanish-Catalan bilinguals, all with early intensive exposure to both languages, sustained throughout their life in everyday usage. Even in the case of highly proficient simultaneous bilinguals, the effects of a language dominance were evident in the vowel discrimination tasks. Differences in early language input apparently can have long-term or permanent effects; a related study on this question by W. Baker and Trofimovich (2005) produced similar findings. In one experiment comparing early simultaneous bilinguals, significant differences were found between adults exposed to both languages from birth depending on whether Catalan or Spanish was the *maternal language*. The precise mechanism responsible for this kind of early cognitive "preference" is still an open question. But what all this suggests is that it may not be restricted to phonology. And such developmental imbalances need not apply to all simultaneous bilinguals (they most probably don't) to require an explanation. Specifically, in these studies (just as in the attrition studies reviewed above) there is no indication that subjects suffered from any SLI-type language impairment. The authors make no mention of this possibility (perhaps because the lack of such impairment seems too obvious to note), underscoring again that the kind of early L_a-L_b differentiation described in the research is evidently one manifestation of normal child bilingual development. Fernald (2006) makes some interesting observations on the Catalan-Spanish studies, as part of a broader discussion on early speech perception research.

In L2 learning, the more consolidated L1 settings become, the more resistant they are likely to be to displacement, and potentially the greater their inhibiting effect may be on "L2 resetting." A progressively stronger L1 filter effect on triggering and resetting would be consistent with findings that analytical abilities and conscious learning strategies come to play a greater role in L2 learning as children's cognitive-general competencies mature (DeKeyser 2000; Harley and Hart 1997).

Recalling Mayberry and Lock's (2003) findings, an instructive apparent contradiction again presents itself. According to their analysis, tentatively accepted here, a complete and fully formed L1, product of normal early childhood language development, sets down an adequate cognitive foundation for successful L2 learning. Deficient L1 learning after the critical period (i.e., language deprivation during the critical period) significantly degrades learning capacity for L2s. At the same time, the suggestion is that a complete and fully formed L1 may filter access to acquisition mechanisms that serve L2 learning, and that the "freeing up" of L1 settings in attrition accompanies (facilitates?) resetting in the L2.[3] However, under this proposal, L2 resetting would not apply to deficient L1 learning in which a true deterioration of language acquisition capacity has resulted from deprivation. L2 resetting would apply fully in cases of RL development, that is, in cases of normal L1 "deficiency" that is the result of attrition/replacement.

Here, the metaphor of "L2 resetting" clearly converges with the Competition Model's linkage between "age-related effects" and transfer, briefly mentioned in chapter 5. Sometimes in comparing observations and explanations it's necessary to not get distracted by the fact that evidence comes from researchers who favor a rival theory. According to Bates, Deveskovi, and Wulfeck (2001) and MacWhinney (2005), also, the L1-L2 attainment difference cannot be accounted for by a "critical age" factor, per se. The use of their concepts of interference and "resisting interference" in bilingual development (Kohnert, Bates, and Hernández 1999) as a way of explaining the shift in dominance ("language reversal") from a former L1 to a new primary language, former L2, is parallel in many ways to the idea of RL development presented here. Even in the absence of significant L1 attrition, "minor shifts in language dominance in childhood can lead to the introduction of strong transfer effects" (MacWhinney 2005, 77, in reference to Döpke 2000). And according to the same logic, L2 is initially parasitic on L1: "the learner's goal is to reduce this parasitism by building up L2 representations as a separate system" (p. 77). For MacWhinney, the L1-L2 difference is also "fundamental" (p. 69), for different reasons and motivated by a different theory; but perhaps it's a point of view that is not entirely divergent from the one favored in this book after all.

One way to take stock of the research considered so far on early imbalances and shifts in dominance among child bilinguals is to revisit how we have been trying to understand the relationship between competence and proficiency. The difference between a bilingual child's dominant and nondominant language might be "simply" a matter of the ability to use one or the other. One could even, perhaps, speak of dominant language in terms of a "preference" (e.g., related to a very strong sociolinguistic constraint). At any rate, the most difficult, and in the long run most interesting, aspect of imbalanced bilingualism involves the possibility of uneven development of competence, as in the cases reviewed here: L1 attrition and early differentiation between a L1 and a L2. In their study of transfer in early asymmetrical bilingual development, Yip and Matthews (2006) propose that dominance should be considered in this more circumscribed way, rather than "merely a measure of performance or language use. . . . Language dominance should be characterized as a property of the [bilingual] mind" (p. 101). We might want to add that a consistent asymmetry in ability (language use of "symmetrically" represented L_a and L_b) is also about properties of the bilingual mind, an important object of study in its own right, especially if "loss of ability" and "loss of competence" are related developmentally. Be that as it may, Yip and Matthews's point is well taken.

Summarizing what could be a promising way forward for research on language attrition, there appear to be two kinds of (L1) language "loss," either of which results in diminished ability in L_a or L_b:

1. Induced by the expanding dominant (or favored) language, inhibition or blocking of access to the lexicon and grammatical subsystems of the nondominant language in performance. Competence in the "weaker" language, however, remains completely intact, the shift being restricted to aspects of processing and use (no replacement).

2. Inhibition that has laid the groundwork for full-fledged RL development, an actual erosion of competence itself in the disfavored language, to some degree. For consistency, then, perhaps we should reserve the term "attrition" for the contraction/displacement of knowledge structures, and for now take "nondominant" as referring to either inhibition in use or erosion of competence. "Attrition" then would refer to contraction of actual linguistic competence; "nondominant" would leave the question open on this score. Note: in both cases, #1 and #2, the "nondominant language" should be UG-constrained. A contracted or early-stabilized L_a or L_b should be so constrained, just as L2 competence appears to be (see the following section).

Scenario #1 has been described extensively in the literature; an example discussed in this chapter is the study by Yukawa (1997, 1998). To deny scenario #2 under all circumstances would lead to a conception of "competence" that veers into the realm of the occult and mysterious; recall the warning about this in the preface. Gürel (2004) and Meisel (2007) take up the relevant research problems and offer different points of view.

6.5 Is Second Language Competence Universal Grammar–Constrained?

In this section, we will see how the facts of early L_a-or-L_b stabilization/L1 attrition in childhood bilingualism should inform the "access to UG in L2 learning" debate. Two proposals follow from the discussion so far: (1) "RL completeness" argues against any version of "language acquisition capacity deterioration"; and (2) "L1 mediation/filtering of L2 development" should prompt us to disfavor strong versions of the "L1 acquisition = L2 acquisition" hypothesis.

Reviewing the pertinent bilingual and L2 phenomena that need to be accounted for, we find that two key dimensions are closely related: levels of L2 development "up" to and including complete, fully formed, native-speaker competence; and levels of attrition of a previously acquired language "down" to and including its complete replacement. To reemphasize, we do not want to deny these two possibilities:

1. L2 learning that attains a complete native-speaker steady state (the view that this is impossible under all circumstances would surely be the most extreme among the strong L1-L2 difference hypotheses);

2. Complete replacement of a L1 or L_a/L_b.

On the other hand, these points may be more controversial:

3. The suggestion that the RL is not a degraded L1. It "reoccupies" the same linguistic knowledge domains (from which the attrited L1 was displaced) that underlie complete native-speaker proficiency. At the same time, it should be kept in mind that there are two possibilities with respect to attrited L1s: complete attrition and replacement in which only a vestige of the former L1 subsystem may remain, or RL dominance coexisting with an attrited former L1 that retains some measure of representation in the linguistic domains (e.g., the same level as that of an advanced L2 interlanguage).

4. The general difference (not contradicted by #1), which we should accept as "fundamental" (Bley-Vroman 2009) in some important way, between universal attainment of completeness in L1 and the wide variation in L2 under comparable conditions of exposure.

5. In early childhood bilingualism, the apparent paradox of balanced development in some children and a disequilibrium (up to and including attrition of L_a or L_b) in others—again, under comparable conditions of exposure. Early differentiation between young bilinguals' languages, "autonomous development" (Meisel 2001), is not called into question by imbalanced acquisition and subsequent attrition.[4]

Considering these five points, we will turn to a discussion of L2 learning, specifically to what appears to be at the center of contention: whether resetting of UG parameters (however these come to be defined) in a L2 is possible after L1 acquisition has successfully run its course. Recall that the idea of parameter resetting might also be relevant to explaining attrition/replacement. A number of convincing objections have been raised regarding how specific parameters are, and how they might be set in the absence of prior grammatical knowledge (Carroll 2001; Newmeyer 1998, 2004).[5] Still, there is something about the idea of deductively "selecting" from a limited array of options that helps us distinguish the preprogrammed unfolding of L1 from inductive learning (S. Anderson and Lightfoot 2002). Jackendoff (2002, 190–193) outlines a possible alternative: an acquisition program characterized more by the gradual emergence of structures in which the predetermined options are less elaborate and less finely tuned than those proposed by most other advocates of parameter-setting theory. A specialized (for language) "toolkit," also less closed off from general cognitive learning mechanisms than in most other theories, is provided prior to experience to strongly bias children's acquisition of grammar. From this point of view, UG is not burdened with setting down every intricate detail of rule-governed knowledge of language—it is not "a highly complex specification of all possible grammars," but a "set of attractor structures that…guide the course of the child's generalizations over the evidence" (p. 426). In practice, pinning down exactly how parameter setting in L1 acquisition works has been difficult. For example, what kind of prior knowledge could young children possess that allows them to recognize the right triggers for language-specific settings in the language data they are exposed to? Therefore, references in the discussion so far to triggering and parameter setting, with the intention of capturing the essence of implicit acquisition of grammatical knowledge, should be taken to be compatible with these critiques. It seems useful to continue using the terms, though, in a nonliteral or figurative sense.

It should be said that some of the credit for this new way of thinking about deductive-type acquisition goes to the critical observations of functionalists, who have called attention to a logical problem with parameter setting as conceived of in the standard model: it presupposes knowledge of grammatical categories on the part of the young child that is too specific—knowing already, so to speak, what he or she has to acquire (Tomasello 2005). Setting aside the debate about whether there is an innate FL or not, these kinds of reappraisal might be better understood by asking *at what level* language development is constrained (Slobin and Tomasello 2005).

In the literature, the different views on whether UG constrains interlanguage grammars are framed in terms of L2 parameter resetting, along two dimensions: (1) full, partial, or no access to UG; and (2) the degree of L1 transfer—full, partial, or none. White (2003) offers the most comprehensive assessment of the alternatives. Starting with dimension #1 (access), theories that conceive of a "global breakdown" in the language-specific acquisition mechanisms would favor a "no (independent) access" or "partial access" view. UG would constrain L2 learning via the L1 in a very narrow way, only through those parameter settings that came to be instantiated during L1 acquisition. Interlanguage grammatical constructions would be learned one by one, and might not necessarily be UG-constrained. According to this view, they might be "defective" from the point of view of underlying properties of natural language. "Local breakdown" would imply a less pervasive impairment of UG and/or the LAD.

Following White's summary, both the "partial access" and "no access" models (implying different degrees of "breakdown") can be contrasted to those that conceive of interlanguage grammars as "unimpaired" – the "full access" hypothesis. If interlanguage grammars develop free of "breakdown" or "impairment" of UG, a broader view of "access via L1" can then be entertained, one that describes learner-language systems as UG-constrained (although parameter resettings will still be restricted). Thus, a "full access" view leaves open the possibility of resetting "new parameters" in the L2. This seems to be the approach favored by White.

Regarding dimension #2 (transfer), White's version of the "full access" possibility accounts for nonnative attainment in L2 by invoking the varying effects of "full transfer," from L1. All of the above, accepting for now White's version of the "full access" position, contrasts with the strong versions of "no transfer/full access" that would seem to discount any FL-internal factor in explaining ultimate attainment shortfalls in L2. Setting this "no transfer" position aside for now, the different hypotheses ascribe varying degrees of importance to the learner's L1 knowledge. For example, L1 transfer provides an initial source of knowledge from which the beginning learner draws. Such cross-linguistic influence continues to affect learning up to and including the learner's final steady-state competence in the L2.

Risking further oversimplification of a complex debate that often turns on very subtle distinctions, we might venture to recategorize the various UG perspectives on L2 learning that flow from our interest in attriting language systems and the development of their RL counterparts:

1. Starting with the L1=L2 model, "no transfer/full access" would predict complete and unfettered participation of all components of UG. In addition to rejecting any sort of "deterioration" or "impairment," the "no transfer/full access" hypothesis predicts that no other FL factor limits access either (as may happen, for example, under the "full transfer/full access" hypothesis).

2. Diametrically contrasting with #1 and the different "unimpaired" grammar views, outlined above, would be a proposal that all or part of the language acquisition capacity withers away, leaving behind only the grammatical knowledge that L1 development has "selected." In this view, unrealized options are stripped away in whole or in part. The L2 learner, laboring with truly impaired acquisition devices, can only call upon the remaining L1 knowledge system, general cognitive learning strategies, and perhaps other residues of UG that have not withered away.

Exhausting the logical possibilities within the framework to which we are provisionally restricting ourselves would be a hypothesis that may cut across many of the established lines of research:

3. This hypothesis rejects both complete, unlimited access to UG, unmediated by L1 transfer (#1, the L1=L2 model), and all versions of UG erosion (#2). Despite differing approaches, a common thread runs through all accounts that propose one degree or another, or one kind or another, of inaccessibility to the special-purpose language acquisition capacity, the relevant obstacle or mediating factor originating within the linguistic domain. One or another component of the FL is placed out of reach or inhibited in some way, but the acquisition capacity of the LAD does not erode. To reemphasize, if access to one or another component is diminished, this diminishing would be a matter of blocking its deployment, not of deterioration of any part of the linguistic knowledge base or any of the acquisition devices themselves. Table 6.1 proposes a way of categorizing the different approaches to the problem of accounting for (1) near-native or native-like attainment of L2 and (2) wide variability in ultimate attainment.

Erosion of language acquisition capacity, even of any one essential subcomponent of the FL, would contradict the "no semilingualism" condition. If child RL development proceeded with a deteriorated UG parameter-resetting-type system (whatever this turns out to be: toolkit, set of attractors, etc.), semilingual—and even monolingual "alingual"—speakers would abound. This would follow, under the nativist account of language development at least, because compensatory cognitive-general strategies, still underdeveloped at this age to be sure, would only partially make up

Table 6.1
Proposed schema for theories of "UG in L2"

	Language acquisition capacity deteriorates, at least in part	Easily accounts for cases of near-native attainment in L2	Easily accounts for variability in L2 ultimate attainment
1. Unimpeded parameter resetting. No transfer/full access.	No	+	−
2. Global or local breakdown of the parameter system. No resetting.	Yes	−	+
3. Contra #1 and #2. No UG or LAD breakdown. L1 "filters" L2 development if L1 is still the primary, unattrited, language.	No (loss of ability to deploy components of language acquisition capacity, to varying degrees)	+	+

for the deficiency. As well, in early sequential bilingualism, we should hesitate to propose that after the "selection" of the child's "first" grammar there is a withering away of the domain-specific acquisition-processing modules that did not participate in fixing the first round of settings (Meisel 2001). None of the other subcomponents of the FL should suffer erosion either (see note 1). Inhibition or blocking may exert a strong effect, but this possibility differs substantially from deterioration of UG, of the LAD, or of any other essential subcomponent of the language acquisition capacity. How pervasive, intrusive, or persistent inaccessibility turns out to be will need to be settled empirically. However, once we discount deterioration of the FL in RL development, we need to discount it for all child L2 learners, and even for adults. If, on the other hand, it can be shown that adult L2 ultimate attainment consistently never surpasses near-nativeness, as Abrahamsson and Hyltenstam (2009) suggest, the "no deterioration of FL" hypothesis would be called into question, at least for late learners.

The idea of a blocking or filtering effect (as opposed to erosion or deterioration) would also be preferable in the face of reports of sequential child bilingualism: L2 learning subsequent to complete acquisition of L1. Often in these cases the L2 develops rapidly, attaining equivalent levels of proficiency, for all practical purposes indistinguishable from the fully developed and undiminished levels in L1. In theory, the effects of L1 filtering can vary all the way to exercising a negligible influence. In chapter 8, in fact, we will consider evidence from the Nahuatl-Spanish study that suggests that under certain conditions of widespread bilingualism at the level of the speech community, these effects might be bypassed or overridden for significant numbers of children. That is, the L1 filter varies in degree of permeability, even perhaps down to a setting of almost completely "open." Again, the hypothesis of erosion or deterioration of the LAD/UG would make it hard to account for sequential bilingualism resulting in balanced L_a+L_b competence (in this case "L_b" stands for a former childhood L2, now with an ultimate attainment equivalent to L_a, formerly the sole L1). Anecdotal reports from widely differing bilingual acquisition situations around the world suggest that this outcome is not as exceptional as it might appear.

Here, even Clahsen and Muysken's (1996) strong "global impairment" theory might not be fundamentally opposed to most of the other "UG access in L2" positions. Arguing against the equivalence of L1 and L2 development, Clahsen and Muysken point out that "once a parameter option...has been chosen, the remaining unexercised options are no longer accessible." Thus, "the grammar of a *particular* language contains less information on parametric options than the initial state." This "no parameter resetting" constraint greatly facilitates the child's language acquisition task because he or she will not "switch parameter values back and forth, *never* settling on a correct grammar." (p. 722). For example, "Once the child has discovered a lexical entry associated with some feature F in his particular language, ... he will determine its feature strength. Subsequently the parameter is set for F and the unexercised option is lost" (p. 723). If we replace "the unexercised option is lost" with "*access to* the unexercised option is lost," and take the liberty of adding emphasis to "particular" and "never" (we would say that in attrition–RL development, values are switched, once), we can pose the key questions differently. What internal dynamics determine diminished *access*, to what degree and involving which modules, and in which circumstances? For example, perhaps once an option is chosen for L1, the nonselected options are no longer accessible ("blocked"), but not forever and not in all circumstances. Similar amendments could be offered to Schachter's (1996) theory, which appears to favor a similar "no parameter resetting" scenario in L2 learning.

In regard to the kind of access to UG that L2 learners can avail themselves of ("full" or "partial"), another question arises that should prompt us to take a less categorical approach to the different hypotheses that have been put forward. White (2000) notes that, in the end, it may not be possible to draw a fine line between the two possible sources of nonlearned, abstract, implicit L2 grammatical knowledge: directly from UG or filtered through the L1. Depending on exactly what the LAD turns out to be responsible for, a filter or mediation by L1 can come to affect access to UG in L2 learning in any number of ways. With this observation in mind, all models that reject both the "no transfer/L1=L2" and the "UG deterioration" theories can profit from a more open discussion of findings. In addition, the growing consensus on critical period effects in L2 (no precipitous age offset, either at age 5 or at puberty; diminishing direct access to UG along modular lines) underscores how the critical period and UG access in L2 questions are related, but also how they are independent of each other. Starting from another assumption, that the poverty-of-stimulus problem applies to L2 learning in some way (probably not in the same way that it does to L1 learning), the field is in a position to accommodate a number of different approaches; Juffs (2002) reviews some of the theoretical foundations to the discussion.

Herschensohn (2000) accounts for the variability and incompleteness of L2 learning by distinguishing between *form* and *strategy*: L1 is fully UG-constrained (form of the grammar) and UG-driven (the acquisition device), while L2 is only fully UG-constrained. The constraints on grammatical form are not depleted or "used up" in L1 acquisition. The idea of filtering/blocking, then, would imply an obstruction or deflection of UG-driven strategies, the LAD component. Similar UG-internal differentiations (e.g., access to principles, but no resetting of parameters) are discussed by Cook (2001), Hawkins (2001, 355–361), Liceras (1996, 23–33), and Tsimpli and Roussou (1991).

The participation of L1 knowledge in L2 development is an important part of the explanation for the variability evident even in advanced L2 end-states (B. Schwartz 1998; Sorace 2003), but intact UG constraints on form make L2 competence "the same type of knowledge. . . . [On] the basis of end-state difference alone, one cannot deduce epistemological non-equivalence" (B. Schwartz 1998, 156). Access to UG and the LAD being plausibly evident in near-native L2 competence, we may want to extend this claim as well, as Schwartz suggests, to lower levels of interlanguage development. The proposal would be, then, that L2 competence is of the same kind as L1 competence, at least in part—that L2 learners know more of the L2 than they should given the limitations of the input they have at their disposal.

6.6 Acquisition and Learning in the Second Language

To say that a bilingual's knowledge of the L2 is epistemologically equivalent to his or her knowledge of L1 is to say that a substantial core of grammatical knowledge has developed implicitly and that it is UG-constrained. The learner's L2, at least in large part, is a natural language conforming to language-specific principles, not a system constructed around a "wild grammar" or the product of exclusively cognitive-general learning strategies. Competence in L2 is built up in large part without deliberate attention to form, with domain-specific acquisition mechanisms playing an important role. L2 knowledge is underdetermined by the input received—in other words, the poverty-of-stimulus problem applies. The same *kind* of knowledge that is part of L1 competence is part of L2 competence even though L2 development rarely achieves completeness (if L1 is maintained as the bilingual's primary language). Interlanguage competence is not determined entirely by target language input and L1 transfer, and it manifests systematicity, "going beyond" both of these sources of evidence.

What appears to account for the loss in L2 of spontaneity, automaticity, and universal completeness is the disabling of one or another component, or network of components, of the language acquisition mechanisms (NB: "disabling" implies something different from "dismantling" or "depleting"). What appears to account for the natural-language systematicity of interlanguage development and input-underdetermined steady-state L2 competence is that whatever comes to be disabled, inhibited, or put out of reach, as the case may be, remains intact. In cases of near-native proficiency of unschooled and uninstructed L2 learners, the idea of an intact acquisition mechanism is most plausible. This proposal is more consistent with the wide variation in L2 end-state competence; the idea of UG or FL erosion is less so. To the category of "equivalent" types of linguistic knowledge, which includes L1-primary language and near-native L2, we should add:

- intermediate/advanced L2,
- all RLs without exception, and
- partially attrited L1s that have not been lost.

To conclude this discussion, we will take up the concept of modularity that has been proposed as part of the explanation for both L1 attrition and L2 learning (Gregg 1996; Sharwood Smith and Van Buren 1991). Here, applied research on L2 learning can potentially be informative on the more basic questions of UG access and how primary languages, L2s, attrited L1s, and RLs are represented mentally. Specifically, what kind of evidence can the language development capacity make use of in constructing an interlanguage or in reconstructing an attrited L1? Can evidence processed by cognitive-general mechanisms contribute to grammatical development? If direct access to UG-guided acquisition procedures is filtered or blocked, can the participation of domain-general learning strategies compensate (in part, for example) for the resulting "inhibited" development?

Again, broadly cutting across theoretical biases, applied research on L2 teaching has focused a good amount of attention on the role of explicit learning, awareness, and corrective feedback (DeKeyser 1998; R. Ellis and Sheen 2006; Gass and Mackey 2006; Long 1996; Loschky and Bley-Vroman 1993; Schachter 1998; Sharwood Smith 1994b). If it can be shown that some variety of focus on form, application of metacognitive operations, inductive learning, meaning-based practice, and provision of negative evidence contribute in some important way to L2 ultimate attainment, the implications should be far-reaching.

Addressing this question, two views on how modularity applies to bilingualism and L2 learning come up with sharply opposing models, a fortuitous opposition that draws the lines clearly for further research and discussion. B. Schwartz (1999) defends a "no interface" hypothesis, associated with Krashen's (1998) strong "comprehensible input" theory, which starkly separates "learning" and "acquisition." According to this view, which appeals to the concept of information encapsulation, the linguistic modules (the motor of "acquisition") are sealed off from Central System learned knowledge. Thus, general cognitive strategies cannot contribute to the development of L2 competence (although they might help the learner develop declarative-type knowledge *about* the L2).

In contrast to Schwartz's strong bottom-up version of modularity in which linguistic modules are highly encapsulated, interactive models allow for the limited operation of top-down connections. Interactive modular approaches (Jackendoff 2002) admit a certain degree of Central System influence in the functioning of lower-level domains. Therefore, in the processing of language for acquisition and learning there would be no reason to exclude the participation of cognitive-general learning in the development of grammatical knowledge (even the kind that is "epistemologically equivalent" to L1 competence). As Clahsen and Muysken (1996, 722) argue (Foster-Cohen (2001) makes a similar point), this version of modularity should apply to L1 acquisition as well:

> It is precisely the division of labour between UG and non-UG learning that is crucial to our understanding of the modular structure of language development. It is implausible that all of L1 development is UG-driven, since it is embedded in a highly intricate process of general cognitive development, involving all kinds of learning. Knowledge of language interacts in yet ill-understood ways with other knowledge-systems, many of which have highly abstract computational properties. . . . Similarly, adult L2 development is plausibly not fully UG-driven.

The case for non-UG acquisition and explicit learning might be strengthened, however, if we are able to distinguish how Central System domains intervene in L1 and L2. For some reason yet to be determined, in primary language acquisition their participation does not result in end-state variation in core grammar. With L2s, on the other hand, the greater recourse to domain-general learning (purportedly, to compensate for a diminished access to UG) would be entirely consistent with wide individual variation. Carroll (2001) and Herschensohn (2000) extensively discuss modular approaches to L2 learning that accept top-down interactions between the Central System and the linguistic subsystems.[6]

A shift of sorts occurs in the balance between UG-driven acquisition and Central System learning mechanisms, assuming for now that both play a role in both L1 and L2 development:

1. In early childhood (for monolingual acquisition and balanced bilingualism), UG plus those Central System operations are universally and uniformly available (Clahsen 1991).

2. In L2 development, proceeding under L1 mediation/filtering/blocking, Central System operations accept a greater and greater burden, because they can (greater maturation) and because they must (diminished access to UG). Crucially, RLs would depart from this scenario, being in essence a kind of extension or continuation of L1 development (Harley and Wang 1997).

In regard to the second case, a balance between domain-specific UG-guided acquisition and general learning (in non-RL/L2 development), a different kind of separation could be considered between acquisition and learning (not as "hard" as Krashen's and rejecting a strong "no interface" separation)—not so much to serve as a bridge between the opposing arguments as to demarcate the lines of discussion more clearly. Over the last four chapters, we have come to adopt a version of modularity that maintains the autonomy of the system of implicit linguistic competence from explicit knowledge systems, of which metalinguistic awareness is a part. Still following closely M. Paradis's (2004) framework, we might propose the outlines of a convergence that could perhaps be compatible with his "non-interface position" (p. 52). Here, a weaker version of the acquisition-learning separation (that allows for a kind of "interface") might be compatible with his overall approach to the problem. The best way to proceed is to start with the assumptions and conclusions from Paradis's chapter 2, "Implicit and Explicit Language Processes." Some of these assumptions we have already covered and tentatively accepted.

• There exist two types of memory: conscious declarative and implicit procedural. What are often termed "unconscious rules of grammar" are implicit computational procedures, themselves inaccessible to awareness.

• The form that a representation takes in the mental grammar is not the same as the overt surface form that is noticeable or a pattern that the learner might have analyzed and uses deliberately in performance. The actual computational procedures, the "rules" of mental grammar, are unavailable to introspection. This applies to both formal learning and naturalistic acquisition. Whatever it is that becomes part of competence is not the same as what is noticed in "comprehensible input."

• The object of metalinguistic awareness and focus on form is the output of linguistic competence, the outcome of procedures. The underlying structures of grammatical knowledge themselves "are nowhere to be noticed" (p. 37). In the following hypothetical mixed Spanish-English utterance, a bilingual who knows both languages would accept it as interpretable (or even "bilingually well-formed") and would recognize the noun phase "the cat on the table with a broken leg" as ambiguous:

The veterinarian examinó el gato sobre la mesa con una pata rota.
[The veterinarian examined the cat on the table with a leg broken].

• However, the actual online computations that signal the impermissible switch points, and the processing mechanisms deploying the speaker's knowledge of Spanish syntax that account for the perception of ambiguity in "el gato sobre la mesa con una pata rota" (e.g., to which node "una pata rota" is attached), are not subject to awareness and reflection.

• In L2 learning (and more obviously in L1 acquisition), metalinguistic knowledge cannot be transformed or converted into implicit grammatical competence. The two kinds of knowledge remain separate—two different memory systems and two distinct neural substrates (p. 45). Acquisition, then, is not a matter of "proceduralizing" explicit rules that were arrived at by means of analysis, inductive learning, memorization, or reflection. Rather, Paradis refers to a continuum of "degree of reliance," in L2 learning (p. 50)—a gradual shift from relying on metalinguistic knowledge to using implicit knowledge. (VanPatten 2003 is a good example of applying these proposals to the problems of L2 teaching.)

• Nevertheless, formal instruction, focus on form, and metalinguistic knowledge contribute to acquisition of linguistic competence (not only learned explicit knowledge about the L2). According to Paradis, the contribution is indirect and secondary: metalevel awareness serves as a model for practice. Practice under the "guidance of explicit knowledge" (p. 50) allows for checking well-formedness and noticing the gap between an interlanguage form and the target form, leading to practice of more correct grammatical patterns and conscious self-correction. Attention can be directed more systematically toward patterns that should be practiced. In this way, then, the use of explicit knowledge "results in" or "leads to" (as opposed being transformed into) competence (p. 52).

Accepting that a contribution from cognitive-general learning to L2 development is indirect and secondary, in this sense, does not mean that the contribution is not important to achieving mastery. An indirect and secondary contribution might even be a necessary one for ensuring the most effective and efficient conditions for learning. From this point of view, there is perhaps a different way to consider the idea of a "noninterface" hypothesis as just outlined.

We might want to consider, now, the possibility that explicit knowledge-learning strategies favor L2 development in more ways than just making practice more productive. There are several possible sources of usable input to the acquisition-processing mechanisms of the LAD in L2 development (to recap: these mechanisms have not atrophied; rather, they may be deflected by L1 filtering/blocking):

1. primary linguistic data in the form of massive doses of positive evidence;

2. especially for L2 learning, positive evidence of the "enhanced input" variety including special modifications associated with "comprehensible input" and active "negotiation of meaning" (in some cultures, early childhood language socialization practices incorporate these interactive discourse features; in many, they do not, yet no demonstrable deficits are evidenced in core-grammar competence); and

3. normal and typical practice and guided/enhanced practice.

Another possible source should not be excluded:

4. metalinguistic learning strategies and systematic focus on form, independently and in addition to #1, #2, and #3. It could be said that this category belongs to an "internal" source, outside the language acquisition modules, involving a "mismatch" between the declarative knowledge domain and the implicit linguistic competence system. But primary linguistic data, comprehensible input, and practice become, or contribute to forming, internal sources of input to the acquisition processor as well. Intake conversions that process entry-level input to serve it up to the LAD in a usable format also transform data from one kind of configuration to another.

Metalinguistic awareness and focus on form also contribute *directly* to constructing an explicit knowledge representation of the L2. This system can be used in performance, and its products are subject to monitoring, analysis, and reflection just like the products of implicit competence. Therefore, there should be no reason to exclude the possibility that the active use of this domain of knowledge also provides input for acquisition. Literate L2 learners exploit texts in the target language extensively as a source of primary linguistic data and comprehensible input, *and* for explicit learning of L2 grammar. Some learners even read L2 grammar books and work in a deliberate and reflective way on written exercises that systematically present language patterns for analysis and guided practice. They then check their responses with the answer key to receive negative evidence unavailable in primary linguistic data. In a popular computer-assisted language-learning program used for providing students with practice after class, learners are asked to listen and type what they hear. Say that in response to the audio prompt "Vous êtes originaire d'où?" a student types, "Vous êtes originaire du?" The student may immediately suspect that something isn't right, because even though this is what she "heard," the question doesn't seem to be well-formed. The automatic corrective feedback function indicates where the error occurred, triggering a reanalysis: "OK, this can't be the preposition+determiner contraction ('du'), because no kind of sentence can end that way. It must be another kind of contraction—yes, of course, with the adverb 'où' (works just like it does in my L1!)."

We wouldn't want to say that only the primary linguistic data and comprehensible input aspects of these L2-learning activities represent usable input to the LAD and that the analytical and focus-on-form aspects only contribute to explicit knowledge. The proposal, then, is that deliberate learning strategies and explicit knowledge make a special contribution to L2 acquisition in the following manner: On the one hand, the input contributes directly to explicit knowledge of the L2 grammar. As such, it is usable in comprehension and production, making all kinds of L2 input more comprehensible. As *language*, it might even serve to trigger domain-specific acquisition modules. In this way, implicit competence and explicit knowledge still maintain their autonomy: no transformation of metalinguistic knowledge into implicit competence, and no access of awareness to underlying structures and computational procedures of the linguistic modules.

6.7 A Wider Discussion: Applying Concepts to New Research

This more heterogeneous view of the FL and how it constructs grammatical competence may help us look afresh at a fundamental distinction made by many linguists that has turned out to be an unnecessary obstacle to the cross-disciplinary exchange of research findings: the now-familiar distinction between competence and performance. Jackendoff (1998, 2002), for one, has argued persuasively along these lines, echoing a long-standing critique of mainstream generative grammar by researchers working from other perspectives, such as Lexical-Functional Grammar (Bresnan and Kaplan 1982). (Kroeger (2004) provides a survey introduction to Lexical-Functional Grammar, and Pinker (1996) applies it to problems of child language development.)

Grammatical knowledge (competence) needs to interface, very closely, with other kinds of knowledge; and all of these, in turn, need to interface with different kinds of processing mechanism in order to deploy this knowledge, very rapidly. So the narrowly circumscribed competence of core grammar is one component in an extensive array of knowledge structures and processors of different kinds. The linguistic competencies (plural) need to make a good fit with the performance components, be embedded in and interconnected with them. The different ways that all these come together in actual language use we have been calling "ability." One way to get a better picture of this componential nature of the language capacity and human language abilities is to try to uncover some of the common underlying mechanisms for the different FL outcomes: primary language, L2, abnormal L1 learning, L1 attrition and replacement.

The starting point for this wide-ranging review of the research, evidence from the study of normal subtractive/imbalanced bilingualism and language replacement in children, has posed questions that should not be put aside by researchers interested in critical period effects and the related "UG in L2" question. In a way, the findings from work on L1 attrition have yet to be reckoned with seriously; the implications for a number of approaches to the study of bilingualism may be far-reaching.

6.7.1 Application of the Attrition/Replacement Concept to a Problem in Language Shift

Explaining early differentiation of L_a+L_b toward L1+L2 might help explain a widely noted sociolinguistic phenomenon: rapid language shift in a situation of minority language bilingualism under strong pressure from a majority national language. The research problems pointed out by heritage speaker studies—most prominently, the question of "incomplete acquisition" of a weaker language in child bilingualism (Domínguez 2009)—are relevant here. In some cases, the rapid pace of displacement and the abrupt turn toward majority language monolingualism is surprising, as recounted by informants in the Mexican study (N. Francis 1997; N. Francis and Navarrete Gómez 2000). For example, in the case of an indigenous language, speakers and nonspeakers alike often perceive it as lacking broad utility and as being associated with low social status. Negative motivational factors affecting bilingual middle-childhood and adolescent speakers, whose indigenous language has attrited from a L_a-or-L_b to a "L2," weigh heavily upon individual language development. This is different from the effect that these external pressures have on a fully formed primary language. The informal observations related in N. Francis 1997 and N. Francis and Navarrete Gómez 2000 are corroborated in other studies in Mexico of the development of Spanish-language dominance among child speakers of Kaqchikel Maya (Heinze 2009) and of Totonac (Lam 2009). But in monolingual L1 development, even sharply adverse conditions of depreciation, prohibition of use outside of the home, degradation of higher-order language use (e.g., loss of the oral tradition), and even low levels of sustained interactive discourse between caregiver and child, will not obstruct the unfolding of the core grammatical competencies. A 5-year-old monolingual indigenous-language speaker may be acutely aware of the subordinate status of his or her language, have little opportunity to engage in extended language use, and show inhibition in normal age-appropriate verbal expression. But clearly none of these external factors would handicap the core grammar acquisition mechanisms of the FL. This same deterministic, modular-type impermeability in development is not available in L2 development—including, or especially, in the case of an attrited L1 or early stabilized L_a or L_b. Again, normal monolingual L1 acquisition is always and in all circumstances unidirectional, inexorably convergent on target language completeness; L2 development is not so.

In cases of rapid language shift of the kind described above, it may appear that an incomplete and degraded form of the vernacular is "passed on to the next generation of speakers" (Seliger 1996, 614). An alternative account, the one being proposed here, highlights the volatility of imbalanced child bilingualism as exemplified by the case studies of L1 attrition reviewed earlier. For example, in a given bilingual speech community many adults may have undergone late attrition of the socially disfavored vernacular, or have elected simply to suppress its use in parent-child interaction. What gets passed on to children is at least one complete well-formed primary language, the national language (now, children's dominant language in actual competence, as well as in terms of parents' and children's preference). Many children, perhaps a majority, will also acquire the vernacular completely, becoming balanced (L_a+L_b) bilinguals. A significant minority will develop an attrited vernacular that coexists, often precariously, with the fully formed L1, the displacer national language. Thus, two or three generations typically suffice for turning the corner toward a definitive demographic shift. However, rather than children passively receiving "fully formed" or "ill-formed" languages from the previous generation, the children's FL effects a kind of selection: L_a dominance, L_b dominance (opening the possibility of attrition of one or the other), or L_a+L_b balanced bilingualism. Clearly, all other things being equal, the "fully formed" primary language of parents will tend to have the inside track (all other things being equal) regarding this "selection"; in child bilingualism, the acquisition mechanisms are able to exercise the option (and in this case they do) of "favoring" the input of one language subsystem over the other. As we saw in the evidence regarding early L1 attrition/stabilization, even a fully formed model can be "disfavored."

Historical evidence from the emergence of creole languages, studies of exceptional L1 and L2 learning (e.g., sign language), and anecdotal accounts of immigrant language transmission suggest that young children do not reproduce the pidginized language system of their parents. If this parental L2 takes on the status of primary L1 for children, even in the absence of a more complete model, a fully formed L1 emerges (Newmeyer 1998). On the other hand, the children might develop an incomplete version of the parent-transmitted interlanguage in a bilingual acquisition context if the other language (the parents' L1) comes to occupy center stage in language socialization. Recall the "no semilingualism" condition. Insufficient or incomplete exposure to a minority/indigenous language, *if it is also the second or weaker language*, often does result in incomplete acquisition of the minority language. But, assuming the broad outlines of the proposal presented in this chapter, the process would not be, strictly speaking, that of "reproducing" or "passing on" an incomplete linguistic system. Recall that even under favorable conditions of would-be additive bilingualism (i.e., sustained and balanced use of two languages in language socialization), there is no guarantee that children will develop balanced and equivalent competence in both. Only one fully formed grammar is "ensured." This proposal is consistent with studies of bilingual socialization that point to a striking asymmetry between minority and majority language regarding the minimum input conditions required for native-speaker ultimate attainment (Gathercole and Thomas 2009; Simpson and Wigglesworth 2008).

In chapter 3, we discussed the possibility that an indigenous language might no longer be used widely by its speech community for higher-order secondary-discourse-related purposes. For example, uses of language associated with the traditional oral genres of formal and elevated discourse might be lost (to literacy practices in the national language, to the school, to radio and television, etc.). These formal and elevated discourse abilities would eventually be practiced by children only in the language of literacy and schooling, the national language. Consequently, aspects of grammar that are associated with these abilities (what in chapter 3 were called the "language-bound" aspects of academic language proficiency) would develop in the national language, and not as robustly in the "nonacademic" vernacular. Chiodi (1993) refers to the frequent observation that aspects of grammar that serve secondary discourse come to be impoverished as the contexts of use of some minority languages come to be progressively restricted to the realm of face-to-face conversational interchange. But to be clear, what we are talking about here is an impoverishment of discourse ability, proficiency in elevated oral genres, literary uses, or peripheral domains of grammar associated with literacy-related language use. The historical decline in these language use contexts in the case of Nahuatl is one of the best-known examples (León-Portilla 1996).

The downgrading of a language's station in society may affect its prestige value, how young people perceive its usefulness, and how they feel about using it in public (see examples in appendix 1). A downgraded "language," in this narrow and very specific sense, might get "passed on" to each generation; but this kind of "incompleteness" should be considered separately from the question of whether the core grammar of the language that children are exposed to is complete and well-formed. The core grammar knowledge of individuals cannot be anything else but complete in the absence of a displacer RL, for example. If this grammar corresponds to the only language children hear, it will normally be complete and well-formed. Again, in the less typical case of primary linguistic data provided by nonnative speakers, the acquisition mechanisms of the children's FL simply upgrade it. If, in a bilingual acquisition scenario (2L1), children are exposed to, for example, a complete well-formed model of the national language and a less-than-complete model of their indigenous language, it is possible, even likely in many situations, that development of the indigenous language will undergo early stabilization or attrition. But the very same imbalanced bilingual outcome is also possible under "additive" conditions of exposure to two complete well-formed sets of language input. In both of these scenarios, then, it is the inhibitory effect of the expanding dominant language that (in the end) accounts for incomplete acquisition of the weaker member of the bilingual L1 pair.

The study of rapid language shift offers an ideal opportunity for collaboration between approaches that analyze external sociolinguistic determinants of L1 erosion and those that try to explain its internal psychological and linguistic correlates. One potential division of labor might distribute the research questions: *which* circumstances and *why* (Crystal 2000; Dorian 2004; Spolsky 2002), complementing the questions of *how* (Allen, Crago, and Pesco 2006; Montrul 2005; and most of the other references in this chapter), and vice versa.

6.7.2 Prospects for Convergence on Some Key Points

As a way to wrap up this discussion of the different ways that grammatical knowledge is constructed in bilingual children, we might consider the following questions posed by our review of the research, in the order in which they appeared. Why, under conditions of adequate/equal exposure to two languages in early childhood, may only one of these develop to form a complete L1? We have to ask this question even if most bilingual children under these conditions might develop native-speaker competence in both languages (that they might is an empirical question at any rate). If in subtractive bilingualism/replacement the "new L1–former L2" attains completeness, implying that UG and the LAD suffer no erosion, what does this "no UG erosion" conclusion imply for "access to UG" in all L2 acquisition/learning situations? If "no UG erosion" turns out to be correct, we can then approach the critical period question in a new way. Apparently there is some kind of fundamental difference between L1 acquisition and L2 learning, accounting for uniform and universal native-speaker attainment in the first case, and wide variation in the second. What might this difference entail for L2-teaching approaches that promote deliberate and explicit learning strategies (over, for example, strong "naturalistic" approaches, which assume some kind of equivalence between L1 acquisition and L2 learning)?

Finally, if Central System/cognitive-general learning mechanisms are shown to play a more prominent role in L2 learning, and the "language modules" are not as encapsulated as some theories of L2 learning would assume, might there be reason to consider a more important role for these mechanisms in L1 acquisition as well? In this way, one version of modularity might contribute to relativizing the competence-performance distinction in a manner more conducive to discussion between less doctrinaire approaches on both sides of the UG/non-UG divide.

7

An Analysis of Academic Language Proficiency

In this chapter, we leave behind the interesting debates on the strictly linguistic aspects of L1 and L2 development. In chapter 6, we focused primarily on the grammatical knowledge side of our theme of bilingual competence and bilingual proficiency: children's competence in two languages, and how this linguistic competence may undergo changes that are sometimes surprising. Now we shift our attention back to proficiency—specifically, to the abilities related to academic uses of language, including the abilities required for reading and writing.

To review chapter 6 briefly, some aspects of grammatical competence unfold spontaneously and without recourse to cognitive-general learning strategies:

1. Whatever "core linguistic knowledge" turns out to be in monolingual speakers and in 2L1 (simultaneous bilingual) development, a part of it at least emerges without deliberate learning and awareness.

2. Even though we are accepting for now that L2 learning does not proceed spontaneously and uniformly in the same way as L1 acquisition, we concluded provisionally that some components of the Language Acquisition Device (LAD), if not all, intervene in L2 development as well. The argument was that if replacing language development shares with typical L1 development the singular hallmark of completeness and uniformity, then the acquisition mechanisms of the Faculty of Language must have remained intact. Following the argument one step further, there is evidence to support the proposal from L2 research that poverty of stimulus is still a problem for the development of L2 grammatical competence. It's still a problem even if the L2 has not taken on the status of a replacing language (i.e., if the learner's L1 has not undergone attrition). This linguistic knowledge, in L1 or L2, is revealed more or less clearly in highly contextualized tasks related to conversational proficiency.

Episodes and encounters from everyday life remind us of the poverty-of-stimulus problem. Shifting attention to command of grammatical patterns by L2 learners of English, we are repeatedly struck by the same phenomenon: accented speech betrays a bilingual competence—specifically, that L1 is probably, almost surely, still complete. Therefore, English is not a replacing language but a true L2. At the same time, we should wonder how it came to pass that some speakers' knowledge of morphology and syntax is as close to complete as it is. Simply put, it isn't likely that cognitive-general learning strategies plus positive transfer from L1 alone account for these observations, and many others like them.

The purpose of this review of chapter 6 is to strike a contrast with the different kind of development we will observe in this chapter in the realm of academic language proficiency. This idea implies that some of the component knowledge structures of academic language proficiency are different in kind, in some important way, from those evidenced in conversational proficiency. One might be tempted to draw a line between the grammatical competencies (spontaneous in development and uniform in ultimate attainment) and the other kinds of competence and processing mechanism that are part of discourse ability. For example, grammatical competence would interface with certain discourse-related competencies in face-to-face conversational ability. Then, the same grammatical competence would be deployed by certain other discourse-related competencies (overlapping, surely, with the first set) for the purpose of performing academic language tasks. While this idea sounds like it's on the right track, it is too simple. Complicating matters in another area of contention, L2 learning, we have found support for the idea that the core grammar of L2 systems, even with the participation of the LAD, might depend on cognitive-general processes of learning in a way that L1 acquisition does not.

These complications notwithstanding, we will now focus on those underlying components of language proficiency that do not follow the deductive-like and universal development that the essential components of grammatical competence follow in early childhood. An interesting question in its own right is this: what is it that makes learning to read, developing advanced comprehension abilities, and developing skill in text construction different from uses of language that do not vary widely from one person to another? One way the two types of language ability may differ has to do with the overused but still meaningful notion of "naturalness" in language learning.

We are also returning here to the topic of chapter 3, where we examined descriptions of bilingual children's abilities in literacy-related skills and considered how these diverge in different ways across the grades. What components make up the different academic language abilities? What is it about these components that may represent a common thread across all the abilities? What features are specific to one component or another? Which are language-specific, and which are not language-specific? At one point, it was suggested that the ability to reflect upon language patterns (the observable ones—on the "surface") and to direct operations upon them has something to do with children's general advancement in academic abilities in both languages. Is this metalinguistic awareness a separate and identifiable dimension of higher-order language proficiency? Discussing these questions will point us in the direction of chapters 8 and 9, where metalinguistic awareness occupies center stage in controlled assessments of students' bilingual reading and writing strategies.

7.1 Secondary Discourse Ability + Metalinguistic Awareness

The description of different aspects of language ability associated with schooling has long been a preoccupation of educators, especially the description of language use related to comprehension of classroom discourse and to academic achievement. Among these aspects of language ability, learning to read and write, and the use of reading and writing for academic purposes, are central to (more precisely: at the very center of) school language development. This brings us back to Cummins (2000) and his model of Cognitive Academic Language Proficiency (CALP). Colombi and Schleppegrell (2002) propose the concept of "advanced literacy," bringing forward some of the same key dimensions of analysis that we found useful in previous chapters. In particular, clarity on the nature of academic language proficiency, and how it develops in children, will help resolve one of the major challenges of multilingual and multicultural school systems: how to provide the most favorable conditions for the development of higher-order academic literacy among children for whom the language of instruction is not the language they understand or understand well.

Two closely related assumptions underlie this discussion: (1) that a distinction can in fact be drawn between advanced literacy-related language proficiencies and other kinds of ability (e.g., abilities that are distributed in such a way that they are not predictive of academic achievement), and (2) that language proficiency, of all kinds and varieties, can be subjected to analysis. As argued throughout this book, the study of CALP reveals component structures that can be investigated: in what way are they independent of each other, and what is the nature of their interfaces and interdependencies?

The goal of the research review in this chapter is a closer, more fine-grained examination of these components. To recap, in the Bilingual Tripartite Parallel Architecture (figure 5.2), the linguistic subsystems L1 and L2, or L_a and L_b, develop autonomously. The Cross-Linguistic Interface connections allow for all kinds of transfer and mutual influence, but they do not result in fusion of L_a and L_b (or L1 and L2) as long as each language continues to develop or maintains a stabilized steady state. If either language undergoes attrition, what has been described as convergence (Myers-Scotton 2002) is entirely possible—thinking in terms of a very one-sided "convergence," that is. However, in regard to the topic of this chapter, it would be advisable to treat language attrition separately. How the loss of L1 and subtractive bilingualism might affect the development of academic language proficiency deserves its own discussion. Another "nonautonomous" possibility might arise in beginning L2 learning. In this case, we may not want to propose a separate L2 representation right from the start. Rather, a parasitical-type dependence in relation to the fully formed L1 might better describe the status of the newly emerging system. These exceptions aside, the basic idea is that the linguistic components develop language-specifically. In contrast, aspects of bilingual proficiency that are shared—knowledge structures that are not linguistic—develop differently. Within the domain of the Central System, the networks of Conceptual Structure (CS) and information processing remain independent from each linguistic subsystem (what we are calling "each language"). Taking a closer look at the modular architecture of bilingual proficiency, and considering some of the finer points and details, should raise a number of helpful questions for future investigations.

In some ways, the study of how two language subsystems interact with the different nonlinguistic components of academic language proficiency complicates the analysis. In other ways, it allows for a privileged view of what academic language proficiency is composed of. In line with a componential approach to studying language ability, we will begin again with Cummins's approach: that some of the competencies and processing mechanisms are independent of linguistic knowledge. In other words, under this proposal, in bilinguals there is one central foundation for CALP, not two separate language-specific academic proficiency domains (CALP-Language 1/CALP-Language 2). Thus, as we will see, all findings from the research on higher-order language abilities in general (e.g., in monolinguals) apply to the development of these abilities in bilingual children. At the same time, we will see how this idea may need to be refined.

One starting point in this line of research is the distinction between secondary and primary discourse proposed by Gee (1996). Secondary discourse ability (SDA) develops from experience in language-learning contexts beyond those associated with primary socialization, in cultural and institutional contexts that extend primary discourse ability. All preschool children exposed to normal primary socialization acquire the prerequisites of SDA; and many start an early apprenticeship that forms the foundation for strong development in this area of literacy-related language ability, years before entering 1st grade (Reeder et al. 1996). With this kind of experience, children learn about an "orientation to meaning" that calls for a "verbal explicitness that is attuned to presumptions of reciprocity of perspectives, and internal coherence" (Blum-Kulka 2002, 113). As one of the components of higher-order reading and writing ability, this orientation to meaning also underlies other kinds of academic language ability. As Gee points out, literacy learning is mastery of one kind of SDA, in this case involving the written modality. This clarification reflects a growing consensus in the field today that broadly qualifies the literacy-SDA connection, obliging us to adopt the cumbersome but more precise formulation: "academic and literacy-related language proficiency." From this point of view, the primary-secondary discourse dichotomy applies broadly, encompassing both written and oral modalities, as well as literate and oral traditions (N. Francis and Navarrete Gómez 2009; Ramey 2007). That is, "primary" does not coincide with "oral," or "secondary" with "literate." Moreover, according to this proposal, the distinction between primary and secondary discourse applies to all cultures and speech communities.[1]

One way to think about this distinction is from the point of view of a deficiency in one case or the other. Deficient primary discourse ability would fall into the category of pathology or intrinsic impairment, a true deficit that is more or less categorical. Deficient SDA would allow for a continuum and would not by itself imply any kind of impairment or abnormal language development. For example, a fully competent native speaker of a language may not be literate or skilled in any oral genre of the formal and monologic type. "Primary" entails universal and uniform attainment; "secondary" does not.

"Universal" here refers to the commonly shared, all-inclusive, invariable access that children have to the core grammatical principles of language and the other basic competencies that underlie different language abilities. Thanks to this access, primary discourse ability unfolds in a spontaneous and exceptionless manner (for children who do not suffer from an intrinsic impairment). Secondary discourses depart from this scenario in all cultures and speech communities. For example, at the individual level, SDA can fail to develop to advanced levels for a number of reasons even among normally developing children with no linguistic deficit. Exceptionally, but again not implying any sort of abnormality, in the case of identifiable groups of individuals, SDA may come to be degraded, fail to develop to advanced levels, or suffer erosion in situations of sharp cultural dislocation (D. Gough and Bock 2001). Under normal circumstances, all societies develop an array of secondary discourses that individuals learn, attaining levels of achievement that vary widely; the primary discourses do not vary in this way. If individuals lose contact with the speech community's established secondary discourses—for example, if they are denied literacy learning and schooling; or if they are dispersed and isolated, resulting in disruption of ties with their oral tradition—the SDAs, for a period of time, may not flourish as they normally do. In contrast, in these same cases, primary discourses remain intact, children being capable even of recreating the grammatical competence components that underpin them in the absence of a reliable or usable adult model, as we saw in chapters 5 and 6.

Among normally developing monolingual children, core linguistic knowledge and primary discourse ability never erode, and they unfold uniformly according to typical developmental milestones. In bilinguals, a L1 may be *displaced* by a L2; but again, the capacity to construct (and reconstruct) linguistic knowledge does not erode. Along these lines, Cummins (2000) points to the widely observed fact that bilingual children may fail to attain adequate levels of advanced literacy-related abilities, as revealed in below-average academic performance in both L1 and L2. But recall that "below-average academic performance in both L1 and L2" does not refer to linguistic competence. Rather, it refers to a specialized set of abilities *revealed in specific contexts of performance*. On the one hand, this kind of below-average academic performance in bilinguals is an unexceptional observation (associated, as it is, with deficient literacy learning in the monolingual condition). At the same time, it highlights the necessity of separating two concepts: the "central" nonlinguistic cognitive domains of discourse ability, and the linguistic representations of the bilingual's L1 and L2 grammars. Again, the underlying linguistic capacity would not suffer an analogous deficiency or erosion. That is, even under the most adverse circumstances of inferior instruction and learning, and failed literacy-SDA development, core grammatical competence in L1 or L2, or even in both, is "sheltered." The relevant modules vigorously resist external influences to which one might be tempted to ascribe determinants of incomplete development or degradation. Only the most egregiously impoverished (abnormal) primary socialization bears negatively upon the specifically linguistic (i.e., grammatical) domains.

All of the authors cited above coincide on the importance of another aspect of advanced literacy-related proficiency: the use of language as an analytic tool of thinking, specifically the development of metalinguistic awareness.

Applying concepts from Vygotsky (1934/1962) and Bernstein (1964), we can say that this dimension stems from advanced conceptions that arise when children begin to systematize the relationship between language use (meaning) and context, and that are then submitted to greater and greater degrees of awareness (Christie 2005; Colombi and Schleppegrell 2002). With this growing awareness of both function and form, children learn to attend to discourse in progressively more abstract ways. They confront text and context in new ways, developing what is commonly called a more "decontextualized" approach to comprehension and expression (Cummins 2000; Olson 2001; Reeder et al. 1996).

Thus, we can identify two broad component categories of academic language proficiency: SDA and metalinguistic awareness. In the next three sections, we will briefly review the research on the development of SDA at three levels: discourse, sentence, and word—examining how metalinguistic awareness works to complete the formation of each kind of ability. As it turns out, this "completion" is just the kind of developmental process in which literacy and schooling can, and should, play a pivotal role.

7.2 The Development of Narrativization and Levels of Narrative Ability

By all accounts, narrative (including the rudimentary prenarrative subgenres that originate in conversational recounts) forms part of the necessary foundation for all subsequent development of independent noninteractive discourse ability. It is inconceivable that a child would skip over this stage. By the same token, a strong development in this domain lays the necessary groundwork for mastering all types of academic language skills, including literacy (Boudreau 2008). Early narrative represents a kind of transitional "interdiscourse" that bridges primary discourse ability and SDA. Itself composed of a network of different kinds of knowledge, the ability to produce a coherent narrative calls upon the meaning-grammar interface in "translating knowing into telling" (Hudson and Shapiro 1991, 89). Miller et al. (2006, 31) point to this ability as a predictor of other literacy-related achievements: "Acquisition of narrative competence is a combination of advanced language skills placed in the service of sharing personal experiences, stories, and other text-level material."

In figure 5.2, the "meaning-grammar interface" is the set of double arrows that depicts the interactions between CS and the grammar components (Phonological Structure (PS) and Syntactic Structure (SS)), the lexicon being the locus of these interactions and interfaces. In the case of narrative ability, this translation of meaning into words is realized in a way that goes beyond typical situation-embedded conversational ability. In reverse, for comprehension, the listener translates a telling, in linguistic form, into a "knowing" in narrative format. In both cases, in both directions, discourse-level constructions are imposed on events (memory sequences of events and linguistic representations of events). This imposition of discourse-level patterning has been described by child language researchers as one of the universal hallmarks of the transition toward true storytelling. Beginning with the growth of more sophisticated conversational skills, children apply previously acquired grammatical knowledge in new ways (Karmiloff and Karmiloff-Smith 2001). For example, the use of pronouns shifts more and more away from exophoric reference toward their use in intratextual cohesion, later alternating with indefinite and definite full noun phrases in a systematic way.

We can, then, view early narrative as a bridge to SDA. Whereas early narrative (Narrative One) represents an unqualified cognitive universal, late narrative (Narrative Two or "schooled narrative"—Fang 2001) begins to differentiate and show greater and greater variation among normally developing children. A number of developments culminating during the period just prior to school entry are part of the transition. Astington (1990, 2002), for one, focuses on Theory of Mind (ToM) and metarepresentational ability. Young children (ages 2–3) already understand human intentionality, can talk about internal mental states, and form hypothetical and counterfactual models (e.g., in pretend play). However, a new stage is inaugurated when children are able to "see that another's belief is . . . his or her representation of reality" (1990, 158). In experiments, children around the age of 4 are successful, for the first time, in attributing false beliefs to others and to themselves: mastering the "appearance-reality" problems, and predicting how dolls will act on the basis of erroneous information (the "Sally-Anne" problem). At about the same time, children become proficient in interpreting mental-state verbs that require subtle distinctions regarding presupposition—for example, the semantic distinctions related to factivity (Astington 1990, 162–166):

(1) The shoemaker doesn't *know* that the elves made the shoes. (factive)
(2) The shoemaker doesn't *think* that the elves came last night. (nonfactive)

Olson (1994) and E. Lee, Torrance, and Olson (2001) review related studies on the "say-mean" distinction. The emergence of second-order metarepresentations is marked first by grasping the idea that belief can be false and later by understanding interpretation, reflecting upon how others think about mental states. In an experiment that depicts Charlie Brown selecting the wrong color shoes because Lucy didn't specify that she wanted the "red ones," when older children are asked, "Does Charlie Brown think he is bringing the shoes Lucy wants?," they reply correctly. Younger children, who still understand false belief only from their own perspective, answer "No" (Olson 1994, 127–131).

These culminating Narrative One acquisitions start to tip development toward the advanced story-telling and story-understanding abilities that require the more active participation of metalinguistic operations, in the transition to Narrative Two. Episodically more complex stories are associated with the confrontations between intentional action and obstacles, conflictual themes, and characters' interacting plans (Stein and Albro 1996). Experience with these kinds of story promotes higher levels of awareness of human intentionality, internal contradiction, false belief, lack states, ambivalence, and goals and plans that enter into conflict.

Recall from chapter 5 that the assessment of ToM was important in describing the unusual pattern of language abilities and deficiencies exhibited by a polyglot savant (N. Smith and Tsimpli 1995). While demonstrating various levels of proficiency in 16 L2s, including an extensive vocabulary and phenomenal mastery of conversational ability, Christopher experienced unusual difficulty with tasks that call upon certain components of discourse ability, even in his native L1. He failed on tasks that young children typically perform successfully by age 6 or earlier. The evidence from this case study that ToM is associated with proficiency in discourse organization, together with the studies of child development in this domain, leads us to categorize ToM development alongside the other intellectual achievements that are part of the transition from Narrative One to Narrative Two.

This view of ToM-related abilities allows us to integrate the findings of Olson and his associates with the perspective outlined by Garfield, Peterson, and Perry (2001) that we considered in chapter 5. According to the view we are considering here, ToM development is open-ended and dependent on learning, not highly encapsulated and innately preprogrammed as a module unto itself. The use of "mental verbs" in chapter 3 as an index of literacy and academic language development is consistent with this approach. Future research on how metalinguistic awareness, ToM-related use of mental state verbs, and the emergence of complex syntax (e.g., sentential complements) are related (Pascual et al. 2008) will help us better understand the componential nature of literacy-related language ability.

Concurrently with the development of these advanced comprehension abilities, children advance in their ability to produce connected and coherent discourse, requiring an assessment of their interlocutor's internal mental state predictively and retrospectively, as opposed to only interactively. Greater independence from conversational support accompanies the shift to themes more and more removed from the immediate situational context (Ninio and Snow 1996), particularly themes removed in time and space from any worldly context or situation. In this regard, the concept of decontextualized discourse is better understood as a *recontextualization* (Hickmann 2003). What level of specificity of shared knowledge can be assumed? In what way should an explanation, for example, be explicit? To what extent is the story-listener (e.g., a hypothetical one) able to align his or her perspective with that of the narrator?

Surely, there is no fine line that marks a boundary between Narrative One and Narrative Two. A crude demarcation that could serve as a starting point might be this: for all normally developing children, Narrative One is universally attainable; Narrative Two is not. Defining features that characterize the transition (which future research could investigate) might include the participation of metalinguistic strategies, transcending dependence on situational context, advanced inferencing, higher-order ToM representations, and the maturation of information-processing capabilities.

As these more advanced productive abilities are applied to narratives of greater complexity and independence from situational context support, children's receptive discourse abilities are put to the test on stories with more elaborate episodic constructions. These kinds of story require active monitoring and a strategic application of attentional resources. Research on discourse comprehension shows how the development of competencies associated with narrative, specifically Narrative Two, lays the foundation for more advanced expository text abilities, such as "essay-text literacy" (Shrubshall 1997). For present purposes, the most relevant aspect of this work focuses on mature comprehension strategies—the kind, for example, that readers engage in when automatic, nondeliberative processing does not suffice to establish coherence (van den Broek 1994). How does the listener or the reader take "transient activations" and build them into a configuration, a "permanent memory representation" (p. 580)? At this point, it would be good to clarify that while the development of rudimentary narrative abilities is an indispensable part of the early transition *toward* higher-order SDA, there is no automatic continuity. That is, there is no assurance that narrative ability leads automatically to the consolidation of abilities related to expository text comprehension. It is in the active building of structure associated with Narrative Two that we can point to a direct continuity with "essay-text literacy."

To help make the distinction between Narrative One and Narrative Two more concrete, we can consider Everett's (2005) claim that the latter is absent as a discourse form that is independently created among the Pirahã. From all descriptions, the community is apparently among the most technologically and materially primitive in existence today. Though the Pirahã have no creation myths or any type of fiction of their own, they know and recite passages of stories from neighboring communities. Because a community that (according to Everett) has access only to the most rudimentary of cultural resources nonetheless engages in Narrative One, which includes extended recounting of immediate experience, we can say that Narrative One reveals itself as a universal of language knowledge and language use. But also, by Everett's account, incipient development of Narrative Two is in evidence as well: initiation of discussions, with researchers, on cosmology; embellishment of nonindigenous creation myths; commentary on stories of other cultures (2005, 632–633); and amalgamation of stories, integrated from fragments or entire narratives, shared with Amazonian mestizo traders (2009, 431). "They are like oral-literary theorists in their telling and discussions of the texts of others" (2005, 633).

With the above examples and proposed distinctions in mind, we could ask, what are the essential foundations of a discourse ability like "narrativity"? Gernsbacher's (1990) Structure-Building Framework begins with the idea that cognitive-general mechanisms, which are independent of language, underlie comprehension. These same mechanisms would therefore subserve discourse production abilities as well. For the bilingual, according to the Bilingual Tripartite Parallel Architecture and similar models, which hold that one central foundation underlies CALP, they would support production and comprehension in both L1 and L2. In the case of narrative, for example, the underlying structure-building strategies of comprehension are "mode-independent," separate from the decoding skills that underlie listening and reading (Walter 2004). In comprehension, activations (from discourse input) of memory nodes build developing mental structures. New information can map onto the developing structure or activate a different set of nodes, forming a new substructure. Skilled comprehension involves the operation of suppression and enhancement mechanisms in such a way that new substructures are not triggered unnecessarily ("shifting too often"). Less-skilled comprehenders fail to establish coherence in large part because access to previous structures is lost or degraded (Gernsbacher and Foertsch 1999; Gernsbacher et al. 2004). Kintsch's (1994) Construction-Integration model describes proficient text comprehension along similar lines: a bottom-up, data-driven activation (associations are "constructed"), followed rapidly by top-down inhibition and deactivation of contextually inappropriate information (integration). In the next section, we will see how this kind of cyclical structure building in discourse comprehension is related to grammatical patterns that children encounter in academic texts, especially when they venture beyond the familiar and highly predictable patterns of standard "early" narrative.

7.3 Language Development—Grammar

Upon mastering the greater part of the phonological system of their native language and acquiring an impressive beginning repertoire of basic vocabulary by age 2 or 3, children rapidly build up a grammar sufficiently approximating a mature steady state so that by age 5, literacy instruction can be initiated universally. The emergence of an elaborate working grammar is so rapid following the two-word stage that beginning literacy learning has been documented well before the average age of entry to kindergarten. For bilinguals, this applies to one of their languages, to the other, or to both. However, we would hesitate to characterize the young child's grammatical abilities (i.e., knowledge + processing capabilities) by 1st grade as complete and fully formed in every way. A final plateau of mature native-speaker competence and oral proficiency is probably not attained until middle childhood. In addition, it appears that some aspects of grammar development during elementary school show a different pattern of emergence than the spontaneous and automatic acquisition of L1 during the preschool years.

If we take as a point of reference UG-based accounts of L1 acquisition (2L1 in the case of early, balanced bilingualism), one approach to grappling with this differentiation is to appeal again to the distinction between core and peripheral grammar. The development of morphology and syntax beyond the core may be governed at least in part by learning mechanisms apart from UG and the LAD. Some aspects of peripheral grammar may be open to individual variation in a way that core grammar is not. Particularly in regard to later stages of language development associated with literacy and academic registers, certain aspects of grammar may be mastered only with the necessary participation of metalinguistic strategies, again unlike core grammar (Foster-Cohen 1993). To date, research has barely scratched the surface of this proposed differentiation within the linguistic subsystems. What independent criteria could we apply in determining to which domain a given principle, rule, or pattern belongs? For example, we would not be satisfied with just designating everything that is universally and uniformly attainable by all normal children as the "core," even though this might be a good place to begin. Are there aspects of peripheral grammar that are attained universally, in a manner analogous to their core counterparts (e.g., exploiting the participation of a subset of domain-general learning mechanisms that are universally available)? Is there a domain of peripheral grammar that may be subject to individual variation, beyond what we would specify as typical, fully formed, complete, native-speaker competence? If so, we would be obliged to propose the participation of cognitive-general learning mechanisms that are not universally available to all children.

In regard to Foster-Cohen's (1993) application of the concept of core and periphery,[2] important questions to address are these: To what extent would late-developing grammar, which evidences non-core-type variation among children, be attributable to actual linguistic knowledge (competence) or to the ability to exploit an early-acquired competence in different contexts of use? How do the development of processing systems, the development of working-memory capacity, and overall cognitive development affect children's ability to call upon their grammatical knowledge? How these extralinguistic factors interact with grammatical competence is of primary interest here because we are focusing now on comprehension abilities. To what extent might a child's difficulty in comprehension be related to incomplete knowledge of some aspect of his or her developing grammar, or to the above-mentioned nonlinguistic factors? A strong version of the "apply early-acquired principles to new uses" hypothesis would indeed reject the suggestion made at the beginning of this section: that some aspects of the knowledge of morphology and syntax may be acquired late (after age 5). First- and 2nd-graders' comprehension failure related to complex grammatical constructions, for example, would then be due exclusively to processing difficulties, that is, to problems of *deploying* a complete and fully formed grammar. Of course, we would want to set aside problems of assigning an interpretation to a sentence because of a lack of concept/vocabulary knowledge:

(3) The marquis returned to settle his account with the cobbler.

or difficulties related to straining working-memory resources in the case of early-developing recursive patterns:

(4) The shoemaker lived in a village [by the river [near the castle [across from a forest [on the side of a mountain]]]].
(5) The man [that the shoemaker's sister thought [she would marry]] is telling the truth.[3]

Recalling our discussion of Gernsbacher's and Kintsch's models of discourse processing, and how children's new set of skills is tied to new sentence patterns, we can again pose these questions: Is the child learning new grammar or learning to apply early-acquired principles to new uses, simply requiring more advanced processing tools? Is it a question of continued development of linguistic competence, or of learning how to marshal the other components of language ability in order to put previously acquired competence to use? For example, in expository texts, clauses are constructed and linked differently from the way they are linked and constructed in both interactive conversational dialog and monologic narrative. Nominalization, for one, is an important resource for establishing links to prior text, a hallmark of academic discourse (Schleppegrell 2001). In addition to dependence on prerequisite prior knowledge (something that one might claim it shares with conversational discourse), this kind of informationally dense text requires a more retrospective and nonlinear kind of processing.[4]

Clearly, unlike the predictive and prospective comprehension strategies typical of Narrative One, these kinds of operation on discourse depend on formal instruction and learning (Schleppegrell 2001; Schleppegrell and Colombi 1997). Proficiency in understanding complex sentence patterns (e.g., heavy noun phrases in subject position) depends on experience in the upper grades with expository registers (especially after 2nd grade). Full mastery of these patterns for comprehension is facilitated by reflective practice with instructive examples. While we can assume broad agreement on these points, the source of the difficulty that children face is still open to debate. There is no question that children do experience comprehension difficulties with such complex grammatical patterns (e.g., in reading) and that these difficulties can be remediated by direct instruction. But again, are children acquiring new grammatical knowledge (i.e., expanding their linguistic competence) or learning how to more effectively process patterns they already know? This question underlies the purposeful ambiguity in such phrases as "development of *grammar*" and "aspects of *grammar*" in this chapter and in previous chapters. This formulation leaves open (where it can be left open) whether we are talking about actual linguistic knowledge or "usage." The latter implies the recruitment of information-processing machinery to put grammatical competence to good use.

In experiments that assessed previously identified skilled readers and unskilled readers, Crain and Thornton (1998) explored this question, comparing their findings with findings from studies of grammatical knowledge of young preschool children. Taking note of studies that show a correlation between reading ability and performance on assessments of syntax, Bar-Shalom, Crain, and Shankweiler (1993) focused on 2nd-graders' knowledge of relative clauses. If appropriate and sufficient contextual support for interpretation is not given, for example, unskilled 2nd-grade readers in fact perform significantly less well than their peers. For example, relevant situational context information would facilitate comprehension of sentences that contain a restrictive relative clause. In example (6), with the nonrestrictive relative clause, it is clear that only one man is involved. By contrast, example (7), with a restrictive relative clause, presupposes the existence of more than one man, only one of whom became wealthy with the help of the elves.

Nonrestrictive relative clause
(6)   The man, who never asked for the elves' help, became very wealthy.

Restrictive relative clause
(7)   The man that the elves helped became very wealthy.

According to the researchers, not depicting more than one man in the experimental workspace leaves unmet, or unsatisfied, a presupposition that (7) normally requires. In contrast, if the pragmatic relations are made explicit by depicting all the figures that might accord with the presuppositions of a restrictive relative clause (in particular, the figures of two men in example (7)), then unskilled readers' performance is comparable to that of skilled readers. These findings favor the Processing Limitation Hypothesis proposed by Bar-Shalom, Crain, and Shankweiler (1993). Failure to provide the relevant contextual support forces the respondent to expend extra computational resources to "accommodate an unmet presupposition" (p. 204). Thus, when unskilled readers' working-memory capacity is strained, comprehension of complex sentence patterns suffers, whereas skilled readers' comprehension of complex sentence patterns does not suffer to the same extent. On the other hand, according to the authors, if the struggling reader is able to interpret and produce complex sentences under more context-embedded conditions, this is evidence that his or her deficiency is not the result of a developmental lag in grammatical competence.

Of course, in the case of beginning or intermediate L2 learners, both incomplete grammatical knowledge of the L2 and processing deficiencies may conspire to block interpretation of complex syntactic patterns.[5] This observation, in turn, suggests the possibility of the same grammatical-competence-related comprehension breakdown in children's primary language. Assuming that children are not born with knowledge of language-specific grammatical rules, and that these unfold maturationally (and not "instantaneously," all at once), for any particular construction, there would be a moment in development at which both immature grammatical knowledge and immature processing capabilities contribute to comprehension difficulties. Thus, there is no reason to exclude the possibility that some of these constructions may be late-developing, maturing during the period of schooled literacy instruction.[6] In any case, the investigations into child language development described above are surely on the right track in their attempt to differentiate the components of sentence comprehension that we can initially categorize along the traditional dimensions of competence and performance (Newmeyer 1998). The only qualification being suggested here is that we should consider competence and performance in less dichotomous terms. Given that literate and highly educated adults experience the same kind of comprehension breakdown with complex sentences even in their primary language (e.g., embedded clauses; see note 5), processing limitations must account for these cases; any version of a Structural Lag Hypothesis must be categorically rejected. By extension, the Processing Limitation Hypothesis cannot be excluded for children either.

Many unanswered questions remain, and just as many await a proper formulation. Again, a key concept that will inform the analysis of future research findings is modularity. Assuming the relative autonomy of the linguistic modules from general cognition, to what extent are they encapsulated? Or, viewed from another angle, how and to what extent are the cognitive-general domains constrained in their interaction with the linguistic modules—for example, developmentally in the acquisition of grammar? It appears that Crain, Thornton, Bar-Shalom, and Shankweiler lean toward the second perspective on modularity, offering a hypothesis that views the processing of language input for acquisition as strictly bottom-up, and the Faculty of Language as sealed off from influence of general cognitive effects and learning. For an alternative view of how modularity might apply to both language development and processing, see Jackendoff 2002 and Pickering, Clifton, and Crocker 2000, respectively.

This consideration of the grammatical aspects of academic discourse ability prompts us to return to the start of this chapter, where one central cognitive domain was assumed to underlie school-related discourse proficiencies. As the argument goes, bilinguals need not store a separate CALP for each language; rather, the same central system is accessible for academic, literacy-related tasks engaged in through L1 or L2. However, since part of academic language proficiency may involve mastering the use of language-specific grammar associated with academic texts, bilinguals may to some degree develop separate representations for these domains, for L1 and L2. As in all comprehension, assigning an interpretation to any potentially meaningful fragment of an academic text calls upon the operation of specific interfaces that connect morphology/syntax and CS, plus the participation of general-purpose interface processors. Recall that this was the suggestion made in chapter 3 to explain an interesting disparity in the performance of the Nahuatl-Spanish bilingual students on literacy assessments in their two languages. Research will need to focus on these interface domains of language use in order to better understand how bilinguals shift between languages when they learn how to use their L1 and L2 in context-reduced, discourse-ability-challenging, academic language tasks.

On the other hand, if it turns out that some aspects of academic-related grammar ability depend on actual late-developing competence (knowledge of peripheral principles, language-specific for the bilingual), these would also be represented within the same SS components in the L1 domain and in the L2 domain, but perhaps in a different way in each one. They would have developed with the participation of central-type learning mechanisms. If this hypothesis is correct, it should prompt us to consider another kind of interaction between the linguistic domains and CS; no neat encapsulation is likely here either. (For a different point of view, see Connor 1996 and Kellerman 2001.)

7.4 Access to Shared Academic Proficiencies in Biliteracy

The research review in this chapter was motivated by the fact that bilingual children in the Nahuatl-Spanish project showed consistently robust performance on academic-literacy tasks in their indigenous language, Nahuatl. Figures 1.2, 3.3, and 3.4 depict comparable performance in Nahuatl and Spanish even though the slope of the "learning curves" for Nahuatl is not as steep as the slope for Spanish. We speculated in chapter 3 about why the children's decoding of Nahuatl texts may not have been as skilled as their decoding of Spanish texts and why their performance on Nahuatl literacy tasks didn't seem to maintain the same rate of improvement across the grades as their performance on Spanish literacy tasks. But whatever lag might have appeared in comparison to Spanish, external constraints, material limitations, and sociolinguistic imbalances did not "short-circuit" access to the relevant processing resources and knowledge structures when literacy tasks were carried out in the socially subordinate language. It is in this sense that we can characterize children's advancing performance in the indigenous language as steady and substantive. In particular, the older children seemed to be able to productively apply decoding and encoding skills learned and practiced in Spanish to the experimental literacy tasks presented to them in the language in which these skills are not practiced. (Recall that one of the notable circumstances of this seemingly favorable outcome was the nature of the instructional program: while teaching of reading and writing was limited, as is customary in this community, to the national language, symbolic recognition is granted to the vernacular.)

Although it did not figure among the objects of our study at the time, the relative facility with which the bilingual students engaged texts in their indigenous, "non-academic" language evokes results from cross-linguistic research on the importance of phonological awareness in skilled reading (Hu 2004; Ibrahim, Eviatar, and Aharon-Peretz 2007). Geva and Wang (2001) review the evidence for underlying universal principles that facilitate children's ability to apply requisite processing strategies in L2 and bilingual literacy learning. Just as in L1 reading (Adams 2004; Perfetti 1994), the rapid and automatized processing of orthographic-phonological correspondences sustains skillful decoding and comprehension. In L2 reading, if word decoding continues to be effortful and laborious, attentional resources cannot be allocated optimally to higher-order, sentence-level processes and to the construction of meaning (Saiegh-Haddad 2003a). (It is important to note, however, that L2 readers' phonological representation of words during decoding need not be native-like or "complete" for the purpose of effecting fast and efficient processing for meaning.)

For cross-language readers, what is most noteworthy is that there are central processing mechanisms that operate within the domain of the Cross-Linguistic Interface, linking the respective phonological structures and their orthographic representations. As depicted in figure 5.2, this is where the L1 and L2 lexicons come into play again, fulfilling their role as linkage and interface, "across" linguistic systems and "downward and upward" with CS and central systems, together, interactively. These processing mechanisms appear to be independent of L1 and L2 and are especially productive in tasks that involve reading; they seem to be accessed readily and applied to decoding in either language when called upon. It also appears that the processing skills that are specific to phonology-orthography mapping are special in some way. Other subsystems (L1-L2 syntax and morphology) do not seem as readily able to take advantage of what researchers term "transfer" (Siegel 2002). For example, not only do phonological processing, phonological awareness abilities, and decoding skills in each language correlate with each other—in fact, these abilities measured in *either L1 or L2* predict decoding skills in beginning L2 reading (Chien, Kao, and Li 2008; Dickinson et al. 2004; Geva and Wang 2001; Leikin, Share, and Schwartz 2005) and maybe even other aspects of L2 learning (Hu 2008). In their large-scale study of bilingual literacy, D. K. Oller and Eilers (2002) refer to what they term "phonological translation" abilities, suggesting similar cross-language effects.

In the Mexican study of cross-language reading and writing, children were applying phonological and orthographic processing skills learned through the medium of the official academic language to an indigenous language that they know. In addition, each set of phoneme-grapheme correspondences for the respective orthographies matches up closely. A separate assessment of children's metaphonological awareness related to their knowledge of each language (N. Francis 1998) provided indices that correlated positively with literacy skills in each language, measured separately. In any case, the pattern of results is consistent with findings from studies of other L2 readers. Some subcomponents that form part of skilled, automatized decoding, applied to the lower-level processes, appear to be learned once and are henceforth available for application to decoding tasks in another language. We would want to accept this principle at least in cases where the orthographies are of the same type (e.g., alphabetic, using the Roman alphabet), as was the case in the Mexican study, in which both orthographies also could be characterized as highly "transparent" or "shallow." Wang, Perfetti, and Liu (2005) studied biliterate readers for whom the two scripts (English and Chinese) represent a contrast of the highest order and concluded, interestingly, that "bilingual reading acquisition is a joint function of *shared* phonological processes and orthographic-specific skills" (p. 83; emphasis added). Further research still needs to explore the question of threshold of competence in the L2. At what minimal level of overall L2 attainment does the application of decoding skills (learned previously through a L1, or taught directly through the medium of L2) become productive? Degand and Sanders (2002) ask the same important question in their investigation of a different level of L1 ↔ L2 interaction: how relational markers in expository text affect comprehension in L1 and L2.

The research on shared processing mechanisms, then, should in no way deny language-specific or script-specific effects (e.g., in the transition from a "shallow" orthography of L1 literacy to a "deep" orthography in L2 literacy). Rickard Liow (1999) reports on differing patterns of decoding strategy among Chinese-English bilingual-biscriptals depending on which language-script was used for initial literacy instruction. In this regard, examples of "strategy transfer" (Rickard Liow 1999, 209) also point to language-specific, script-dependent factors that deserve further investigation (Bialystok 2002). Along these lines, in a critique of whole-language approaches to L2 reading, Birch (2002) points out how the view that the reading process is "unitary" and not amenable to analysis into "separate skills" leads holistic-oriented practitioners to overstate the similarity in processing strategies common to all languages and scripts. To be fair, the degree to which bottom-up mechanisms are neglected in L2 literacy teaching probably varies according to how strongly holistic an application of whole-language philosophy turns out to be in practice.

Transfer of lower-level processing strategies that are language-specific, and transfer of strictly linguistic features, should also be taken into account; these will vary widely depending on the typological differences between L1 and L2. A good starting point for research would be to compare decoding strategies for different pairs of languages and scripts that differ maximally (L1 literacy in Chinese—L2 literacy in a shallow alphabetic script). Subsequent comparisons could focus on scripts that differ in other ways, and then on scripts that differ minimally.

A number of practical applications could follow from these comparisons. For example, in bilingual literacy-learning situations in which a new orthography is proposed for initial reading instruction in an indigenous language, how closely should the new writing system adhere to the standard system of the national language (to facilitate, for example, productive "strategy transfer")? The preliminary results from the studies of Mexican children's Spanish and Nahuatl writing seem to suggest that a close orthographic match might be in the best interests of emerging biliterates (N. Francis 2005); López (2001) presents an alternative point of view. At the same time, the wide-ranging evidence for the existence of central processing mechanisms that operate within or upon the phonological system holds important implications for understanding how the components of bilingual proficiency interact in reading. To repeat, it appears that these processing mechanisms are not bound to the specific phonological representations of either L1 or L2. The identification of lower-level cross-language skills in orthographic and phonological processing makes for an interesting parallel with the higher-order abilities that are more obviously cross-language in how bilingual readers access them. None of this, however, should lead us to discount the operation of language-specific lower-level processors. That there might be a mix of language-specific and language-independent components at each level simply reflects the componential nature of reading ability. This is just what we would expect from a system that is internally diverse, instead of undifferentiated and homogeneous.

What is interesting about these findings regarding the components of reading ability in bilinguals is the apparent dissociation in regard to how the subsystems of L1 and L2 interact. While it may be easy to see why discourse-organizing schemas are relatively freely accessible to both L1 and L2 (Pearson 2002) because they are clearly not language-specific, a different picture emerges when we consider the phonological and syntactic systems. Why would the processing interfaces that serve phonological abilities allow more unfettered cross-linguistic access than appears to be the case for syntax? Recall that skilled phonological processing in L1 predicts skilled decoding in L2, while measures of performance related to L1 syntax have not shown the same kind of universal cross-linguistic tendency (Pearson 2002; Siegel 2002).

In bilingual literacy, not all language-related competencies, processing mechanisms, and other necessary kinds of knowledge structure are "accessed" and "shared" in the same way between L1 and L2. This follows from modular approaches to analyzing reading ability, as outlined by Perfetti (1994). Thus, questions about degree of autonomy, interdependence, and language (and script) dependence need to be asked one at a time, component by component. All of this leads to the hardest question of all: how does one relationship of autonomy, interdependence, or dependence interact with others? A case in point: we considered the evidence that common underlying processors (to paraphrase, on purpose, Cummins's Common Underlying Proficiency) facilitate decoding in beginning L2 readers. Such facilitated decoding outpaces learners' actual L2 phonological knowledge, not to mention the development of other linguistic subsystems. This was taken as evidence in favor of its "central" and language-independent nature. We also should suspect that, in reading comprehension, the intervention and integration of other components will bear on how productive L2 phonological processing will turn out to be. Some of these components are more or less autonomous (from L1 and L2); others will be more highly language-dependent.

One working hypothesis would predict that the ability to take advantage of a given lower-level phonological processing skill or higher-order discourse-organizing skill in L2 will be conditioned to some degree by overall L2 linguistic competence. To this point, Bialystok (2001a, 152–181) reminds investigators that studies that assess the ability to apply decoding strategies cross-linguistically cannot bypass two critical factors: (1) the reader's actual level of linguistic knowledge of the L2, and (2) the reader's level of literacy skills previously attained through a L1. Indeed, a serious methodological defect of many studies of L2 literacy is the failure to specify the first factor, often designating study participants simply and indistinctively as "English as a Second Language (ESL)," for example.

Few L2 literacy researchers today hold to early simplistic models of the "mother tongue advantage" that mechanically prescribed a kind of "natural order–stages approach" of L1 oral proficiency → L1 literacy (implying exclusion of L2 literacy instruction) → L2 oral proficiency → L2 literacy. Literacy ability does not always follow oral language ability in a one-to-one fashion: bilingual children often attain a higher level of literacy ability in the language they do not speak fluently (Moll, Sáez, and Dworin 2001; Rubin and Galván Carlan 2005). However, attempts to set aside the factor of L2 linguistic competence in the study of L2 reading will surely not prosper either. Recall that it was with this idea that we began discussing L2 literacy in chapter 2. An important curriculum question in bilingual teaching situations is, at what level of general L2 grammatical competence can L2 literacy learning be undertaken productively? It is a question of far-reaching practical implications, for example, in the case of children who speak a vernacular language as their L1 and must learn literacy in a L2 of wider communication without unnecessary delay during the elementary grades. The research questions are actually rather straightforward; but the relevant comparisons would necessarily have to identify and separate out several child bilingual circumstances:

1. L2 literacy learning for mature L1 literates,
2. L2 literacy learning for developing L1 literates,
3. L2 literacy learning for young nonliterate children.

Then, for cohorts #1/#2 and for cohort #3, one would have to ask, what level of overall L2 grammatical competence has been achieved? For example, a series of experiments might be designed for cohort #3 (initial literacy learning in a nonprimary language) as follows. The rate of literacy achievement in L2 could be assessed first for subgroups of learners, beginning with those comprised of subjects who possess *no knowledge of the L2*. Then a comparison could be made with the rate of achievement of subgroups with progressively more advanced initial levels of L2 linguistic competence. Short of such an ambitious research design, findings that indicate diminished automaticity of processing even in advanced L2 reading

(Bialystok 2001a, 178–179; Fraser 2004) offer an initial framework for formulating the right questions. And for a perspective on the special circumstances of L2 literacy in an alphabetic script for deaf learners, see the interesting discussion regarding bilingual/bimodal teaching approaches in DeLuca and Napoli 2008; Mayer and Akamatsu 2000; Supalla, Wix, and McKee 2001; and Swanwick and Watson 2005. (In regard to this aspect of biliteracy, see again the discussion of sign language bilingualism in chapter 5.)

7.5 Linking Secondary Discourse Ability and Metalinguistic Awareness at the Discourse, Sentence, and Word Levels

We began this chapter with the proposal that the study of the components of academic language proficiency can be divided, for analytic purposes, along two dimensions: secondary discourse ability (SDA) and metalinguistic awareness (MA). We then focused on three different levels of SDA: the narrative/discourse level (section 7.2), grammar at the sentence level (section 7.3), and the processing skills specific to reading at the phonological level (section 7.4). To each of these correspond aspects of MA that complement them. Fully developed academic language proficiency (which in today's world includes skilled reading comprehension) necessarily implies this correlation, without exception. Another way of looking at this relationship might be that SDA and the competencies and skills associated with it begin to develop independently of MA, attaining a rudimentary status. They then develop toward higher, more advanced stages concurrently with emerging metacognitive strategies that operate upon the three levels of language use just mentioned: discourse, sentence, and word.

To recapitulate, narrative emerges early from children's first attempts to mentally organize, recount, or understand experience, sometimes at first with extensive interactive scaffolding from an adult interlocutor. Competencies (knowledge structures) in the domain of discourse develop: the reorganization of memory activations into coherent integrated representations, and the acquisition of mental schemas of forms, in addition to the content schemas of general world knowledge. Information-processing skills develop, augmenting the ability to analyze, integrate, categorize, infer, and conduct different logical operations applied to problem solving. Metalinguistic abilities advance hand in hand with these competencies and processing skills.

In practice, it would be hard to draw a fine line between emerging SDA and emerging MA. Awareness of and attention to discourse patterns (e.g., focused reflection on how parts of stories go together) (MA) becomes necessary when comprehension (SDA) is challenged. Under the category of the pragmatics of discourse comprehension and production, context is taken into account strategically. Children learn to identify and use different kinds of context, and learn to evaluate their relevance, suspending the effects of context and previous expectations when necessary. Monitoring of comprehension, for example, is more controlled and deliberate. In sum, as discourse processing becomes more demanding, metacognitive operations directed at this level of language use become more indispensable.

This relationship between text difficulty and monitoring helps us untangle a controversy over the relative contributions of context, previous knowledge, and bottom-up decoding. Top-down processes obviously facilitate comprehension. Even further, we could argue that normal comprehension would not be possible without some interaction between text information and previous knowledge. But readers, for example, can depend on top-down information unreflectively only to the extent that there is a close match between previous knowledge and text information. In fact, they would be ill-advised to depend on previous knowledge too much when the going gets rough—for example, when new concepts start to be introduced with greater frequency and *pre*conceptions are no longer as dependable. Decoding now gets the recognition it deserves; reading slows down, and preconceived ideas, from "previous knowledge," might even have to be overturned.

Turning now to the next level down, grammar and sentence comprehension, we contrasted two proposals:

- for complex syntax, typical of academic texts, the difficulties that children experience can be traced to demands placed on working-memory resources and processing mechanisms (only), or
- they can be traced to these same performance factors plus incompletely attained, late-developing grammatical knowledge.

In either case, strategies that children learn, primarily through reflective experience in parsing complex sentences in reading, have been shown to provide for significant improvements in decoding and comprehension. Applying analogous monitoring strategies from discourse comprehension to the sentence level, skilled readers self-correct and scan text in a nonlinear fashion to check for (among other things) well-formedness of syntax and for semantic relationships that are to be expressed obligatorily. Controlled, or selective, attention to grammatical patterns that are difficult to process develops in response to reflection upon comprehension failure, ambiguity, and so on. (We will see examples of this kind of reading strategy in chapter 9.)

The phonological level departs in at least one important way from the other two. Advanced SDA-related and MA attainments at the discourse and sentence levels are applicable in a useful and practical way to both oral and written modalities, in comprehension and production. For phonology, the application is to reading and writing, to graphemes (although one interesting possible exception in the oral modality, in the realm of the aesthetic genres, does come to mind). That is, phonological processing skills and the separate but related development of phonological awareness are largely specific to literacy, and both can be objects of direct instruction. We could also add here the "word analysis skills" that are part of morphological awareness (Rispens, McBride-Chang, and Reitsma 2008; Siegel 2008). For L2 learners, in particular, sharpening their ability to direct attention to aspects of these developing skills is one way of boosting comprehension and expression beyond their current stage of mastery. And the development of this kind of language awareness appears to be especially amenable to the effects of properly designed focus-on-form instruction. For example, Packard et al. (2006) have demonstrated the effects of early direct teaching (in 1st grade) of word morphology and orthographic elements on writing ability in Chinese. Likewise, W. Li et al. (2002) showed that morphological awareness predicts reading ability. Not surprisingly, a bidirectional causal relationship between awareness of morphemes and literacy learning for alphabetic systems has been demonstrated as well (Nunes, Bryant, and Bindman 2006). That is, as with the other levels of MA, *initial literacy* may provide children with the most important early opportunity to develop morphological awareness, then becoming a critical component of subsequent literacy learning (for further relevant findings and discussion, see Chung and Hu 2007). This view is different from one that would propose that preliterate metalevel language abilities are a *prerequisite* for literacy learning.

One way to put this summary into perspective would be to see how the SDA counterparts of their respective primary domains fit into the picture. Beginning again at the top, recall that Narrative Two and advanced expository discourse abilities are supported by development in metalinguistic awareness, and vice versa. In contrast, basic conversational ability and Narrative One, while they may provide some contexts for early MA development and may involve the beginnings of reflection and awareness of language forms, do not depend on it in the fully reciprocal way that has been proposed for the secondary domains. In the case of L1 core grammar competence and L1 phonological knowledge, the separation between secondary and primary domains is more clear-cut. Awareness of and attention to morphological and syntactic patterns appear to help children process complex sentences that they encounter in academic-type discourse; and phonological awareness helps children learn how to read and write.

On the other hand, acquisition of core grammatical competence, evidenced in primary discourse tasks, unfolds autonomously from the metalinguistic domains. Similarly, children's L1 phonological knowledge attains completeness through simple exposure to positive evidence. Metaphonological abilities and discrete processing skills that require manipulations of isolated phonemes may contribute to developing abilities related to the performance of specialized oral genres. But nonliterate children and adults normally have no use for them (ludic and aesthetic functions aside). They are literacy-specific, for the most part. A noteworthy consensus in the work on metalinguistic abilities (Brockmeier 2000; Gee 2001; Olson 1996), cutting across theoretical models of language development, is that they are most profitably studied as they intervene in the learning of academic-type, literacy-related proficiencies. Among the promising candidates for cross-paradigm convergence, this one should surely go toward the top of a short list. Thus, corresponding metalevel knowledge intervenes at each level or subsystem of language: text/discourse, sentence/phrase, morphology, and phonology. Nuances aside, the role of MA in the development of literacy-related language proficiencies proposed in this chapter is broadly consistent with the most recent report of the National Early Literacy Panel, *Developing Early Literacy* (Lonigan, Schatschneider, and Westburg 2008).

Many of the proposals in this conclusion, for which evidence is still tentative, should be taken as hypotheses for further research. They are especially relevant for studies of child bilingualism because of the questions of how knowledge and skills are "accessed by L1 and L2" and which components of these competencies and skills might be "shared." For L2 educators, an accounting of which knowledge structures and processing skills are not "language-bound" and which are more language-specific will contribute to the important task of designing more efficient language-teaching programs. This leads back to the proposed model of how some components of language proficiency are represented differently from others. Figure 5.2, the Bilingual Tripartite Parallel Architecture, helps us think about how the different aspects of "complex grammar ability" might be divided up for bilinguals and monolinguals. ("Complex grammar ability" is shorthand for "ability to comprehend and use expressively complex grammar typical of academic discourse.") In the case of children, for those constructions whose difficulty is caused strictly by strains on information processing we can "locate" the domain easily and straightforwardly. Setting aside for now the L2 learner with incomplete linguistic representations, the difficulty would not be traced to a deficiency or developmental lag associated with SS; rather, it would be traced to the processing interfaces that connect the grammatical modules and CS. These would be associated with the sentence- and discourse-processing skills that children *learn* over their years of contact with abstract concepts, problem solving, higher-order discourse, and academic texts, especially of the essay/expository type. In figure 5.2, specifically, we would focus primarily on the CS "base" and the CS-language interfaces (the double arrows connecting upward to the linguistic domains). This approach has the virtue of keeping the linguistic modules and Central System domains separate, especially for purposes of the hypothesis that there will never be any structural lag or developmental "immaturity" in relation to grammar knowledge (e.g., a strong version of the Processing Limitation Hypothesis).

Different versions of the Structural Lag Hypothesis would also accept the idea that, for "complex grammar" difficulties occasioned not by incomplete linguistic competence but by processing factors, the relevant components would be within the domain of the CS ↔ language interface. On the other hand, for comprehension failure related to "complex grammar" that does have its origin in a developmentally immature/incomplete knowledge of some subcomponent of morphology and syntax, modeling this scenario is slightly more complicated. The hypothetical boundaries and encapsulations are not as easily drawn on any model, including figure 5.2. If certain aspects of grammatical knowledge (beyond "core grammar") develop in later childhood in response to contact with school literacy, then these components of linguistic knowledge would not emerge in the same way that core grammar did in early childhood. Specifically, cognitive-general learning mechanisms would play a more prominent role. There would even be a greater degree of individual variation from one native speaker to another. The grammatical knowledge that would come to be constructed, even though it might be a different kind of knowledge from the knowledge that was set down with the guidance of the LAD, would still form part of the same component of SS. To what other kind of knowledge structure could it belong? But what we would have to allow for then would be a SS that was built by UG and the LAD along with the participation of domain-general learning. That is, development of linguistic knowledge would not be parameter-setting-type development all up and down the line. This model would then also have to admit greater degrees of interactivity between the CS domains and the linguistic domains. If we accept the hypothesis (from chapter 6; Clahsen and Muysken 1996) that L2 learning draws more heavily from CS than L1 acquisition does, then the question of the participation of domain-general learning in L1 versus L2 is really a matter of degree.

The depiction in figure 5.2 of two linguistic subsystems of the same kind then is also correct, even if one turns out to be a L1 and the other a L2. This is because L1s and L2s, during the course of their development, both draw from CS. If L2s were built with completely different mechanisms than L1s, we would be compelled to represent them in a completely different way. Recall from chapter 6 that we are also accepting the position of other researchers (Herschensohn 2000; White 2003) that UG continues to play a role in L2 learning, another reason to keep depicting the two sides of the bilingual's linguistic competence with the same shapes.

8
Metalinguistic Awareness, Bilingualism, and Writing

Chapter 7 returned to the primary focus of our study of bilingual competence and proficiency: the abilities that develop in school associated with learning how to read and write. As we saw, some of these abilities are observable in other kinds of language use, in problem solving and creative endeavor. Some of the same component knowledge structures and skills are shared with abilities related to listening comprehension and oral expression. As Cummins (2000) points out, Cognitive Academic Language Proficiency is not the same as literacy ability. Along the same lines, research has shown that as children become skilled in decoding, measures of reading comprehension correlate highly with measures of oral comprehension (Gernsbacher 1990). Thus, just as we propose that in bilingualism, these "central" knowledge structures are not language-specific, so we can propose the same, to a certain extent, for modality: they are not completely specific to written language either. But for a number of good reasons, how children develop advanced academic abilities is most amenable to study in the area of literacy. Literacy is the primary learning objective of schooling in the elementary grades and should be prominent among the concerns of child language researchers for this reason alone. This chapter will present findings from another phase of the Mexican study on the development of academic language proficiency, children's writing ability—and in particular one aspect of this ability, children's correction, revision, and editing of their own compositions.

A second theme explored in chapter 7 was how academic language proficiency can be analyzed along two dimensions: secondary discourse ability and metalinguistic awareness. With this possible connection (between the two dimensions) in mind, the project looked to the analysis of self-correction strategies as a good place to begin in designing the assessments. One might argue that attention to language forms is an integral part of successful performance in writing (as opposed to in reading, for example); or perhaps attention to form is more important in writing than in reading (chapter 9 will return to this idea). So asking children to reread their compositions for the purpose of revising them should bring this kind of awareness about language, and the ability to perform operations on language form, to the forefront even more. The children were asked to do this in both of the languages that they know. (We also had the good fortune of possessing adequate writing samples on which to base this experiment.) The findings will be reviewed in the order in which the studies were conducted: first the results from Spanish writing and then the results from Nahuatl writing.

The sections that describe the assessments go into some detail, though without most of the tables and statistical details that can easily be obtained elsewhere (N. Francis 2004, 2005). Since this is the first study to be carried out that involves correction of writing samples from an indigenous language, our goal is to provide enough information for replicating it. More importantly, given this study's limitations as an exploratory assessment restricted to the description of correlations and tendencies, a new series of studies, implementing a more powerful design, might pick up where it left off. For now, the results are interesting because they shed some light on the relationship between secondary discourse ability and metalinguistic awareness. Chapter 9, which will describe a parallel assessment of self-correction in reading, will leave some room for cautious speculation in chapter 10 about where this line of research might lead, and where it shouldn't lead.

8.1 Metalinguistic Development and Bilingualism

In one way or another, the role of focus on language form has been a recurring theme in all of the subdisciplines of language learning. For some time, researchers have been interested in the possible connections between metalinguistic awareness and literacy (Garner 1992; Morais 2003) and bilingualism (M. Schwartz, Leikin, and Share 2005; Swain 1998; Wenden 1998). As suggested in chapter 7, all of the research on language awareness and literacy applies to bilingual learners. A related question (surely more controversial) is whether bilingualism and L2 learning might be causally related to some aspect of metalinguistic development. The question can also be asked about the relationship between metalinguistic awareness and L2 learning in the other direction. Chapters 6 and 7 touched on some ways of approaching this issue, which has been debated for a number of years now: can metalinguistic knowledge boost or accelerate L2 learning? Sharwood Smith (2004) raises this possibility, applying a modular approach similar in some ways to the one considered here.

The objectives that motivated this series of literacy assessments were (1) to describe the tendencies across the grades that emerged in an inventory of corrections and revisions of first-draft writing samples; (2) to compare these tendencies with the findings of previous evaluations of the children's awareness of language forms; and (3) to propose a framework for further research on bilingualism, literacy, and metalinguistic awareness. Objective #1 is exploratory and descriptive, with an eye to the key developmental trends. In some respects, the ability to reflect upon and manipulate one's own written expression marks the highest level of literacy development. As expected, measures of children's awareness of language form correlated with literacy assessment (objective #2). The analysis of these data suggests that continued research on the possibility that metalinguistic awareness is related in some important way to literacy development would be a good idea. In regard to objective #3, the findings from the literacy assessment study did not support or disconfirm any current hypotheses. But the wide-ranging discussion on the relationship between bilingualism and metalinguistic awareness stands as an important backdrop to the problem of improving literacy learning for L2 students.

Over the years, a widely cited approach to examining the metalinguistic dimensions of bilingualism has been that of Bialystok (1991, 2007). A brief review is in order. To start with, in Bialystok's view, monolingual and bilingual children solve metalinguistic problems in basically the same way. However, bilinguals may tend to approach these tasks with higher initial levels of mastery of analysis and control of language processing. This advantage that bilinguals purportedly enjoy, then, seems to reflect a difference in underlying processing abilities, one that in turn should be reflected in higher levels of performance in other "advanced uses of language."[1] The contexts of language use from which this difference in underlying proficiencies may emerge include (1) the experience of applying communicative strategies to conversation in a L2 in which higher levels of processing control are required; (2) situations where the child must attend to the language code itself (e.g., where the child must choose which language to use when addressing speakers with varying levels of proficiency in L1 and L2); (3) literacy tasks involving both languages (i.e., if the bilingual becomes literate and is afforded the opportunity to use both languages in literacy tasks, he or she might be able to submit language patterns to inspection and analysis with greater facility). The opportunity to engage in a kind of contrastive analysis of the grammar of L1 and L2 might enhance awareness of how different forms can express similar thoughts, how subtle differences change meaning, and so on (e.g., parsing sentences to express the same idea: "I don't like talking dolls," an English pattern, contrasted to "do not appeal to me the dolls that talk" [no me gustan las muñecas que hablan], in Spanish). These metalinguistic aspects of language use imply the development of explicit mental representations about forms, and how it is that they are related to meanings. Bialystok and Hakuta (1994, 122) proposed one possible strong hypothesis for consideration: certain aspects of bilingualism and L2 learning "create new ways of thinking and new mental organizations. The result of this is that the mind of a bilingual speaker has a different structure than the mind of a monolingual."

But in a subsequent review of the research on bilingualism and metalinguistic development, Bialystok (2001b) called attention to mixed findings. While bilinguals outperform monolinguals on some metalinguistic tasks, a bilingual superiority across the board does not appear to hold up. Studies often show no differences between bilinguals and monolinguals, or short-term advantages that diminish over time (Goetz 2003); D. K. Oller and Eilers (2002) discuss related comparative measures. Thus, it may not be the knowledge of two languages, by itself, that contributes to higher levels of metalinguistic awareness. In line with the approach we have been following so far, implicit linguistic competence (in one, two, or three languages) is a different kind of knowledge from that involved in metalinguistic awareness. In this view, more advanced metalevel knowledge in bilingual children results from specific uses of the two languages (for relevant findings, see Le Pichon Vorstman et al. 2009). Conceivably, then, certain uses of bilingual competence would strongly favor metalinguistic awareness, some only marginally, and others hardly at all.

8.2 Metalinguistic Awareness in Literacy and Second Language Learning

With all this in mind, we can again consider the linkage between the "secondary" attainments of literacy and L2 learning, on the one hand, and metalinguistic awareness, another "nonprimary" development in children, on the other. What should be interesting to any observer of the debates on literacy learning and L2 learning is that similar terms and categories come up in each discussion. In the development of literacy skills, what role do explicit and analyzed representations play? In studies of L2 writing, a recurring research question has been the degree of effectiveness of corrective feedback and related focus-on-form learning tasks (Bitchener and Knoch 2009; Frodesen and Holten 2003; Heift and Rimrott 2008; Hyland and Hyland 2006; I. Lee 2007; Polio, Fleck, and Leder 1998; Raimes 2002). Critiques of exclusively communicative and input-based approaches to L2 learning turn on the same question (DeKeyser 1998; Loschky and Bley-Vroman 1993; Swan 2005; Vignola and Wesche 1991).

Can positive evidence alone ("rich immersion," to borrow Gee's (2001) term) suffice for optimal rates of learning and high levels of ultimate attainment? For example, researchers who have studied the role of individual differences and learning context (DeKeyser 2005; Peter, Hirata-Edds, and Montgomery-Anderson 2008) have pointed out that extensive exposure to comprehensible input and "input flooding" restricted to positive evidence are insufficient for maximizing the learning of L2 grammar. In a major investigation that addressed this question, Norris and Ortega (2001) analyzed 77 studies that focused on direct instruction in L2 learning. What may appear sufficient for L1 acquisition falls short for L2 learners, who (1) appear to substantially benefit from the opportunity to engage in the analysis of language patterns; (2) may profit from explicit knowledge and reflection upon negative evidence; and (3) need to be able to test out interlanguage forms in active negotiation of meaning,[2] and monitor their production, when this is possible (Doughty 2001; Laufer 2009). Lyster (2004) goes further, making the case that L2 learners benefit most when negative evidence is provided explicitly (e.g., "prompts" that direct learners' attention to form more systematically, as opposed to "recasts"). R. Ellis, Loewen, and Erlam (2006) present confirming findings; and Nichols, Lightbown, and Spada (2001) review the literature specifically on recasts as negative evidence. Hale (2001) argues that the learning context of late L2 immersion differs from the kind of "immersion" that young children experience in L1 acquisition. Thus, in L2 learning, recourse to deliberate learning strategies, including the participation of metalinguistic abilities, might compensate for no-longer-privileged and no-longer-unimpeded access to the Language Acquisition Device. Fortunately for the more mature language learner, advanced learning capabilities continue to develop, making it possible to apply analytic and metacognitive approaches more successfully. Sharwood Smith (1994a) and Schachter (1998) offer similar arguments.

In the research on literacy learning, the fundamental issues in contention seem to echo these same points. Is the participation of higher-order metalevel learning strategies a necessary component of reading and writing development beyond the beginner stages (Carson 2001; Ferris 2010; Hyland 2003; I. Lee 2004; Peregoy and Boyle 2008)? The text-processing skills that are called upon in self-correction and revision would seem to demand the highest levels of reflective and analytical thinking about written language. This is one reason why it was selected as an object of study, in the hope that it might shed some light on how children engage abilities associated with advanced literacy.

8.3 A Study of Children's Perceptions of Focus on Form

8.3.1 The Participants

Participants in this study of revision and correction were the same 45 children who formed the cohort of bilingual 2nd, 4th, and 6th graders followed throughout the book. Here, a few details regarding their language ability profile will be relevant. They were selected by their teachers as having at least oral comprehension ability in both languages and adequate grade-level achievement in reading. To get an approximate idea about the children's language-learning history, parents were interviewed. The interviews suggested the following categories of preschool bilingualism and L2 learning: 13 children were identified as Spanish speakers (among bilinguals and "monolinguals"), 12 as having low-intermediate level ability in Spanish, and 20 as beginners. Our own testing of proficiency in both languages, however, suggested a higher overall entry-level comprehension ability in Spanish than was indicated by the parents. In fact, on conversational, context-embedded tasks it was not possible to unequivocally categorize any of the 45 children as interlanguage speakers of Spanish. Thus, for the majority of children, Spanish is their L2; however, all demonstrated intermediate, near-native, or native conversational fluency in Spanish by 2nd grade. Assessment in Nahuatl identified 4 students (3 in 2nd grade, 1 in 4th grade) as "passive bilinguals" (native speakers of Spanish, intermediate/advanced to near-native comprehension abilities in Nahuatl, with varying levels of expressive ability).

8.3.2 The Assessments

The Spanish Revision/Correction Task To begin with the Spanish version of the assessment: First drafts produced by children of a version of "El cazador de venados" [The Deer Hunter] were the object of scrutiny. This was the story that children had composed earlier for the writing assessment discussed in chapter 1 (figure 1.2). Each writing sample was typed, double-spaced, and returned to the student who wrote it. After a brief demonstration of the use of standard editing marks and of options available when correcting and revising, students were asked to make any changes to their drafts that they deemed necessary. Given present-day instructional practices in rural, indigenous, community schools in Latin America (Feldsberg 1997; Hamel 2009; Hamel et al. 2004; López and Jung 2003; Merkx and Pichún Seguel 1998; Vargas Ortega 1996), confirmed by extensive classroom ethnographic data from our own study, we could assume that this text-editing/correction task was novel for the students.

Categories of Analysis for the Revision/Correction Task Corrections and revisions were categorized along two dimensions: (I) level or subsystem of language (or orthographic pattern) that corresponds to the change, and (II) effectiveness of the change.

First, all attempts at revision and correction were coded for level or subsystem (I).

1. Orthographic correction: overall grapheme/phoneme correspondence, word segmentation, and accent placement

ya nomas le   ba a estar
~~llanomasle~~ ponemos la carne y en un momento ~~bastar~~ listo
(HF604) 6th grade

HF has corrected the segmentation in both cases. [all we have to do is put (in) the meat and in a moment it will be ready]

como pajáros
(PA201) 2nd grade

PA has inserted a missing accent; however, it should appear over the first syllable ("pájaros").

2. Morphosyntactic or semantic pattern at the sentence level

no lo oyo
lo desperto so esposa pero ~~olo oyo~~ so esposa
(MR404) 4th grade

Corrected version: [his wife woke him up but *she didn't hear him* (instead of *or hear him*) his wife]

3. Insertion of punctuation/capitalization, and discourse-level revisions

su   . el joven
El joven ya se iba para ~~so~~ casa se iba muy triste proque no lo mato ^ ~~El venado~~ ~~y~~ estaba cansado y tenia anbre
(HP410) 4th grade

HP inserts a period after "mato" presumably because "porque no lo mato El venado" [because not it killed the deer = because he didn't kill it the deer] contains a redundant element, either "lo" [it] or "El venado" [The deer]. Having eliminated the redundancy ("El venado"), HP repeats "el joven" [the young man] to clarify that it was he, and not the deer, that was tired and hungry, in the process omitting "y" [and].

All attempts were then coded for the resulting effectiveness of correction (II).

Noneffective Attempts

1. *No change:* Original sequence is replaced by the same sequence of letters or words.

2. *Correct → Correct (–):* No orthographic or grammatical errors are introduced into the revised version; however, the revised version is now unclear, results in a loss of coherence, or the like.

3. *Correct → Error:* An error-free original is changed; the revision results in an error.

4. *Error → Error or Error (–):* An original sequence that contains an error is changed; the resulting sequence is equally or more difficult to understand, is equally ungrammatical or ungrammatical to a greater degree, or results in an orthographic pattern that departs from the conventional form equally or to a greater degree than it did in the original version.

Effective Attempts

1. *Correct → Correct or Correct (+):* An original sequence that contains no errors is revised; the revised version contains no errors, or represents an improvement of some kind over the original.

2. *Error → Corrected or Improved:* An original sequence that contains an error or errors is significantly improved in some way, sometimes resulting in a conventional form or a correct grammatical sequence.

Analyzing corrections and revisions along these two dimensions allowed us to examine general developmental trends across the grades (in which categories could we identify systematic trends? in which could we not?), and provided indices to compare with other measures of academic language ability and metalinguistic awareness.

The Language and Literacy Assessments In addition to the new results from (1) the Revision/Correction task, data were available from an earlier battery of language and literacy assessments in (2) Reading, (3) Oral Narrative, and (4) Writing (figure 1.2), and (5) Metalinguistic Awareness (MA) related to bilingualism. MA scores were combined from a series of estimates of bilingual children's awareness of different aspects of language form and language use patterns (appendix 1 describes each of these tasks in detail):

a. provide a conventional name for both languages children speak or understand (2 points);

b. correctly identify the language(s) that the student customarily uses in class when speaking to the teacher (1 point);

c. correctly identify the language (Nahuatl or Spanish) of a series of short written texts, "text identification" (10 points);

d. correctly identify the language of individual lexical items, "words out of context" (18 points).

8.4 Children's Development of a Reflective Posture toward Writing: Results from Spanish

Findings are reported here in two parts, corresponding to two objectives:

1. a description of both global and grade-level tendencies along the two dimensions of analysis outlined above;

2. a comparison of the response patterns with the five measures of literacy and literacy-related language proficiency, with special attention to the assessment of metalinguistic awareness.

8.4.1 Objective #1: Tendencies in Revision/Correction from 2nd to 6th Grade

In all, 479 attempts at revision/correction were made by the 45 children; all typewritten copies of first drafts that were returned reflected some effort to revise or correct the text in some way. On average, older students made more attempts (6th grade—13.4, 4th—10.7, 2nd—7.9); however, 4th- and 6th-graders' written samples were also longer.

Rather than number of attempts, it was effectivity of corrections or revisions that distinguished beginners from more mature writers. Noteworthy is the result that even among 2nd graders, the majority of attempts (54.2%) fell into one of the effective categories. The 4th-graders' rate increased to 76.4%, and the 6th-graders' to 82.6%. For now, note the curve for percentage of effective revisions/corrections for Spanish in figure 8.1.

When corrections were examined according to subsystem of language, other contrasts between beginners (2nd grade) and more experienced writers (4th and 6th grades) became apparent. Counting the number of children who made at least one successful attempt under different categories, word segmentation and the

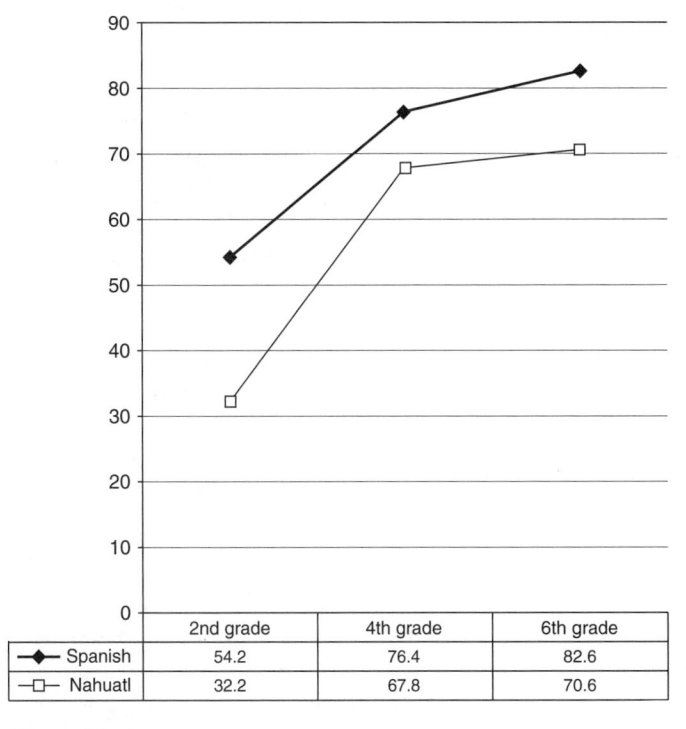

	2nd grade	4th grade	6th grade
◆ Spanish	54.2	76.4	82.6
□ Nahuatl	32.2	67.8	70.6

Figure 8.1
Percentage of effective corrections/revisions compared with total attempts in Spanish and Nahuatl

combination punctuation/capitalization+discourse appear to be late-developing. Older students were more likely to successfully attempt corrections or revisions at the higher levels of language processing.

8.4.2 Objective #2: Comparisons with Other Measures of Literacy and Metalinguistic Awareness

The results of the MA evaluation revealed interesting patterns in and of themselves. The subtest that we can characterize as more contextualized ("text identification"—5c) showed a slight upward trend but not a significant variation from 2nd grade to 6th grade. In contrast, the "words out of context" assessment (5d) showed both significant differences between grade levels and positive correlations with all the academic language abilities. This result, of course, was predictable. Older, more highly literate children do better on any kind of academic language assessment than younger children, and they should perform better on any kind of literacy-related language task, including the ones we invented for them on the bilingual awareness test. The interesting contrast was "degree of decontextualization." Abilities associated with highly contextualized language awareness tasks appear to be "early-developing," show little variation across grade levels, and do not correlate with Reading, Writing, and Oral Narrative as do the "late-developing" decontextualized abilities.

These results are also consistent with the research on one particular aspect of metalinguistic development: phonological awareness and related phonological/orthographic skills have been shown to be among the strong predictors of reading achievement in the early elementary grades (Perfetti 1994). On our measure, the largest subtest (5d—"words out of context") effectively required children to attend to the phonological and morphological features of the test items to be able to respond correctly. Items were chosen that did not have translation equivalents across the two languages (appendix 1). Therefore, the critical features for responding correctly were structural—in this case, structural at the word level since sentence context was removed.

As it turned out, MA correlated moderately with Oral Narrative, more highly with Reading, even more highly with Writing, and highest ($r = .69$, $p < .001$) with Effectivity of Revision/Correction. We could say that the MA measure (whose most important component was a test of phonological/morphological awareness—the most "decontextualized" of the measures) is more closely related to literacy tasks that require more attention to language forms and patterns—that is, the assessment of revision and correction in writing. (As an aside, to address the older-students-excel-in-everything-academic issue, the calculation was done for each grade separately. MA correlated significantly with Effectivity of Revision/Correction in 2nd grade and in 4th grade. It might have for 6th graders also, were it not for the fact that they uniformly scored too high—at ceiling—on the MA measure. A follow-up study might be able to confirm this suggestion.)

8.5 Metalinguistic Awareness as a Component of Literacy Ability—Writing in Particular

We can now look more closely at the research objectives outlined in section 8.1, beginning with a description of what the students took note of in their attempts at correction or revision (Objective #1).

The Effectivity of Revision/Correction measure revealed children's developing awareness of grammatical patterns and their ability to apply this awareness to a practical literacy task. In addition to an increase in general effectivity from 2nd to 6th grade, older children are more likely to focus attention on sentence and discourse levels beyond the local level of orthographic correction. In fact, the development of academic language proficiency implies an ability to begin consciously reflecting upon patterns that involve successively longer sequences of text. The grade-level tendencies that emerge, especially the appearance that the qualitative growth in the higher-order revision/correction strategies occurs between 2nd and 4th grade, is in line with Karmiloff-Smith's (1986) view of cognitive/discourse development after age 5:

> The most fundamental feature of later language development concerns the change of function of linguistic categories from the local sentential level to the level of extended spans of discourse. . . . [Children] first seem to concentrate on building up what might be termed an "utterance grammar." This seems to be mastered around the age of 5. They then go on, until 8 years or beyond, to reorganize its components and to acquire procedures for operating on spans of coherently related utterances, thereby changing the functions of the earlier mastered categories. This involves fundamental changes in children's underlying representations. (p. 474)

The new period of development reveals the application of grammatical competence to the processing not only of consecutive or juxtaposed utterances (as in conversation), but also of more complex sequences, aspects of coherence, and text organization. "And if age 8 represents the beginning of a further period, it may be related to the over-8 year old's capacity to cope abstractly with language" (p. 474). Other relevant studies are Karmiloff-Smith et al. 1993 (on children's awareness of discourse functions) and Rojas-Drummond et al. 1999 (on the development of "self-regulation," a metalinguistic ability at the text level). As children begin to gain control over letter formation, segmentation and spelling, and the marking of grammatical patterns at the sentence level, they can shift attention more and more to discourse patterns: cohesive ties across sentences, coherence, and aspects of narrative organization.

These grade-level trends suggest an interesting research question: to what extent is the writer's ability to focus on higher-order patterns dependent on control over lower-level skills? In the samples from the study it appears—impressionistically, from inspection alone—that the children with greater control over orthographic conventions were more successful in their attempts at the syntactic, semantic, and discourse levels. In addition, younger writers, who demonstrated the least control over word segmentation, rarely attempted corrections at this level, despite having many more opportunities to do so as compared with more skilled writers. Parenthetically, it is not a coincidence that when children attempted the highest-level (i.e., discourse-level) revisions, the resulting change was always effective. The idea is that mastery over the lower levels might free up processing resources for higher-level operations. It is important not to get the wrong idea here. The fact that 4th and 6th graders tended to attempt, and be successful at, a greater number of higher-level revisions in no way implies that the categories of word- and sentence-level correction are somehow less important for literacy development, or that they belong to an early, more immature stage of writing ability. In fact, we now turn to a late-developing spelling pattern, which continues to pose significant difficulties even among the most skilled 6th-grade writers.

8.5.1 Mastering a Spelling Pattern

Another revealing aspect of the effectivity of corrections was analyzed. This was a subset of grapheme/phoneme correspondence that represents a closed category, thus permitting a comparison between opportunities to correct and the actual number of effective corrections: the common spelling error involving the substitution of "o" for "u" and vice versa. Nahuatl-speaking bilingual children might be more prone to commit this error because of the "subdifferentiation" in speech, in reference to the Spanish vowel system (Flores Farfán 1992), of the phonemes /o/ and /u/. In fact, the tendency to "(con)fuse" these vowels seems to be one of the most visible features, at the phonological level, of beginning L2 Spanish learners whose L1 is Nahuatl. In particular, the analysis sought to confirm the observation that even among mature school-age writers this highly stigmatized phonological transfer feature represents a persistent problem in spelling. Older children even misspell their own last name when it involves this alternation: for example, Conde → Cunde, Bueno → Boeno. This particular feature of L2 Spanish—a seemingly minor discrete point of pronunciation and spelling—is cause for great consternation among local teachers. It reveals one's ethnic identity in a way that reinforces the popular association, based on deep-rooted prejudice, between indigenous-language bilingualism and deficient literacy learning.

Even students in the higher grades in the school experienced persistent difficulties with this spelling pattern. A pilot test of editing skills and orthographic knowledge focusing specifically on this feature was given to all 35 of the 6th graders. They were asked to identify all the incorrectly spelled words in a two-paragraph text. Among the errors introduced into the passage were "mochas" (for "muchas" [many]), "mochacho" (for "muchacho" [boy]), "moi" (for "muy" [very]), and "utras" (for "otras" [others]), misspelled high-frequency words that typically form part of younger children's spelling error inventories. Sixth-graders' performance on this task indicated a markedly low level of awareness regarding the graphic representation of this particular sound pattern in Spanish. Only 3 students identified all four errors. The majority, 18 students, identified only one, and 6 students identified none. Here is another example of uneven development: while some aspects of writing show consistently upward trends from 2nd grade to 6th grade (text-level organization, coherence, use of discourse markers, cohesive devices, and various orthographic skills), this particular feature, perhaps related to interlinguistic transfer, appears relatively stable.

In regard to the "Deer Hunter" compositions, the frequency of effective corrections in comparison to opportunities suggests a certain opaqueness of this feature. Among the 6th graders (in other respects the most skilled writers, superior on virtually all other indices), 128 opportunities to correct the /o/ - /u/ error were counted, yet only 2 corrections were attempted (successfully). Of the 15 students in 6th grade who wrote "Deer Hunter" compositions, only 2 were able to avoid the error in their first draft.

Of the possible interpretations of this result, the interesting one to discuss here is related to the Output Hypothesis (Morgan-Short and Bowden (2006) review the research). "Input flooding" (massive amounts of comprehensible input over an extended period spanning several years) restricted to positive evidence (in this case, in the form of reading—exposure to the words in meaningful contexts, but without systematic corrective feedback) may fail to result in significant improvements in accuracy with the /o/ - /u/ pattern. We can be relatively confident of the characterization of "input flooding" given that virtually all of the misspelled words are high-frequency sight-word-type items that the average 6th grader has seen a very large number of times in print since 1st grade. Such categories of transfer error (hypothetically) are clearly not impervious to correction. Analogous to the case of fossilized interlanguage forms in speech, for example, L2 writing development may have a tendency to stabilize around (nontarget) grammatical patterns that happen to "satisfy communicative need." On the other hand, it has been proposed that deliberate attention to grammatical patterns in comprehension and production, abstracted from meaning and communication, begins to set the stage for "destabilizing" such learner-language forms.

This point leads to the second objective of the study: the relationship between metalinguistic awareness and different aspects of literacy learning. The point of reference for strong versions of the "natural approaches" to language learning (including literacy) is L1 acquisition. That is, in this view learning to read and write is more like what occurs when young children acquire their primary language. Two perspectives on metalinguistic awareness might follow from this view: (1) that focus on form and conscious learning play a marginal role, and/or (2) that metalinguistic awareness should not be viewed as a separate development. Thus, "natural approaches" would tend to see a continuity between literacy and primary language acquisition. Proponents of language-teaching models that have emphasized the role of direct instruction and provision of negative evidence would differ with both #1 and #2.

8.5.2 Metalinguistic Awareness and Context

Recall that comparing the correlations between MA and different aspects of literacy ability suggests that *degree of decontextualization* is a factor to explore in further studies. To repeat: context-reduced language tasks may depend to a greater degree on metalinguistic awareness. Intuitively, the notion is attractive: the less extralinguistic context support is available for comprehension and expression, the more "abstract" the task becomes. Focus on form involves contemplating and manipulating language patterns, "abstracted" from context to a greater degree. In comprehension, for example, if less information is available from situational context or prior knowledge, or if the available contextual information is irrelevant or misleading, more attention must be directed to *textual* information.

Of the five literacy and literacy-related measures that were correlated with MA, Oral Narrative seems to stand apart ($r = .32$). In fact, Oral Narrative was by far the most context-embedded task: students narrated a short story based on illustrations that immediately before had provided the visual context support for a conversational-type dialog. The Reading ($r = .52$) and Writing ($r = .59$) evaluations focused on text comprehension and completeness/coherence. In both of these assessments, the task was strictly textual (illustrations that accompanied both tasks provided only minimal context support). For the Revision/Correction task ($r = .69$), students were given typewritten versions of their first draft and instructions on how to correct and revise texts, but they received no extratextual information of any kind (no illustrations or review of the "Deer Hunter" story). Especially among the 2nd and 4th graders, children who were most successful on the Revision/Correction task were the ones who earlier had scored higher on the MA test. Considering another dimension of decontextualization, note that the self-correction task calls on writers to "step back from" and objectify their own words, separating the intended meaning of a passage from its present form. Could another presentation of this segment be more explicit or grammatically acceptable, make a better connection with an antecedent, or conform more closely to a convention of writing? From this point of view, the Revision/Correction task falls at the most context-reduced end of the context-reduced—context-embedded continuum.

However, a simple comparison of *r* values does not indicate decisively that there exists a "closer relationship" between certain measures than between certain other measures or that one factor predicts one outcome more strongly than another. Thus, the suggestion that metalinguistic awareness is more closely related to performance in written expression than in reading, for example, needs to be studied further. The present limited findings do suggest, however, that this line of investigation might shed light on the relevant categories and research questions. The difference in requirements for comprehension and production might be especially relevant for L2 learners. However, production in one's L2 would tend to be more controlled and deliberate, L2 learners being forced to devote more attention to grammar patterns. In addition, they should be able to profit from explicit reflection on those patterns that correspond to aspects of grammar they have not completely mastered. Where grammatical knowledge is far from native- or target-like, the same distinction explains why a wider gap exists between comprehension and production abilities for L2 learners than for native speakers. But again, more work is needed on these proposed divergences between reading and writing in L2.

8.6 Possible Implications for Teaching Writing Skills

Findings from the study of children's corrections and revisions are compatible with the view that both literacy and L2 learning might find points of support in focused attention on language patterns. As Wenden (1998, 532) suggests, applying strategies that require reflection on the process of language learning helps students "become more autonomous in their approach to the learning of their new language"; and errors can be a window into their developing interlanguage system (Raimes 2002). Thus, language teachers might want to take a second look at learning activities that direct students' attention to language patterns, especially to contrasts between target forms and incomplete learner-language forms. Inductive methods that exploit the cognitively more mature school-age child learner's ability to process both positive and negative evidence could, in appropriate language-learning contexts, turn a developmental necessity into a learning opportunity. For literacy teachers, focus-on-form research offers similar kinds of opportunity at all levels, including phonological awareness. For example, direct instruction on language-specific elements of L2 orthography appears to help learners block interference from L1 (Rolla San Francisco et al. 2006). Just as decoding skills at the word level may benefit from explicit instruction, so too, if not more so, may the higher-level proficiencies (Taylor, Stevens, and Asher 2006).

The descriptions of self-correction strategies in this chapter, while they should be of interest to educators who favor focus-on-form instruction, do not yet provide evidence in favor of this teaching approach—over, say, "naturalistic" methods that rely exclusively on enriched immersion. In chapter 6, we looked at some theoretical arguments for why such "natural approaches" might be inadequate for L2 learning. In chapter 10, we will review evidence for why they would fall short of expectations in literacy learning as well. But again, despite the bias in this discussion in favor of form-focused instruction and development of metalinguistic awareness, the tendencies and correlations associated with children's self-monitoring that are reported here are only *compatible* with this bias. To gauge the state of the controversy on the role of negative evidence in L2 literacy development, see the exchange among Chandler (2003), Ferris (2010), and Truscott (2004, 2009) and numerous relevant articles in the *Journal of Second Language Writing*.

8.7 Children's Development of a Reflective Posture toward Writing: Results from Nahuatl

We now turn to the Revision/Correction assessment in Nahuatl. When children engage in this kind of specialized literacy task, what tendencies might be revealed if it is the indigenous language that is the object of reflection? Some of the questions are the same as those regarding the Spanish Revision/Correction assessment, and some are different. First, it is important to confirm or disconfirm that the same overall trends reappear. Second, the Revision/Correction assessment allows us to more directly compare performance between the languages. Recall that we hesitated to make this comparison in discussing the previous assessments because we weren't sure that certain intervening factors depressing Nahuatl performance could be controlled. This time, the uncertainty about task equivalence is partially resolved (it never is completely). The same students worked under the same conditions on their own first-draft compositions, twice, once in each language. There was no reason to suppose that the Nahuatl compositions would be much more difficult to reread and reflect upon than the Spanish compositions (since they were the children's own words). In addition, both compositions offered children more opportunities for correction than any of them could come close to exploiting fully. On the other hand, the external factors that can be accounted for (the sociolinguistic imbalance between national and indigenous languages, which implies vastly differing opportunities for practicing literacy skills in each) do make for an interesting comparison. How might the social inequalities be manifested? Are bilinguals in situations similar to this one able to apply non-language-specific competencies and skills to tasks in either language in ways that are comparable, at least minimally? This is related to a question that we already touched on in chapter 3: what might be the limits of access to the Common Underlying Proficiency (CUP)?

Over the years, the following version of Cummins's Interdependence Hypothesis has been widely cited in the bilingual education literature:

> To the extent that instruction on Lx is effective in promoting proficiency in Lx, transfer of this proficiency to Ly will occur provided there is adequate exposure to Ly (either in school or environment) and adequate motivation to learn Ly. (1999, 32)

How the related concepts of CUP and interdependence might apply (or how not) in the case of the more atypical circumstances of national language (NL)—indigenous language (IL) bilingualism is the question that comes up again. As formulated, the Interdependence Hypothesis leaves open the possibility that it may not apply or may apply in an attenuated way. Possibly, access to these underlying proficiencies might come to be obstructed or blocked such that any practical benefit accruing to the IL-speaking bilingual turns out to be of little consequence.

On the basis of findings from studies of the effectiveness of bilingual instruction, Cummins (2000) elaborates on the notion of interdependence. Recall that under the CUP model, literacy-related academic proficiencies maintain a degree of independence from both the language through which they may have been learned and the bilingual child's other language. In addition, some components of these higher-order analytic abilities, comprehension strategies, conceptual schemas, and information-processing skills develop through experiences completely independent of language. Thus, a three-way interdependence allows bilinguals to access both interlinguistic (L1 ↔ L2) resources and the literacy-related (largely nonlinguistic) "underlying" proficiencies that are common to both L1 and L2.

> We can talk of the influence of these factors loosely in terms of "transfer," although in reality they form the underlying cognitive apparatus that is used to interpret textual meaning rather than being "transferred" directly across languages. Linguistic knowledge, on the other hand, does transfer across languages in a more direct way than underlying operational or conceptual knowledge. Letter recognition among languages that share a Roman orthography is one example. Clearly, cognate relationships across languages also provide opportunities for transfer of linguistic knowledge. (Cummins 2000, 190)

This view of how bilingual children avail themselves of the peculiar internal differentiation of proficiency in two languages finds parallels in the work on L2 learning (Eubank and Gregg 1999; Sharwood Smith 1993), the psycholinguistics of bilingual proficiency (C. Baker 2006; Grosjean 1995; M. Paradis 2004), and L2 reading (Verhoeven 2007). It is compatible with Bialystok and Cummins's (1991) earlier proposal about modularity cited in chapter 4; and it is the basis for the successive models of bilingual proficiency that we have been discussing, culminating with the Bilingual Tripartite Parallel Architecture (figure 5.2). The Interdependence

Hypothesis also explains why access to the CUP, or Central Processing System, is not "automatic" (Cummins 2000, 191–194). Language-specific (i.e., specific to L1 or L2) knowledge, language-specific abilities, and external circumstances that differentially bear on L1 and L2 will represent limiting factors, for example, on performance on this or that academic task in a weaker or disfavored language.

Again, because the Nahuatl and Spanish Revision/Correction assessments were as parallel as one could hope for, we were able to test the predictions from chapters 1 and 3. The predictions are repeated here. In comparison to the expected ascending indices of performance across the grades in Spanish, two logical outcomes in response to the parallel Nahuatl assessments are predicted, both equally plausible:

1. Performance in the sociolinguistically disfavored IL, virtually excluded from day-to-day literacy instruction and practice, will show weak, nonsignificant advances across the grade levels, or none at all.

2. Performance in Nahuatl will show statistically significant ascending curves, commensurate with the achievement curves in Spanish, despite the sociolinguistic imbalance.

8.8 The Revision/Correction Assessment in Nahuatl

In contrast to the Reading and Cloze tests, which all 4 "Nahuatl language learners" attempted, 2 of them elected to complete the Nahuatl Writing assessment entirely in Spanish, hence the difference in number of participants: Spanish Writing ($N = 45$), Nahuatl Writing ($N = 43$).

For comparison purposes, a model was chosen for the Nahuatl writing task that was similar in its narrative organization to "El cazador de venados" [The Deer Hunter]. "Tecuani uan coneme" [The Lion and the Children], a Hansel and Gretel–type story, consists of three episodes: abandonment of the children by their father and stepmother, sojourn in the wilderness under the care of a wild beast, return to their community and family. Also, the two narratives both follow a clear logical-causal pattern (in contrast to, for example, a temporal-arbitrary pattern). The resulting student texts in both languages were comparable in length, and qualitatively, in regard to indices of coherence and narrative organization. All first drafts contained more than enough opportunities for revision and correction, only a fraction of which were exhausted during the first attempt at editing.

As in the Spanish version of the assessment, the children worked on their revisions and corrections from typewritten copies; and the same evaluation rubric was applied. The following are examples of changes that the children attempted, arranged by level/subsystem:

1. Orthographic correction

guan   oquin
~~guano quin~~ guicac y leonyninchan
(JP209) 2nd grade

Revised version: [and they take them to the lion's house]. JP209 corrects the segmentation error ("o" belongs to "oquin").

2. Morphosyntactic or semantic pattern at the sentence level

in kokone oqui temoto tekuani ako okacique in tekuani piltontzitzin oyaque

tepetl
~~altepetl~~
(LM605) 6th grade

Revised version: [the children looked for the lion they didn't find him the lion the children went to the mountain]. LM605 substitutes "mountain" for "town."

    ocholo
catcolin leon ^ oauitemototlen coakque
(NP414) 4th grade

Revised version: [there was the lion he fled he looked for something to eat]. NP414 inserts "he fled."

3. Insertion of punctuation/capitalization and discourse-level revisions

              . FIN
huan in yolkatl o kuikak yn coneme ^ ^
(JA405) 4th grade

Revised version: [and the animal took the children with him]. JA405 inserts a missing period and the word "FIN" ["END" in Spanish].

The following Nahuatl substitutions for Spanish loanwords could be categorized as a kind of discourse-level revision. Using Spanish words did not introduce grammatical errors, and replacing the Spanish words with Nahuatl words does not affect sentence-level meaning or grammar. Therefore, a teacher of Nahuatl might argue that such revisions represent an attempt to make the text more coherent or consistent, from a pragmatic point of view.

                            uan
guan oktaquien se tekuani guan quistuan ~~pero~~ quienen se tekuien
                    tatsitsiuan   nanatsin
kin noxasquien nochtin y no ~~papan~~ guan ni ~~mamas~~
(HF604) 6th grade

Revised version: [and they saw a lion and they said and how can a lion come with two children and they said to call all the fathers and mothers]. HF604 changes Spanish "pero" [but] to Nahuatl "uan" [and], Spanish "papan" [fathers] to Nahuatl "tatsitsiuan" [fathers], and Spanish "mamas" [mothers] to Nahuatl "nanatsin" [mothers].

8.9 A Comparison of Performance between the Languages

8.9. Parallel Tendencies and Correlations

At first glance, the patterns of correction and revision on the Nahuatl writing samples indicate broad parallels with those in Spanish. The average number of attempts in the two languages is similar: 479 in Spanish (average 10.6), 438 in Nahuatl (average 10.2). As in the Spanish task, it is in the rate of effectivity where a difference is apparent between younger and older students.

The effectivity rates were 32.2% for 2nd graders, 67.8% for 4th graders, and 70.6% for 6th graders, statistically significant between 2nd and 4th and between 2nd and 6th grades (figure 8.1). In general, as the correlations indicate, students more skillful in correcting and revising their Spanish texts tended to carry these skills over to their Nahuatl texts. As well, the percentage of effectivity in Nahuatl correlated positively with other measures of academic language proficiency: overall coherence in Nahuatl Writing, and MA. On the other hand, as figure 8.1 depicts, overall effectivity of correction/revision was significantly higher for Spanish than for Nahuatl. For example, while 46% (21 out of 45) of the children successfully attempted revisions at the highest level in Spanish (punctuation/capitalization+discourse level), this percentage fell to 21% in Nahuatl (9 out of 43).

8.9.2 Borrowing and Language Switch

As reported in previous chapters, the most visible index of the social disparity between IL and NL is found in children's writing: all Nahuatl compositions except that of one 6th grader contained borrowed material from Spanish, whereas (historical loanwords aside) no borrowing or codeswitching occurred in any of the children's Spanish "Deer Hunter" stories.

Faced with revising their Nahuatl first draft, students were therefore presented with a good number of opportunities to switch back to the "selected" language. Although few children elected to attend to this feature, making a quantitative analysis difficult and any interpretation entirely speculative, the distribution of these choices is interesting. For example, only among the oldest and more experienced novice writers did any effective revisions involving a switch from Spanish to Nahuatl occur. Of the 17 total attempts, all 11 effective switches were made by 6th graders. Of the few attempts at switching from Spanish to Nahuatl made by 2nd and 4th graders, none was effective. Clearly, no definitive conclusion is warranted given the small number of these interlinguistic revisions. However, this observation does coincide with previous analyses of the same children's performance on different language tasks and observed activities related to language choice: (1) As grade level increases, students begin to prefer Nahuatl over Spanish in peer conversation. (2) In contrast to younger bilinguals, in their writing, 4th and 6th graders begin to favor Nahuatl content words over Spanish borrowings. (3) The same tendencies are evident in the children's oral narratives. Sixth graders resorted to borrowing Spanish content less frequently than both 2nd and 4th graders. Appendix 2 and table A.2 summarize these tendencies, evidenced in the shifting "balance" of children's bilingual proficiency, stated language preference, and actual use toward a more equal distribution between the two languages.

Further study might explore the connection between language awareness and ability to pay attention to features related to interlinguistic influences and L1-L2 transfer of different kinds. The data from this study are also too sparse in regard to this question. Nevertheless, the few indications of a possible relationship suggest that a more closed-ended task might provide data that reveal systematic tendencies across grade level regarding awareness of differences between Spanish and Nahuatl. Among the 6th graders, for example, the 3 students with the highest scores on the MA measure all attempted "corrections" of Spanish borrowings. Again, the relatively low frequency of attempts, interesting as it may be, prevents us presently from drawing any hard conclusions from the findings as they stand.

8.10 Internal Resources and External Factors

One suggestion from the results that deserves further study is that engaging in advanced literacy tasks that require reflection need not be restricted to the language that is by custom, official policy, or expediency associated with schooling. Taken together with the results from chapter 3, the fact that the children's performance on the Nahuatl Revision/Correction task was commensurate with their performance on the same task in Spanish is consistent with prediction #2: performance on tasks of advanced literacy improves significantly across the grades in the socially disfavored extracurricular language. The findings point to untapped possibilities for promoting additive bilingual development, but, at the same time, to certain limitations. What are the factors that affect access to the CUP? (NB: Not all the factors imply limitations.)

As a proposal for further research, the potentially limiting and facilitating factors fall into two categories:

1. Factors related to how the language is processed in written form related to knowledge representations and skills that students can draw on in performance

a. Under this category, the proximity of the orthographic systems of Spanish and Nahuatl, and students' mental model of each, is a good place to begin. The adoption of an alphabetical system for Nahuatl closely following the grapheme-phoneme correspondences of Spanish naturally facilitates all writing tasks in the IL. It is this orthographic affinity, noted in previous work, that may be responsible in large part for the consistently strong performance of bilingual children from other indigenous communities on this kind of assessment (N. Francis 2004). While the orthographic factor logically facilitates access to at least lower-level writing skills, the absence of standardization might introduce a degree of confusion among young beginning writers. Competing orthographies currently in circulation represent the same phonological patterns differently, one particularly salient divergence being that between the orthography introduced in the sixteenth century by the Spanish, and attempts over the years to "reform" it (e.g., "Quetzalcoatl"—"Ketsalkouatl").

b. Given that virtually all practice in writing, in and outside of school, is in Spanish, diminished automaticity in regard to a number of sentence- and word-level skills in Nahuatl is to be expected—for example, uncertainty about spelling patterns and segmentation. Word boundaries follow different morphological patterns in Nahuatl and Spanish, which children have knowledge of (as revealed in speech), but which they only practice, with rare exceptions, in writing, in Spanish.

c. While students possess complete knowledge of the core grammatical system of Nahuatl, sentence-level grammar that serves the requirements of academic text construction is rarely, if ever, practiced. These discourse-serving aspects of grammar are practiced to varying degrees in Spanish, mainly in school. Passive exposure to these patterns is more extensive through reading and studying school texts, again only in Spanish.

d. Transfer from Spanish (e.g., borrowing and codeswitching), to partially compensate for the imbalance in #1c, might cut both ways. On the negative side, hesitations regarding the appropriate use of loanwords, as well as interference from Spanish at the phonological/orthographic level, could affect performance in writing. On the other hand, a possible facilitative effect might apply to young bilinguals whose fluid command of codeswitching strategies allows them to make use of this interlinguistic resource freely in their written expression.

2. Attitudes and motivational perspectives related to the sociolinguistic context—how the IL and the NL are portrayed to children in regard to actual language use patterns, and how they are perceived

a. Spanish being the unmarked language of literacy, perceptions about the appropriateness of Nahuatl for tasks related to writing may affect productivity.

b. The perceived utility of IL writing could conceivably be related to motivational postures. As a rule, literacy is learned through Spanish; thus, it is assumed that a speaker of Nahuatl who is literate is also bilingual. In other words, a written message in Spanish could always be read by any literate person in the indigenous communities of this region. The same cannot be assumed about a written message in Nahuatl, and monolingual speakers of the IL are likely not to be literate. This aspect of audience awareness, which would be part of school-age children's sociolinguistic knowledge, might suggest the idea that writing in Nahuatl (unlike in the past) has become superfluous from a purely instrumental/communicative point of view. The Preference for Writing/Utility subtest on the MA assessment (appendix 1) attempted to gauge this perception.

c. School language policy, overt assertions and observations, and implicit messages of the "hidden curriculum" sort about the value of literacy in Nahuatl would interact in different ways with the above factors. The available evidence points to a certain advantage for this particular cohort of bilinguals. Teachers and principals are usually bilingual themselves, lead students weekly in the Nahuatl-language version of the national anthem, and help sponsor and organize periodic cultural events that validate and honor the linguistic heritage of the community. In their personal conduct, in and outside of the classroom (e.g., with parents), they exhibit the same respect for and recognition of the IL. Teachers and principals freely comment to parents and children that the school adheres to official Secretariat of Public Education policy on bilingual education (CONAFE 2000; DGEI 1999); Cárdenas Demay and Arellano Martínez (2004) and Hamel (2003) comment on this important contextual factor.

To reiterate one last time, the limiting condition of less-than-native-speaker grammatical competence in the IL did not obtain in this population of bilingual children. Thus, explanations for the gap in performance on the Nahuatl Writing task should be sought among the above written-language-processing and motivational factors. The present findings do not favor any one set or combination over another. In the future, investigators in this particular kind of bilingual instructional setting could design more controlled experiments to specify the weight to be assigned to different limiting and facilitative conditions. For example, if it turned out that grammatical aspects of academic discourse ability do not develop as rapidly and completely in the IL as they do in the NL (factor #1c), we could ask how such an imbalance might be remediated. This question is pertinent to curriculum planning in IL developmental/additive bilingual programs, surveyed in Hinton and Hale 2001. A hypothesis to explore could be this: learning the special grammatical patterns associated with academic discourse in the disfavored vernacular is a far less formidable undertaking than learning the core grammar of an IL that was not acquired during the preschool years. For the indigenous student whose primary language is the NL, and whose exposure to the IL has been minimal, learning the

IL as a L2 in late childhood will likely come up against an entire array of limiting circumstances, some of which were alluded to earlier: motivation related to relative prestige and utility, language prejudice and discrimination, and so on. While L1 acquisition during early childhood is ensured under the circumstances of *any* normal pattern of socialization, high levels of L2 attainment even as "early" as late childhood are not. This was the factor related to intergenerational language shift that we considered in chapter 6.

In contrast, learning the "academic discourse grammar" of the IL (for "IL," feel free to substitute "any other disfavored language of a bilingual child") requires sustained experience with secondary discourses associated with the elevated genres of the oral tradition or written texts. In this case, no critical period effect or L1 blocking/filtering effect would apply, as it might to the development of core grammatical competence. The same hypotheses would apply to factors #1a (orthographic abilities), #1b (automaticity of writing skills), and #1d (metalinguistic awareness related to borrowing and codeswitching). The rationale would be that these are secondary-type language-learning objectives, subject to standard teaching methods of the kind that children can normally profit from in school. Parenthetically, this proposed distinction between one kind of knowledge and another would also be a test of the degree of modularity of the type of three-component model (L1-L2-CUP) of bilingual proficiency discussed so far. If the emergence of different kinds of grammatical competence is tied to language use in different domains, this might be revealed in the way that these kinds of knowledge of language develop in bilingual children (e.g., in the *uneven* way that they may develop under certain circumstances). The Bilingual Tripartite Parallel Architecture depicted in figure 5.2 is also a three-component model in fundamentally the same way.

In regard to factors #2a–c, the sociolinguistic conditions that may either inhibit or facilitate access to CUP, research could begin to explore how different levels of recognition and integration of an IL in school affect performance on bilingual literacy tasks. Two candidates for research sites, and a hypothetical third, might provide for a number of critical comparisons.

1. Across the state line from the Spanish-Nahuatl bilingual school where the study was carried out, the "Escuela B. Juárez" serves a population characterized by similarly high levels of both Nahuatl linguistic competence and ethnolinguistic vitality. Informal observation in recent years, however, has suggested a divergence: the beginnings of a noticeable language shift toward Spanish monolingualism. While children are not prohibited from speaking the IL in private conversation, no recognition, symbolic or otherwise, is afforded to the language. Fewer teachers are bilingual themselves, and cultural events and activities confer no status (by systematic omission) to the IL.

2. The "Escuela H. Cortés," from the same region, shares most of the characteristics of the "Escuela B. Juárez," with the exception of an explicit Spanish-only policy, including a prohibition against using the IL in school for any purpose.

3. The orientation of the hypothetical "Academia Bilingüe Nezahualcóyotl" coincides with the positive valorization of bilingualism at our present research site. In addition, a modest enrichment component to the Language Arts curriculum introduces higher-order literacy-related learning activities in the IL, aligned with the academic content objectives of the school program.

The interesting questions here are these: How robust are the psycholinguistic mechanisms of transfer and access to CUP such that they may resist greater and greater degrees of adverse social circumstance (as in cases #1 and #2)? On the other hand (in relation to the more facilitative conditions of case #3), what is the minimal threshold "time on task" in the disfavored language that may result in any measurable closing of the gap in performance between the two languages? Recall that the gap tends to widen in figures 1.2, 3.3, and 3.4. For example, would a "time on task" distribution of 10% IL – 90% NL produce any significant narrowing of the divergent curves and a closing of the gap?

8.11 Applying Different Kinds of Knowledge in Literacy Development

Previous studies that have provided evidence for a CUP and interdependence have compared bilingual children's performance on measures of academic achievement typically between two languages of "NL status," each with no shortage of written language resources at their disposal (Modiano's (1972) study of Tzotzil, Tzeltal, and Spanish, which could be taken as a precursor to this line of research, did focus on an IL/NL comparison). In addition, the variable of interest most often has been linguistic knowledge: a L1 and a L2 far short of native-level competence. Our study of Spanish-Nahuatl bilingualism held linguistic competence between L1 and "L2" constant (as it turned out), while attending to the effect of the social imbalances that separate the two languages. These imbalances, it is proposed, affect the normally free access to CUP. Given that exposure to Nahuatl literacy is so minimal, the evidence of access to CUP during the Nahuatl Writing and Revision/Correction assessments lends support of a new kind to the Interdependence Hypothesis. Access to CUP is not blocked and interdependence is not shut down. At the same time, the lag in performance on the Nahuatl writing tasks confirms that this access is not automatic. Nonnative levels of competence in the L2 (e.g., beginner levels) also restrict access. Logically, no competence in or Level 0 beginner knowledge of a L2 blocks access to CUP completely (e.g., recognizing cognates and guessing what an article from a journal in one's field of study is about don't count). Nonexposure, unavailability of written texts, exclusion from school, lack of opportunity to practice, sociolinguistic inequalities, and the like, limit access in a different way.

The idea of interactivity among the three domains—the L1 linguistic subsystem, the L2 linguistic subsystem, and the components of the largely nonlinguistic CUP—offers the beginning of an explanation. In turn, it calls our attention to several ongoing research problems that we have been pursuing since chapter 1:

• How is each domain structured internally?

• How does each domain process the information that corresponds to that domain?

• What exactly is the nature of the different interfaces and connections?

• Are some subcomponents more interactive than others (the others being more "encapsulated"—another concept in need of more precision)?

• How does the participation of the different components get integrated in actual performance in real time?

These questions, and others that may be even more interesting, may someday come to be settled empirically. In the meantime, a more manageable, more immediately applicable project related to these questions could look like this. A L2 teacher copies an article from the Internet to serve as language-learning material for her Level 1 beginner students. What should she consider in the design of a group activity in regard to these factors?

• L1-L2 transfer,

• requisite overall L2 proficiency,

• mastery of specific grammatical patterns that may be obligatory for the selected text,

• task demands related to processing mode (receptive, expressive, written, oral, etc.),

• requisite discourse abilities and advanced literacy skills,

• access to relevant content and formal (discourse-type) schemas, and

• situational constraints related to diglossia and other sociolinguistic factors.

The other areas of investigation mentioned in the review of research should also benefit from such an applied research program. For example, to which aspects of language learning is the development of metalinguistic awareness especially relevant, and to which aspects might it be less so? One application of the metalinguistic awareness discussion is to the question of focus on form, and the usefulness of positive and negative evidence, in L2 learning. Here it might be helpful to consider the discussion in parts, separating learning the L2 grammar from those aspects of L2 learning that are related to literacy. This leads us back to the principal object of the Nahuatl-Spanish study: literacy development in bilingual circumstances. The students in the study were responding to their own perceptions of structural accuracy and coherence, rather than teachers' observations and notations. Thus, the findings are neutral in regard to the debate over the efficacy of teacher-initiated corrective feedback. That students found this focus-on-form task to be appropriate and meaningful in both languages suggests that attention to this kind of literacy-learning objective might promote more advanced reflection on texts. Attending to it through the medium of both languages that bilinguals speak might even maximize the benefits. These are research questions for which empirical studies still need to be carried out.

Taking together the discussions of chapters 7 and 8, a proposal for further investigation that we are gradually converging upon is that metalinguistic knowledge about language plays an integral role in literacy-related abilities at all levels. In the initial stages of learning how to read, phonological awareness may indeed emerge as one of the fundamental components, not necessarily as a prerequisite, but as an indispensable component for continued development. In addition, as we saw in chapter 7, each subsystem of language knowledge calls upon its parallel explicit (metalevel) knowledge structure in advanced literacy tasks. Chapter 9 will look at a metalinguistic ability also related to monitoring and self-correction, applied to a different literacy skill.

9
Metalinguistic Awareness, Bilingualism, and Reading

Continuing on the theme of literacy and metalinguistic awareness, we now examine another way that the self-monitoring of text processing may be related to this connection. Chapter 8 described how children reflect on language forms when they revise and correct their own writing. This chapter looks at how self-monitoring works in reading. Again, it is error correction that offers a window into the mechanisms of this kind of attention to text patterns. Here we will focus on reading comprehension: what kinds of strategy do children make use of when they commit a reading error or "miscue" and notice the error, prompting them to self-correct? An important distinction will be made between two types of self-correction: one for which context prior to the miscue did not provide a prompt to self-correct, and one that does have the benefit of prior context.

One of the original objectives of this assessment was to propose an outline for a typology of oral-reading self-correction strategies. Conceivably, a metalinguistically aware posture toward the decoding of texts should be related in some way to effective comprehension. So the question was, what is the profile of this kind of skilled reading? Recall that the participants in these studies had been selected to take a random sample of average to above-average achievement levels among children who knew both languages of the community. Related to this selection was the need to exclude children with serious vision problems (we realized that this would be a potentially confounding factor when it came to our attention that none of the children at the school wore glasses), dyslexia, and other unidentified disabilities. Thus, our interest in the self-correction study was in describing a strategy that characterizes the best readers among the 45 children who participated in the project, themselves part of a preselected group. Note that in this study, differences in self-correction strategy (e.g., how context is utilized by the reader) are being considered as a contributing factor in sentence comprehension, not primarily as a direct indicator of how readers make use of context for lower-level decoding (word identification). Without a doubt, higher-order comprehension and lower-level decoding are related in many important ways. But since a different set of component structures and processors intervene in each case, the questions of how context affects sentence comprehension and what role it plays in word identification should be considered separately. Serious work on this distinction awaits further study.

9.1 Modular Approaches to the Study of Reading

Sadowski and Paivio's (1994) Dual Coding Theory (DCT) of reading comprehension, and Paivio's (1991) bilingual version of the DCT, offer a perspective that coincides in a number of ways with the bilingual proficiency models discussed so far. Sadowski and Paivio distinguish between verbal and nonverbal systems, which are separate but interconnected. Central to the DCT is the idea that this distinction flows from two different kinds of mental representation and from the different ways in which verbal and nonverbal information are processed. The former is organized into units that are more discrete and separable; the latter is "stored in a more continuous, integrated way" (p. 585). Extending this idea to biliteracy (as the DCT suggests), the two verbal subsystems, which share similar mental representations, maintain one kind of interaction with each other and a different kind of interaction with the less modular nonverbal (or shared conceptual) system. To the latter correspond, in addition to concepts, those literacy-related proficiencies that are not strictly language-bound, such as certain key components of discourse ability and metalinguistic awareness. So, to be sure, the awareness of language forms is a kind of knowledge that is different from the knowledge that the verbal systems are built from. One way to think of the difference is in terms of explicit versus implicit knowledge (the distinction that came up in the discussion of M. Paradis's (2004) model in chapter 6). Perfetti's (1994) componential framework and Stanovich's (2000) modular approach to the study of reading ability are other important points of reference.

In regard to our object of study, reading self-correction, another possible starting point is the concept of nonlinear processing. Online reanalysis that compels the reader to return to previously decoded text for the purpose of rectifying an error should be one aspect of academic language proficiency. The more cognitively demanding the comprehension task becomes, the more retrospective reading needs to be, not just for error correction. It happens that among the receptive language skills, it is only in reading (exceptional circumstances aside) that this kind of monitoring and retrospection can be fully exploited. As previous knowledge support diminishes, in "difficult texts," attention to language patterns (focus on form) becomes more important for comprehension (Morrison 2004). Predictable text can be read quickly, with less need or occasion for retrospection. In contrast, academic text that involves understanding new concepts and building new schemas cannot be read (meaningfully) in this "context-dependent" way. At the same time, it is important to note that only the kind of strategic monitoring we are talking about here is potentially productive. A high frequency of regression in reading, when it is symptomatic of inaccurate and inefficient decoding, should be considered separately. (For a discussion of factors that affect reading rate and fluency in L2 reading, consult Fraser 2004.)

Introductory surveys of the psycholinguistic research on language comprehension provide numerous examples of how within the overall sequential and serial progression of comprehension, processing of discourse is also nonlinear. Comprehension involves both "looking ahead" and "backtracking" (Akmajian et al. 2001; Field 2004; Scovel 1998). What is interesting about the notion of nonlinear processing is that there appear to be two kinds of nonlinearity: one category that is represented by examples that are so automatic and mandatory that they are not available to introspection, and another that can be subject to attention and monitoring. As noted in the earlier discussion of the computational procedures for implicit competence and explicit knowledge, nonlinear processes internal to the domain of the implicit system cannot be monitored. In contrast, the product of these procedures, in comprehension and production, should be accessible to monitoring, to one degree or another.

Thus, the highly modular types of nonlinearity that are impervious to introspection can be contrasted to the accessible (to awareness) kind, of which we can in turn distinguish two subcategories:

1. language processing that is accessible but normally effected without attention, and

2. comprehension strategies that require, or greatly benefit from, deliberate reflection.

We could propose that the "higher" the level, the greater the participation of top-down strategies, drawing more and more from the nonlinguistic domains. Conversely, the "lower" the level, the more modular and encapsulated nonlinear processing should be. From this point of view, examining the role of metalinguistic awareness in reading development belongs to subcategory #2: a kind of nonlinear approach to texts as an aspect of comprehension strategy. This approach to reading will reveal itself more prominently when texts present some kind of difficulty in decoding, word identification, or understanding. It is this type of decoding, which requires retrospection, that showed itself to be most interesting in the analysis of the students' oral-reading miscues and self-corrections.

In fluent, proficient reading, the high degree of interactivity among the subsystems obscures their autonomy. By contrast, when decoding is inefficient, unskilled, or dysfunctional to some degree, when comprehension fails, the relationship between compartmentalization and interactivity is unveiled. As a result of the strain on text processing, readers tend to commit miscues more frequently, evidencing a greater or lesser breakdown in the interaction of the different subsystems. Most readers are familiar with the phenomenon of decoding (on some level) all the words of a long passage of text, and realizing upon reflection that the cognitive domain of real-world knowledge has been completely or partially disengaged. Processing at levels of syntax and below apparently must have taken place, but in such a manner as to be detached from the intervention of meaning construction. Looking back to figure 5.2, we might say that the interface components that connect Conceptual Structure to the linguistic modules were not activated, were temporarily out of service, or were diverted toward some other cognitive activity (something in the text itself may even have triggered the diversion). In the case of language production, Garrett (2007) gives examples of this kind of temporary "disconnect" between semantics and the other components of grammar in the analysis of speech errors.

Morphosyntactic or phonological processing apart (i.e., disjoined) from the semantic subsystem is commonly observed in readers' miscues, and is at least implicitly recognized in studies based on oral miscue analysis (Y. Goodman 1995; Y. Goodman and Goodman 1994). This was the methodological approach assumed in the assessment discussed here. The objective was to describe two types of monitoring of these miscues, with one suggesting a greater degree of nonlinear strategy than the other. To repeat, retrospection and a predisposition toward integrating constituents and propositions should be an aspect of advanced comprehension strategies, especially for the kinds of reading task that are decontextualized. By their very nature, these strategies should require higher levels of metalinguistic awareness. (Recall the discussion in chapters 7 and 8 on the relationship between levels of context-embeddedness of the different metalinguistic awareness tasks and performance on measures of literacy (also appendix 1): the less context-embedded they are, the more closely they are related to literacy.)

9.2 A Study of Focus on Form in Reading

A pilot study at the same bilingual school examined the reading self-correction patterns of 6 students. Two contrasting profiles emerged:

1. The three students (dubbed the "low-language-awareness" readers) who received the three lowest scores among the 4th and 6th graders on the Metalinguistic Awareness test described in chapter 8, and
2. Three students from the same classes (the "high-language-awareness" readers) who scored in the upper 25%.

In an analysis of successful attempts at self-correction (defined as repair attempts that did not result in another miscue), three categories emerged from coding the first 30 oral reading miscues committed by each reader:

1. *Type-A*: self-corrections resulting from a possible retrospection. The subsequent context of the passage following the miscue provides the cue to correct. At the sentence level, the miscue forms part of a sentence pattern that is syntactically and semantically compatible with the entire fragment immediately preceding the miscue.
2. *Type-B*: self-corrections that are potentially triggered at the point of the miscue. The previous context (a syntactic pattern and/or semantic constraint that turns out to be incompatible with the miscue), inadmissible word-level pattern, or resulting nonword provides a sufficient cue to self-correct.
3. *Type-C*: "unnecessary" self-correcting of a dialect miscue, transfer of a L1 phonological feature, or other miscue completely compatible with sentence- and text-level context.

The idea that reading comprehension is related to metalinguistic ability in some way led the researchers to ask what aspect of reading behavior could be shown to be associated with a reflective posture toward language. Oral reading appeared to offer a useful research site, and we hoped that focusing on readers' self-corrections would provide a measure of reflection and monitoring. As Y. Goodman, Watson, and Burke (1987) suggest, responses to texts that are highly transparent and easy to decode obscure the differences in strategy between readers of different proficiency levels. When texts are easy (readers have complete access to background knowledge, and decoding is cognitively undemanding), reading calls on metacognitive skills to a lesser degree. On the other hand, when texts are sufficiently difficult, readers begin to commit more miscues, and they resort to other means (some more effective than others) to parse and reparse sentences. One hypothesis to consider could be this: different kinds of repair attempt that are applied to more difficult passages might help differentiate among degrees of proficiency in reading.

Among the high-language-awareness readers, we observed a good number of type-A self-corrections. A miscue that prompts a type-A self-correction creates an incompatible sequence with the subsequent fragment. On occasion, the incompatibility is not as straightforward as it might first appear. Consider these two self-corrections, for example:

Sus guardianes eran dos serpientes: una tenía dos cuernos y
otro^(self-corrected)
un dibujo blanco en forma de cruz en la frente: era Masakoatl; la otra era Tlilkoatl.
[Their guardians were two snakes: one had two horns and a white design in the form of a cross on its forehead: (it) was Masakoatl, the other was Tlilkoatl.]
(ML411) 4th grade
Ellos le respondieron que no podían hablar con él porque era
el^(self-corrected)
del mundo de arriba y ellos del corazón del mundo.

[They responded that they couldn't speak to him because (he) was from the world of above and they (were) from the heart of the world.]
(JA405) 4th grade

The initial fragment of the passage read by ML411, including the miscue "otro" [other] for "un" [a], is grammatically acceptable ("Their guardians were two snakes: one had two horns and [the] *other*. ..."). The second fragment is grammatical as well ("... *other* white design in the form of a cross on the forehead"). Only when one attempts to combine the fragments does the entire sequence show itself to be malformed, something that ML411 perhaps detected upon attempting to integrate "otro dibujo blanco" with the initial sequence. The self-correction by JA405 involves a similar operation: "porque era *el (the substitution miscue)* mundo de arriba" [because (he) was *the* world of above], by itself, is syntactically well-formed. Here, perhaps the cue to reconstruct the phrase was semantic. We could say that readers who are indeed monitoring their own text processing are compelled to return to the miscue or to the beginning of the phrase.

In cases where the disconfirming context follows the miscue immediately—as in the passage read by PA201, "She got very angry ..." (original text) → "She got *ready to* angry ..."—both the miscue itself and the subsequent context cue may be an integral part of the same visual fixation. Thus, no regression would be materially observable.

    a^(self-corrected)

Se puso muy enojada y empezó a batir las alas y quejarse como un guajolote.
[(She) got very angry and started to flap her wings and cry out like a turkey.]
(PA201) 2nd grade

In contrast, the low-language-awareness readers made few type-A self-corrections (2 out of 10). The typical response was that the reader did not return to a miscue after subsequent context should have signaled either that the sentence was not well-formed or that something didn't make sense. The following examples are characteristic of an almost exclusively linear "zero-monitoring" mode (Hutchinson et al. (2004, 189–192) report a similar finding). Opportunities are neglected to correct even the more "visible" type-B miscues; all the substitutions (except "el" [the]) are phonologically or morphologically admissible nonwords:

    brillado   *flofuera el*
Los cuernos le brillaban como si fueran   de

crista   *sabro*
cristal. Comenzó a correr por el sendero
(CG409) 4th grade

Original text: [The horns shined as if (they) were of glass. (He) began to run down the path.]

Hypothetically, type-A self-corrections reflect a broader-based strategy that is sensitive to both syntactic patterns and meaning relationships; moreover, it is sensitive to these constraints both before the miscue and after. Type-B self-corrections also exploit meaning and form (including word-level cues related to morphological and phonological patterns) but are cued at the point of the miscue itself. To repeat, *both* type-A and type-B self-corrections favor comprehension. For example, RG415 proceeds as follows, effecting two type-B self-corrections:

    andas$^{(self\text{-}corrected)}$ *tierras*$^{(self\text{-}corrected)}$
Decidió andar por todos lados en la tierra.
(RG415) 4th grade
Original text: [(He) decided to walk all over on the Earth.]

For substitution miscues "andas" [(you) walk] and "tierras" [lands], previous context ("Decidió" [(He) decided], "en la" [on the]) is sufficient to self-correct immediately.

Notably, the number of readers who self-corrected "high-quality" miscues (Y. Goodman, Watson, and Burke 1987, 60–74), type-C, was both low and unrelated to grade level or general reading proficiency, a finding we will return to in the following sections.

In sum, the appearance of a relationship between metalinguistic awareness and proficient reading strategies suggested the following informal hypothesis for the next phase of this assessment: a more deliberate approach to comprehension—the ability to mentally step back from "what words say" and contemplate "how words are used"—should be evidenced in an approach to the reading task that is less "linear." It is as if the less proficient (less reflective) reader applies a strategy based on an expectation that meaning will unfold in a completely serial, word-by-word fashion. The working assumption here is that language comprehension of the highly context-embedded and cognitively undemanding variety requires less nonlinear-type processing than comprehension of the more context-reduced variety. The latter, although it is usually associated with comprehension abilities in reading, also characterizes academic-type oral discourse (Cummins 2007). Writing simply puts at the disposal of the listener/reader the ideal (sometimes indispensable) tool for reckoning with discourse that requires both looking ahead and recuperating previous text passages.

9.3 The Development of a Reflective Posture toward Reading Comprehension

The typology of self-corrections proposed from the results of the pilot study was applied to the entire group of 2nd, 4th, and 6th graders, 45 students in all. For each reader, the total number of successful self-corrections effected within the first 30 miscues was tabulated, so as not to inflate the ratings of the most proficient readers.[1] Self-corrections were then categorized as type-A, -B, or -C.

As is typical of oral-reading miscue studies, the data made available from performance is of a strictly naturalistic-observational nature, with all the limitations that this method implies. The findings to be reported in the self-correction phase of the study call attention to broad tendencies across grade levels and to descriptive correlations. Thus, the objectives of the analysis are modest, and discussion of the findings will emphasize the provisional nature of the interpretations of the data. We will first briefly review the results of the previous language and literacy assessments, and then proceed to analyze the self-corrections in Spanish reading. The parallel assessment in Nahuatl is projected for future study.

9.3.1 Performance on the Metalinguistic Awareness Tasks

From the comparisons examined in chapter 8, what appears to be another fruitful avenue of research is the correlation between degrees of decontextualization in the MetalinguisticAwareness tasks and literacy abilities—in particular, the most advanced literacy skills. Recall from appendix 1 that the relatively context-embedded Metalinguistic Awareness subtests, Language Naming and Written Message Identification, did not correlate with Reading and Writing performance, in either language. That the closest relationship was found between the Metalinguistic Awareness assessment, overall, and written composition should not be surprising either (if confirming research in fact bears this out—review results from chapter 8). In writing, since greater attention appears to be devoted to language patterns, high levels of both proficiency in the language itself and metalinguistic awareness would seem to contribute strongly to skilled performance in the composing tasks that were presented to the students.

Nevertheless, receptive tasks such as reading comprehension should also be related to the ability to reflect upon and to mentally manipulate language, to shift attention to patterns and forms. Metalinguistic development related to reading encompasses awareness of linguistic and discourse patterns at all levels from "metaphonological" to "metapragmatic" (Gombert 1992). Perhaps even, context-embeddedness is more important than factors related to the receptive-expressive distinction, as suggested above. For example, a highly decontextualized *reading* comprehension activity (studying a textbook) might depend on metalinguistic abilities to a greater degree than a highly context-embedded and interactive *writing* task.

9.3.2 Self-Correction Strategies

A total of 158 oral-reading repairs were tabulated and coded as type-A, -B, or -C. As figure 9.1 shows, the average number of effective self-corrections (total) appears

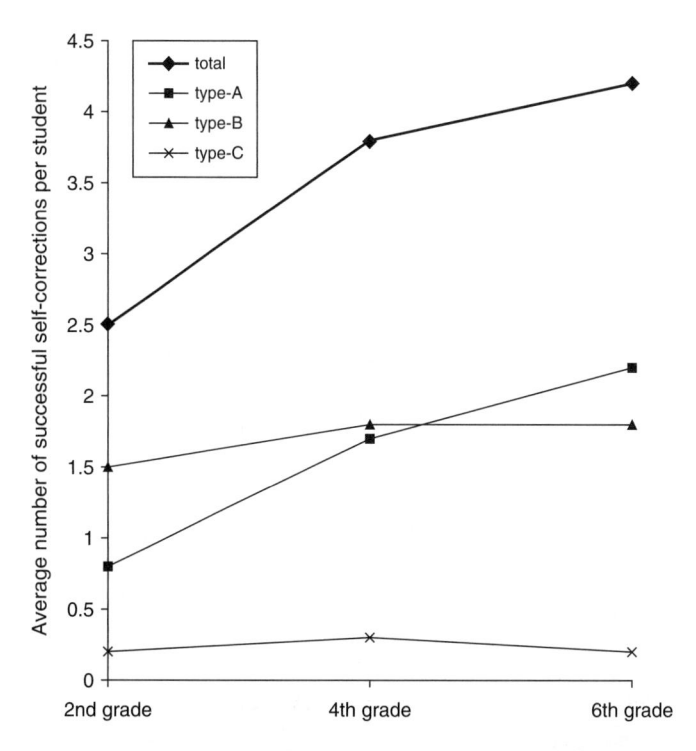

1. *Type-A*: Self-corrections resulting from a possible retrospection. The subsequent context of the passage following the miscue provides the cue to correct. At the sentence level, the miscue forms part of a structure that is syntactically and semantically compatible with the entire fragment immediately preceding the miscue.
2. *Type-B*: The previous context (a syntactic pattern and/or semantic constraint that turns out to be incompatible with the miscue), inadmissible word-level pattern, or resulting nonword provides a sufficient cue to self-correct.
3. *Type-C*: "Unnecessary" self-correcting of a dialect miscue, transfer of a L1 phonological feature, or other miscue completely compatible with sentence- and text-level context.

Figure 9.1
Average number of successful self-corrections per student effected upon the first 30 miscues: total number of self-corrections, type-A, -B, and -C

to increase with grade level, as might be expected, from 2.5 in 2nd grade to 4.1 in 6th grade. However, the difference falls short of being significant. Note that type-B self-corrections (cued by prior context) unambiguously show no ascending tendency across the grade levels. Only the frequency of type-A self-corrections increases significantly among the more mature readers, providing support for the suggestion that emerged from the pilot study. Older, more experienced readers, who may also approach the reading task in a more reflective way, will take advantage of type-A opportunities more often. That is, they may be more sensitive to disconfirming cues that follow the miscue than beginners. While 2nd graders as a group successfully attempted 12 type-A self-corrections, 6th graders did so on 33 occasions. Readers who are attentive to type-A opportunities monitor grammar for acceptability and semantic patterns for meaning and coherence, with this level of monitoring continuing to be active before *and* after miscues. Correlations calculated for type-A and type-B self-corrections with other indices lend support to this distinction. Type-B did not correlate at a significant level with any of the principal measures of academic language proficiency. Type-A correlated positively (albeit moderately) with all: Reading, Completeness of Retelling, Writing, Oral Narrative, and Metalinguistic Awareness.

9.4 One Way in Which Children Learn to Use Context Strategically

In this section, we will consider some tentative implications of the findings, particularly in reference to the special status proposed for self-corrections cued after the reading error (type-A). Turning first to children's reading self-corrections overall (on figure 9.1, the curve marked "total"), it appears that monitoring and repairing in general are components of readers' decoding/comprehension strategies from the beginning—an early-developing aspect of proficient reading. The antecedents of metacognition applied to reading can be traced to the early development of abilities related to discourse comprehension (S. J. Samuels et al. 2005). Total successful attempts did not differ significantly between 2nd and 6th grade, and only 2 students (out of 45) were observed to abstain throughout from correcting their miscues. As a universal predisposition toward forming grammatical sentences and meaningful propositions in reading, self-correction probably emerges spontaneously and intuitively, without the aid of any kind of direct instruction. In their study of children's speech repairs, Karmiloff-Smith et al. (1993) point to a related distinction between early-developing reflection (the access that native speakers have to linguistic intuitions) and higher levels of reflection, which involve attempts at metalinguistic explanation. Consider also Comeau, Genesee, and Mendelson's (2007) interesting study of 2;7- to 3;7-year-old bilingual children's repairs that required a language switch, giving us a glimpse into key aspects of an early-developing metalinguistic awareness related to knowledge of two languages.

In any case, *both* type-A and type-B repairs form part of readers' inventories of productive and necessary monitoring strategies. Again, no implication follows from these findings that because type-B did not correlate with any other index of literacy development, this type of self-correction is unrelated to proficient reading. Perhaps another study could be designed with a different set of measures (e.g., indices that might be more sensitive to the lower, more incipient levels of development) that would reveal repairs signaled prior to the miscue to be predictive of proficient reading as well. Rather, type-A, reflecting a more "context-sensitive" and deliberate decoding strategy, might turn out to be the better predictor of proficient reading. When readers are more attentive to type-A opportunities (the disconfirming context cue does not present itself until after the miscue), they appear to be monitoring sentence grammar and meaning in a more active way. It is as if their "monitor" were instructing them to be conscious of applying a particular strategy: "The entire sentence, not just a fragment of it, should be grammatically well-formed and interpretable." Readers who can be described as metalinguistically aware have developed strategies that include (1) reliable decoding, (2) confirming/disconfirming, (3) deliberately continuing to read or regressing, and (4) reflecting and integrating. These strategies, unlike the less reflective approach to text, may not emerge spontaneously and intuitively. Herein, perhaps, lies a difference between readers who are able to monitor type-B opportunities, but still may not have advanced to a more nonlinear approach to texts, and those who are able to exploit both types of repair opportunity.

This proposed distinction is consistent with trends in the development of metalinguistic awareness in children. Earlier, incipient forms of this awareness emerge in the course of everyday conversational language use and first exposure to highly context-embedded written messages. On the other hand, fully developed awareness of language and reflective engagement of oral and written discourse are not expected to follow a universal and invariable course of development in all children. This interpretation certainly must be qualified, given the descriptive nature of the data, which simply indicated an overall tendency for more proficient readers to engage in a broader array of self-correction strategies. But it does coincide with other distinctions that also revolve around the participation of metalinguistic awareness. Recall the proposal for distinguishing between Narrative One and Narrative Two (chapter 7), and the tentative conclusion that certain localized self-corrections are "early-developing" while others are "later-developing" (chapter 8).

This brings us to another aspect of monitoring and reflective reading: selective attention. Recall that type-C repairs occur when the reader self-corrects a mispronunciation or other miscue that would not have affected meaning or grammar. Many students ignore this type of miscue, passing over L1 phonological transfer and dialect features, for example. Judiciously directing attention exclusively toward miscues that generate inadmissible or meaning-changing sequences may form part of our hypothetical proficient reader's profile. On the other hand, many L1 transfer miscues interfere with comprehension, especially at beginner L2 proficiency levels. Thus, enhanced awareness about how certain aspects of L1-L2 transfer may interfere, and how other aspects may not, might help readers to be more selective and strategic. This type of awareness should help bilingual readers differentiate more successfully between the two kinds of L1 transfer miscue: (1) mispronunciations that, in effect, do result in change of meaning, and (2) features related to cross-linguistic influence that do not alter text meaning.

As a final example, note the parallels between 6th graders JL612 and LM605 in regard to how miscues are self-corrected selectively and strategically. First, JL612:

Tenía por esposa a una mujer ya anciana, de cabellos

      canosos^(not self-corrected)

largos y canos a la que llamaban Tlalocan Nana.

   grandes^(self-corrected)   *cuerpos*^(not self-corrected)
Sus guardianes eran dos serpientes: una tenía dos cuernos
y un dibujo blanco en forma de cruz en la frente.
(JL612) 6th grade

[(He) had as a wife a woman that was already old, of long white hair, who was called Tlalocan Nana.

Their guardians were two snakes: one had two horns and a white design in the form of a cross on its forehead.]

"Sus *grandes* eran dos serpientes," while not strictly ungrammatical (the phrase can be understood as "His *big ones* were two snakes"), is not compatible, semantically, with subsequent context. Most selectively attentive readers here would have expected a noun to precede or follow the adjective miscue "grandes" [big] instead of the immediately following verb "eran" [were], which in this case may have signaled the miscue. "Canosos" is synonymous with "canos," ["white" (haired)], and mythical serpents can sport two bodies ("cuerpos") as easily as they can grow horns ("cuernos"). Neither of these type-C miscues is corrected.

Sixth grader LM605 ignores all of her "dialect miscues" (recall this feature from chapter 7 in the analysis of children's spelling):

"gubernaba" for "gobernaba" [was governing]
"juven" for "joven" [young man]

Chamaco cabeza "dora" for "dura" [hard-headed boy]
However, she is attentive to the substitution of "a" for "o" in
    mucha^(self-corrected)
ponerse mucho maíz

because in this case the miscue results in a lack of grammatical concordance ("maíz" is masculine in "mucho maíz" [lots of corn]). Here again, subsequent context prompts nonlinear processing, related in this example to gender marking that is required in one of LM605's languages (Spanish) but not the other (Nahuatl). Perhaps not coincidentally, this student is the 6th grader with the highest Metalinguistic Awareness score and the third-highest overall rating for reading comprehension. Note again, though, that even beginner and nonproficient readers apparently devote little attention to this class of miscue.

This leads us to an alternative interpretation of the importance of type-C self-corrections and the miscues that might prompt them (deviations that affect neither meaning nor syntactic well-formedness). The findings, in fact, indicate the need to reevaluate the incidence of this class of miscue in skilled and unskilled readers. Are these "high-quality" miscues more, less, or equally frequent among skilled readers? Do skilled readers, in fact, tend to self-correct them less frequently? For example, included among the measures in an earlier assessment of reading ability was an evaluation of the syntactic and semantic compatibility of each of the first 30 miscues committed. Predictably, degrees of compatibility correlated with other measures (Completeness of Retelling and a Cloze test). However, from simple inspection it was evident that the readers with the highest comprehension scores committed, quantitatively, fewer miscues, and vice versa, irrespective of miscue type. In other words, skilled readers tend to decode more accurately, across the board.

In teacher-training programs, the distinction between "high-quality" and "low-quality" miscue is a useful way of helping teachers distinguish between different kinds of error or mistake. In particular, in remedial work with young beginning readers who still are not skilled in decoding, and whose miscue frequency is high, it is recommended that teachers call attention to these miscues selectively. For example, when a reader completes a malformed sentence occasioned by an uncorrected substitution miscue, the teacher may provide a prompt to get the reader to reflect on what the sentence meant, or whether or not it "sounded right." Such direct correction prompts cannot be applied to all miscues, the "high-quality" miscues being good candidates for nonintervention; and no sane remediation program would direct teachers to prompt readers to correct simple type-C dialect miscues that do not affect sentence comprehension. Labov and Baker (2010) discuss relevant findings from a study that used an approach similar to the one used in the study of reading miscues reported on here.

However, for research purposes, different considerations may come into play. A more streamlined assessment of miscues, dispensing with deep analyses of each individual deviation from the printed text, may result in measures that are just as useful. Qualitative methods suffer from their own deficiencies, one of which our initial analysis may have fallen prey to as well: attributing too much importance to the interesting observation regarding the frequency of type-C self-corrections. The resistance to recognizing the usefulness of quantitative methods on the part of many practitioners, who insist on miscue-analysis-type procedures for all literacy assessment, often stems from deeply ingrained methodological prejudices. But this is a topic for another book. (Further discussion of alternative assessment procedures based on samples of oral reading and cloze-type measures can be found in Fuchs, Fuchs, and Hosp 2001 and H. Wiley and Deno 2005.) Objective comparisons that weigh the relative merits of different research tools will help investigators design more accurate measures, one of the basic requirements of valid interpretation. But despite the limitations of oral-miscue analysis, the examination of self-correction strategies offers promising new directions for the study of decoding strategies. Repairs of all types and varieties provide a "natural unit of metalinguistic exploration" (Karmiloff-Smith et al. 1993).

In all of this, I don't want to make the claim that metalinguistic awareness is a prerequisite for beginning to develop effective comprehension abilities or that a one-way causal relationship is involved here. Metalinguistic awareness, quite a mixed bag itself, is best viewed as one component of a broader complex of secondary discourse abilities and information-processing mechanisms. Into this confederation of modules and interfaces the ability to strategically call upon general world knowledge intervenes, altogether resulting in what experienced teachers recognize as proficient reading.

9.5 Future Research on Literacy Learning, Metalinguistic Awareness, and Bilingualism

The last two sections indirectly posed questions about the effectiveness of focus on form in language instruction, centered in this case on sentence-level reading strategies, and how metalinguistic awareness and bilingualism may be related. Regarding the first question, it is worth noting, one last time, the limitations of the findings so far. Settling the debates on instructional applications will require large-scale experimental designs. Regarding the second question, recall that a more complete discussion was left pending in chapter 8. Some speculation on these topics is presented here as part of a proposal for future research.

Regarding the effectiveness of form-focused instruction, a wider agreement perhaps exists on the necessity of developing metalinguistic abilities at the text/

discourse level and in relation to the higher-order comprehension skills (Carrell, Gajdusek, and Wise 1998; Valdez Pierce 2001). At the discourse level, "rudimentary strategies" (Garner 1992) emerge in early childhood, without explicit tutoring (e.g., the ability to use prediction on the basis of experience with basic narrative genres). But more analytical and heterogeneous strategies (required for comprehending less uniform and less predictable nonnarrative texts) seem more dependent on direct instruction of some kind. What the research findings suggest, tentatively, is that pedagogical approaches that promote control of processing and monitoring can be applied effectively at the sentence level as well. That is, teaching methods that favor the development of a kind of metalinguistically aware decoding, including the more advanced levels of phonological awareness tied to knowledge of orthography (Bialystok 2006), could be an effective component of literacy instruction.

Part of becoming literate is learning to be aware of the special features of writing that afford certain advantages in language processing (which may imply limitations in other kinds of language use). These features are different in some critical respects (not all) from features of oral discourse, which offer the speaker/listener a different set of advantages and limitations. Looking at the problem from this point of view, the development of a kind of *metapragmatics of literacy* may help children to maximize modality-specific resources that they can exploit in reading and writing. Olson (1994) discusses at length the information-processing innovation that represents language visually, invented and/or perfected in all technologically advanced cultures. The resource of deliberate and systematic reflection on language patterns, which is not as productive in oral discourse, and which does not seem to emerge spontaneously and uniformly among all children, has been shown to be an ideal candidate for direct instruction—for example, in remedial programs modeled after Reading Recovery (Clay 1993; Hiebert 1994). Such approaches based on active monitoring have been shown to be effective in reading instruction for some time now. From this point of view, the ability to perform operations on language itself appears to be an essential component of literacy development. This was one of the arguments advanced in chapter 7; in chapter 6, it was suggested that this ability might be an important component of L2 learning as well. In regard to learning how to read and write, Wells (1987, 110) alludes to broader objectives in the development of metalinguistic awareness:

At each of the preceding levels . . . , the concern is with literacy as a mode of communication. However, to focus only on the interpersonal communicative functions of literacy is to fail to recognize the changes that reading and writing can make in the mental lives of individuals and, by extension, of the societies to which those individuals belong. To be literate, according to this . . . perspective, is to have available ways of acting upon and transforming knowledge and experience that are, in general, unavailable to those who have never learned to read and write. From the curricular point of view, literate behavior is seen as simultaneously both a mode of language use and a mode of thinking, and the attitudes to be encouraged are those of creativity, exploration, and critical evaluation.

Since the participants in the Nahuatl-Spanish study were bilingual, the relationship between L2 learning and metalinguistic development comes up again. On this point, L2 literacy may turn out to be an especially informative object of study for future research. Let us conclude this section with some further thoughts on this widely noted relationship, picking up from where we left off in chapter 8.

Perhaps in reaction to early theories that ascribed deficits to child bilingualism, studies began to suggest not only that the deficit theories were incorrect, but that bilingualism might even accelerate metacognitive development. (C. Baker (2006) surveys the evolution of the research, and Genesee (2002) reviews important related issues.) Some evidence even pointed to the possibility that bilingual children enjoy at least a potential advantage in this area. The bilingual child's constant comparing and contrasting of the L1 and L2 grammars, and the cognitive "imbalance" related to the struggle to comprehend texts with less than complete linguistic knowledge (Bialystok 1991), have been proposed as factors that might foster the development of a more analytical stance toward language.

Another possibility would be that it is specifically biliteracy (using two languages in cognitively demanding reading and writing tasks) that facilitates the development of metalinguistic awareness. Without taking up the broader debate on orality and writing (Jahandarie 1999), we might speculate that the written modality offers greater opportunities for bilinguals to analyze and monitor language patterns: bilingual children have two languages in which to carry out such analysis and monitoring, which involve contrasts and comparisons that don't come up in monolingual literacy and that are difficult to direct awareness toward in oral discourse. In the case of bilingual and L2 readers, who have this kind of special opportunity at their disposal, the connection between bilingualism and metalinguistic awareness deserves further study. Regarding our miscue correction study, a comprehensive analysis with a more controlled experimental design, involving a greater number of self-corrections, might explore this link more thoroughly. For example, for different cohorts, type-A and type-B self-corrections could be compared with their respective sets of missed opportunities. Metalinguistic awareness related to L2 learning and bilingualism could represent a factor around which other academic, literacy-related language proficiencies might cluster as well.

But clearly, bilingualism is not a necessary condition for developing advanced levels of metalinguistic awareness, and it would be difficult to demonstrate that across the board bilinguals achieve superior levels as compared to monolinguals. Even more difficult would be to show that bilingual children enjoy inherent or unique advantages in cognitive development. In fact, bilingualism per se may turn out to be related to metalinguistic awareness only indirectly. Rather, it has been suggested that metalinguistic development may be fostered in specific *learning* situations in which L2 learners apply higher-order cognitive strategies to the tasks of

- comparing and contrasting grammatical features of L1 and L2,
- focusing attention on their own errors and noticing differences between native-speakers' speech and their own interlanguage patterns,
- "negotiating meaning" with native speakers and more advanced L2 learners, and
- learning to apply strategies of selective attention in reading and writing.

L2 reading, in some circumstances, might call greater attention to certain forms.

These and other similar "nonprimary" language-learning strategies have been proposed as necessary components of optimal L2 development (R. Ellis 2005; Gass and Mackey 2006; Pica and Washburn 2002; Schachter 1998; Schmidt 2001). Thus, perhaps, only certain aspects of bilingualism may be relevant to the question at hand (Le Pichon Vorstman et al. 2009), such as *L2 learning* that involves the above cognitive demands and the use of two languages for higher-order problem-solving tasks.

Now, it should be apparent that monolingual children might also be fortunate enough to be exposed to cognitively challenging language use. Each of the above points has its counterpart in reflective use of language involving early literacy experiences, negotiation of meaning with more mature speakers, and analyzing, comparing, and contrasting patterns related to different genres, all within the confines of a monolingual speech community. In L1 reading, attention needs to be shifted from one level to another, and monolingual readers and writers also selectively attend to linguistic forms. But then, all things being equal, certain aspects of using two languages may also be among the factors that contribute to higher-order cognitive development, alongside and in combination with other kinds of higher-order language use. Among these one might include literacy, rich immersion in an oral tradition, and cultural practices that challenge young children's language abilities (like solving very hard riddles). The discussion among researchers on this question has in fact taken a turn toward considering new and interesting aspects (and some that are old and still interesting) of the relationship between bilingualism and metacognition, and more broadly between language and thought.

9.6 Does the Use of Context Contradict Modularity in Reading?

To conclude this chapter properly, an important clarification is in order on the use of methods borrowed from miscue analysis in the evaluation of the bilingual students' self-corrections. Associated as our choice of method is with the whole-language outlook on literacy learning, one might infer that it flows from a top-down,[2] or holistic, perspective on the role of context in skilled reading. According to strong versions of this perspective, reading ability depends less on precision in decoding than on prediction and "sampling" (a kind of "guessing" strategy constrained by cueing systems based on the subsystems of language). That is, what characterizes the strategy of good readers is less reliance on "visual information" and more on top-down interpretation and the use of previous knowledge. Effective self-correction conceivably would then shift resources away from decoding and toward greater reliance on context. For a comprehensive exposition of different whole-language approaches to L2 and bilingual literacy, not all of which are strong versions, see Carrasquillo 1993; Hudelson 1994; Krashen 2002; and Hadaway, Vardell, and Young 2002.

On the contrary, though, a closer examination of self-correction strategies that children apply to oral-reading miscues (including the ones examined in this chapter) does not support the holistic, top-down, context-dependent view of reading. Reflecting on the successful self-corrections observed among readers in the Mexican study could just as easily lead one to conclude that efficient and precise processing of orthographic information is the foundation (a bottom-up foundation) for effective monitoring and sentence comprehension. Of course, another series of studies would be required to marshal supporting evidence for this claim. Such studies would, for example, control for factors that we did not attend to in our naturalistic assessment of oral-reading miscues.

Before we speculate on the problems that the readers in this study encountered when they were faced with the task of self-correction, note that it is important not to confuse the two related but different senses of the term "context": previous background knowledge ("nonvisual information") and textual context (e.g., at the sentence level). So far, I have been using the term in both senses without signaling the difference. The two get confounded somewhat when we consider "previous knowledge just acquired" in an earlier passage of the text being read; but for now, let us work with the two clearly contrasting senses. Importantly, "sentence-level context" includes both semantic and syntactic constraints. With respect to making a type-B self-correction (cued by the preceding segment), it would be previous context within the sentence in which the miscue occurs that provides the most relevant information. Secondarily, semantic, discourse-level information in preceding sentences could be useful. Previous background knowledge (extratextual) might also constrain decoding to some extent, but again, the most useful information is to be found in the immediate sentence-level context and in the orthographic information of the target word itself.

In line with a componential perspective on decoding and comprehension, Perfetti (1994) points out that discourse context (and previous knowledge) provides the wrong kind of data for fast and reliable word identification. For word identification to be rapid and accurate, the components of reading ability that are most useful are the ones specialized for linking phonological forms to orthographic patterns. Efficient and effective self-correction strategies utilize contextual information to monitor grammatical form and meaning, but if word identification is slow and inaccurate, these strategies tend to be reduced to unreliable guessing. So for type-B self-correction, the reader needs to apply one strategy above all others: accurately decoding the pre-miscue sequence and refocusing attention reliably on the "visual information" in the misread word. Even one uncorrected error in the pre-miscue sequence can short-circuit any relevant support from previous sentence-level context. And even a well-formed pre-miscue sequence cannot compensate very well for inconsistent mapping between orthography and phonology in word identification. In fact, depending on the circumstances, the pre-miscue sentence-level context could turn out to be less useful than one might assume. This alternative hypothesis could be a candidate for testing in future studies.

Turning to type-A self-correction (cued by subsequent context), how does the reader recover from grammatically incompatible miscues or miscues that alter text meaning? Here, readers who are overly dependent on context clues, or who utilize context in the wrong way because their graphophonic skills are deficient, run into trouble. The miscue, which is now part of a well-formed sequence, is providing contextual information that potentially leads the (overly) context-dependent reader down the wrong path. Successful recovery from this type of error requires a kind of suspension of the influence of context (which is now providing misinformation). Self-correction now, as the alternative hypothesis claims, would benefit from renewed attention to decoding at the word level that brings the break in grammar pattern or the anomalous semantic relation up to awareness, without undue delay.

Experienced remedial-reading teachers are familiar with the type-A phenomenon. If the reader is able to "suppress" the effect of the misleading context (the miscue now embedded in a well-formed initial sentence fragment) and refocus attention on bottom-up processing, recovery from the error is often spontaneous, without need for any external corrective feedback. On the other hand, if the error is taken as good coin and integrated into the new sentence pattern that is now being *reconstructed* (all still grammatically well-formed), new errors can build upon old. From this perspective, a truly interactive model of reading shows how context cuts both ways. A suggestive analogy is the seemingly contradictory double effect of background knowledge in discourse comprehension that was mentioned in chapter 7. The construction of meaning is impossible without it; but overdependence leads to a different kind of breakdown. Gernsbacher and Foertsch (1999) discuss a related phenomenon in describing comprehension difficulty: unskilled readers tend to shift prematurely to new substructures. Here, an overreliance on prospective strategies short-circuits retrospection and the integration of new propositions into current substructures when this is still necessary. In other words, "shifting" too frequently or inconsistently disrupts the construction of coherent constituent "subpatterns" of discourse.

Interestingly, research evidence suggests that the *word recognition* skills of proficient readers are not characterized by a greater reliance on context than those of poor readers. In their review of the literature, Stanovich and Stanovich (1999) emphasize that to understand the results from studies on the use of context, it is important to be clear about which level of processing is being considered. Studies have shown that proficient readers are in fact better able to utilize contextual information to facilitate *comprehension*, an ability related to postlexical identification processes of integration and interpretation. This is the sense in which we may want to refer to the most proficient readers in the Mexican study as applying strategies that are more "context-sensitive" in their self-corrections. Sensitivity to context of this kind would also imply the application of decoding strategies that are more "deliberate," for more effective recovery from miscues that should be self-corrected. Thus, the findings from this self-correction study cannot be generalized to the word recognition level, to lexical access itself. "Efficient word-recognition has the properties of autonomous, or modular, processing...properties of speed, low capacity usage, and obligatory execution, free from interference by ongoing operations" (Stanovich and Stanovich 1999, 18). The authors point out that previous studies that have looked at the use of context by analyzing reading errors and self-corrections did not distinguish between the use of context before and after word recognition. Miscues and self-corrections reflect the application of sentence-level comprehension strategies as well as word recognition skills. Thus, the assumption made by holistic top-down models that contextual dependency is a key characteristic of proficient reading is too simplistic. For impaired readers and immature nonproficient readers, contextual facilitation compensates (precariously most of the time) for deficient/incipient and inefficient decoding skills. Skilled readers, on the other hand, actually are able to free themselves more easily from this dependence, especially when they have to. In decoding words, they are less likely to be "fooled by unpredictability" (Perfetti 1994, 865). From another perspective, P. Gough and Wren (1999) make a similar point in their discussion of the role that decoding plays in text comprehension.

When it comes to studying the more wide-ranging subject of reading comprehension, Perfetti (1994, 868) sums up the problems facing researchers in a way that leaves much room for discussion on how the subsystems of reading ability interact:

A descriptively coherent view of comprehension comprises an interactive model with constraints on interactions. It continues to be plausible to view the linguistic components, but not the knowledge components, as autonomous. . . . A reader, as well as a listener, accesses words and parses sentences, rapidly and without undue influence from higher-level knowledge. However, the construction of message representations is the result of interactions between local semantic representations (propositions) and knowledge that the comprehender has about a number of relevant things, some obtained from the discourse, some from outside the discourse. In processing terms, there appear to be some constraints on how rapidly knowledge outside the local linguistic representation can be made useful. The existence or perhaps the strength of these constraints is what divides models into modular and interactive models respectively.

Along these lines, the analysis of any kind of language proficiency in terms of components and subsystems helps us describe, and eventually understand better, the different types of self-correction strategy in reading. The bigger idea is, perhaps, that a componential approach to understanding a given language proficiency (especially since we are talking about the interaction of all kinds of competencies and processors in performance—as in reading) can also be interactive as long as the concept of interaction is not that of a top-down free-for-all. Chapter 10 will pick up on this theme again and conclude with a broader assessment of whole-language theory.

In closing this chapter, it's important to reemphasize that the findings from the assessments of the Mexican bilingual students' literacy-related abilities do not count as hard evidence supporting any of the hypotheses presented so far. In some chapters, to be sure, I have attempted to suggest that a componential approach will help us understand better the problems of bilingualism in school. But clearly, the arguments have served at most to chart out some possible ways of asking the right research questions for the future.

10
Conclusion
Results and Prospects

In this concluding chapter, we will see how the theme of modularity might help put a coherent framework around some outstanding questions that were touched on in the previous chapters, but now require some closure: (1) a critique of whole-language and naturalistic approaches to literacy and L2 learning; (2) a retrospective assessment of how the proposed model of bilingual competence and bilingual proficiency has fared so far; and (3) concluding thoughts on aspects of language loss, not as we considered them earlier in regard to changes in linguistic competence, for the individual child, but as a shift affecting an entire speech community.

Section 10.1 picks up where we left off in chapter 9. Just from the everyday, commonsense understandings of "modular" and "holistic," one might think that whole-language approaches to literacy learning would be antithetical to the approach taken so far in this book. In fact, this is almost completely correct. And perhaps it isn't a coincidence that a parallel debate exists about the effectiveness of naturalistic and holistic approaches to L2 learning. As hinted several times earlier, then, there is something interesting about the connection between literacy learning and L2 learning. Taking a last look at this controversy will tie together common threads going back to chapter 6. This review of where things stand in a practical application of research leads us in section 10.2 to consider future prospects for advances in the field of bilingualism. What are the prospects for research within the framework of the componential models proposed in chapters 3–5?

In section 10.3, an interesting question that has been ignored since being mentioned in chapter 2 will receive the attention it deserves, serving as a case study for some broader questions. We have exploited the bilingual circumstance of an indigenous community to exemplify concepts and to speculate about new directions in research. It could be said that, aside from the peculiar sociolinguistic imbalances that affect language development in indigenous communities, any other bilingual setting would have provided examples of the same concepts. However, the possibility of language shift in many of these language communities, some that are down to their last surviving speakers, also raises a special question. The shift to a majority language often implies an extinction. What is lost, precisely, when a language is no longer spoken or understood by any of its former speakers? At least for a period of time, the same population of speakers usually remains intact, its culture undergoing a concurrent shift. How does the evolution toward bilingualism, and then toward a new monolingualism, affect domains of knowledge associated with the displaced language? (So as not to prejudice the question, I avoid for now the formulation "domains of knowledge *embedded in* the displaced language.") Some interesting parallels come to mind from the earlier review of the research on language attrition in bilingual children. Nothing less than the long-standing question of the relationship between language and thought comes up, one that a discussion of modularity cannot avoid for too long. In this way, this concluding chapter will take up unfinished business from chapter 9 and work backward.

10.1 Parts to Whole: What's Natural and What's Unnatural in Language Learning?

We have noted how modular approaches to studying the processes of reading and writing appear to contradict the admonitions of whole-language philosophy not to break language up into its component parts, apparently for any purpose. A componential approach, according to Edelsky (2006, 82), is the "fundamental problem with the various versions of Cummins's THEORY...based on an erroneous, psychologically derived 'theory' of the nature of literacy—a conception of reading and writing as consisting of separate skills involving discrete components of language." The next point of contention that we examined was related to how readers use context in sentence comprehension. In this regard, Edelsky contrasts the "decoding orientation" and "skills orientation" with the "whole-language orientation." The latter, in the assessment of literacy abilities, "requires observing the entire (whole) context-bound purpose-driven language-using activity within a particular situation" (p. 82). This rejection of the analysis of the component processes of reading is also consistent with the whole-language approach's general inclination toward models that minimize bottom-up processes. The notion of "natural acquisition" is tied to literacy learning as a "top-down process" (Hudelson 1994, 132).

Of special interest here is how this perspective on literacy development appears to find common cause with "natural approaches" to L2 learning. This coincidence, in turn, allows us to revisit the research on literacy development in bilingual and L2 learners. In fact, a widely held view among practitioners in the field of bilingual education argues that naturalistic, whole-language-type methods are uniquely well-suited for young L2 learners, both for learning the L2 itself and for L2 literacy. Krashen (1999), for one, is consistent in his endorsement of this coincidence.

In regard to what "natural" development of language abilities refers to, we should admit a wide range of possibilities: even complex skills learned through arduous training are natural for humans. Only thanks to our unique genetic endowments, which underlie development in the relevant cognitive domains, are we able to compose symphonies and epic poems, design orbiting space stations, and understand complex logical problems. Just because an ability develops with the strong participation of domain-general learning capacities associated with complex cognition doesn't mean that it isn't natural and dependent on specific human faculties. Species-specific innate capabilities underlie all kinds of human cognitive achievement, including both abilities that emerge universally without deliberate learning and those that develop unevenly from direct instruction. Some depend more directly on dedicated, domain-specific modules, and others—to a greater extent, or even completely perhaps—on cognitive-general learning. To the first category would belong spontaneous acquisition of L1 (at least those aspects of it that are spontaneous and automatic); to the second, development of aspects of academic language proficiency that are learned.[1]

With literacy in mind, then, the question should be reformulated: do the skills of reading and writing develop naturally in the same way as L1s unfold naturally in young children? Here, an analogy to the primary and secondary discourse abilities (from chapter 7) is helpful. Rather than positing a seamless continuity between L1 acquisition and literacy, we should approach the problem of understanding how children learn to read and write in terms of an important distinction: the former is primary; the latter, secondary. The difference is between an evolutionary and a historical emergence, universal attainment versus uneven distribution. Unlike L1 acquisition, all normal children do not learn literacy skills spontaneously and effortlessly by means of simple immersion. The key distinction cannot be oral-visual, either. The linguistic competencies and processing mechanisms that underlie sign language development are primary; literacy, for deaf and hearing children alike, is secondary.

This is a good place to begin to unravel the fundamental differences that punctuate the debate on literacy learning. Whole-language philosophies present a counterposition on virtually every important question in the research literature, taking as their point of departure the notion of a strong continuity between primary-language acquisition and literacy, coupled with an aversion to modular approaches to the study of language overall. The lines of discussion are clearly drawn.

10.1.1 Universal Principles across Languages and Orthographies

Summarizing a number of key studies, Perfetti (2003, 4) begins with the idea that "reading is defined by a language and by the writing system that encodes the language." The language part consists of abstract competencies distributed among well-structured subcomponents. All writing systems, today, represent language; that is, none bypass it to construct an independent system of signs that directly encodes meaning. And findings from cross-linguistic/scriptural research go even further: no writing system is processed without the participation of phonological structure, at one stage or another. This idea follows from the proposed Universal Writing System Constraint and the Universal Phonological Principle (Perfetti and Liu 2005).

For example, comparing (alphabetic/morphophonemic) English and (logographic/morphosyllabic) Chinese writing systems, in both cases readers activate phonological representations even when they read for meaning, silently. The difference between how this occurs in English and how it occurs in Chinese shows how writing systems do affect processing. In English, phonological forms are activated pre- or sublexically in a rapid manner, "cascading to word identification." Grapheme-phoneme correspondences activate phonological patterns from the first segments of visual input. In Chinese, on the other hand, pre- or sublexical activation of phonological forms normally occurs only when pronunciation is required. When reading for meaning, the evidence suggests that phonology is activated in a "graphic-threshold style," awaiting a threshold level of graphic recognition before coming online. The phonological structures of English, for example, intervene in a prelexical manner:

in that the grapheme-phoneme connections drive phonology from the first moments of visual processing. Chinese [writing] does not have prelexical phonology. The phonology that corresponds to a component is syllable-size and morphemic (i.e. the component is also a word). Thus its effect can be considered not prelexical but lexical. (Perfetti 2003, 14)

So writing systems do affect the way the different subsystems of language enter into processing (on a related note, Koda (2000) and Wang, Koda, and Perfetti (2003) discuss nonalphabetic "first literacy" effects in L2 reading involving an alphabetic orthography). But in the final analysis, even nonalphabetic systems do not circumvent phonology.

This cross-linguistic and cross-writing-system research has pointed to universal principles of phonological processing in reading. Previously, phonological information had been assigned a marginal role in nonalphabetic writing systems; in these deep orthographies, decoding of text was assumed to proceed primarily by directly linking characters and semantic information. Subsequent studies have strongly suggested that this view is incorrect (Geva and Wang 2001). Perfetti (2003, 16–17) concludes that the task before the child is to learn how his or her writing system works, in all cases and without exception, "in the details of its orthographic implementation, ... supported by a learned sensitivity to spoken language units." For all literacy learners, in one way or another, "learning to read requires mastering the system by which print encodes oral language" (Geva and Wang 2001, 184).

For children learning how an alphabetic system encodes oral language, research has converged on the importance of one component of awareness of language form in particular: phonological awareness that is related to alphabetic knowledge (Ehri 2005; Goswami 2001; Shankweiler and Fowler 2004; Share 2004). Skillful processing of orthographic patterns appears to be closely related to the development of this kind of knowledge, which happens not to be a necessary, spontaneously unfolding, and universally accessible component of phonological structure. That is, it appears to be separate from phonological competence, per se. Typically, *awareness* of phonology develops during the early stages of literacy learning or begins during the early stages of literacy-related language use (e.g., involving traditional poetic genres that children in many cultures are exposed to). For children learning how a nonalphabetic system encodes oral language, on the other hand, the degree of participation of phonological awareness in reading ability might be different. In Chinese, for example, L. H. Tan et al. (2005, 8784) conclude that it is "minor and fragile, depending on age, grain size of sound units and their interactions with other factors. . . . [The] predictive power of phonological awareness is secondary and complex." In any case, there exists a lively ongoing discussion on the importance of phonological awareness in early reading; for example, Chow, McBride-Chang, and Burgess (2005) and McBride-Chang and Zhong (2006) appear to differ with Tan et al.'s conclusion.

There appear to be two responses among whole-language proponents to this line of research: a strong top-down hypothesis; and a weaker version, in appearance more interactive. The former favors the view that general previous knowledge and contextual information penetrate all lower-level processes in a thorough-going manner, in effect obliterating any compartmentalization or independent operation of components. The strongest whole-language hypothesis would deny even that there are such things as components or modules. Fluent readers purportedly start with predictions and utilize text mainly to confirm them (Krashen 1999). If skilled reading is context-dependent in this way, attention to accurate decoding and precision in word identification, conceivably, may actually disrupt the context-driven prediction/confirmation cycle. According to this view, skill in phonological/orthographic processing and the early development of phonological awareness linked to early exposure to print are not fundamental attainments of literacy learning and should not be a priority in any initial literacy-teaching program. The weak whole-language hypothesis tends to recognize a certain psychological reality in the linguistic subsystems (termed "cueing systems"), including phonology. However, the weak whole-language hypothesis appears to maintain that phonological "cues" make an equal contribution to skilled reading in concert with the others: syntax, semantics, general world knowledge, and cultural context. None of these "cueing systems," then, is deemed more important than any of the others. A seemingly reasonable and defensible position, the weak whole-language hypothesis too fails to reckon with mounting evidence that efficient phonological/orthographic processing and automatized knowledge of grapheme-phoneme mappings are a foundation of skilled reading. These components of reading ability are not an option that can be easily compensated for at other levels of processing (Chiappe and Siegel 2006; Ehri et al. 2001; Rayner et al. 2001; Stanovich 2000); for an opposing view, in defense of whole-language theory, see K. Goodman 2005 and Krashen 2004.

Surely, it would be incorrect to deny all top-down influences in decoding and word identification. Strong serial-processing and highly encapsulated bottom-up models have not stood up to disconfirming evidence. Context effects do in fact facilitate lower-level processing, but not in an all-encompassing and unconstrained way. Stanovich's (2000) Interactive-Compensatory Hypothesis, for example, refers to a "trade-off" between the quality of the incoming message and top-down information that can be called upon to support decoding. Thus, context supports decoding, but it can compensate for deficient lower-level processing only to a limited extent. Depending on the circumstances, it may compensate only to a very limited extent, and sometimes not at all in any reliable way. For beginning readers with incipient decoding skills and a rudimentary "sight vocabulary," overdependence on context support, for the purpose of making up for weak lower-level processing, results in decoding that tends to be inefficient and inaccurate. Unskilled decoding in nonproficient readers is often marked by dependence on context as a compensatory strategy that is overapplied, so to speak. Since top-down information can only provide limited support for decoding, the unskilled reader's compensatory strategy leads to more frequent misidentifications. The miscues actually degrade context support, in turn making it more difficult to depend on it for both accurate word recognition and meaning construction. Only if efficient bottom-up decoding strategies are deployed can context be called upon effectively; proficient readers "depend" on it in the right proportion. This means not allowing the effect of context to override or substitute for accurate word recognition.

As a number of the researchers cited so far have emphasized, contextual information, including previous knowledge, plays a more prominent role in *text comprehension*, just as a modular approach to reading would predict (for more discussion, see P. Gough, Hoover, and Peterson 1996; Leikin, Share, and Schwartz 2005; Shatil and Share 2003). Meaning construction draws on the Central System domains, just the kind of information that the *discourse*-processing task at hand requires. In text comprehension, of academic texts in particular, deficient prior knowledge results in a familiar dissociation in normal reading, one that metacognitively immature children may still have difficulty in monitoring. In this case, decoding may proceed without the complete integration of semantic information. On the other hand, readers who are skilled at applying contextual information and prior knowledge have less trouble with texts that contain high frequencies of new vocabulary, for example. In addition, remedial-reading teachers are familiar with the compensatory strategy of nonproficient decoders who have learned to monitor their own comprehension and use it to identify known lexical items encountered in print. Only the most rigidly bottom-up serial-processing model would deny the facilitative effect of contextual information on word identification. Many readers who suffer from nondebilitating processing deficits, for example, learn to apply top-down strategies to boost their word identification skills. But these strategies only compensate partially. For sublexical processing and word recognition, background knowledge and other higher-order schemas do not provide, for the most part, the right kind of information where the premium is on precision—on fast and reliable application of decoding skills. Here, it is important to note that componential approaches to the study of reading difficulty and impairment do not attribute poor comprehension ability exclusively to deficient lower-level skills, as is sometimes the impression. Among readers with adequate decoding skills, comprehension breakdown has been traced to deficits in other components, associated with conceptual knowledge domains, for example (Landi and Perfetti 2007).

But even at the discourse level, where we should expect whole-language theories to provide sounder advice, their strong top-down perspective still leads us astray sometimes. For example, it is not uncommon for reading teachers to be admonished for checking that students understand text meaning, or to be cautioned against approaches that involve correct interpretation and "right and wrong answers" in comprehension assessment (e.g., Hudelson 1994). The most extreme relativist/context-dependent theories place little importance on notions such as "literal comprehension," leading to an important debate on broader questions of the nature of understanding, and of progress in scientific knowledge. Sokal (2008) and Gottschall (2008) offer wide-ranging critiques of radical social constructivism from the perspective of the natural sciences and the humanities, respectively.

10.1.2 Reading Subskills and Specific Reading Disability

Reviewing the research on exceptional bilingualism in chapter 5 made it possible to differentiate among domains of language ability that are sometimes hidden from view. Studying the breakdown of normal reading ability does the same. The competence-proficiency distinction, which has already proven useful in a number of ways, can now be applied to another area of literacy research: specific reading disability, or dyslexia. At the same time, findings from the basic research should have important practical applications. By the very nature of their object of study, investigators of reading disability have taken seriously an analytic approach toward the subcomponents of reading. In contrast, it should come as no surprise that strong whole-language theories have no place for an inquiry into component subskills. If some children in fact do suffer from one or another kind of deficit that affects reading ability specifically (e.g., other language abilities are spared and intellectual development is normal), the disability in question might be traced to specific dysfunctions. If the impairment corresponds to cognitive domains that disrupt the deployment of identifiable subskills of literacy, the holistic view of literacy would have to be fundamentally questioned. However, simplistic critiques of the research on dyslexia (see, e.g., F. Smith 2004, "On Seeing Backwards") might be answered more effectively if investigators clarify which subcomponents of reading ability are the focus of scrutiny. For example, are the affected subcomponents part of the domain of competence (e.g., knowledge of phonology), or are they part of an aspect of proficiency that encompasses processing modules or other nonlinguistic subskills necessary for performance on specific literacy tasks? The approach to this problem taken by Bar-Shalom, Crain, and Shankweiler (1993) and Crain and Thornton (1998) that we examined in chapter 7 is one that is applicable here as well.

As many as 20% of children experience persistent difficulties in profiting from normal and typical literacy instruction. It is estimated that between 1.5% and 4% of the school population suffers from actual disabilities specific to reading. Taking dyslexia as an intrinsic disability, logically speaking, L2 learners should be afflicted in the same proportion, assuming a universal neurological basis for this disability, the Central Deficit Hypothesis (Oren and Breznitz 2005). Within the broader category, L2 learners probably make up a disproportionate fraction of all nonproficient readers, inadequate instruction figuring among the primary causal factors. Aside from the theoretical importance of distinguishing disabilities rooted in cognitive impairment from learning failure caused by extrinsic factors, identifying the core characteristics of truly disabled readers will help practitioners design more effective remedial programs for *both* groups. To reiterate, the study of imbalances and defects sheds light on how complex, internally diverse systems function normally. Identifying patterns of selective breakdown and specific impairment help us understand how a language ability consists of interfacing components and how it is put to use through the interaction of these components. Investigations of reading disability are not of one mind on all the empirical questions, hardly a reason to disqualify findings from any one current or another. But as research in this field continues to advance, it becomes more and more difficult to dismiss empirical findings out of hand. For overviews from different perspectives, see Grigorenko 2001, Shaywitz, Mody, and Shaywitz 2006, and Vellutino et al. 2004; and for research on developmental dyslexia involving a nonalphabetic system, specifically on how components of reading ability can be selectively impaired, see Ho et al. 2004 and H. Li et al. 2009.

Beginning with the multivariate nature of reading, its uneven development and selective breakdown, research has focused on linguistic knowledge components, processing mechanisms and related subskills, and explicit awareness of language forms. In regard to work on breakdown in reading development involving alphabetic systems, a consensus has formed around the importance of the child's ability to acquire a functional use of the principles of grapheme-phoneme correspondence. Proficiency in decoding implies the deployment of component subskills of word identification. The skills in question require the active engagement of metalinguistic analysis related to orthographic knowledge. Importantly, this is a specific type of sublexical knowledge, which is not a prerequisite for speaking and understanding words in speech, but is apparently necessary for the development of proficient reading: an *awareness* that spoken words consist of phonemes and how their patterns are mapped onto an orthography (Vellutino et al. 2004). In a morphosyllabic system, this awareness would focus on syllables and morphemes and how they are mapped onto the orthography.

This distinction between metalevel knowledge about an aspect of phonology and phonological competence per se calls for an important point of clarification in the research. A good place to begin is to differentiate among different combinations of underlying factors that might be related to reading disability—for example:

1. impaired decoding skill, associated with phonological processing difficulties mainly specific to written forms among children who manifestly show no sign of abnormal language development in any linguistic subsystem, including ("primary") phonological competence;

2. dyslexia in children who can also be unambiguously diagnosed as suffering from one type or another of Specific Language Impairment, in particular a deficit specific to phonological competence or phonological processing, manifested in abnormal speech or audition;

3. within the broad category of SLI,, an impairment affecting one or another or a combination of linguistic modules (van der Lely 2005). Children afflicted by a specific linguistic deficit might nevertheless have had their word-decoding skills spared. This possibility should not be excluded. For a discussion of language-impaired children's abilities, see Genesee, Paradis, and Crago 2004; and note the glossary entry for SLI.

The critical differentiation seems to be the first one. If a reading-disabled child shows no symptom of defective speech or of impaired ability to understand sentences embedded in typical conversational discourse, the starting point should be that phonological competence is unimpaired or developing normally. A complete (or age-appropriate, normally developing) mental representation of phonological knowledge is indispensable for adequate performance in both oral expressive and receptive abilities. Just as grammatical sentences are not produced simply by calling upon stored sequences of words, so abstract and complex linguistic knowledge underlies phonologically well-formed speech. Even malformed speech or impaired auditory perception does not automatically implicate an incomplete or defective mental representation of phonological knowledge, because the impairment may be restricted to a processing domain. In studies that correlate mastery in "phonological tasks" and reading among non-language-impaired children (Wang, Perfetti, and Liu 2005), for example, what is measured is typically the ability to *manipulate* and differentiate phonological units in a deliberate way, to *detect* contrasts reflectively, and to *attend to* spoken word forms. Castles and Coltheart (2004) make a related methodological observation regarding correlational studies that have attempted to demonstrate that phonological awareness directly facilitates literacy learning. Leikin, Share, and Schwartz (2005, 469) conclude their study of child L2 readers by emphasizing:

the need to distinguish between what might be termed "basic" phonological processing abilities that are intrinsic to spoken language development as opposed to the literacy-related metalinguistic ability required to manipulate meaningless phonological segments of speech—phonological awareness. The former can be regarded as a truly *linguistic* competence—one that is not primarily dependent on literacy acquisition, whereas the latter is best conceived as a *metalinguistic* skill closely tied to alphabetic literacy development.

Returning now to the issue of dyslexia, remediation-resistant decoding impairments have been associated with deficient performance on a number of early diagnostic measures: awareness of rhyming, segmentation abilities such as adding or deleting initial consonants, blending speech sounds, decoding nonwords, and other abilities to manipulate or attend to the internal patterns of words. In addition, naming-speed deficits may be caused by a disruption of timing mechanisms that make it more difficult to map segments of speech onto orthographic patterns (Vellutino et al. 2004). Even illiterate adults, who are perfectly competent speakers of their native language and surely possess a mature and fully formed mental representation of phonological structure, may experience difficulty with some of the above tasks. Thus, for category #1 of dyslexia (normal speech and auditory speech perception spared), a focus on processing deficits and metalevel knowledge specific to print decoding would make for a sharper demarcation than speculation about broad and less well-defined deficiencies in linguistic competence within the domain of phonology. In addition, it is important to specify more clearly how phonological knowledge is represented and how it is related to different kinds of phonological ability. Of course, competence-based factors involving actual deficits in phonological knowledge are entirely pertinent to cases falling under categories #2 and #3.

The multivariate nature of reading ability also helps us understand some of the seemingly unusual dissociations that researchers uncover (Obler and Gjerlow 1999). And from the applied subfield of remedial instruction comes indirect evidence for an interactive model that takes modularity as a starting point but recognizes that constrained top-down processes are not shut out completely from penetrating downward. In regard to this point, Vellutino et al. (2004) review studies that consider at-risk children who suffer from varying degrees of disability, suggesting that literacy-related deficits fall along a continuum rather than being all or nothing, normal versus abnormal. The most interesting cases were those of children who were identified as high-risk prior to school entry, but who nevertheless attained reading ability outcomes within the normal range by 2nd grade. Although they scored within acceptable grade-level norms in reading, their achievement was significantly lower than that of the low-risk control group, and they still experienced difficulty on some assessments of phonological processing. Thus, it is arguable that these high-risk but unimpaired readers might share some of the cognitive dysfunctions with their high-risk impaired counterparts. Now the question is, how was it that they appeared to have compensated for their weak phonological/orthographic processing skills? Vellutino et al. point to interacting effects involving other subcomponents that, while they may play a secondary role in fluent decoding, intervene to "bootstrap" inefficient decoding skills.

Further research needs to account for two things: (1) the fact that high-risk children, some of whom suffer serious reading failure and others of whom attain adequate levels of proficiency, nonetheless share characteristics rooted in poor phonological processing; and (2) why the former succumb to actual reading impairment and the latter do not. One conclusion could be that what is broadly termed as dyslexia "is a multifactorial trait in which basic constitutional (genetic) vulnerabilities (notably in phonological skills) interact with other cognitive skills and environmental factors to produce an increased risk of dyslexia in a continuous way." This would be especially true when considering the "varying degrees of subclinical impairment" (Vellutino et al. 2004, 24). Mild impairments are often masked by the effects of strong and effective instructional programs—again, in a continuous way.

The bootstrapping hypothesis (suggested in the above cases) could receive confirming evidence from studies of adult readers who had childhood diagnoses of dyslexia. Citing work by Bruck (1992), Vellutino et al. point to findings similar to those regarding the child high-risk unimpaired readers. Despite showing reading comprehension skills that were comparable to those of age-matched controls, the "dyslexic" college students scored significantly lower in spelling skills, evidenced "inaccurate and dysfluent word recognition," and even performed poorly on measures of phonological awareness. Here, a strong bottom-up serial model would have trouble explaining how these students, who all continued to be affected by a phonological processing deficit, attained levels of reading ability that approached those of nondyslexic college-level readers. Bruck scrutinized this divergence further by differentiating the dyslexic students into less and more proficient comprehenders. Comparison of these two groups showed that the latter had higher childhood IQs and more robust development of vocabulary knowledge, even though their decoding skills were equally deficient. Apparently, superior domain-general cognitive abilities "pulled up" reading comprehension, other processing strategies compensating in part for deficiencies in phonological processing, which persisted far beyond the childhood years.

10.1.3 Second Language Literacy

In L2 reading, the compensatory effect of top-down prediction strategies should not be overstated either. To start with, we need to specify a whole range of intervening factors. For example, the resources available to the highly literate (from L1) intermediate L2 learner, who is able to draw upon advanced text comprehension and metalinguistic abilities, intervene in a way that complicates the research question and analysis of findings. In some ways, the more interesting case is the young nonliterate beginning L2 learner with access to only immature higher-order cognitive strategies. And not to forget, if the literate L2 learner's first and second orthographies are alphabetic, part of his or her metalinguistic advantage takes the form of advanced awareness of grapheme-phoneme correspondences plus highly efficient bottom-up processing strategies that are carried over, so to speak, from L1 reading.

Among L2 literacy teachers and learners alike, the effect of extensive background knowledge on reading comprehension of L2 texts is well-known. Even learners with the most basic beginner-level L2 grammatical competence are able to glean the main idea of expository texts by identifying key content words and inferring how those words fit into a conceptual schema that they already possess. In fact, we could all probably agree that providing younger, less metacognitively aware L2 readers with this kind of "predictable" text material is a good way to get things started (especially if for them, L2 reading is also initial literacy learning). Many autodidact polyglots, especially those who prefer books for language learning, often start with reading material that they find interesting and for which relevant background knowledge enables easy comprehension and quick access to the new language's grammar. But metalinguistically sophisticated adult learners are not fooled for long; and teachers of child L2 readers should not mislead their pupils on this score, either. If the ultimate or medium-term objective of developing L2 literacy is using it for academic purposes, the limits of relying on top-down strategies become apparent as soon as texts are no longer highly predictable. Independent of genre, students will be working with texts that provide significant amounts of new content, incorporating conceptual frameworks that may also be new. Typical academic text comprehension is cognitively demanding precisely because previous knowledge schemas can no longer easily assimilate the unfamiliar concepts that are introduced with greater and greater frequency. Background knowledge often must be overturned or deliberately set aside. Under these conditions, deficient mastery of lower-level grammatical patterns in L2 cannot be compensated for in any consistent and effective way. Readers who rely heavily on prediction now run the risk of simply confirming what they think they know, or being led down garden paths triggered by "contextually compatible" miscues that are left uncorrected.

For child preliterate beginning L2 learners, models of reading that downplay the importance of linguistic knowledge (in particular, command of L2 phonology and morphology/syntax) would seem to be even more problematic. To begin with, at the grapheme-phoneme level, we can point to weak phonological representations in addition to low levels of relevant metaknowledge and inadequate processing skills as factors contributing to reading failure. Beginner interlanguage competence in the domain of morphology and syntax affects L2 readers' bottom-up processing severely or moderately depending on access to other sources of information from the lexicon. On these points, whole-language-inspired proposals that claim that lower-level competence factors are inconsequential or that L2 literacy development can support itself adequately by recourse to top-down mechanisms have yet to be put to the test.[2] If strong top-down holistic models are holding up poorly for L1 reading, there should be less reason to take them seriously for beginning readers, whose tenuous control over their L2 grammar would make prediction strategies even less reliable for both decoding and comprehension. The "sampling" notion—that "visual information" in reading is secondary—is even less applicable to situations in which context is called upon to support decoding of text in a language that the beginning reader doesn't understand. Efficient fixation and regression (as in the type-A self-corrections examined in chapter 9) are obstructed if competence in the language of the text falls below a certain threshold (Birch 2002, 64–71).

With these and related factors in mind, from an ethnographic perspective, Tabors and Snow (2001) make a strong case for not excluding the beginning reader's L1 from the beginning literacy-teaching program. Commenting on their review of the literature on initial exclusive L2 reading instruction, the authors conclude:

[Studies] indicate that young emergent bilingual children can and do engage in a wide variety of literacy-related activities in English, such as developing concepts about print, naming and writing letters of the alphabet, and, in some cases, developing impressive sight word vocabularies. Difficulties arise, however, when more sophisticated linguistic knowledge is required. . . . [E]arly accomplishments of the children seem almost language free. (p. 173)

These observations (also see Aarts and Verhoeven 1999; Abu-Rabia 2004) suggest that both exclusive L1 literacy (and postponed L2 learning in general) and early all-L2 reading instruction offer less than optimal models for preliterate child beginning L2 learners. In the case of exclusive L2 reading instruction, minimizing the role that linguistic competencies play in learning to read would also be the wrong way to approach the problem of how to maximize initial L2 literacy learning when objective limitations exclude the possibility of L1 literacy.

As noted in earlier chapters, exclusive L2 literacy instruction may be the only program model available to preliterate L2 beginners in multilingual classrooms. But it would be an error to ignore the objective difficulties that this approach implies in the teaching of initial reading skills. Recognizing these challenges allows them to be factored into L2 curriculum design in a systematic way. Monolingual L1 speakers with limited extracurricular access to the L2 would be among the prime beneficiaries. Add to this group L2 learners who may also be laboring under the effects of dyslexia, subclinical processing deficits, or general garden-variety reading comprehension problems, and the prerequisites for initial literacy that educators must take into account multiply. In an important series of studies, Oren and Breznitz (2005) and Breznitz, Oren, and Shaul (2004) examine the factor of specific reading disability in L2 reading. Findings show, again, how different combinations of imbalance and stress on a bilingual system uncover interesting aspects of the inner workings of language processing.

Back in chapter 1, an unlikely convergence of modular and connectionist perspectives regarding certain applied research problems was suggested. It is in the field of literacy learning where one such possibility has actually come up. Despite an affinity that one might assume between holistic theories and connectionist models, research on reading development has drawn the lines of debate differently. Regarding the role that phonology plays in word identification and in the learning of grapheme-phoneme correspondences, connectionist and modularity-oriented researchers tend to come to the same conclusion: strong top-down constructivist theories, which minimize the importance of orthography-phonology mapping, are seriously flawed (Rayner et al. 2001; Seidenberg 2005). That diverging paradigms have coincided in this way should motivate reflection on what aspects of each approach lead to this kind of coincidence on a specific empirical question. One possibility to explore might be related to the distinction, mentioned in chapter 9, between interactive models and integrativist (strongly holistic) theories.

10.2 Versions of Modularity and Pending Questions in Bilingual Research

In an overview of the research on modularity and related issues, Marcus (2004) suggests that it will be the study of how the components of language are interconnected and how they interact that will set the stage for the next advances in understanding this aspect of mental architecture. Such an approach may not depend on localizing regions of the brain that contain one or another discrete knowledge component. Accordingly, the most interesting investigations will probably involve studying the interconnections and interactions between the language subsystems and the other cognitive systems. And surely, whatever the contours of the networks of linguistic and conceptual knowledge and their designated processors turn out to be, they are not likely to look like bubbles and triangles, overlapping in the manner of icebergs connected by double-sided arrows. Alternatively, this more cautious hypothesis may be too weak; and a stronger version of modularity, in which the linguistic subsystems are neurologically segregated and localizable, will conform better to the evidence (Grodzinsky and Friederici 2006).

For now, how does our distinction between bilingual competencies and bilingual proficiencies, in the particular way it has been drawn in this book, hold up? And how does the bilingual version of Jackendoff's Tripartite Parallel Architecture (TPA) square with some of the leading research on the way that knowledge is represented in bilinguals? From the way that competencies and proficiencies are being conceived here, the Bilingual TPA (figure 5.2) should be able to do double duty, as a model of both bilingual competence and bilingual proficiency, of knowledge structures and other aspects of ability.

Reviewing the literature on "bilingual memory," Heredia and Brown (2004) trace the history of this concept from the early "coordinate-compound distinction" to the current discussion about how bilingual lexicons are organized in relation to the conceptual system. A summary of their overview will point us in the right direction for formulating research questions for future studies. We can begin with the apparently contradictory findings that supported either the shared- or the separate-memory hypothesis. The mixed results have led to the view that some aspects of bilingual competence must be represented separately and that other components are shared between L1 and L2. The findings of Kroll and her associates on the relative strength of connections between words in L1 and L2 and how they are in turn connected to the conceptual system are depicted in the now widely accepted Revised Hierarchical Model (RHM) (Sunderman and Kroll 2006). The Bilingual TPA model, and all its predecessors discussed so far from Cummins's CUP to Jackendoff's TPA to M. Paradis's Three-Store Hypothesis, should be taken as being broadly compatible with the RHM. If this chapter makes any contribution to the discussion on mental representation in bilinguals, I hope it will be that some of these researchers might find the others' work interesting in some way. My impression (though I may have missed something in the literature search) is that none of the four just-mentioned authors has considered especially pertinent the recent work of the other three.

10.2.1 First Language–Second Language Autonomy and First Language–Second Language Interaction

To review, all the above-mentioned models assume that the bilingual's lexicons are best conceived as separate (Werker and Byers-Heinlein 2008), with a nonlinguistic conceptual system that is shared. The models also account for the interactions, directly, between the L1 and L2 linguistic domains through the Cross-Linguistic Interfaces (CLIs) that link one lexicon to the other, comprising a vast number of interconnections. In other words, interfacing is what lexicons do (Jackendoff 2002). One class of interface mechanism enables communication among modules within each language subsystem; another, the CLI, takes care of the interfaces between language subsystems. So when we refer to influences "between language subsystems" the proposal is that two independent mental representations actually coexist within the larger linguistic domain, separate in turn from the domain of Conceptual Structure (CS). The evidence for stronger links from L2 to L1 than in the reverse direction (the "translation asymmetry") is consistent with findings from studies of all kinds of L1-L2 interaction, from the language-mixing and codeswitching research in particular. Typically in imbalanced bilinguals, and often among balanced bilinguals (because of external sociolinguistic pressures, for example), there is an asymmetry in language mixing. The four models also seem to view the interfaces that connect the L1 and L2 lexicons (the "lexical links") as different in kind from the "conceptual links" that connect linguistic entries in the lexicons with their CS counterparts.

Here, one particularly interesting question for future research is how separation is achieved developmentally. If L2 representations in beginning learners are parasitic on the L1 (for example, in the very early stages all new L2 lexical items are linked to their L1 translation equivalent), how does the L2 develop toward autonomy? We would have to admit that at some early stage of interlanguage development there is still just one language system; the second system is still not separate, only establishing its autonomy in stages, at least for an initial period. Hypothetically, this separation-by-stages development of L2s would be different from how L_a and L_b are differentiated in simultaneous bilingual development (2L1) as described by Meisel (2004).

M. Paradis (2004) addresses the problem of how the L2 subsystem maintains its autonomy (from the L1 subsystem). The above example of incipient L2 learning aside, he proposes two kinds of "interference": static and dynamic. "Dynamic interference" refers to performance transfer or incidental cross-linguistic influence, as in a "dynamic interference error" (p. 188). In static interference, on the other hand, actual representations from one language subsystem are integrated into the other. For example, representations from the L1 may be integrated into L2 grammatical knowledge. In this case, regardless of the degree of static interference in the L2, each language subsystem will be treated as separate. Identical structures will be redundantly represented in each language subsystem. Similarly, in more balanced bilingualism, linguistic structures that appear to be "shared" are stored independently and separately, twice (pp. 212–216). Hypothetically, this kind of redundancy would apply equally to L1-L2 pairs that are typologically "similar" and to L1-L2 pairs that are "distant."

Like all "hierarchical" models, De Groot's (2002) "distributed model of bilingual memory" distinguishes between the lexical and conceptual levels. It also elaborates on how semantic features can be "distributed" across the bilingual's languages in different ways for different pairs of lexical items. Along similar lines, Heredia and Brown (2004), following Altarriba (2003), offer a more interesting example than the comparison of (English) "sleep," (Spanish) "dormir," and (French) "dormir/endormir" in chapter 5. They demonstrate how complex the distribution of semantic features between L1 and L2 can be, underlying subtle but important differences in meaning. For example, even advanced Spanish-English bilinguals sometimes stumble over the distinctions between the high-frequency pairs "love"/"like" and "amor (n.)/amar (v.)"/"querer." Just to scratch the surface: English "love" can be used interchangeably for animate and inanimate entities, but Spanish "amar" cannot be used for the latter—nor, typically, for nonhuman animals (neither "I love chocolate ice cream" nor "I love my kitty" can be translated word for word using "amar"). Among humans, "amar" is appropriate for a nonfamily boyfriend or girlfriend, but it is used only between husband and wife within the family. "Amor" (noun) can be used in descriptions of a type of love such as "fatherly love" [amor paternal], but "amar" (verb) cannot normally be used to express the English equivalent of "I love my father" [amo a mi padre] (Heredia and Brown 2004, 240–241). Along these lines, both the RHM and the distributed model should be able to account for all of the different kinds of link between L1-L2 pairs in the lexicon:

- translation equivalents for which all semantic features are the same and cognates are related closely also at the lexical level,
- translation pairs that share certain core features but not others,
- false cognates,
- homographs and homophones.

The last two, hypothetically, are linked only at the lexical level, and sometimes precariously at that (e.g., homographs: English noun "hay"—Spanish verb "hay" [there is], English adverb "quite"—Spanish noun "quite" [removal or dodge]). The basic idea is that "[w]ords from different languages will share semantic features thus providing a bridge between languages through the conceptual system" (de Bot 2004, 24).

Future research will continue the important work on the related question of bilingual lexical access in language processing. To what extent is information retrieved in a language-selective or -nonselective way? And how can the contextually "inappropriate" language be kept in the background, as if it were "switched off"? (This question does not imply that all interference from the nonselected language can be shut out completely; rather, it asks how bilinguals inhibit the activation of L1 or L2 as effectively as they do.) De Groot (2002) reviews the research and suggests some alternatives for sorting out the findings. The question is familiar here from the discussion of the effect of context on decoding. In lexical decision tasks involving homographs, for example, investigators found that initial processing is nonselective. That is, in comprehension, both L1 and L2 are activated. But it's not likely that both languages maintain the same level of uninhibited activation in actual sentence and discourse processing of monolingual input. In production, a strong nonselective model might favor the view that the two language subsystems actively "compete" in some way, a highly unlikely possibility (for one, making simultaneous translation very difficult). Even though much of the evidence for nonselectivity involves experimental tasks that do not take sentence-level grammar into account (resulting in findings that seem counterintuitive), we still need to not only explain them but also integrate them into a comprehensive model of bilingual processing. How the L1 and L2 lexicons are interconnected, including how interconnections are inhibited in actual comprehension and production, will surely turn out to be more complex than anyone suspects.

A bilingual processing model that minimizes the importance of the CLI would have a hard time interpreting the evidence that the two languages are simultaneously available to some degree, in some way, during comprehension and production. It should be clear, then, since the CLI figures prominently in most approaches to the problem of bilingual processing, that evidence for nonselective lexical access is entirely compatible with the autonomy of two separate linguistic subsystems. Arguments that favor a single undifferentiated bilingual or multilingual network might be encouraged by findings of non-target-language activation—but not for long, because all theoretical frameworks will have to be reconciled with evidence for both selective and nonselective access. Both can be correct, about different things, in the same way that the four mutually compatible models discussed above have reconciled the conflicting findings on whether bilingual memory is shared or separate.

Similarly, codeswitching and other kinds of L1-L2 alternation, interference, and transfer, far from being evidence of the fusion of L1 and L2, are better understood from the point of view of the systematic interaction between two autonomous grammatical subsystems. In the research on both lexical access and codeswitching, what needs to be explained is what kind of mental representation and what kinds of processing mechanism allow bilinguals to alternate and transfer between L1 and L2, and at the same time inhibit these kinds of cross-linguistic influence. If, in performance, access to all the lexical items of L1 or L2, including idioms and bound morphemes, can be blocked, especially if it's a dominant L1 that is being inhibited, this strongly suggests that each lexicon is part of a distinct system.

One possibility to explore is a context-free, nonselective access at the initial stages of processing. For comprehension, this access could be either total or partial, depending on various factors (e.g., how constraining the grammatical context is). A tight preselection that puts up a firewall against all interference from the nontarget language would be discarded, as findings from the research are showing. That is, a proactive hard "switch-off" is not an option available to the bilingual. However, as De Groot (2002) cautions, the research on production has arrived at results that are less conclusive on this point. Inhibitory control, then, becomes the focus of inquiry: for example, how might the nontarget language be suppressed differently in comprehension and in production? Especially when performance is governed by the "monolingual mode" (Grosjean 2001), in which proactive control appears to inhibit interference from the nontarget language completely, what mechanisms account for this? Recall the sharp differentiation in monolingual and bilingual mode in the bilingual narrators in the Mexican study as a function of initial language choice: Spanish or Nahuatl. When inhibitory control is being exercised, in what way or in what sense does the nontarget language still remain activated (if at all, as for example in production)?

Just as the interference from a nontarget language in child codeswitching reveals how each language subsystem actually maintains its integrity, so reports of early fusion of the L_a and L_b grammars, leading to significant developmental delays, have been shown to be unfounded. (Cases of "bilingual SLI" should be considered separately here.) As we saw in chapter 6, even in cases of early L1 attrition, in which the dominant replacing language is progressively imposing structures in domains ceded by the attriting language, transfer or interference is not random and unsystematic. In language replacement, the attriting language does not simply get progressively dissolved around the edges into the soon-to-be-sole-remaining primary language. The evidence for early differentiation in child bilingualism, in all its variations, stands as the most important indication of separate grammatical representations and separate lexicons in all cases of dual-language knowledge. The fact that this separation is achieved by the cognitively immature child in the face of confusing and conflicting primary linguistic data (a good example of the poverty-of-stimulus problem) strongly supports this view. Separation is very unlikely to be a consequence of the development of metalinguistic awareness that imposes order from above over a homogeneous and undifferentiated "two-language" network. Rather, it appears that the developing linguistic competencies in L_a and L_b or L1 and L2 are based on their respective early-emerging neural representations (Genesee 2003; Meisel 2004). Here again, we have the beginnings of a strong proposal from the study of bilingualism for grappling with Plato's allegory of the cave and Descartes's observations about knowledge and experience, discussed in chapter 1.

What is it about the Language Acquisition Device that allows for such flexibility? It appears to be programmed to guarantee the development of at least one primary language ("Knowledge of Language" with a capital "K" and capital "L" ensures this). At the same time, it is poised to make very fine differentiations in development, making it possible for the child to spontaneously construct separate networks of linguistic knowledge, what we call "languages" (lowercase; mental representations that, externally, are designated as English, Navajo, Spanish, Nahuatl, and so on). Only one language is absolutely guaranteed, in all cases, to reach native-speaker completeness, as the facts of L1 attrition and imbalanced early bilingualism suggest. But the Language Acquisition Device appears also to be equipped to guide early child bilingualism toward equivalent native-speaker completeness in two. As we saw in chapter 6 on language attrition and the critical period in L1 acquisition, there is another way of thinking about the Language Acquisition Device. Why is "Language" so resistant to variation in experience up to and including what would seem to be seriously adverse conditions for healthy language development, while "languages" (L1s and L2s alike) are so much more "unsteady" in comparison (more sensitive to environmental variation)?[3]

10.2.2 Language–Conceptual Structure Autonomy, Language–Conceptual Structure Interaction

In chapter 5, it was proposed that the idea of a L1-L2 separation—modularity applied "crosswise" between the representations of the linguistic subsystems—is independent of the argument in favor of the "up-and-down" relation of autonomy of CS from language. The tentative argument was that one form of autonomy does not necessarily and forcibly follow from the other, although admittedly we have tried hard to consider the validity of both dimensions of differentiation. But perhaps there might be, after all, a logical necessity in tying these two dimensions of modularity together, a reconsideration that now introduces the rest of this concluding chapter. Recall the CS domain in the Bilingual TPA model. The conceptual features that combine to form concepts are part of a system whose primitives are unlike those that any of the linguistic modules make use of. Then how could there be, or why should there be, parallel CS networks for each language we acquire or learn? As we saw in the discussion of L1-L2 autonomy in the previous section, redundancy in a model would not be, by itself, a convincing argument against proposing parallel networks in this instance.

But there are other good reasons for preferring a shared conceptual system, the relative ease of translation and other kinds of interlinguistic communication, notwithstanding glitches and disconnects of all sorts, being one that immediately comes to mind (Jackendoff 1997). Thinking now of the language modules, note that bilingualism doesn't just bring together structurally similar languages. The L1 and L2 morphology/syntax structures, the ones that interface most directly with CS, can vary radically, as the languages of the world actually do in real life. To date, there is little hard evidence that in the latter case access to concepts varies in a radical and fundamental way depending on which language the bilingual is using as a tool of thought. P. Li and Gleitman (2002) discuss an interesting related question: how linguistic differences might affect the ways that speakers of different languages apply reasoning strategies to nonlinguistic problems; also, see Au 2006 on counterfactuality in Chinese.

The example of access to concepts via two languages most familiar to bilingual educators is that of two L2 learners of English, one whose L1 is a closely related European language and another whose L1 is distantly related. Let us assume that both students, prior to their contact with English, had received extensive and rigorous academic preparation in mathematics and the natural sciences. There is no evidence in the educational research literature that the student whose L1 is more closely related to English should have freer access to mathematical and scientific concepts through the medium of English than the student whose L1 is distantly related.

We shouldn't deny any facilitative effect of language either. Undoubtedly, specialized vocabulary helps us frame problem-solving tasks and categorize ideas, and discourse patterns are a part of our culture. On the other hand, the arguments that syntax determines thought are on much shakier ground, often not based on empirical evidence, and sometimes tilting unintentionally toward linguistic and ethnocentric biases. For an example, see Chamberlain and Medinos-Landurand's (1991, 123) contrastive analysis of the seemingly equivalent expressions "We missed the bus" (English) and "Se nos fue el autobús" [more or less: "left us the bus"] (Spanish). The authors speculate that, in the latter case, "the language reflects the outside focus of control. The strong contrast of belief systems between fate (or greater force) versus individual responsibility creates serious problems for students and educators in North American mainstream classrooms." While this last bit of advice to teachers is clearly over the top, the research on how conceptual structures are mapped onto linguistic structures at the syntax-semantics interface raises hard questions not easily dispensed with. Resorting to simple approaches that radically compartmentalize language and thought doesn't get us very far, especially with the more difficult cases.

Along the syntax-semantics interface (figure 5.1), dedicated correspondences match up knowledge systems and processors that have to work together in performance. CS is still independent of language, with the interfaces for L1 and L2 converging on the same sets of semantic features. But between language and thought, semantic features are associated with words in what Jackendoff (1996) terms *Lexical Conceptual Structure* (LCS), "piece[s] of CS associated with linguistic expression[s]":

LCS can be thought of as "tools" for building an infinite variety of meanings dynamically in the course of language production and comprehension. . . . In speech production, a thought (a composite conceptual structure) is divided up into LCSs, whose words can then be mapped into syntactic and phonological structure. . . . In speech perception, noises physically drive the ear to activate the auditory system. Auditory signals are mapped into phonological representations which can then be parceled into words (the process of "lexical access"). . . . In linguistic imagery, or "inner speech," thoughts are mapped into phonological structures, but the mapping to motor interactions does not take place. . . . [I]nner speech" consists of speech production minus motor activity. (p. 204)

From this perspective, the discussion on "how language helps us think" should still be considered wide open; and the renewed interest in aspects of the Sapir-Whorf hypothesis should not be viewed as a bad thing either, even if its original claims still fail to muster reliable evidence.

While differing on a number of points from Jackendoff's approach to the problem of how language is recruited in thought, Carruthers (2002) lays out key working assumptions in a way that can keep the discussion going:

• For the purpose of operating on conceptual reasoning tasks, central cognition exploits the resources of the language system.
• Normal language ability is necessary for at least some kinds of reasoning and problem solving, and for intellectual development in children.
• Thought is independent of natural language, even though certain cognitive achievements depend on it. (Parenthetically, Pinker and Jackendoff (2005, 206) observe that "there are domains of human concepts which are probably unlearnable without language.")
• Central cognition is in part organized along modular lines, not sweepingly holistic and integrative.

Carruthers goes on to argue that there is a non-domain-specific central arena that collates and integrates outputs from participating modules. More controversially, he claims that the central-process integration cannot operate without accessing the resources of language—that language is the medium of cross-modular thought. This is a much stronger claim regarding how central cognition makes use of the resources of the language system than the one advanced so far in this book. The Bilingual TPA maintains more of a separation between the linguistic domains and CS. But there is clearly room for weighing the arguments and considering a good number of intermediate claims that stay clear of the implausible extremes. As Carruthers correctly charts out the territory: language is nothing more than an input-output system for central cognition, at one extreme—language is the medium of all thinking, at the other.

10.2.3 Central Processes and Periphery: Pending Discussion

Among researchers who reject the strong social-constructivist and holistic view of language, the discussion on modularity should be considered wide open as well, to be approached anew with an eye toward avoiding premature disqualifications. The modularity hypothesis should still be viewed as a recently formulated idea, with decisive empirical evidence favoring one version or another yet to be forthcoming. With research still offering conflicting results, it's difficult to clearly draw the sharp distinctions that some authors insist on. Among the questions around which the debate should *not* polarize are:

1. the nature of the central domains (if they are not completely diffuse, global, and horizontal, what is it that distinguishes them from the kind of processing and the kind of knowledge structures that we find in the "periphery"?) and

2. the degree of encapsulation of the lower-level modules (the idea that we can admit to degrees of openness to top-down processes (Jackendoff 2002) doesn't appear to be incompatible with Fodor's (1990) view that modules are not hermetically impenetrable, but rather that access to higher-level information is "constrained by general features of cognitive architecture . . . relatively rigidly and relatively permanently constrained" (p. 3)).

Continued discussion, inclined toward a more convergent tenor, along the lines of #1 and #2, is what Coltheart (1999) and Marcus (2006) seem to be advocating. As proposed earlier, such a discussion might also make for a more generous assessment of work outside the inner circles of UG-oriented cognitive science. The main idea is that such an interdisciplinary discussion would be favored by a working conception of modularity that includes the idea that components and domains are of different kinds, not all only one kind of module. This would be a good way to think about the concluding topic of this chapter.

10.3 Language Diversity, Cognition, and Culture

10.3.1 Forgetting Isn't Random

M. Baker (2001) concludes his discussion of the parametric theory of language diversity with an apparently unrelated point, calling attention to the erosion of indigenous languages. It seems fitting that we do the same. Baker also avails himself of numerous samples and examples from languages that are in danger of extinction. For students of language and cognition, the loss of linguistic diversity results in an impoverishment of a patrimony of humanity. In a narrow sense, it is a loss in the same way that the destruction of temples and artifacts by the European conquerors in the New World is for the archeologist. At the same time, it is almost impossible to not address broader consequences.

Concretely, what is lost when a language undergoes displacement? When we asked our Mexican bilingual students what would happen if one day people no longer spoke Nahuatl in their town because it had been replaced by Spanish, the responses of those who viewed this possibility as lamentable fell into two categories (appendix 1): (1) a loss of communicative ability (inability to talk with a grandfather or grandmother who has not learned Spanish, or with someone from another town where Nahuatl is still spoken), and (2) a more fundamental loss related to the students' sense of identity as members of a community, or even as a people. As one 4th grader put it, "Porque todos lo hablan y somos mexicanos" [Because everyone speaks it and we are Mexicanos] ("Mexicano" refers either to belonging to the Mexican nation or to belonging to the Nahua people). Another student replied, "It is the language of our great-grandparents"; it would be the loss of a language that has been spoken for so long, "a mother tongue." Sixth grader Fidel went so far as to say that "now everything was forgotten."

Just as language attrition in the individual must be accompanied, in normal circumstances, by language replacement (recall chapter 6), so minority languages that suffer extinction are displaced by expanding languages. And by the same token, language obsolescence does not proceed unsystematically, precisely because rather than fading through simple "loss," the lexicon and the grammatical systems of the receding language progressively cede domains to a replacing language. The displacement evidences grammatical innovation, even "enrichment" (Aikhenvald 2002), because new knowledge is developing; language loss/replacement is not a "random forgetting" (Seliger 1996).

In regard to such displacement, are differences between languages commensurable, or are they so deep that language shift might affect the very expressive capabilities of speech communities and their ability to understand things in the same way as before? Linguists agree that the grammatical systems of all languages are comparable, equal in their capabilities, this assessment being independent of the number of entries in each dictionary. Related to this idea is the question of translatability: Can the content of messages (all relevant contextual factors being accounted for) be interpreted in the same way when they are translated? Will some aspect of meaning inevitably be changed? We could agree perhaps that language systems interface with conceptual representations in different ways. The semantic features are nonlinguistic, but the way they are "distributed" or "bundled" may be, in some way, language-specific. In this way, language "organizes conceptual material" and participates in the formation of new concepts (M. Paradis 2004, 202). Thus, how far any variation resulting from this interaction between grammatical structures and concepts can be taken is still worthy of thoughtful inquiry. But for this most difficult question we should set aside the more straightforward aspects of language displacement: loss of communicative ability and the loss of language as emblem of ethnic/national identity. For these, arriving at agreement on contributing factors and consequences should not be too hard. Since displaced languages never leave a vacuum, and over time emblems and identities change, we can say that a new relative equilibrium will eventually be achieved, sooner or later.

It is Fidel's assertion that "everything would be forgotten," that touches on the most difficult question: how language and thought (knowledge of language and knowledge of almost everything else) are related. Might the differences among languages be so fundamental that the replacement of a "mother tongue" with a "foreign" one would change the community's culture—how people perceive the world, solve problems, and think about themselves and other people? "Everything" wouldn't be forgotten; but might the shift to the new language result in the forgetting of many important things, and might other aspects of knowledge and cognition change in a fundamental way? Specifically related to one of the principal objects of this study, the narrative genre, what effect would language shift have on a community's oral tradition: might no part of it survive the transition/translation, or might some of it survive, or all of it? From the point of view of the concerned minority-language speaker, the question should be framed in a coherent way with an eye toward an objective assessment of the problem. Tsunoda (2005) examines the different points of view at length and concludes, "[I]t seems unjustifiable to say that when a language is lost, the culture is lost entirely" (p. 163). So being more precise about what may be endangered, and what may remain intact, helps pose problems and remedies in a more credible way, and helps direct language revitalization efforts more effectively. In the event that revitalization is not practicable or possible, as is often the case, documentation projects can proceed more deliberately.

10.3.2 A Language-Specific Verbal Art Form

To help sort out what is at stake in the displacement of a language, let us look at an inverse example—that is, what is *preserved* when a minority language does not undergo rapid extinction. The example suffers from an exceptional circumstance: it involves a variety of a major world language, Spanish. But because in this case Spanish became a minority language in the host cultures that came to envelop it, the example serves to illustrate some of the key aspects of the problem just posed. The discovery in the early twentieth century by investigators of the oral tradition, most prominent among them R. Menéndez Pidal, of how extensively the fifteenth-century *romances* (ballads) came to be preserved among the Sephardic communities of North Africa and the Near East is still a subject of considerable interest. This story of unrequited ethnolinguistic loyalty, compelling in its own right, highlights an important aspect of the question we are considering.

Banished from Spain in 1492, the dispersed Jewish communities carried with them the oral tradition of the *romances* just at the time when they were at a high point of development on the Iberian Peninsula. For a number of interesting historical reasons, they had survived longer there than in the rest of Europe. From nearby Tangier across the Strait of Gibraltar to Constantinople and Palestine to the east, and north to one of the cradles of the Eastern European oral tradition in Bosnia, the Sephardic diaspora maintained both its ancestral language and the poetic traditions of medieval Spain, in large part as a consequence of its dispersion and its peculiar manner of integration into the receiving communities. Occasional reports filtered back to Spain, such as the version of the sea captain Domingo de Toral who, upon paying a visit to Aleppo (Syria) in 1634, found a settlement of 800 Sephardim families. Among them he encountered assiduous readers of Lope de Vega and Luis de Góngora, known for incorporating the romance tradition into their work. In the cities of the Ottoman Empire, it was common to find pamphlets and booklets printed in Hebrew script (but in Ladino)[4] of romances that narrated events that had occurred after 1492, evidence that the diaspora communities continued, for many years, to receive the oral tradition from their mother country (Menéndez Pidal 1945; and see Minervini 2006 for some historical background).

However, Menéndez Pidal's discovery 300 years later was the most interesting. Not only had the fifteenth-century ballads stood the test of time, but a number of the preserved diaspora versions had apparently been lost to memory back in Spain. More complete versions of some ballads were still being performed among the Sephardim, recuperating material that had fallen away over the years in Spain, as in the case of the celebrated "Song of Count Arnaldos" (Menéndez Pidal 1938). A similar phenomenon is found in remote regions of Mexico. Musical forms introduced from the European tradition during the sixteenth century now accompany traditional indigenous dances, having been conserved by the autochthonous communities, and are still performed by adults and young people today (another entry of miscellaneous unpaid debt that can be entered into the ledger of the Old World).

Speculating now on the relationship between the loss of a language and the traditional knowledge of the people who speak it, what does this account of language and genre preservation suggest? Menéndez Pidal observes that the traditional romances availed themselves of a medium more effective than the printing press: music and song. The poetry being inseparable from the ballad's tonal patterns, a reciter often cannot execute the verse unless he or she can sing it. It is the special linguistic features connected to the verse's poetic forms that forge the link between language and knowledge—in this example, knowledge of a genre. Indirectly, the narrative content of the ballad is carried along with it.

Citing examples from Dante, Shakespeare, Milton, Mohawk oration, and West African folktales, M. Baker (2001) makes a related observation. Languages differ in how they fix alternatives that are universally available; linguistic differences arise from the ways basic elements are combined. In acquiring a particular language, what children must have is a kind of prior (to experience) knowledge that is substantial enough to overcome the poverty-of-stimulus problem. At the same time, these capabilities need to be open-ended enough to construct a specific grammatical system from among all the possibilities. But at the core, all languages share the same acquisition mechanisms, whatever, precisely, these turn out to be. It might be true that some languages facilitate performance of certain tasks, like counting and memorizing numbers in series (Marcus 2004, 126). And while the same ideas can be expressed by all languages, perhaps not all ideas can be expressed with the same facility from one language to another. But the deep core shared by all languages allows for a broad equivalence in the capacity of each one to serve as a tool of thinking. The CS systems that also cut across all cultures, and that are shared by all normally developing children, maintain an alignment with the linguistic subsystems, thus ensuring this broad equivalence in cognitive capacity. (Everett's (2005) strong version of the "cultural constraint on linguistic structure" can be taken as a contrasting view.)

Following this line of argument, Baker proposes that the loss that accompanies language shift lies, not in the capacity to express propositions, understand concepts, or reflect on meanings (not even culturally specific concepts and meanings), but in the domain of the aesthetic genres, primarily affecting the preservation of poetic forms. Verbal art forms tied to language-specific grammatical features (including phonology) are then the most vulnerable in the transition to a replacing language. The more language-dependent the genre (in this sense), the more endangered it is—poetry much more so than narrative, for example. The more that traditional narrative depends on the resources of poetry and other musical aspects of language, the more it is at risk—at least in its complete and fully formed versions—during the displacement of the indigenous language with which it is associated. In contrast, we can now propose, the most prosaic discourse forms, along with all those aspects of cultural knowledge that are associated with them, would be the most resistant to loss. In other words, they would be among the most easily "translatable." The basic concept underlying this idea, the distinction between aspects of literary tradition that are more language-specific and those that are more easily translatable, has been well understood for some time now (Sapir 1921).

This idea is compatible with the model of a single underlying CS domain, serving separate linguistic subsystems in the bilingual. In the same way, traditional knowledge associated with an endangered language is not all of one kind. Under this view, specific literary and aesthetic genres, for example, would be affected by a shift to the replacing language differently according to how dependent each one is on the Syntactic Structure and Phonological Structure of the attriting language. This is the inverse of our example of the preservation of specific poetic genres tied to the survival of linguistic knowledge.

10.3.3 A Final Thought on Language and Culture

All of this brings us to one of the enduring puzzles in the language sciences: How closely are language and culture related? How might linguistic forms determine thought and cultural knowledge? Plotkin (2001) and Sperber and Hirschfeld (2004) take up the broader question that bears on this discussion as well: the cognitive underpinnings of cultural knowledge. Here again (and for the last time), a modular approach might help us get some traction on all these interesting and as yet unresolved problems. And contrary to perception, the strong tendency on the part of UG-oriented researchers to keep language and thought compartmentalized does not allow them to easily dispatch the problem. Since "language" is not all of one piece, we can proceed to examine, without prejudice, how "intimately tied with" or how "autonomous from" each other language and culture are, part by part. Where they are related, closely or otherwise, the question can then be asked, how or in what way? Restricting the debate to language competencies (because we could agree that language abilities and performances really are inseparable from cultural knowledge), a different approach can then be taken for each component domain of linguistic knowledge. A different kind of relationship with culture will obtain when we consider the component knowledge structures that participate in discourse ability, in the use of grammar in sentences, and in word usage. Thinking about how language is related to other things, part by part, allows for discussions that are, if nothing else, more manageable.

Appendix 1: Assessment of Metalinguistic Awareness Related to Bilingualism

1. Language Naming (LN)

As an introduction to the interview, the examiner commented to the child that students at the Xicohtencatl school speak two languages and then pointed out, "You also know how to speak (or understand) two languages." Responses were recorded to the questions, "What languages do you know? What are they called?" If the child indicated only one, or was unsure of how to respond, the same questions were repeated after he or she completed the Written Message Identification Test (WMI), and the Preference for Writing/Utility interview (PWU).

2. Written Message Identification (WMI)

The purpose of the WMI was to make a preliminary estimate of language awareness based on five short written texts (a shopping list, a message for a family member, a note passed to a friend in class, a sign advertising chicken for sale, the first line of a story). Each text was presented in two versions, Spanish and the translation equivalent in Nahuatl, for a total of 10 items. After explaining that some cards "will have something written in Spanish and some will have something written in Nahuatl," and after confirming that the child could read each card, the experimenter presented the same cards again, in random order, asking the child to identify the language in which each text was written. The score was the number of correct responses.

3. Preference for Writing/Utility Interview (PWU)

In bilingual communities marked by an imbalance between the indigenous language and the national language, even in many bilingual schools, all written texts and literacy materials are in Spanish. As a rule, and regardless of the circumstances, initial literacy is taught in Spanish. The aim of the PWU was to examine students' perspectives on written language in Spanish and Nahuatl. Children were presented with pairs of flash cards from the previous test (WMI) (both shopping lists, both story fragments, etc.) and were asked to choose which would be better for each purpose. For each of the five choices, Spanish, Nahuatl, or Undecided was recorded. See examples below of the "Shopping list" item and the "Story" item.

Shopping List
Now I am going to show you two cards with different things written on them, and you are going to choose which one is better. Let's say that you are going to send a friend of yours to the market to buy some things that your mom needs. You are going to make a list of the things you want him (or her) to buy for you so that he (or she) doesn't forget anything. Which one of these is better for making a list?

tuna	tloal
hongo	yetl
durazno	tenoxtle
maíz	xokotl
frijol	nanakatl
calabaza	ayotl
zapote	tsapotl

Story
You are going to write a story that another child will read. Which one of these is better for starting to write a story?

Itech se altepetsintli	En un pueblito
ochantia se tlakatsintli	vivía un señor que
okipiaya se ichpokaua, …	tenía una hija, …

4. Language Loyalty/Attitude/Usage (LLAU)

Using a conversational format, children were asked to discuss a series of topics related to language loyalty, attitudes, and everyday usage, including personal examples and rationales:

1. Language choice: which language is normally spoken to siblings, cousins, friends at home, with the teacher at school, parents and grandparents, ritual kin, and at the store.

2. Personal preference and fluency ("Which do you like better? Which is easier when talking with a friend?").

3. Public perception: what affective factors are associated with speaking Nahuatl or Spanish in "public" situations (e.g., feeling embarrassed when others have overheard you speak in Spanish, in Nahuatl).

4. Conservation/Loss of the indigenous language (e.g., "Might it be possible that someday people in this town will not speak Nahuatl anymore, because they forgot it, and then only speak Spanish? Which languages will you teach to your own children?").

Representative Negative Responses to Language Preservation Question
Following question #4, children were asked, "Let's imagine that this *could* happen, that everyone in San Isidro now only speaks Spanish because they forgot Nahuatl. How would you feel? What would happen?"

Sixth grade
Román: "Fastidiado, que todos han olvidado del lenguaje de nuestro pueblo" [Annoyed, that everyone has forgotten the language of our town].

Fermín: "Dar pena, si alguien diría algo en mexicano no entendería" [Embarrassed, if someone would say something in Nahuatl, I wouldn't understand].

Flavio: "Muy mal, por ejemplo si yo quería hablar con otra persona en náhuatl, no me entendería" [Very bad, for example if I wanted to speak to another person in Nahuatl, he wouldn't understand].

Mónica: "Mal, porque todos hablan en español y solamente yo hablo en náhuatl, porque es difícil hablar con las otras personas que solamente hablan español" [Bad, because everyone speaks Spanish and only I speak Nahuatl, because it's difficult to speak with other people who only speak Spanish].

Beatriz: "Muy mal, porque por mucho tiempo han hablado náhuatl" [Very bad, because for a long time they have spoken Nahuatl].

Imelda: "Me sentiría orgullosa por no olvidar esa lengua; les diría a otras personas, ¿por qué olvidaron?" [I would be proud for not forgetting that language; I would say to other people, why did you forget?].

Pascual: "Triste, porque se perdió una lengua madre, porque se olvidaron del náhuatl" [Sad, because a mother tongue was lost, because Nahuatl was forgotten].

Alfredo: "Mal, porque ya no me van a hacer caso cuando hablo con ellos" [Bad, because they won't pay attention to me anymore when I speak to them].

Fourth grade
Zacarías: "Muy feo, los demás hablan español y yo hablo náhuatl" [Very bad, the others speak Spanish and I speak Nahuatl].

Alvaro: "Mal, voy a hablar mucho con la gente y preguntarles por qué se olvidaron de hablar en náhuatl" [Bad, I will talk to the people a lot and ask them why they forget how to speak Nahuatl].

Second grade
Natalia: "Me sentiría avergonzada porque haber cambiado de voz me equivocara de hablar en náhuatl o en castilla" [I would feel ashamed because having changed voices, I would make mistakes speaking in Nahuatl or in Spanish].

Macario: "Mal, porque ya no hablan mi lengua, fueron nuestros tatarabuelitos" [Bad, because they don't speak my language anymore. They were our great-grandfathers (with diminutive marker for respect/endearment)].

Fidel: "Mal, porque ya se olvidó todo" [Bad, because now everything was forgotten].

Esperanza: "Muy triste, ya no pueden hablar en mexicano*, lloraba porque ya no pueden hablar" [Very sad, they can't speak in Nahuatl anymore, I (or the people) were crying because they can't speak anymore].

Sergio: "Mal, olvidaron nuestra propia lengua" [Bad, because they forgot our own language].

Sample Responses of Students Who Indicated That They Will Teach Both Languages to Their Own Children When They Are Adults

Sixth grade
Alfredo: "Para que, en algunas partes, le preguntan en mexicano*, le contesta" [So that, in some parts, they ask him in Nahuatl, he answers].

Alicia: "Porque algunos de nuestros abuelitos no saben hablar en español" [Because some of our grandparents don't know how to speak Spanish].

Pascual: "El español les va a servir en la escuela, el náhuatl les va a servir para platicar con nosotros y para un concurso de náhuatl" [Spanish will be useful to them in school, Nahuatl will be useful to them to speak with us and for a Nahuatl contest].

Fourth grade
Marta: "Para que aprendan a hablar, porque todos lo hablan y somos mexicanos*" [So that they learn how to talk, because everyone speaks it and we are Mexicanos].

Alvaro: "Para entender todo" [To understand everything].

Claudia: "Dice mi abuela, porque a veces cuando vamos a Puebla tienen que hablar español" [My grandmother says because sometimes when we go to Puebla they have to speak Spanish].

Second grade

Nazario: "Porque nosotros hablamos otra lengua y en San Pablo hablan otra lengua, en español" [Because we speak another language and in San Pablo they speak another language, in Spanish].

Sergio: "Me gustan las dos aunque no sepa hablar bien el náhuatl, porque no van a saber en qué están hablando" [I like both although I don't know how to speak Nahuatl well, because they won't know which they are speaking].

Natalia: "Porque cuando vamos a Puebla tenemos que decir buenas cosas allí y traer algo para comer" [Because when we go to Puebla we have to say good things there and bring (home) something to eat].

*Depending on the context, "mexicanos" refers either to Mexicans (citizens of the country of Mexico) or speakers of "mexicano" (traditional or colloquial term for Nahuatl).

5. **Language Awareness Test (LAT)**

A list of 25 individual words was presented on flash cards, and children were asked to read each word and to indicate in which language it was written. This assessment differed from the WMI in that the items would normally form part of the speaking vocabulary of all local adult residents (monolingual Spanish, monolingual Nahuatl, and bilingual), and in everyday conversation translation equivalents do not normally occur. Students were making a judgment regarding the "linguistic origin" of words that form part of their Nahuatl and Spanish lexicons based on their knowledge of phonological and morphological patterns of each language.

Appearing individually, items on the LAT did not have the benefit of context that made a similar determination on the WMI straightforward for all 6th graders, almost all 4th graders (93% of all items correct), and most 2nd graders (75%). Of the 25 words, presented in random order, 18 were of Nahuatl origin, 7 Spanish.

The LAT was scored by counting the number of Nahuatl terms correctly identified minus the number of Spanish terms misidentified as Nahuatl.

Language Awareness Test (LAT) items
1. XICOHTENCATL
2. RESURRECCION
3. HUAMANTLA
4. POPOCATEPETL
5. SANTISIMA
6. SEMPOALXOCHITL

7. SITLALI
8. BENITO JUAREZ
9. MARGARITAS
10. GORDITA
11. MALINTZIN
12. CUAUHTEMOC
13. TLALOC
14. METZLI
15. AMOZOC
16. INDEPENDENCIA
17. XOXTLA
18. GUADALUPE
19. POXCATZI
20. YOLOTZIN
21. IZTACCIUATL
22. COMAL
23. METLAPIL
24. TEMASCAL
25. TAMAL

18 items of Nahuatl origin
XICOHTENCATL—official name of the elementary school in San Isidro
HUAMANTLA, AMOZOC, XOXTLA—nearby towns
POPOCATEPETL, IZTACCIUATL, MALINTZIN—nearby volcanoes
SEMPOALXOCHITL—marigold ("caléndula" in Peninsular Spanish)
SITLALI, METZLI, YOLOTZIN—common Mexican given names [Star, Moon, Little Heart]
CUAUHTEMOC—street named after a prominent Aztec leader
TLALOC—Aztec god of rain, common metaphor for precipitation
POXCATZI—nearby ravine
COMAL, METLAPIL—common household items
TAMAL—popular food item (familiar to English speakers in its plural form)
TEMASCAL—traditional steam bath

7 items of Spanish origin
RESURRECCION, SANTISIMA, MARGARITAS—names of local neighborhoods
BENITO JUAREZ—official name of the elementary school in neighboring San Miguel

INDEPENDENCIA—street name in San Isidro
GORDITA—popular food item
GUADALUPE—popular Mexican given name for both boys and girls

6. The Expressive Vocabulary Section of the Bilingual Interview

This assessment was not originally part of the Metalinguistic Awareness study. It was administered earlier as part of the evaluation of children's oral language skills: informal conversation and formal interview based on illustrations depicting a short narrative; independent narrative based on the same illustrations; and an

Table A.1
Responses to Expressive Vocabulary section of the Bilingual Interview (Felícitas, 2nd grade)

Nahuatl application	Spanish application
cama	cochinos
chichi	toro
silla	silla
canasta	cubeta
mesa	trastes
tasa	venden
casuela	mesa
xochitl	bebé
piltontsitsi	burro
naranja	perro
sombrero	nopal
cuaderno	chivo
tlajkuilotok	niño
tlakualchiua	sol
burro	conejo
uva	flores
tototsintle	árbol
okotl	pájaro
volcán	mamá
tonaltsin	hongos
kali	agua
mili	taza
kajkoke	casa
itskuintle	señor
Nahuatl 12	muchachos
Spanish 12	Spanish 25

OVERALL TOTALS: Nahuatl 12, Spanish 37

assessment of Expressive Vocabulary, each administered in parallel in Spanish and Nahuatl.

Expressive Vocabulary was assessed by an open-ended procedure: Four scenes of everyday life, two for Spanish (interior of house, market) and two for Nahuatl (exterior of house, cornfield), were presented to each child by teachers who spoke exclusively in Spanish or Nahuatl, respectively, during the sessions. Each child named as many items in each scene as he or she could, with one prompt each time to help exhaust all possibilities. For each language session or application, children were specifically instructed to name items in the selected language.

Scoring was as follows: (1) list all words produced for each language session (Nahuatl application and Spanish application) separately; (2) eliminate repeated words, but not translation equivalents, within the list for each application separately; (3) count the total number of items in Nahuatl and in Spanish for each list and add the separate totals for each language to obtain an overall total for that language. The example in table A.1 is from 2nd-grade student Felícitas.

Response patterns for Expressive Vocabulary across grades made for an interesting comparison with the Metalinguistic Awareness scores. As exemplified in Felícitas's responses, children tended to produce a larger number of items in Spanish than in Nahuatl (see chapter 5 for a discussion of this tendency). More importantly, older children produced vocabulary samples that were, on average, significantly more balanced than those of younger children. Subtracting the number of Nahuatl responses from the number of Spanish responses, the grade-level averages fall from 24.2 in 2nd grade to 9.5 in 6th grade. In addition, comparing each child's "balance score" with his or her score on the LAT, we find a modest correlation (N. Francis 1998). As children's performance on this subtest of the Metalinguistic Awareness assessment (awareness of differences between Spanish and Nahuatl) improves, so does their ability to comply with the instructions on the Expressive Vocabulary assessment (to name items in Nahuatl or Spanish when asked to do so).

The LN, WMI, and LAT assessed metalinguistic awareness in the more narrow sense (discriminating between the two languages at different levels and in reference to different contexts). The PWU and LLAU, while they were primarily designed to examine students' attitudes and perceptions, involved categories of awareness as well, but along a different dimension. Again, as an evaluation of language dominance, the Bilingual Interview followed the standard procedure of assessing each language separately, with items administered monolingually, by two separate persons, in each section.

Appendix 2: Indices of Additive Bilingualism

Chapters 5 and 9 refer to apparent trends in how the children in the Mexican study used both languages they know and how they perceived the relationship between them. Some of the trends were barely noticeable, as in the case of the choices for revision/correction in their Nahuatl compositions; others were strikingly evident, observable immediately from visual inspection alone (e.g., the patterns of lexical borrowing when writing in each language). All, however, showed the same trend, in the same direction. This leads us to speculate that even in the domains of language interaction and language contact where the apparent tendency could not be shown to be statistically significant, it fell into line with the same course of bilingual development, typical perhaps for children in this particular community. These tendencies are summarized in table A.2. The overall trend can be characterized informally as a kind of additive bilingual development, perhaps restricted to the bilingual school and community that was the site of this investigation. In fact, recent informal observation in the neighboring indigenous town (in the state of Puebla) has suggested the beginnings of a gradual shift away from Nahuatl in neighboring localities in the immediate vicinity that is not as apparent in the community where the research project was located.

Although Nahuatl is mainly restricted to symbolic recognition at school, children's linguistic competence in the language continues to develop, most visibly among children who are Spanish-dominant upon entering 1st grade. Sociolinguistic factors that can be suggested as possible explanations include (1) the continuing strong presence in the community of the indigenous language in all realms of social life, confirmed in the national census report of 2000 (INEGI 2000), conferring upon it broad utility among all age groups; and (2) the school's positive disposition (symbolic though it may be) toward expressions of children's bilingual identity, and its promotion of enrichment activities related to Nahuatl language and culture. What is interesting is that these conditions seem to be consistently reflected in performance on language assessment measures, controlled observations, and formal interviews among children and their parents (N. Francis 1997; N. Francis and Navarrete

Table A.2
Comparing younger and older children on measures of language proficiency, preference, and use

Measure	Tendency as children attain higher grade levels (4th and 6th)
Borrowing in Nahuatl writing	Lower frequency of borrowed Spanish content words
Borrowing in Nahuatl oral narrative	Lower frequency of borrowed Spanish content words
Revision/Correction of borrowed items in Nahuatl compositions	Successfully attempted corrections of Spanish borrowings in Nahuatl writing made only by 6th graders
Bilingual Interview: Vocabulary	Higher percentage of Nahuatl expressive vocabulary as a function of grade level
Bilingual Interview: Language dominance	Children with less than complete Nahuatl conversational fluency: 2nd grade—3, 4th grade—1, 6th grade—0
Observation of language use in conversation with peers	Increasing preference for Nahuatl with grade level
Sociolinguistic interview	Indices of ethnolinguistic loyalty/preference for Nahuatl higher for 4th and 6th graders

Gómez 2003), tendencies consistent with recent field observations by Nava Nava (2010). The right-hand column of table A.2 lists the language assessment, the in-school observation of language use, or interview conducted with each of the 45 child participants in the study. The left-hand column lists the tendency of results that support the characterization of additive bilingual development. The following sections of the appendix briefly describe each measure.

Borrowing in Nahuatl Composition and in Nahuatl Oral Narrative

As figure A.1 shows, total frequency of borrowing does not vary with grade level. Rather, the measure of interest is a decrease in the frequency of borrowing of Spanish content words among 4th and 6th graders. Borrowing of discourse connectors—"hasta" [as far as, up to, until], "por" [in order to, because of], "para" [in order to, so that], "pero" [but], "entonces" [then], and so on—actually increases, reflecting the widespread use of these loanwords from Spanish among all Nahuatl speakers, even older adults with little knowledge of Spanish. A similar overall trend and relation between content word and discourse connector borrowing was evidenced in children's oral narratives. As table A.2 indicates, this apparent tendency

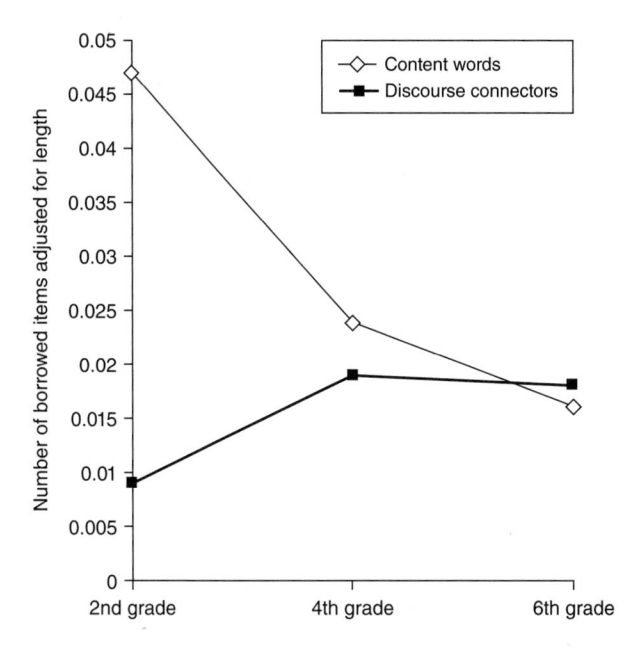

Index of borrowing from Spanish: Total number of content words and discourse connectors from Spanish divided by total number of running words.

Figure A.1
Borrowing from Spanish when writing in Nahuatl

on the part of older students to begin to "avoid" Spanish borrowing of content words, replacing them with their Nahuatl counterparts, is consistent with all the other related measures. Torres's (2006) study of "bilingual discourse markers" focuses on this same differentiation by lexical category. In addition, the decrease in content word borrowing is negatively correlated with Metalinguistic Awareness. All of this is also consistent with the parenthetical observation made in chapter 3 that 5th graders tend to be more "congruent" in their choice of language in the Story Stem assessment. Specifically, of the 35 children in 3rd grade who participated in this assessment, 6 completed the Nahuatl story stem in Spanish and 29 did so in Nahuatl. None of the 5th graders made this "switch," all 34 of them electing to complete the Nahuatl story stem in Nahuatl.

Beyond simply registering the tendency on the part of older students to prefer a more "purist style" in regard to content words, and beyond describing the correlations with the other language choice indices, a common factor appears to underlie these parallel tendencies: metalinguistic development, a factor that further research might continue to explore. The children's growing awareness of language form and language use (related to bilingualism in the community) may explain in large part the patterns of responses summarized in table A.2. Schooling and literacy, by all accounts, is a major contributor to this apparent tendency in language development. The children's developing proficiency in Nahuatl across the grades, evidenced in measures of both conversational ability and literacy-related abilities, probably also accounts for the tendency toward separating the languages when children are called upon to do so. Level of proficiency in a L2 (or socially subordinate L1) appears to be related to the ability to control cross-language competition. That is, interference from the nonselected language decreases in highly proficient bilinguals (Costa et al. 2003).

Revision/Correction of Borrowed Items in Nahuatl Compositions

Recall the results outlined in chapter 8: only 6th graders successfully attempted revision/correction of their Nahuatl compositions that involved a language switch (i.e., changing a borrowed Spanish item to its Nahuatl translation or an equivalent term).

Bilingual Interview: Expressive Vocabulary

In the open-ended Expressive Vocabulary task described in appendix 1, children's production in Spanish shows no upward trend across the grades (see figure A.2), as was predicted since this task tapped everyday conversational discourse and semantic networks that are nonacademic. If the participants had been beginning or intermediate L2 learners of Spanish, then progressive mastery of these items would have been expected; but all were fluent Spanish speakers. The Nahuatl curve, on the other hand, does indicate an apparent progressive mastery. Recall that in chapter 5 we tentatively attributed this result to factors including (1) L2 learning of Nahuatl by children who were at one time Spanish-dominant 1st graders; (2) more advanced metalinguistic awareness on the part of Nahuatl speakers in regard to the separation of the languages they speak; and (3) the learning of new Nahuatl vocabulary (by the L1 speakers) that may replace earlier borrowed items from Spanish in the appropriate language use context.

Bilingual Interview: Language Dominance

Unlike the Expressive Vocabulary measure, which cannot estimate language dominance because of different perceptions of loanword inclusion by younger and older bilingual speakers, conversational interviews that require question comprehension and acceptable grammatical response provide a better measure of relative linguistic competence in each language (N. Francis and Reyhner 2002, 175–179, 247–252). The following are results from this part of the Bilingual Interview:

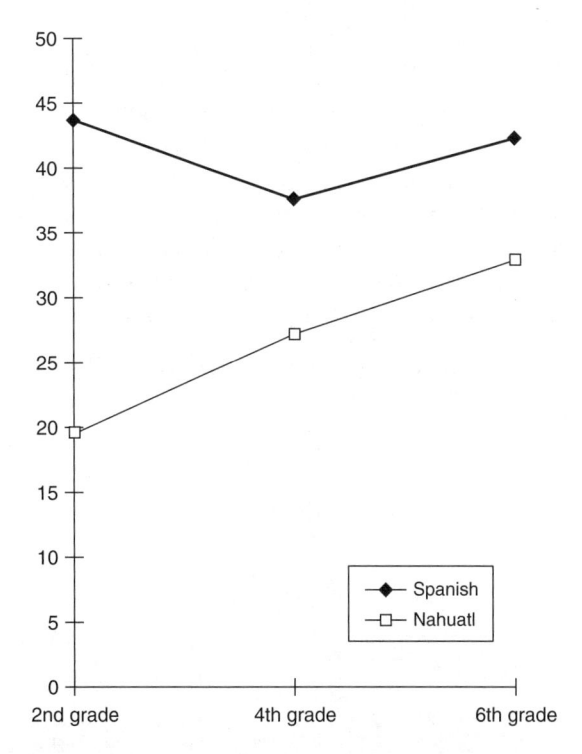

Figure A.2
Expressive Vocabulary: Section 1 of the Bilingual Interview

2nd grade: balanced bilingual—12, Spanish-dominant—3
4th grade: balanced bilingual—14, Spanish-dominant—1
6th grade: balanced bilingual—15, Spanish-dominant—0

Observation of Language Use in Conversations

Participants in the 2nd-, 4th-, and 6th-grade cohort were observed in small groups during recess and lunch break in the school library while they engaged in cooperative activities that required conversation (board games and picture card games); children were grouped by grade level. Each conversational turn was recorded as either Spanish, Spanish-Nahuatl (frequent intersentential switching), or Nahuatl (monolingual or language mixing in which Nahuatl was clearly the matrix language). The results were as follows:

2nd grade—(Spanish) 6, (Spanish-Nahuatl) 8, (Nahuatl) 1
4th grade—(Spanish) 1, (Spanish-Nahuatl) 8, (Nahuatl) 6
6th grade—(Spanish) 0, (Spanish-Nahuatl) 4, (Nahuatl) 11

Sociolinguistic Interview

Children were interviewed on a wide range of topics concerning their perceptions of Spanish and Nahuatl in their community and their views on different aspects of language use in school and in the community. One purpose of the interview was to gauge ethnolinguistic loyalty. The measures that emerged from the child interviews were compared with those from interviews with the children's parents and other adult family members (N. Francis and Navarrete Gómez 2003). Among the responses that indicated an additive bilingual trend are the ones to the following questions:

1. In which language do you speak with your friends? Responded "Nahuatl":
   2nd—7
   4th—10
   6th—13

2. Which is easier when speaking with a friend? Responded "Spanish":
   2nd—8
   4th—4
   6th—4

3. Which do you like better? Responded "Spanish":
   2nd—10
   4th—6
   6th—3

Interestingly, when asked, "In which language do you speak with your parents and grandparents?" (the familial counterpart to question #1), children responded uniformly (no differences of note across grades), as would be expected, despite children's stated preferences and self-estimates of facility.

4. Might it be possible that someday people in this town will not speak Nahuatl anymore, because they forgot it, and then only speak Spanish?
   2nd—9
   4th—3
   6th—2

5. How would you feel about this (refers to question #4)? Responded "badly" or "unhappy":
   2nd—11
   4th—11
   6th—all 15

Compare these responses with similar trends in the Metalinguistic Awareness assessment (appendix 1 and chapter 8).

Appendix 3: Early Childhood Borrowing and Codeswitching

The following transcription of mixed English-Spanish utterances by a bilingual child ("Elizabeth"), recorded sporadically from age 2 years 2 months (2;2) through 4 years 11 months (4;11) is offered here as a corpus for further analysis. Students of early childhood codeswitching should find it interesting for the patterns that might be revealed. The total expressive vocabulary at age 1;9 is also included as a beginning reference point. The sample is relatively small, with obvious gaps in the record (these clearly do not indicate a diminution in mixing during these months; rather, they derive from a lapse in annotations by Elizabeth's parents). However, the sample does represent the complete and unselected available data during this period of early bilingual development.

Background Information

Elizabeth is representative of nonbalanced bilingual development, typical of many young immigrants to the United States from Spanish-speaking countries (in this case at age 2;5). Despite greater total exposure to Spanish (in quantitative terms) through at least age 3 (including television) in her bilingual home, English rapidly becomes the dominant primary language in all respects. English language development is normal at all stages from age 3 on, while expressive abilities in Spanish unambiguously and unmistakably indicate nonnative grammatical competence (confirmed subsequently in middle childhood). See chapter 6 for discussion and similar case study reports.

From a cursory examination of the mixing patterns—in particular, the predominance of English as the matrix language from an early stage—one is tempted to propose (with the benefit of hindsight) a similarly early divergence/imbalance in which only one language begins to take on the status of a fully formed primary-L1. Not revealing itself clearly in either monolingual L_a or L_b utterances, this kind of emerging imbalance might be indicated much sooner by early mixing patterns. Cross-linguistic influence is not without its effects in the opposite direction (from the developing nondominant language to the developing dominant primary-L1), as evidenced occasionally in what appear to be possible "loan translations"; examples are shown below. I leave these assessments, highly speculative as they are, open to other interpretations.

Total Expressive Vocabulary—Age 1;9

Spanish
nena
mamá
papá
abui
agua
otro
ven
éste
popó
tú
yo
e-gangan
má[s]
English
nose
boo[k]
mo[re]
bau [ball]
chee[se]
ca[r]
Indeterminate
no
[a]way -or- [f]ue

Mixed Utterances Subsequent to Onset of Two-Word Stage

Age 2;2
Come pan, b[r]ead.
[*Eats bread*, bread.]

Dos doggie.
[*Two* doggie.]

Otro flower.
[*Other* flower.]

A [s]nake, *otro*.
[A snake, *other*.]

Off this, *feo*.
[Off this, *ugly*.]

This *pone*.
[This *put*.]

Mami *bobo*, here.
[Mami *balloon*, here.] ("bobo" = "globo")

A [s]nake *come*, careful.
[A snake *eats*, careful.]

A [s]nake, a [s]nake *come* lelephant.
[A snake, a snake, *eats* elephant.]

[S]nake *come* me.
[Snake *eats* me.]

Age 2;3
Mira, todos sleep.
[*Look, everyone* sleep]

This, *todo*.
[This, *all (of it)*.]

Otro slide, big one, round and round and round.
[*Other* slide, big one, round and round and round.]

Azul ball, *azul* ball.
[*Blue* ball, *blue* ball.]

Muchos leaves, *todos* leaves.
[*Many* leaves, *all* leaves.]

Catch the ball Big Bird; no there, *arriba*.
[Catch the ball Big Bird; no there, *up (there)*.]

Wet, *pelo* wet.
[Wet, *hair* wet.]

Vamos a copies.
[*Let's go to* copies (the copy store).]

Casa far away?
[*House* far away?]

Here ya go, *ten*, *una más*, there *todos*, there.
[Here you go, *here* (directive, imperative form of verb "tener" = to have), *one more*, there *all (of them)*, there.]

Come; good?
[*Eat* (directive to doll); good?]

Age 2;4
Así, *eso*, a little bit.
[*In this way, right*, a little bit.]

Muchos frogs.
[*Many* frogs.]

Ojo, *otro* eye, mouth, *otro* man eye, *ojo*.
[*Eye*, *other* eye, mouth, *other* man eye, *eye*.]

No water, *agua*, water, *agua*, Mami.
[No water, *water*, water, *water*, Mami.]

Age 2;5
This *azul*; Yani like blue.
[This *blue*; Yani like blue.]

Vamos outside.
[*Let's go* outside.]

No vayas, close the door.
[*Don't go*, close the door.]

Me buy *chita*.
[Me buy *milk*.] ("chita" = "lechita," diminutive of "leche")

Otro me hand.
[*Other* me hand.]

Find the *queso*.
[Find the *cheese*.]

Titas de agua in the baby tree.
[*Little drops of water* in the baby tree.] ("titas" = "gotitas," "gotas" + diminutive)

This *mis* sticks.
[This *my* sticks.]

One *arriba*, one *abajo*, one *abajo*, one *arriba*, one here.
[One *up*, one *down*, one *down*, one *up*, one here.]

Ahí va Papi's *cama*.
[*There goes* Papi's *bed*.]

Kitty cat *no vayas*.
[Kitty cat *don't go*.]

I see *niños*.
[I see *children*.]

You fall you *pelo*?
[You fall you *hair*?]

No *pica* that chile.
[(It's) not *spicy* that chile.]

Papi *sube* a plane.
[Papi *get on* a plane.]

You *misa* same color.
[You *shirt* same color.] ("misa" = "camisa")

Mami, *fría chita*; Papi say milk.
[Mami, *cold milk*; Papi say milk.]

Me room *mucho* dark, here no.
[Me room *much* dark, here no.]

Papi drink coffee *todo*.
[Papi drink coffee *all (of it)*.]

Mina me eye.
[*Look at* me eye.] ("mina" = "mira")

Oo ta Papi's coins?
[*Where is* Papi's coins?] ("oo ta" = "¿dónde está?")

Age 2;6
Put you *leche* on the table, and *luego* back.
[Put you *milk* on the table, and *then* back.]

No, off *besos*.
[No, off *kisses*.]

Así is.
[*That's the way it* is.]

Sí tiene little bit.
[*Yes (he or she) has* little bit.]

Me /*prend*/ that.
[Me *light* that.] (pointing to lamp; "prend" = verb stem missing Spanish inflection for 1st person)

Papi, *uvas* there.
[Papi, *grapes* there.]

Age 2;7
See *muchos* in there.
[See *many* in there.]

A pretty one, no a *feo* one.
[A pretty one, no an *ugly* one.]

No, I'm a girl, Mommy say *niña*, Papi say girl.
[No, I'm a girl, Mommy say *girl*, Papi say girl.]

Age 2;8
Take me toys *a* bed.
[Take me toys *to* bed.]

Here *bubú aquí*. Here *bubú aquí*.
[Here *boo-boo here*. Here *boo-boo here*.]

I like *dulces*.
[I like *candies*.]

Age 2;9
Father: What do you see?
Elizabeth: *Más*, more snow, falling down.
[Elizabeth: *More*, more snow, falling down.]

A *pluma*, a little feather for a little eagle.
[A *feather*, a little feather for a little eagle.]

Spanish say *rosa*, English say pink.
[Spanish say *rosa (pink)*, English say pink.]

Look, a little *uva*.
[Look, a little *grape*.]

Ice me want, *hielo*.
[Ice me want, *ice*.]

He like *dulce*, he like candy.
[He like *candy*, he like candy.]

Me want the *moño*, thank you.
[Me want the *hair ribbon*, thank you.]

What put the sand for *la nieve*.
[What put the sand for *the snow*.]

I'll get another *yoyo*.
[I'll get another (bathroom tissue) *roll*.] ("yoyo" = "rollo")

That's *feo*, turn it off.
[That's *ugly*, turn it off.]

Ten, here one.
[*Here* (directive, imperative form of verb "tener" = to have), here (locative adverb) one.]

Me no like that song, that *feo* song.
[Me no like that song, that *ugly* song.]

Mother (playing "restaurant"): ¿Qué le podemos servir? [What can we serve you?]
Elizabeth (speaking for each of four dolls): Grandma—water, Grandpa—water, *Abui—agua, Buito—agua*, because they speak Spanish.
[Elizabeth: Grandma—water, Grandpa—water, *Grandma—water, Grandpa—water*, because they speak Spanish.]

Age 2;10
That will be a good *día*.
[That will be a good *day*.]

Let's be the three bears; you be *papi oso*.
[Let's be the three bears; you be *Papa Bear*.]

Donde está el pelo like the baby upstairs?
[*Where is the hair* like the baby upstairs?]

This *comida*.
[This *food*.]

Papi how you eat *dulces*, how you eat candy!
[Papi how you eat *candies*, how you eat candy!]

Eating *papas*.
[Eating *potatoes*.]

I want *hongos*.
[I want *mushrooms*.]

Ellos on the table.
[*They* on the table.]

Look Mami, *zafó*.
[Look Mami, *ran away*.] (verb "zafarse"/"se zafó" would normally be reflexive in this context)

Age 2;11
I saw the *luz* in there.
[I saw the *light* in there.]

You buy *pavo* and *dulce* bread.
[You buy *turkey* and *sweet* bread.]

What you say *papa oso* in English?
[What you say *Papa Bear* in English?]

Ten Papi, put up there.
[*Here (take this)* Papi, put up there.]

Me want *hielo*.
[Me want *ice*.]

That *chueco*.
[That *crooked*.]

Me want *huevos* Mami.
[Me want *eggs* Mami.]

Timothy no like the *nieve*.
[Timothy no like the *snow*.]

Put the little *jabón* up there.
[Put the little *soap* up there.]

You *ya sabe*?
[You *already know*?]

The *luz* come in your eye.
[The *light* come in your eye.]

Sí, I say *sí*.
[*Yes*, I say *yes*.]

I eat *huevo*.
[I eat *egg*.]

Age 3;0
Me go to *México*.
[Me go to *Mexico*.]

He have *colita*.
[He have *backside*.]

Here is *colita*.
[Here is *backside*.]

Here Papi, this part is his *panza*, this is his arm.
[Here Papi, this part is his *tummy*, this is his arm.]

Mami, I want *chile* on my *huevos*.
[Mami, I want *chile* on my *eggs*.]

The doggie get the string for *los dos*.
[The doggie get the string for *the two (of them)*.]

Age 3;1
That a *paleta*.
[That an *ice cream pop*.]

Father: What are you looking for?
Elizabeth: *A sillas*, the chairs.
[Elizabeth: *To chairs*, the chairs.]

Come the *duende*, he promise.
[Come the *elf*, he promise.]

It's on his *panza*.
[It's on his *tummy*.]

He's pushing the bear on *jabón*.
[He's pushing the bear on *soap*.]

Give me that, the *jarrocitos*.
[Give me that, the *little jugs*.] ("jarro" + diminutive = "jarrocitos")

That say *china* food
[That say *Chinese* food.]

Age 3;7
He is big and *gordo*.
[He is big and *fat*.]

I was *chuping* it all up.
[I was *sucking* it all up.]

/Lans/ it to the sky.
[*Throw* it to the sky.] ("lans" = verb stem missing inflection for imperative)

Age 3;8
He gave me *cariñitos* on my foot.
[He gave me *tickles* on my foot.]

You can /prest/ it to me.
[You can *lend* it to me.] ("prest" = verb stem missing Spanish infinitive affix)

Age 3;9
That is a *fishote*.
[That is a *big fish*.] ("fish" (Eng.) + augmentative (Sp.) = fishote)

They are *mexicanos*.
[They are *Mexicans*.]

Nina and George, they *nace* [to]gether.
[Nina and George, they *is born* together.]

You put some carrots and some onions and you mix it and make *japopona* food.
[You put some carrots and some onions and you mix it and make *Japanese* food.]

Age 4;11
She has a sewing *máquina*.
[She has a sewing *machine*.]

Otro por favor, with *más* cream.
[*Another one please*, with *more* cream.]

Possible Loan Translations/Transfers (Influence of Spanish)

Manys papers. (2;6)
Those rabbits funnys. (2;6)
This big, these tinies. (2;7)
There is. (2;8)
I put him his name. (2;9)
I cut them and you form them up. (3;7)
I can pass this to you. (3;8)
Father: Who can help me?
Elizabeth: I. (3;9)
What you prepare? (3;9)

Of particular interest is the apparent imposition of "English" modifier placement (but note that in Spanish, modifiers that precede the noun are often a grammatical option):

Azul ball, *azul ball*. (2;3)
[*Blue* ball, *blue ball*.]

Ahí va Papi's cama. (2;5)
[*There goes* Papi's bed.]

Mami, *fría chita*; Papi say milk. (2;5)
[Mami, *cold milk*; Papi say milk.]

Look, a <u>little *uva*</u>. (2;9)
[Look, a <u>little *grape*</u>.]

Me no like that song, that <u>*feo* song</u>. (2;9)
[Me no like that song, that <u>*ugly* song</u>.]

That will be a <u>good *día*</u>. (2;10)
[That will be a <u>good *day*</u>.]

Put the <u>little *jabón*</u> up there. (2;11)
[Put the <u>little *soap*</u> up there.]

You put some carrots and some onions and you mix it and make <u>*japopona* food</u>. (3;9)
[You put some carrots and some onions and you mix it and make <u>*Japanese* food</u>.]

She has a <u>sewing *máquina*</u>. (4;11)
[She has a <u>sewing *machine*</u>.]

However, the last series of examples highlights the problem that all Spanish-speaking children, bilingual and monolingual alike, encounter in acquiring the word order patterns for nouns and their modifiers. And in fact, we might want to hesitate to point to these examples as evidence for an early imposition of English syntax. For balanced Spanish-English bilinguals, the available positive evidence is clearly dauntingly impoverished considering their eventual mastery of the respective word orders in this case. And for monolingual Spanish-speaking 2-year-olds, with no competing input from another language, the task is not as straightforward either. Modifiers only follow nouns most of the time, the (frequent and ubiquitous) "exceptions" being related to very subtle semantic distinctions: "bonito niño" [pretty baby], "hermoso bebé" [beautiful baby], "profundo mar" [deep sea], "fuerte viento" [strong wind], "jóvenes poetas poblanos" [young Puebla poets]. What is the evidence in the primary linguistic data that "casa blanca" [house white] and "cara roja" [face red] cannot be inverted, in contrast to "niño bonito" [baby pretty], which can be? Examples of adjective+noun (Adj+N ⇒ N) compounds are

"mediodía" [mid+day],
"medianoche" [mid+night],
"altavoz" [high/loud+voice ⇒ loudspeaker].

And examples of noun+adjective compounds (N+Adj ⇒ N) are

"cabezadura" [head+hard ⇒ hardhead],
"camposanto" [field+holy ⇒ cemetery],
"aguardiente" [water+burning ⇒ alcoholic beverage].

Not to make things any easier, Spanish-speaking preschoolers know the Brothers' Grimm character Snow White as "Blanca Nieves"! (Perhaps offsetting some of the potential indeterminacy in this instance is the fact that "Blanca" is a common given name.) Hualde, Olarrea, and Escobar (2001) provide more examples and a discussion of the poverty-of-stimulus problem in the acquisition of Spanish. Nicoladis (2006) does the same in a study of the same "input ambiguity" hurdle involving adjective-noun order that French-English bilingual children must overcome.

Students of early child bilingualism will note another interesting feature that deserves further investigation and conceptual clarification: What significance should be attributed to the frequency of translation equivalents (TEs) in this sample of Elizabeth's speech? Not only do we observe a number of TEs in this small sample, but they often present themselves within the same utterance (starting at age 2;4). The sample contains 21 TE pairs, but this clearly represents a fraction of the total, as we do not have a full record of unmixed speech in each language. Holowka, Brousseau-Lapré, and Petitto (2002) review the relevant research. Early studies, which extended a "principle of contrast" to bilingualism, found evidence for an undifferentiated lexicon in the apparent avoidance of TEs by young bilinguals. Later studies contradicted this finding, and reasoned that the principles of contrast apply within each language subsystem, separately, in turn supporting the claim for early differentiation between L_a and L_b. But even from the restricted sample presented here, the question arises, how late into development can we interpret the appearance of TEs as an indication of separation? At some point, children's *awareness* of translation, and its subtleties, requires a different approach to the problem. For example, what is the difference between an early intrautterance TE at age 2;4 (*oyo*—eye) and a TE separated by 12 months (*comida*, 2:10—food, 3;9), attested later in development?

Appendix 4: Writing Samples, including the Assessment of Revision/Correction

In "Tetsitsilintlan" (Nahuatl), by Pascuala (figure A.3), note the following borrowed words from Spanish (refer to the discussion of borrowing and codeswitching in section 5.3):

Line 1	den cuando
Line 2	papán
Line 3	den cuando
Line 4	cuando
Line 8	pero, culpable, porque, pronto
Line 9	doktor
Line 11	luego
Line 13	peligroso, pero
Line 14	luego

In "El señor Tlalocan y la señora Tlalocan" (Spanish), by Margarito (figure A.4), as is typical for all children in the study, no borrowed material from Nahuatl (apart from historical loanwords) is in evidence.

In "El cazador de venados" (Spanish), by Rosalinda (figures A.5, A.6), note the following representative examples of revision/correction (refer to categories of analysis for the Revision/Correction task in section 8.3.2):

Lines 2/3	orthographic correction
Line 7	orthographic correction
Line 11	discourse-level correction
Line 15	sentence-level correction
Line 17	discourse-level revision

308   Appendix 4

Tetsitsilintlan

Ika miek yolkokolistli tikualkaktiuej tlen tech ual tlajtlapoijtiue:

Mijtoa se tlakatl okipiaya nitajtsin omokokoaya ye uejkan. Amo omomatia keman omomikiliskia okilnamik ika tlakayajkayotl kiuikas Zongolica uan ompa kikajkauas.

Nitajtsin omoyolkokoaya tleka okitaya nitelpoch amo kuali okimokuitlauiaya uan ako oknekia kitas nik itlakayo okpiaya tlajtlakosauatl uan yopotonia ako ouelitia meuas. In ye omoyolpachiui kampa ompa ixpojpoliuis.

Nitelpoch omoyolnonots uan otlajto inauak itajtsin.
— Okili notajtsin ¿amo tikonneki tonmopajtiti? Nimitsonuikas Zongolica, ompa katej kuajkuali tepajtijkej, akin kixmatij kuajkuali pajmej uan kimatiskej mitsompaj tiskej.
— Nitajtsin okinankili, amo nikneki ximo kuatotoni tla ako niuejkauas, poliui se, ome, yei, tonal uan ye nimikis, uan nik neki nimikis kampa onitlakat, kan amo niktemakas tekipachol inauak akin amo kenin nikinita nijki nik neki manechtlaltokakan innauak in nokojkoltsitsiuan uan innauak in nokniuan, nikan toteopan kalten.

— Notajtsin nik neki xompajnamiki — kon neki uan amo, itelpoch okikuik se kuajpal uan okimomemelti uan ope nejnemi imelajki altepetl, tlajko ojtli oajsia uan okiseui nitlamemel oktlali ipan se tetl tlen ompa okajsik. Kuak yomoseui okuel okikuik in ojtli, kampa oajsito Zongolica.

in TaTazin o mit guan ni cone den cuando ogualo in ni papán yomit guan ok tocato guan in piltontli nik omit guan dencuando in ni Tazin omit ompacot ca se tetl guae cuando omit in ye Tatazin in tetl onen zilinia gan ogualo in piltontli onen chocalla guan ompa in piltontli ocho calla oktonya tleca nomik in no Tazin pero oye niculpable porque amo pronto onicualik in doktor guan yenonikomit guan luego in telpocatl omo chokiliaya tleca opanok in non peligroso pero luego in Telpocatl

Figure A.3
Pascuala (359)—3rd grade

El señor Tlalocan y la señora Tlalocan

En un pueblito de la región de la Malintzin, sus habitantes escogieron a un muchacho de una familia muy pobre para que se presentara ante el señor Tlalocan y la señora Tlalocan llevándoles un pequeño mensaje. En él pedían muchas cosas que necesitaban.

Los ancianos educaron al muchacho para que pudiera hacer ese trabajo. Le decían que tenía que salir brincando por un sendero en una noche de luna llena, con unos cuernos de venado blanco en la cabeza.

Llegó el día en que debía partir y comenzaron a arreglarlo para que al ponerle en la cabeza los cuernos pareciera un venado de verdad. Los cuernos le brillaban como si fueran de cristal.

Comenzó a correr por el sendero que lo conduciría a un sótano muy profundo. Decían que por allí se entraba al corazón de la tierra, o sea al lugar donde mandan los señores Tlalocan.

Descendió, se metió al sótano y llegó a una ciudad subterránea muy grande y muy bella que tenía grandes campos con milpas de maíz y muchas otras cosas.

Seguía su camino de repente vio plantas extrañas y se asusto porque en su pueblo no sembraban o no abia plantas de esa clase por eso se asusto entonses siguio caminando rrumbo a su destino para cumplir con su trabajo Saltando como si fuera un real Venado banco Su destino era endonde gobernaban el señor y la señora Tlalocan para que cuando lleque les dier el mensaje Siguio y siguio brincando por el cendero de ese gran y bello mundo del señor y la señora Tlalocan. Faltaba mucho para lleqar en ese reino Se dijo el muchacho Cuando caminaba tenia miedo de que no le darian todo lo que decian en el mensaje pero sigio tambien contento porque

Figure A.4
Margarito (523)—5th grade

Nombre: Rosalinda   Edad: 8

Un día El casador de venados
se levanto a la cinco de la maña
na y le dijo a somoger que te a
lloden para aser el cardo para El
venado y el casador se fue aca
sar en el monte y llevo so escape
to y un señor llevaba so borrito
El señor casador le pergonto a
donde dormia el venado
en un una troca a y estaba
el conejo el señas tenia mucha
anmer y no lo encontro
y llego a so casa y somoger
le dijo adonde esta el vendo
que nos pormetiste tengo mocha
anmer dame unas trotilla y
el cardo

Figure A.5
Rosalinda (203)—2nd grade

Rosalinda (203)   Second grade   Age: 8

un día El casador de venados
se levanto a la cinco de la mañano
~~pa~~ y le dijo a so mojer que te a
lloden para aser el cardo para El
venado y el casador se Fue aca
sar en el monte y llevo so escope
ta y ~~un~~ un señor llevaba so borrito
El señor casador le pergonto a
donde dormia el venado
en un una rroca a y estaba
el ~~conejo~~ vehado el señor tenia mucha
anmer y no lo encontro
y llego a so casa y so moger
le dijo adonde esta el vendo
que nos pormetiste tengo mocha
anmer dame unas trotilla y
el cardo esta sabroso. dijo el señor con nun pelazo de carhe

Figure A.6
Rosalinda (203)—2nd grade

Glossary

Ability: Synonymous with *proficiency*. A given language ability can never consist of a single module or processing mechanism by itself. Knowledge structures, information-processing components, and different kinds of subskill come together in performance of language-related tasks. See also *competence*.

Additive bilingualism: Usually refers to sequential bilingualism in children, in which the L2 develops without resulting in any erosion of the L1. In contrast, *subtractive bilingualism* proceeds toward the development of one dominant/primary language (normally a rapidly developing L2) and the early stabilization or attrition of the other. It is important to emphasize that subtractive bilingualism does not typically imply any variety of *semilingualism*, and that it is a normal language development outcome among children exposed to two languages.

Aphasia: Loss, impairment, or disruption of language ability as a result of trauma to the brain. Impairment may be partial and/or temporary and may affect only specific domains or functions. Also, impairment may affect an underlying linguistic knowledge structure or a language-processing component.

Attrition: Erosion, loss of competence. In this book, when referring to language, the term implies (language impairment aside) replacement of one language subsystem by another.

Autochthonous: Indigenous.

Awareness: Refers to perception, or to another kind of mental product that undergoes processing and that is subject to deliberate reflection, sensible in some way, or available to introspection. "Awareness" implies that attention may be brought to bear on a mental product or activity.

Bilingualism: Knowledge of two languages that is significant in some sense (e.g., beyond beginning L2 learning). In bilingualism, one language may be weaker or less complete than the other; that is, "bilingualism" does not refer only to balanced bilingualism or equivalent proficiency in two languages, which is the other possible outcome of exposure to two languages. This definition is preferable to restricting the term to the select subset of persons who possess complete native-like abilities in two languages.

Bootstrapping: From the metaphorical use of the name of the strap sewn at the rear of a boot to help in pulling it up, as in "pulling yourself up by your own bootstraps." It implies the ability to carry out a task by relying on one's own resources. In language acquisition and learning, the idea is that children call upon existing knowledge structures or abilities to intervene in the acquisition or learning of another competence or ability. One knowledge structure or ability that is more highly developed may "pull up" another. Pinker (1994, 385) proposes that children "lift themselves up by their bootstraps at the very outset of language acquisition, and make the first basic discoveries about the grammar of their language." They "get syntax acquisition started" by making inferences, for example, about subjects based on the position of the agent of an action in simple declarative active sentences.

Bottom-up: See *top-down*.

Codeswitching: See *mixing*.

Coherence/Cohesion: "Coherence" is the characteristic of a *discourse* or *text* whereby its elements are organized in a logical or structured manner; the parts are connected in a meaningful way—for example, chronologically in the case of narrative. In the case of argumentative discourse, one might ask, are points and counterpoints pertinent? Meanings in a text or discourse are linked, as in a dialog for example, where shared knowledge might indicate the relationship between the elements in question. A coherent discourse takes the form of a dialog (as in a conversation), a monolog (as in a speech or lecture), or a text. "Cohesion," on the other hand, refers to a specific relationship between elements in a text (e.g., between two words; between a word and a phrase; or between a word or a phrase and a "deleted" element, as in ellipsis). Cohesion and coherence work together in an interdependent way.

Competence: A knowledge system or knowledge structure that underlies *ability*. Processing mechanisms (which also underlie ability), which control or put competence to use in actual performance, should be considered separately. According to this view, an ability depends on the coming together of competencies and processing mechanisms. That is why competence is revealed only indirectly in performance. Even within the linguistic domain there are different kinds of "knowledge of language," different kinds of competence.

Componential: Refers to cognitive components or structures. Shatil and Share (2003, 25), for example, propose that "[a] componential approach to reading allows us to categorize reading processes as either modular or nonmodular." In this book, a "componential approach" to studying language is the same as a "modular approach." See *modularity*.

Conceptual Structure (CS): See *semantics*.

Context-embedded/Contextualized: Refers to comprehension, for example, that depends to a significant degree on the physical situation in which the message occurs. A less obvious variety of context-embedded communication occurs when prior knowledge, background information, or shared assumptions are so complete that comprehension of the message requires less processing of new information in the message or text itself. Comprehension in this example depends less on the actual words that make up the *discourse* and more on access to contextual information. "Decontextualized" language use, therefore, does not imply that all contextual information (including all relevant previous knowledge) has been stripped away; under such circumstances, comprehension would be impossible. Rather, in this case, the comprehender is not able to depend on context in the way that one normally can in typical face-to-face conversation. Discourse is always "contextualized" or "decontextualized" to some degree.

Creole: A language that has emerged from a *pidgin* to become the primary language of a speech community. The creole becomes the L1/native language of children acquiring their mother tongue. In this way, a creole is a fully formed language. See *pidgin*.

Decontextualized: See *context-embedded*.

Cross-linguistic influence: See *interference, transfer*.

Deficit: An inherent impairment, disability, or internal dysfunction that affects ability and performance (in speech comprehension or production, literacy learning, etc.). The term does not apply to extrinsic learning difficulties that are amenable to instructional treatment and can be remediated completely. Deficits are intrinsic handicapping conditions. "Deficit" should not be confused with "deficient," which does not necessarily describe an intrinsic impairment or disability.

Dialect: A variation in language, among native speakers of a language, associated with regional, ethnic, or social differences. Contrasts with the kind of variation in *register* and *interlanguage*.

Diglossia: Whereas *bilingualism* is used to describe how two languages coexist or interact within an individual, this term refers to the relationship between two languages in contact in society. For example, it is applied to situations where it is likely that one language is associated with certain social functions, uses, circumstances, and/or purposes and the other is associated with different ones.

Discourse: Speech or writing about a topic, subject, or theme that is treated at some length; usually speech or writing beyond the sentence level. Discourse can be interactive, as in a conversation (dialog), or produced by a single speaker or writer (in a monologic fashion). The critical feature of discourse is that the sequence of sentences or utterances forms an integrated whole. They are related to one another in some coherent way, and they constitute a recognizable instance of language that is, as a unit, meaningful. A specific discourse ability is composed of components (knowledge structures and processing mechanisms). In the case of Cummins's (2000) differentiation between Basic Interpersonal Communication Skills and Cognitive Academic Language Proficiency, the first describes a type of discourse ability that is required for normal, culturally appropriate conversational uses of language; rules (specific to one's speech community) related to social interaction in face-to-face communication play an important role. CALP, which shares a number of underlying components with conversational ability, can be described as a discourse ability, or complex of abilities, that relies on a different set of knowledge structures, including metalinguistic awareness, in this case related to literacy, artistic genres, formal speech, and academic uses of language.

Domain: In this book, "domain" refers to mental structures and processes in the cognitive sphere, as in the case of a distinctly delimited component of knowledge, a processing mechanism, or a network of structures and processors that underlie a specific ability. So as not to confuse things, "domain" does not refer here to realms of language use as it normally does in the field of sociolinguistics.

Dominant language: In bilinguals and multilinguals, the language subsystem that has attained native-speaker completeness (or in the case of young children, is marking the typical developmental milestones on schedule toward completeness). A dominant language contrasts with a language that has either stabilized in development at a stage short of native-speaker completeness or undergone attrition. Thus, a nondominant language could be an early-stabilized (fossilized) L2 or an attrited one-time primary language. In normally developing bilingual children, either (1) one language is dominant, or (2) development in both language subsystems indicates balanced acquisition and equivalent ability. In the field of sociolinguistics, "dominant" may also refer to aspects of unequal patterns of language use, socially, in a speech community, as in most situations of *diglossia*.

Double dissociation: A relationship of mutual autonomy between two cognitive structures. For example, in a given individual one language ability may be disrupted as a result of brain damage, but another language ability may be spared, while a different affected individual may suffer the reverse pattern of disrupted and spared abilities.

Dyslexia: A specific reading disability independent of general learning difficulty. Dyslexia is an intrinsic *deficit* related to specific cognitive and/or linguistic dysfunction. Thus, it is also independent of extrinsic factors such as inadequate literacy instruction (at the same time, children suffering from a dyslexic condition often do not receive adequate instruction in reading and writing).

Focus on form: In regard to language teaching, methods that draw learners' attention to grammatical forms or discourse patterns, either explicitly and directly or indirectly. In the literature, "focus on form" sometimes implies that students' attention is shifted to language patterns within the framework of a meaning-based teaching approach—for example, if a problem of miscommunication is perceived. Focus-on-form approaches contrast with "focus-on-meaning" approaches. However, most L2 educators who favor direct instruction of grammar-learning objectives would maintain that form-focused instruction is most effective when it is part of a meaning-based approach that includes a strong communicative component.

Fossilization: An outcome of language acquisition or learning that applies to L2s or attriting languages, when development in certain domains of linguistic competence fails to advance despite adequate exposure, relevant instruction, and so on. "Stabilization" is preferred by some authors to avoid the connotation that such a plateau in development remains permanent.

Higher-order: Refers to language ability in comprehension and production that requires the integration of specific knowledge structures, processing mechanisms, and other necessary component subskills. Implies the participation, on some level, of metacognitive operations (reflection on meaning and sometimes even on language forms). In problem solving, language serves as a tool to direct attention to pertinent aspects of the task and facilitates awareness of thinking and learning strategies. "Higher-order" also refers to processing of larger units of language involving sentence-level and discourse-level comprehension, for example, in contrast to language processing below the sentence level. Word and letter recognition (e.g., in reading) and phonological processing are examples of processing at a "lower-order" level.

Input: Language data to which a language learner is exposed. Input can be visual or auditory. Implicit in the definition is that input is potentially processible—that the learner can actually use the data in some way (e.g., to build up knowledge of a language). The stage when input is processed by a learning or acquisition mechanism, leading to the formation of knowledge, is sometimes referred to as "intake" (Sharwood Smith 1994a). See *primary linguistic data*.

Integrativist model: An approach to the study of cognition that rejects any notion of isolable components, autonomous mental structures, or modules. While some modular approaches conceive of domains or mental operations that may be highly interactive and "permeable," as opposed to others that are self-contained to a greater degree, integrativist models propose an unconstrained integration of mental representations and processes. In the study of language ability related to literacy, strong versions of the "whole-language" philosophy tend to be integrativist as the term is used in this discussion.

Interdependence Hypothesis: "To the extent that instruction on Lx is effective in promoting proficiency in Lx, transfer of this proficiency to Ly will occur provided there is adequate exposure to Ly (either in school or environment) and adequate motivation to learn Ly" (Cummins 1999, 32).

Interference: See *transfer* (cross-linguistic influence). In the literature, "interference" typically indicates a kind of cross-linguistic influence that results in grammatical error or the participation of L1 phonological features in L2 language production (as in "accented speech").

Interlanguage: Synonym: "learner language." An "approximative system" that develops in L2 learning. The L2 competence that learners construct, which approaches the target language system in a systematic way. "Approaches" implies incompleteness in comparison to the fully formed grammar of normal L1 acquisition. Interlanguage is different from approximative systems in child L1 acquisition because of the prior existence of, and continuing interaction with, the L2 learner's primary language. Interlanguage is "rule-governed" (like L1 acquisition), because the Faculty of Language plays a role in its development, even in the evolution of error patterns and in the formation of a stabilized nonnative grammar—sometimes termed *fossilization*.

Intransitive: See *transitive*.

Language Acquisition Device (LAD): A set of processing mechanisms specialized for language acquisition, in children especially, that allows them to build up a complete native-speaker competence in their primary language. Acquisition is guided by the principles of *Universal Grammar* and does not require deliberate analysis of language forms, awareness of grammatical patterns, corrective feedback, or any other kind of *negative evidence*. In L2 learning, this book proposes that the mechanisms of the LAD are still available for processing language input for the purpose of constructing implicit grammatical knowledge. They have not atrophied, nor have they been dissolved, even if their deployment might come to be blocked or deflected under certain circumstances. See *parameter setting*.

Language awareness: See *metalinguistic awareness*.

Language shift: Language erosion or loss socially; displacement of one language by another at the level of a community. The expanding language is almost always a language of wider communication. Not to be confused with other kinds of language change such as the evolution of the grammar of a language over time.

Language-specific: Refers to a cognitive structure that is associated with or linked to the specific linguistic representation of one language subsystem or another (in a bilingual/multilingual, the specific language subsystems of L1, L2, etc.). This idea assumes that each language subsystem of a bilingual is a separate cognitive entity. Other authors use the term "language-specific" to indicate association or linkage to Language (with a capital "L") in general.

Learner language: See *interlanguage*.

Marked: Used in this book only in the sociolinguistic sense indicating language use that is atypical, unexpected, or extraordinary in some way (as opposed to normal, customary, or unexceptional). Contrasts with "unmarked."

Metacognition: See *metalinguistic awareness*.

Metalinguistic awareness: The awareness of language itself, especially attention to its outward forms and observable patterns in speech and writing. More specifically, viewing language as an object of reflection or study in which the learner deliberately manipulates or attends to the forms of the language. For example, when children successfully focus attention on word and sentence patterns for the purpose of correcting spelling and grammar errors, they are displaying metalinguistic awareness. Children appear to spontaneously manifest the beginnings of this aspect of language development when they experiment with rhymes and invent jokes involving wordplay. Young bilingual children often compare forms of one language and another, or refer to interesting phenomena related to knowledge of two languages such as translation equivalents. Metacognition is a more general concept that refers to thinking about and reflecting upon mental processes. Metalinguistic awareness is therefore a kind of metacognition. In this book, "language awareness" = "metalinguistic awareness."

Miscue: In oral reading, an "unexpected response" in which the decoded words produced by the reader differ from the text. Examples are substituting one word for another, omitting part of a text, or inserting something that does not occur in the text.

Mixing: For purposes of consistency, Muysken's (2000) terms for different intrasentential language interaction phenomena are adopted in this book: (1) "code-mixing"—a general cover term referring to all cases in which words, longer sequences, and grammatical features from two languages appear in one sentence (note that "mixing" does not imply unsystematic or grammatically degraded bilingual speech); (2) "insertion"—a term referring to cases in which words or longer constituents from one language are embedded into a pattern from the other language; (3) "alternation"—a term akin to Poplack's (1980) "codeswitching" that refers to cases in which two languages alternate (a sentence beginning in one language switches to the other, from the syntactic pattern of one to that of the other). In this book, the more common term "codeswitching" refers to the same idea of "alternation." The more general term "switching" is synonymous with "mixing."

Modularity: The property of a cognitive system such that it is composed of autonomous components. Within the realm of language, for example, independent modules, self-contained to some degree, are specialized for representing different kinds of linguistic knowledge. Others may be specialized for processing certain kinds of information. "Specialization" means that the cognitive structure in question is "domain-specific" in some way. Comprehension and production are implemented by the activity of these dedicated components, each with its own internal structure and accompanying interface connections. See *componential*.

Negative evidence: Provides information to the learner calling attention to a grammatical pattern that does not conform to the target-language system. Corrective feedback is one kind of negative evidence. When learners reflect on their own language production ("inner speech" included), conceivably they might provide themselves with negative evidence.

Parameter setting: In language acquisition, a hypothesis about how the "learning burden" may be reduced for young, cognitively immature children. In some current proposals, *Universal Grammar* provides parameters (sets of options) for how grammatical principles are realized. Each "choice point" has a limited number of settings (e.g., two) from which the child "selects" on the basis of limited evidence available in the input; see *poverty of stimulus*. This is one way of thinking about how human languages are based on a universal design: any given language (an instantiation of Language) is the product of setting innately given parameters in one way or another (M. Baker 2001). In this book, "parameter setting" refers to the deductive-type acquisition guided by the *Language Acquisition Device*.

Phonological Structure (PS): See *phonology*.

Phonology: The component of grammar that establishes the distinctive sound units (phonemes) of a language and how they combine with other linguistic sound units. Phonological Structure (PS) is the linguistic knowledge structure dedicated to the encoding of the sound patterns of a language.

Pidgin: A pidgin is a "streamlined" language system with a reduced grammar, used by speakers who already have knowledge of a complete primary language (i.e., normally a person would not be a monolingual speaker of a pidgin, though this is possible in cases of extreme language deprivation). Pidgins emerge from the need to construct a system for intercultural and interlinguistic communication by simplifying a target language. See *creole*.

Poverty of stimulus: In reference to language acquisition, the evidence that children receive in the *input* is not sufficient for them to be able to construct a complete grammar. In particular, information about which patterns do not conform to the target language is not available in any reliable way from experience. Nevertheless, children do not have to learn the grammar of their primary language by trial and error, forming hypotheses, trying them out with native speakers, and receiving usable corrective feedback, a kind of *negative evidence*. Young children appear to be able to construct the grammar of their L1 using positive evidence alone. An important discussion in the field of L2 learning is whether the poverty-of-stimulus problem applies to *interlanguage* development in L2s.

Primary linguistic data: Language *input* that a child or L2 learner receives that contains positive evidence about the grammar from examples of well-formed sentences in the target language. From these examples, the acquirer or learner constructs a linguistic knowledge system.

Primary language: A first language (L1) that has not undergone attrition, or the *dominant language* of a bilingual speaker. Thus, a second language (L2) can become the primary language under the circumstances of language attrition/replacement. Bilinguals can also have two primary languages (neither is the dominant or the weaker language).

Proficiency: Skill in using language for a specific purpose, synonymous in this book with *ability* and *performance*. While knowledge (synonymous with *competence*) might be revealed indirectly in some aspect of a language user's proficiency, proficiency itself is revealed directly by performance on a given set of tasks. A particular proficiency, or ability, is made up of closely interacting components: competence structures and processing mechanisms.

Recursion: In language, the property of syntax that allows for the embedding of a constituent inside a constituent of the same kind. For example, in English a noun phrase must contain a noun; may be preceded by a determiner, an adjective phrase, or both; and may be followed by a prepositional phrase: NP → (Det)-(AP)-N-(PP). In turn, a prepositional phrase consists of a preposition followed by a noun phrase: PP → Prep-NP. Thus, NP can be embedded below NP, and this "pattern embedded within a pattern" can be repeated indefinitely. For example:

The elves made the shoes [by the fireplace [in the old shop [next to the bakery [on the town square]]]].

Another example is the embedding of relative clauses inside relative clauses:
[the shoes [that were made by the elves [that were sold to the marquis [who paid the shoemaker in gold]]]]

Register: A situationally determined stylistic variety (e.g., reflecting degrees of formality), or variation according to specific communicative purpose. Also, a speaker of a language may develop proficiency in uses of language related to different fields or endeavors (e.g., academic discourse). Not to be confused with dialectical variation.

Representation: A mental entity or structure that is postulated as part of a psychological theory: a knowledge structure, a schema, a processing module, an interface, or the like. In this sense, "a representation" does not necessarily imply that the mental entity in question is "a model of" or "a representation of" something existing outside the mind, "in the world."

Sapir-Whorf hypothesis: The widely debated hypothesis associated with E. Sapir and B. L. Whorf, which argues that perception and concept formation depend on the grammar of the particular language people speak—that each language imposes on its speakers a particular "world view." The related "linguistic relativity principle" holds that "users of markedly different grammars are pointed by their grammars toward different types of observations and different evaluations of externally similar acts of observation, and hence are not equivalent as observers but must arrive at somewhat different views of the world" (Whorf 1956, 221).

Schema: A mental *representation* of complex patterns of events, scenes, different kinds of knowledge, and so forth. Knowledge that is stored, or represented, in the mind and that is connected to networks of related categories of knowledge.

Semantics: The cognitive domain, separate from syntax and phonology, responsible for the organization of thoughts and concepts that can be expressed linguistically. In Jackendoff's (2002) model, the thoughts and concepts expressed by language are organized in a cognitive domain independent from language. Conceptual Structure (CS) is the (nonlinguistic, Central System) knowledge structure dedicated to the encoding of meanings.

[The] thoughts expressed by language are structured in terms of a cognitive organization called conceptual structure. Conceptual structure is not part of language per se—it is part of thought. It is the locus for understanding of linguistic utterances in context, incorporating pragmatic considerations and "world knowledge"; it is the cognitive structure in terms of which reasoning and planning take place. (Jackendoff 2002, 123)

[The] units of CS are entities like conceptualized physical objects, events, properties, times, quantities, and intentions. These entities . . . are always assumed to interact in a combinatorial system. Unlike the combinatorial systems of (narrow) syntax and phonology, this system is usually assumed to be purely relational, in the sense that linear order plays no role. (Jackendoff 1998, 30)

Conceptual structure, the representational system in which linguistic meanings are expressed, is highly structured and principled, and the structure and principles of CS are present in the learner prior to the task of language acquisition. (Culicover and Nowak 2003, 11)

Semilingualism: An abnormal condition that may affect children exposed to two languages in which neither language attains a complete native-speaker level of *competence*. Circumstances that may lead to this condition include brain damage, severe deprivation during the critical period of language acquisition, denial of access to processible language input during the critical period (as in the case of some deaf children), or an intrinsic language deficit such as *Specific Language Impairment* that would typically affect a bilingual child's ability in both languages. Semilingualism is not to be confused with *subtractive bilingualism*. Nor should the concept of semilingualism be applied to failed or below-average achievement in literacy-related language abilities that might be manifested "in both languages" if a bilingual student is evaluated for these abilities in L1 and L2.

Simultaneous bilingualism: In the research on child bilingualism, the acquisition of two languages during the critical period of primary language development. Both languages are considered as primary L1, sometimes designated L_a and L_b (as in this book) to avoid the misleading indication of a L1 and a L2. While one can easily imagine a language-learning situation in which a child develops ability in two languages concurrently after acquiring a primary L1, the term "simultaneous bilingualism" is usually restricted to early childhood acquisition of two primary languages. Simultaneous bilingualism may evolve toward either balanced competence in two languages or an imbalanced relationship between the language subsystems in which only one may come to be primary. See *additive bilingualism, bilingualism, dominant language, primary language, semilingualism.*

Skill: In this book, synonymous with *ability*. Sometimes has the connotation of referring to a component part of a more complex ability, as in "microskill." In language teaching, reading, listening, speaking, and writing are often referred to as the four language skills.

Specific Language Impairment (SLI): A deficit in grammatical competence or basic-level processing functions specific to language production and comprehension. Because it is an intrinsic handicapping condition, bilingual children afflicted with SLI manifest the disability in both languages. SLI should be considered independently from *dyslexia*, which involves dysfunctions related to the decoding of written language, although SLI by itself can negatively affect literacy learning depending on which subcomponents of grammatical competence and processing have been impaired and which have been spared.

Stabilization: See *fossilization.*

Subtractive bilingualism: See *additive bilingualism.*

Syntactic Structure (SS): See *syntax.*

Syntax: The component of grammar that determines how words and morphemes combine in such a way that a speaker/listener is able to construct phrases, clauses, and sentences that are grammatical and interpretable. It serves as a "way-station between phonology and semantics, making the mapping between them more articulate and precise." Syntax is "special in the sense that it is the most 'isolated' component" (Jackendoff 2002, 126). It is "the solution to a basic design problem: semantic relations are recursive and multidimensional but have to be expressed in a linear string. . . . [It] is a sophisticated accounting system for marking semantic relations so that they may be conveyed phonologically" (Jackendoff and Pinker 2005, 223). Syntactic Structure (SS) is linguistic knowledge structure that participates in the construction of well-formed constituents at the sentence level, which can be deployed in both comprehension and expression.

Text: A meaningful instance of language, typically beyond the single-word level. In this book, "text" is used to refer to written language. Other authors define "text" more broadly, using it synonymously with "discourse," oral or written. Expository text is a prose genre, usually associated with the general category of nonfiction, used to communicate ideas; transmit information; explain concepts; relate events; analyze phenomena, ideas, propositions; and so forth. "Expository" often refers to the kind of written discourse, or genre, that is characteristic of textbooks on social studies, science, and mathematics. The essay is a typical example of expository text, in contrast to narrative.

Top-down: Refers to processing (e.g., of language). Top-down processes progress from larger units and proceed "downward" toward smaller units. In reading, for example, word recognition might be affected (e.g., facilitated) by sentence-level grammar patterns involving semantic and syntactic information. In listening, one might be able to make use, to a certain degree, of previous knowledge ("higher-level" knowledge structures) in processing information that is received. In the other direction, so to speak, bottom-up processes progress from lower-level units "upward" toward larger units. In reading, for example, word recognition would begin with the recoding of spellings into pronunciations, and the reader would then build progressively larger constructions to achieve text comprehension.

Transfer: Synonymous with "cross-linguistic influence." In the research literature, the term "transfer" is often used more broadly to encompass interactions and interfaces among linguistic and nonlinguistic components alike. In this book, when the term refers to this research and the respective authors' use of the term in this broader sense, it has been placed in quotation marks: "transfer."

Transitive: Refers to a property of verbs that requires or allows them to take two semantic arguments (e.g., agent and patient: "The elves made the shoes"). An intransitive verb does not require or cannot take a second argument ("The shoemaker slept"). For example, in English, the verb "walk" has two senses: one associated with the transitive feature and the other with the intransitive feature (respectively: "The shoemaker walked his wife to the workshop" and "The shoemaker walked to the workshop"). The Spanish verb "caminar" [walk] has the same intransitive sense as the English intransitive "walk" but normally not the same transitive sense of "accompanying another person walking." Conversely, Spanish "dormir" [sleep] has two meanings, one associated with the intransitive feature, as in English; and one associated with the transitive feature ("to put someone to sleep" as in "tuck in at night"), which English "sleep" does not have. Transitiveness-intransitiveness, then, is part of the essential meaning of verbs; and "argument structure" (how a verb's semantic arguments and their syntactic realization are related) is an aspect of the syntax-semantics interface (Jackendoff 2002, 132–134).

Universal Grammar (UG): General principles specific to linguistic knowledge structures that are not violated by any particular language; also, design features common to all languages. For example, operations of movement and ordering that language systems allow are structure-dependent; and languages are category-based (have distinctions that include nouns, verbs, adjectives, etc.). The term refers to the constraints on language variation that are universal, set down by the human genetic endowment. In this sense, UG is a kind of innate knowledge that allows L1 acquirers and L2 learners to deduce a grammar using language input. See *Language Acquisition Device, parameter setting, poverty of stimulus*.

Universal Writing System Constraint: All full writing systems encode spoken language; they do not encode meaning independently of language. In no modern writing system does reading implement a direct visual-to-meaning interface that allows the reader to by-pass language. The related Universal Phonological Principle proposes that for skilled readers the activation of word pronunciation occurs across all writing systems. Phonology is activated at the lowest level specified by the script—for example, phonemes in an alphabetic system, syllables in a morphosyllabic system (Perfetti and Liu 2005).

Vernacular: A mother tongue of a language community that is spoken on a daily basis within a defined region, locality, or group of localities, especially for interpersonal communication. "Vernacular" usually refers to a local or regional language, in contrast to a language of wider communication that is also associated with formal uses and institutional contexts. The latter may also enjoy official status; a vernacular usually does not.

Vocabulary: Term traditionally used in language teaching that refers to an aspect of lexical knowledge—that is, a learner's ability to make an association between a word's phonological form and its meaning and grammatical function. For a literate L2 learner, it refers to the ability to connect the written form of a word with certain semantic and grammatical features and with an approximation to its phonological form. In this sense, the L2 learner's knowledge of basic vocabulary items can consist of partial representations, in contrast to the typically fully formed lexical entries of native speakers of the language.

Notes

Chapter 1

1. In this book, the Faculty of Language will be taken to encompass the totality of the human language capacity, including (1) the principles of Universal Grammar; (2) an acquisition mechanism (a special-purpose language acquisition processor or Language Acquisition Device); and (3) general-purpose processing and acquisition mechanisms from the domain of General Cognitive Competencies. Herschensohn (2000) and Jackendoff (2002) explain the details of this approach. A related concept is Pinker and Jackendoff's (2005) distinction between Faculty of Language-broad (FLB) and Faculty of Language-narrow (FLN). Fitch, Hauser, and Chomsky (2005) offer an alternative (though not entirely different) conception of FLB and FLN.

2. In Mexico, federal public schools that serve indigenous communities, supervised by the Dirección General de Educación Indígena (DGEI), are officially designated as bilingual. In most places, however, implementation of official school language policy (DGEI 1990) can best be described as partial or minimal. For example, in the school where our study was conducted, almost all teachers, together with the principal, are bilingual or have some knowledge of Nahuatl. In school, the indigenous language is accorded prominent symbolic recognition. However, these exceptions aside, and despite the important shift from the previous exclusionary model, the school's curriculum and actual practice during the period of the study was virtually all Spanish. In a sociolinguistic assessment of the larger Nahuatl-speaking region in Tlaxcala and Puebla states, Messing (2007) concurs with previous analyses regarding the rapid shift to Spanish monolingualism, leaving little doubt that the same tendencies will soon be observed in the most linguistically conservative communities of San Isidro Buensuceso and San Miguel Canoa. At the same time, Messing points to the resurgence, incipient though it is, of a culturally conscious layer of language revitalization promoters—in large part, local bilingual teachers. Special historical circumstances of the Nahuatl language (lingua franca of both the Aztec empire and the post-Conquest evangelization in Central Mexico) set it apart. A significant literary heritage and a certain privileged status in Mexican academic and cultural circles, among other factors, suggest that it is premature to project a complete and final displacement of the language. An interesting contrast is the more rapid and complete shift to Spanish involving smaller languages in the greater Puebla region (Lam 2009).

Chapter 2

1. The proposal in this chapter on promoting the L2 learning of languages-of-wider-communication in multilingual states would be strongly questioned by many authors who also favor linguistic pluralism (see, e.g., Phillipson 2001; Ricento 2000 and numerous citations therein). On the one hand, it remains unclear what alternative language policies would be implied in the downgrading of English teaching, for example, in Anglophone countries such as Nigeria, Ghana, and South Africa. (Phillipson (2001) seems to object even to the category "Anglophone"—and by extension, "Francophone," "Lusophone," and so on.) Along similar lines, language policy proposals that express varying degrees of ambivalence toward or outright opposition to the expansion of the former colonial languages in Africa appear to represent a growing consensus (Banda 2000; Mansour 1993; Mwansoko 1994; Omoniyi 2003; Stroud 2001). Omoniyi draws out the logic of this perspective explicitly. In contrast to both the "neutrality paradigm, which purports to manage problems of multiethnicity and multilingualism by installing so-called neutral Eurolanguages" and the "imperialism paradigm, which interprets the pressure and dominance of excolonial languages as part of a greater global hegemonic scheme," the alternative is the "anti-imperialist paradigm, which pursues the institutionalization of indigenous languages as a cause, almost to the total exclusion of the excolonial languages" (Omoniyi 2003, 146). A less extreme but equally utopian proposal to downgrade the use of the former colonial language is made by Neke (2003, 264), in relation to language policy in Tanzania: "[M]ake Kiswahili the medium of instruction at all levels of education," with English remaining a "reference reading language."

On a more fundamental note, what appears to be at the heart of the critiques by many ideologically preoccupied theorists is the need to challenge an "autonomous" and "positivistic" linguistics (Ricento 2000, 14–15) caricatured as "defined by standard grammars" and embracing theories based on "prescriptivism." Without representative citations of the work of "positivist" and "autonomous" linguists, who purportedly espouse prescriptivism, it remains unclear how one is to interpret the distinctions posed by the various "critical" theories.

2. The unwieldy "national-official-language-of-wider-communication" will be abbreviated "NL" for "national language." Because of its many uses, this term can cause confusion. Often, it refers to a country's majority, or most widely spoken/understood, language of national communication. In Latin America, the language of the former colonial power (e.g., Spanish) commonly receives the designation "national" or "official" nationwide, with major indigenous languages also being recognized as "national" or even "co-official" (see INALI 2003 for the case of Mexico). In Paraguay, exceptionally, Spanish and Guarani are both official. Another distinction is made in West Africa: for example, French—"official," African languages—"national." Here, the continued expansion of the former colonial languages may indeed render "former colonial" as outdated as it is today in the "New World."

3. "Insufficiency" of a language for specific academic and scientific fields refers only to availability of specialized texts. That publishing and dissemination come to be restricted in this way from one epoch to another is arbitrary from a linguistic point of view. The short-lived experiment in the Americas during the sixteenth century in which some of the major indigenous languages were elevated to written lingua franca and academic discourse status (León-Portilla 1996; Lerner 2000), subsequently to be completely driven out of the higher-order realms of literacy, testifies to the arbitrariness of such allocation. The fact remains that there

is a need for standardization, modernization, and graphicization of indigenous languages in order to include them in tertiary-level academic programs, if such an objective comes to form part of a multilingual state's new language policy, as it has in South Africa since 1996. The grammatical underpinning of all languages is "sufficient" for any purpose. Peripheral shortcomings (e.g., in vocabulary) can always be remedied by utilizing the language's internal morphological resources.

4. From http://www.tanzania.go.tz/educationf.html:

> Medium of Instruction: The main feature of Tanzania's education system is the bilingual policy, which requires children to learn both Kiswahili and English. English is essential, as it is the language which links Tanzania and the rest of the world through technology, commerce and also administration. The learning of the Kiswahili enables Tanzania's students to keep in touch with their cultural values and heritage. English is taught as compulsory subject in the primary education whereas at post primary education is the medium of instruction. With regard [to] Kiswahili, it is the medium of instruction at primary education while at tertiary education is taught as compulsory subject at secondary education and as option at tertiary education.

A discussion of the constraints on policy and planning in regard to the promotion of Kiswahili in neighboring Kenya can be found in Ogechi 2003.

5. The problem of the development and revitalization of indigenous languages in the context of competing language-learning policies that prioritize languages of international and regional importance presents difficult choices for educational planners. Hamel (2001) reviews trends among the Mercosur countries (Brazil, Argentina, Uruguay, and Paraguay) toward a new valorization of L2 learning of Spanish and Portuguese by their respective national-language speakers, and how this new regional language-learning awareness squares with the continuing inroads of English. The dilemma is sharpest for Paraguay, which has taken on the historic challenge of revitalizing and normalizing the now co-official indigenous language, Guarani, still spoken by a majority of the population. On a related note, Anamalai (2003) comments on the widely reported ambivalence on the part of indigenous- and minority-language-speaking communities toward language education proposals that downgrade the teaching of languages of wider communication.

Chapter 3

1. The controversy surrounding the construct of Cognitive Academic Language Proficiency dates back at least to the investigations of Bernstein (1964), who differentiated between situation-dependent discourses (supported by extralinguistic context) and discourses associated with academic language use. The latter are characterized by comprehension strategies based on the ability to modify previous knowledge schemas by incorporating new information, a kind of "bottom-up" type strategy that depends less on prediction. Also relevant here is Vygotsky's (1934/1962) discussion of the development of writing: language use that is more abstract and deliberate, without an interlocutor's interactive support, related in turn to the distinction between monolog and dialog.

2. In the final analysis, models of language comprehension that claim to be exclusively "top-down" (or exclusively "bottom-up," for that matter) are impossible. After reviewing studies of L2 reading and listening, Field (2004) proposes that "top-down" and "bottom-up"

are better understood in terms of "directions of processing." For example, the effect of vocabulary knowledge on a listener's interpretation of a string of phonemes would be a top-down effect, and how lower-level units are progressively built up to form higher-level structures would be bottom-up. Also, it is useful to keep separate the two kinds of "context" (the influence of world knowledge, and the influence of information within the discourse or text itself). What is interesting is that contextual cues appear to be exploited by listeners in a compensatory way similar to that used by readers. As in reading, in listening a heavy dependence on top-down strategies, to compensate for inadequate lower-level information, allows beginner L2 learners to construct meaning (though often at the expense of literal comprehension).

3. As a result of 500 years of language contact, Nahuatl has incorporated an increasing number of words from Spanish (in a similar way, despite some interesting differences, Mexican Spanish has been influenced by Nahuatl). All of the students' Nahuatl writing samples incorporate this borrowed material (see examples in appendix 4). In addition, the distinction should be made between established loanwords and extemporaneous or nonce borrowings (Dolitsky 2000), the former usually (but not always) integrated phonologically and/or morphologically into Nahuatl. The frequency of the latter, often difficult to distinguish from codeswitching per se (Hill and Hill 1986; Poplack, Sankoff, and Miller 1988), varies widely, language choice being an important factor (as exemplified in the all-Spanish responses to the Nahuatl writing task by some of the 3rd graders). Callahan (2004) analyzes codeswitching specifically in written expression, concluding that the same models developed from work based on oral corpora are applicable.

4. Caution is always advised when comparing scores on literacy assessments from two languages in contact that are distributed, socially, in such an imbalanced manner. Several intervening factors are relevant: novelty of the indigenous-language reading and writing tasks, students' expectations regarding demarcations of appropriate language use, and lack of standardization of the indigenous language. Since the text passages cannot be translations of each other (in assessments for comparative purposes), equivalence of difficulty level can be affected by any number of unforeseen variables.

5. Note Schachter's (1992) objection, even here, to applying the concept of transfer. Instead, Schachter proposes a set of constraints "imposed by previous knowledge on a more general process, that of inferencing" (p. 44)—pointing out, for example, that adult L2 learning approximates general concept learning, that the L2 learner tests alternatives, makes inferences, and samples from a universe of hypotheses drawn from previous learning and from the new learning situation itself.

6. In a related study (N. Francis 2001) involving the cohort of 2nd-, 4th-, and 6th- grade bilingual students who participated in the studies discussed in the text, the mean length of utterance (MLU) was calculated for samples from three different language tasks: Written Narrative, independently produced Oral Narrative responding to a series of illustrations, and Conversation (interview/dialog type) based on the same illustrations. MLU indices across grade levels showed a significant increase for Written Narrative and Oral Narrative, as would be expected. Notably, MLU indices for Conversation did not vary significantly across grade levels, nor did they correlate with any other measure of academic discourse. Grammatical/Discourse features such as subordination, complement clauses, appositives, constituents conjoined in series, and reported speech (Chafe 1985), cataloged more frequently in 4th and 6th grades, develop as children apply them to new contexts of language use.

Chapter 4

1. "Vertical" processes interface with components that are highly domain-specific, innately specified, neurologically hardwired, and computationally autonomous; these processes are mandatory and fast. Systems that are nonmodular (or modular to a lesser degree) depend more on "horizontal" processes, are interactive to a greater degree, and integrate information across domains to a greater extent, as in problem solving. Maratsos (2005, 494) gives an instructive analogy from the animal kingdom:

> Basically we proposed a metaphorical translation of Isaiah Berlin's distinction between foxes and hedgehogs. Berlin classified intellectual theories as being either hedgehogs or foxes. Hedgehogs do one big thing well (quills), and hedgehog figures like Plato have one big idea (eternal ideas). Foxes succeed by doing many different things well, and fox-like intellectual systems…do the same. We suggested that psychological systems can also be classified into hedgehog systems, which work off relatively few big principles and can be algorithmized, and fox systems, which are hard to describe explicitly and involve a great variety of processes. In language, Chomskyan core grammar is clearly a hedgehog. By contrast, peoples' pragmatic use of language to achieve social goals stands squarely in the fox domain, consisting of a great variety of abilities and processes.

2. Siguán (1987) clarifies that Vygotsky's concept of "inner speech" is not the same as "language of thought" or "mentalese" (Fodor 1975; Pinker 1997), the latter referring to structures for information processing and abstract conceptual structures governed by "rules of concept formation" (Jackendoff 1992). About these Vygotsky, strictly speaking, had little to say. On the other hand, nondialogic and noncommunicative language use is a kind of performance (that only one person is aware of). Siguán's understanding of Vygotsky's "inner speech" suggests that it is complementary with "mentalese"—"inner speech" referring to the end product, minus the motor activity, of linguistic encoding (subject to awareness and reflection), "mentalese" to the inner workings of Conceptual Structure.

3. Part of the difficulty in the discussion about the autonomy, interdependence, or integration of language and thought flows from how these two constructs are understood by different authors. Regarding the former, are we considering knowledge of language or language use? Even setting usage aside, approaches will vary depending on which linguistic knowledge subsystem is on the language side of the interaction. Similarly regarding thought, with the way in which concepts are represented and subjected to mental operation, one can speculate about how literacy, for example, contributes to the "development of distinctive modes of thought" (Olson 1994, 17). In this case, reference to "thought" would probably not be to the inner workings of Conceptual Structure. When we speak of "modern scientific thought," "narrative thought," "logical/mathematical thought," or "higher-order thinking," we probably also have something else in mind, and speculation about the dependence of thought (understood in these terms) on language, and even literacy, becomes more interesting. Regarding the tools of thought, thinking here of both senses, certain aspects of "language" are among those that come preprogrammed, together with the primitives of Conceptual Structure. Language-processing technologies (like writing) belong to the cultural innovations that extend language abilities, of which our given capacities are also a part.

4. Even scratching the surface of the wide-ranging debate on the cognitive correlates of orality and literacy would take us far afield. Nonetheless, a few remarks are in order.

We can catch a glimpse of a consensus (e.g., Olson 1991) around the suggestion that writing is neither the source of higher-order thinking nor the only underpinning for the development of secondary discourse ability and metalinguistic awareness. The ethnographic study of oral genres and analyses of verbal art and oratory (Finnegan 1988; Goody 1987; Hill 1995; Lord 1991; Tannen 1992) settled the question some time ago. Earlier, Vygotsky recognized, in what he cataloged as "oral monologic discourse," the features that are prototypically associated with writing. From the poetic and ceremonial genres to the prosaic forms, levels of complexity are attained that are commensurate with that of written text. Requiring deliberate attention to form, and often requiring long periods of apprenticeship, productive mastery of the oral genres is not universally accessible to all native speakers of a language in any culture. From the point of view of child language development, it would be safe to say that children tutored in the oral tradition of any speech community begin to construct the same discourse-processing skills that underlie the development of CALP. The short conclusion is, no "Great Divide" between orality and writing.

In addition to the above, evidence has accumulated regarding the numerous continuities between oral discourse development and literacy (Bamberg and Moissinac 2003; Stein and Albro 1996—namely, that early preliterate narrative and certain interactive verbal discourses that actively engage child language learners represent an essential platform for the development of academic-type language proficiency.

However, it would be an error, especially on the part of bilingual educators working in communities in which the traditional oral genres retain a strong presence, to draw a broad and far-reaching equivalence between the surviving oral genres and literacy. Denny (1991, 80) points out that decontextualization is "not an effect directly produced by writing" and that "literacy is only an amplifier of the tendency to decontextualize thought." In this regard, "amplify" is the key idea. Relativizing the importance of literacy (as if proficiency in reading and writing were merely one option, among other equivalent means, for the development of higher-order academic abilities) is not likely to contribute to narrowing the achievement gap between indigenous-language- and national-language-speaking children.

5. Primary discourse abilities are abilities related to conversation, which include rudimentary interactive narrative. All normally developing children have access to these abilities–which is why, in assessment, core grammatical competence is revealed more unambiguously in types of performance that call upon one of the primary discourses. Uniformity of access to their underlying component competencies and processing mechanisms diminishes the possibility that performance is compromised by extraneous factors.

6. In contrast to ("narrow") grammatical competence, the competencies that are specific to pragmatic knowledge should be considered separately, apart from the strictly linguistic subsystems; see Blakemore 2001 for a modular approach to the study of pragmatics. On a related note, Gregg (1996) criticizes the concept of "communicative competence." It will be easier to understand all around if we think in terms of "communicative *ability*" when thinking about aspects of this kind of performance. Abilities are composed of networks of underlying competencies and processing mechanisms. Some of these cognitive structures are domain-specific and others more open-ended.

7. To reiterate, we need to consider Cummins's differentiation between academic discourse and basic interpersonal communicative discourse separately from the distinction made by linguists between competence and performance. Cummins distinguishes between two kinds of language *ability*, in both cases aspects of *performance*. Each kind of ability involves the

participation of different networks of knowledge and processing mechanism (with components shared in common): competencies related to pragmatic knowledge, restrictions on information processing, analytical operations, text-coherence-building skills, world knowledge schemas, knowledge of vocabulary and grammar, and so forth.

8. The distinction adopted in this discussion between acquisition and learning is that of López (1993), who differentiates between L1 *acquisition*, which "proceeds parallel to the primary socialization of the child," (p. 93) and L2 *learning* (both formal and informal). For the development of secondary discourses and metalinguistic awareness, in L1 and L2 (literacy-related language abilities), López also reserves the term "learning." López's distinction between acquisition and learning is related to Krashen's (1991, 1998) but differs from it in a number of respects.

9. L1 grammatical competence is acquired incidentally and its actual mental representation is not subject to awareness. Speakers cannot reflect upon the internal computational procedures that operate on the primary linguistic data in language input. As M. Paradis (2004, 35) points out, "What is noticed is not what is internalized."

> Explicit knowledge is qualitatively different from implicit competence. Explicit knowledge is conscious awareness of some data and/or of their explicit analysis. Implicit competence, on the other hand, is a set of computational procedures (of which the speaker is unaware) that generates sentences. (p. 47)

> Implicit linguistic competence and metalinguistic knowledge are distinct, as suggested by neurofunctional, neurophysiological, and neuroanatomical evidence, and recently confirmed by a number of neuroimaging studies on bilinguals. They have different memory sources, each subserved by neuroanatomical structures and neurophysiological mechanisms that differ from those subserving the other. (p. 61)

Chapter 5

1. Very much to the point regarding possible quasi-modular aspects of certain Central System competencies (open to interaction to a degree that non–Central System modules are not) is the fact that Christopher did succeed in passing some Theory of Mind tasks. On these tests, he was apparently able to call upon other general cognitive knowledge sources to compensate for his impaired Theory of Mind abilities (N. Smith and Tsimpli 1995, 6–7).

2. In his study, Meisel (2001) restricts the evaluation of findings to early balanced bilingualism in which neither language exercises a measurable dominance over the other. This is surely a good place to begin, regardless of one's view on the relative prevalence of balanced versus nonbalanced early childhood bilingualism. The latter presents a more exacting test case of the early differentiation hypothesis. For example, sometimes a weaker language, stabilized in development far from native-speaker competence, is termed "subordinate" to a complete L1. In the end, "subordinate" may not be the most adequate term if it can be shown that the weaker L2 subsystem is still autonomous from the L1 subsystem.

3. As a shorthand, unfortunate though it is, I often use "speech" to mean "speech and/or sign." All references in this book to "bilingual speech," "monolingual speech," "inner speech," and the like, apply as well to the visual modality counterpart in all respects. The Faculty of Language is tuned to language-like patterns in both auditory and visual modalities. "The main adaptation of sign languages is replacing the distinctive features of vocal articulation by distinctive features of manual and facial articulation" (Jackendoff 1994, 97).

4. Persistent confusion over the applicability of the concept of semilingualism (e.g., Toukomaa 2000) flows from the failure to differentiate between the specifically linguistic components of language (the core grammatical modules) and the wider network of competencies and processing mechanisms that together constitute a particular language ability. In this confusion, the particular ability in question usually involves an academic language proficiency. But it is not coherent to describe deficiencies in bilingual children's performance on a literacy-related language assessment in terms of semilingualism. Under normal conditions, such assessments may indeed show evidence of below-average achievement "in both languages." But to call this kind of learning difficulty "semilingualism" is completely incorrect. The term may properly refer to deficient development in the domains of core grammatical competence, though clearly the range of conditions to which it should apply is quite restricted. Examples may include genetically transmitted dysfunctions of the Specific Language Impairment (SLI) type, or consequences of extreme input deprivation as when deaf children are isolated from sign language input during the critical period. Unfortunately, research on bilingual SLI is sparse and of uneven quality. For example, in their study of bilingual SLI, Crutchley, Conti-Ramsden, and Botting (1997) fail to provide assessment results in both of the subjects' languages, rendering the data uninterpretable. In contrast, see Genesee, Paradis, and Crago 2004, Håkansson, Salameh, and Nettelbladt 2003, and Thordardottir et al. 2006 for scientific guidelines for evaluating linguistic abilities in bilingual children suspected of suffering from language impairment, and van der Lely 2005 for a discussion of the "components of language and SLI."

Chapter 6

1. The notion of completeness should be taken to refer to the steady state in language development that native speakers typically attain: knowledge of the core grammatical system and the ability to put it to use in performance. Not included are aspects of language ability associated with literacy-related academic-type proficiencies or other higher-order uses of language. These should be considered peripheral domains of language knowledge and language use beyond the universal attainment of all native speakers. In this sense, the core grammar would be a kind of "closed" system (and would reach an early developmental plateau). The peripheral grammar, aspects of lexical knowledge, many processing capabilities, and discourse-related competencies would be more "open-ended." Hopper (1998) presents an alternative view of completeness and modularity in a version of the "emergent grammar" hypothesis.

2. Hyltenstam and Abrahamsson (2003, 570), approaching the evidence on early L_a-L_b asymmetry from a different angle, also allude to the possibility that "maturational effects are noticeable as early as from *birth* in both L1 and L2 acquisition" (emphasis added).

3. The possibility that in language replacement L1 settings are "freed up" and thus might facilitate parameter resetting in the L2 is a working hypothesis that merits further study. Mistakenly, some proponents of exclusive L2-medium instruction for L2 learners might try to find some comfort in this idea, in particular those who view children's L1 abilities as an obstacle to "complete" acquisition of the official language of schooling. However, no support for exclusionary monolingual school language policy can be garnered from this hypothesis. In the first place, the possible reciprocal relationship between L1 knowledge that is lost in attrition and "special" L2 acquisition is proposed as an explanation for the completeness of

replacing languages. As such, it suggests nothing interesting about which pedagogical approach should be taken to maximize L2 learners' academic achievement and literacy learning. Even in the hypothetical case where L1 maintenance might be a factor that inhibits the "complete" acquisition of one or another grammatical feature in the L2, no academic disadvantage presents itself as a plausible outcome. There is no reason to believe that L2 learning would be significantly retarded or rendered deficient for academic purposes by the preservation of a fully formed L1 grammatical system. Perhaps for purposes of "linguistic cleansing," for which any remaining vestige of children's L1 grammatical competence in their L2 performance is to be extinguished, an actively subtractive educational policy might be indicated. But this kind of instructional program flows from a political objective that actually contradicts the optimal learning conditions for L2 learners.

Parenthetically, it should also be clear that the idea behind the "replacing language/no semilingualism" condition is not the same as the Limited Capacity Hypothesis discussed by Genesee, Paradis, and Crago (2004); in fact, it is very different. Rather, the proposals made in chapter 6 should be taken as favoring a somewhat weaker version of the Dual Language System Hypothesis developed by Genesee (2001, 2002).

4. The questions of autonomous development in early L_a-L_b differentiation and the possibility of imbalanced early bilingualism should be considered separately, evidence for the latter not really bearing on the former. The observation of extensive interference of an emerging, stronger, primary language on a weaker language would not be incompatible with the hypothesis of autonomous development. The separation of two linguistic subsystems would not be called into question by evidence of L_a structures that have been integrated into the L_b subsystem, or vice versa ("static interference"; M. Paradis 2004, 187–191), less so by evidence of interference across the CLI that connects the respective lexicons. In a review of the research, Meisel (2004) considers whether L2 learners, including children beyond an "optimal age period," have full access to the language-making capacity that guides L1 acquisition. As a preliminary hypothesis, Meisel suggests that child L2 acquisition might share properties of adult L2 acquisition: "the tentative conclusion which may thus be suggested here claims that successive acquisition of bilingualism results in qualitative differences, as compared to monolingual as well as bilingual L1 development, if the onset of acquisition falls into an age period after the optimal age for language learning" (p. 109). These qualitative differences, Meisel proposes, are tied to maturational changes occurring around the age of 5, related to the possibility that "settings" not activated during L1 acquisition are no longer available. This hypothesis is not the same as the one proposed in chapter 6. Rather than arguing for a maturational offset, evidence of early L_a or L_b stabilization/attrition and replacing-language completeness argues for a different mechanism, one that blocks or filters access to the language-making capacity. Regardless, Meisel's suggestion that access to the Language Acquisition Device may be inhibited even among child language learners as young as 6 or 7 allows for a strong alternative proposal for further research.

5. Critiques of the parameter-setting approach to language acquisition have pointed to a number of potentially serious flaws, under two main categories:

1. The idea that a finite set of innate parameters, each with a binary setting for example, is ready and available to the child assumes a fine-tuning and precision in UG that seems improbable, especially considering the conceivably very large number of parameters that would be needed to account for linguistic variation. The genetic program of UG cannot be that elaborate ("rich") or that specific and detailed in how it guides language acquisition.

2. How do children detect triggers in the environment? Presumably, for children to be able to set a parameter to one value or another, structure must somehow be assigned to raw linguistic input in the first place. What might this preexisting language-specific grammatical knowledge consist of? For discussion of some of these problems, see Culicover and Nowak 2003, Maratsos 1999, and Newmeyer 2004; and from a Construction Grammar point of view, Goldberg 2003. In a major reformulation of his Fundamental Difference Hypothesis, Bley-Vroman (2009) calls attention to some of the same considerations, arguing that the original conception of parameter setting is no longer useful in understanding how L1 and L2 development differ.

While it may be necessary to back away from the exacting specificity of triggering preprogrammed values, the basic idea of parameter setting (as a figure of speech or image perhaps) speaks to an important problem in child language acquisition that should not be thrown out with the bathwater. How do children converge so rapidly and completely on the right rule systems without costly trial-and-error and "wild" intermediate grammars, on the basis of positive evidence alone? Inductive learning typically results in degrees of individual variation in ultimate attainment. Deductive processes, on the other hand, based on prior-knowledge structures, yield the kind of uniform attainment characteristic of core grammatical competence. Poverty of stimulus is still a problem for language acquisition; a kind of narrowing or selection from a human language "template" is a model that still appears to be viable.

In bilingualism, the poverty-of-stimulus problem appears to be even more insurmountable, the evidence for early L_a-L_b differentiation and early preference for one subsystem over the other in nonbalanced development being especially difficult to account for by appealing to inductive learning mechanisms. In both cases, certain "selections" appear to be blocked, and alternative options appear to be rapidly and systematically eliminated, all of this vastly underdetermined by available evidence. How do we explain the phenomenon of "continuity" (e.g., its weak version): that even in the immature non-target-like performance of young children, intermediate/incomplete grammars conform to patterns that are consistent with adult-like grammar? Neither monolingual nor bilingual children seem to pass through a stage in which they experiment with highly divergent hypotheses, receive negative evidence, and then retreat to the smaller target grammar (Meisel 1995).

6. A related line of research on the "dual-mechanism" model of inflection (as opposed to "single-mechanism" models) attempts to explain the dissociation between regular and irregular verb inflection in child L1 acquisition (Clahsen, Aveledo, and Roca 2002; Pinker 1999). Two systems are proposed: one for lexical entries that are listed associatively, another for a rule-based system. Weber-Fox and Neville (2001) present evidence along the same lines: that the neural processes associated with access to open- and closed-class words are affected differently by delays in L2 exposure. Likewise, Norton, Kovelman, and Petitto (2007) examine the evidence for "dual-route" versus "single-route" models in literacy. Here is another arena for promising dialog. Commenting on the debate over how regular and irregular past tense inflection is processed, Pinker and Ullman (2002, 462) concede that connectionist models are:

> deservedly influential ... because [they capture] a real phenomenon. The persistence of families of irregular verbs with overlapping partial similarities, and people's use and occasional generalization of these family patterns according to similarity and frequency, can be simply explained by the assumption that human memory is partly superpositional and associative. Theories that try to explain every instance of redundancy among words using the same combinatorial mechanism used for productive syntax and regular morphol-

ogy require needless complexity and esoteric representations, and fail to capture the many linguistic, psychological, and neuropsychological phenomena in which irregular forms behave like words.

Chapter 7

1. For further discussion of conversational and academic registers and how this dimension intersects with the features and resources of written and spoken forms, see Biber et al. 2002, Gee 2001, Jahandarie 1999, Olson 2001, and Stein and Albro 2001. In her discussion of the different ways in which context and background knowledge are taken into account in both comprehension and expression, Schleppegrell (2004) argues that

> [s]chool-based registers typically do not emerge through the active interaction of interlocutors. While they also have elements that construe the speaker/writer's awareness of audience, these are different from the give and take of conversational interaction. (p. 59)

> School disciplines are not about everyday knowledge. They construe specialized knowledge and a specialized grammar is part of that construal. This is true of all the subject areas of schooling. Even mathematics, often considered a school subject that depends less on language, has its own academic register features, and a considerable amount of the knowledge required for success in higher levels of mathematics is construed through language. (p. 138)

2. In discussing how grammar develops in children, so far I have used the terms "core" and "periphery" differently from other authors. In the traditional, or more technical, sense, "core grammar" refers to the invariant properties of grammar, the centric and nuclear regularities governed directly by UG. "Periphery" usually refers to the local idiosyncrasies and marked exceptions that account for variation from one speaker (or speech community) to another. In this book, "core grammar" refers to the primary or substantive child grammar secured developmentally by simple exposure to primary linguistic data—an "invariant" UG core in a developmental sense. In this view, peripheral grammar emerges with the necessary participation of domain-general learning mechanisms, in a manner different from automatic and spontaneous acquisition. It is not considered "invariant" in the way that core grammar is—that is, it is not attained spontaneously, completely, and universally without exception by all children. The notion of "core" used in this book comes from a differentiation suggested by Foster-Cohen (1990, 166):

> [It] is important to reiterate that research into UG only concerns certain parts of the grammar. UG is claimed to embody information that will allow the child to formulate the *core grammar* of the language. The remainder of the grammar—the peripheral grammar—as well as the pragmatic rules for language use, involve a variety of different underpinnings—some linguistic innate knowledge, and some information from the input.

This distinction is also related to Clahsen and Muysken's (1996) proposal of a "division of labor between UG- and non-UG learning" that was quoted in chapter 6: "It is implausible that all of L1 development is UG-driven, since it is embedded in a highly intricate process of general cognitive development, involving all kinds of learning" (p. 722).

Culicover and Jackendoff (2005) have argued that the traditional differentiation between core and periphery (what was just referred to as the "more technical sense") does not hold up to scrutiny in any event—for example, from the point of view of language acquisition. Young children may require more time to sort out which verbs are irregular, for example;

but by the age of 10 or 11, complete attainment of this aspect of grammar and most of the rest of the traditionally defined "periphery" is as invariant as the "deep regularities." Put another way, "the periphery presents as much of a problem for acquisition as does the core" (p. 26). Starting with the idea that peripheral phenomena (in this sense) are inextricably interwoven with the core, Culicover and Jackendoff propose that a "learning theory adequate for the lexicon and the 'periphery' rules would, with only moderate adjustments or amplification, be able to learn the 'core' as well" (p. 26). The fact that we observe no appreciable interindividual variation in middle childhood in the irregular grammatical patterns of everyday speech would appear to be consistent with the workings of the same basic "learning theory."

The idea behind the differentiation between core and periphery adopted in this book, then, is part of a still-vague proposal that some aspects of grammar development do not proceed to completeness spontaneously and universally, without exception. Under this view, these domains of the knowledge of language would develop under the guidance of a different kind of balance between UG and "non-UG learning" and might involve a "variety of different underpinnings." Development in this domain might depend on experience in a different way than development does in the core. In other words, the grammatical knowledge ("broad") of *all* late-elementary-age children, speakers of a given language, would not be equivalent in *every* way. As a rough approximation, it would be equivalent in every way in the domain of the core, having attained completeness spontaneously from exposure to primary linguistic data alone. It would not be equivalent in every way in the domain of the periphery.

The core-periphery distinction, as outlined here, has the advantage of allowing us to better integrate the findings from research inspired by nongenerative theoretical frameworks. One example, especially pertinent to the discussion in this chapter, is Diessel's (2004) study of the development of complex sentences in young children, which applied a usage-based approach and complemented Schleppegrell's (2004) study of the "language of schooling," for older children. Complex sentences pose comprehension difficulties for children well into the school years, development proceeding gradually and incrementally. Unlike mastery of core grammar, development in this area depends on the frequency of particular constructions in the ambient language. Diessel points to the findings of his study as contradicting the Continuity Hypothesis (that children's grammatical representations are the same as adults'); Tomasello (2000) argues along similar lines. We might speculate that the findings show that strong versions of the Continuity Hypothesis must be reexamined.

3. The difficulty that L2 learners and native speakers alike experience with so-called center-embedding cannot simply be a matter of taxing working memory, of too much information to process. Consider the sentence "Elves elves help help make shoes." For most speakers of English, it's only after inserting the optional complementizer "that" between "elves" and "elves" or bracketing [elves help] that a meaningful interpretation is possible. For an interesting discussion of how grammatical knowledge and parsing are related, see N. Smith 1999.

4. Chafe (1985) catalogs the grammatical devices that writing, in particular, places at the service of expository discourse for the purpose of expanding the size and complexity of "idea units." Academic writing calls on students to apply their grammatical knowledge with an eye not only on well-formed sentences, but also on how they contribute to constructing coherent texts of a new kind (Celce-Murcia 2002), different from narrative and conversation.

5. Jacobs (1995) explains why different kinds of dependent clause (e.g., subordinate vs. embedded) pose different kinds of comprehension difficulty, especially for L2 learners.

Subordinate clauses generally present fewer problems than embedded clauses. A subordinate clause functions as an adjunct and is often introduced by semantic markers that serve as useful signposts for processing. In contrast, as an argument of a predicate, the embedded dependent clause requires the listener/reader to sort out which arguments go with which predicates. Again, complexity and comprehension difficulty are not just a matter of size, not just a question of the amount of information that might tax working memory. Academic discourse is replete with such phrases and sentence patterns, requiring even highly literate native speakers to reread and reanalyze, shifting to a metalinguistic mode of processing. If the content of the message is important, *readers* can count their blessings that they have a text to go back to. Creative L2 teachers exploit the possibilities that written language offers (for focused reflection and explicit attention to grammatical patterns) to help students apply inductive learning strategies to these kinds of problem-solving task.

On a related point, Noguchi (2003) discusses an interesting paradox that English teachers encounter in the domain of writing. Forming grammatical sentences in writing—that is, avoiding "fragments"—appears to be another late-developing ability. ("Run-on" sentences we should consider separately. Strictly speaking, they are not usually syntactically malformed sentences; rather, they mark a discourse-level or stylistic infelicity.) In the case of "fragments," native speakers' grammatical competence should, it would seem, serve as a better corrective monitor than it usually does. However, the way sentence boundaries are marked in writing is a question of learned conventions that do not line up in any straightforward manner with the way sentence boundaries are marked in speech; often, there is no audible signal of any kind. Moreover, slips and performance mistakes aside, "sentence fragments" in speech are not necessarily syntactically malformed; as such, they conform to native speakers' implicit grammatical knowledge. As a language use requirement, the "complete sentence" belongs to specific categories of written discourse and formal speech, and to a school register characteristic of certain kinds of teacher-student interaction.

6. Implicit in the idea that children are not born with knowledge of language-specific grammatical structures is that "knowledge of grammar" also refers to competencies that are specific to languages (with a lowercase "l"). This means that grammar knowledge corresponds to patterns in a given language, not only to universal principles. Perhaps it is the study of bilingualism in particular that suggests this idea: the evidence that early simultaneous bilinguals construct separate representations for French and English, Spanish and Nahuatl, and so on (chapter 4). The evidence from bilingual aphasics of selective loss and recovery (chapter 5) also suggests separate networks for each language. From another point of view, "knowledge of language" might also refer to non-language-specific capacities of the Faculty of Language. This potential point of confusion perhaps could be corrected by standardizing the usage of terms; in the meantime, we should be attentive to the different senses of "knowledge of language."

Chapter 8

1. Although Bialystok suggests that her "metalinguistic dimensions of bilingual proficiency" model is neutral with respect to the role of modular and central processes, she does set aside the components of language ability that are "automatic processes involved in low-level aspects of language processing." These are "fast processes...essentially inaccessible to study and impervious to development" (1991, 116). This useful distinction places the development

of metalinguistic awareness within a domain that allows the question of the possible cognitive benefits of bilingualism to be examined in a more coherent way. Sharwood Smith (1994b) draws the distinction more explicitly. Referring to the later stages of language development, he states that "new representations may be reformatted so they are accessible to conscious introspection. . . . This optional, final, stage [is tied to] metalinguistic representations [that] are also qualitatively different from the representations that are the outcome of earlier processes" (p. 40). Along the same lines, Schachter (1990, 41) distinguishes between grammatical competence and certain aspects of lexical knowledge:

> [This] latter knowledge may form part of a conceptual system which constitutes part of some other faculty of mind that provides common sense understanding of the world. These two systems are said to interact, but a great deal of work must go into the delineation of what properly belongs to conceptual knowledge and what to linguistic, and to the question of how these interact.

By now, the basic affinity between Cummins's "three-component" model (L1–L2– Common Underlying Proficiency) and the Bilingual Tripartite Parallel Architecture from chapter 5 should be abundantly clear: (1) that to some extent L1 and L2 (or L_a and L_b) are represented autonomously, in a way that also allows for cross-linguistic influence; (2) that CUP, or Conceptual Structure in the Bilingual TPA, is composed of cognitive structures that are non-language-specific. In both cases, concepts are "shared"; the bilingual has access to them through the medium of either L1 or L2. CUP is contrasted with a hypothetical Separate Underlying Proficiency (SUP) model (Cummins 1981). Informally, SUP supposes that all aspects of language ability, including the skills of reading and writing, are language-specific. Unlike CUP, SUP implies that no knowledge component, skill, or ability is shared or is autonomous from the grammar of L1 and L2. In its strongest version, all concepts are also language-specific.

2. Discussing social-interactionist models of language acquisition and language learning would take us far afield from the objectives of this chapter. However, the debate is pertinent to the role that reflection on language form plays in regard to different aspects of language development. Swain (1995) speculates on the shortcomings of input-based theories of L2 learning "in light of the Vygotskian theory which argues that individual knowledge is socially and dialogically derived" (p. 138), and that "interaction drives language development" (p. 136). In an effort to sort out the relevant arguments, we might propose that a broader consensus has emerged around this aspect of Vygotsky's theories as it is applied to *L2 learning* and the *learning of higher-order language abilities*, less so in regard to the social, dialogic, and interactionist determinants of L1 acquisition.

Chapter 9

1. Comparisons based on students' first 30 miscues represent a more exigent measure than the fraction of each type of self-correction in relation to all miscues committed by the reader. The reason for adopting this more stringent measure is that the most proficient readers committed fewer miscues. The 2 students with the highest overall reading scores among the 4th and 6th graders both fell short of 30 miscues (24 and 9, respectively). All of the top 3 readers among the 2nd graders also fell short of 30 (16, 24, and 12 miscues each). Comparing the test scores of all 10 students who committed fewer than 30 miscues with those of their peers who committed 30 or more ($N = 35$) suggests a clear difference in overall reading ability: on

the cloze measure, the former achieved an average of 64.9%, the latter, 46.6%, a difference significant at $p<.01$, $t = 3.06$. Less skilled readers, especially at the lower grade levels, tended to commit large numbers of miscues; and more often than not, few were corrected.

2. The literature on L2 reading often refers to "top-down" and "bottom-up" processing. Van Dijk and Kintsch (1983, 25) remind us that "pure top-down models have never really existed, strictly speaking, because pure top-down processing is psychologically absurd." Purely bottom-up processing might be like what happens when someone "reads" or "listens" to a text and recognizes it as language (even specifically a language he or she knows), but is engaged concurrently in some other mental activity. The skilled L2 reader shifts back and forth, strategically, between relying on linguistic knowledge and bottom-up processing when background knowledge is scarce, and relying on content and formal schemas. "Short-circuiting" occurs when either one or the other does not come online, for whatever reason. For example, less skilled L2 readers may be characterized by an *over*reliance on context and previous knowledge. Conversely, students who experience difficulties in comprehension may have trouble applying relevant background knowledge to what they glean from a text, leaving fragments of information unconnected. Droop and Verhoeven (2003) present relevant research findings on the interrelationship between oral-language and literacy skills in a L2.

For clarity, the concept "interactive" is different from "integrative" as it is applied to the description of processing in holistic models. In reading, for example, some components may be more encapsulated and others more open; and all modular approaches to the study of language ability imply interactivity and interface. From their study of the antecedents of reading ability in kindergarten and 1st-grade children, Shatil and Share (2003, 25) conclude:

> An immediate implication of cognitive modularity in word recognition relates to the classification of poor readers. A componential approach to reading allows us to categorize reading processes as either modular or nonmodular. This has far-reaching implications for the taxonomy of reading disability syndromes. For example, . . . such terms as developmental dyslexia may be less precise than unambiguous labels such as "specific decoding impairment." Greater specification might include the source of the word-reading deficit such as phonological or orthographic.

Chapter 10

1. References to "naturalness," on all sides, may not be very useful in clarifying the key points in contention. Certain approaches to language learning have been characterized as "natural"—but no one, pro or con, has ever described "skill-building" methods as "unnatural." All acquisition and learning involving language and literacy, implicit or deliberate, is species-specific in one way or another. To paraphrase an observation once made by Noam Chomsky (1979): to claim that birds and humans are endowed with the same kind of musical faculty would be akin to describing jumping in humans, up to and including the most formidable Olympic performance, as a kind of flying. Expert musical ability, even though it requires years of focused learning and practice, is built upon natural, biologically determined competencies, part of a specifically human genetic endowment. The capacity for flight depends on a specific genetic endowment of other species. Even partisans of the strongest version of behaviorism would concede that some kind of innate cognitive machinery underlies

abilities that only humans are capable of mastering; what they seem to reject is any version of modularity. Fodor (1983) made this observation a long time ago.

In regard to literacy learning, again, Liberman and Whalen (2000, 192–193) ask the right question:

> How do we account for the biological gulf that separates speech from the reading and writing of its alphabetic transcription? The preliterate child is a prodigy of phonological development. Commanding thousands of words, he readily produces their phonological structures when speaking, and just as readily parses them in listening. Thus, he exploits the particulate principle quite naturally, without its ever having been taught to him, and without his having to be aware of the principl. . . . For the skillful use of that principle in speech, it is enough to be a normal member of the human race and to have been exposed to a mother tongue. By contrast, applying the particulate principle to the task of reading and writing is not an automatic outgrowth of the natural capacity for language but an achievement of a distinctly intellectual kind. . . . To develop the phonemic awareness that reading and writing call for, the child must therefore learn to put his attention where it has never had to be.

2. Beyond a basic introduction to phonics (not necessarily from phonics lessons in school), extensive practice with continuous text is universally recognized as a requirement for the consolidation of reading skills. And it cannot be excluded that many emergent readers induce an initial platform of alphabetic principles without any direct instruction focused on grapheme-phoneme pairings. But a core acquisition of alphabetic principles does take place on one level or another, whether through direct instruction, through systematic shared reading that calls attention to sublexical elements, or even by means of "simple immersion" and untutored experience with written language. Only a small fraction of the hundreds of mappings of phonology to orthography (in English, for example) can be introduced through direct phonics teaching. Building on this observation, Rayner et al. (2001, 66) point out, "Because of the sheer number of these connections, self-teaching is hypothesized as the mechanism by which children continue their reading achievement beyond the basic levels. . . . Self-teaching assumes a foundation of phonological awareness and decoding skill upon which to bootstrap new orthographic information." This would apply with equal force to bilingual or L2 readers. Access to decodable texts, which *progressively* introduce greater grammatical complexity and greater proportions of low-frequency vocabulary, should then figure among the most useful resources for developing skill in decoding, sentence-level processing, and text comprehension for L2 learners. On this question, the widespread opposition by whole-language advocates to modified (simplified) decodable texts for L2 learners, following their negative assessment of graded anthologies for beginning L1 readers (Hadaway, Vardell, and Young 2002, 55–56), is difficult to justify. The objection to graded texts for beginning L2 readers is supported mainly by anecdotal accounts and impressionistic and selective analyses of poorly written basal reader anthologies.

Returning to the bootstrapping notion, that children are able to induce the orthographic patterns of their writing system through immersion is an important research problem. They must be able to do so, because large numbers of them learn how to read without direct phonics instruction, and many become proficient readers without the benefit of effective instruction of any kind. Therefore, the role of top-down conceptual-domain factors should not be minimized in explaining how beginning readers learn efficient decoding skills. Again, it's important to emphasize that research findings on *learning* do not automatically translate into conclusive recommendations for *teaching*.

3. In the summary of their large-scale study of bilingualism in the Miami area, D. K. Oller and Eilers (2002) present an interesting description of some aspects of imbalanced development in L1 and L2. In the context of discussing interdependence (Cummins 2001) and the factor of "time on task/frequency of input" in language learning, they propose a "distributed characteristic of bilingual knowledge." In the case of vocabulary knowledge (here the authors refer to Pearson, Fernández, and Oller 1993), it would not be surprising to observe a "distribution" of L1 and L2 words in bilingual children. Some knowledge domains associated with L1 use would be linked to L1 vocabulary, while development of the lexicon in the L2 would be both complementary and overlapping. Measured separately, each lexicon might appear limited in comparison with the respective monolingual norm. In a bilingual assessment of lexical knowledge, this could be demonstrated by administering in the L2 test items missed in L1, and vice versa. In this way, among normally developing and appropriately matched populations, it would also be easy to demonstrate the effective equivalence between monolinguals and bilinguals. On some level, this "distributed imbalance" might even be observed as a stable feature of bilingual competence in some bilinguals. But in any case, a distribution of this kind would not be cause for categorizing it as abnormal or as an example of semilingualism.

D. K. Oller and Eilers (2002) go on to ask, to what extent might this kind of "incompleteness" in L1 and L2, complementary when "combined," apply to domains beyond vocabulary?

> The distributed characteristic may represent a sort of compromise achieved by default due to time constraints and differences in day-to-day environments of exposure to the two languages. The compromise is that since not every word, and perhaps not every grammatical construction, needs to be learned in both languages, the learner may acquire the two languages with limitations in each, minimizing learning costs. (pp. 286–287)

In our discussion of attrition/language replacement in chapter 6, we accepted the possibility of such a stable "overlap" in lexical knowledge, but implied that the linguistic subsystems of phonology and morphology/syntax would develop toward completeness independently, following the results of the studies of autonomous grammatical development by J. Paradis and Genesee (1996) and Meisel (2001). Completeness in the domains of phonology and morphology/syntax would apply to the 2L1 scenario, to either L_a or L_b in imbalanced bilingualism, and to any replacing language. This was the "no semilingualism" condition. The idea was that a fully distributed grammatical competence would only normally be observed, and not necessarily, in transitory phases of subtractive bilingualism. So, in what way might the proposal for a distributed characteristic be compatible with the "no semilingualism" condition? Alternatively, would it represent falsifying evidence; i.e., that such imbalances in bilingual competence might extend beyond vocabulary? For starters, we would want to exclude temporary delays in developing child grammars that appear to show "overlap" or "distribution," and put aside consideration of those domains beyond the core grammar that are tied to school achievement, academic discourse, and literacy. Perhaps another way of proceeding would be to demonstrate first *how* the distributed characteristic might apply to these circumstances, thus helping us delimit the question. More directly, interesting findings from a study of ultimate attainment in the replacing language (Swedish) of child adoptees who had undergone long-term and absolute L1 (Spanish) attrition (Hyltenstam et al. 2009) appear to contradict the "no semilingualism" condition. A difficult conceptual problem for future work, which this study highlights, remains that of making more precise the criteria for "completeness" and "nativelikeness," so far based on measures that may not have been sufficiently exacting.

4. One could say that Ladino, the dialect of Spanish spoken by the Sephardim that conserves many archaic features, survived long enough to serve as a vehicle for preserving certain artistic genres. Today, of course, it faces an uncertain future along with the other minority European languages and dialectal variants of the major languages (Czöndör 2008). And as a result, who knows which poetic forms were not in a position to take advantage of the uniquely productive vehicles of the oral tradition and music, missing the train, as it were.

References

Aarts, R., and L. Verhoeven. 1999. Literacy attainment in a second language submersion context. *Applied Psycholinguistics* 20:377–393.

Abrahamsson, N., and K. Hyltenstam. 2009. Age of onset and nativelikeness in a second language: Listener perception versus linguistic scrutiny. *Language Learning* 59:249–306.

Abu-Rabia, S. 2000. Effects of exposure to literary Arabic on reading comprehension in a diglossic situation. *Reading and Writing: An Interdisciplinary Journal* 13:147–157.

Abu-Rabia, S. 2004. Reading ability in Ethiopian learners of Hebrew: How important is phonemic awareness? *Language, Culture and Curriculum* 17:196–202.

Adams, M. J. 2004. Modeling the connections between word recognition and reading. In *Theoretical models and processes of reading*. 5th ed., ed. R. Ruddell and N. J. Unrau, 1219–1243. Newark, DE: International Reading Association.

Aikhenvald, A. 2002. Traditional multilingualism and language endangerment. In *Language endangerment and language maintenance*, ed. D. Bradley and M. Bradley, 24–33. London: Routledge.

Akmajian, A., R. Demers, A. Farmer, and R. Harnish. 2001. *Linguistics: An introduction to language and communication*. Cambridge, MA: MIT Press.

Allen, S. 2007. The future of Inuktitut in the face of majority languages: Bilingualism or language shift? *Applied Psycholinguistics* 28:515–536.

Allen, S., M. Crago, and D. Pesco. 2006. The effect of majority language exposure on minority language skills: The case of Inuktitut. *International Journal of Bilingual Education and Bilingualism* 9:578–596.

Altarriba, J. 2003. Does "cariño" equal "liking"? A theoretical approach to conceptual nonequivalence between languages. *International Journal of Bilingualism* 7:305–322.

Anamalai, E. 2003. Reflections on a language policy for multilingualism. *Language Policy* 2:113–132.

Anderson, J. 2008. Towards an integrated second-language pedagogy for foreign and community/heritage languages in multilingual Britain. *Language Learning Journal* 36:79–89.

Anderson, R. 2004. First language loss in Spanish-speaking children: Patterns of loss and implications for clinical practice. In *Bilingual language development and disorders in Spanish-English speakers*, ed. B. Goldstein, 187–212. Baltimore, MD: Brooks Publishing.

Anderson, S., and D. Lightfoot. 2002. *The language organ: Linguistics as cognitive physiology.* Cambridge: Cambridge University Press.

Artigal, J. M. 1997. The Catalan immersion program. In *Immersion education: International perspectives*, ed. R. Johnson and M. Swain, 133–150. Cambridge: Cambridge University Press.

Astington, J. 1990. Narrative and the child's theory of mind. In *Narrative thought and narrative language*, ed. B. Britton and A. Pellegrini, 151–171. Mahwah, NJ: Lawrence Erlbaum.

Astington, J. 2002. The ongoing quest to explain false-belief understanding. Review of P. Mitchell and K. Riggs, Children's reasoning and the mind. *Contemporary Psychology* 47:761–763.

Au, T. K.-F. 2006. The relationship between language and cognition. In *The handbook of East Asian psycholinguistics*. Vol. 1, *Chinese*, ed. P. Li, L.-H. Tan, E. Bates, and O. J. L. Tzeng, 281–286. Cambridge: Cambridge University Press.

Baker, C. 2003. Education as a site of language contact. *Annual Review of Applied Linguistics* 23:95–112.

Baker, C. 2006. *Foundations of bilingual education and bilingualism.* Clevedon: Multilingual Matters.

Baker, M. 2001. *The atoms of language.* New York: Basic Books.

Baker, M. 2003. Linguistic differences and language design. *Trends in Cognitive Sciences* 7:349–353.

Baker, W., and P. Trofimovich. 2005. Interaction of native and second-language vowel system(s) in early and late bilinguals. *Language and Speech* 48:1–27.

Bamberg, M., and L. Moissinac. 2003. Discourse development. In *Handbook of discourse processes*, ed. A. C. Graesser, M. A. Gernsbacher, and S. R. Goldman, 395–437. Mahwah, NJ: Lawrence Erlbaum.

Bamgbose, A. 2000. *Language and exclusion: The consequences of language policies in Africa.* Hamburg: Lit Verlag Münster.

Banda, F. 2000. The dilemma of the mother tongue: Prospects for bilingual education in South Africa. *Language, Culture and Curriculum* 13:51–66.

Bardovi-Harlig, K. 2000. *Tense and aspect in second language acquisition: Form, meaning and use.* Oxford: Blackwell.

Barrett, H. C., and R. Kurzban. 2006. Modularity in cognition: Framing the debate. *Psychological Review* 113:628–647.

Bar-Shalom, E., S. Crain, and D. Shankweiler. 1993. A comparison of comprehension and production abilities of good and poor readers. *Applied Psycholinguistics* 14:197–228.

Bates, E. 2001. Tailoring the emperor's new clothes. *Aphasiology* 15:391–395.

Bates, E., A. Devescovi, and B. Wulfeck. 2001. Psycholinguistics: A cross-language perspective. *Annual Review of Psychology* 52:369–396.

Benson, C. 2002. Real and potential benefits of bilingual programmes in developing countries. *International Journal of Bilingual Education and Bilingualism* 6:303–317.

Bernstein, B. 1964. Elaborated and restricted codes, their social origins and some consequences. *American Anthropologist* 66:55–67.

Bersten, J. 2001. English in South Africa: Expansion and nativization in concert. *Language Problems and Language Planning* 25:219–235.

Bialystok, E. 1991. Metalinguistic dimensions of bilingual language proficiency. In *Language processing in bilingual children*, ed. E. Bialystok, 113–140. Cambridge: Cambridge University Press.

Bialystok, E. 2001a. *Bilingualism in development: Language, literacy and cognition.* Cambridge: Cambridge University Press.

Bialystok, E. 2001b. Metalinguistic aspects of bilingual processing. *Annual Review of Applied Linguistics* 21:169–181.

Bialystok, E. 2002. Acquisition of literacy in bilingual children: A framework for research. *Language Learning* 52:159–199.

Bialystok, E. 2006. Bilingualism at school: Effect on the acquisition of literacy. In *Childhood bilingualism: Research on infancy through school age*, ed. P. McCardle and E. Hoff, 107–124. Clevedon: Multilingual Matters.

Bialystok, E. 2007. Acquisition of literacy in bilingual children: A framework for research. *Language Learning* 57:45–77.

Bialystok, E., and E. Cummins. 1991. Language, cognition, and education. In *Language processing in bilingual children*, ed. E. Bialystok, 222–231. Cambridge: Cambridge University Press.

Bialystok, E., and K. Hakuta. 1994. *In other words: The science and psychology of second language acquisition.* New York: Basic Books.

Biber, D., S. Conrad, R. Reppen, P. Byrd, and M. Helt. 2002. Speaking and writing in the university: A multidimensional comparison. *TESOL Quarterly* 36:9–48.

Birch, B. 2002. *English L2 reading.* Mahwah, NJ: Lawrence Erlbaum.

Birdsong, D. 2006. Age and second language acquisition and processing: A selective overview. *Language Learning* 56 (S1):9–49.

Birdsong, D., and M. Molis. 2001. On the evidence for maturational constraints in second-language acquisition. *Journal of Memory and Language* 44:235–249.

Bitchener, J., and U. Knoch. 2009. The relative effectiveness of different types of direct written corrective feedback. *System* 37:322–329.

Blakemore, D. 2001. Discourse and relevance theory. In *The handbook of discourse analysis*, ed. D. Schiffrin, D. Tannen, and H. Hamilton, 100–118. Oxford: Blackwell.

Bley-Vroman, R. 2009. The evolving context of the fundamental difference hypothesis. *Studies in Second Language Acquisition* 31:175–198.

Bloom, P. 1994. Recent controversies in the study of language acquisition. In *Handbook of psycholinguistics*, ed. M. Gernsbacher, 741–779. San Diego, CA: Academic Press.

Bloom, P. 2000. *How children learn the meanings of words.* Cambridge, MA: MIT Press.

Bloom, P. 2001. Précis of *How children learn the meanings of words. Behavioral and Brain Sciences* 24:1095–1103.

Bloom, P. 2004. *Descartes's baby: How the science of child development explains what makes us human.* New York: Basic Books.

Blum-Kulka, S. 2002. "Do you believe that Lot's wife is blocking the road (to Jericho)?": Co-constructing theories about the world. In *Talking to adults: The contribution of multi-party discourse to language acquisition*, ed. S. Blum-Kulka and C. E. Snow, 85–115. Mahwah, NJ: Lawrence Erlbaum.

Bolonyai, A. 1998. In-between languages: Language shift/maintenance in childhood bilingualism. *International Journal of Bilingualism* 2:21–43.

Bongaerts, T., S. Mennen, and F. van der Slik. 2000. Authenticity of pronunciation in naturalistic second language acquisition: The case of very advanced late learners of Dutch as a second language. *Studia Linguistica* 54:298–308.

Bosch, L., and N. Sebastián-Gallés. 2003. Simultaneous bilingualism and the perception of a language-specific vowel contrast in the first year of life. *Language and Speech* 46:217–244.

Boudreau, D. 2008. Narrative abilities: Advances in research and implications for clinical practice. *Topics in Language Disorders* 28:99–114.

Bourdereau, F. 2006. Politique linguistique, politique scolaire: La situation du Maroc. *Le Français Aujourd'hui* 154:25–34.

Bourhis, R., E. Montaruli, and C. Amiot. 2007. Language planning and French-English bilingual communication: Montreal field studies from 1977 to 1997. *International Journal of the Sociology of Language* 185:187–224.

Bresnan, J., and R. Kaplan. 1982. Introduction: Grammars as mental representations of language. In *The mental representation of grammatical relations*, ed. J. Bresnan, xvii–lii. Cambridge, MA: MIT Press.

Breznitz, Z., R. Oren, and S. Shaul. 2004. Brain activity of regular and dyslexic readers while reading Hebrew as compared to English sentences. *Reading and Writing* 17:707–737.

Brockmeier, J. 2000. Literacy as symbolic space. In *Minds in the making: Essays in honor of David R. Olson*, ed. J. Astington, 43–60. New York: Blackwell.

Bruck, M. 1992. Persistence of dyslexics' phonological deficits. *Developmental Psychology* 28:874–886.

Bruner, J. 1975. Language as an instrument of thought. In *Problems of language and learning*, ed. A. Davies, 61–82. London: Heinemann.

Bylund, E. 2009. Maturational constraints and first language attrition. *Language Learning* 59:687–715.

Callahan, L. 2004. *Spanish/English codeswitching in a written corpus*. Amsterdam: John Benjamins.

Cárdenas Demay, A., and A. Arellano Martínez. 2004. Hacia la definición de una política del lenguaje en México. In *Endangered languages and linguistic rights: On the margins of nations*, ed. J. Argenter and R. McKenna Brown, 67–72. Bath: Foundation for Endangered Languages.

Carrasquillo, A. 1993. Whole native language instruction for limited-English-proficient students. In *Whole language and the bilingual learner*, ed. A. Carrasquillo and C. Hedley, 3–19. Norwood, NJ: Ablex.

Carrell, P., L. Gajdusek, and T. Wise. 1998. Metacognition and EFL/ESL reading. *Instructional Science* 26:97–112.

Carrillo Avelar, A. 2004. Cultura académica instituyente e instituida en las escuelas indígenas hñähñús. Unpublished doctoral dissertation in Ciencias Antropológicas. México DF: Universidad Autónoma Metropolitana.

Carroll, S. 2001. *Input and evidence: The raw material of second language acquisition*. Amsterdam: John Benjamins.

Carruthers, P. 2002. The cognitive functions of language. *Behavioral and Brain Sciences* 25:657–674.

Carruthers, P. 2003. Moderately massive modularity. In *Minds and persons*, ed. A. O'Hear, 67–89. Cambridge: Cambridge University Press.

Carruthers, P. In press. Language in cognition. In *The Oxford handbook of philosophy and cognitive science*, ed. E. Margolis, R. Samuels, and S. Stich. Oxford: Oxford University Press.

Carson, J. 2001. Second language writing and second language acquisition. In *On second language writing*, ed. T. Silva and P. Matsuda, 191–199. Mahwah, NJ: Lawrence Erlbaum.

Castles, A., and M. Coltheart. 2004. Is there a causal link from phonological awareness to success in learning to read? *Cognition* 91:77–111.

Celce-Murcia, M. 2002. On the use of selected grammatical features in academic writing. In *Developing advanced literacy in first and second languages: Meaning and power*, ed. M. J. Schleppegrell and M. C. Colombi, 143–158. Mahwah, NJ: Lawrence Erlbaum.

Chafe, W. 1985. Linguistic differences produced by differences between speaking and writing. In *Literacy, language, and learning: The nature and consequences of reading and writing*, ed. D. Olson, N. Torrance, and A. Hildyard, 105–123. Cambridge: Cambridge University Press.

Chamberlain, P., and P. Medinos-Landurand. 1991. Practical considerations for the assessment of LEP students with special needs. In *Limiting bias in the assessment of bilingual students*, ed. E. Hamayan and J. Damico, 111–156. Austin, TX: Pro-ed.

Chandler, J. 2003. The efficacy of various kinds of error feedback for improvement in the accuracy and fluency of L2 student writing. *Journal of Second Language Writing* 12:267–296.

Cheung, H., and A. M.-Y. Lin. 2005. Differentiating between automatic and strategic control processes: Toward a model of cognitive mobilization in bilingual reading. *Psychologia* 48:39–53.

Chiappe, P., and L. Siegel. 2006. A longitudinal study of reading development of Canadian children from diverse backgrounds. *Elementary School Journal* 107:135–152.

Chien, C.-N., L.-H. Kao, and W. Li. 2008. The role of phonological awareness development in young Chinese EFL learners. *Language Awareness* 17:271–288.

Chiodi, F. 1993. Los problemas de la educación bilingüe intercultural en el area de lenguaje. In *Pedagogía intercultural bilingüe: Fundamentos de la educación bilingüe*, ed. W. Kuper, 173–206. Quito: Ediciones Abya-Yala.

Chomsky, N. 1979. *Language and responsibility: Based on conversations with Mitsou Ronat*. New York: Pantheon Books.

Chomsky, N. 1999. On the nature, use, and acquisition of language. In *Handbook of child language acquisition*, ed. W. Ritchie and T. K. Bhatia, 33–54. San Diego, CA: Academic Press.

Chow, B. W.-Y., C. McBride-Chang, and S. Burgess. 2005. Phonological processing skills and early reading abilities in Hong Kong Chinese kindergarteners learning to read English as a second language. *Journal of Educational Psychology* 97:81–87.

Christie, F. 2005. Using the functional grammar to understand children's written texts. *Australian Review of Applied Linguistics* 19:9–22.

Chung, W.-L., and C.-F. Hu. 2007. Morphological awareness and learning to read Chinese. *Reading and Writing* 20:441–461.

Clahsen, H. 1991. *Child language and developmental dysphasia: Linguistic studies of the acquisition of German.* Amsterdam: John Benjamins.

Clahsen, H., F. Aveledo, and I. Roca. 2002. The development of regular and irregular verb inflection in Spanish child language. *Journal of Child Language* 29:591–622.

Clahsen, H., and P. Muysken. 1996. How adult second language learning differs from child first language development. *Behavioral and Brain Sciences* 19:721–723.

Clark, E. 2003. *First language acquisition.* Cambridge: Cambridge University Press.

Clark, E., and A. Wong. 2002. Pragmatic directions about language use: Offers of words and relations. *Language in Society* 31:181–212.

Clay, M. 1993. *Reading recovery: A guidebook for teachers in training.* Portsmouth, NH: Heinemann.

Colombi, M. C., and M. J. Schleppegrell. 2002. Theory and practice in the development of advanced literacy. In *Developing advanced literacy in first and second languages: Meaning and power*, ed. M. J. Schleppegrell and M. C. Colombi, 1–20. Mahwah, NJ: Lawrence Erlbaum.

Coltheart, M. 1999. Modularity and cognition. *Trends in Cognitive Sciences* 3:115–120.

Coltheart, M. 2006. The genetics of learning to read. *Journal of Research in Reading* 29:1224–1232.

Comeau, L., F. Genesee, and M. Mendelson. 2007. Bilingual children's repairs of breakdown in communication. *Journal of Child Language* 34:159–174.

Connor, U. 1996. *Contrastive rhetoric: Cross-cultural aspects of second-language writing.* Cambridge: Cambridge University Press.

Consejo Nacional de Fomento Educativo (CONAFE). 2000. *Didáctica bilingüe: Alfabetización en lengua materna.* México, DF: Secretaría de Educación Pública.

Cook, V. 2001. Linguistics and second language acquisition: One person with two languages. In *The handbook of linguistics*, ed. M. Aronoff and J. Rees-Miller, 488–511. Oxford: Blackwell.

Cormier, M., and M. Turnbull. 2009. Une approche littératiée: Apprendre les sciences et la langue en immersion tardive. *Canadian Modern Language Review* 65:817–840.

Costa, A. 2004. Speech production in bilinguals. In *The handbook of bilingualism*, ed. T. Bhatia and W. R. Ritchie, 201–223. Oxford: Blackwell.

Costa, A., A. Colomé, O. Gómez, and N. Sebastián-Gallés. 2003. Another look at cross-language competition in bilingual speech production: Lexical and phonological factors. *Bilingualism: Language and Cognition* 6:167–179.

Crain, S., and P. Pietroski. 2002. Why language acquisition is a snap. *Linguistic Review* 19:163–183.

Crain, S., and R. Thornton. 1998. *Investigations in Universal Grammar: A guide to experiments on the acquisition of syntax and semantics.* Cambridge, MA: MIT Press.

Crutchley, A., G. Conti-Ramsden, and N. Botting. 1997. Bilingual children with Specific Language Impairment and standardized assessments: Preliminary findings from a study of children in language units. *International Journal of Bilingualism* 1:117–134.

Crystal, D. 2000. *Language death.* Cambridge: Cambridge University Press.

Culicover, P., and R. Jackendoff. 2005. *Simpler Syntax.* Oxford: Oxford University Press.

Culicover, P., and A. Nowak. 2003. *Dynamical grammar: Minimalism, acquisition, and change.* Oxford: Oxford University Press.

Cummins, J. 1979a. Cognitive/academic language proficiency, linguistic interdependence, the optimum age question and some other matters. *Working Papers in Bilingualism* 19:197–205.

Cummins, J. 1979b. Linguistic interdependence and the educational development of bilingual children. *Review of Educational Research* 49:222–251.

Cummins, J. 1981. The role of primary language development in promoting educational success for language minority students. In *Schooling and language minority students: A theoretical framework,* ed. California State Department of Education, 3–49. Los Angeles: National Dissemination and Assessment Center.

Cummins, J. 1991. Language development and academic learning. In *Language, Culture and Cognition,* ed. L. Malavé and G. Duquette, 161–175. Clevedon: Multilingual Matters.

Cummins, J. 1999. Alternative paradigms in bilingual education research: Does theory have a place? *Educational Researcher* 28:26–41.

Cummins, J. 2000. *Language, power and pedagogy: Bilingual children in the crossfire.* Clevedon: Multilingual Matters.

Cummins, J. 2001. *Negotiating identities: Education for empowerment in a diverse society.* Los Angeles: California Association for Bilingual Education.

Cummins, J. 2007. Review of F. Genesee, K. Lindholm-Leary, W. Saunders, and D. Christian, eds., *Educating English language learners: A synthesis of research evidence. Language and Education,* 21:87–92.

Cummins, J., and M. Swain. 1983. Analysis-by-rhetoric: Reading the text or the reader's own projections? A reply to Edelsky et al. *Applied Linguistics* 4:23–41.

Cummins, J., and M. Swain. 1986. *Bilingualism in education: Aspects of theory, research and practice.* New York: Longman.

Curtain, H., and C. Dahlberg. 2010. *Languages and children: Making the match.* 4th ed. New York: Allyn & Bacon.

Curtiss, S. 1994. Language as a cognitive system: Its independence and selective vulnerability. In *Noam Chomsky: Critical assessments,* ed. C. Otero, 211–255. London: Routledge.

Czöndör, K. 2008. La escritura de la lengua Judeo-Española. *Verbum Analecta Neolatina* 10:79–97.

Damico, J. S. 1991. Descriptive assessment of communicative ability in limited English proficient students. In *Limiting bias in the assessment of bilingual students*, ed. E. V. Hamayan and J. S. Damico,157–218. Austin, TX: Pro-ed.

Davies, J., S. Sandstrom, A. Sharrocks, and E. Wolff. (2006). *The world's distribution of household wealth*. Study released by the World Institute for Development Economics Report. Helsinki: United Nations University, http://www.wider.unu.edu/.

De Bot, K. 2000. A bilingual's production model: Levelt's "speaking" model adapted. In *The bilingualism reader*, ed. L. Wei, 420–442. London: Routledge.

De Bot, K. 2004. The multilingual lexicon: Modeling selection and control. *International Journal of Multilingualism* 1:17–32.

De Bot, K., and M. Hulsen. 2002. Language attrition: Tests, self-assessments and perceptions. In *Portraits of the L2 user*, ed. V. Cook, 253–274. Clevedon: Multilingual Matters.

Degand, L., and T. Sanders. 2002. The impact of relational markers on expository text comprehension in L1 and L2. *Reading and Writing* 15:739–757.

De Groot, A. 2002. Lexical representation and lexical processing in the L2 user. In *Portraits of the L2 user*, ed. V. Cook, 32–63. Clevedon: Multilingual Matters.

De Groot, A., and I. Christoffels. 2006. Language control in bilinguals: Monolingual tasks and simultaneous interpreting. *Bilingualism: Language and Cognition* 9:189–201.

De Houwer, A. 2006. Le développement harmonieux ou non harmonieux du bilinguisme de l'enfant au sein de la famille. *Langage & Société* 116:29–49.

DeKeyser, R. 1998. Beyond focus on form: Cognitive perspectives on learning and practicing second language grammar. In *Focus on form in classroom second language acquisition*, ed. C. Doughty and J. Williams, 42–63. Cambridge: Cambridge University Press.

DeKeyser, R. 2000. The robustness of critical period effects in second language acquisition. *Studies in Second Language Acquisition* 22:499–533.

DeKeyser, R. 2005. What makes learning second-language grammar difficult? A review of the issues. *Language Learning* 55:1–25.

Dekydtspotter, L., R. Sprouse, and K. Swanson. 2001. Reflexes of mental architecture in second-language acquisition: The interpretation of combien extractions in English-French interlanguage. *Language Acquisition* 9:175–227.

DeLuca, D., and D. J. Napoli. 2008. A bilingual approach to reading. In *Signs and voices: Deaf culture, identity, language, and arts*, ed. K. Lindgren, D. DeLuca, and D. J. Napoli, 150–159. Washington, DC: Gallaudet University Press.

Denny, J. P. 1991. Rational thought in oral culture and literate decontextualization. In *Literacy and orality*, ed. D. Olson and N. Torrance, 66–89. Cambridge: Cambridge University Press.

Descartes, R. 1984. *The philosophical writings of Descartes*, vol. 2. Trans. J. Cottingham, R. Stoothoff, and D. Murdoch. Cambridge: Cambridge University Press.

Deuchar, M., and S. Quay. 2000. *Bilingual acquisition: Theoretical implications of a case study*. Oxford: Oxford University Press.

Díaz-Rico, L., and K. Z. Weed. 2001. *The crosscultural, language, and academic development handbook*. Boston: Allyn & Bacon.

Dickinson, D., A. McCabe, N. Clark-Chiarelli, and A. Wolf. 2004. Cross-language transfer of phonological awareness in low-income Spanish and English bilingual preschool children. *Applied Psycholinguistics* 25:323–348.

Diessel, H. 2004. *The acquisition of complex sentences*. Cambridge: Cambridge University Press.

Dijkstra, T., and W. van Heuven. 2002. The architecture of the bilingual word recognition system: From identification to decision. *Bilingualism: Language and Cognition* 5:175–197.

Dirección General de Educación Indígena (DGEI). 1990. *Fundamentos para la modernización de la educación indígena*. México DF: Secretaría de Educación Pública.

Dirección General de Educación Indígena (DGEI). 1999. *Lineamientos generales para la educación intercultural bilingüe para las niñas y los niños indígenas*. México DF: Secretaría de Educación Pública.

Dolitsky, M. 2000. Codeswitching in a child's monologues. *Journal of Pragmatics* 32:1387–1403.

Domínguez, L. 2009. Charting the route of bilingual development: Contributions from heritage speakers' early acquisition. *International Journal of Bilingualism* 13:271–287.

Döpke, S. 2000. Generation of and retraction from cross-linguistically motivated structures in bilingual first language acquisition. *Bilingualism: Language and Cognition* 3:209–226.

Dorian, N. 2004. Minority and endangered languages. In *The handbook of bilingualism*, ed. T. Bhatia and W. Ritchie, 437–459. Oxford: Blackwell.

Doughty, C. 2001. Cognitive underpinnings of focus on form. In *Cognition and second language instruction*, ed. P. Robinson, 206–257. Cambridge: Cambridge University Press.

Doughty, C. 2003. Instructed SLA: Constraints, compensation, and enhancement. In *The handbook of second language acquisition*, ed. C. J. Doughty and M. H. Long, 256–310. Oxford: Blackwell.

Droop, M., and L. Verhoeven. 2003. Language proficiency and reading ability in first- and second-language learners. *Reading Research Quarterly* 38:78–103.

Echevarría, J., and A. Graves. 2007. *Sheltered content instruction: Teaching English language learners with diverse abilities*. Boston: Allyn & Bacon.

Edelsky, C. 1996. *With literacy and justice for all: Rethinking the social in language and education*. London: Taylor & Francis. [3rd ed. (2006), Mahwah, NJ: Lawrence Erlbaum.]

Edelsky, C., S. Hudelson, B. Flores, F. Barkin, B. Altwerger, and C. Jilbert. 1983. Semilingualism and language deficit. *Applied Linguistics* 4:1–22.

Edwards, H., and A. Kirkpatrick. 1999. Metalinguistic awareness in children: A developmental progression. *Journal of Psycholinguistic Research* 28:313–329.

Ehri, L. 2005. Learning to read words: Theory, findings, and issues. *Scientific Studies of Reading* 9:167–188.

Ehri, L., S. Nunes, D. Willows, B. Schuster, Z. Yaghoub-Zadeh, and T. Shanahan. 2001. Phonemic awareness instruction helps children learn to read: Evidence from the National Reading Panel's meta-analysis. *Reading Research Quarterly* 36:250–287.

Eisenbeiss, S. 2009. Generative approaches to language learning. *Linguistics* 47:273–310.

Ellis, N. 2008. The dynamics of second language emergence: Cycles of language use, language change, and language acquisition. *Modern Language Journal* 92:232–249.

Ellis, R. 2005. Principles of instructed language learning. *System* 33:209–224.

Ellis, R., S. Loewen, and R. Erlam. 2006. Implicit and explicit corrective feedback and the acquisition of L2 grammar. *Studies in Second Language Acquisition* 28:339–368.

Ellis, R., and Y. Sheen. 2006. Reexamining the role of recasts in second language acquisition. *Studies in Second Language Acquisition* 28:575–600.

Emmorey, K., H. Borinstein, R. Thompson, and T. Gollan. 2008. Bimodal bilingualism. *Bilingualism: Language and Cognition* 11:43–61.

Epstein, S., S. Flynn, and G. Martohardjono. 1996. Second language acquisition: Theoretical and experimental issues in contemporary research. *Behavioral and Brain Sciences* 19:677–758.

Errihani, M. 2008. *Language policy in Morocco: Implications of recognizing and teaching Berber*. Saarbrücken: VDM Publishing.

Eubank, L., and K. Gregg. 1999. Critical periods and (second) language acquisition: Divide et impera. In *Second language acquisition and the critical period hypothesis*, ed. D. Birdsong, 65–99. Mahwah, NJ: Lawrence Erlbaum.

Everett, D. 2005. Cultural constraints on grammar and cognition in Pirahã: Another look at the design features of human language. *Current Anthropology* 46:621–646.

Everett, D. 2009. Pirahã culture and grammar: A response to some criticisms. *Language* 85:405–442.

Fabbro, F. 1999. *The neurolinguistics of bilingualism: An introduction*. London: Taylor & Francis.

Fabbro, F. 2001. The bilingual brain: Cerebral representation of languages. *Brain and Language* 79:211–222.

Fabbro, F., M. Skrap, and S. Aglioti. 2000. Pathological switching between languages after frontal lesions in a bilingual patient. *Journal of Neurology, Neurosurgery, and Psychiatry* 68:650–652.

Faiq, S. 1999. The status of Berber: A permanent challenge to language policy in Morocco. In *Language and society in the Middle East and North Africa*, ed. Y. Suleiman, 137–153. Surrey: Curzon Press.

Falk, Y. 2001. *Lexical-Functional Grammar: An introduction to Parallel Constraint-Based Syntax*. Stanford, CA: Center for the Study of Language and Information.

Faltis, C. 2001. *Joinfostering: Teaching and learning in multicultural classrooms*. Columbus, OH: Prentice Hall.

Fang, Z. 2001. The development of schooled narrative competence among second graders. *Reading Psychology* 22:205–223.

Feldman, C. 1991. Oral metalanguage. In *Literacy and orality*, ed. D. Olson and N. Torrance, 47–65. Cambridge: Cambridge University Press.

Feldsberg, R. 1997. Fronteras socioculturales: Usos y prácticas de lectura y escritura de alumnos de la comunidad boliviana en la escuela pública argentina y en el hogar. *Lectura y Vida* 18:5–12.

Ferguson, C. 1959. Diglossia. *Word* 15:325–340.

Fernald, A. 2006. When infants hear two languages: Interpreting research on early speech perception by bilingual children. In *Childhood bilingualism: Research on infancy through school age*, ed. P. McCardle and E. Hoff, 19–29. Clevedon: Multilingual Matters.

Ferris, D. 2010. Second language writing research and written corrective feedback in SLA. *Studies in Second Language Acquisition* 32:181–201.

Field, J. 2004. An insight into listeners' problems: Too much bottom-up or too much top-down. *System* 32:363–377.

Fillol, V., and J. Vernaudon. 2004. Les langues kanakes et le français, langues d'enseignement et de culture en Nouvelle-Calédonie: D'un compromis à un bilinguisme équilibre. *Etudes de Linguistique Appliquée* 133:47–59.

Finnegan, R. 1988. *Literacy and orality*. Oxford: Blackwell.

Fishman, J. 1967. Bilingualism with and without diglossia: Diglossia with and without bilingualism. *Journal of Social Issues* 23:29–38.

Fitch, W. T., M. D. Hauser, and N. Chomsky. 2005. The evolution of the language faculty: Clarifications and implications. *Cognition* 97:179–210.

Flores Farfán, J. A. 1992. *Sociolingüística del náhuatl: Conservación y cambio de la lengua mexicana en el Alto Balsas*. México DF: Centro de Investigaciones y Estudios Superiores en Antropología Social.

Fodor, J. 1972. Some reflections on L. S. Vygotsky's *Thought and language*. *Cognition* 1:83–95.

Fodor, J. 1975. *The language of thought*. New York: Crowell.

Fodor, J. 1983. *The modularity of mind*. Cambridge, MA: MIT Press.

Fodor, J. 1990. Précis of *The modularity of mind*. In *A theory of content and other essays*, ed. J. Fodor, 195–206. Cambridge, MA: MIT Press.

Fodor, J. 1998. *In critical condition: Polemical essays on cognitive science and the philosophy of mind*. Cambridge, MA: MIT Press.

Foster-Cohen, S. 1990. *The communicative competence of young children: A modular approach*. London: Longman.

Foster-Cohen, S. 1993. Directions of influence in first and second language acquisition research. *Second Language Research* 9:140–152.

Foster-Cohen, S. 1996. Modularity and principles and parameters: Avoiding the "cognitively ugly." *First Language* 16:1–16.

Foster-Cohen, S. 2001. First language acquisition...second language acquisition: What's Hecuba to him or he to Hecuba? *Second Language Research* 17:329–344.

Francis, D. J., N. Lesaux, and D. August. 2006. Language of instruction. In *Developing literacy in second-language learners: Report of the National Literacy Panel on Language-Minority Children and Youth*, ed. D. August and T. Shanahan, 365–413. Mahwah, NJ: Lawrence Erlbaum.

Francis, N. 1997. *Malintzin: Bilingualism y alfabetización en la Sierra de Tlaxcala*. Quito: Ediciones Abya-yala.

Francis, N. 1998. Bilingual children's reflections on writing and diglossia. *International Journal of Bilingual Education and Bilingualism* 1:1–29.

Francis, N. 2001. Complejidad sintáctica - ¿competencia lingüística o competencia discursiva?: Análisis de narrativas infantiles orales y escritas. *Memorias del V Encuentro Internacional de Lingüística en el Noroeste*, ed. G. López Cruz and M. Morúa Leyva, 15–38. Hermosillo: Departamento de Letras y Lingüística, Universidad de Sonora.

Francis, N. 2004. Estrategias de autocorrección en la lectura y la escritura. *Lectura y Vida* 25: 26–35.

Francis, N. 2005. Bilingual children's writing: Self-correction and revision of written narratives in Spanish and Nahuatl. *Linguistics and Education* 16:74–92.

Francis, N., and P. R. Navarrete Gómez. 2000. La narrativa como sitio de intercambio entre el náhuatl y el español: Un análisis de la alternancia lingüística. *Estudios de Cultura Nahuatl* 31:359–391.

Francis, N., and P. R. Navarrete Gómez. 2003. Language interaction in Nahuatl discourse: The influence of Spanish in child and adult narratives. *Language, Culture and Curriculum* 16:1–17.

Francis, N., and P. R. Navarrete Gómez. 2009. Documentation and language learning: Separate agendas or complementary tasks? *Language Documentation and Conservation* 3:176–191.

Francis, N., and R. Nieto Andrade. 1996. Stories for language revitalization in Nahuatl and Chichimeca. In *Stabilizing indigenous languages*, ed. G. Cantoni, 163–173. Flagstaff: Northern Arizona University.

Francis, N., and C. Paciotto. 2004. Bilingüismo y diglosia en la Sierra Tarahumara: Fundamentos de la evaluación del lenguaje. *Pueblos Indígenas y Educación* 55:57–82.

Francis, N., and J. Reyhner. 2002. *Language and literacy teaching for indigenous education: A bilingual approach*. Clevedon: Multilingual Matters.

Fraser, C. 2004. Lire avec facilité en langue seconde. *Canadian Modern Language Review* 61:135–160.

Frodesen, J., and C. Holten. 2003. Grammar and the ESL writing class. In *Exploring the dynamics of second language writing*, ed. B. Kroll, 141–161. Cambridge: Cambridge University Press.

Fuchs, L., D. Fuchs, and M. Hosp. 2001. Oral reading fluency as an indicator of reading competence: A theoretical, empirical, and historical analysis. *Scientific Studies of Reading* 5:239–256.

Garfield, J. 1987. Introduction: Carving the mind at its joints. In *Modularity in knowledge representation and natural language understanding*, ed. J. Garfield, 1–36. Cambridge, MA: MIT Press.

Garfield, J., C. Peterson, and T. Perry. 2001. Social cognition, language acquisition and the development of the Theory of Mind. *Mind & Language* 16:494–541.

Garner, R. 1992. Metacognition and self-monitoring strategies. In *What research has to say about reading instruction*, ed. S. J. Samuels and A. E. Farstrup, 236–252. Newark, DE: International Reading Association.

Garrett, M. 2007. Speech error research: Comments on the state of the art. In *The state of the art in speech error research*, ed. C. Schütze and V. Ferreira, 395–405. MIT Working Papers in Linguistics 53. Cambridge, MA: MIT, MIT Working Papers in Linguistics.

Garrod, S., and M. Pickering. 2004. Why is conversation so easy? *Trends in Cognitive Sciences* 8:8–11.

Gass, S., and A. Mackey. 2006. Input, interaction and output. *AILA Review* 19:3–17.

Gathercole, V., and E. Thomas. 2009. Bilingual first-language development: Dominant language takeover, threatened minority language take-up. *Bilingualism: Language and Cognition* 12:213–237.

Gee, J. P. 1996. *Social linguistics and literacies: Ideology in discourses*. London: Taylor & Francis.

Gee, J. P. 2001. Educational linguistics. In *The handbook of linguistics*, ed. M. Aronoff and J. Rees-Miller, 647–663. Oxford: Blackwell.

Genesee, F. 2001. Bilingual first language acquisition: Exploring the limits of the language faculty. *Annual Review of Applied Linguistics* 21:153–168.

Genesee, F. 2002. Portrait of the bilingual child. In *Portraits of the L2 user*, ed. V. Cook, 170–196. Clevedon: Multilingual Matters.

Genesee, F. 2003. Rethinking bilingual acquisition. In *Bilingualism: Beyond basic principles, Festschrift in honour of Hugo Baetens Beardsmore*, ed. J. Dewaele, A. Housen, and L. Wei, 204–228. Clevedon: Multilingual Matters.

Genesee, F., E. Nicoladis, and J. Paradis. 1995. Language differentiation in early bilingual development. *Journal of Child Language* 22:611–632.

Genesee, F., J. Paradis, and M. Crago. 2004. *Dual language development and disorders: A handbook on bilingualism and second language learning*. Baltimore, MD: Paul Brooks.

Gernsbacher, M. A. 1990. *Language comprehension as structure building*. Mahwah, NJ: Lawrence Erlbaum.

Gernsbacher, M. A., and J. A. Foertsch. 1999. Three models of discourse comprehension. In *Language processing*, ed. S. Garrod and M. Pickering, 282–299. London: Taylor & Francis.

Gernsbacher, M. A., R. Robertson, P. Palladino, and N. Werner. 2004. Managing mental representations during narrative comprehension. *Discourse Processes* 37:145–164.

Gerrans, P., and V. Stone. 2008. Generous or parsimonious cognitive architecture? Cognitive neuroscience and Theory of Mind. *British Journal for the Philosophy of Science* 59:121–141.

Geva, E., and M. Wang. 2001. The development of basic reading skills in children: A cross-language perspective. *Annual Review of Applied Linguistics* 211:182–204.

Glastra, F., and P. Schedler. 2004. The language of newcomers: Developments in Dutch citizenship education. *Intercultural Education* 15:45–57.

Goetz, P. 2003. The effects of bilingualism on theory of mind development. *Bilingualism: Language and Cognition* 6:1–15.

Goldberg, A. 2003. Constructions: A new theoretical approach to language. *Trends in Cognitive Sciences* 7:219–224.

Goldin-Meadow, S. 2000. Learning with and without a helping hand. In *Perception, cognition, and language: Essays in honor of Lila Gleitman*, ed. B. Landau, J. Sabini, J. Jonides, and E. Newport, 121–137. Cambridge, MA: MIT Press.

Goldin-Meadow, S. 2005. What language creation in the manual modality tells us about the foundations of language. *Linguistic Review* 22:199–225.

Gombert, J. E. 1992. *Metalinguistic development*. Chicago: University of Chicago Press.

Goodman, K. 2005. Making sense of written language: A lifelong journey. *Journal of Literacy Research* 37:1–24.

Goodman, Y. 1995. Miscue analysis for classroom teachers: Some history and some procedures. *Primary Voices K–6* 3: 2–9.

Goodman, Y., and K. Goodman. 1994. To err is human: Learning about language processes by analyzing miscues. In *Theoretical models and processes of reading*, ed. R. B. Rudely, M. R. Rudely, and H. Singer, 104–123. Newark, DE: International Reading Association.

Goodman, Y., D. Watson, and C. Burke. 1987. *Reading miscue inventory*. New York: Richard Owen Publishers.

Goody, J. 1987. *The interface between the written and the oral*. Cambridge: Cambridge University Press.

Goswami, U. 2001. Early phonological development and the acquisition of literacy. In *Handbook of early literacy research*, ed. S. Neuman and D. Dickinson, 111–125. New York: The Guilford Press.

Gottschall, J. 2008. *Literature, science, and the new humanities*. New York: Palgrave Macmillan.

Gough, D., and Z. Bock. 2001. Alternative perspectives on orality, literacy and education: A view from South Africa. *Journal of Multilingual and Multicultural Development* 22:95–111.

Gough, P., W. Hoover, and C. Peterson. 1996. Some observations on a simple view of reading. In *Reading comprehension difficulties: Processes and intervention*, ed. C. Cornoldi and J. Oakhill, 1–13. Mahwah, NJ: Lawrence Erlbaum.

Gough, P., and S. Wren. 1999. Constructing meaning: The role of decoding. In *Reading development and the teaching of reading: A psychological perspective*, ed. J. Oakhill and R. Beard, 59–78. Oxford: Blackwell.

Grabe, W. 2002. Reading in a second language. In *The Oxford handbook of applied linguistics*, ed. R. Kaplan, 49–59. Oxford: Oxford University Press.

Grantham-McGregor, S., Y. B. Cheung, S. Cueto, P. Glewwe, L. Richter, and B. Strupp. 2007. Developmental potential in the first five years for children in developing countries. *Lancet* 369:60–70.

Gregg, K. 1989. Second language acquisition theory: The case for a generative perspective. In *Linguistic perspectives on second language acquisition*, ed. S. M. Gass and J. Schachter, 15–40. Cambridge: Cambridge University Press.

Gregg, K. 1996. The logical and developmental problems of second language acquisition. In *Handbook of second language acquisition*, ed. W. Ritchie and T. Bhatia, 49–81. New York: Academic Press.

Grigorenko, E. 2001. Developmental dyslexia: An update on genes, brains, and environments. *Journal of Child Psychology and Psychiatry, and Allied Disciplines* 42:91–125.

Grodzinsky, Y., and A. Friederici. 2006. Neuroimaging of syntax and syntactic processing. *Current Opinion in Neurobiology* 16:240–246.

Grosjean, F. 1995. A psycholinguistic approach to code-switching: The recognition of guest words by bilinguals. In *One speaker, two languages: Cross-disciplinary perspectives on code-switching*, ed. L. Milroy and P. Muysken, 259–275. Cambridge: Cambridge University Press.

Grosjean, F. 1997. Processing mixed language: Issues, findings, and models. In *Tutorials in bilingualism: Psycholinguistic perspectives*, ed. A. de Groot and J. Kroll, 225–254. Mahwah, NJ: Lawrence Erlbaum.

Grosjean, F. 2001. The bilingual's language modes. In *One mind, two languages: Bilingual language processing*, ed. J. Nicol, 1–22. Oxford: Blackwell.

Gross, S. 2004. A modest proposal: Explaining language attrition in the context of contact linguistics. In *First language attrition: Interdisciplinary perspectives on methodological issues*, ed. M. Schmid, B. Köpke, M. Keijzer, and L. Weilemar, 281–297. Amsterdam: John Benjamins.

Guglielmi, R. S. 2008. Native language proficiency, English literacy, academic achievement, and occupational attainment in limited-English-proficient students: A latent growth modeling perspective. *Journal of Educational Psychology* 100:322–342.

Gürel, A. 2004. Selectivity in L2-induced L1 attrition: A psycholinguistic account. *Journal of Neurolinguistics* 17:53–78.

Hadaway, N., S. Vardell, and T. Young. 2002. *Literature-based instruction with English language learners*. Boston: Allyn & Bacon.

Haeri, N. 2003. *Sacred language, ordinary people: Dilemmas of culture and politics in Egypt*. New York: Palgrave Macmillan.

Håkansson, G., E. Salameh, and U. Nettelbladt. 2003. Measuring language development in bilingual children: Swedish-Arabic children with and without language impairment. *Linguistics* 41:255–288.

Hale, K. 2001. Linguistic aspects of language teaching and learning in immersion contexts. In *The green book of language revitalization in practice*, ed. L. Hinton and K. Hale, 227–235. San Diego: Academic Press.

Haley, M., and T. Austin. 2004. *Content-based second language teaching and learning: An interactive approach*. Boston: Allyn & Bacon.

Hall, J. K., A. Cheng, and M. Carlson. 2006. Reconceptualizing multicompetence as a theory of language knowledge. *Applied Linguistics* 27:220–240.

Halliday, M. 1978. *Language as social semiotic: The social interpretation of language and meaning*. London: Edward Arnold.

Hamel, R. E. 2001. L'apparition de nouvelles politiques linguistiques dans les blocs régionaux: Le cas du Mercosur en Amérique du Sud. *Terminogramme* 99–100:129–160.

Hamel, R. E. 2003. El papel de la lengua materna en la enseñanza: Particularidades en la educación bilingüe. In *Abriendo la escuela: Lingüística aplicada a la enseñanza de lenguas*, ed. I. Jung and L. E. López, 248–260. Madrid: Morata.

Hamel, R. E. 2008. Bilingual education for indigenous communities in Mexico. In *Encyclopedia of language and education*, vol. 5, ed. J. Cummins and N. Hornberger, 311–322. New York: Springer.

Hamel, R. E. 2009. La noción de calidad desde las variables de equidad, diversidad y participación en la educación bilingüe intercultural. *Revista Guatemalteca de Educación* 1:177–230.

Hamel, R. E., M. Brumm, A. Carrillo Avelar, E. Loncón, R. Nieto Andrade, and E. Silva Castellón. 2004. ¿Qué hacemos con la castilla? La enseñanza del español como segunda lengua en un currículo intercultural bilingüe de educación indígena. *Revista Mexicana de Investigación Educativa* 9:83–107.

Hamel, R. E., and N. Francis. 2006. The teaching of Spanish as a second language in an indigenous bilingual intercultural curriculum. *Language, Culture and Curriculum* 19:171–188.

Hamers, J. 1991. L'ontogénèse de la bilingualité: Dimensions sociales et trans-culturelles. In *Bilingualism, multiculturalism, and second language learning*, ed. A. Reynolds, 127–144. Hillsdale, NJ: Lawrence Erlbaum.

Hamers, J., and M. Blanc. 2000. *Bilinguality and bilingualism*. Cambridge: Cambridge University Press.

Hansen, L. 2001. Language attrition: The fate of the start. *Annual Review of Applied Linguistics* 21:60–76.

Harley, B., and D. Hart. 1997. Language aptitude and second language proficiency in classroom learning of different starting ages. *Studies in Second Language Acquisition* 19:379–400.

Harley, B., and W. Wang. 1997. The critical period hypothesis: Where are we now? In *Tutorials in bilingualism: Psycholinguistic perspectives*, ed. A. de Groot and J. Kroll, 19–51. Mahwah, NJ: Lawrence Erlbaum.

Harris, P., M. de Rosnay, and F. Pons. 2005. Language and children's understanding of mental states. *Current Directions in Psychological Science* 14:69–73.

Hawkins, R. 2001. *Second language syntax: A generative introduction*. Oxford: Blackwell.

He, D., and D. Li. 2009. Language attitudes and linguistic features in the 'China English' debate. *World Englishes* 28:70–89.

Heift, T., and A. Rimrott. 2008. Learner responses to corrective feedback for spelling errors in CALL. *System* 36:196–213.

Heinze, I. 2009. Bilingual acquisition in Kaqchikel Maya children and its implications for the teaching of indigenous languages. In *Language is life: Proceedings of the 11th Annual Stabilizing Indigenous Language Conference,* ed. W. Leonard and S. Gardner, 13–25. Berkeley: University of California.

Herdina, P., and U. Jessner. 2002. *A dynamic model of multilingualism: Perspectives of change in psycholinguistics*. Clevedon: Multilingual Matters.

Heredia, R., and J. Altarriba. 2001. Bilingual language mixing: Why do bilinguals code-switch? *Current Directions in Psychological Science* 10:164–168.

Heredia, R., and J. Brown. 2004. Bilingual memory. In *The handbook of bilingualism*, ed. T. Bhatia and W. R. Ritchie, 225–249. Oxford: Blackwell.

Hernández, A. 2005. Making content instruction accessible for English language learners. In *English learners: Reaching the highest level of English literacy*, ed. G. García, 125–149. Newark, DE: International Reading Association.

Hernández, A., P. Li, and B. MacWhinney. 2005. The emergence of competing modules in bilingualism. *Trends in Cognitive Sciences* 9:220–225.

Herrera, S., and K. Murry. 2005. *Mastering ESL and bilingual methods: Differentiating instruction for culturally and linguistically diverse students*. New York: Pearson.

Herrera, S., D. Pérez, and K. Escamilla. 2010. *Teaching reading to English language learners: Differentiated literacies*. New York: Pearson.

Herschensohn, J. 2000. *The second time around: Minimalism and L2 acquisition*. Amsterdam: John Benjamins.

Hickmann, M. 2003. *Children's discourse: Person, space and time across languages*. Cambridge: Cambridge University Press.

Hiebert, E. 1994. Reading recovery in the United States: What difference does it make to an age cohort? *Educational Researcher* 23:15–25.

Hill, J., and K. Hill. 1986. *Speaking Mexicano: Dynamics of syncretic language in central Mexico*. Tucson: University of Arizona Press.

Hill, J. 1995. The voices of Don Gabriel: Responsibility and self in a modern Mexicano narrative. In *The dialogic emergence of culture*, ed. D. Tedlock and B. Mannheim, 97–147. Champaign: University of Illinois Press.

Hinton, L., and K. Hale, eds. 2001. *The green book of language revitalization in practice*. San Diego: Academic Press.

Ho, C. S.-H., D. W.-O. Chan, S.-H. Lee, S.-M. Tsang, and V. H. Luan. 2004. Cognitive profiling and preliminary subtyping in Chinese developmental dyslexia. *Cognition* 91:43–75.

Hogan-Brun, G., U. Ozolins, M. Ramoniene, and M. Rannut. 2007. Language politics and practices in the Baltic states. *Current Issues in Language Planning* 8:469–631.

Holowka, S., F. Brosseau-Lapré, and L. Petitto. 2002. Semantic and conceptual knowledge underlying bilingual babies' first signs and words. *Language Learning* 52:205–262.

Holtzheimer, P., W. Fawaz, C. Wilson, and D. Avery. 2005. Repetitive transcranial magnetic stimulation may induce language switching in bilingual patients. *Brain and Language* 94:274–277.

Hopper, P. 1998. Emergent grammar. In *The new psychology of language: Cognitive and functional approaches to language structure*, ed. M. Tomasello, 155–175. Mahwah, NJ: Lawrence Erlbaum.

Hornberger, N. 2002. Multilingual language policies and the continua of biliteracy: An ecological approach. *Language Policy* 1:27–51.

Hovens, M. 2002. Bilingual education in West Africa: Does it work? *International Journal of Bilingual Education and Bilingualism* 5:249–266.

Hu, C.-F. 2004. The development of phonological representations among Chinese-speaking children. *Taiwan Journal of Linguistics* 2:103–130.

Hu, C.-F. 2008. Rate of acquiring and processing L2 color words in relation to L1 phonological awareness. *Modern Language Journal* 92:39–52.

Hualde, J., A. Olarrea, and A. Escobar. 2001. *Introducción a la lingüística hispánica*. Cambridge: Cambridge University Press.

Hudelson, S. 1994. Literacy development of second language children. In *Educating second language children: The whole child, the whole curriculum, the whole community*, ed. F. Genesee, 129–158. Cambridge: Cambridge University Press.

Hudson, J., and L. Shapiro. 1991. From knowing to telling: The development of children's scripts, stories, and personal narratives. In *Developing narrative structure*, ed. A. McCabe and C. Peterson, 89–135. Mahwah, NJ: Lawrence Erlbaum.

Hulk, A., and N. Müller. 2000. Bilingual first language acquisition at the interface between syntax and pragmatics. *Bilingualism: Language and Cognition* 3:227–244.

Hulstijn, J. 2002. Towards a unified account of the representation, processing and acquisition of second language knowledge. *Second Language Research* 18:193–223.

Hutchinson, J., H. Whiteley, C. Smith, and L. Connors. 2004. The early identification of dyslexia: Children with English as an additional language. *Dyslexia (Chichester, England)* 10:179–195.

Hyland, K. 2003. *Second language writing*. Cambridge: Cambridge University Press.

Hyland, K., and F. Hyland. 2006. Feedback on second language students' writing. *Language Teaching* 39:83–101.

Hyltenstam, K., and N. Abrahamsson. 2003. Maturational constraints in SLA. In *The handbook of second language acquisition*, ed. C. Doughty and M. Long, 539–588. Oxford: Blackwell.

Hyltenstam, K., E. Bylund, N. Abrahamsson, and H.-S. Park. 2009. Dominant-language replacement: The case of international adoptees. *Bilingualism: Language and Cognition* 12:121–140.

Iazzi, E. 1998. Amenagement linguistique: Cas de l'amazighe (berbère) marocain. *Plurilinguismes* 16:53–88.

Ibrahim, R., and J. Aharon-Peretz. 2005. Is literary Arabic a second language for native Arab speakers? Evidence from a semantic priming study. *Journal of Psycholinguistic Research* 34:51–70.

Ibrahim, R., Z. Eviatar, and J. Aharon-Peretz. 2007. Metalinguistic awareness and reading performance: A cross-language comparison. *Journal of Psycholinguistic Research* 36:297–317.

Instituto Nacional de Estadística Geografía e Informática (INEGI). 2000. *XII Censo general de población y vivienda (Tlaxcala)*. México DF: INEGI.

Instituto Nacional de Lenguas Indígenas (INALI). 2003. *Ley general de derechos lingüísticos de los pueblos indígenas y reforma a la fracción cuarta del artículo séptimo de la ley general de educación*. México DF: INALI.

International Reading Association. 2001. *Second language literacy instruction: A position statement*. Newark, DE: International Reading Association.

Isurin, L. 2005. Cross-linguistic transfer in word order: Evidence from L1 forgetting and L2 acquisition. In *Proceedings of the 4th International Symposium on Bilingualism*, ed. by J.

Cohen, K. McAlister, K. Rolstad, and J. MacSwan, 1115–1130. Somerville, MA: Cascadilla Press.

Jackendoff, R. 1987. *Consciousness and the computational mind.* Cambridge, MA: MIT Press.

Jackendoff, R. 1992. *Languages of the mind.* Cambridge, MA: MIT Press.

Jackendoff, R. 1994. *Patterns in the mind: Language and human nature.* New York: Basic Books.

Jackendoff, R. 1996. Preliminaries to discussing how language helps us think. *Pragmatics & Cognition* 4:197–213.

Jackendoff, R. 1997. *The architecture of the language faculty.* Cambridge, MA: MIT Press.

Jackendoff, R. 1998. The architecture of the language faculty: A neominimalist perspective. In *The limits of syntax*, ed. P. Culicover and L. McNally, 19–46. Syntax and Semantics 29. New York: Academic Press.

Jackendoff, R. 2002. *Foundations of language: Brain, meaning, grammar, evolution.* Oxford: Oxford University Press.

Jackendoff, R., and S. Pinker. 2005. The nature of the language faculty and its implications for evolution of language (reply to Fitch, Hauser & Chomsky). *Cognition* 97:211–225.

Jacobs, R. 1995. *English syntax: A grammar for English language professionals.* Oxford: Oxford University Press.

Jahandarie, K. 1999. *Spoken and written discourse: A multi-disciplinary perspective.* Stamford, CT: Ablex.

Johnson, D. C. 2009. The relationship between applied linguistic research and language policy for bilingual education. *Applied Linguistics* 31:72–93.

Johnson, K., and M. Swain, eds. 1997. *Immersion education: International perspectives.* Cambridge: Cambridge University Press.

Juarros-Daussà, E., and T. Lanz. 2009. Re-thinking balanced bilingualism: The impact of globalization in Catalonia. *Language Problems and Language Planning* 33:1–21.

Juffs, A. 2002. Formal linguistic perspectives on second language acquisition. In *The Oxford handbook of applied linguistics*, ed. R. Kaplan, 87–103. Oxford: Oxford University Press.

Jusczyk, P. 2001. Learning language: What infants know about it, and what we don't know about that. In *Language, brain, and cognitive development: Essays in honor of Jacques Mehler*, ed. E. Dupoux, 363–377. Cambridge, MA: MIT Press.

Kamwangamalu, N. 2003. Social change and language shift: South Africa. *Annual Review of Applied Linguistics* 23:225–242.

Karmiloff-Smith, A. 1986. Some fundamental aspects of language development after age 5. In *Language acquisition*, ed. P. Fletcher and M. Garman, 455–474. Cambridge: Cambridge University Press.

Karmiloff-Smith, A. 1991. Beyond modularity: Innate constraints and developmental change. In *The epigenesis of mind: Essays on biology and cognition*, ed. S. Carey, 171–197. Hillsdale, NJ: Lawrence Erlbaum.

Karmiloff-Smith, A., H. Johnson, J. Grant, M. C. Jones, Y. N. Karmiloff, J. Bartrip, and P. Cuckle. 1993. From sentential to discourse functions: Detection and explanation of speech repairs by children and adults. *Discourse Processes* 16:565–589.

Karmiloff, K., and A. Karmiloff-Smith. 2001. *Pathways to language.* Cambridge, MA: Harvard University Press.

Kaufman, D., and M. Aronoff. 1991. Morphological disintegration and reconstruction in first language attrition. In *First language attrition,* ed. H. Seliger and R. Vago, 175–188. Cambridge: Cambridge University Press.

Kaufman, D. 1995. Where have all the verbs gone? Autonomy and interaction in attrition. *Southwest Journal of Linguistics* 14:43–66.

Kaufman, D. 2001. Tales of L1 attrition—evidence from pre-puberty children. In *Sociolinguistic and psycholinguistic perspectives on maintenance and loss of minority languages,* ed. T. Ammerlaan, M. Hulsen, H. Strating, and K. Yagmur, 185–202. Berlin: Waxmann.

Kegl, J., A. Senghas, and M. Coppola. 1999. Creation through contact: Sign language emergence and sign language change in Nicaragua. In *Language creation and language change,* ed. M. DeGraff, 179–237. Cambridge, MA: MIT Press.

Kellerman, E. 2001. New uses for old language: Cross-linguistic and cross-gestural influence in the narratives of non-native speakers. In *Cross-linguistic influence in third language acquisition,* ed. J. Cenoz, B. Hufeisen, and U. Jessner, 170–191. Clevedon: Multilingual Matters.

Kenneally, C. 2007. *The first word: The search for the origins of language.* New York: Penguin.

Kim, E. J. 1997. The sensitive periods for the acquisition of L2 lexico-semantic and syntactic systems. In *Proceedings of the 21st Annual Boston University Conference on Language Development,* ed. E. Hughes, M. Hughes, and A. Greenhill, 354–365. Somerville, MA: Cascadilla Press.

King, K. 2004. Language policy and local planning in South America: New directions for enrichment of bilingual education in the Andes. *International Journal of Bilingual Education and Bilingualism* 7:334–347.

Kintsch, W. 1994. The psychology of discourse processing. In *Handbook of psycholinguistics,* ed. M. A. Gernsbacher, 721–739. New York: Academic Press.

Koda, K. 2000. Cross-linguistic variations in L2 morphological awareness. *Applied Psycholinguistics* 21:297–320.

Kohnert, K., E. Bates, and A. Hernández. 1999. Balancing bilinguals: Lexical-semantic production and cognitive processing in children learning Spanish and English. *Journal of Speech, Language, and Hearing Research* 42:1400–1413.

Köpke, B. 2001. Quels changements linguistiques dans l'attrition de la L1 chez le bilingue tardif? *Travaux Neuchâtelois de Linguistique* 34/35:355–368.

Köpke, B. 2004. Neurolinguistic aspects of attrition. *Journal of Neurolinguistics* 17:3–30.

Köpke, B., M. Schmid, M. Keijzer, and S. Dostert, eds. 2007. *Language attrition: Theoretical perspectives.* Amsterdam: John Benjamins.

Köppe, R., and J. Meisel. 1995. Codeswitching in bilingual first language acquisition. In *One speaker, two languages: Cross-disciplinary perspectives on codeswitching,* ed. L. Milroy and P. Muysken, 276–301. Cambridge: Cambridge University Press.

Kovelman, I., S. Baker, and L. Petitto. 2008. Age of first bilingual language exposure as a new window into bilingual reading development. *Bilingualism: Language and Cognition* 11:203–223.

Krashen, S. 1991. Bilingual education: A focus on current research. *Focus: Occasional Papers in Bilingual Education*, no. 3. Washington, DC: National Clearinghouse for Bilingual Education.

Krashen, S. 1998. Comprehensible output? *System* 26:175–182.

Krashen, S. 1999. *Three arguments against whole language and why they are wrong*. Portsmouth, NH: Heinemann.

Krashen, S. 2002. Defending whole language: The limits of phonics instruction and the efficacy of whole language instruction. *Reading Improvement* 39:32–42.

Krashen, S. 2004. False claims about literacy development. *Educational Leadership* 61:18–21.

Kroeger, P. 2004. *Analyzing syntax: A lexical-functional approach*. Cambridge: Cambridge University Press.

Kroll, J., and N. Tokowicz. 2001. The development of conceptual representation for words in a second language. In *One mind, two languages: Bilingual language processing*, ed. J. Nicol, 49–71. Oxford: Blackwell.

Kuhl, P., B. Conboy, D. Padden, T. Nelson, and D. Pruitt. 2005. Early speech perception and later language development: Implications for the "critical period." *Language Learning and Development* 1:237–262.

Labov, W., and B. Baker. 2010. What is a reading error? *Applied Psycholinguistics* 31:735–757.

Lam, Y. 2009. The straw that broke the language's back: Language shift in the Upper Necaxa Valley of Mexico. *International Journal of the Sociology of Language* 195:219–233.

Landi, N., and C. Perfetti. 2007. An electrophysiological investigation of semantic and phonological processing in skilled and less-skilled comprehenders. *Brain and Language* 102:30–45.

Language Plan Task Group. 1996. *Towards a national language plan for South Africa: Final report of the Language Plan Task Group (LANGTAG)*. Pretoria: Government Printer.

Lanza, E. 1997. *Language mixing in bilingual children*. New York: Oxford University Press.

Lasagabaster Herrate, D. 1998. *Creatividad y conciencia metalingüística: Incidencia en el aprendizaje del inglés como L3*. Bilboa: Universidad del País Vasco.

Laufer, B. 2009. Research timeline: Second language acquisition from language input and from form-focused activities. *Language Teaching* 42:341–354.

Laurence, S., and E. Margolis. 2001. The poverty of stimulus argument. *British Journal for the Philosophy of Science* 52:217–276.

Lebrun, Y. 2002. Implicit competence and explicit knowledge. In *Advances in the neurolinguistics of bilingualism: Essays in honor of Michel Paradis*, ed. F. Fabbro, 299–313. Udine, Italy: Forum.

Lee, E., N. Torrance, and D. Olson. 2001. Young children and the say/mean distinction: Verbatim and paraphrase recognition in narrative and nursery rhyme contexts. *Journal of Child Language* 28:531–543.

Lee, I. 2004. Error correction in L2 secondary writing classrooms: The case of Hong Kong. *Journal of Second Language Writing* 13:285–312.

Lee, I. 2007. Assessment for learning: Integrating assessment, teaching, and learning in the ESL/EFL writing classroom. *Canadian Modern Language Review* 64:199–214.

Leikin, M., D. Share, and M. Schwartz. 2005. Difficulties in L2 Hebrew reading in Russian-speaking second graders. *Reading and Writing* 18:455–472.

León-Portilla, M. 1996. *El destino de la palabra: De la oralidad y los códices mesoamericanos a la escritura alfabética*. México DF: Fondo de Cultura Económica.

Le Pichon Vorstman, E., H. De Swart, V. Ceginskas, and H. Van den Bergh. 2009. Language learning experience in school context and metacognitive awareness of multilingual children. *International Journal of Multilingualism* 6:258–280.

Lerner, I. 2000. Spanish colonization and the indigenous languages of America. In *The language encounter in the Americas, 1492–1800*, ed. E. Gray and N. Fiering, 281–291. New York: Berghahn Books.

Lessow-Hurley, J. 2009. *The foundations of dual language instruction*. Boston: Pearson.

Levelt, W. 1999. Producing spoken language: A blueprint of the speaker. In *The neurocognition of language*, ed. C. Brown and P. Hagoort, 83–122. Oxford: Oxford University Press.

Li, H., H. Shu, C. McBride-Chang, H. Y. Liu, and J. Xue. 2009. Paired associate learning in Chinese children with dyslexia. *Journal of Experimental Child Psychology* 103:135–151.

Li, P., and L. Gleitman. 2002. Turning the tables: Language and spatial reasoning. *Cognition* 83:265–294.

Li, W., R. C. Anderson, W. Nagy, and H. Zhang. 2002. Facets of metalinguistic awareness that contribute to Chinese literacy. In *Chinese children's reading acquisition: Theoretical and pedagogical issues*, ed. W. Li, J. S. Gaffney, and J. L. Packard, 87–106. Boston: Kluwer.

Liberman, A., and D. Whalen. 2000. On the relation of speech to language. *Trends in Cognitive Sciences* 4:187–196.

Liceras, J. 1996. *La adquisición de las lenguas segundas y la Gramática Universal*. Madrid: Editorial Síntesis.

Lidz, J., and L. Gleitman. 2004. Argument structure and the child's contribution to language learning. *Trends in Cognitive Sciences* 8:157–161.

Lillo-Martin, D. 1999. Modality effects and modularity in language acquisition: The acquisition of American Sign Language. In *Handbook of child language acquisition*, ed. W. Ritchie and T. Bhatia, 531–567. New York: Academic Press.

Long, M. 1996. The role of the linguistic environment in second language acquisition. In *Handbook of second language acquisition*, ed. W. Ritchie and T. Bhatia, 413–468. New York: Academic Press.

Lonigan, C., C. Schatschneider, and L. Westburg. 2008. Identification of children's skills and abilities linked to later outcomes in reading, writing, and spelling. In *Developing early literacy*, ed. National Early Literacy Panel, 55–106. Washington, DC: National Institute for Literacy.

López, L. E. 1993. Lengua e individuo. In *Didáctica del quichua como lengua materna*, ed. T. Valiente, 73–81. Quito: Ediciones Abya-Yala.

López, L. E. 2001. Literacy and intercultural bilingual education in the Andes. In *The making of literate societies*, ed. D. Olson and N. Torrance, 201–224. Oxford: Blackwell.

López, L. E. 2008. Top-down and bottom-up: Counterpoised visions of bilingual intercultural education in Latin America. In *Can schools save indigenous languages? Policy and practice on four continents*, ed. N. Hornberger, 42–65. New York: Palgrave Macmillan.

López, L. E., and I. Jung. 2003. "Hay que terminar este chiquitito cuentito": Informe de un estudio piloto comparativo sobre la relación entre el habla y la escritura en el aprendizaje de una segunda lengua. In *Abriendo la escuela: Lingüística aplicada a la enseñanza de lenguas*, ed. I. Jung and E. López, 118–134. Madrid: Ediciones Morata.

Lord, A. 1991. *Epic singers and oral tradition*. Ithaca, NY: Cornell University Press.

Loschky, L., and R. Bley-Vroman. 1993. Grammar and task-based methodology. In *Tasks and language learning: Integrating theory and practice*, ed. G. Crookes and S. M. Gass, 123–167. Clevedon: Multilingual Matters.

Louw, P. 2004. Anglicising postapartheid South Africa. *Journal of Multilingual and Multicultural Development* 25:318–332.

Lüdi, G. 2003. Code-switching and unbalanced bilingualism. In *Bilingualism: Beyond basic principles, Festschrift in honour of Hugo Baetens Beardsmore*, ed. J. Dewaele, A. Housen, and L. Wei, 174–188. Clevedon: Multilingual Matters.

Luria, A. R. 1981. *Language and cognition*. New York: Wiley.

Luria, A. R. 1994. Scientific perspectives and philosophical dead ends in modern linguistics. In *Noam Chomsky: Critical assessments*, vol. 2, ed. C. P. Otero, 320–330. London: Routledge.

Lyster, R. 2004. Differential effects of prompts and recasts in form-focused instruction. *Studies in Second Language Acquisition* 26:399–432.

MacLean, M., and A. d'Anglejan. 1986. Rational cloze and retrospection: Insights into first and second language reading comprehension. *Canadian Modern Language Review* 42:814–826.

MacSwan, J. 1999. *A minimalist approach to intrasentential code switching*. New York: Garland Publishing.

MacSwan, J. 2000. The threshold hypothesis, semilingualism, and other contributions to a deficit view of linguistic minorities. *Hispanic Journal of Behavioral Sciences* 22:3–45.

MacSwan, J., and K. Rolstad. 2006. How language proficiency tests mislead us about ability: Implications for English language learner placement in special education. *Teachers College Record* 108:2304–2328.

MacSwan, J., and K. Rolstad. 2008. Semilingualism. In *Encyclopedia of bilingual education*, ed. J. González, 737–739. Los Angeles: Sage.

MacWhinney, B. 2005. Extending the competition model. *International Journal of Bilingualism* 9:69–84.

MacWhinney, B. 2006. Emergentism: Use often and with care. *Applied Linguistics* 27:729–740.

Maddy-Weitzman, B. 2006. Ethno-politics and globalization in North Africa: The Berber culture movement. *Journal of North African Studies* 11:71–83.

Mansour, G. 1993. *Multilingualism and nation building*. Clevedon: Multilingual Matters.

Maratsos, M. 1992. Constraints, modules, and domain specificity: An introduction. In *Modularity and constraints in language and cognition*, ed. M. Gunnar and M. Maratsos, 1–23. Mahwah, NJ: Lawrence Erlbaum.

Maratsos, M. 1999. Some aspects of innateness and complexity in grammatical acquisition. In *The development of language*, ed. M. Barrett, 191–228. East Essex: Psychology Press.

Maratsos, M. 2005. Review of *How children learn the meanings of words*, by P. Bloom. *Language* 81:495–498.

Marcus, G. 2004. *The birth of the mind: How a tiny number of genes creates the complexities of human thought*. New York: Basic Books.

Marcus, G. 2006. Cognitive architecture and descent with modification. *Cognition* 101:443–465.

Marinova-Todd, S., D. Bradford Marshal, and C. Snow. 2000. Three misconceptions about age and L2 learning. *TESOL Quarterly* 34:9–34.

Marley, D. 2005. From monolingualism to multilingualism: Recent changes in Moroccan language policy. In *Proceedings of the 4th International Symposium on Bilingualism*, ed. J. Cohen, K. McAlister, K. Rolstad, and J. MacSwan, 1487–1500. Somerville, MA: Cascadilla Press.

Martin-Jones, M., and S. Romaine. 1986. Semilingualism: A half-baked theory of communicative competence. *Applied Linguistics* 7:26–37.

Martohardjono, G., and S. Flynn. 1995. Is there an age factor for Universal Grammar? In *The age factor in second language acquisition*, ed. S. D. Singleton and Z. Lengyel, 135–153. Clevedon: Multilingual Matters.

Mayberry, R., and E. Lock. 2003. Age constraints on first versus second language acquisition: Evidence for linguistic plasticity and epigenesis. *Brain and Language* 87:369–384.

Mayberry, R. 2007. When timing is everything: Age of first-language acquisition effects on second-language learning. *Applied Psycholinguistics* 28:537-549.

Mayer, C., and T. Akamatsu. 2000. Deaf children creating written texts: Contribution of American Sign Language and signed forms of English. *American Annals of the Deaf* 145:394–401.

McBride-Chang, C., and Y. Zhong. 2006. Emergent literacy skills in Chinese. In *The handbook of East Asian psycholinguistics*, ed. P. Li, L. H. Tan, E. Bates, and O. J. L. Tzeng, 81–89. Cambridge: Cambridge University Press.

McCormack, B. 2004. Methodological aspects of a generative-based attrition study. In *First language attrition: Interdisciplinary perspectives on methodological issues*, ed. M. Schmid, B. Köpke, M. Keijzer, and L. Weilemar, 243–257. Amsterdam: John Benjamins.

McDonald, J. 2000. Grammaticality judgments in a second language: Influences of age of acquisition and native language. *Applied Psycholinguistics* 21:394–423.

McGroarty, M. 2006. Neoliberal collusion or strategic simultaneity? On multiple rationales for language-in-education policies. *Language Policy* 5:3–13.

McLaughlin, B., A. Gesi Blanchard, and Y. Osanai. 1995. *Assessing language development in bilingual preschool children*. Washington, DC: National Clearinghouse for Bilingual Education.

Meisel, J. 1994. Codeswitching in young bilingual children: The acquisition of grammatical constraints. *Studies in Second Language Acquisition* 16:413–439.

Meisel, J. 1995. Parameters in acquisition. In *The handbook of child language*, ed. P. Fletcher and B. MacWhinney, 10–35. Oxford: Blackwell.

Meisel, J. 2001. The simultaneous acquisition of two first languages: Early differentiation and subsequent development of grammars. In *Trends in bilingual acquisition*, ed. J. Cenoz and F. Genesee, 11–42. Amsterdam: John Benjamins.

Meisel, J. 2004. The bilingual child. In *The handbook of bilingualism*, ed. T. Bhatia and W. R. Ritchie, 91–113. Oxford: Blackwell.

Meisel, J. 2007. The weaker language in early child bilingualism: Acquiring a first language as a second language. *Applied Psycholinguistics* 28:495–514.

Menéndez Pidal, R. 1938. *Flor nueva de romances viejos*. Madrid: Espasa-Calpe.

Menéndez Pidal, R. 1945. *La epopeya castellana a través de la literatura española*. Madrid: Espasa-Calpe.

Merkx, A., and R. Pichún Seguel. 1998. El lenguaje integral en al educación intercultural bilingüe: Implicancias en la formación de maestros bilingües en Ecuador. *Lectura y Vida* 19:23–32.

Messing, J. 2007. Ideologies of public and private uses of language in Tlaxcala, Mexico. *International Journal of the Sociology of Language* 187/188:211–227.

Milicevic, M. 2007. Modularity in SLA: Transfer, innate mechanisms and input in the L2 acquisition of Italian reflexive and reciprocal constructions. *EUROSLA Yearbook* 7:89–120.

Miller, J., J. Heilman, A. Nockerts, A. Iglesias, L. Fabiano, and D. Francis. 2006. Oral language and reading in bilingual children. *Learning Disabilities Research & Practice* 21:30–43.

Minervini, L. 2006. El desarrollo histórico del judeoespañol. *Revista Internacional de Lingüística Iberoamericana* 8:13–34.

Mishina-Mori, S. 2002. Language differentiation of the two languages in early bilingual development: A case study of Japanese/English bilingual children. *International Review of Applied Linguistics* 40:211–233.

Modiano, N. 1972. *Indian education in the Chiapas highlands*. New York: Holt, Rinehart & Winston.

Moll, L. C., R. Sáez, and J. Dworin. 2001. Exploring biliteracy: Two student case examples of writing as a social practice. *Elementary School Journal* 101:435–449.

Molyneux, P. 2009. Education for biliteracy: Maximising the linguistic potential of diverse learners in Australia's primary schools. *Australian Journal of Language and Literacy* 32:97–117.

Montrul, S. 2004. Subject and object expression in Spanish heritage speakers: A case of morphosyntactic convergence. *Bilingualism: Language and Cognition* 7:125–142.

Montrul, S. 2005. Second language acquisition and first language loss in adult early bilinguals: Exploring some differences and similarities. *Second Language Research* 21:199–249.

Montrul, S. 2008. *Incomplete acquisition in bilingualism: Re-examining the age factor.* Amsterdam: John Benjamins.

Morais, J. 2003. Levels of phonological representation in skilled reading and in learning to read. *Reading and Writing* 116:123–151.

Morford, J., and J. Kegl. 2000. Gestural precursors to linguistic constructs: How input shapes the form of language. In *Language and gesture*, ed. D. McNeill, 358–387. Cambridge: Cambridge University Press.

Morgan, G., and J. Kegl. 2006. Nicaraguan Sign Language and Theory of Mind: The issue of critical periods and abilities. *Journal of Child Psychology and Psychiatry, and Allied Disciplines* 47:811–819.

Morgan-Short, K., and H. Bowden. 2006. Processing instruction and meaningful output-based instruction: Effects on second language development. *Studies in Second Language Acquisition* 28:31–65.

Morrison, L. 2004. Comprehension monitoring in first and second language reading. *Canadian Modern Language Review* 61:77–106.

Morrow, L. M. 1988. Retelling stories as a diagnostic tool. In *Reexamining reading diagnosis: New trends and procedures*, ed. S. M. Glazer, L. W. Searfoss, and L. M. Gentile, 128–149. Newark, DE: International Reading Association.

Mostari, H. A. 2004. A sociolinguistic perspective on Arabisation and language use in Algeria. *Language Problems and Language Planning* 28:25–43.

Muñoz, C. 2006. *Age and the rate of foreign language learning.* Clevedon: Multilingual Matters.

Muñoz-Sandoval, A., J. Cummins, C. Alvarado, and M. Ruef. 1998. *Bilingual verbal ability tests.* Itasca, IL: Riverside Publishing.

Muysken, P. 2000. *Bilingual speech: A typology of code-mixing.* Cambridge: Cambridge University Press.

Muysken, P. 2004. Two linguistic systems in contact: Grammar, phonology and lexicon. In *The handbook of bilingualism*, ed. T. Bhatia and W. R. Ritchie, 147–168. Oxford: Blackwell.

Mwansoko, H. 1994. The post-primary Swahilisation scheme in Tanzania: From debate to struggle. In *Teaching and researching language in African classrooms*, ed. C. M. Rubagumya, 15–23. Clevedon: Multilingual Matters.

Myers-Scotton, C. 2002. *Contact linguistics: Bilingual encounters and grammatical outcomes.* Oxford: Oxford University Press.

Myers-Scotton, C. 2006. *Multiple voices: An introduction to bilingualism.* Oxford: Blackwell.

Nakamoto, J., K. Lindsey, and F. Manis. 2008. A cross-linguistic investigation of English language learners' reading comprehension in English and Spanish. *Scientific Studies of Reading* 12:351–371.

Nava Nava, R. 2010. Las primeras etapas del desplazamiento lingüístico náhuatl-español en San Isidro Buensuceso, Tlaxcala. In *Memorias del XI Encuentro Nacional de Estudios en Lenguas*, ed. R. Domínguez Angel and L. Pérez Sánchez, 391–400. Tlaxcala: Universidad Autónoma de Tlaxcala.

Navés, T., I. Miralpeix, and M. Celaya. 2005. Who transfers more...and what? Cross-linguistic influence in relation to school grade and language dominance in EFL. *International Journal of Multilingualism* 2:113–134.

Neke, S. M. 2003. English in Tanzania: An anatomy of hegemony. Doctoral dissertation. Faculteit van de Letteren en Wijsbegeerte, Universiteit Gent.

Newmeyer, F. 1998. *Language form and function*. Cambridge: Cambridge University Press.

Newmeyer, F. 2004. Against a parameter-setting approach to typological variation. *Linguistic Variation Yearbook* 4:181–234.

Newmeyer, F. 2008. Conceptualization, communication, and the origins of grammar. In *Origin and evolution of languages: Approaches, models, paradigms*, ed. B. Laks, 112–132. London: Equinox.

Newport, E. 1990. Maturational constraints on language learning. *Cognitive Science* 14:11–29.

Newport, E. 1991. Contrasting conceptions of the critical period for language. In *The epigenesis of mind: Essays on biology and cognition*, ed. S. Carey and R. Gelman, 111–130. Mahwah, NJ: Lawrence Erlbaum.

Nicholas, H., P. Lightbown, and N. Spada. 2001. Recasts as feedback to language learners. *Language Learning* 51:719–758.

Nicoladis, E. 2006. Cross-linguistic transfer in adjective-noun strings by preschool bilingual children. *Bilingualism: Language and Cognition* 9:15–32.

Nicoladis, E., and F. Genesee. 1997. Language development in preschool bilingual children. *Journal of Speech-Language Pathology and Audiology* 21:258–270.

Ninio, A., and C. E. Snow. 1996. *Pragmatic development*. Boulder, CO: Westview Press.

Noguchi, R. 2003. Run-ons, comma splices, and native-speaker abilities. In *Teaching grammar: A reader and workbook*, ed. J. Hagemann, 138–146. New York: Allyn & Bacon.

Norris, J., and L. Ortega. 2001. Does type of instruction make a difference? Substantive findings from a meta-analytic review. *Language Learning* 51:157–213.

Norton, E. S., I. Kovelman, and L. A. Petitto. 2007. Are there separate neural systems for spelling? New insights into the role of rules and memory in spelling from functional magnetic resonance imaging. *Mind, Brain, and Education* 1:48–59.

Nunes, T., P. Bryant, and M. Bindman. 2006. The effects of learning to spell on children's awareness of morphology. *Reading and Writing* 19:767–787.

Obler, L., and K. Gjerlow. 1999. *Language and the brain*. Cambridge: Cambridge University Press.

Odlin, T. 2002. Language transfer and cross-linguistic studies: Relativism, universalism, and the native language. In *The Oxford handbook of applied linguistics*, ed. R. Kaplan, 253–261. Oxford: Oxford University Press.

Ogechi, N. O. 2003. On language rights in Kenya. *Nordic Journal of African Studies* 12:277–295.

Oller, D. K., and R. E. Eilers. 2002. Balancing interpretations regarding effects of bilingualism: Empirical outcomes and theoretical possibilities. In *Language and literacy in bilingual children*, ed. D. K. Oller and R. E. Eilers, 281–292. Clevedon: Multilingual Matters.

Oller, D. K., B. Pearson, and A. Cobo-Lewis. 2007. Profile effects in early bilingual language and literacy. *Applied Psycholinguistics* 28:191–230.

Oller, J. 2008. El coneixement de la llengua catalana i la llengua castellana per part de l'alumnat estranger escolaritzat a l'educació primària de Catalunya: Factors explicatius i relacions d'interdependència lingüística. Doctoral dissertation, Universitat de Girona.

Oller, J., and I. Vila. 2010. Effects of sociolinguistic environment and the length of residence on the linguistic performance in Catalan and Spanish of sixth grade immigrant pupils in Catalonia. *Sociolinguistic Studies* 4:63–84.

Olson, D. 1977. From utterance to text: The bias of language in speech and writing. *Harvard Educational Review* 47:257–281.

Olson, D. 1991. Literacy and metalinguistic activity. In *Literacy and orality*, ed. D. Olson and N. Torrance, 251–270. Cambridge: Cambridge University Press.

Olson, D. 1994. *The world on paper*. Cambridge: Cambridge University Press.

Olson, D. 1996. Language and literacy: What writing does to language and mind. *Annual Review of Applied Linguistics* 16:3–13.

Olson, D. 2001. What writing is? *Pragmatics & Cognition* 9:239–258.

Omoniyi, T. 2003. Local policies and global forces: Multiliteracy and Africa's indigenous languages. *Language Policy* 2:133–152.

Ong, W. J. 1992. Writing is a technology that restructures thought. In *The linguistics of literacy*, ed. P. Downing, S. D. Lima, and M. Noonan, 293–319. Amsterdam: John Benjamins.

Oren, R., and Z. Breznitz. 2005. Reading processes in L1 and L2 among dyslexic as compared to regular bilingual readers: Behavioral and electrophysiological evidence. *Journal of Neurolinguistics* 18:127–151.

Ovando, C., M. Combs, and V. Collier. 2006. *Bilingual and ESL classrooms: Teaching in multicultural contexts*. Boston: McGraw Hill.

Packard, J. 2000. *The morphology of Chinese: A linguistic and cognitive approach*. Cambridge: Cambridge University Press.

Packard, J., X. Chen, W. Li, X. Wu, J. Gaffney, H. Li, and R. Anderson. 2006. Explicit instruction in orthographic structure and word morphology help Chinese children learn to write characters. *Reading and Writing* 19:457–487.

Paivio, A. 1991. Mental representation in bilinguals. In *Bilingualism, multiculturalism, and second language learning*, ed. A. Reynolds, 113–125. Mahwah, NJ: Lawrence Erlbaum.

Paivio, A. 2007. *Mind and its evolution: A dual coding theoretical approach*. Mahwah, NJ: Lawrence Erlbaum.

Pallier, C. 2007. Critical periods in language acquisition and language attrition. In *Language attrition: Theoretical perspectives*, ed. B. Köpke, M. Schmid, M. Keijer, and S. Dostert, 155–168. Amsterdam: John Benjamins.

Pallier, C., S. Dehaene, J.-B. Poline, D. LeBihan, A.-M. Argenti, E. Dupoux, and J. Mehler. 2003. Brain imaging of language plasticity in adopted adults: Can a second language replace the first? *Cerebral Cortex* 13:155–161.

Paradis, J., M. Crago, and F. Genesee. 2005. Domain-general versus domain-specific accounts of Specific Language Impairment: Evidence from bilingual children's acquisition of object pronouns. *Language Acquisition* 13:33–62.

Paradis, J., and F. Genesee. 1996. Syntactic acquisition in bilingual children. *Studies in Second Language Acquisition* 18:1–25.

Paradis, M. 1997. The cognitive neuropsychology of bilingualism. In *Tutorials in bilingualism: Psycholinguistic perspectives*, ed. A. de Groot and J. Kroll, 331–354. Mahwah, NJ: Lawrence Erlbaum.

Paradis, M. 2001. Bilingual and polyglot aphasia. In *Handbook of neuropsychology*, vol. 3, ed. S. Sloan Berndt, 69–91. 2nd ed. New York: Elsevier.

Paradis, M. 2004. *A neurolinguistic theory of bilingualism*. Amsterdam: John Benjamins.

Pascual, B., G. Aguado, M. Sotillo, and J. C. Masdeu. 2008. Acquisition of mental state language in Spanish children: A longitudinal study of the relationship between the production of mental verbs and linguistic development. *Developmental Science* 11:454–466.

Pavlenko, A., and S. Jarvis. 2002. Bidirectional transfer. *Applied Linguistics* 23:190–214.

Pearson, B. Z. 2002. Narrative competence among monolingual and bilingual school children in Miami. In *Language and literacy in bilingual children*, ed. D. K. Oller and R. E. Eilers, 135–174. Clevedon: Multilingual Matters.

Pearson, B. Z., S. Fernández, and D. Oller. 1993. Lexical development in bilingual infants and toddlers: Comparisons to monolingual norms. *Language Learning* 43:93–120.

Peregoy, S. F., and O. F. Boyle. 2008. *Reading, writing and learning in ESL*. New York: Pearson.

Perfetti, C. 1994. Psycholinguistics and reading ability. In *Handbook of psycholinguistics*, ed. M. A. Gernsbacher, 849–885. New York: Academic Press.

Perfetti, C. 2003. The Universal Grammar of reading. *Scientific Studies of Reading* 7:3–24.

Perfetti, C., and Y. Liu. 2005. Orthography to phonology and meaning: Comparisons across and within writing systems. *Reading and Writing* 18:193–210.

Peter, L., T. Hirata-Edds, and B. Montgomery-Anderson. 2008. Verb development by children in the Cherokee language immersion program, with implications for teaching. *International Journal of Applied Linguistics* 18:166–187.

Petitto, L. 1992. Modularity and constraints in early lexical acquisition: Evidence from children's early language and gesture. In *Modularity and constraints in language and cognition*, ed. M. Gunnar and M. Maratsos, 25–59. Mahwah, NJ: Lawrence Erlbaum.

Petitto, L. 1997. In the beginning: On the genetic and environmental factors that make early language acquisition possible. In *The inheritance and innateness of grammars*, ed. M. Gopnick, 45–69. Oxford: Oxford University Press.

Petitto, L., and I. Kovelman. 2003. The bilingual paradox: How signing-speaking bilingual children help us resolve bilingual issues and teach us about the brain's mechanisms underlying all language acquisition. *Learning Languages* 8:5–18.

Pfaff, C. 1999. Changing patterns of language mixing in a bilingual child. In *Bilingualism and migration*, ed. G. Extra and L. Verhoeven, 97–121. New York: Mouton de Gruyter.

Phillipson, R. 2001. English for globalisation or for the world's people? *International Review of Education* 47:185–200.

Pica, T., and G. Washburn. 2002. Negative evidence in language classroom activities: A study of its availability and accessibility to language learners. In *Working papers in educational linguistics 18*, ed. K. Daniel-White, 1–28. Philadelphia: University of Pennsylvania, Graduate School of Education.

Pickering, M., C. Clifton, and M. Crocker. 2000. Architectures and mechanisms in sentence comprehension. In *Architectures and mechanisms for language processing*, ed. M. Crocker, M. Pickering, and C. Clifton, 1–29. Cambridge: Cambridge University Press.

Pinker, S. 1994. How could a child use verb syntax to learn verb semantics? *Lingua* 92:377–410.

Pinker, S. 1996. *Language learnability and language development.* Cambridge, MA: Harvard University Press.

Pinker, S. 1997. *How the mind works.* New York: Norton.

Pinker, S. 1999. *Words and rules: The ingredients of language.* New York: HarperCollins.

Pinker, S. 2002. *The blank slate: The modern denial of human nature.* London: Penguin Books.

Pinker, S., and R. Jackendoff. 2005. The faculty of language: What's special about it? *Cognition* 95:201–236.

Pinker, S., and M. Ullman. 2002. The past-tense debate: The past and future of the past tense. *Trends in Cognitive Sciences* 6:456–463.

Piper, T. 2007. *Language and learning: The home and school years.* 4th ed. Upper Saddle River, NJ: Pearson.

Plato. 1941. *The republic.* Trans. F. M. Cornford. London: Oxford University Press.

Plotkin, H. 2001. Some elements of a science of culture. In *The debated mind: Evolutionary psychology versus ethnography*, ed. H. Whitehouse, 91–112. Oxford: Berg.

Polinsky, M. 1995. Cross-linguistic parallels in language loss. *Southwest Journal of Linguistics* 14:87–121.

Polio, C. G., C. Fleck, and N. Leder. 1998. "If I only had more time:" ESL learners' changes in linguistic accuracy on essay revisions. *Journal of Second Language Writing* 7:43–68.

Poplack, S. 1980. Sometimes I'll start a sentence in Spanish y termino en español: Toward a typology of codeswitching. *Linguistics* 18:581–618.

Poplack, S., D. Sankoff, and C. Miller. 1988. The social correlates and linguistic processes of lexical borrowing and assimilation. *Linguistics* 26:47–104.

Proverbio, A. M., R. Adorni, and A. Zani. 2007. The organization of multiple languages in polyglots: Interference or independence? *Journal of Neurolinguistics* 20:25–49.

Raimes, A. 2002. Errors: Windows into the mind. In *Dialogue on writing: Rethinking ESL, basic writing, and first-year composition*, ed. G. DeLuca, L. Fox, M. Johnson, and M. Koen, 279–287. Mahwah, NJ: Lawrence Erlbaum.

Ramey, P. 2007. Studies in oral tradition: History and prospects for the future. Master's thesis, University of Missouri-Columbia.

Rayner, K., B. Foorman, C. Perfetti, D. Pesetsky, and M. Seidenberg. 2001. How psychological science informs the teaching of reading. *Psychological Science in the Public Interest* 2:31–74.

Reagan, T. 2001. The promotion of linguistic diversity in multilingual settings: Policy and reality in post-apartheid South Africa. *Language Problems and Language Planning* 25:51–72.

Reeder, K., J. Shapiro, R. Watson, and H. Goelman. 1996. From communication to literacy. In *Literate apprenticeships: The emergence of language and literacy in the preschool years*, ed. K. Reeder, J. Shapiro, R. Watson, and H. Goelman, 13–28. Norwood, NJ: Ablex.

Ricento, T. 2000. Historical and theoretical perspectives in language policy and planning. In *Ideology, politics and language policies: Focus on English*, ed. T. Ricento, 9–23. Amsterdam: John Benjamins.

Rickard Liow, S. 1999. Reading skill development in bilingual Singaporean children. In *Learning to read and write: A cross-linguistic perspective*, ed. M. Harris and G. Hatano, 196–213. Cambridge: Cambridge University Press.

Rispens, J., C. McBride-Chang, and P. Reitsma. 2008. Morphological awareness and early and advanced word recognition in Dutch. *Reading and Writing* 21:587–607.

Rojas-Drummond, S., L. Gómez, M. Peón, A. M. Márquez, A. Olmos, and M. Vélez. 1999. El desarrollo de macroestructuras en niños de primaria. *Estudios de Lingüística Aplicada* 29:13–32.

Rolla San Francisco, A., E. Mo, M. Carlo, D. August, and C. Snow. 2006. The influences of language of literacy instruction and vocabulary on the spelling of Spanish-English bilinguals. *Reading and Writing* 19:627–642.

Romaine, S. 1995. *Bilingualism*. Oxford: Oxford University Press.

Romaine, S. 2001. Multilingualism. In *The handbook of linguistics*, ed. M. Aronoff and J. Rees-Miller, 512–532. Oxford: Blackwell.

Rondal, J. 1995. *Exceptional language development in Downs Syndrome*. Cambridge: Cambridge University Press.

Rossell, C. 2005. Teaching English through English. *Educational Leadership* 62:32–36.

Rubin, R., and V. Galván Carlan. 2005. Using writing to understand bilingual children's literacy development. *Reading Teacher* 58:728–741.

Ryan, E., and G. Ledger. 1984. Learning to attend to sentence structure: Links between metalinguistic development and reading. In *Language awareness and learning to read*, ed. J. Downing and R. Valtin, 149–172. Berlin: Springer-Verlag.

Sacks, O. 1990. *Seeing voices: A journey into the world of the deaf*. New York: Basic Books.

Sadowski, M., and A. Paivio. 1994. A dual coding view of imagery and verbal processes in reading comprehension. In *Theoretical models and processes of reading*, ed. R. B.

Ruddell, M. R. Ruddell, and H. Singer, 582–601. Newark, DE: International Reading Association.

Saiegh-Haddad, E. 2003a. Bilingual oral reading fluency and reading comprehension: The case of Arabic/Hebrew (L1)-English (L2) readers. *Reading and Writing* 16:717–736.

Saiegh-Haddad, E. 2003b. Linguistic distance and initial reading acquisition: The case of Arabic diglossia. *Applied Psycholinguistics* 24:431–451.

Samuels, R. 2006. Is the human mind massively modular? In *Contemporary debates in cognitive science*, ed. R. J. Stainton, 37–56. Oxford: Blackwell Publishing.

Samuels, S. J., K. A. Ediger, J. R. Willcutt, and T. J. Palumbo. 2005. Role of automaticity in metacognition and literacy instruction. In *Metacognition in literacy learning*, ed. S. Israel, C. Collins Block, K. Bauserman, and K. Kinnucan-Welsch, 41–60. Mahwah, NJ: Lawrence Erlbaum.

Sánchez, L. 2003. *Quechua-Spanish bilingualism: Interference and convergence in functional categories*. Amsterdam: John Benjamins.

Sandler, W. 2003. On the complementarity of signed and spoken languages. In *Language competence across populations: Towards a definition of SLI*, ed. Y. Levy and J. Schaeffer, 383–409. Mahwah, NJ: Lawrence Erlbaum.

Sapir, E. 1921. *Language: An introduction to the study of speech*. New York: Harcourt, Brace.

Schachter, J. 1990. Communicative competence revisited. In *The development of second language proficiency*, ed. B. Harley, P. Allen, J. Cummins, and M. Swain, 39–49. Cambridge: Cambridge University Press.

Schachter, J. 1992. A new account of language transfer. In *Language transfer in language learning*, ed. S. M. Gass and L. Selinker, 32–46. Amsterdam: John Benjamins.

Schachter, J. 1996. Maturation and the issue of Universal Grammar in second language acquisition. In *Handbook of second language acquisition*, ed. W. Ritchie and T. Bhatia, 159–193. New York: Academic Press.

Schachter, J. 1998. Recent research in language learning studies: Promises and problems. *Language Learning* 48:557–589.

Schaengold, C. 2003. The emergence of bilingual Navajo: English and Navajo languages in contact regardless of everyone's best intentions. In *When languages collide: Perspectives on language conflict, language competition, and language coexistence*, ed. B. Joseph, J. DeStefano, N. Jacobs, and I. Lehiste, 235–254. Columbus: Ohio State University Press.

Scherag, A., L. Demuth, F. Rösler, H. Neville, and B. Röder. 2004. The effects of late acquisition of L2 and the consequences of immigration on L1 for semantic and morpho-syntactic language aspects. *Cognition* 93:B97–B108.

Schleppegrell, M. J. 2001. Linguistic features of the language of schooling. *Linguistics and Education* 12:431–459.

Schleppegrell, M. J. 2004. *The language of schooling: A functional linguistics perspective*. Mahwah, NJ: Lawrence Erlbaum.

Schleppegrell, M. J., and M. C. Colombi. 1997. Text organization by bilingual writers: Clause structure as a reflection of discourse structure. *Written Communication* 14:481–504.

Schlyter, S. 1993. The weaker language in bilingual Swedish-French children. In *Progression and regression in language: Sociocultural, neuropsychological, and linguistic perspectives*, ed. K. Hyltenstam and Å. Viberg, 289–308. Cambridge: Cambridge University Press.

Schmid, C. 2008. Ethnicity and language tensions in Latvia. *Language Policy* 7:3–19.

Schmid, M. 2009. On L1 attrition and the linguistic system. *EUROSLA Yearbook* 9:212–244.

Schmidt, R. 2001. Attention. In *Cognition and second language instruction*, ed. P. Robinson, 3–32. Cambridge: Cambridge University Press.

Schmitt, E. 2000. Overt and covert codeswitching in immigrant children from Russia. *International Journal of Bilingualism* 4:9–29.

Schwartz, B. 1998. The second language instinct. *Lingua* 106:133–160.

Schwartz, B. 1999. Let's make up your mind: "Special nativist perspectives on language, modularity of mind, and nonnative language acquisition. *Studies in Second Language Acquisition* 21:635–655.

Schwartz, M., M. Leikin, and D. Share. 2005. Bi-literate bilingualism versus mono-literate bilingualism: A longitudinal study of reading acquisition in Hebrew (L2) among Russian-speaking (L1) children. *Written Language and Literacy* 8:179–206.

Scovel, T. 1998. *Psycholinguistics*. Oxford: Oxford University Press.

Scovel, T. 2000. A critical review of the critical period research. *Annual Review of Applied Linguistics* 20:213–223.

Scribner, S., and M. Cole. 1981. *The psychology of literacy*. Cambridge: Harvard University Press.

Sebastián-Gallés, N., S. Echevarría, and L. Bosch. 2005. The influence of initial exposure on lexical representation: Comparing early and simultaneous bilinguals. *Journal of Memory and Language* 52:240–255.

Seidenberg, M. 2005. Connectionist models of word reading. *Current Directions in Psychological Science* 14:238–242.

Seliger, H. 1996. Primary language attrition in the context of bilingualism. In *Handbook of second language acquisition*, ed. W. Ritchie and T. Bhatia, 605–625. New York: Academic Press.

Senghas, A., and M. Coppola. 2001. Children creating language: How Nicaraguan Sign Language acquired a spatial grammar. *Psychological Science* 12:323–328.

Senghas, R., A. Senghas, and J. Pyers. 2005. The emergence of Nicaraguan Sign Language: Questions of development, acquisition, and evolution. In *Biology and knowledge revisited: From neurogenesis to psychogenesis*, ed. J. Langer, S. Parker, and C. Milbrath, 287–306. Mahwah, NJ: Lawrence Erlbaum.

Shankweiler, D., and A. Fowler. 2004. Questions people ask about the role of phonological processes in learning to read. *Reading and Writing* 17:483–515.

Share, D. 2004. Orthographic learning at a glance: On the time course and developmental onset of self-teaching. *Journal of Experimental Child Psychology* 87:267–298.

Sharwood Smith, M. 1991. Language modules and bilingual processing. In *Language processing in bilingual children*, ed. E. Bialystok, 10–24. Cambridge: Cambridge University Press.

Sharwood Smith, M. 1993. Input enhancement in instructed SLA. *Studies in Second Language Acquisition* 15:165–179.

Sharwood Smith, M. 1994a. *Second language learning: Theoretical foundations*. New York: Longman.

Sharwood Smith, M. 1994b. The unruly world of language. In *Implicit and explicit learning of languages*, ed. N. Ellis, 33–44. New York: Academic Press.

Sharwood Smith, M. 2004. In two minds about grammar: On the interaction of linguistic and metalinguistic knowledge in performance. *Transactions of the Philological Society* 102:255–280.

Sharwood Smith, M., and P. van Buren. 1991. First language attrition and the parameter setting model. In *First language attrition*, ed. H. Seliger and R. Vago, 17–30. Cambridge: Cambridge University Press.

Shatil, E., and D. L. Share. 2003. Cognitive antecedents of early reading ability: A test of the modularity hypothesis. *Journal of Experimental Child Psychology* 86:1–31.

Shaywitz, S., M. Mody, and B. Shaywitz. 2006. Neural mechanisms in dyslexia. *Current Directions in Psychological Science* 15:278–281.

Short, D., and S. Fitzsimmons. 2007. *Double the work: Challenges and solutions to acquiring language and academic literacy for adolescent English language learners—A report to the Carnegie Corporation*. Washington, DC: Alliance for Excellent Education.

Shrubshall, P. 1997. Narrative, argument and literacy: A comparative study of the narrative discourse development of monolingual and bilingual 5–10-year-old learners. *Journal of Multilingual and Multicultural Development* 18:402–421.

Siegel, L. 2002. Bilingualism and reading. In *Precursors of functional literacy*, ed. J. Verhoeven, C. Elbro, and P. Reitsma, 287–302. Amsterdam: John Benjamins.

Siegel, L. 2008. Morphological awareness skills of English language learners and children with dyslexia. *Topics in Language Disorders* 28:15–27.

Siguán, M. 1987. El lenguaje interior. In *Actualidad de Lev Vigotski*, ed. M. Siguán, 136–159. Barcelona: Anthropos.

Siguán, M. 1991. La langue dans le système d'enseignement de la Catalogne. *Le Français dans le Monde*, février/mars, numéro spécial, 91–99.

Simos, P., R. Billingsley-Marshal, S. Sarkari, E. Pataraia, and A. Papanicolaou. 2005. Brain mechanisms supporting distinct languages. *Learning Disabilities Research & Practice* 20:31–38.

Simpson, J., and G. Wigglesworth. 2008. *Children's language and multilingualism: Indigenous language use at home and school*. London: Continuum International.

Singleton, D. 2001. Age and second language acquisition. *Annual Review of Applied Linguistics* 21:77–89.

Skutnabb-Kangas, T. 2000. *Linguistic genocide in education or worldwide diversity and human rights?* Mahwah, NJ: Lawrence Erlbaum.

Skutnabb-Kangas, T. 2003. Revitalization of indigenous languages in education: Contextualizing the Papua New Guinea experience. *Language and Education* 17:81–85.

Slobin, D., and M. Tomasello. 2005. Thirty years of research on language, cognition, and development: The legacy of Elizabeth Bates. *Language Learning and Development* 1:139–149.

Smith, F. 2004. *Understanding reading: A psycholinguistic analysis of reading and learning to read.* 6th ed. Mahwah, NJ: Lawrence Erlbaum.

Smith, N. 1999. *Chomsky: Ideas and ideals.* Cambridge: Cambridge University Press.

Smith, N., and I. Tsimpli. 1995. *The mind of a savant: Language learning and modularity.* Oxford: Blackwell.

Snow, M. A. 2001. Content-based and immersion models for second and foreign language teaching. In *Teaching English as a second or foreign language,* ed. M. Celce-Murcia, 303–318. London: Heinle & Heinle.

Sokal, A. 2008. *Beyond the hoax: Science, philosophy and culture.* Oxford: Oxford University Press.

Solé i Durany, J. R. 2004. Obstacles in the recovery of Catalan. In *Endangered languages and linguistic rights: On the margins of nations,* ed. J. Argenter and R. McKenna Brown, 109–116. Bath: Foundation for Endangered Languages.

Sorace, A. 2003. Near-nativeness. In *The handbook of second language acquisition,* ed. C. Doughty and M. Long, 130–152. Oxford: Blackwell.

Sorace, A. 2004. Native language attrition and developmental instability at the syntax-discourse interface: Data, interpretations and methods. *Bilingualism: Language and Cognition* 7:143–145.

Sperber, D. 2001. In defense of massive modularity. In *Language, brain, and cognitive development: Essays in honor of Jacques Mehler,* ed. E. Dupoux, 47–57. Cambridge, MA: MIT Press.

Sperber, D., and L. Hirschfeld. 2004. The cognitive foundations of cultural stability and diversity. *Trends in Cognitive Sciences* 8:40–46.

Spolsky, B. 1999. Language in Israel: Policy, practice, and ideology. In *Georgetown University Round Table on Languages and Linguistics,* ed. J. Alatis and A. H. Tan, 164–173. Washington, DC: Georgetown University Press.

Spolsky, B. 2002. The development of Navajo-English bilingualism. In *Opportunities and challenges of bilingualism,* ed. L. Wei, J. M. Dewaele, and A. Housen, 171–198. Berlin: Mouton de Gruyter.

Stanovich, K. 2000. *Progress in understanding reading: Scientific foundations and new frontiers.* New York: Guilford.

Stanovich, K., and P. Stanovich. 1999. How research might inform the debate about early reading acquisition. In *Reading development and the teaching of reading: A psychological perspective,* ed. J. Oakhill and R. Beard, 12–41. Oxford: Blackwell.

Stein, N., and E. Albro. 1996. Building complexity and coherence: Children's use of goal-structured knowledge in telling stories. In *Narrative development: Six approaches,* ed. M. Bamberg, 5–44. Mahwah, NJ: Lawrence Erlbaum.

Stein, N., and E. Albro. 2001. The origins and nature of arguments: Studies in conflict understanding, emotion, and negotiation. *Discourse Processes* 32:113–133.

Stoller, F. 2004. Content-based instruction: Perspectives on curriculum planning. *Annual Review of Applied Linguistics* 24:261–284.

Stoller, F. 2007. Project-based learning: An effective means for promoting purposeful language use. In *Selected papers from the Sixteenth International Symposium on English Teaching*, ed. Y.-N. Leung, 139–152. Taipei: English Teachers' Association.

Stowe, L., M. Haverkort, and F. Zwarts. 2005. Rethinking the neurological basis of language. *Lingua* 115:997–1042.

Stroud, C. 2001. African mother-tongue programmes and the politics of language: linguistic citizenship versus linguistic human rights. *Journal of Multilingual and Multicultural Development* 22:339–355.

Sunderman, G., and J. Kroll. 2006. First language activation during second language lexical processing. *Studies in Second Language Acquisition* 28:387–422.

Supalla, S., T. Wix, and C. McKee. 2001. Print as a primary source of English for deaf learners. In *One mind, two languages: Bilingual language processing*, ed. J. Nicol, 177–190. Oxford: Blackwell.

Swain, M. 1995. Three functions of output in second language learning. In *Principle and practice in applied linguistics: Studies in honor of H. G. Widdowson*, ed. G. Cook and B. Seidlhofer, 125–143. Oxford: Oxford University Press.

Swain, M. 1998. Focus on form through conscious reflection. In *Focus on form in classroom second language acquisition*, ed. C. Doughty and J. Williams, 64–82. Cambridge: Cambridge University Press.

Swan, M. 2005. Legislation by hypothesis: The case of task-based instruction. *Applied Linguistics* 26:376–401.

Swanwick, R., and L. Watson. 2005. Literacy in the homes of young deaf children: Common and distinct features of spoken language and sign bilingual environments. *Journal of Early Childhood Literacy* 5:53–78.

Tabors, P., and C. Snow. 2001. Young bilingual children and early literacy development. In *Handbook of early literacy research*, ed. S. Neuman and D. Dickinson, 159–178. New York: Guilford Press.

Tager-Flusberg, H. 1999. Language in atypical children. In *The development of language*, ed. M. Barrett, 311–348. East Sussex: Psychology Press.

Tan, C. 2006. Change and continuity: Chinese language policy in Singapore. *Language Policy* 5:41–62.

Tan, L. H., J. Spinks, G. Eden, C. Perfetti, and W. T. Siok. 2005. Reading depends on writing. [in Chinese] *Proceedings of the National Academy of Sciences of the United States of America* 102:8781–8785.

Tannen, D. 1992. How is conversation like literary discourse? The role of imagery and details in creating involvement. In *The linguistics of literacy*, ed. P. Downing, S. Lima, and M. Noonan, 31–46. Amsterdam: John Benjamins.

Tarone, E. 2002. Frequency effects, noticing, and creativity: Factors in a variationist framework. *Studies in Second Language Acquisition* 24:287–296.

Taylor, A., J. Stevens, and J. Asher. 2006. The effects of explicit reading strategy training on L2 reading comprehension. In *Synthesizing research on language learning and teaching*, ed. J. Norris and L. Ortega, 213–244. Amsterdam: John Benjamins.

Thordardottir, W., A. Rothenberg, M. Rivard, and R. Naves. 2006. Bilingual assessment: Can overall proficiency be estimated from separate measurements of two languages? *Journal of Multilingual Communication Disorders* 4:1–21.

Tilmatine, M., and Y. Suleiman. 1996. Language and identity: The case of the Berbers. In *Language and identity in the Middle East and North Africa*, ed. Y. Suleiman, 165–179. Surrey: Curzon Press.

Tomasello, M. 2000. The item-based nature of children's early syntactic development. *Trends in Cognitive Sciences* 4:156–163.

Tomasello, M. 2005. Beyond formalities: The case of language acquisition. *Linguistic Review* 22:183–197.

Tong, F., B. Irby, R. Lara-Alecio, and P. Mathes. 2008. English and Spanish acquisition by Hispanic second graders in developmental bilingual programs: A three-year longitudinal randomized study. *Hispanic Journal of Behavioral Sciences* 30:500–529.

Torrance, N., and D. Olson. 1985. Oral and literate competencies in the early school years. In *Literacy, language, and learning: The nature and consequences of reading and writing*, ed. D. Olson, N. Torrance, and A. Hildyard, 256–284. Cambridge: Cambridge University Press.

Torres, L. 2006. Bilingual discourse markers in indigenous languages. *International Journal of Bilingual Education and Bilingualism* 9:615–624.

Toukomaa, P. 2000. The linguistic problem child has many names. In *Rights to language: Equity, power, and education*, ed. R. Phillipson, 214–218. Mahwah, NJ: Lawrence Erlbaum.

Towell, R. 2004. Representational modularity and second language acquisition research. *Transactions of the Philological Society* 102:281–305.

Troike, R. 1984. SCALP: Social and cultural aspects of language proficiency. In *Language proficiency and academic achievement*, ed. C. Rivera, 44–54. Clevedon: Multilingual Matters.

Truscott, J. 2004. Evidence and conjecture on the effects of correction: A response to Chandler. *Journal of Second Language Writing* 13:337–343.

Truscott, J. 2009. Dialogue: Arguments and appearances: A response to Chandler. *Journal of Second Language Writing* 18:59–60.

Truscott, J., and M. Sharwood Smith. 2004. Acquisition by processing: A modular perspective on language development. *Bilingualism: Language and Cognition* 7:1–20.

Tsimpli, I., and A. Roussou. 1991. Parameter-resetting in L2? UCL Working Papers in Linguistics 3:149–169.

Tsimpli, I., and N. Smith. 1998. Modules and quasi-modules: Language and theory of mind in a polyglot savant. *Learning and Individual Differences* 10:193–215.

Tsunoda, T. 2005. *Language endangerment and language revitalization*. Berlin: Mouton de Gruyter.

Tunmer, W. E., and E. Myhill. 1984. Metalinguistic awareness and bilingualism. In *Metalinguistic awareness in children*, ed. W. E. Tunmer, C. Pratt, and M. L. Herriman, 169–187. New York: Springer-Verlag.

UNESCO. 1953. *The use of vernacular languages in education,*. Paris: United Nations.

UNESCO. 2003. *Education in a multilingual world*. Paris: United Nations.

UNESCO. 2007. *Education for all by 2015: Will we make it?* Paris: United Nations.

Valdez Pierce, L. 2001. Assessment of reading comprehension strategies for intermediate bilingual learners. In *Literacy assessment of second language learners*, ed. S. Rollins Hurley and J. Villamil Tinajero, 64–83. Boston: Allyn & Bacon.

Van Boxtel, S., T. Bongaerts, and P.-A. Coppen. 2005. Native-like attainment of dummy subjects in Dutch and the role of the L1. *International Review of Applied Linguistics* 43:355–380.

Van de Craats, I. 2003. L1 features in L2 output. In *The interface between syntax and the lexicon in second language acquisition*, ed. R. van Hout, A. Hulk, F. Kuiken, and R. Towell, 69–95. Amsterdam: John Benjamins.

van den Broek, P. 1994. Comprehension and memory of narrative texts. In *Handbook of psycholinguistics*, ed. M. A. Gernsbacher, 539–588. New York: Academic Press.

van der Lely, H. K. J. 2005. Domain-specific cognitive systems: Insight from grammatical-SLI. *Trends in Cognitive Sciences* 9:53–59.

Van Dijk, T., and W. Kintch. 1983. *Strategies of discourse comprehension*. New York: Academic Press.

VanPatten, B. 2003. *From input to output: A teacher's guide to second language acquisition*. Boston: McGraw Hill.

Vargas Ortega, R. 1996. El inicio de la alfabetización en niños tzotziles. *Lectura y Vida* 17:27–35.

Vellutino, F., J. Fletcher, M. Snowling, and D. Scanlon. 2004. Specific reading disability (dyslexia): What have we learned in the past four decades? *Journal of Child Psychology and Psychiatry, and Allied Disciplines* 45:2–40.

Verhoeven, L. 2000. Components of early second language reading and spelling. *Scientific Studies of Reading* 4:313–330.

Verhoeven, L. 2007. Early bilingualism, language transfer, and phonological awareness. *Applied Psycholinguistics* 28:425–439.

Versteegh, K. 2001. *The Arabic language*. Edinburgh: Edinburgh University Press.

Vignola, M. J., and M. Wesche. 1991. L'écriture en language maternelle et en langue seconde chez les diplomés d'immersion française. *Etudes de Linguistique Appliquée* 82:94–115.

Vygotsky, L. 1934/1962. *Thought and language*. Cambridge, MA: MIT Press.

Wagner, D. 1993. *Literacy, culture, and development: Becoming literate in Morocco*. Cambridge: Cambridge University Press.

Wagner, D. 1998. Putting second language first: Language and literacy learning in Morocco. In *Literacy development in a multilingual context: Cross-cultural perspectives*, ed. A. Durgunoglu and L. Verhoeven, 169–184. Mahwah, NJ: Lawrence Erlbaum.

Wagner, D., J. Spratt, and A. Ezzaki. 1989. Does learning to read in a second language always put the child at a disadvantage? Some counterexamples from Morocco. *Applied Psycholinguistics* 10:31–48.

Walter, C. 2004. Transfer of reading comprehension skills to L2 is linked to mental representations of text and to L2 working memory. *Applied Linguistics* 25:315–339.

Walter, C. 2007. First- to second-language reading comprehension: Not transfer, but access. *International Journal of Applied Linguistics* 17:14–37.

Walter, C. 2008. Phonology in second language reading: Not an optional extra. *TESOL Quarterly* 42:455–474.

Wang, M., K. Koda, and C. Perfetti. 2003. Alphabetic and nonalphabetic L1 effects in English word identification: A comparison of Korean and Chinese English L2 learners. *Cognition* 86:129–149.

Wang, M., C. Perfetti, and Y. Liu. 2005. Chinese-English biliteracy acquisition: Cross-language and writing system transfer. *Cognition* 97:67–88.

Weber-Fox, C., and H. Neville. 2001. Sensitive periods differentiate processing of open and closed class words: An ERP study of bilinguals. *Journal of Speech, Language, and Hearing Research* 44:1338–1353.

Wei, L. 2002. The bilingual mental lexicon and speech production process. *Brain and Language* 81:691–707.

Wells, G. 1987. Apprenticeship in literacy. *Interchange* 18:109–123.

Wenden, A. 1998. Metacognitive knowledge and language learning. *Applied Linguistics* 19:515–537.

Werker, J., and K. Byers-Heinlein. 2008. Bilingualism in infancy: First steps in perception and comprehension. *Trends in Cognitive Sciences* 12:144–151.

Wesche, M., ed. 2001. French immersion and content-based language teaching in Canada. Special issue, *Canadian Modern Language Review* 58 (1).

Wesche, M., and P. Skehan. 2002. Communicative, task-based, and content-based language instruction. In *The Oxford handbook of applied linguistics*, ed. R. Kaplan, 207–228. Oxford: Oxford University Press.

White, L. 2000. Second language acquisition: From initial to final state. In *Second language acquisition and linguistic theory*, ed. J. Archibald, 130–155. Oxford: Blackwell.

White, L. 2003. *Second language acquisition and Universal Grammar*. Cambridge: Cambridge University Press.

Whorf, B. L. 1956. *Language, thought, and reality: Selected writings of Benjamin Lee Whorf*. Cambridge, MA: MIT Press.

Wiley, H., and S. Deno. 2005. Oral reading and maze measures as predictors of success for English learners on a state standards assessment. *Remedial and Special Education* 26:207–214.

Wiley, T. 2002. Accessing language rights in education: A brief history of the U.S. context. In *Language policies in education*, ed. J. Tollefson, 39–64. Mahwah, NJ: Lawrence Erlbaum.

Williams, J., and G. Snipper. 1990. *Literacy and bilingualism*. New York: Longman.

Wilson, D. 2005. New directions for research on pragmatics and modularity. *Lingua* 115:1129–1146.

Wright, S. 2007. The right to speak one's own language: Reflections on theory and practice. *Language Policy* 6:203–224.

Yamada, J. 1990. *Laura: A case for the modularity of language*. Cambridge, MA: MIT Press.

Yeh, H., H. Chan, and Y. Cheng. 2004. Language use in Taiwan: Language proficiency and domain analysis. *Journal of Taiwan Normal University: Humanities and Social Sciences* 49:75–108.

Yeni-Komshian, G., J. Flege, and S. Liu. 2000. Pronunciation proficiency in the first and second language of Korean-English bilinguals. *Bilingualism: Language and Cognition* 3:131–148.

Yip, V. 2006. Early bilingual acquisition in the Chinese context. In *The handbook of East Asian Psycholinguistics*. Vol. 1, *Chinese*, ed. P. Li, L.-H. Tan, E. Bates, and O. J. L. Tzeng, 148–157. Cambridge: Cambridge University Press.

Yip, V., and S. Matthews. 2006. Assessing language dominance in bilingual acquisition: A case for mean length utterance differentials. *Language Assessment Quarterly* 3:97–116.

Yip, V., and S. Matthews. 2007. *The bilingual child: Early development and language contact*. Cambridge: Cambridge University Press.

Youssef, V. 2002. Issues of bilingual education in the Caribbean: The cases of Haiti, and Trinidad and Tobago. *International Journal of Bilingual Education and Bilingualism* 5:182–193.

Yukawa, E. 1997. L1 Japanese attrition of a 5 year-old bilingual child. *Japan Journal of Multilingualism and Multiculturalism* 3:1–22.

Yukawa, E. 1998. *L1 Japanese attrition and regaining: Three case studies of two early bilingual children*. Tokyo: Kurosio Publishers.

Zentella, A. C. 2005. Perspectives on language and literacy in Latino families and communities. In *Building on strength: Language and literacy in Latino families and communities*, ed. A. C. Zentella, 1–12. New York: Teachers College Press.

Zwanziger, E., S. Allen, and F. Genesee. 2005. Crosslinguistic influence in bilingual acquisition: Subject omission in learners of Inuktitut and English. *Journal of Child Language* 32:893–909.

Index

Academic achievement, 18–19, 27–28, 34, 40, 46, 56–57, 80, 103, 179–181, 227, 231, 330, 333, 341
Academic language ability, 4, 8, 12, 25–47, 51–60, 79–80, 85–106, 210–213, 255. *See also* Cognitive Academic Language Proficiency
  assessment, 65–77
  bilingual, 14–21
  classroom discourse, 179
  components of, 177–201
  debate on, 327, 332
  mean length of utterance, 328
  narrative, 329
  oral tradition, 330
  writing, 6, 219–227
Aesthetic genre, 199, 279, 315, 330, 342. *See also* Ballad; Music; Poetry
Affirmative action, 30–31, 35
African languages, 35–38, 326–327
Allegory of the cave, 4–5, 8, 271
Alphabetic system, 193–194, 197, 199, 224, 256–257, 260, 262, 264, 322, 340
American Sign Language, 109–112
Aphasia, 4, 89, 133, 313
Arabic, 38–44
Armenian, 32
Assessment
  attrition, 149–150
  in bilingual education, 105
  Bilingual Interview (*Entrevista bilingüe*), 287–288, 290–291, 292–293
  comprehension, 259
  discrete point, 53, 55, 77
  grammar, 330, 332
  Language Naming, 281
  Language Awareness Test, 285–287
  language dominance (native-speaker ability), 17–18, 100
  Language Loyalty/Attitude/Usage, 282–285
  language mixing, 120, 124
  literacy, 53, 60, 205, 210, 216, 254, 328
  metalinguistic awareness, 120, 179, 193, 212, 237–238, 248
  Nahuatl and Spanish, 19, 63, 94, 97, 118, 191, 208, 218–220
  narrative, 200
  open-ended, 78
  phonological processing, 263
  Preference for Writing/Utility interview, 87, 225, 281–282
  reading, 42, 61, 65, 189, 231, 237, 242–244
  standardized, 55
  vocabulary, 97, 99, 341
  writing, 61, 203–205, 208–210
  Written Message Identification, 281
Associative learning, 11, 93, 134, 334
Attention, 59–60, 74, 82, 241–243, 313, 318, 330. *See also* Selective attention
  to discourse patterns, 197–199
  to grammar patterns, 122, 170, 198, 207, 215–217, 223, 247, 316, 337
  and monitoring, 131, 166, 185
  in reading and writing, 192, 203, 212–213, 216, 231–233, 238, 249, 257, 340

Index

Attrition (of language ability or language knowledge), 20, 22, 141–176, 177–180, 254, 271–272, 276, 313, 315, 319, 332–333, 341
Autochthonous language. *See* Indigenous language
Automaticity, 72, 84, 110, 117, 152, 166, 185, 187, 192–193, 196, 224, 226, 233, 255, 258
Awareness, 3, 8, 59, 86–89, 91, 122–124, 131, 167–169, 177, 182, 184, 205, 223, 225
Aztecs, 325

Ballad, 277–278
Baltic languages, 30–32, 36
Basic Interpersonal Communication Skills (BICS), 53–55, 84, 87, 104
Behaviorism, 339
Berber, 38–44
Bilingual acquisition in early childhood (2L1), 91, 116–117, 133, 154, 175, 177, 187, 268, 341
Bilingual (balanced), 92, 116–117, 133, 141–144, 148, 154, 168, 172–173, 175, 187, 268, 331, 341
  imbalanced, 96, 116–117, 141–144, 148, 155–158
  Spanish-Nahuatl, 17–18, 97
Bilingual Dual Coding model (Paivio), 88, 90, 92, 107, 127
Bilingual (exceptional), 109–112, 113–115, 125, 133–134, 174, 259
Bilingual interview (Entrevista bilingüe). See Assessment, *Bilingual Interview*
Bilingualism (additive), 22–23, 36, 45, 98, 141, 146, 174–175, 223, 225, 289–294, 313
Bilingualism (subtractive), 22, 100, 103, 141, 143, 146, 172, 175, 180, 313, 320, 333, 341
Bilingual memory, 267–268, 270
Bilingual (sequential), 1, 90–91, 164
Bilingual (simultaneous), 23, 91–92, 95, 133, 143, 154, 156–157, 177, 268

Biliteracy, 44, 192–201, 232, 246
  second language literacy, 23, 29, 38–44, 51, 74, 103, 194–197, 218, 248, 254–265
Bootstrapping, 262, 313–314
Borrowing. *See* Mixing, borrowing
Bottom-up processing, 54–55, 60, 73, 130, 321–322, 327–329
  Construction-Integration model, 187
  literacy, 194, 198, 248–249, 254, 258–259, 263–265, 339
  and modularity, 93, 101, 125, 167, 191

Canada, 32
Central processes, 23, 90, 98–99, 101–102, 108, 113–114, 127, 132, 180, 182, 200, 258, 274–275, 331, 337
Central Processing System, 14, 49, 57–58, 80
Common Underlying Proficiency, 191–195, 220
Conceptual Structure, 320
domain-general learning, 77–78, 167–168, 176,
interactivity, 93, 110
not language-specific, 203
Chinese, 256–257, 273
Closed-ended, 223
Cloze, 55, 61–65, 68–69, 220, 243, 244
Codeswitching. *See* Mixing, codeswitching
Cognate, 269
Cognitive Academic Language Proficiency (CALP), 84
  and Common Underlying Proficiency, 53–59, 186
  compared to Basic Interpersonal Interactive Skills, 87–88, 315, 330
  and literacy, 179–180
  in second language, 72–76, 104–105
Cognitive-functional theories, 15, 20, 82, 145, 161
Cognitive mobilization, 59
Cognitive verb, 67–68, 78, 184–185
Coherence, 63, 80, 94, 180, 186–187, 209, 213, 215–216, 220, 222, 229, 240, 314, 331

Cohesion, 183, 314
Colonial language, 38, 45, 326
Common Underlying Proficiency, 14, 21, 53, 56, 59–60, 68, 70–72, 76, 80, 88, 96, 195, 219–220, 223, 226–228, 267, 338
Communicative (aspects of language use), 53, 84, 87, 105, 130, 205, 225, 329
Communicative language teaching, 206, 215, 245, 330
Compartmentalization
  in cognition, 78, 88–94
  in language use, 36, 41, 45–46, 76
Compensatory strategy, 163, 258, 264, 266
Competence, 73–74, 85–89, 103–104, 113, 116, 141–145, 187–192, 314
  compared to proficiency, 1–15, 141
  lexical, 99–101, 138–139
  mental representation, 60
  multicompetence, 124, 149
  native-speaker, 92, 95, 188
  and performance, 81
  in two languages, 76–78, 131, 138–139, 149–153, 156–171, 177–178
Competition model (MacWhinney), 123, 156, 158
Completeness (of language knowledge), 115, 141–159, 261, 272, 331–336, 341–342
  in first language, 90, 95, 104–106, 117
  in first language or second language, 124, 164–175
  lexicon, 100, 136
  non-native (incomplete) knowledge, 88
Complex cognition, 82–83, 86
Componential, 9, 11, 13, 23, 33–35, 55, 59–60, 71, 76–77, 79–106, 107, 114, 180, 185, 195, 253–254, 259, 339. *See also* Modularity
Comprehensible input, 73, 167, 169–171, 206, 215
Concept formation, 320, 329
Conceptualizer, 122, 130–131
Conceptual Structure, 71, 135, 320, 329, 338. *See also* Semantics
  in bilinguals, 108, 113–114, 180, 268
  and interfaces, 104, 125–128, 272–280
  in the lexicon, 137–138

Connectionism, 15, 132, 266, 334
Construction Grammar, 334
Construction-Integration model (Kintch), 187
Construction of meaning, 89, 193
Content-based instruction, 32, 34, 45–47
Context, 106, 205, 330
  in assessment, 210, 212
  contextualized tasks, 177, 182, 197–198
  in discourse/text processing, 187, 327–328, 339
  and metalinguistic awareness, 216–217
  in reading, 231–251
  situational context and scaffolding, 113, 119, 185, 189
  sociocultural, 77, 83
Context-embedded and context-reduced, 53–56, 72–75, 84–87, 93–94, 99, 124, 190–191, 207, 216, 237, 314
Continuity Hypothesis, 91–92
Convergence (in cross-linguistic influence), 148
Conversational discourse, 8–9, 17–18, 33, 61, 66–67, 96, 113–114, 119, 133, 261, 314–315, 328
  compared to nonconversational discourse, 53, 55, 73–75, 77, 79, 84–87, 93–94, 178, 183–185, 189, 199, 335–336
  not the same as grammatical competence, 103, 177
Core grammar, 72, 91, 95, 97, 106, 166, 170, 177–178, 199, 329
  in assessment, 330
  completeness, 100, 142, 146, 150–151, 168, 175
  and interfaces, 172–173
  and the lexicon, 99, 124, 136
  peripheral grammar, 187–188, 201, 334–336, 341
  and semilingualism, 332
  and universals, 181–182
Corrective feedback, 116, 167, 171, 206, 229, 249
  prompt, 207
  recast, 207
Creole, 44–45, 110–113, 151, 174, 314, 319

Critical period, 22, 92, 100, 105, 110–112, 117, 132–133, 141–176, 272, 320–322
Cross-linguistic influence (or interaction), 51, 59–60, 68–71, 88–89, 96, 108, 117–118, 125, 129, 162, 195–196, 268, 270, 315, 317, 322, 338. *See also* Transfer
Cross-Linguistic Interface, 122, 128–129, 131–132, 179, 193, 267–268, 270, 333
Culture, 9, 27–28, 30, 38, 40, 74–75, 83, 142, 152, 170, 226, 245, 247, 289, 329–330
  cultural constraint on linguistic structure, 279
  and language, 54–56, 86, 180–181, 254, 273, 275–280
  and narrative, 186
  pragmatics, 97–99, 315
Curriculum design, planning, and teaching
  bilingual, 2, 21, 23, 49, 57, 196–197
  direct instruction, 199–200, 216, 226, 340
  grammar, 6
  language policy, 25–47
  reading, 243–245, 257, 265–266
  second-language instruction, 73, 78, 167, 169, 176, 194
  writing skills, 217–218

Deafness, 100, 102, 109–112, 115, 133, 152, 197, 255, 332
Declarative memory/knowledge, 90, 167, 169–170
Decoding, 217, 243–245, 254, 256–269, 340
  and comprehension, 186, 198, 203, 240–241
  and context, 248–250
  metalinguistic awareness, 231–235
  in two languages, 192–196
Decontextualized, 53, 55, 67, 73, 93, 182, 185, 212, 234, 238, 314, 330
"Deer Hunter" stories, 208, 215–216, 220, 222
Defective lexical entry, 136, 138
Deficit theory, 54–56, 104–105, 181
Democracy, 35–38
Dependent clause, 336–337

Deprivation, 100, 112, 133, 151, 158, 319–320, 332
Descartes, René, 7, 10, 272
Developing countries, 26, 33
Dialect, 41–42, 85–86, 104, 131, 235, 239, 242–243, 315, 320
Diaspora, 278
Didactic materials, 26–27
Differentiation
  kinds of knowledge and ability, 77, 82, 88, 90, 93, 165, 187, 261, 271–272, 315, 330–331, 335–336
  language subsystems, 7, 12–13, 91–92, 93, 109–110, 115–118, 133, 144, 157, 159–160, 172, 333–334
Diglossia, 26, 29–32, 44–47, 98–100, 122, 228
Dirección General de Educación Indígena, 325
Disability/impairment, 2, 13, 56, 105, 115, 154, 259–264, 266, 315–316, 321, 339
Discourse ability, 12, 18, 66–67, 82, 88, 100, 113–114, 134, 314–315, 327–328, 336–337, 341. *See also* Narrative; Primary discourse ability; Secondary discourse ability
  bilingual, 118–121
  and grammatical competence, 28, 58, 280
  and literacy, 35, 51, 54–56, 70–78, 79–80, 91, 108, 258–259, 261, 330–332
  and metalinguistic awareness, 23, 93–97, 177–201
Discourse connector, 75, 120–121, 290–291
Discrete point measure, 53, 55, 77
Dissociation, 12–13, 78, 85, 101, 109, 112–113, 121, 136, 195, 258, 262, 316, 334
Distributed characteristic of bilingual knowledge, 99, 341
Distributed model of bilingual memory (De Groot), 14, 130, 268–269, 276
Distribution (allocation in language use), 26, 44–46, 86–87, 98, 116, 119, 223, 227, 328
Domain-specific, 10, 77, 79, 102, 106, 112, 114, 166, 168, 171, 255, 274, 318, 329

Dominant language, 8, 40, 68, 116–118, 134, 315–316, 319
  balanced/imbalanced bilingualism, 96, 116–118, 141, 144, 295–296, 313
  replacing language, 146–151, 158–159, 173, 175, 270–271
  Spanish-Nahuatl, 17–20, 74, 134
Double-iceberg model (Cummins), 52, 56–57, 92
Dual-formulator, 130–131
Dual Language System Hypothesis (Genesee), 333
Dual-system, 91
Dyslexia, 259–263, 266, 316, 321, 339

Embedded language, 148
Embedding, 191, 319, 336–337
Emergentism, 15, 145, 332
Encapsulation, 71, 90, 93, 96, 99, 101, 106, 110, 114, 123, 138, 167, 185, 191–192, 201, 258, 275, 339
English, 7–8, 16, 26, 28, 30–31, 34–37, 41–42, 44–45, 75, 92, 95, 109, 113–114, 120, 129–130, 146–151, 156, 169, 177–178, 193–194, 196, 256, 265, 269, 273, 295–296, 305–306
English as a Second Language (ESL), 68, 73, 196
Environmental print, 19
Essentialist conceptual system, 7
Ethnocentric, 273
Ethnography, 55, 208, 265, 330
Ethnolinguistic vitality. *See* Assessment
Evolution, 255
Exceptional bilingualism, 109–110, 113–115, 125, 133–134
Exclusion, 27–28, 32, 37–40, 43, 47. *See also* Inclusion
Explicit knowledge, 89–90, 167–171, 176, 205–207, 216–217, 229, 232–233, 260, 331, 337. *See also* Declarative memory/knowledge

Faculty of Language, 7, 76, 96–100, 331
  and bilingualism, 96, 129, 142, 144–145, 150–151, 154–155, 161–164, 166, 171–173, 175, 177, 317

broad, 191, 325, 337
  and communication, 81
  narrow, 78, 100, 104, 113, 191, 325
First language acquisition, 1–3, 11–15, 136, 173, 176, 187, 255, 331
  critical period, 100, 112
  Language Acquisition Device, 96, 165, 177–178, 272
  and language policy, 34
  and L2 learning, 143, 150, 152–156, 160–161, 168–169, 201, 317, 333–334
  negative evidence, 116
  parameter-setting, 90–91
  social interactionist theory, 338
Focus on form (form-focused instruction), 98, 167, 169–171, 197, 199, 203–229, 231–251, 316, 318, 337, 340
Formulator, 130–131
Fossilization. *See* Stabilization
French, 30, 32, 44–45, 92, 95, 113, 130, 269, 326
Functionalism, 15, 20, 82, 145, 161
Fundamental Difference Hypothesis (Bley-Vroman), 143, 160, 176, 334

Genetic, 83, 105, 137, 255, 263, 322, 332–333, 339
Geometry, 7
Gesture, 110–111
Globalization, 26, 326
Grapheme, 193, 198, 208, 214, 224, 256, 261, 265–266. *See also* Orthography
Graphophonic skills, 249
Great Divide theory (orality-writing), 330
Guarani, 326–327

Haitian Creole, 44–45
Hebrew, 146–147, 278
"Hegemonic scheme," 326
Heritage language, 146, 172
Higher education, 33, 36–37, 327
Higher order, 55, 96, 101, 103, 113, 133, 192, 195–196, 219, 259, 264, 316, 326, 329–330, 332
  academic-related proficiencies, 73, 75, 179–180, 227, 338
  discourse, 70, 91, 173–174, 200, 245

Higher order (*cont.*)
  lower level, 231
  metalinguistic awareness, 207, 213–214, 247
  Theory of Mind, 185–186
  thinking, 82–88, 329–330
Holistic models, 54–55, 60, 77–78, 102, 112, 114, 124–125, 194, 248, 250, 253, 260, 265–266, 274–275, 339
Homesign, 110–112
Horizontal process, 81, 93, 191, 329
Human/language rights, 26–27, 29–31, 33, 35–37, 40
Hungarian, 147–148

Iconicity, 110
Idioma de Signos Nicaragüense, 111
Immersion, 32, 39, 45–47, 104, 111, 134, 149–150, 340
Impairment (SLI), 112, 117–118, 133, 144, 154, 157, 181, 313, 320, 321
  deficit, 56, 105, 315
  reading, 259–263, 339
  semilingualism, 103, 105
"Imperialist paradigm," 326
Implicit knowledge, 13, 60, 86, 90, 99, 104, 123, 161, 165–166, 168–171, 317, 337
Inclusion, 28, 32, 40, 44. *See also* Exclusion
Indigenous language, 12, 16–20, 50, 61–68, 86, 94–101, 108, 118–124, 192–193
  loss of, 172, 175, 275–277
  and national language, 20, 27–30, 172, 175, 214
  writing, 194, 204, 207–210, 214–228
Individual differences, 85, 93
Inductive learning, 71, 153, 161, 167, 169
Inhibitory control, 129–130, 269–271
Inhibitory process, 119, 122–123, 131–133, 155, 157, 159, 163–164, 166–167, 173, 175
Inner speech, 81–85, 131, 274, 318, 329, 331

Input, 54, 60, 70, 102, 130, 142, 169–171, 186, 191, 256, 270, 274. *See also* Comprehensible input; Primary Linguistic Data
  input competition, 156–157
  positive evidence, 90–93
  sign language, 110–112
  in two languages, 95–96, 116–117, 133–134, 144, 150–152, 154, 166–167, 174–175
Input-based teaching approach, 206
Input flooding, 206
Instructional program design, 28, 31–32, 35–37, 39–40, 44–47, 225, 227–228. *See also* Curriculum design, planning, and teaching
Integrativist models, 55, 78, 82, 102, 124–125, 266, 316–317, 339
Interaction hypothesis, 155
Interactive-Compensatory Hypothesis (Stanovich), 258
Interdependence principle, 14, 49–53, 60, 68–76, 122, 133, 195, 219, 227, 317, 329, 341
Interface components, 70–71, 77, 108, 127–128, 136–137, 172, 178–179, 191, 195, 200, 272, 329. *See also* Cross-Linguistic Interface
  and integration, 131–132
  and modularity, 93, 125
Interface (syntax-semantics), 104, 126, 130, 183, 201, 273, 276
Interference, 92, 96, 98, 117, 129, 150, 158, 217, 224, 250, 268–271, 317. *See also* Transfer
Interlanguage (learner language), 60, 129, 131, 134, 136, 138, 144, 150–151, 153, 160–162, 166–167, 170, 174, 265, 317
Interview (ethnolinguistic vitality). *See* Assessment
Inuktitut, 120, 129
IQ, 55

Japanese, 149

Ladino, 278, 342
LANGTAG, 35

Language Acquisition Device (LAD), 91, 96, 100, 117, 177, 187, 201, 207, 317–318, 322, 325
  bilingualism and L2 learning, 142, 145, 154, 162–166, 170–171, 175, 271, 333
  critical period, 112
Language-bound, 22, 53, 58, 74–76, 78, 96, 174, 195, 200
Language contact, 20, 24, 26–27, 30, 41, 50, 76
Language dominance, 17–18, 23, 61, 97, 116, 141, 144, 146–151, 155, 157–160, 173, 175, 270–271, 315–316, 319, 331
Language loyalty, preference, and choice, 282–283, 290–293
Language of wider communication, 27–31, 35, 37, 326–327
Language policy and planning, 25–27, 31–33, 35–39, 44, 47
Language preservation (revitalization), 28, 31, 44, 146, 277–279, 325, 327
Language shift (displacement, loss), 22–23, 25, 27, 36, 123, 141, 147–150, 155–159, 172–175, 253–254, 276–277, 279, 317
Language socialization, 76, 142, 148, 152, 170, 174, 331
Language-specific, 12, 14, 16, 19, 75–76, 95, 116, 145, 156, 178, 180, 190–191, 217–218, 220, 317, 334, 337–338
  and language-independent, 52, 56–57, 119, 127, 138, 194–195, 200, 203
  language separation, 129–130, 133
  parameter-setting, 161
  sign language, 109
  verbal art form, 277–279
Language Threshold Hypothesis, 51
Langue des signes québécoise (LSQ), 109–110
Late-developing, 94–96, 188, 190–191, 198, 212, 337
  early-developing, 96
Lemma, 131
Lexical conceptual structure, 273
Lexical-Functional Grammar, 126, 172
Lexicon(s), 76, 119, 126–128, 136–138, 183, 265, 276, 336
  bilingual, 97–100, 122, 131, 134, 193, 267–271, 333, 341

Lingua franca, 28, 36, 325–326
Literacy, 4, 13–15, 20, 27–38, 54, 56, 83, 85, 254–259
  advanced literacy, 26, 136, 179, 192, 201, 223, 228, 246
  assessment of 16–20, 53–55, 192, 207, 216, 234–244
  initial literacy, 30, 32, 38–42, 194, 196, 199, 229
  literacy-related abilities, 54–55, 59, 70, 79–80, 84, 86, 88, 90–91, 101–106, 108, 178–201
  reading, 231–251
  second language literacy, 6, 21, 23, 29, 39–44, 47, 51–53, 60–78, 94–101, 264–266 (see also Biliteracy)
  subskills and components, 13, 49, 51, 53–55, 70–71, 74, 186, 192–197, 198–199, 259–264
  written expression, 203–229
Literary forms, 42, 75, 186
Literary tradition, 30, 279, 325
Loanwords, 98, 119, 221–224
Loan translation, 295–296, 304
Love (in English and Spanish), 269

Massive modularity, 101–102
Matrix Language Frame Model (Myers-Scotton), 147–148
Maturational factors (in language acquisition), 145, 151–153, 168
Maturational hypothesis (Schachter), 91–92
Mean Length of Utterance, 328
Medium of instruction, 21–41, 45–47, 51, 72–73, 76
Mentalese, 329
Mental representation, 4–5, 14, 60, 68–71, 84, 101–102, 182–186, 193, 197, 261–262, 265, 320, 331, 336–338
  explicit knowledge, 171
  of lexical knowledge, 99, 126–127
  orthographic, 136–138, 256
  of two languages, 57, 88–93, 113, 119, 129, 156, 160, 180, 191, 195, 200, 267–268, 270–273

Mercosur, 327
Metacognition, 84–88, 240, 247, 317, 261–265, 271
Metalinguistic awareness, 23, 73, 78, 86–98, 115, 131, 168–171, 318
  assessment, 120, 122–124
  language mixing, 66
  literacy-related abilities, 59–60, 102–106, 203–229, 231–251
  and secondary discourse ability, 80, 179–201
Metapragmatics of literacy, 245
Mexicano, 283–285
Mexico, 16–20, 29, 43, 49, 80, 94, 108, 124, 325–326
Minority languages, 25, 27–33, 37–40, 327, 342
Miscue analysis, 55, 61
Mismatch (language), 25
Mixing, 2, 8, 96, 131, 133–134, 268, 318, 295–306
  in attrition, 147–148, 155
  borrowing, 7, 23, 66, 69, 75–76, 108, 118–120, 122, 124–125, 151, 222–223, 295–306, 328
  codeswitching, 8, 16, 23, 66, 108, 118, 120–121, 123–125, 129, 142, 147–148, 155, 268, 270–271, 295–306, 328
  grammatical patterns, 70, 107, 118–123
  input for language acquisition, 115–116
Modularity, 11–15, 59–60, 71, 77–78, 79–85, 110–139, 191, 204, 219, 226, 314, 318, 329–332
  components of bilingualism, 88–106, 180, 226
  critique of, 53
  and holistic models, 253–275
  interactivity, 339–340
  language and thought, 280
  reading, 195, 232–234, 247–251
Monitor, 59, 122, 124, 131, 171, 185, 198, 207, 218, 229, 231–236, 240–241, 245–249, 259, 337
Monolingual model and bilingual model, 116, 130, 271
Morocco, 38–44

Morphology, 59, 99–100, 113, 122, 129–130, 134, 136, 147, 178, 187–188, 191, 193, 199–201, 212, 224, 236–237, 265, 272, 327–328, 335, 341
Mother tongue, 1, 16, 28–31, 36–37, 40, 43, 45–46, 83, 276–277, 340
Motivation, 28, 41, 172, 192, 227
  symbolic valorization, 18, 325
Multicompetence, 149
Music, 278–279, 339, 342

Nahuatl, 16–23, 49–51, 60–78, 80, 94–100, 108, 118–124, 191–194, 203–214, 218–229, 271–272, 275–276, 281–288, 289–294, 325, 328
Narrative, 12, 18–20, 61–62, 65, 68, 71, 74–75, 96–97, 118–121, 189, 210, 212–213, 220, 223, 314, 321, 330, 336
  advanced narrative ability, 56, 74–75, 94, 183–185, 197–199
  and aesthetic genres, 277–279
  development of, 183–187
  and metalinguistic awareness, 216
  primary, 94, 183–185
  story structure, 59, 61, 62–63
  Sense of Story Structure (assessment), 65–68
  traditional narrative, 71
National identity and ethnic identity, 29, 214, 289–290, 293–294
National language, 25–38, 41, 45–46, 51, 95–97, 108
Native language magnet theory (Kuhl), 156
Natural Approach (Krashen), 83, 143, 176, 253, 254–266
Negative evidence, 90–91, 116, 167, 171, 206–207, 216–218, 228, 318, 334
  corrective feedback, 116, 167, 171, 206, 215, 229, 249
Negotiation of meaning, 84, 170
Neurology, 12, 84, 89, 122, 132, 260, 267, 329, 331, 335
Nicaragua, 110–112
No interface hypothesis, 167–170
Nominalization, 189
Nonbalanced bilingualism, 295
Nonlinear processing, 232–234, 237, 241, 243

Normalization (standardization), 31–34, 46, 327
North Africa, 38–44
Noticing, 122, 169–170, 231, 247

Official language, 26–27, 30–31, 33, 35–38, 41, 44, 325–327, 332
Oral tradition, 12, 44, 62, 71, 74–75, 104, 118, 226, 247, 257, 277–279, 330, 342
Oration, 278
Orthography/orthographic form, 23, 135–138, 208–209, 226, 248–249, 339–340
  alphabetic, 18, 193–194, 197, 199, 224, 256–257, 260, 262, 264–265, 340
  comparison of orthographies, 255–259
  graphicization, 327
  literacy learning, 40, 42, 69, 72, 192–195, 199, 261–266
  and metalinguistic awareness, 212–219, 221, 245
  morphosyllabic, 255–261
Overlapping representations, 56–57, 71, 92, 127, 129

Parallel Architecture. See Tripartite Parallel Architecture
Parameter setting, 15, 90–91, 106, 117, 143–145, 152–155, 160–165, 201, 318, 332–334
Pedagogical implications. See Curriculum design, planning, and teaching
Peripheral grammar, 174, 187–188, 191, 332, 335–336
Phonological awareness, 191–200, 212, 217, 229, 256–257, 260–266
Phonological processing, 42, 59, 194–200, 224, 260–266, 339
Phonological Structure, 113, 117, 125–130, 135–138, 157, 183, 193, 256, 260–266, 273–274, 279, 319, 328, 340–341
Phonological transfer, 61, 69, 85, 89, 100, 134, 146, 214
Pidgin, 110–112, 138, 151, 174, 314, 319
Pirahã study (Everett), 20, 186
Plato, 4–10, 271
Pluralism, 26, 47, 326

Poetry, 12, 257, 278–279, 330, 342
Positive evidence, 90–91, 95, 116, 155, 170, 199, 206, 215, 217, 228, 319, 334
Positivism, 326
Poverty of Stimulus problem, 14–15, 21, 81, 153, 271, 279, 319, 322, 334
  in bilingual development, 10–11, 24, 92, 95, 115, 165–166, 177
  in language attrition, 143
  sign language, 111–112
Pragmatic knowledge/ability, 72, 84, 87–88, 97, 99, 101, 113–114, 127, 130, 133, 190, 197, 221, 238, 245, 320
Prescriptive, 34, 44, 54
Prescriptivism, 326
Presupposition, 184, 190
Primary discourse ability, 77, 87, 95–100, 103–104, 180–181, 183, 199, 330
Primary linguistic data, 10, 90–91, 100, 142, 152, 155, 170–171, 175, 271
Problem solving, 71, 83, 102, 197, 200, 273–274
Processing deficit, 89, 105, 114, 259, 261–263, 266, 339
Processing Limitation Hypothesis, 190–191, 200
Proficiency, 3–10, 71–76, 94–101, 179–187, 192–201, 214–218, 240–244
Puebla, 17, 325
Purism, 46

Qualitative methods, 220, 244
Quebec, 31, 36

Rationalism, 7
Reading, 32, 49, 56–57, 61, 71–74, 83, 177, 180, 189, 192, 199, 330, 340
  bilingual and second language, 18, 34, 39, 47, 59, 63–65, 100, 179, 192–196, 264–266, 327, 339
  components of, 13, 254–263
  comprehension, 8, 19, 62, 96, 136, 189, 203, 231, 235
  decoding and word identification, 42, 46, 186, 197–198, 203, 254–255, 340
  disability, 4, 259–264, 339
  prediction strategy, 70, 245, 248

Reading (cont.)
  self-correction, 231–251
  and sign language, 93
Reading Recovery, 245
Reasoning, 11, 84, 86, 273–274. See also Problem solving
Recontextualization, 185
Recursion, 11, 20, 188, 319
Register, 74, 85, 187, 189, 320, 335, 337
Relative clause, 189–190, 319
Relativism, 54, 60, 259
Remediation, 134, 152, 243, 262
Repair, 234–235, 238, 240–241, 244
Replacing language, 141–146, 150–151, 162–168, 172, 271–277, 279, 332–333, 341
  completeness, 155, 158–160, 175
Retrospection, 232–235, 239, 249
Revised Hierarchical Model (Kroll), 267
Revitalization, 28, 31, 44, 277, 325, 327
Romances, 277–278
Russian, 30–32

Sapir-Whorf hypothesis, 274, 320
Savant, 113
Say good things (in Puebla), 285. See also Spanish, speaking Spanish
Scaffolding, 113, 197
Schema, 70, 196–197, 219, 228, 232, 259, 264, 327, 331, 339
Scissors effect, 20, 65–66, 71, 74, 76
Secondary discourse ability, 83–88, 91, 93–97, 103–106, 179–187, 197–201, 226, 255
  contrast to "primary," 74, 77
  and metalinguistic awareness, 80, 203–204, 206, 244, 330–331
Second language learning, 1–3, 10–11, 15, 21–23, 39, 45–47, 100–103, 131–136, 174–176, 177–180, 204–207, 217–219, 245–247, 253–255. See also Comprehensible input; Transfer
  access to UG in second language, 141–145
  critical period, 150–171
  language policy, 27–36
  metalinguistic awareness, 91
  ultimate attainment, 90, 112

Second language literacy. See Literacy; Reading
Secretaría de Educación Pública, 225
Selective attention, 198, 241–243, 247
Self-correction, 203–251
Semantics, 126, 129, 136–138, 143, 184, 198, 209, 221, 234–236, 239–243, 248–249, 251, 256–258, 268–269, 273, 320, 337. See also Conceptual Structure
  semantic feature, 127, 129–130, 138, 276
Semilingualism, 2, 22, 100, 103, 105, 142, 146, 155, 163, 174, 313, 320, 332–333, 341
Sense of story. See Narrative
Sentence fragment, 5–6, 235–236, 239, 241, 249, 337
  sentence run-on, 337
Sentence grammar, 8, 11, 64, 75–76, 86, 97, 104, 112–113, 126–129, 143, 161, 164–165, 174
  core grammar, 36, 73, 100, 104, 142, 168–170, 173, 175, 178, 225
  interfaces, 183, 234
  metalinguistic knowledge of, 197–201, 205, 240–242, 249
  second language (and incomplete) grammar, 6, 12, 34–35, 44, 88, 111, 131, 136–138, 162, 171–172, 182, 206, 217, 228, 246, 264–265
  separate mental grammars (L1 and L2), 10, 12, 89, 92, 115, 120, 123–124, 134, 271
  teaching of, 45–46
  usage/processing (compared to "competence"), 9, 71–74, 187–192, 224, 226, 270, 280
  weaker grammar subsystem (in bilinguals), 148–151
Sephardim, 277–278, 342
Shared domains, 12, 14, 16
Sleep (in English, French, and Spanish), 129–130, 269
Snow White (Blanca Nieves), 305
Social-constructionism, 82, 85, 259, 274
Social inequality, 16, 19–20, 26, 40, 54, 76, 86, 104, 108, 192, 218, 222–223, 227
Social-interactionist theory, 53–54, 338

Sociolinguistic imbalance/asymmetry, 19–20, 26, 37, 39–40, 43, 63, 72, 76, 95, 98, 119, 192, 218, 220, 224–228, 253, 268, 325
Sociolinguistics, 21, 27, 44–47, 108, 116
Sociopolitical issues, 25–27, 30, 32, 37, 39–40, 43
Song, 12, 277–278
South Africa, 26, 35–38
Soviet Union (former), 30–32
Spain, 30, 32, 277–278
Spanish, 7–8, 16–20, 30–32, 49–52, 57–78, 84–85, 94–100, 118–124, 157, 169, 203–229, 231–251, 269, 273, 277, 295–306
 speaking Spanish (and perception of), 281–288, 289–294
Specialization, 8–13, 60, 71, 77, 79, 89, 93, 99, 110–112, 114, 125, 156, 161, 163, 182, 199, 273, 278, 325, 335
Specific Language Impairment. *See* Impairment (SLI)
Speech production model (Levelt), 130
Spelling, 69, 213–215, 224, 242, 263
Stabilization (fossilization), 141, 144, 151, 153, 156, 159, 174–175, 315–316
Stages theory (of L2 literacy), 40, 47, 196
Standard (and nonstandard) dialect, 41–42, 45, 85–86, 104, 194
Standardization. *See* Normalization
Standardized tests, 54–55
Static interference, 268
Structural Lag Hypothesis, 191, 200–201
Structure Building Framework (Gernsbacher), 186–187
Submersion, 103
Subsystems hypothesis, 89, 333
Subtractive bilingualism, 22, 100, 103, 141, 143, 146, 172, 175, 175, 180, 313. *See also* Attrition
Swahili, 326–327
Syntactic Structure, 125–132, 134–139, 183–184, 187–192, 279, 321

Tanzania, 31, 326
Target language, 33–34, 41, 44, 60, 88, 111, 129, 134, 136, 166, 170–171, 173

Teaching applications. *See* Curriculum design, planning, and teaching
Testing, 18, 53, 53–54, 61. *See also* Assessment
test-wiseness, 54–55
Text comprehension, 58, 70, 74, 105, 186–187, 216, 250, 258, 264, 322, 340
Text (expository), 103, 185–186, 189, 194, 199–200, 264, 321, 336
Theory of Mind, 11, 78, 113–114, 183–185, 331
Thought
 Common Underlying Proficiency, 57
 and language, 67, 82–83, 101–102, 125, 127, 254, 272–274, 277–280
 language and culture, 280
 literacy, 330
 "mentalese," 329
 Theory of Mind, 113–114, 183–185
Three Stores Hypothesis (Paradis), 107, 267
Time on task, 227
Tlaxcala, 17, 325
Top-down processes
 central system, 110, 167–168
 compare to bottom-up, 60, 125, 321, 327–328, 339–340
 context and prediction, 54–56, 198, 264–266
 modularity, 99, 262, 275
 previous knowledge, 198, 232, 248, 257–258, 264, 327–328, 339
 in reading, 247–248
 whole-language, 103, 250–251, 254, 257–259, 264–266
Transfer, 22, 75, 148, 150, 158–166, 193–194, 219, 227–228, 268, 270–271, 322, 328. *See also* Cross-linguistic influence
 Competition Model, 158
 different senses of the term, 49–50, 53, 56–61
 between first and second language, 68–71, 88, 96, 114, 117–118, 129, 132, 136, 178–179, 223–224
 reading, 235, 239, 242
 spelling, 214–215
 theories of Universal Grammar access in second language, 145, 161–166

Transfer and conservation hypothesis (Van de Craats), 13, 138
Transitional bilingual education, 31–32, 36, 44
Transitive, 130, 322
Translation equivalent, 127, 129, 268–269, 306
Triggering, 152–153, 156–157, 161, 171, 334
Tripartite Parallel Architecture (Jackendoff), 125–132, 267
  Bilingual Tripartite Parallel Architecture, 125–139, 148, 267, 272, 274, 338

UG lexicon (Smith and Tsimpli), 127
Ultimate attainment, 147–148, 151–155, 162–164, 167, 174, 334, 341
UNESCO, 28, 38–39, 47
Uneven development, 34, 132–139, 158, 215, 260
Universal Grammar (UG), 14–15, 72, 91, 100, 103–106, 112, 141–143, 159–172, 175–176, 187, 201, 322, 325, 333–336
  mainstream UG, 102, 145, 172
Universals, 22, 81, 168, 178, 195, 260, 278
  completeness, 152–153, 160, 166
  concept of Cognitive Academic Language Proficiency, 52
  of language acquisition, 54, 71, 76–77, 79, 124
  primary abilities, 181, 183, 185–188, 192, 255–257
Universal Writing System Constraint (Perfetti and Liu), 256
  Universal Phonological Principle, 256
Usage (grammar). *See* Sentence grammar

Variation
  dialect, 85–86
  in language development (in general), 79, 168, 187–188, 201
  in language use, 119–120
  in the lexicon, 124–125
  in literacy-related abilities, 18, 77, 95–97, 103–105, 183
  in second language, 153, 160, 166, 176

Verbal art, 277–279, 330
Vernacular languages, 27–29, 38, 40–47, 322
Vertical process, 81, 90, 329
Vocabulary, 72, 92, 94, 97–100, 105, 113–114, 120, 124, 134, 136, 138, 184, 187–188, 323

Whole language, 53–54, 103, 194, 247–248, 251, 253–259, 265, 340
Wild grammar, 166
Word recognition, 72, 192, 199, 217, 224, 231–233, 248–251, 256–261, 262–266
Working memory, 188, 190, 198, 336–337
World Englishes, 34
Writing development, 18–20, 62–78, 203–229
Writing systems, 194, 223–224, 255–259